T0330655

Production, Distribution and Trade: Alternative Perspectives

This collection brings together significant new contributions to the Sraffa-based theories of production and distribution, from post-Keynesian arguments concerning monetary and macroeconomics to the history of thought and methodology. All of the authors are well-established authorities in their field, and in this book they add stimulating and original pieces of analysis to the contemporary literature.

Production, Distribution and Trade: Alternative Perspectives is divided into three parts. The first explores analytical issues in production and exchange theory, the second examines post-Keynesian macroeconomics and the final part includes essays on the history of economic thought and methodology. This collection has been written in honour of Sergio Parrinello and is a fitting tribute to his untiring efforts to stimulate discussion among classicists, Marxists, post-Keynesians, and evolutionists.

The book is a clear and convincing attempt to prove that an alternative paradigm to mainstream economics is alive and thriving and to argue that these perspectives shed better light on current economic problems, both as diagnosis and in terms of policy conclusions. The book will be of interest to Economics postgraduate students and researchers working in the classical and post-Keynesian tradition.

Adriano Birolo is Associate Professor at the University of Padua, Italy. **Duncan K. Foley** is Leo Model Professor of Economics at the New School for Social Research, New York, US. **Heinz D. Kurz** is Full Professor of Economics at the University of Graz, Austria and Director of the Graz Schumpeter Centre. **Bertram Schefold** is Professor of Economic Theory at the Goethe-University Frankfurt, Germany. **Ian Steedman** is Emeritus Research Professor at Manchester Metropolitan University, UK.

Routledge studies in the history of economics

Production, Distribution and Trade: Alternative Perspectives

Essays in honour of Sergio Parrinello

**Edited by Adriano Birolo,
Duncan K. Foley, Heinz D. Kurz,
Bertram Schefold and Ian Steedman**

Routledge
Taylor & Francis Group

LONDON AND NEW YORK

First published 2010
by Routledge
2 Park Square, Milton Park, Abingdon, Oxon, OX14 4RN

Simultaneously published in the USA and Canada
by Routledge
270 Madison Avenue, New York, NY 10016

Routledge is an imprint of the Taylor & Francis Group, an informa business

Typeset in Times by Wearset, Tyne and Wear

British Library Cataloguing in Publication Data
A catalogue record for this book is available from the British Library

Library of Congress Cataloging in Publication Data
Production, distribution and trade: alternative perspectives: essays in
honour of Sergio Parrinello / edited by Adriano Birolo ... [et al.].
p. cm.
Includes bibliographical references and index.
1. Production (Economic theory) 2. Distribution (Economic theory)
3. Macroeconomics. 4. Economics—History. I. Birolo, Adriano.

HB241.P739 2010
338.5—dc22   2009053400

ISBN13: 978-0-415-55723-8 (hbk)
ISBN13: 978-0-203-84845-6 (ebk)

Contents

Contributors

Amit Bhaduri is Professor Emeritus at Jawaharlal Nehru University, Delhi and Professor of Political Economy at the University of Pavia, Italy.

Adriano Birolo is Associate Professor in the Department of Management of Industrial Systems, University of Padua, Italy.

Guglielmo Chiodi is Professor of Economics in the Department of Innovation and Society, University of Rome 1, Italy.

Leonardo Ditta is Professor of Economics in the Department of Economics, Finance and Statistics, University of Perugia, Italy.

Amitava Krishna Dutt is Professor of Economics and Political Science in the Department of Political Science and in the Faculty of Economics, Fellow at the Kroc Institute of International Peace Studies and Kellogg Institute of International Studies, Indiana, US.

Duncan K. Foley is Leo Model Professor of Economics in the Department of Economics, New School for Social Research, New York, US.

Takao Fujimoto is Professor of Economics in the Faculty of Economics, Fukuoka University, Japan.

Pierangelo Garegnani is Emeritus Professor of Economics in the Department of Economics, University of Rome 3, Italy.

Claudio Gnesutta is Professor of Economic Policy in the Department of Public Economy, University of Rome La Sapienza, Italy.

Eiji Hosoda is Professor of Economics in the Faculty of Economics, Keio University, Kanekiyo, Kensuke and Managing Director of the Institute of Energy Economics, Japan.

Grazia Ietto-Gillies is Emeritus Professor of Applied Economics and Director at the Centre for International Business Studies, London South Bank University, UK.

J. A. Kregel is Professor at the Levy Economics Institute of Bard College and Center for Full Employment and Price Stability, Kansas City, US.

Heinz D. Kurz is Full Professor of Economics in the Department of Economics at the University of Graz, Austria and Director of the Graz Schumpeter Centre.

Lynn Mainwaring is Emeritus Professor of Economics at the University of Wales and a part-time Research Professor at Swansea Law School, UK.

Angelo Marzollo is Professor of Applied Mathematics in the Department of Mathematics and Computer Science at the University of Udine, Italy.

Stan Metcalfe is Stanley Jevons Professor of Political Economy and Cobden Lecturer at the University of Manchester, Centre for Research on Innovation and Competition (CRIC), University of Manchester, UK.

Edward J. Nell is Malcolm B. Smith Professor of Economics in the Department of Economics, New School for Social Research, New York, US.

Massimo Pivetti is Professor of Economics in the Department of Law, Section of Economics and Finance, University of Rome La Sapienza, Italy.

Flavio Pressacco is Professor of Financial Mathematics in the Department of Finance at the University of Udine, Italy.

Alessandro Roncaglia is Professor of Economics in the Department of Social and Economic Studies, University of Rome La Sapienza, Italy.

Annalisa Rosselli is Professor of the History of Political Economy in the Department of Economia e Istituzioni, University of Rome 2, Italy.

Neri Salvadori is Professor of Economics in the Department of Economic Science, University of Pisa, Italy.

Bertram Schefold is Professor of Economics at the Fachbereich Wirtschaftswissenschaften, Johann Wolfgang Goethe-University, D-60054 Frankfurt am Main, Germany.

Ian Steedman is Emeritus Professor of Economics in the Department of Economics, Manchester Metropolitan University, UK.

Introduction

The path of a scholar

Adriano Birolo

1 The context

This collection of essays is a tribute to the academic career of Sergio Parrinello,[1] a scholar whose research has focused in particular on the strand of neo-Ricardian and post-Keynesian studies as developed in Italy in the 1960s, influenced by the post-war debate between the two Cambridge Schools on the theory of capital and distribution.[2] Unlike other young scholars of the time, as a graduate from a peripheral university no opportunity came his way for a scholarship for specialisation in a university abroad, such as the University of Cambridge, which was accorded the greatest favour at the time.[3] Thus the early years of his postgraduate education continued in the same university where he had taken his degree.

The 1960s saw great ferment in theoretical research. There was a distinct perception in much of Italy's academic world that, subsequent to cogent criticism of the Cambridge School, certain of the foundations of neoclassical economic theory now had to be replaced with material produced in the new field of "classical" economics. The demolition, the *pars destruens* of criticism, was to be followed by the *pars costruens* (Sylos Labini 1973).

In many areas of research, reconstruction was awaited on the basis of the new, scant but fundamental, material produced. The aim was to build a new theoretical "paradigm" to contrast the neoclassical model at all its various levels, from theory to applications and economic policies.

As we know, this ferment did not lead to the expected results – the eagerly awaited reconstruction of political economy on non-neoclassical foundations.

By the mid-1970s the scene was already changing and the typically "Sraffian" components dropped away: the wind of research was blowing in another direction. The causes were manifold, some extraneous to the discipline. But the sluggish approach to the original themes of research, to shaping the "core", the founding propositions, the aptitude for exegesis of the texts and criticism, resulted in ever-increasing distance from the goal of the *pars costruens*.[4]

In this state of affairs Sergio Parrinello took on a singular role. He was one of the few scholars of the second[5] "generation" to dedicate almost all his research activity to extending the original founding "core" of the new paradigm, demonstrating its flexibility in absorbing, in different forms and with new significance, themes and theories discussed solely with the new classical paradigm or applying analytic tools typical of that paradigm.

In the language of Lakatos, it may reasonably be argued that Parrinello strove to produce and organise part of those "auxiliary theories" that are fundamental to render a new paradigm acceptable and power its circulation within a community of scholars. His was a somewhat solitary labour, much like that of an explorer who discovers new lands and makes them known by tracing out conceptual maps. He may have developed this aptitude through having, in his early years of (self) tutoring,[6] undergone the influence of the Cambridge School only at a mediated level[7] and shown a degree of resistance to certain dogmas that immediately arose in that School and that subsequently held many of the adherents back from straying out of that familiar territory. He had retained the curiosity of his early years and the freedom to strike out in new directions, albeit within the terms of the same paradigm, without being restrained by the fear of sliding into syncretism.[8] Some bricks were missing from the paradigm being built, limiting its interpretative scope vis-à-vis the neoclassical scheme – the role of demand, of expectations – and on these he has worked over time. His efforts have focused not only on broadening the limits of the new paradigm, but also on the critical reappraisal of certain of the "struts" including, for example, the precise nature of the concept of equilibrium contained in "long-period position".

2 The background

Parrinello's early contributions reflect the major lines of research of the time. He addressed them applying the most advanced analytic methods – activity analysis, linear programming, input–output ([1], [2]). The third work [3] is of particular interest for the subsequent developments in the course of his research. Here reference becomes explicit to a classical economic growth scheme, albeit more Marxian in conception than explicitly Sraffian. The article, *inter alia*, contains a critical discussion of the then recent Pasinetti model with vertically integrated sectors. He grasped with clear insight the essentially normative nature of "how it must be" rather than "how it is" in accounting for the nature of the full employment assumption. Setting the "rank condition" is a technical artifice that allows for full employment dynamic equilibrium but deprives the model of the capacity to interpret a capitalistic growing economy. This criticism was developed in depth in a subsequent work [5] which was not published but circulated "underground".[9]

A note on the theories of induced inventions [4] was followed by a co-authored article [6] on the criteria for choice in investments in research. In the part he authored, Parrinello provided a critique of the aggregate growth models in vogue at the time, and the associated notion of productivity. He also set out the reasons for moving on to a more disaggregated approach. Furthermore, he offered a critical discussion of the international trade models utilised in a context of growth, and his incisive criticisms anticipated developments in the neo-Ricardian models of international trade that were to come.

His contribution [7] on the relationship between "objective" prices and growth out of equilibrium completed and closed the preparatory stage in the construction of the "new" theories inside the classical–Ricardian paradigm. In this work he returned to discussion of the Pasinetti model, examining the function of the vertically integrated sectors in the models of non-balanced growth and inquiring into which restrictive hypotheses, the principal one being the shortsightedness of the entrepreneurs' expectations, must be placed in order to be able to determine the "objective" prices independently of the demand conditions during the traverse process. So he raises some doubts about the adequacy of the "Sraffian" theory of prices to interpret situations of non-equilibrium dynamics. Thus arises the interpretative and analytic problem of whether, and if so how, to introduce some model of non-shortsighted expectations violating to the nature of the equilibrium in the system of prices in the "classical" approach. This was to become a recurrent concern, tackled with successive approximations but never finally settled in many of his subsequent writings.

The following years saw the birth of the "constructive" theories: "international trade", "exhaustible resources", "institutions" and "non-material goods". At the same time certain fundamental elements of the paradigm were being conceptually enhanced and refined: the composition of demand and its relation with the price system, uncertainty, market forms, and the role of returns to scale. However, significant and in many cases innovative contributions were to appear touching on the paradigm or in culturally contiguous areas of research on the concept of equilibrium in economics, for example, on post-Keynesian theory, and on the history of economic thought and analysis. Last but not least, there were also contributions in the didactic field, in criticism within the field of welfare economics and, in the early 1970s, contributions in both theoretical and applied areas regarding socialist economies.[10]

Sergio Parrinello published contributions in Italian emerging from his first 15 years of research in the major Italian academic economic journals. This was very much the common practice of the time, but it did mean only limited circulation[11] for certain of his fundamental contributions, reaching only the very few economists who could read Italian in the Anglo-Saxon world. Subsequently his publications were written in English[12] and the main lines of his research thus received recognition abroad among scholars taking neo-Ricardian, post-Keynesian approaches, or at any rate those critical of neoclassical theory.

In the following section we will look into two "constructive" theories of the neo-Ricardian paradigm associated in their entirety or in part with his name. We will then go on to consider the essence of various other writings of his on the subject of institutions, the production of material goods and the composition of demand within the neo-Ricardian scheme of determination of relative prices, as well as offering some remarks on matters of theory, method and overall evaluation of Sraffian economics. To conclude, we will outline the important role played by Parrinello as founder and organiser of the Trieste Summer School and in the management of *Metroeconomica*, first as co-editor and subsequently as managing editor for about 30 years. (From 1967 to 1982 as assistant and subsequently co-editor, and from 1983 to 1997 as managing editor.)

3 The "constructive" theories

3.1 Foreign trade

Sergio Parrinello published the first article [8] on extension to the open economy of the Sraffian model.[13] In this article the exposition and method of analysis showed the considerable influence of the lesson to be drawn from activity analysis and linear programming. The starting point is a scheme of general equilibrium which is not neoclassical because certain hypotheses are introduced including positive wages with labour unemployment and the absence of a theory of demand, which are simply taken as given.

Balanced growth is assumed for the whole of the international economy. The concept of "return of specialisation" is defined as an explicit extension of the technology choice problem of the closed economy, and proof is offered that the wage–profit frontier of an open economy is not always necessarily decreasing, the result depending on the choice of numeraire. The analytic novelty of the neo-Ricardian approach lies in specification of the criterion to measure the advantage or disadvantage of an economy in transition from autarky to international trade, which takes form in the comparison between two growth rate–wage curves one of autarky, the other of openness to foreign trade.

It was not until some years later that explicit expression was given to the awareness that such systems *à la* Sraffa amount to theorisation of an observable system of production of goods operating in a historical time that has already reached a non-momentary equilibrium of its own, also in terms of quantity. In a few words, this is a contribution which, on the basis of the critical developments contained in the *Production of Commodities*, lays the alternative analytic foundations on the basis of which the principal propositions of the neoclassical theory of international trade are called into question.

In the following work ([10], [16]) Parrinello rewrote the Ricardian theory of trade and comparative advantage. As with the method adopted in the first work equilibrium (accounting) conditions are set and from them are drawn constraints on the variables in order to arrive at an economically significant solution. This is practically a normative approach: once the parameters are established a relation of equilibrium is set between the significant variables, some given, others adjustable. The variables left endogenous are determined by the accounting relation of system consistency. There is continual reference to competition as the institutional mechanism implying a cost-minimising behaviour of the classical type which, if not obstructed, brings the endogenous variables to the accounting equilibrium which is subsequently interpreted as long-period position. The subsequent, fruitless debate on gravitation serves to point out that there is, indeed, a "problem" in this approach. Significantly enough, many years later Parrinello began to investigate other notions of equilibrium and the various mechanisms that bring it about ([40], [45], [60]).

The model provides solutions for productive specialisation between the two countries in relation to the real wages in each of them. The specialisation chosen is that which affords one country or both the highest growth rate. The relative size of the countries, the large and the small, is determined endogenously. On the basis of the hypothesised propensity to save it is possible to deduce the rates of profit in each country. The value system and the quantity system are thus linked up. It is demonstrated that opening up to trade is not always profitable for all the countries or for all the social classes within each country. Adjusting the model to neoclassical hypotheses, Parrinello formulated an analytic critique of Heckscher–Ohlin's theorem enlarging upon the findings already arrived at for the closed and open economy.[14] The contribution [10] appeared in English, in a version only slightly modified [16], in a volume of essays on international trade (Steedman 1979).

Apart from a valuable introduction [13] to the first of the five *Essays on Some Unsettled Questions of Political Economy* by J. S. Mill, it would be some years before Parrinello returned to the issue in an article published in *JPKE* [30]. Taking a non-technical approach he raised an issue that was only apparently a matter of the history of analysis. The question was whether the positions taken by Smith with the "productivity doctrine" and Ricardo with the "comparative costs doctrine" on foreign trade did in fact conflict with one another or whether, on the other hand, a certain complementarity between the two positions might be proved, the latter being the thesis to demonstrate. Returning to some propositions already advanced in [10] and [16], Parrinello argued that Ricardo's theory of comparative costs was compatible with various hypotheses on returns to scale, was not associated with full labour employment equilibria, and that the gains from trade were not to be interpreted as reallocation of given resources. On the strength of his interpretation, he was able to demonstrate the non-incompatibility of the theory of comparative costs with Smith's theory of the extension of markets. In any case the explicative scope of the Ricardian theory, as it is reinterpreted at textbook level, is limited by the assumptions of constant returns, but one factor of production, labour, and of perfect competition and full employment. The critical analysis which Parrinello formulates in this work leads to the conclusion that the "gains from trade" indicated by the original Ricardian model are at best only partial. The total effects of opening up to international trade must also include the impact of trade on the degree of utilisation of the productive capacity of the countries involved, and the lasting effect brought about by trade on technological change. In this way the theory of comparative costs can serve as a logical basis on which to graft the Keynesian principle of effective demand and the theories derived from the Smithian "vent-for-surplus" and "widening the extent of the market".

In an article of 2001 published in 2002 [56] Parrinello turned his attention once again to international trade. The article consists of a brief critical review dealing in particular with the role of the institutional factors in the New Trade Theory (NTT),[15] to point out a certain complementarity of the NTT with the neoclassical tradition. They have in common certain basic hypotheses, but the emphasis in the

NTT is placed on increasing returns and imperfect competition. The institutional factors modify neither the method of analysis nor the structure of the traditional model; they only affect certain parameters. The main point of criticism is that, if explaining means predicting, the NTT models do not yield a general theorem serving to predict the pattern of trade on the evidence of given structural characteristics of the countries involved in trade. Instead of "causal relations" NTT models go no further than establishing correlations between the structural data and the endogenous variables. Thus, much as is the case with the theory of general equilibrium, in the NTT models the patterns of specialisation can take manifold forms starting from the same set of structural data. Parrinello argues that, in contrast with attempts applying the NTT, the institutional factors can easily be included in trade models that do not belong to the Walrasian tradition – models constructed along neo-Ricardian and neo-Marxist lines – given their open nature. A further point in the article, namely that globalisation is not necessarily favourable for all the countries involved in it, was taken up from the analytic viewpoint in a final contribution on trade [68]. With a very simple version of the neo-Ricardian model, with fully mobile financial capital and labour unemployment, Parrinello demonstrates without any particularly restrictive assumptions that absolute productivity and advantages can prevail over relative productivity and comparative advantages in determining the pattern of specialisation to the point of delineating positions such that can exclude from international trade a country's productive sectors as a whole. Thus a theoretical basis is provided for explanation of the growth or decline of the countries involved in global trade. This is a further example of the capacity of the neo-Ricardian framework to endow insights or facts observable in the global arena with theoretical substance.

3.2 Exhaustible natural resources

Parrinello came to this topic rather later than the other neo-Ricardian economists. In 1982 he published in Italian the entry "Terra" (Land) in *Dizionario di Economia Politica* [20], a critical discussion of how the role of exhaustible natural resources had been dealt with by the neoclassical and neo-Ricardian authors. The other neo-Ricardian scholars[16] had written on the subject of "land" starting from Sraffa's presentation in chapter XI of *Production of Commodities* and tracing out the foundations for subsequent reflection.

In 1983 the part of the entry *Terra* [20] dedicated to the neo-Ricardian approach appeared in English [23]. A foreword had been added to the original text on the role of natural resources as a limit to growth processes. Parrinello argued that the authors who had first analysed chapter XI of *Production of Commodities* had, erroneously, bundled together with the Sraffian "land" the exhaustible resources in general, such as mineral resources. This way of placing on the same plane "land" and exhaustible natural resources was, Parrinello believed, implicitly suggested by Sraffa himself. Here lay the novelty of Parrinello's text ([20], [23]) departing from the contributions that had so far appeared in chapter XI of *Production of Commodities*.[17]

As Parrinello saw it, in chapter XI Sraffa interpreted the coexistence of two methods of cultivation on pieces of land of the same quality as if it were the result of a process of decreasing productivity occurring historically within a model that finds no place among steady-state models.

He develops his analysis with an exhaustible natural resource (inventory) and the model determines the prices of the resource in the subsoil in two contiguous periods. The solution depends upon the temporal distribution of the exhaustible resource being known or governed by a long-period expectations model. The consequence is that the entire system of prices cannot be accounted for solely by the technology and distribution within the self-contained period of time; determination of the prices also comes to depend upon the quantity of natural resources in short supply. Thus a certain affinity emerges between the surplus approach and the neoclassical approach, but the affinity is limited since in the former the rate of profit, whose value is confined by the technological limits, is the result of an incomplete theory of distribution whereas in the neoclassical approach the rate of interest is characterised as a rate of intertemporal preference.

The basic issue that Parrinello's exhaustible natural resources model highlights is whether the classical method of long-period positions is compatible with an excessively fast historical process of decreasing productivity of an intensive or extensive nature associated with progressive exhaustion of natural resources yielding increasing rent. Sooner or later the scant resource is exhausted and some change in the productive methods becomes imperative. At the economic level, a system of long-period prices with a scant natural resource can persist if the changes in relative prices occurring as the resource dwindles are not anticipated.

Parrinello revised and enlarged his original model ([20], [23]) in a symposium on "Exhaustible Natural Resources and Sraffian Analysis" organised by Ian Steedman for *Metroeconomica* ([54]). He rewrote his model in such a way as to allow for structural change and determination of the price system in each of the periods preceding exhaustion of the natural resource, unlike the other similar models (Bidard and Erreygers, Kurz and Salvadori, Schefold all in the 2001 *Metroeconomica* Symposium) in which the price system solution, arrived at through "backward induction", is made to depend upon a backstop technology known *a priori* in which "the future influences the past". To obtain this result he sets a "rank condition" on the system establishing, from the economic point of view, that changes in the methods of production or in the rate of interest must be consistent with the revaluation of the exhaustible resource in each period at a rate equal to the current rate of interest. And again, changes in the quantities produced, even though exogenous, must not be arbitrary. Admittedly, these conditions cannot simply be assumed. However, following the constructive methodology of proof adopted by Sraffa in the *Production of Commodities*, they can be interpreted as the result of an observed historical sequence, a moving equilibrium, in which the "given" quantities which structure the solution for prices together with technology are the result of the arbitrage between the real returns among various assets realised through the endogenous shifts of capitals.

Actually the producers' expectations do exert some weight, but only within each single period, and without extending to the prices of the following periods.

In a subsequent work, Parrinello ([59]), responding to the objections of some critics (Bidard and Erreygers 2002) who interpreted the "rank condition" of the "oil–corn" model solely as a mathematical constraint guaranteeing solution, abandoned the "rank condition" to replace it with the notion of "effectual supply" of the exhaustible natural resource. The fact was that the "rank condition" hid the variables that adjusted the system to the long-period position. For the solution of the model thus modified it is necessary for the "given" quantities of goods in each period to include also the exhaustible resource flow magnitude, the "effectual supply", and not the entire stock of resource in the subsoil. The theory of "normal prices" functions perfectly in the modified model. Parrinello's interpretation is that Sraffa's system of given quantities represents theoretical reconstruction of a production system observable and at work. This in turn derives from the assumption that the production system is the outcome of the choice of profit maximisation in conditions of competition in a long-period context. The output accomplished is assumed to satisfy a given "effectual demand" or path of "effectual demand". The given quantities of the Sraffian system of prices must now also satisfy a certain path of "effectual supply" of the exhaustible resource, the amount of which can reflect the behaviour of the investors in moving between various productive processes and the conservation process applied to the exhaustible resources to gain on the difference between the rate of profit and the rate of appreciation of the exhaustible resource.

It is worth noting that, albeit indirectly, Parrinello's argumentation in his various contributions on the issue of "exhaustible natural resources" as a whole seems to hark back to the demonstrative method of an algorithmic nature followed by Sraffa in *Production of Commodities*, subsequently termed "constructive methodology" by Velupillai (1989, 2008).

4 Inside the neo-Ricardian "core" and other "constructive" theories

4.1 The long-period positions

A constant feature evident in the writings of Parrinello on natural resources but also cropping up in a great many of his contributions in the neo-Ricardian area is deliberation on the economic meaning of the specific notion of equilibrium, the "long-period positions" (LPPs),[18] which supports the models of neo-Ricardian conception. This is the notion of equilibrium[19] that would give economic meaning to the prices and distributive variables stemming from the solution of a system of apparently "accounting" relations.

Parrinello deals with the concept of equilibrium in many of his writings: reference is provided for twelve of them in note 10. Even before 1970 he had addressed the topic in contributions [3], [5] and in particular [7]. The relations that seem, perhaps, to reflect his approach to the topic best are [40], [51] and [55].

In [40] Parrinello stepped in to defend the LPPs, but taking a line that enhanced their interpretative capacity. He succeeded in precisely identifying the pre-analytic conditions that endow LPP equilibrium with meaning and the type of adjustment that creates the possibility for convergence of market prices to normal prices or, at any rate, not systematic divergence. He analysed the positions of the critics who called for a completely dynamic approach to adjustment, highlighting the problematic aspects of these criticisms. He also drew attention to the risk that the specific analytic method proposed by the critics to "prove" the stability of long-period prices might deprive the very concept of LPPs of meaning, together with the underlying classical model. The path of adjustment would trace out a model of perfect disequilibrium, a sort of stable moving equilibrium, and the attractors, the LPP prices, would lose the role assigned to them by classical theory. There would be a risk of confusion between classical model and neoclassical model.

Parrinello's position is that "the difference in the two rival theories of prices require also a different approach to the analysis of convergence and to the kind of empirical correlates on which each theory of prices must be founded". Thus he set about analysing the notion of the attractor, reutilising the notions of statistical equilibrium,[20] the nature of expectations, the empirical correlates to the "normal states" and the role of random disturbances[21] in defining the "fundamentals" of the normal states, arguing that all these aspects can usefully be incorporated into the classical Sraffian model, reinforcing its foundations.

In a subsequent work [51] of markedly methodological conception which focused on the role of the normal states produced by the theory, seen as contrasting alternatives in explanation–interpretation of historical events, Parrinello returned to discussion of the meaning of normal prices (LPP prices). He interpreted them explicitly as benchmarks produced by a specific theory.[22] Thus the normal prices become a yardstick for the effective prices, seen as resulting from specific historical conditions. On the basis of a rule of correspondence between normal prices and effective prices, their divergence could be accounted for. For example, when temporary conditions of monopoly prevail in a specific sector the price in that sector diverges from the normal price associated with conditions of competition in [21]. This marked a step further in extending the interpretative capacity of the LPPs.

At the end of his contribution [55], consisting in valuable critical commentary on some essays contained in Kurz (2000), Parrinello seems to have accepted Garegnani's position of the two levels of analysis in definition of the equilibrium in the classical Sraffian scheme: the system of prices, accounted for by the fundamental theory in which the quantities are given, postulated as necessary to avoid the trap of constant returns; the quantities, i.e. level and composition, of demand, accounted for by a separate theory showing a less abstract, more inductive approach than the theory of prices; and the suggestion that linkage and integration between the two levels of analysis may be reached through an iterative procedure on quantities, prices and so forth. At the same time, however, he expressed regret that since the publication of *Production of Commodities* no contribution had appeared that adopted this promising procedure in various stages. Practically dismissing that theory and equilibrium as little more than "wishful thinking", he noted that:

> the Sraffian side continue to develop the criticism of marginalism or they pertain to the history of economic thought. This attitude contrasts in some respects with the works of the Classics which are taken as a benchmark. The latter were actively concerned with applying their theories to the important economic problems of their own time. Ricardo and Marx, in particular, did not wait until the defects of the theory of value (of which they were indeed aware) were overcome before dealing with the problems of growth, innovation and distribution of the nineteenth century.... [They] have only occasionally followed the Classics in trying to apply Sraffa's approach to the contemporary problems of growth, innovation, distribution and globalization. The reason for this different attitude can be traced back to the priority that they assign to the task of dismantling the consolidated neoclassical system on the basis of a pure theoretical and methodological criticism. It seems as if they were engaged in a sort of division of labour and as if they say: we have done our critical work and we are still doing it; others, perhaps more expert in the fields of historical studies and of non-economic social sciences, should make the rest of the work in order to explain the level and the structure of economic activity and the evolution of these phenomena relative to historically determined factors. But why does such a second field of enquiry not emerge in a complementary way with the Sraffian theory of prices and the assumed methodology of Sraffa? This is a legitimate question 40 years after the publication of Sraffa's book.... At the same time Sraffa's Legacy suggests why a theoretical controversy, not accompanied with a parallel development of a positive alternative theory of the economic process as a whole, can be stimulating indeed, but in a certain sense it leaves only losers and nonwinners on the ground.[23]

4.2 Other "constructive" theories

Parrinello has provided many more contributions extending the interpretative capacity of the Sraffian model. This constant endeavour to plant new seeds has not so far been consistently rewarded with the fruit of new contributions by other scholars along the lines traced out. This may be due to the greater aptitude of members of the Sraffian tribe, as previously noted, for critical rather than constructive work.

As early as 1982 he published an essay [21] pointing out the possible compatibility of a case of the productive process being performed in monopoly with the notion of long-period equilibrium. In doing so he demonstrated on the one hand the possibility of persistence in the differential between rates of profit and, on the other hand, the non-independence between system of prices and system of quantities inasmuch as an individual producer can swell his profit through change in the level of demand for the commodity which he produces with change in the monopoly price.

The period 1981–4 saw no fewer than five ([18], [22], [24], [25], [26]) contributions from him dedicated to examination of the elements that determine the composition of demand, and to endogenous preferences and adaptive behaviours. His approach involved pointing out that the "individual tastes" that play a part in the formation of demand are still anchored to the system of production and the functions the individuals perform within it. At the analytic level, the aim is to show the influence of the system of production on demand which determines the "given" long-period equilibrium quantities.

Parrinello traced out another new path with a series of contributions – [29], [31], [35] and [39] – with the introduction of social norms into the Sraffian model. Unlike the traditional theory according to which the production technology is independent of the various institutional structures that govern the technology of trade, in the model proposed by Parrinello the choice of techniques is the joint result of technology conditions and the actual pattern of social norms. In a capitalist economy with competition prevailing systems of production and systems of negotiation will emerge that tend to minimise the overall costs of both production and trade.

In articles [36] and [43] he enters the notion of efficiency wage within the neo-Ricardian framework. In these articles we witness the endeavour to theorise inductively a factual situation, namely the existence of sectoral wage structures differing for similar work typologies.

In 1993 Parrinello published a work [42] introducing for the first time the distinction between "private goods" and "non pure private goods" within the Sraffian framework. Nonrival inputs are considered as possible origins of increasing returns and analytic tools to extend neo-Ricardian theory beyond the limits of constant returns and find room within it also for "public goods". As a partial extension of this work, in [44] and [47], Parrinello returned to one of the pillars of the neo-Ricardian "core", namely part III of *Production of Commodities* on the choice of techniques. He demonstrates that the Sraffian method of choice of techniques is compatible only with locally constant returns, and that if the variable returns are allowed in association with economies or diseconomies outside the firms, then the sequence of techniques introduced subsequent to an increase in demand or under the effect of technological change can entail persistent adoption of inefficient techniques and a lower level of the endogenous distributive variable. In his analysis the existence of externalities on the side of production has significant social effects on the choice of techniques when the choice remains governed solely by minimisation of private costs.

In more recent years (2003–7), with a series of contributions ([57], [61], [64]) Parrinello opened a further new front for neo-Ricardian analysis, extending the original scheme to an economy that sees processes producing material goods and processes providing services working side by side.

One of the aims pursued in these works is to provide theoretical support for the thesis denying that *per se* the expansion of services and consequent apparent "dematerialisation" of the economy is associated with increasing generation and dissemination of knowledge. The statistical classification between production of commodities and production of services reflects the evolution in the organisation and division of labour, coming about through a continual decomposition and recomposition of processes in the production of services and intermediate goods. This "reshuffling" is not necessarily correlated with an expansion of the knowledge economy which influences material and immaterial production without distinction. Goods and services are not rival products but complementary, and a new role of knowledge should therefore be duly divorced from the dichotomy between goods and services. Thanks to the innovative contents of the contributions listed above, with analytic distinction between processes producing goods (serial processes) and processes producing services (parallel processes), another way is opened within the neo-Ricardian logical framework for generalisation of the choice of techniques to theory of choice of techniques and organisation of the economy in terms of processes, firms and markets. One of the findings thus obtained is that a capitalist economy cannot be an economy of pure services.

4.3 Keynesian contributions

Sergio Parrinello has not confined his attention solely to issues within the classical theory of value and distribution, or issues that revolve about it. In the early 1970s he also wrote two theoretical contributions on the self-managed enterprise in the Yugoslav model ([9] and [11]) and an empirical contribution on EEC–COMECON trade [12], while the late 1980s saw a critical contribution [38] on the use of probabilities as a measure of uncertainty.

He also took part in the debate of the 1970s–1980s on the reinterpretation of Keynes's thought. His first contribution [14] took on the critique of overdetermination and the antithesis between causality and interdependence between the endogenous variables in the Keynesian model. His argument ran that criticism along these lines shifted attention from the true weaknesses of the model, which lie in the hypotheses of homogeneity of physical capital and labour, and the method of short-period general equilibria. Strict causality or interdependence are, he holds, of no real relevance as means to account for the principle of effective demand. What is indispensable, on the other hand, is that there be a monetary economy, uncertainty, separation between investment decisions and saving decisions and the role of income as adjustment variable.

In contributions [17] and [19] Parrinello raises the question as to which prices and which quantities are implicit in the aggregate demand function as defined in chapter 3 of the *General Theory*, and which are the microeconomic foundations underlying the point of intersection between aggregate supply and demand. He argues that effective demand is an expected magnitude consisting in the compound product of price and quantity. The expectations apply to positions of equilibrium in which a certain amount of product and a level of prices are implicit. The classical method of equilibrium taken as a centre of gravity thus appears compatible with Keynesian methodology if equilibrium is understood in terms of equilibrium of equilibrium expectations.

Analytical investigation of effective demand continues in [28] and [37]. Parrinello sets the principle of effective demand back on Marshallian microeconomic bases and points out that the method adopted by Keynes in chapter 3 of the *General Theory* is in fact a hybrid obtained by superimposing on Marshall's static analysis of equilibrium a dynamic analysis of the adjustment process.

5 Sergio Parrinello: scientific organiser

5.1 The Trieste Summer School[24]

Sergio Parrinello has not only produced theoretical innovations and traced out new paths in the area of the neo-Ricardian paradigm, but has also shown unflagging zeal as an organiser of scientific events. The "Trieste Summer School"[25] is among the fruits of these activities.

As a venture at the international level, the "Trieste Summer School" is virtually unique of its kind. It sees between twenty to forty scholars (depending on the year) of Sraffian and post-Keynesian inspiration – the great twofold core of the Cambridge tradition – coming together from many and varied major centres of culture and learning in a score of different countries to spend ten days teaching and discussing with between thirty and fifty students, young university researchers.

The school pursued two principal aims. The first was to promote debate among exponents of the two theoretical strands to investigate the extent to which Keynesian analysis of effective demand in a monetary production economy can be integrated with revival of classical economics along Sraffian lines. An important aspect of the debate [32] lay in verifying whether the theoretical "facts" of the two strands have the capacity to interpret the facts of the real economy and the contingent problems of economic policy, applying these also to countries with various levels of development. With this approach there was no risk of debate being confined solely to comparison of the terms of the two research programmes. The "theories" came under discussion on the plane of empirical interpretations, also in relation to those deriving from traditional theory. The debate did not lead to the two strands, the post-Keynesian and neo-Ricardian programmes, being woven into one. As Parrinello saw it [32], their incompatibility lies in the "concept of uncertainty and the way of theorising a world in which individuals act in conditions of uncertainty.... Clearly, it follows that, while Keynesian criticism of the tradition of economy focuses on the role of uncertainty, the criticism of the theoreticians of surplus revolves around a theory of capital that has nothing to do with the existence of uncertainty."

The debate did, nevertheless, bear fruits in the articles and conference proceedings produced (in particular Kregel 1983).

The second objective of the school was to stimulate and disseminate ideas, and generate interaction among international groups of young scholars interested in heterodox approaches to political economy. His purpose was achieved to the full, and young scholars from peripheral countries who would otherwise have worked in isolation joined in with interpersonal circuits of great utility for their future research work. Many have gone on to successful careers in academia and other fields.

About halfway through the School's decade of activity the debate between post-Keynesians and neo-Ricardians reached the stage of decreasing returns. The question arose as to whether the School of Trieste was to be transformed from an arena for comparison and contrast to a school of thought, be it post-Keynesian or neo-Ricardian, or indeed open up to other theoretical approaches that could fertilise both the didactic activity and the debate with new ideas. Urged by certain members of the Summer School who took a critical line on the less robust aspects of the two strands of thought, the choice fell on opening up to new influences. As from 1985,[26] alongside the post-Keynesian and neo-Ricardian positions, other approaches critical of neoclassical theory, like the evolutionist and institutionalist approaches, found room in both the teaching and the internal debate.

5.2 Metroeconomica

The name of Sergio Parrinello is associated with the name of a journal, *Metroeconomica*, whose official editor he was for 15 years, having for the previous 15 years been co-editor and assistant editor, amounting to 30 years of editorial responsibility. *Metroeconomica*[27] was founded in 1949 by Eraldo Fossati,[28] who then held the chair of Political Economy at Trieste.[29] In the editorial of the first issue of the journal it was proclaimed that the founding members were "bound together by a tie of adhesion to the econometrical principle" and that the title of the journal had been conceived "to fix and explain its aim as well its method". *Metroeconomica*, it was stressed, is "open to every scholar, who appreciates the quantitative reach of economic science to its full value". The most important economists of the day sat on the editorial board: to begin with C. Bresciani-Turroni, L. Dupriez, R. Frisch, G. Lutfalla, A. Marget, U. Papi, E. Schneider, J. Tinbergen, G. Tintner and F. Zeuthen, and later on R. Roy, W. Leontief, J. Marschak and G. L. S Shackle.

In the first ten years of activity it published theoretical articles by G. Debreu, K. Arrow, M. Allais, R. Roy, M. Morishima, H. Nikaido, T. Negishi, D. Patinkin, G. L. S. Shackle and R. Frisch. Later on contributions also came from F. Hahn, R. Kuenne and P. Newman. Further important contributions were in the sphere of econometrics and applied research. The most renowned authors included R. Frisch, J. Tinbergen, G. Tintner and H. Theil.

As from 1962 editorship was taken over by Manlio Resta, with no change to the editorial line. This period saw a burgeoning of studies on growth models. The journal accepted neoclassical contributions as well as contributions running on the lines traced out by von Neumann. The authors included L. McKenzie, K. Shell, D. Levhari, K. I. Inada, K. Kurihara, A. Takayama, M. Shubik and many others. The early 1970s saw contributions by Kamien and Schwartz, Diewert and Takayama. Most of the contributions still belonged to "mainstream economics", but the occasional "Sraffian" article began to appear, like the articles by L. Pasinetti on vertical integration and B. Schefold on fixed capital.

Close as he was to Resta, Sergio Parrinello found himself directly drawn into the atmosphere of his contributions and, as from 1967, worked alongside Resta in running the journal, first as assistant editor and subsequently, as he advanced in his academic career in Italy, as co-editor. By now Parrinello's unique "classical Ricardian" leaning had found full expression through his writings. The editorial line of the journal was about to change direction while, in keeping with its tradition, continuing to favour contributions of particular rigor in terms of analytic tools. It was the contents that changed. As from the beginning of the 1980s Parrinello accorded ever more room to contributions along neo-Ricardian lines (including, among many others, articles by I. Steedman, S. Metcalfe, N. Salvadori, L. Mainwaring and P. Garegnani). In 1983 Parrinello took over sole editorship of *Metroeconomica*. The 1980s were also the years that witnessed the School of Trieste. *Metroeconomica* opened up an increasing number of pages to "mainstream" critical contributions, reflecting the debates that were held within the annual Summer Schools. Various contributions appeared by leading post-Keynesian exponents including S. Weintraub, T. Asimakopulos and H. Minsky, in addition to the flow of contributions following the diverse neo-Ricardian strands. The journal progressively extended its range to take in other mainstream critical contributions including articles of evolutionist and institutionalist inspiration.

A new phase, with a number of co-editors now working alongside the editor, began in 1998. The volume of that year was introduced by an editorial that drew an end to one period and set out to open a new one. Many of the remarks contained therein faithfully reflected the positions that Parrinello had arrived at vis-à-vis the "critical" theories in the course of the School of Trieste debates. It begins by proclaiming that "Economic theory is in a state of flux"; neoclassical theory was multifarious and many other theories clashed with it mostly on specific issues, but as yet there was no "alternative" theory. The editors deemed that in this state of affairs "the present debate among conflicting ideas and theories should be encouraged and their supporters should be offered an appropriate international forum". Parrinello's attitude emerged clearly and boldly as he asserted that

> those economists who disagree with the dominant doctrines have insisted too much on purely methodological and critical arguments. This line of action soon reached diminishing returns to effort, and we believe that critical arguments are far stronger when they open the way to constructive suggestions, leading to more satisfactory explanations of relevant economic questions and more reliable predictions of economic facts.

This was the same position that he took in a critical comment [32] on his experience with the School of Trieste. Looking forward to more positive developments he insisted:

Furthermore, we would hope to publish works trying to incorporate into economic analysis the role of institutions, beyond the traditional emphasis on markets alone. This, by the way, might give the system greater structure and reduce the degree of indeterminateness in the economic agent's behaviour.

This is part of the research programme that Parrinello was conducting in his field.

To extend the range of contributions accepted by *Metroeconomica* in the following years, Parrinello opted for an active editorial policy, not simply waiting for material to arrive. He encouraged contributions that he held to be interesting, and organised conferences (1991, Production organization, efficiency and social norms) and workshops (1993, The notion of competition and cooperation in economics; 1995, Theoretical bases for employment increasing policies) which bore fruit in special issues of the journal while drawing further articles from yet more scholars.

In keeping with his penchant for dialogue and keen interest in "other" theories, Parrinello decided to open up the board of editors to the major exponents of the alternative theoretical approaches, in 1989 taking B. Schefold and I. Steedman on board, in 1992 R. Arena, D. Foley, H. Kurz and N. Salvadori. Subsequently he took on A. Bhaduri, A. K. Dutt, R. Frenke, W. Guth, H. Hosoda and S. Metcalfe, and in the space of a few years he had brought the board back to the sanguine conditions it had enjoyed in the first years of the life of the journal.

At the beginning of the 1990s Parrinello's great editorial endeavours hit a bottleneck in a system of circulation no longer adequate to the reputation acquired.[30] At the end of 1992 *Metroeconomica* became a journal of Blackwell Publishers entailing a great boost to its circulation and prestige.

At the end of 1997, after 30 years of direct editorial responsibility, in the knowledge of having carried out an enormous task, as the journal was entering into its fiftieth year of life Parrinello deemed that the time had come to bow out to a new managing editor; the board called on Heinz Kurz, who is still editing *Metroeconomica*[31] with undiminished enthusiasm.

6 The organisation of the volume and the contributions

The contributions collected in the volume reflect in their various ways the scientific interests that Sergio Parrinello has cultivated during his career.

6.1 Analytical issues in production and exchange theory

This first section consists of nine contributions which can be grouped within three broad fields.

The first three are highly technical. Eiji Hosoda discusses a specific issue of production diseconomy, looking into the introduction of processes for the abatement and recycling of the bads of production processes in a linear model with linked production, examining its conditions of reproducibility when specific constraints apply on the use of manufacturing residuals. Ian Steedman demonstrates that the assumption of the quasi-concavity of preferences applied to the characteristics does not necessarily transfer to the preferences derived from the goods. This casts serious doubts on the standard assumption of quasi-concavity for the curves of indifference in consumer theory. Duncan Foley analyses the results of a model of trade with disequilibrium prices or without recontracting, applying Edgeworth box construction, and demonstrates that agents of the same type can arrive at different final consumption baskets although they have the same final supply prices. The second group contains four contributions that address, in the case of the first two, aspects of capital theory from a Sraffian viewpoint and, the second two, critical appraisal of the relevance of the category of studies harking back to *Production of Commodities*.

Pierangelo Garegnani analyses the shortcomings of the concept of "quantity of capital" which led the Hicks of *Value and Capital* to adopt a Walrasian representation of capital as a physical vector of factors. In the neoclassical theory this representation became dominant only three decades later, when the final conclusions of the controversy of the 1960s on capital proved the absolute unsustainability at the level of pure theory of the notion of capital as a single magnitude. In more recent years, however, capital taken as a "single commodity" once again found a basic role in the saving–investment process associated with determination of distribution in terms of factor substitution.

Heinz Kurz and Neri Salvadori return to the topic of heterogeneous capital taking their cue from chapter 21, "The marginal equalities", of C. Bidard's *Prices, Reproduction, Scarcity*. They insist, with reference to P. H. Wicksteed, who is cited by Sraffa (1960, pp. v–vi), that one ought to be careful in distinguishing between "spurious margins" and the "genuine thing", and that a careless use of the term "marginal" is a source of "dire confusion". They stress, contrary to Bidard, that the finding of an equality between the rate of profits and the marginal productivity of capital, appropriately defined, implies nothing whatsoever as regards the determination of the level of the rate of profits. "Marginal equalities" must not be mistaken for substantive explanations of economic phenomena, that is, they must not be taken for the "genuine article".

Lynn Mainwaring raises the question as to whether Sraffian theory could serve as a guide for policymakers tackling the problems of the contemporary world, to come up with a negative answer because the "objective" nature of the classical theory, perfectly suited to addressing problems of "long-period analysis", implies a marginal role for "individual or social behaviours", while many of the problems of the contemporary world arise on account of the ways individuals and organisations respond to rapid changes. Guglielmo Chiodi and Leonardo Ditta concur to some extent with Mainwaring's thesis but reject his pessimistic conclusions because, following the drift of a contribution by Parrinello himself, they argue that there is in fact a practicable way out from the problems posed by Mainwaring.

The third group consists of two contributions, both on the pure theory of international trade. Stan Metcalfe outlines an evolutionary theory of international trade linking the changeable structure of distribution of the production at the worldwide level to changes in the pattern of world trade. A static theory of comparative advantages is of little use in such a context. In its place we have a theory of comparative advantages taken as a dynamic process in which the "patterns of trade" are the result of the different dynamics of production and consumption. Takao Fujimoto presents a linear model with linked production and heterogeneous labour in which he analyses the connection between labour value and prices with an extension to unequal trade between countries.

6.2 Post-Keynesian macroeconomics

This second section contains six contributions: the first three set out in their various ways to interpret the present crisis, while the second three address basic aspects of post-Keynesian economic theory.

Amit Bhaduri constructs a model on the basis of which he is able to analyse the connection between the financial sector and the real sector in the recent crisis. Given that the cultural background to the crisis consists in free-market monetarist ideology, the model explores the basic mechanism behind the fluctuation of debt and gains driven by opposing currents deriving from growth in demand supported by credit and growth in service on the accumulated debt.

Claudio Gnesutta analyses the effects of redistribution of the financial risk on the trend in gains on the basis of a given financial structure which is the product of the rules adopted. The author demonstrates that advanced financial systems do not in themselves constitute a guarantee of efficient allocation of financial assets in support of the stable growth of productive capital.

Jan Kregel analyses the "Triffin paradox" and suggests that a similar dilemma is implicit in the present form of globalisation of the international financial and trade system. Recent developments suggest that the doubts about the sustainability of the system were not misplaced.

In his contribution Massimo Pivetti compares the relationship between the monetary interest rate and the general level of prices as taken in "inflation targeting" theory, on the one hand, and in monetary distribution theory on the other hand, with interesting implications.

Amitava Dutt introduces two characteristics into a Harrodian model and a Kalecki–Steindl model. The first is the existence of bands within which the agents cannot change their type of behaviour, while the second states that the agents react in more than one way to a particular disequilibrium. The author demonstrates that not only is path dependence generated with the introduction of these characteristics but also that new elements emerge to meet certain criticisms of this model typology.

Ed Nell's contribution closes the second section. He discusses the circulation of "real and fiat money" in new economies in which the bank system and government operate, distinguishing two different sorts of impact of demand on the economy – with either essentially an effect on prices, or an effect on quantities. In the former case we have "flex-price" economies, in the latter "fix-price" economies, that are adjusted through the multiplier. The different result in terms of demand variation is accounted for by the different technological and cost structures. Nell demonstrates that "real money" functions effectively in a "flex-price" system but generates recession in a "fix-price" system. On the other hand, "fiat money" would destabilise a "flex-price" system because it tends to generate inflation, although it is appropriate for a "fix-price" system.

6.3 History of economic thought and methodology

The third section in the volume contains four contributions. Two deal with the history of thought and two with the appraisal of research in economics, the latter being an issue that Sergio Parrinello has recently been involved in, attempts at an evaluation similar to the research assessment exercise of the United Kingdom having also been undertaken in Italy.

The first contribution is by Alessandro Roncaglia, who looks into the origins of social inequality. After William Petty, he points out, it was Adam Smith who saw the division of labour as the source not only of growth in productivity but also of social stratification, between the classes and within the working classes. Roncaglia investigates as to whether social stratification is indeed a natural phenomenon, looking back to Plato and Aristotle, and on to Paul Samuelson. Smith's thesis is found to be in conflict with the conception that prevailed in classical antiquity and which also underlies the marginalist approach.

Bertram Schefold appraises the figure of the German economist J. H. Von Thünen, looking into the contents of his major works, and also offers some formalisations of his theory of value, adopting both a marginalist and a classical Sraffian framework.

Grazia Ietto-Gillies opens her contribution with some serious criticisms of the evaluation system based on peer review, and goes on to propose an alternative system for assessment of academics which she refers to as the "*ex-post bottom-up Peer Comments system*": an open access system which exploits the new information technologies and multiplies the possibilities for interaction between the members of the academic communities.

Adriano Birolo and Annalisa Rosselli present the findings of their research on a vast database containing the relevant information on the scientific characteristics of the three cohorts of assistant professors recruited in Italy in the early 1980s, the 1990s and the first few years of the new millennium. Their first objective is to trace out the scientific profile of the assistant professor in the early 1980s and the changes that came about in the following 25 years due to general changes in the profession and in the specific conditions of the Italian academic market. The second aim is to see what turn in direction the scientific standard has taken for access to a career as a young professor of economics, the number and typology of publications, the fields of research.

Closing this last section are two brief memoirs casting light on the cultural context that saw Sergio Parrinello's scientific progress grow to maturity. The first, by Flavio Pressacco, depicts Parrinello as professor at the University of Trieste, while the second, by Angelo Marzollo, illustrates the background to the launch of the happy venture of the Trieste Summer School.

Acknowledgements

A great many people, colleagues and in some cases friends, have made this volume possible. In the first place, all those who agreed to contribute with their writings to it. A great deal of the merit for this volume goes to Nicola Acocella and Cristina Marcuzzo, who insisted so forcefully as eventually to persuade me that organising a collection of writings in honour of Sergio Parrinello was not outside my capabilities. Bertram Schefold, Heinz Kurz and Richard Arena succeeded in dispelling my remaining doubts.

Nicola Acocella and the editors shared with me the task of identifying possible contributors, while Nicola Acocella and I jointly undertook the job of inviting contributors and securing their commitment. Heinz Kurz played a key role in picking out the publisher and convincing him that publishing this volume would be an excellent decision.

Nicola Acocella, Claudio Gnesutta, Heinz Kurz and Bertram Schefold read and commented upon an earlier draft of this introduction. Their advice has proved crucial to improving it.

Thanks are also due to the many people who have helped me in reconstructing Sergio's scientific development and career history. Snatches of memoirs, records and documents have been combined to produce a coherent composition. Thus our thanks go, in geographical order, hoping not to have left anyone out, to: in Trieste, Gabriella Benedetti, Sergio Bartole, Mario Petrucco, Linda Livia, Mario Cogoy and Attilio Wedlin; in Udine, Angelo Marzollo and Flavio Pressacco; again in Trieste, but as "Trieste Summer School", Jan Kregel and Bertram Schefold; in Florence, Claudio Cecchi, Marco Dardi and Giandomenico Majone; in Manchester, Ian Steedman, Stan Metcalfe and Takao Fujimoto; in Rome, Nicola Acocella, Claudio Gnesutta, Alberto Himler, Grazia Ietto-Gillies, Cristina Marcuzzo and Alessandro Roncaglia. Special thanks go to Giuli Liebman Parrinello, whom I eventually had to involve to help me fill in the picture.

Appendix A

Sergio Parrinello

A biography

Sergio Parrinello was born in Trieste (in the northeast of Italy) in the late summer of 1935. He studied for his degree in economics at the University of Trieste, where he graduated in 1962, with Mario Arcelli as his supervisor with a thesis in applied economics on the use of Leontief matrices in interregional analysis. Given the academic hierarchy, he embarked on his training and career under the guidance of Manlio Resta, then full professor in the chair of political economy. In the years he spent in Trieste his studies led him to the issues, then looming large in the major international economics journals, of economic growth and structural change, examined in the analytical aspects and policy implications. Resta's cultural disposition kept him at a distance from the critical movement that was growing at the time; nevertheless, he did not discourage his young pupil from following the new paths (indeed, he indirectly encouraged him) leading him in the direction of the critiques being raised by the Cambridge School against the neoclassical theory of capital and distribution. He was immediately appointed temporary assistant, then (1963–5) *tecnico laureato* (a special type of assistant professor) and by 1965–6 he had already begun in his first lectureship, on the history of economic thought. In these early years he also collaborated on the courses that Resta was holding at the newly fledged faculty of economics of Verona, at the time an annex of the University of Padua.

In 1966, having been shortlisted some time before among the candidates for a post as assistant at the University of Rome, he was called as tenured assistant to the chair of political economy occupied by Resta, shortly after moving from Trieste to Rome. In 1968 he qualified as a university lecturer.

He did not abandon the University of Trieste. In the period 1969–72 he held a temporary professorship in economic policy at Trieste.

In 1972 he won a competitive examination to become full professor, and in November of the same year was called to the faculty of economics at the University of Florence. Here he found a decidedly lively cultural environment, with Pierangelo Garegnani and Giacomo Becattini incarnating the lay spirit while Piero Barucci and Piero Tani represented the Catholic persuasion. At the time Florence was frequented by a great many foreign scholars (Ian Steedman, Nicholas Georgescu Roegen, John Eatwell, Richard Kahn and Joan Robinson, to name but a few). Sergio stayed on in Florence until 1978, when he was called to the University of Rome faculty of engineering as the first economist to be assigned the chair in economics applied to engineering. Again, the engineering faculty offered a stimulating environment and Sergio formed a research group on institutionalism. After only a few years, however, the sirens were luring him back to the faculty of economics. In 1981 he returned to the Rome faculty of economics which he had left as assistant in 1972. In November of 1986 he moved to the University of Venice, Economics faculty, but by the November of 1989 he was on his way back to the Rome faculty as professor of mathematical economics and political economy, where he remained until 2006, the year of his retirement.

In 1968–9, on the strength of a scholarship, Parrinello was able to spend some months in London and Cambridge, where he met Sraffa. However, it took another decade for him, by then professor, to begin his travels at the invitation of foreign universities on either side of the Atlantic and weave together that network of acquaintances that proved fundamental for the development of the Summer School of Trieste. In the US he was visiting professor at Rutgers University in 1978. In the early 1980s he went on to hold a number of seminars in various US universities: at Washington University in St Louis, at the University of Colorado at Boulder, at Los Angeles Riverside and at Stanford. In 1982 he became Simon Fellow at the University of Manchester, the years 1984–5 saw him at the J. W. Goethe-Universität of Frankfurt am Main, before going on to spend short periods at the University of Graz, followed by a stint in Berlin and in 1989 at the Wissenschaftszentrum. In 1985 he was at the Italian University of Mogadishu, and in the early 1990s he was visiting professor at the University of Okayama in Japan.

Parrinello was certainly not averse to working in the field of applied economics. In the mid-1970s he coordinated research on the economy of the Trieste area on behalf of the Province of Trieste, then governed by the centre-left, to draw up a plan for the economic development of the area. The network of contacts with the local government was again to prove useful some time later when the Summer School of Trieste was under way, from 1980 to 1990. Sergio managed to obtain local logistic and financial support to organise and run the Summer School, with Pierangelo Garegnani and Jan Kregel assisting Sergio in coordination at the scientific level. The "Scuola di Trieste" is of its kind a virtually unique international venture. Scholars of Sraffian and post-Keynesian backgrounds from many and varied major centres of cultural research met up for ten days of teaching and discussion with young student researchers from various European and American universities.

Sergio Parrinello proved an indefatigable scientific organiser. Indeed, many years before the Trieste School, when still a very young man, he found himself from 1967 sharing the management of *Metroeconomica*, with Mario Resta, with increasing responsibilities, to become the single editor in 1983. In the 1980s the journal served to some extent as a cultural showcase for the Trieste School. As editor he promoted and organised various workshops and conferences. In the 1990s the labours of so many years were crowned with success when *Metroeconomica* was taken up by a major international publisher, guaranteeing its circulation and a more prominent role.

Appendix B

Sergio Parrinello's publications (updated July 2009)[32]

[1] 1965 "L'ottimizzazione della produzione e degli scambi in un sistema pluriregionale: un approccio dinamico", *Economia internazionale*, No. 4.

[2] 1966 "L'indice delle variazioni strutturali nell'analisi della produttività globale", *Giornale degli economisti e annali di economia*, No. 5/6.

[3] 1966 "Alcune implicazioni della diffusione del progresso tecnologico in uno schema classico di crescita economica", *Metroeconomica*, No. 3.

[4] 1966 "Una nota sulla teoria delle invenzioni indotte", *Rivista di politica economica*, No. 12.

[5]   1967 *Alcune considerazioni critiche sul modello disaggregato di L. Pasinetti*, mimeo, delivered at the "Gruppo CNR per lo studio dei problemi economici della distribuzione, del progresso tecnico e dello sviluppo".

[6]   1967 "Le scelte degli investimenti nella ricerca: alcuni problemi metodologici", *Rivista di politica economica*, No. 6 (with G. Majone).

[7]   1970 "Analisi a livello oggettivo e sviluppo economico non bilanciato", *Giornale degli economisti e annali di economia*, No. 5/6.

[8]   1970 "Introduzione ad una teoria neoricardiana del commercio internazionale", *Studi Economici*, No. 2.

[9]   1971 "Un contributo alla teoria dell'impresa jugoslava", *Est-ovest*, No. 3.

[10] 1973 "Distribuzione, sviluppo e commercio internazionale", *Economia-Internazionale*, No. 2.

[11] 1974 "Una nota su alcune recenti teorie dell'impresa jugoslava", *Est-ovest*, No. 1

[12] 1975 "Alcune considerazioni sulla cooperazione Cee-Comecon in relazione alla congiuntura economica dell'Europa occidentale", *Est-ovest*, No. 2

[13] 1975 "Introduzione", *John Stuart Mill, Saggi su alcuni problemi insoluti di economia politica*, ISEDI, Milan.

[14] 1976 "Aspetti controversi del modello keynesiano", *Politica ed Economia*, No. 6.

[15] 1977 "Note sulla nozione di equilibrio nell'economia politica", *Giornale degli Economisti e Annali di Economia*, No. 1–2.

[16] 1979 "Distribution, Growth and International Trade", in Steedman, I. (ed.), *Fundamental Issues in Trade Theory*, Macmillan, London.

[17] 1980 "The Price Level Implicit in Keynes' Effective Demand", *Journal of Post-Keynesian Economics*, No. 3(1).

[18] 1981 *La teoria delle scelte: azioni presenti e gradi di libertà di azioni future*, discussion paper R 81–05, Istituto di Automatica, Facoltà di Ingegneria, Università di Roma.

[19] 1981 "I prezzi impliciti nel principio keynesiano della domanda effettiva", in Graziani, A. (ed.), *Essays in honor of A. De Luca*, Liguori, Naples (revised Italian version of the article [17]).

[20] 1982 "Terra", entry in Lunghini, G. (ed.), *Dizionario di Economia Politica*, Boringhieri, Turin.

[21] 1982 "Some Notes on Monopoly, Competition and the Choice of Techniques", *Manchester School of Economic and Social Studies*, No. 3.

[22] 1982 "Flexibility of Choice and the Theory of Consumption", *Metroeconomica*, No. 1–3.

[23] 1983 "Exhaustible Natural Resources and the Classical Method of Long-Period Equilibrium", in Kregel, J. (ed.), *Distribution, Effective Demand and International Economic Relations*, Macmillan, Basingstoke.

[24] 1984 "La composizione della domanda nel lungo periodo: flessibilità nelle scelte e adattamento all'ambiente", in *I problemi economici della tutela ambientale*, Giuffrè, Milano.

[25] 1984 *On the Role of Demand Schedules: A Comment*, mimeo, Rome.

[26] 1984 "Adaptive Preferences and the Theory of Demand", *Journal of Post-Keynesian Economics*, No. 6(4).

[27] 1984 "In Memory of Manlio Resta", *Metroeconomica*, No. 2–3.

[28] 1985 "Le noyau marshallien de la Théorie Générale", in Barrére, A. (ed.), *Keynes Aujourd'hui: Théories et Politiques*, Economica, Paris.

[29] 1987 *Comparative Institutional Analysis and the Cost of Running the Economy*, mimeo, delivered at the "International Workshop on Income Distribution", University of Tennessee, Gatlingburg, July.

[30] 1988 "On Foreign Trade and the Ricardian Model of Trade", *Journal of Post-Keynesian Economics*, No. 10(4).

[31] 1988 *Costi comparati e norme sociali*, mimeo, "Società Italiana degli Economisti, XXIX Riunione", Rome, 28 October.

[32] 1988 "Il ruolo di una scuola estiva di economia", *Economia Politica*, No. 3.

[33] 1989 "Individualismo metodologico contro altri 'ismi' in economia: un commento", *Economia Politica*, No. 1.

[34] 1989 "Individualismo metodologico ed equilibrio: una replica", *Economia Politica*, No. 1.

[35] 1989 "Norme sociali, fluttuazioni e moneta nel modello $(1 + r)\,Ap + wl = Bp$", *Economia Politica*, No. 2.

[36] 1989 "The Efficiency Wage Hypothesis and the Representation of the Production Process", discussion paper FS 190–3, Wissenschafts-zentrum Berlin fur Sozialforschung.

[37] 1989 "The Marshallian Core of the General Theory", in Barrère, A. (ed.), *Money, Credit and Prices in Keynesian Perspective*, Macmillan, London.

[38] 1989 "Uncertainty and the Residual Hypothesis", in Kregel, J. A. (ed.), *Inflation and Income Distribution in Capitalist Crisis: Essays in Memory of Sidney Weintraub*, New York University Press, New York.

[39] 1989 "Social Norms, Fluctuations and Money in a Linear Model of Prices", in Sebastiani, M. (ed.), *The Notion of Equilibrium in the Keynesian Theory*, St Martin's Press, New York (English version of [35]).

[40] 1990 "Some Reflexions on Equilibrium, Expectations and Random Disturbances", *Political Economy, Studies in the Surplus Approach*, special issue, No. 1–2(6).

[41] 1991 "On Foreign Trade and the Ricardian Model of Trade", in Blaug, M. (ed.), *David Ricardo (1772–1823), Elgar Reference Collection series. Pioneers in Economics series*, vol. 14, Edward Elgar, Cheltenham (previously published [30]).

[42] 1993 "Non Pure Private Goods in the Economics of Production Processes", *Metroeconomica*, No. 3.

[43] 1995 "The Efficiency Wage Hypothesis in the Long Period", in Harcourt, G., Roncaglia, A. and Rowley, R. (eds), *Income and Employment in Theory and Practice: Essays in Memory of Athanasios Asimakopulos*, St Martin's Press, New York; Macmillan Press, London.

[44] 1995 "Rendimenti di scala, effetti esterni e scelta delle tecniche", *Economia Politica*, No. 1

[45] 1995 *"Some Notes of the Transfer of Statistical Equilibrium from Physics to Economics"*, Working Paper, No. 6, Dipartimento di Economia Pubblica, Università di Roma "La Sapienza".

[46] 1996 "Equilibri Statistici e Nuovi Microfondamenti della Macroeconomia", in Gnesutta, C. (ed.), *Incertezza, Moneta, Aspettative ed Equilibrio: saggi in onore di Fausto Vicarelli*, Il Mulino, Bologna.

[47] 1997 "Returns to Scale, Externalities and the Choice of Techniques", *Manchester School of Economic and Social Studies*, No. 3

[48] 1998 "Equilibrium", entry in Kurz, H. and Salvadori N. (eds), *The Elgar Companion to Classical Economics*, Edward Elgar, Cheltenham.

[49] 1998 "The Second Fundamental Theorem of Welfare Economics: A Pedagogical Note", *Economia Politica*, No. 2.

[50] 1998 *Sraffa's Quantities and the Method of Separate Stages of Analysis*, mimeo, delivered at the Conference "Sraffa and Modern Economics", Rome, October.

[51] 1999 "Explaining and Understanding Economic Events by Contrasting Alternatives", *Metroeconomica*, No. 3

[52] 1999 "Supply Constraints on Employment and Output: NAIRU versus Natural Rate: Comment", in Gandolfo, G. and Marzano, F. (eds), *Economic Theory and Social Justice*, St Martin's Press, New York; Macmillan Press, London.

[53] 2000 *Linguaggio e Realtà in Economia*, Esculapio, Bologna

[54] 2001 "The Price of Exhaustible Resources", *Metroeconomica*, No. 3

[55] 2002 "Sraffa's Legacy in Economics: Some Critical Notes", *Metroeconomica*, No. 3

[56] 2002 "The 'Institutional Factor' in the Theory of International Trade: New vs. Old Trade Theories", in Boehm, S. *et al.* (eds), *Is There Progress in Economics? Knowledge, Truth and the History of Economic Thought*, Edward Elgar, Cheltenham and Northampton, MA.

[57] 2003 *The Myth of the Service Economy*, Working Paper, No. 55, Dipartimento di Economia Pubblica, Università di Roma "La Sapienza", June.

[58] 2003 *Exhaustible Natural Resources, Normal Prices and Intertemporal Equilibrium*, Working Paper, No. 57, Dipartimento di Economia Pubblica, Università di Roma "La Sapienza", December.

[59] 2004 "The Notion of Effectual Supply and the Theory of Normal Prices with Exhaustible Natural Resources", *Economic Systems Research*, No. 3.

[60] 2004 *Intertemporal Competitive Equilibrium: A Reappraisal of a Basic Source of Instability*, Working Paper, No. 67, Dipartimento di Economia Pubblica, Università di Roma "La Sapienza", April.

[61] 2004 "The Service Economy Revisited", *Structural Change and Economic Dynamics*, No. 4.

[62] 2005 "Intertemporal Competitive Equilibrium, Capital and the Stability of Tatonnement Pricing Revisited", *Metroeconomica*, No. 4.

[63] 2006 *National Competitiveness and Absolute Advantage in a Global Economy*, Working Paper No. 95, Dipartimento di Economia Pubblica, Università di Roma "La Sapienza", November.

[64] 2007 "Introduction: A Note on Goods and Services and Input–Output Analysis", *Metroeconomica*, No. 3.

[65] 2008 "The Stability of General Intertemporal Equilibrium: A Note on Schefold", *Metroeconomica*, No. 2.

[66] 2008 "A Reply to the Comment by Duncan Foley", *Metroeconomica*, No. 2.

[67] 2008 "A Reply to Schefold", in Chiodi, G. and Ditta, L. (eds), *Sraffa or An Alternative Economics*, Palgrave Macmillan, Basingstoke.

[68] 2009 "The Notion of National Competitiveness in a Global Economy", in Vint, J., Metcalfe, J. S., Kurz, H. D., Salvadori, N. and Samuelson, P. (eds), *Economic Theory and Economic Thought, Essays in Honour of Ian Steedman*, Routledge, London.

Notes

1 A biography of Sergio Parrinello appears in the appendices to this introduction, together with a list of his publications. Text citations to his works refer to a number in square brackets, the format used in the appendices.

2 Porta (2000, 2004). An inside reconstruction of the Italian debate on the new paradigm in the 1960s and 1970s is offered by one of its protagonists, Pierangelo Garegnani (Garegnani 1984). Interesting evidence was also provided by Paolo Sylos Labini (Sylos Labini 1984).

3 The destination preferred by young scholars following in the wake of Garegnani and Pasinetti in the 1960s (Casarosa 2004 and Ciocca 2004).

4 Some hints for interpretation can be found in Marcuzzo and Rosselli (2002), and the clear, well-structured position in Mainwaring (2009).

5 The first included Pierangelo Garegnani, Luigi Pasinetti and, to some extent, the young Luigi Spaventa.

6 Those who lacked the right sort of support in Italy to obtain scholarships to study abroad had no choice but to follow the traditional postgraduate academic path, pursuing some lines of research with the – at times distant – guidance of the professor with whom graduation was normally completed, without following any formalised line of study. In the following passage, drawn from a note drafted for the conference "In ricordo di Manlio Resta nel centenario della nascita" (In memory of Manlio Resta on the hundredth anniversary of his birth) (Rome, ABI, November 2008), Sergio Parrinello offers an autobiographical example of this practice and at the same time reference to his early topics of research and the origins of his interest in Sraffian theory. He writes:

> At the beginning of the 1960s Manlio Resta had sensed the importance of a slender volume little known in Italy entitled "Production of Commodities by Means of Commodities". I remember how we gathered round to read it and the discussions on each page of that enigmatic text by Sraffa, which Resta tackled together with a quartet of us young assistants on the winter evenings in Trieste. We would spend long evenings in his room in the Institute of Trieste deep in discussion.... Outside the cold northeast wind was blowing and we could hear it whistling through the triple glaze of the windows on the top floor of the Faculty. Here was prompted my interest in certain not exactly orthodox contributions on economics, which I tracked down with great curiosity among the shelves of the

Institute library: Marx, Keynes and Schumpeter, but also Simon, Boulding, Baumol and Hirschman were among the authors I read most keenly, stimulated by those evening meetings with Resta, while the hurdle represented by Sraffa's slim volume was always there as an intellectual challenge.

And again, we read in this passage [27]:

With regard to Resta's tendency to give preference to the theory of production and efficient distribution of resources, I well remember the intense discussions that he loved to encourage among his students, at the beginning of the Sixties in Trieste on models of linear programming applied to the allocation of resources, on models of optimum growth and on the analysis of technical progress.... I shall not forget the genuine interest for the science that induced Resta, during his time in Trieste, Verona and Rome, to go deeply in his writings and in his discussions with students, into the theories of von Neumann and Sraffa and to face up to considerable mathematical difficulties.

7 He made only fleeting visits to Cambridge.
8 It is in fact difficult to situate his work within one of the three Sraffian schools of thought (Roncaglia 1991).
9 The Pasinetti model was also criticised on the grounds that in general different "horizontal" matrices can generate the same set of vertically integrated sectors.
10 Listed below by broad content typologies are Sergio Parrinello's contributions as from 1970.

1 "Constructive" theories of the paradigm

- foreign trade   [8], [10], [16], [30], [41], [56], [63], [68]
- exhaustible natural resources [20], [23], [54], [58], [59]
- institutional analysis   [29], [31], [35], [36], [39], [42], [43], [57], [61], [64]

2 Themes within the neo-Ricardian paradigm

- demand composition and   [18], [22], [24], [25], [26], [38], [51]
  uncertainty
- market forms   [21]
- returns to scale   [44], [47]

3 Methodology and economic theory

- equilibrium   [15], [33], [34], [40], [45], [46], [48], [50], [60], [65], [66], [67]
- keynesian themes   [14], [17], [19], [28], [37], [52]
- history of economic analysis [13], [55]

4 Miscellany   [26], [32], [49], [53]
5 Socialist economies   [9], [11], [12]

His contributions before 1970 could be grouped in the rough category of "Growth" themes.
11 [8] and [10], for example.
12 As from 1980 about 20 per cent of his contributions are in Italian.
13 In a footnote at the end of the article, he pointed out that he had received from Ian Steedman and Stan Metcalfe two manuscripts addressing similar problems with a neo-Ricardian approach, albeit starting from different hypotheses, when he had already finished the article. The manuscripts bore the titles "A Ricardian Model of Trade and Income Distribution" and "On Trade between Countries with the same Ricardian Technology". In the course of 1970–1, the second manuscript was presented by Ian Steedman in a scientific assembly of the "Gruppo C.N.R. per lo studio dei problemi

economici della distribuzione, del progresso tecnico e dello sviluppo" and discussed by the participants. As from 1972 Metcalfe and Steedman published various articles on international trade taking a neo-Ricardian approach, collected in Steedman (1977, 1979).

14 Garegnani (1970), Metcalfe and Steedman (1972).

15 P. Krugman, G. Grossman and E. Helpman are the leading representatives of the NTT.

16 See the references contained in [20] and [23].

17 Schefold (1989, chapter 19.b) finds in Parrinello [20] the first attempt to deal with exhaustible natural resources within a neo-Ricardian framework, thereby deriving the Hotelling rule. The appraisal is repeated in Schefold (2001, p. 319, note 2): "The pioneer of the approach was Parrinello (1982)."

18 We owe to Garegnani (1976, 1983) conceptual depiction of the equilibrium as "long-period positions" in the models of classical derivation.

19 Strictly speaking this position is attributable to one of the three schools of Sraffian derivation (Roncaglia 1991), namely that of Garegnani.

20 A notion subsequently developed in [45] and [46].

21 A topic already addressed in [39].

22 In an unpublished text [50] Parrinello offers an incisive outline of the theoretical function of the "core" of classical theory:

> In a general sense, an economic magnitude is defined "normal" within the classical approach because it is supposed to be theoretical outcome of the power, force, capacity of the free competition and wealth seeking behaviour, once these explanatory factors have been isolated by others. Therefore a normal magnitude is not *defined* as an average over its actual values.... The field of useful application of the wealth seeker and free competition assumptions ... it is not confined to the unknowns of equation $(1 + r) \mathbf{A}p + w\mathbf{l} = \mathbf{B}p$.... the same basic assumptions can be also used to theorize part of the quantity side. In this sense, beside normal prices and normal rate of profits, we can conceive a normal output, a normal real wage, a normal technique (i.e. cost minimizing technique), a normal employment and a normal degree of capacity utilization etc.

23 He returned to the theme of equilibrium in the Sraffian model in subsequent texts ([60], [62], [65], [66], [67]), but within a context of intertemporal equilibrium in which a heterodox *tatonnement* process is at work.

24 I owe much of the information on the School of Trieste to the reminiscences of Jan Kregel, who was good enough to send me a written record. In a series of telephone conversations Angelo Marzollo also offered me some further useful references. For the contents of the School I drew upon contributions by Arena (1987) and Parrinello himself [32].

25 The Trieste Summer School was the fruit of an idea shared by P. Garegnani, J. Kregel and S. Parrinello. The first step, in 1980 in Udine, was to organise a conference under the auspices of Angelo Marzollo and the Centre for Mechanical Science (CISM). Over 30 economists from 15 countries having direct or indirect interest in the Cambridge School met and decided to create, for the summer of the following year, an international summer school. The Centre for Advanced Economic Studies was constituted, to become subsequently the Centre for the Study of Political Economy, with premises in Trieste, and a board formed by Angelo Marzollo, Giampaolo de Ferra, Pierangelo Garegnani, Jan Kregel and Sergio Parrinello, the three last named, the economists, constituting the Scientific Committee which organised the first edition of the Trieste Summer School in the late summer of 1981. The School went on from year to year until 1990. Each edition of the School was regularly followed by an international conference open to all. The scientific committee dealt with the didactic planning: it decided on the programmes, professors, students and foreign and Italian graduates entering upon university careers, in such a way as to preserve a certain

equilibrium between the various strands of the Cambridge tradition. The lectures and workshops were held in the morning and early afternoon in the right conditions to favour full and general discussion. Sergio Parrinello was the key figure and kept in touch with the local authorities for logistic and financial support, securing further funds from the economic committee of the CNR (National Research Council) and supervising all the organisational aspects of the school.

26 In the last years of the School's activity, attesting to the widening range of theoretical orientations, there came to work side-by-side with the five original members of the Centre for the Study of Political Economy G. Becattini, G. Borruso, A. Graziani, L. Pasinetti, A. Roncaglia and P. Sylos Labini.

27 Kurz and Gehrke (1999) outline the history of the journal.

28 A critical re-evocation of this important scholar is to be seen in Pomini (2009) and in Shackle (1965).

29 The publisher of the journal was the Casa Editrice Cappelli with a registered office in Bologna and operational base in Trieste where it ran the eponymous Cappelli bookshop. *Metroeconomica* came to light as a publication of the Trieste bookshop, which was already acting as publisher for texts edited by professors of the local university. In 1962, on the death of its founder, who had in fact moved on to the University of Genoa in the mid-1950s, the publisher Cappelli, owner of the journal, invited Manlio Resta, who had succeeded Fossati to the Chair in Political Economy in Trieste, to take over editorship of the journal.

30 Cappelli was a small publisher working on the Italian market alone, without the scope for circulation that can only be achieved by an international publisher specialising in scientific material.

31 In the last few years he has enjoyed the support of Neri Salvadori as second managing editor.

32 This bibliography has been collected consulting the databases "Econlit", "Essper" and other minor sources.

References

Arena, R. (1987), "L'école internationale d'été de Trieste (1981–1985): vers une synthèse classico-Keynesienne?", *Oeconomica*, No. 7.

Bidard C. and Erreygers, G. (2002), "A Critique of Post-Sraffian Approaches to Exhaustible Resources", Montréal, mimeo.

Casarosa, C. (2004), "Gli studi nel Regno Unito della seconda generazione" in Garofalo, G. and Graziani, A. (eds), *La formazione degli economisti in Italia, 1950–1975*, Bologna, Il Mulino.

Ciocca, P. L. (2004), "Il contributo di via Nazionale", in Garofalo, G. and Graziani, A. (eds), *La formazione degli economisti in Italia, 1950–1975*, Bologna, Il Mulino.

Garegnani, P. (1970), "Heterogeneous Capital, the Production Function and the Theory of Distribution", *Review of Economic Studies*, No. 3.

Garegnani, P. (1976), "On a Change in the Notion of Equilibrium in Recent Work on Value: A Comment on Samuelson", in Brown, M., Sato, K. and Zarembka, P. (eds), *Essays in Modern Capital Theory*, Amsterdam, North Holland.

Garegnani, P. (1983), "The Classical Theory of Wages and the Role of Demand Schedules in the Determination of Relative Prices", *American Economic Review (Paper and Proceedings)*, No. 2.

Garegnani, P. (1984), "Su alcune questioni controverse circa la critica della teoria della distribuzione dominante e lo sviluppo di una teoria alternativa", *Quaderni di storia dell'Economia Politica*, No. 2.

Kregel, J. (ed.) (1983), *Distribution, Effective Demand and International Economic Relations*, Macmillan, Basingstoke.

Kurz, H. D. (ed.) (2000), *Critical Essays on Piero Sraffa Legacy in Economics*, Cambridge, Cambridge, University Press.

Kurz, H. and Gehrke, C. (1999), "Metroeconomica at 50", *Metroeconomica*, No. 3.

Mainwaring, L. (2009), "Can Sraffa Point Us to a Better Future?", this volume.

Marcuzzo, M. C. and Rosselli, A. (2002), "Economics as History of Economics: The Italian Case in Retrospect", *History of Political Economy*, Vol. 34, pp. 98–109, Supplement.

Metcalfe, J. S. and Steedman, I. (1972), "Heterogeneous Capital and the HOS Theory of Trade", in Parking, J. M. and Nobay, A. R (eds), *Essays in Modern Economics*, London, Longman.

Metcalfe, J. S. and Steedman, I. (1973), "On Foreign Trade", *Economia Internazionale*, Nos 3–4.

Pomini, M. (2009), "A Note on Metroeconomica: Shackle's Contribution", *Metroeconomica*, No. 2.

Porta, P. L. (2000), "Europe and the Post-1945 Internationalization of Political Economy: The Case of Italy", in Coats, A.W. (ed.), *The Development of Economics in Western Europe since 1945*, London, Routledge.

Porta, P. L. (2004), "Tradizione e innovazione negli studi economici nell'Italia del Novecento", in Garofalo, G. and Graziani, A. (eds), *La formazione degli economisti in Italia, 1950–1975*, Bologna, Il Mulino.

Roncaglia, A. (1991), "The Sraffian Schools", *Review of Political Economy*, Vol. 3, No. 2; English translation of "Le scuole sraffiane", in Becattini, G. (ed.), *Il pensiero economico: temi, problemi e scuole*, Turin, Biblioteca dell'economista, ottava serie, UTET, pp. 233–74.

Schefold, B. (1989), *Mr. Sraffa on Joint Production and Other Essays*, London, Unwin Hyman.

Schefold, B. (2001), "Critique of the Corn–Guano Model", *Metroeconomica*, No. 3.

Shackle, G. L. S. (1965), "Eraldo Fossati, 1902–1962", *Econometrica*, No. 3.

Sraffa, P. (1960), *Production of Commodities by Means of Commodities. Prelude to a Critique of Economic Theory*, Cambridge, Cambridge University Press.

Steedman, I. (ed.) (1977), *Saggi sulla teoria del commercio internazionale*, Venice, Marsilio Editori.

Steedman, I. (ed.) (1979), *Fundamental Issues in Trade Theory*, London, Macmillan.

Sylos Labini, P. (1984), "L'attività svolta nel periodo 1964–1982 dal gruppo di Economia costituito presso il C.N.R.", *Quaderni di storia dell'Economia Politica*, No. 2.

Sylos Labini, P. (ed.) (1973), *Prezzi relativi e distribuzione del reddito*, Turin, Boringhieri.

Velupillai, K. Vela (1989), "The Existence of the Standard System: Sraffa's Constructive Proof", *Political Economy Studies in the Surplus Approach*, No. 1.

Velupillai, K. Vela (2008), "Sraffa's Mathematical Economics: A Constructive Interpretation", *Journal of Economic Methodology*, No. 4.

Part I

Analytical issues in production and exchange theory

1 Bads as joint products in a linear production system

*Eiji Hosoda**

1 Introduction

The classical economic theory rehabilitated by Sraffa (1960) has had a great impact on economists who work on the reproducibility of a capitalist economy and distribution of income. It is really amazing to see that not only non-mainstream economists but mainstream ones are deeply affected by the rehabilitation of classical economics. It is quite natural to develop further the idea of reproducibility of a pure capitalist economy in order to capture more complicated aspects of a modern capitalist economy where environmental issues among others are gaining more serious attention. Obviously, sustainable development has become an unavoidable concept for human beings, and sustainability is a natural extension of reproducibility of a capitalist economy.

To develop an economic theory in this direction, one important problem must be sorted out and answered; how one deals properly with residuals, which may be required neither for consumption nor for production, in an economic model. The purpose of this chapter is to consider this problem following the classical tradition, and demonstrate how a linear production model based upon the tradition can contribute to the understanding of sustainable development.

This problem has been ignored for such a long time, evidenced by the fact that the assumption of free disposal has been adopted. It is quite interesting to see that this assumption was adopted by both mainstream and non-mainstream economists. It was such a convenient assumption that it was hard for quite a few economists to dispense with it.

It must, however, be remembered that such a distinguished scholar as Debreu (1962) tackles the problem in a rather early stage of the history of the general equilibrium analysis. He proves the existence of an equilibrium solution without depending upon the free-disposal assumption in an abstract economic model. Quite a few researchers follow his research agenda, and develop an elegant model without the assumption (Hart and Kuhn 1975; Bergstrom 1976; and Gay 1979). One common feature of their highly sophisticated general equilibrium models is that prices of commodities which are disposed of must be negative.[1] Consequently, they have shown that commodities in a broad sense consist of not only goods but also bads.

A further important contribution to the problem comes from a different school, namely, a modern classical economist. Franke (1986) analyzes a Sraffian type of general joint production model, using the concept of a cost-minimizing system. He tries to show that a classical notion of equilibrium holds valid in a more general setting which reflects realities, getting rid of the assumption of free disposal. As in the cases above, it is shown that prices of some commodities may be negative, when an equality system is adopted for description of a quantity aspect of an economy.

He notices the significance of negatively priced commodities (discommodities) more than the mainstream economists we have mentioned above, and explains the meaning of negative prices. Since negatively priced commodities, namely bads, are given more concrete meaning as waste than the previous studies, costly disposal processes and demand for bads are naturally introduced and well explained in his model.

To the best of the author's knowledge, Lager (2001) is one of the most comprehensive studies on reproducibility of a capitalist economy in this line.[2] Although he inherits the spirit of modern classical economists, he is more conscious of the problem of bads as an environmental issue, and deals with the long-run classical equilibrium with costly disposal processes more elegantly than previous researchers by means of a linear complementary theory.

One of the characteristics of his model is that restriction of free disposal is carefully introduced into his model, in the sense that a certain amount of disposal of residuals may be allowed instead of zero emission, although free disposal is restricted. Thus, whether some commodities may be goods or free goods is endogenously determined.

Yet, a more interesting feature of this chapter is that whether commodities in a broad sense may be goods or bads is shown to depend upon economic parameters as well as being endogenously determined. This means that residuals from production processes may possibly be resources which are positively priced, just like ordinary resources. Clearly, some residuals are bads or more simply waste which must be treated properly on a daily basis. In this way, the relativity of residuals' nature is revealed in a very persuasive way.

Kurz (2006) surveys the goods/bads problem in the traditional theory of joint production, demonstrating that quite a few classical economists have noticed that some commodities may be negatively priced and they have tried to formulate the problem in one way or another. It is revealed that, although the existence of bads and activation of costly disposal processes have not been satisfactorily theorized, the problem itself has been debated among some classical economists.

By means of basic concepts and elementary diagrams, he also shows how one can deal with the costly disposal problem, following the classical tradition. From his argument, he concludes as follows:

> One of the lessons the above example teaches us is that there is generally no *a priori* distinction possible between goods or commodities on the one hand and bads or discommodities on the other. Whether a product belongs to one

class or the other depends not only on the needs and wants of society but also on the technical alternative available to producers. What in one system of production-cum-disposal is a bad, might in another one be good.

(Kurz 2006, p. 295)

Basically, we follow Lager (2001) in formalizing the following economic model. Although we share the fundamental spirit of pursuing the problem with him, there are some differences between his model and ours. First, he assumes that the requirements for consumption denoted by f are given, following the Sraffian tradition. On the other hand, we assume that consumption depends upon both activity and price levels. Second, we explicitly consider a savings–investment relationship, which is not taken into account in his model. Third, we study a relationship between the binding disposal restriction and inferiority of processes, and explore how tightening the restriction affects per capita consumption. Fourth, being related to the first and second points, we prove the existence of equilibrium, using a different mathematical method from Lager's. Since per capita consumption depends upon prices and so linearity collapses in the consumption side, a linear complementary theory cannot be utilized here. Instead, the Gale–Nikaido–Debreu lemma is fully exploited. Altogether, it might be said that the present model is slightly inclined to a linear production model *à la* Morishima though Lager is more loyal to the original Sraffian style.[3]

In the next section, we present the basic assumptions and show the simple model in which costly disposal processes, whether they be recycling processes or waste treatment processes, satisfy some inferiority criterion. Then, the conditions to guarantee the existence of equilibrium are shown. At the same time, we explore characters of the set of a disposal constraint vector which is compatible with equilibrium solutions. It is also studied how tightening the constraint affects per capita consumption. In section 3, we generalize the model, handling the case in which commodities in a broad sense may be goods, free goods, or bads depending upon economic circumstances. The final section gives some concluding remarks.

2 The basic settings

In this section, the basic model and some assumptions are presented. In order to make the explanation precise, an inequality system is utilized rather than an equality system. In the process of transformation of mathematical expressions, we gradually introduce an equality system to utilize a square matrix theory. A more general model will be shown in section 3.

2.1 The basic model and assumptions

Let us suppose there are n normal commodities (goods), whose production creates k residuals. Those residuals are supposed to affect the natural environment if they are disposed of freely without proper treatment. Residuals are defined as "bads" when free disposal of those residuals is restricted by a binding constraint and negatively priced. Bads are joint products of normal commodities or goods. Each commodity (good) is assumed to be produced by a unique technique: there is no choice of technique. This assumption is not essential, and choice of technique can be easily introduced into the model. However, we assume only one technique for each commodity just for simplicity.

It is supposed that there are abatement or recycling processes (which are called AR processes for short) in an economy. The former processes input commodities and residuals, transforming residuals into substances which are not harmful to nature and human beings. The latter processes input commodities (goods) and residuals, transforming residuals into commodities usable for consumption or production, namely goods. Some of the residuals may be bads. We do not exclude the case where some residuals may be goods, although we deal with this case later (in section 3). First, it is assumed that all the residuals are bads.

Then input and output matrices as well as a labor input vector can be written as follows:

$$\tilde{A} = \begin{pmatrix} \overbrace{A}^{n} & \overbrace{A_W}^{k} \\ O & I_k \end{pmatrix} \begin{matrix} \}n \\ \}k \end{matrix} \quad \tilde{B} = \begin{pmatrix} \overbrace{I_n}^{n} & \overbrace{B_W}^{k} \\ W & O \end{pmatrix} \begin{matrix} \}n \\ \}k \end{matrix} \quad l = (\overbrace{l_A}^{n}, \overbrace{l_W}^{k}).$$

Following conventional notation, A is an input matrix ($n \times n$) in a production sector which is assumed to be indecomposable. This means that all goods are basic commodities in Sraffa's sense (Sraffa 1960). Matrix A_W denotes an input matrix ($n \times k$) of AR processes. Since it is assumed that only one abatement or recycling process corresponds to one type of residual, a k-dimensional identity matrix I_k is denoted under A_W. This assumption can also be relaxed without difficulty as shown in section 3. It must be noted that residuals are supposed to be inputs in AR processes.

Since a possibility of joint production of normal commodities is excluded here, an n-dimensional identity matrix I_n appears in the upper left corner of $\tilde{B}$. Matrix W is an output matrix ($k \times n$) of residuals. Each column and row of W is supposed to have at least one positive component. B_W is an output matrix of AR sectors. If a process is an abatement process, the column of B_W corresponding to the process is zero. As for a recycling process, the corresponding column of B_W has a positive component. For simplicity, let us assume that a recycling process produces only one commodity, and then the column of B_W has at most one positive component. Assuming that abatement or recycling processes output no residuals, we put a zero matrix in the lower right corner of $\tilde{B}$. This is not assumed in section 3. Vector l_A is an n-dimensional labor input vector of production sectors, and l_W a k-dimensional labor input vector of AR processes. It is assumed $l = (l_A, l_W)$ is positive.

Then a cost–price relationship and a supply–demand relationship are expressed as

$$\left|\begin{array}{rcl} p\tilde{B} & \leq & (1+r)p\tilde{A} + wl \\ p\tilde{B}x & = & (1+r)p\tilde{A}x + wlx \\ x_A + B_W x_W & \geq & (1+g)(Ax_A + A_W x_W) + C \\ p_A(x_A + B_W x_W) & = & (1+g)p_A(Ax_A + A_W x_W) + p_A C \\ Wx_A & \leq & (1+g)x_W + q \\ p_W W x_A & = & (1+g)p_W x_W + p_W q \end{array}\right.$$

which will be analyzed in detail in the following. Here, $p = (p_A, p_W)$, $x = \begin{pmatrix} x_A \\ x_W \end{pmatrix}$, r, g, w and $\tilde{C} = \begin{pmatrix} C \\ q \end{pmatrix}$ are a price vector of goods (p_A) is an n-dimensional row vector) and C, residuals (p_W is a k-dimensional row vector), an activity vector of normal production processes (x_A is an n-dimensional coloumn vector) and AR processes (x_W is a k-dimensional column vector), a rate of profit, a growth rate, a wage rate and a vector of consumption (C is an n-dimensional column vector) and restriction on disposal of residuals (q is a k-dimensional column vector), respectively.

The above expression implies that the following must hold in an equilibrium. There is no extra profit in any process (the first inequality), and a process which runs a deficit is not activated (the first equality). There is no excess demand for any commodity (the second inequality), and a price of any overproduced commodity is zero (the second equality).[4] Finally, the total amount of each residual disposed of must not be greater than that which is treated by AR processes and, in addition, allowed to be discharged to the environment (the third inequality), and if the former is strictly smaller than the latter, the disposal fee is zero (the third equality).

In the first half of the chapter, we mainly deal with the case in which all the activities are utilized. Hence, there might not seem to be any problem even if cost–price and supply–demand relationships are expressed by equalities instead of inequalities. Yet, since some subtleties occur when a binding constraint on residuals takes a specific vector, and since inequality expressions are consistent with the treatment taken in the second half of the chapter, we dare to express the relationships by inequalities here.

For an economy to be productive, the following must hold:[5]

Assumption 1 $\exists x_A \geqslant 0$ s.t. $(I - A)x_A \geqslant 0$.

Assumption 1 means that matrix A satisfies the Hawkins–Simon condition. This assumption, however, does not guarantee that the whole system including AR processes is reproducible. Hence, an extended Hawkins–Simon condition must be introduced to guarantee reproducibility of the whole system.

When an activity level is $x = (x_A^T, x_W^T)^T$, the input and output are expressed as $Ax_A + A_W x_W$ and $x_A + B_W x_W$, respectively.[6] Suppose that disposal of residuals is constrained by vector q with equality, i.e. $Wx_A = q + x_W$. Then final demand vector d^f is expressed as

$$d^f = (I - A, B_W - A_W) \begin{pmatrix} x_A \\ x_W \end{pmatrix}.$$

Substituting $x_W = Wx_A - q$ into the above equation, the following is obtained:

$$d^f = (I - A^+)x_A - (B_W - A_W) q$$

where $A^+ \equiv A - (B_W - A_W)W$. For the above equation to have a non-negative solution for sufficiently small non-negative q and any non-negative d^f, matrix A^+ satisfies the Hawkins–Simon condition. Hence, we assume

Assumption 2 A^+ is indecomposable, $A^+ > 0$ and $\exists x_A > 0$ s.t. $(I - A^+)x_A \geqslant 0$.

The assumption that A^+ is indecomposable is just for simplicity.

If Assumption 2 is satisfied, there is positive x_A and x_W for sufficiently small q from $x_W = Wx_A - q$.[7] Then it is clear that there exists a positive rate of growth g such that $[I - (1 + g)A]x_A + [B_W - (1 + g)A_W]x_W \geqslant 0$ for some positive $x = (x_A^T, x_W^T)^T$.

Since we would like to describe an economy as simply as possible, we adopt the easiest assumption on saving behavior: capitalists do not consume and workers do not save. Therefore, the profit rate equals the growth rate, i.e. $r = g$.

Let us make a remark here. It is assumed that each component of q is small enough so that equation $Wx_A = q + x_W$ holds. Since we are considering a growing economy where free disposal is restricted, this assumption is justified. Yet, it may be possible to suppose the restriction is not binding for some residuals, and the constraint holds with inequality, instead of equality, i.e. $Wx_A < q + x_W$. This possibility will be taken into account in section 3.

2.2 The price side

In this subsection, we discuss how an economy can be reproducible when a constraint on disposal of residuals is binding, using a square matrix theory. For a while, we proceed with the analysis, assuming that the wage rate is positive. In the final part of this subsection, we briefly refer to the case in which it is zero.

Now the cost–price equations are expressed as follows:

$$\begin{cases} p_A + p_W W = (1 + r)p_A A + wl_A \\ p_A B_W = (1 + r)(p_A A_W + p_W) + wl_W. \end{cases} \tag{1}$$

Suppose, for an explanatory reason, that AR processes are not activated. Then, we can set $p_W = 0$ in (1), and have

$$p_A = (1 + r)p_A A + wl_A,$$

a conventional cost–price equation. From this, the following is obtained:

$$1 = wl_A [I - (1 + r)A]^{-1}d, \tag{2}$$

where d denotes numeraire basket and $pd = 1$. Equation (2) expresses the wage–profit frontier.

Since AR processes are not supposed to be activated in this case, residuals are freely disposed of into the natural environment. As the amount of residuals increases in the natural environment, it will have a negative effect on human economic activities. If disposal of residuals continues without any constraint, even workers' health will be damaged. Thus, the reproducibility of an economy will surely be disturbed.

Although this negative effect may possibly be foreseen by capitalists, they may be reluctant to take definite action to reduce disposal of residuals, since the reduction of residuals should definitely mean reduction of their profits, as actually seen in the real world. Moreover, the negative effect of free disposal of residuals on an economy will possibly be future matter. In such an instance, the government must control the amount of residuals disposed of, imposing some constraints on them. This restriction is expressed by q in the present model. We will explicitly consider the restriction in subsection 2.3.

When all AR processes are activated by government restriction, the following can be obtained from (1):

$$p_A \left(I + \frac{B_W W}{1 + r} \right) = (1 + r)p_A \left(A + \frac{A_W W}{1 + r} \right) + w \left(l_A + \frac{l_W W}{1 + r} \right). \tag{3}$$

Before we begin the analysis of the price formation represented by (1), let us make important definitions for the later argument in this section. Since the possibility that some residuals may become goods or free goods is basically excluded in this section, certain conditions are required for the disposal constraint to be meaningful and, thus, for negativity of prices of residuals to be guaranteed.

Let us make the following two matrices:

$$\Upsilon^{(i)}(r) \equiv \begin{pmatrix} I - (1 + r)A & [B_W -(1 + r)A_W]^{(i)} \\ W & -(1 + r)I_k \\ -l_A & -l_{wi} \end{pmatrix},$$

and

$$\Upsilon^{+(i)}(r) \equiv \begin{pmatrix} \left[\left[I + \frac{B_W W}{1 + r} \right] - (1 + r) \left[A + \frac{A_W W}{1 + r} \right] \right] & [B_W - (1 + r)A_W]^{(i)} \\ 0 & - (1 + r) \\ -\left[l_A + \frac{l_W W}{1 + r} \right] & -l_{wi} \end{pmatrix},$$

where $[B_W - (1 + r)A_W]^{(i)}$ and l_{wi} denote the i-th column of $[B_W - (1 + r)A_W]$ and the i-th component of l_w, respectively.

The former matrix, namely $\Upsilon^{(i)}(r)$ refers to the original price system (1), while the latter, namely $\Upsilon^{+(i)}(r)$, to the integrated system where (3) is considered instead of the first equation of (1).

Then, the following definitions are made:

Definition 1 (Modified F-inferiority of AR processes) *If there exists a non-negative n dimensional column vector y such that*

$$\Upsilon^{(i)}(r)\begin{pmatrix} y \\ -1 \end{pmatrix} \geqslant 0$$

for i, the i-th process is said to satisfy modified F-inferiority.

This definition means that the i-th AR process is F-inferior, although the definition of F-inferiority here is a little different from the conventional one, since the rate of profit appears in the matrix $\Upsilon^{(i)}(r)$.[8] Thus, the inferiority definition here is not only on a technical condition but on an economic condition since the expression of $\Upsilon^{(i)}(r)$ contains a profit factor.

Definition 2 (Modified F-inferiority of AR processes in the integrated system)

$$\Upsilon^{+(i)}(r)\begin{pmatrix} y' \\ -1 \end{pmatrix} \geqslant 0$$

for i, the i-th process is said to satisfy modified F-inferiority in the integrated system.

This definition means that the i-th AR process is F-inferior in a modified form in the integrated system. Here, the *integrated system* refers to the one in which AR processes are consolidated into activities of the normal production processes.

As we have made preparation sufficient for the following argument, let us proceed to the analysis of the price formation. To solve the above for p_A, the nature of the following matrix must be known:

$$\left[I - \left\{ (1+r)\left(A + \frac{A_W W}{1+r}\right) - \frac{B_W W}{1+r} \right\} \right].$$

Actually, the following important result is obtained.

Lemma 1 *The components of* $\left[I - \left\{ (1+r)\left(A + \frac{A_W W}{1+r}\right) - \frac{B_W W}{1+r} \right\} \right]$ *is non-positive unless they are diagonal components, which are positive. Furthermore, it has a positive inverse matrix.*

Proof. See Appendix.

From Lemma 1, one knows

$$p_A = w\left(l_A + \frac{l_W W}{1+r}\right)\left[I - \left\{(1+r)\left(A + \frac{A_W W}{1+r}\right) - \frac{B_W W}{1+r}\right\}\right]^{-1} \tag{4}$$

is positive. Thus, the following result is obtained:

Proposition 1 *Under Assumption 2, even if abatement or recycling processes are activated, prices of normal commodities are positive, provided that the wage rate is positive.*

Now, let us refer to a price vector of residuals which are supposed to be bads in this section. From (1) and (4),

$$p_W = w\left(l_A + \frac{l_W W}{1+r}\right)\left[I - \left\{(1+r)\left(A + \frac{A_W W}{1+r}\right) - \frac{B_W W}{1+r}\right\}\right]^{-1}$$
$$\left[B_W - (1+r)A_W\right] - w l_W$$

must hold.

Although it might seem hard for us to get information on the sign of p_{Wi} from the above, the following result can be obtained by means of the two definitions above:

Proposition 2 *Suppose all residuals are treated by AR processes. Then, under Assumption 2, (i) prices of residuals are negative if and only if all the AR processes satisfy the modified F-inferiority in the integrated system, and (ii) prices of residuals are negative if all the AR processes satisfy the modified F-inferiority in the original system and each component of W is sufficiently small, provided that the wage rate is positive.*

Proof. See Appendix.

Remark 1 *Notice that we have made a hypothesis that all residuals are treated by AR processes in Proposition 2. This means that the disposal constraint is supposed to be binding for all residuals although the constraint is not explicit so far. Yet, it might be possible to consider the case in which it is binding only for some residuals and not for others. In this case, the prices corresponding to non-binding residuals are zero. This implies that the corresponding price–cost inequalities hold with strict inequalities, for, otherwise, $(p_A, p_{Wi}, w)\Upsilon^{+(i)}(i) = 0$ should have a semi-positive solution, and this should contradict the modified F-inferiority in the integrated system. Thus, the corresponding AR activities are zero. Consequently, Proposition 2 may be a little relaxed to the case in which the disposal constraint is non-binding for some residuals, and in this case, it can be said that prices of residuals are non-positive.*

The residuals whose prices are negative are regarded as bads. If the productivity of a recycling sector is sufficiently high, the price of a residual may turn out to be positive. Then the residual is not bads, but goods, since the recycling process which uses the residual and produces a commodity is profitable just as are other production processes, even when the process uses residual with a positive price. Profitability depends upon the rate of profit. Although how residuals are traded as goods will be considered in section 3, it is assumed for the time being that all the residuals are bads.

Now, from (4), the wage–profit relationship can be obtained when abatement and recycling processes are activated:

$$1 = w\left(l_A + \frac{l_W W}{1+r}\right)\left[I - \left\{(1+r)\left(A + \frac{A_W W}{1+r}\right) - \frac{B_W W}{1+r}\right\}\right]^{-1} d. \qquad (5)$$

If the productivity of recycling processes is sufficiently small, i.e. b_{ij}^W (ij component of B_W) is small, then the wage–profit frontier expressed by (5) is completely inside the one expressed by (2). This means that neither abatement nor recycling processes are activated in a competitive equilibrium without environmental restriction (insofar as recycling processes are not so productive).

Yet, in order to maintain the reproducibility of an economy, some constraints on disposal of residuals are necessary, and the frontier expressed by (5) is valid in an economy where there is an environmental restriction or a restriction on free disposal of residuals. Otherwise the wage–profit frontier expressed by (2) should shift inward someday, and the shift cannot be stopped by belated treatment. The final frontier may be completely inside the frontier expressed by (5).

Let us briefly refer to a special case in which the wage rate is zero. The solution for p_A is obtained as an eigen vector of

$$p_A\left[I - (1+r)\left\{\left(A + \frac{A_W W}{1+r}\right) - \frac{B_W W}{(1+r)^2}\right\}\right] = 0.$$

Thus, when the maximum rate of profit equals $R \equiv 1/\lambda^\dagger - 1$ where $\lambda^\dagger$ is the Frobenius root of the matrix inside the curly brackets in the above, it is known that p_A is positive. Hence, p_W is negative if all the AR processes satisfy the modified F-inferiority in the integrated system. Thus, it is proved that Propositions 1 and 2 are extended to the case where $w = 0$.

2.3 The quantity side

Next, let us turn to the quantity side. Here, we assume that the government imposes a certain constraint on disposal of residuals or bads. More concretely, we assume that the government allows disposal of bads only in the amounts expressed by vector q.

At this point, one must be very careful, since bads have (negative) prices. If all bads are abated by abatement or recycling processes, there is no problem. But if some amount of bads is emitted into the environment, part of the costs of the bads must be paid to someone by capitalists, since bads have negative value. Larger (2001) interprets this as the payment of emission permits or entitlements. Surely, this interpretation is applicable to emission of some sorts of aerial residuals, particularly such as sulfur dioxide, carbon dioxide and so on, since trade of emission permits or entitlements has been implemented for those gases.

Another interpretation is that the payment is for disposal in landfill sites. If capitalists would like to have residuals treated in landfill, they have to pay some amount of money to landfill owners, and this amount must be equal to the unit treatment cost of AR processes by arbitrage. Clearly, if there is oversupply of landfill space relatively to the amount of residuals which must be treated in landfill in equilibrium, they are treated freely in landfill sites. Obviously, this interpretation is suited very much to the emission of solid waste.

Whichever interpretation one might adopt, one has to determine, in the present model, how the money paid by capitalists should be distributed. We assume that this value is attributed to workers. This may be justified, because residuals disposal comes only from production and not from consumption.[9]

Under this assumption, workers' income consists of wages and the amount of money paid by capitalists for waste emission, namely, $\{w\ (l_A x_A + l_W x_W) - p_W q\}$. It is assumed that all the workers' income is spent on consumption and not saved, and that the consumption proportion of goods depends only upon prices of normal commodities, being expressed as a vector $c(p_A)$.

As for the consumption proportion vector, the following assumption is adopted:

Assumption 3 *A consumption proportion vector $c(\cdot)$ is defined on $\mathbb{R}^n_+ \backslash \{0\}$, non-negative, continuous and homogeneous of degree zero. Moreover, there exists positive ϵ such that $P_A c(p_A) > \epsilon$ for any P_A which belongs to a simplex.*

The above assumption says that workers spend at least a certain amount of money on consumption of some goods. This assumption is a little technical but required to prove the existence of equilibrium solution. Unless it is assumed, the proof should be too complicated.

Then, consumption demand is expressed as $\{w\ (l_A x_A + l_W x_W) - p_W q\}$ $\{1/p_A c(p_A)\} c(p_A)$ and investment demand as $(1 + g)\ (A x_A + A_W x_W)$. Hence, a supply–demand balance of normal commodities is

$$x_A + B_W x_W = (1 + g)\ (A x_A + A_W x_W) + \{w(l_A x_A + l_W x_W) - p_W q\}$$
$$\frac{1}{p_A c(p_A)} c(p_A). \tag{6}$$

As a normalization of an activity vector, we adopt the total labor force as a unit, and so put $l_A x_A + l_W x_W = 1$.

If a constraint on disposal of residuals is not strict and components of q are very large, abatement or recycling processes are not activated. In this case, some residuals are freely disposed of. Since we are dealing with a problem caused by emission of bads in this section, we suppose that components of q are relatively small, and a constraint of disposal of residuals is binding, i.e.

$$q = Wx_A - (1 + g)x_W \text{ where } x_A \geq 0 \text{ and } x_W \geq 0. \tag{7}$$

Equation (7) implies that a constraint is binding for all the residuals. This seems a very strong assumption, and although this assumption is adopted in this section, it will be relaxed later.

Then, substituting $x_W = (Wx_A - q)/(1 + g)$ into (7), we obtain

$$\left(I + \frac{B_W W}{1 + g}\right)x_A = (1 + g)\left(A + \frac{A_W W}{1 + g}\right)x_A + \frac{B_W - (1 + g)A_W}{1 + g}q$$

$$q + (w - p_W q)\frac{1}{p_A c(p_A)}c(p_A),$$

from which

$$x_A = \left[I - \left\{(1 + g)\left(A + \frac{A_W W}{1 + g}\right) - \frac{B_W W}{1 + g}\right\}\right]^{-1}\left[\frac{w - p_W q}{p_A c(p_A)}c(p_A)\right.$$

$$\left. + \frac{1}{1 + g}\{B_W - (1 + g)A_W\}q\right] \tag{8}$$

is obtained.

Notice

$$\left[I - \left\{(1 + g)\left(A + \frac{A_W W}{1 + g}\right) - \frac{B_W W}{1 + g}\right\}\right]^{-1} \geqslant 0$$

due to Assumption 2. (The same argument which proves the positivity of p_A is applicable here.) Clearly, x_A is positive when q is zero insofar as $w > 0$. Therefore, by continuity, if $q_i(i = 1, ..., k)$ is small enough, vector x_A is positive.

On the other hand, from the constraint of waste disposal $x_W = (Wx_A - q)/(1 + g)$, an activity vector of the abatement or recycling sector is expressed as

$$x_W = \frac{1}{1 + g}W\left[I - \left\{(1 + g)\left(A + \frac{A_W W}{1 + g}\right) - \frac{B_W W}{1 + g}\right\}\right]^{-1}$$

$$\left[\frac{w - p_W q}{p_A c(p_A)}c(p_A) + \frac{\{B_W - (1 + g)A_W\}q}{1 + g}\right] - \frac{q}{1 + g}. \tag{9}$$

This vector is also positive if $q = 0$, and so it is also positive if $q_i(i = 1, ..., k)$ is sufficiently small, provided that $w > 0$.

Consequently, the following result is obtained:

Proposition 3 *Suppose productivity of recycling processes is so low that residuals are valued negative. Furthermore, suppose the disposal constraint* *vector is sufficiently small. Then, under Assumptions 2 and 3, activity vectors of the production process are non-negative and AR processes are also non-negative, provided that the wage rate is positive. All the activity vectors are positive if the disposal constraint vector is zero, provided that the wage rate is positive.*

Let us mention briefly the case in which $w = 0$. In this special case, put q as $q = 0$. Then, x_A is an eigen vector of the following matrix equation:

$$\left[I - (1 + g)\left\{ \left(A + \frac{A_W W}{1 + g} \right) - \frac{B_W W}{(1 + g)^2} \right\} \right] x_A = 0.$$

Thus, if the maximum rate of growth is set as $1/\lambda^\dagger - 1$, $x_A^\dagger$ is positive, where $x_A^\dagger$ denotes an eigen vector, and so, corresponding $x_W^\dagger$ is positive.

So far, it has been assumed that the disposal constraint expressed by q is so tight that it is binding to all residuals and (7) holds. But one question remains: How small must q be in order for the constraint to be binding? This question naturally leads us to exploration of a set of q which makes an equilibrium with the binding constraint meaningful. Let me consider this problem in a special case in the following subsection.

2.4 The binding disposal constraint in a special case

In the following, we would like to explore effects of the binding constraint changes upon equilibrium values. Since things become significantly simpler when we assume that a consumption proportion vector is constant, let us assume $c(p_A) = c$ (constant) for a while, and analyze how a change in the binding constraint affects the equilibrium circumstances, particularly per capita consumption in the following subsection. Notice that, even if we assume a consumption proportion vector as given, the basket itself is dependent upon the price vector (p_A, p_W).

In order to examine how a change in q affects equilibrium values, let us define $c(p_A, p_W; q)$ as

$$c(p_A, p_W; q) \equiv \frac{w - p_W q}{p_A c} c.$$

Here, labor is adopted as numeraire and $w = 1$ holds.

As a benchmark, consider a case in which q is at a specific value such that (7) holds with $x_W = 0$. Very interestingly there are two different situations where $x_W = 0$ holds; the one where $p_W = 0$, and the other where $p_W \leq 0$. Of course, the latter include the extreme situation where $p_W \ll 0$. It is quite obvious that the equilibrium price vector of normal goods corresponding to the former is different from that corresponding to the latter. Furthermore, since a consumption basket is affected by the change of the equilibrium price vector through two channels, that is, through a change in income and one in a consumption proportion, it is also different in two situations.

In the first situation ($p_W = 0$), the price vector of goods and the activity vector of the normal processes are expressed as follows:

$$\begin{cases} p_A^* = l_A[I_n - (1 + r)A]^{-1} \\ x_A^* = [I_n - (1 + g)A]^{-1} c(p_A^*, 0; q^*), \end{cases}$$

where q^* is defined as $q^* \equiv Wx_A^*$. It is clear that for this q^* the price vector $(p_A^*, 0)$ and the activity vector $((x_A^*)^T, 0)^T$ are the equilibrium vectors.

Due to the above equations, the following must hold:

$$\Phi(g) \begin{pmatrix} x_A^* \\ 0 \end{pmatrix} = \begin{pmatrix} c(p_A^*, 0; q^*) \\ q^* \end{pmatrix},$$

where $\Phi(g)$ is defined as

$$\Phi(g) \equiv \begin{pmatrix} I_n - (1 + g)A & B_W - (1 + g)A_W \\ W & - (1 + g)I_k \end{pmatrix}.$$

Now, let us consider the second situation ($p_W \leq 0$), and denote the price vectors of goods and bads as p_A^{**} and p_W^{**}. Here, some components of p_W^{**} are negative, i.e. $p_W^{**} < 0$. Clearly, $p_W^{**} \ll 0$ is a special case as we have already mentioned.

Then the following lemma can be proved:

Lemma 2 *There exists $x_A^{**} > 0$ and $q^{**} > 0$ such that*

$$\Phi(g) \begin{pmatrix} x_A^{**} \\ 0 \end{pmatrix} = \begin{pmatrix} c(p_A^{**}, p_W^{**}, q^{**}) \\ q^{**} \end{pmatrix}$$

holds.

Proof. See Appendix.

This lemma tells us that the price vector (p_A^{**}, p_W^{**}) and the actitivity vector $((x_A^{**})^T, 0)^T$ are equilibrium vectors when the disposal constraint is q^{**} and it is binding. Hence, some or all prices of residuals can be negative *and* no AR process is activated even if the disposal constraint is binding.

Proposition 4 *The following equations hold:*

$$x_A^* = x_A^{**}, q^* = q^{**}, \frac{1}{p_A^* c} = \frac{1 - p_W^{**} q^{**}}{p_A^{**} c}, \text{ and } c(p_A^*, 0; q^*)$$

$$= c(p_A^{**}, p_W^{**}; q^{**}) \text{ with } p_W^{**} < 0.$$

Proof. See Appendix.

This result is remarkable, since it means that, when the constraint is q^* ($= q^{**}$), there are two types of equilibria; one in which all the residual prices are zero with a binding constraint, and the other in which some or all residual prices are negative with the same binding constraint. Moreover, in both cases, the equilibrium activity vector and real income distribution are completely the same. It must be noticed that this lemma holds only if the consumption proportion is constant.

Before we go further on examining how a change in the constraint q affects equilibrium values, we would like to explore the nature of a set of q which makes an equilibrium solution exist with a binding constraint. For this purpose, a set Q is defined as follows:

$$Q \equiv \left\{ q \in \mathbb{R}^k_+ \middle| \Phi(g) x = \left(\frac{c(p^{**}_A, p^{**}_W; q)}{q} \right) lx = 1 \text{ and } x \geq 0 \right\}.$$

Then, one can obtain the following property of Q.

Proposition 5 *(1) Q is compact and convex.*
(2) $\exists \epsilon > 0$ s.t. $\|q\| < \epsilon \Rightarrow q \in Q$.
(3) $x(q) \gg 0$ for $q \in int\ Q$.[10]
(4) $q^* (= q^{**}) \in Q$.

Proof. See Appendix. (Here, int Q implies interior of Q.)

From the third and fourth properties, clearly $q^* (= q^{**})$ is on the boundary of Q. Furthermore, $0 \in Q$, and so, from the first property, it is easily understood that the line segment $\overline{O_q^*}$ is entirely in Q, and its extension in either direction is not in Q. Hence, it is known that $tq^* (= tq^{**}) \in Q$ for all $t \in [0, 1]$. Consequently, the following corollary can be obtained:

Corollary 1 *Suppose t satisfies $0 \leq t \leq 1$. Then, for a disposal constraint vector $q = tq^*$, equations (8) and (9) have positive activity vectors.*

We have found positive activity vectors of normal production processes and AR processes *either* when q is sufficiently small *or* when q is expressed as $q = tq^*$. If q is not small *and* not proportional to q^* so that it is not in Q, one cannot find non-negative activity vectors insofar as we assume a binding constraint expressed by $Wx_A = q + x_W$. If one component of q, say, q_i, is very small and q_j ($j \neq i$) is rather large, a binding constraint by q_i may be inconsistent with a binding constraint by q_j, as far as one keeps activity vectors non-negative.

To clear this point, i.e. to take any non-negative q into account, we have to introduce an inequality constraint instead of an equality constraint, i.e. $Wx_A \leq q + x_W$. We will do this in section 3.

2.5 An effect of tightening of q on consumption

Finally, let us briefly refer to the effect of the tightening of disposal constraint q on consumption. Suppose $q = tq^* (= tq^{**})$ and decrease the value of t from unity to zero. Then, the constraint becomes stronger. Notice that price vector (p_A^{**}, p_W^{**}) is fixed and independent of t. Other variables are invariant, while the transfer income from the government to workers decreases. Thus, per capita consumption decreases.

It must, however, be remembered that per capita consumption does not go to zero, and has a lower bound, which is expressed by $1/(p_A^{**}c)c$. In other words, per capita consumption moves in the following range:

$$\frac{1}{p_A^{**}}c \leq c(p_A^{**}, p_W^{**}; tq^*) \leq \frac{1}{p_A^{*}}c \text{ for } t \text{ such that } 0 \leq t \leq 1.$$

As t gets close to zero (i.e. nearly zero emission of bads), an activity vector of normal production processes converges to the following vector:

$$x_A = \left[I - \left\{(1+g)\left(A + \frac{A_W W}{1+g}\right) - \frac{B_W W}{1+g}\right\}\right]^{-1} \frac{w}{p_A^{**}}c.$$

It is clear that there is a trade-off between per capita consumption and an environmental constraint to *a certain extent*.

2.5.1 Some remarks

Before we proceed to generalization of the basic model, we would like to make some brief remarks on the results we have obtained so far.

In the basic model, we have considered the price aspect independently of the quantity aspect. This is possible since it is assumed that all the AR processes satisfy the modified F-inferiority in the integrated system and $q \in Q$ holds. The former implies that the AR processes are dominated by the normal production processes in terms of production of net products. The latter implies that the disposal constraint is binding for all the residuals.

What happens if some AR processes do not satisfy the modified F-inferiority in the integrated system? Let us remember that, insofar as Proposition 2 (i) is concerned, the modified F-inferiority in the integrated system is a necessary and sufficient condition for negativity of the i-th AR processes. If the inferiority condition is not satisfied for a certain AR process, the price of the residual corresponding to this process turns to be positive. Then, the residual is goods instead of bads, and this requires that the disposal constraint should not be applied to this commodity.

Next let us consider the meaning of $q \in Q$. Due to this condition, we are allowed to utilize an equality system, instead of a complicated inequality system. This condition, in addition to the modified F-inferiority in the integrated system, makes us regard residuals as bads, and thus it is possible for us to separate the price system from the quantity system. Notice that *non*-inferiority for a certain process in the present sense is not compatible with a binding disposal constraint for the corresponding residual.

Altogether, it may be said that the basic model we have presented so far is an extension of the so-called non-substitution theorem. Given the binding constraint with $0 \ll q \in Q$, the price formation is consistent in itself and independent of the quantity system when the inferiority condition is satisfied. Once $q \notin Q$ holds, such simplicity is lost, and a certain complexity must be handled. We do this in the next section.

3 A more general case: relativity of goods and bads

3.1 A possibility that a disposal constraint is not binding

A basic model is presented in section 2, based upon rather strict assumptions. Generalization is tried in this section. Let us take into account the possibility that the disposal constraint is not binding for some residuals ($q \notin Q$). Hence, some residuals may be free goods or even goods. This means that a constraint for residuals disposal is expressed by inequality instead of equality.

This line of analysis is carried out by Lager (2001) elegantly by means of a linear complementary theory. Yet, this method is not applicable to the present model where consumption depends upon not only activity levels but also prices. Hence, a different approach must be taken.

Before we show the technical aspects of the generalized model, we would like to describe the main modifications of the basic model step by step.[11] First, let us relax the restrictive assumption that AR processes input residuals which are specific to those processes. In this section, it is assumed that AR processes input plural residuals as inputs. We denote this input matrix as $E_k(> 0)$, instead of I_k in the previous section. Each column and row is assumed to have at least one positive component.

Second, we avoid using the binding condition of residuals expressed as (7) since $q \notin Q$ may hold. The (7) must be rewritten as follows:

$$q \geq Wx_A - (1 + g)E_k x_W. \tag{10}$$

Third, we also drop the restrictive assumption that AR processes do not produce residuals. That is, we assume that residuals are obtained from AR processes as joint products, too. This means that the output matrix has some positive components in the lower right part of matrix $\tilde{B}$. Let us denote residual output matrices in normal processes and AR processes as W_A and W_W respectively.

Then the constraint (10) must be changed to

$$q \geq W_A x_A + W_W x_W - (1 + g) E_k x_W.$$

We have to take another important point into consideration. Since an equality constraint of residuals is relaxed to inequality, there is a possibility that residuals are goods, instead of bads, and positively valued in a market. When residuals are goods, then outputs of those residuals must not be smaller than inputs. Thus, inequality (10) must be modified to the following inequality:

$$q \geq W_A x_A + W_W x_W - (1 + g) E_k x_W \geq 0. \tag{11}$$

Improvement of this treatment is essential. If a strict equality holds in the left-hand side inequality of (11) for some residuals, they are bads, and negatively valued. If a strict inequality holds in both the left-hand and right-hand side inequality of (11) for some residuals, then they are neither goods nor bads; namely, they are free goods. If a strict equality holds in the right-hand side inequality of (11) for some residuals, they are goods, and positively valued.

In this way, one can deal with the possibility that residuals are goods (free goods) or bads, depending upon how the constraint on residuals is satisfied. Precisely speaking, one cannot identify whether residuals are goods or bads if q_i (the i-th component of q) is zero, just by looking at (11). Yet, as will be shown later, the goods/bads character of residuals is uniquely determined.

To deal with this case easily, however, let us rearrange input and output matrices as follows: Regard outputs of residuals of a production sector as inputs, and inputs of residuals of an abatement or recycling sector as outputs. Then one can have

$$\tilde{A} = \begin{pmatrix} A & A_W \\ \dfrac{W_A}{1+g} & \dfrac{W_W}{1+g} \end{pmatrix} \quad \tilde{B} = \begin{pmatrix} I_n & B_W \\ O & (1+g)E_k \end{pmatrix}.$$

Since residuals become goods or bads depending upon how a residuals constraint is satisfied, an equilibrium condition is a little more complicated than conventional expression. Let us introduce the following matrices:

$$\hat{A} = \begin{pmatrix} A & A_W \\ \dfrac{W_A}{1+g} & \dfrac{W_W}{1+g} \\ -\dfrac{W_A}{1+g} & -\dfrac{W_W}{1+g} \end{pmatrix} \quad \hat{B} = \begin{pmatrix} I_n & B_W \\ O & (1+g)E_k \\ O & -(1+g)E_k \end{pmatrix}$$

and

$$\Omega(g) \equiv \hat{B} - (1+g)\hat{A} = \begin{pmatrix} I_n - (1+g)A & B_W - (1+g)A_W \\ -W_A & (1+g)E_k - W_W \\ W_A & -(1+g)E_k + W_W \end{pmatrix}.$$

The price and quantity systems are expressed as follows:

$$\begin{cases} p\hat{B} \le (1+r)p\hat{A} + wl \\ p\hat{B}x = (1+r)p\hat{A}x + wlx \\ \hat{B}x \ge (1+g)\hat{A}x + (c(p_A, \tilde{p}_W; q)^T, -q^T, 0)^T \\ p\hat{B}x = (1+g)p\hat{A}x + p(c(p_A, \tilde{p}_W; q)^T, -q^T, 0)^T \\ r = g \\ p \equiv (p_A, \tilde{p}_W, \upsilon_W) > 0 \quad \tilde{p}_{Wi} \cdot \upsilon_{Wi} = 0 \quad x > 0, \end{cases} \tag{12}$$

where $\tilde{p}_{Wi}$ and υ_{Wi} are the i-th components of $\tilde{p}_W$ and υ_W respectively, $l = (l_A, l_W)$ and $c(p_A, \tilde{p}_W; q) = (w + \tilde{p}_W q) \frac{1}{p_A c} c(p_A)$. It is easy to see that $\tilde{p}_W$ corresponds to $-p_W$ which is defined in the previous section. We return to the assumption that c is dependent upon p_A and a semi-positive vector, i.e. $c = c(p) > 0$.

Let us assume

Assumption 4 $\exists x = (x_A^T, x_W^T)^T > 0$ *and* $\exists g > 0$ *such that*
$$\{I - (1+g)A\} x_A + \{B_W - (1+g)A_W\} x_W \gg 0 \text{ and } W_A x_A + W_W x_W = (1+g)E_k x_W$$

which corresponds to Assumption 2. It is clear that, if the above assumption is not satisfied, there is no equilibrium when $q = 0$.

Before we prove the existence theorem of solution, we would like to explain the subtleties of the problem. Let us refer to the second and third matrix inequalities contained in the third expression of (12), which express inequality (11). Unless q_i (the i-th component of q) is zero, corresponding rows of those matrices do not satisfy the third expression of (12) with strict equality simultaneously. Namely, both $(1+g)E_k^i x_W - W_A^i x_A - W_W^i x_W = -q_i$ and $(1+g)E_k^i x_W - W_A^i x_A - W_W^i x_W = 0$ do not hold simultaneously, where E_k^i, W_A^i and W_W^i denotes the i-th row vectors of E_k, W_A and W_W respectively. If $(1+g)E_k^i x_W - W_A^i x_A - W_W^i x_W = -q_i$ and $(1+g)E_k^i x_W - W_A^i x_A - W_W^i x_W < 0$ hold, the corresponding residuals are bads, and $-\tilde{p}_{Wi}$ (the i-th component of $-\tilde{p}_W$) is the non-positive price of the residuals, or bads. In this case, υ_{Wi} (the i-th component of υ_W) is zero from the fourth expression of (12).

If $(1+g)E_k^i x_W - W_A^i x_A - W_W^i x_W > -q_i$ and $(1+g)E_k^i x_W - W_A^i x_A - W_W^i x_W = 0$ hold, the residuals are utilized as inputs without any disposal constraint. Thus, υ_{Wi} means the non-negative price of the residuals or goods. In this case, $\tilde{p}_{Wi}$ is zero from the fourth expression of (12).

When both $(1+g)E_k^i x_W - W_A^i x_A - W_W^i x_W > -q_i$ and $(1+g)E_k^i x_W - W_A^i x_A - W_W^i x_W < 0$ hold, part of the residuals are utilized as inputs, but those residuals are partly disposed of without infringing on the disposal constraint. The corresponding prices are zero from the fourth expression of (12). Thus, they are neither goods nor bads; they are free goods.

We can show that (12) has a solution, assuming that $q \gg 0$. It is possible to relax the assumption of this inequality and to show the existence of a solution when $q \ge 0$. We would like to relegate the proof to the Appendix, since it is lengthy. Anyhow, the following can be obtained:

Proposition 6 *Suppose q is a positive vector. Then, inequality system (12) has a solution under Assumptions 3 and 4 if r (= g) is sufficiently small.*

Proof. See Appendix.

Proposition 7 *Even if some or all components of q are zero, there exists a solution to (12) under Assumptions 3 and 4.*

Proof. See Appendix.

Remark 2 *Notice that for residuals whose disposal constraint q_i is zero, either p_{Wi} is positive with v_{Wi} being zero or v_{Wi} is positive with p_{Wi} being zero, unless $p_{Wi} = v_{Wi} = 0$. The reason is as follows: for δ defined in Appendix C, $p_{Wi\delta} > 0$ and $v_{Wi\delta} = 0$ hold, or $p_{Wi\delta} = 0$ and $v_{Wi\delta} > 0$ hold, unless $p_{Wi\delta} = v_{Wi\delta} = 0$. Thus, $p_{Wi\delta} \cdot v_{Wi\delta} > 0$ for any positive δ is impossible. Therefore, $p_{Wi0} \cdot v_{Wi0} > 0$ is also impossible.*

From the above, one knows the following: Clearly, p_A^* is an equilibrium price vector of normal goods. If p_{Wi}^* is positive and v_{Wi}^* is zero, the residuals are bads with the price being $-p_{Wi}^*$, negative. If v_{Wi}^* is positive and $-p_{Wi}^*$ is zero, they are goods, and traded without any constraint. If both p_{Wi}^* and v_{Wi}^* are zero, the residuals are neither goods nor bads; they are free goods. Thus, the property of residuals is determined endogenously in the supply–demand conditions with a disposal constraint on residuals.

3.2 Further generalizations

Finally, let us refer to the possibility of further generalizations. We have assumed so far that each sector has one process, whether it be the production sector or the AR sector. In this sense, there is no problem regarding the choice of technique, although whether AR processes are activated or not is determined endogenously.

If the choice of technique is introduced into a model, the input and output matrices are no longer square. Yet, it is quite easy to introduce the choice of technique in a conventional sense into the present model. Indeed, the model which is described in subsection 3.1 is applicable to this case. One problem to be solved is that W_A and W_W are not square any more. Yet, since we do not have to utilize the nature of squareness of the matrices in the proof of the generalized model, this does not become any serious problem.

Another generalization: We have assumed that all the profit income is spent on investment and all the workers' income (the wage payment and the reimbursement from the government) on consumption, and thus, $g = r$ holds. We can weaken the assumption, for example, to the extent that part of the profit income is spent on consumption. In this case, $g = s_p r$ holds, where s_p denotes as the propensity to save from profit income. Altough $\Omega(g) \neq \Omega(r)$ holds, the proof in Appendix B is still valid with minor modifications. The key point for the proof is utilization of the Walras Law. Insofar as the law holds, $g \neq r$ does not seem to create a serious problem. Yet, things should be very complicated and the existence proof should become difficult once we allow the possibility that there is a switch between Pasinetti and anti-Pasinetti equilibria.[12]

Moreover, general joint production can also be introduced into the present model without difficulty, insofar as the mathematical aspect is concerned. But such generalization might negate the simplicity of the model.

4 Concluding remarks

We have presented a reproduction model with residuals, or bads, which are joint products of goods, utilizing a classical type of linear production model *à la* Morishima. As an economy is to be reproducible or sustainable in the long run, disposal of residuals, or bads, must be restricted, and thus, an assumption of free disposal should be abandoned. If disposal of some residuals is restricted with a binding constraint, prices of those residuals are valued negatively.

In this chapter, first we have shown the negativity of prices of residuals or bads by means of a square matrix theory, when disposal of all the residuals are restricted with a binding constraint. It has also been proved that there exists a non-negative equilibrium vector of production activities in such an economy.

Some residuals, however, may be disposed of freely into the environment without any restriction. Hence, a binding constraint for disposal holds for some residuals and not for others. Some residuals may even be inputted to a production process in the same way as normal goods. In this case, a square matrix theory cannot be used. To cope with this circumstance, we have utilized a famous lemma, namely, the Gale–Nikaido–Debreu Lemma. It is proved that residuals can be bads, free goods or goods, depending upon how a disposal constraint of residuals is satisfied.

Finally, let us make a remark on a disposal constraint given by q. The constraint vector q is given on a per capita basis. This means that total disposal of residuals increases in a growing economy, unless q equals zero. Clearly, such a situation will surely be intolerable. Hence, some components of q must be reduced as an economy grows. Since Propositions 6 and 7 hold for any non-negative q, this circumstance does not matter, apart from a stability argument. A study on stability is, however, beyond the scope of this chapter.

Appendix A

Proof of Lemma 1. Let us first show that $[(1 + r)A + A_W W - B_W W/(1 + r)]$ is a non-negative matrix. Actually, one can have

$$(1 + r)A + A_W W - \frac{B_W W}{1 + r} = rA + A + A_W W - \frac{B_W W}{1 + r}$$
$$\geqq rA + A + A_W W - B_W W$$
$$= rA + A^+ > 0$$

due to Assumption 2. Clearly its diagonal components are smaller than unity.

Next, since $I - A^+ = (I - A) + (B_W - A_W)W$ holds, thanks to Assumption 2 again, one knows that there is a positive scalar r and a semi-positive vector x_A such that

$$[I - (1 + r)A]x_A + \frac{1}{1+r}[B_W - (1 + r)A_W] Wx_A \geqslant 0, \tag{13}$$

holds. Consequently, $\left[I - \left\{(1 + r)\left(A + \frac{A_W W}{1+r}\right) - \frac{B_W W}{1+r}\right\}\right]$ has a positive inverse matrix.

Proof of Proposition 2. (i) Equation (1) holds if and only if $(p_A, p_{Wi}, w) \Upsilon^{+(i)}(r) = 0$ holds for $i = 1, \ldots, n$ and the second equality of (1) holds as well. From the condition of the modified F-inferiority in the integrated system, one knows that $(p_A, p_W, w)\Upsilon^{+(i)}(r) = 0$ has no semi-positive solution (Gale 1960, p. 48, Theorem 2.9). Hence, (3) and

$$p_A B_W^{(i)} = (1 + r) p_A A_W^{(i)} + (1 + r)p_{Wi} + wl_W$$

have no semi-positive solution for all i, where $A_W^{(i)}$ and $B_W^{(i)}$ are the i-th columns of A and B respectively. Since one knows that $p_A \geqslant 0$ from Proposition 1, one knows that $p_{Wi} < 0$ for all $i = 1, \ldots, n$.

(ii) Suppose that each w_{ij} is sufficiently small. Then, $\Upsilon^{(i)}(r) (y^T, -1)^T = 0$ with $y > 0$ implies $\Upsilon^{+(i)}(r) ((y')^T, -1)^T = 0$ with $y' > 0$.

Proof of Lemma 2. Define Γ as $\Gamma \equiv \{x_A | x_A > 0$ and $l_A x_A = 1\}$. Clearly, Γ is convex and compact. Choose arbitrary x_A' from Γ and set $q = Wx_A'^T$. Then, c $(p_A^{**}, p_W^{**}; q$ $(x_A'))$ is a function of x_A', where c $(p_A^{**}; p_W^{**}, q$ $(x_A')) = \{(1 - p_W^{**}q (x_A'))/p_A^{**}c\}$ c. Next define Ψ (x_A') as

$$\Psi (x_A') \equiv (1 + g)Ax_A' + c (p^{**}, p_W^{**}; q (x_A')). \tag{14}$$

Then, $x_A' \equiv \frac{1}{l_A \Psi (x_A')} \Psi (x_A')$ is a continuous mapping from Γ to itself. Brauwer's fixed point theorem guarantees that there exists a fixed point x_A^{**} in Γ, and the following holds:

$$x_A^{**} = \frac{1}{l_A \Psi (x_A^{**})} \Psi (x_A^{**}) \text{ with } q^{**} \equiv Wx_A^{**}. \tag{15}$$

Multiply p_A^{**} to (15) from the left, one can have

$$p_A^{**}x_A^{**} = \frac{p_A^{**} \Psi (x_A^{**})}{l_A \Psi (x_A^{**})}. \tag{16}$$

One can calculate as

$$\begin{aligned}
p_A^{**} \Psi (x_A^{**}) &= (1 + g)p_A^{**}Ax_A^{**} + (1 - p_W^{**} q^{**}) \\
&= (1 + r)p_A^{**}Ax_A^{**} + (l_A x_A^{**} - p_W Wx_A^{**}) \\
&= [(1 + r)p_A^{**}A + (l_A - p_W W)] x_A^{**} \\
&= p_A^{**}x_A^{**}.
\end{aligned}$$

Coupling this with (16), one can have $l_A \Psi (x_A^{**}) = 1$. From (15) and the definition of Ψ, finally one can obtain

$$x_A^{**} = (1 + g) A x_A^{**} + c (p_A^{**}, p_W^{**}; q^{**}) \text{ with } q^{**} = W x_A^{**}$$

which is nothing but $\Psi (x_A^{**}, 0) = \left(c(p_A^{**}, p_W^{**}; q^{**})^T, (q^{**})^T \right)^T$.

Next, we show that $x = (x_A^T, x_W^T)^T$ expressed by (8) and (9) satisfies $l_A x_A + l_W x_W = 1$. But this is easily checked as follows: from (8) and (9), one can have

$$l_A x_A + l_W x_W = \left(l_A + \frac{l_W W}{1 + g} \right) \left[I - \left[(1 + g) \left(A + \frac{A_W W}{1 + g} \right) - \frac{B_W W}{1 + g} \right] \right]^{-1}$$

$$\left[\frac{w - p_W q}{p_A c} c + \frac{\{B_W - (1 + g) A_W\} q}{1 + g} - \frac{l_W q}{1 + g} \right]$$

$$= \frac{p_A}{w} \left[\frac{w - p_W q}{p_A c} c + \frac{\{B_W - (1 + g) A_W\} q}{1 + g} - \frac{l_W q}{1 + g} \right] \text{ (from (4) and } g = r)$$

$$= \frac{w - p_W q}{w} + \frac{p_A}{w} \frac{\{B_W - (1 + g) A_W\} q}{1 + g} - \frac{l_W q}{1 + g}$$

$$= 1 - \frac{p_W q}{w} + \frac{1}{1 + g} \left[\frac{(1 + g) p_W}{w} + l_W \right] q - \frac{l_W q}{1 + g} \text{ (from (1) and } g = r)$$

$$= 1.$$

Proof of Lemma 4. Since $l_A^* x_A^* = l_A^{**} x_A^{**} = 1$ holds and consumption baskets are proportional, one knows that $x_A^* = x_A^{**}$ holds. (Notice that $x_W^* = x_W^{**} = 0$.) Since $x_A^* = x_A^{**}$ holds, one has $\Phi(g) ((x_A^*)^T, 0)^T = \Phi(g) ((x_A^{**})^T, 0)^T$. By construction, one has

$$\left(\begin{matrix} c(p_A^*, 0, q^*) \\ q^* \end{matrix} \right) = \left(\begin{matrix} c(p_A^{**}, (P_W^{**}, q^{**}) \\ q^{**} \end{matrix} \right).$$

Proof of Proposition 5. (1) (*Compactness*) Let us first show that Q is bounded from above. Suppose not. Then, one can choose a sequence $\{q_v\}$ from Q such that at least one component of q_v, say, q_{iv} goes to infinity. Since

$$q_v = W x_{Av} - (1 + g) x_{Wv}$$

must hold for any v, some components of x_{Av} must go to infinity as $v \to \infty$. This is, however, incompatible with $l_A x_{Av} + l_{Wv} = 1$. Hence Q is bounded. Closedness is clear.

(*Convexity*) Let us first show that the interior of Q ($\equiv$ int Q) is convex. It is easy to show that

$$\text{int } Q = \left\{ q \in \mathbb{R}_+^k \middle| \Phi(g) x = \left(\begin{matrix} c(p_A^{**}, p_W^{**}; q) \\ q \end{matrix} \right) lx = 1 \text{ and } x \gg 0 \right\} (\equiv Q_+).$$

Suppose $q^o = (q^o_1, ..., q^o_k) \in \text{int } Q$, and x^o is a corresponding solution to q^o.[13] Then, $q^o_\epsilon \equiv (q^o_1 \pm \epsilon_1, ..., q^o_k \pm \epsilon_k) \in Q$ for sufficiently small $\epsilon_i > 0$ $(i = 1, ..., k)$. Yet, if some component of x^o, say x^o_i or, is zero, then either $q^o_j + \epsilon_j$ or $q^o_j - \epsilon_j$ for some $j = 1, ..., k$ makes x^o_i negative since x linearly changes with respect to q. A contradiction. Thus, $x^o \gg 0$, and so int $Q \subset Q_+$.

Suppose $q^o \in Q_+$. Then, for q^o_ϵ with sufficiently small positive ϵ_i $(i = 1, ..., k)$, there exists a solution $x^o_\epsilon \gg 0$, since x changes linearly with respect to q and $x^o \gg 0$. Hence, $q^o \in \text{int } Q$. Consequently, int $Q = Q_+$.

Choose q^o arbitrarily from int Q. Then, a corresponding solution satisfies $x^o \gg$, and thus, $p^{**}_W \ll 0$. This p^{**}_W is the same for all $q^o \in \text{int } Q$. Therefore, x^o_A and x^o_W change linearly with respect to $q^o \in \text{int } Q$. This implies that any convex combination of two points in int Q exists in int Q.

Finally, note that the boundary of Q consists of the points such that some components of a solution x corresponding to q are zero. Suppose that q^b is an arbitrary point on the boundary. Then, one can choose a sequence of $\{q^o_v\} \in \text{int } Q$ and $\lim_{v \to \infty} q^o_v = q^b$. Thus, any convex combination of the points of the boundary can be expressed as a limit point of certain convex combinations of two interior points. This implies the former convex combination is in Q, since Q is closed.

(2) This is clear of the construction of a solution $(x^T_A, x^T_W)^T$.
(3) This is proved in the above (1).
(4) This is clear from $q^* = q^{**}$ which is proved in Lemma 4.

Appendix B

Proof of Proposition 6. To show that there is a solution to (12), one can utilize the method adopted by Bidard and Hosoda (1987).[14]

Step 1. Define $Y_{n+2k} \equiv \{y | y \geq 0 \text{ and } ye = 1.\}$ where $y \equiv (y_A, y_W, u_W)$ and $e \equiv \overbrace{(1,..., 1)}^{n+2k}$. We will show that there exists $y^* \in Y_{n+2k}$ such that y^* multiplied by a certain scalar is actually an equilibrium price vector with an equilibrium activity vector.

To facilitate the following proof, we also define

$$Y^\epsilon_{n+2k} \equiv \{y | y \geq (\overbrace{\epsilon e_n}^n, \overbrace{0}^k, \overbrace{0}^k) \text{ and } ye = 1.\} \text{ where } e_n \equiv \overbrace{(1,..., 1)}^n.$$

Choose arbitrary y from Y^ϵ_{n+2k}. There exists positive and finite $\lambda(y)$ and r such that

$$\lambda(y)y \, \Omega(r) \leq l$$

holds with equality for at least one component. Notice that $\Omega(r)$ is defined as

$$\Omega(r) = \hat{B} - (1 + r) \, \hat{A} = \begin{pmatrix} I - (1+r)A & B_W - (1+r)A_W \\ -W_A & (1+r) E_k - W_W \\ W_A & -(1+r) E_k + W_W \end{pmatrix}.$$

For any $y \in Y^{\epsilon}_{n+2k}$, $y\Omega(r) < 0$ does not hold. Otherwise one would have $y\Omega(r)x \leq 0$ for any $x \in \{x | lx = 1 \text{ and } x > 0.\}$. But from Assumption 4, one knows that there are non-negative x and positive r such that the first n components of $\Omega(r)x$ are all positive and others non-negative. A contradiction.

Hence, one can define a unique positive and finite λ for $y \in Y^{\epsilon}_{n+2k}$. Clearly,

$$\lambda : y \in Y^{\epsilon}_{n+2k} \to \lambda(y) > 0$$

is continuous.

Step 2. Denoting p as $p = \lambda(y)y$, we define $X(y)$ as follows:

$$X(y) \equiv \{x \mid x > 0,\ lx = 1 \text{ and } x \text{ satisfies}$$
$$p\Omega(r)x = lx = 1 \text{ with } p = \lambda(y)y \text{ for } y \in Y^{\epsilon}_{n+2k}.\ \}.$$

Let us prove the following lemma.

Lemma 3 *The correspondence* $y \in Y^{\epsilon}_{n+2k} \to X(y) \in X_L$ *is non-empty, convex and compact valued, and upper hemi-continuous, where* $X_L \equiv \{x | x > 0 \text{ and } lx = 1.\}$.

Proof. The first two properties are clear. Consider two sequences $\{y^v\}$ and $\{x^v\}$ which belong to Y^{ϵ}_{n+2k} and X_L respectively, and converge to y^0 and x^0, with $x^v \in X(y^v)$. There exists a sequence $\{p^v\}$ corresponding to $\{y^v\}$, which converge to p^0 that satisfies $p^0\Omega(r) \leq i$. Since $p^v\Omega(r) \leq l$ and $p^v\Omega(r)x^v = l$ hold for all $\{p^v\}$ and $\{x^v\}$, they must hold for p^0 and x^0, also. This means $x^0 \in X(y^0)$.

The following is a very famous and useful lemma, which is fully utilized:

Lemma 4 (Gale–Nikaido–Debreu) *Let K be a convex and compact subset of* $\mathbb{R}^n_+$, *and* $z: p \in K \to z(p) \in \mathbb{R}^n$ *an upper hemi-continuous correspondence with non-empty convex and compact values in a compact set; if* $pz(p) \leq 0$ *for any* $p \in K$, *then*

$$\exists p^* \in K, z^* \in z(p^*) \text{ s.t. } z^* \in K^o,$$

where $K^o \equiv$ *polar cone of* $K \equiv \{z | zK \leq 0\}$.

Proof. See Debreu (1982).

Remark 3 *An excess demand vector is defined as* $z\ (y_{\epsilon}) = (c(p_A, \bar{p}_W;\ q)^T,$ $-q,\ 0)^T - \Omega(g)x_{\epsilon}$. *Clearly, $z\ (y_{\epsilon})$ is well defined for* $y_{\epsilon} \in Y^{\epsilon}_{n+2k}$. *Due to Lemma 4, it is known that there exists y_{ϵ} such that $y_{\epsilon}z^*_{\epsilon} \leq 0$ for all* $y_{\epsilon} \in Y^{\epsilon}_{n+2k}$ *where* $z^*_{\epsilon} \in z\ (y_{\epsilon})$. *It is also known, by construction, that the following holds:*

$$\forall \epsilon,\ \exists x_{\epsilon} \in X_L \text{ and } \exists p_{\epsilon} > 0 \text{ with } p_{A\epsilon} \gg 0 \text{ s.t. } p_{\epsilon}\Omega(r) \leq l \text{ and } p_{\epsilon}\Omega(r)x_{\epsilon} = lx_{\epsilon} = 1 \tag{17}$$

where $p_{A\epsilon}$ is a vector of the first n components of p_{ϵ}, and $p_{\epsilon} \equiv \lambda(y_{\epsilon})y_{\epsilon}$.

As ϵ gets close to zero, x_ϵ and y_ϵ admit accumulation points x_0 and y_0, to which p_0 corresponds.

Notice that $(e_{(i)}, 0, 0) \in Y_{n+2k}^\epsilon$, where $e_{(i)}$ denotes a vector whose i-th component is unity and others are zero ($i = 1, \ldots, n$). Since $(e_{(i)}, 0, 0) z_\epsilon^* \leq 0$, one can have $z_{\epsilon i}^* \leq 0$, which is the i-th component of z_ϵ^*. Therefore, $z_{\epsilon i}^* \leq 0$ is bounded from above. Thus, at least one component of $p_{A\epsilon}$ does not go to zero, and $p_{A0} > 0$. (Otherwise, $c(p_A, \tilde{p}_W; q)$ should go to infinity.)

Let us get ϵ closer and closer to zero. Denote y_0 and x_0 as accumulation points of y_ϵ and x_ϵ with $p_0 = \lambda(y_0)y_0$. From the above argument, p_{A0}, which is the vector of the first n components of p_0, has at least one positive component.

Step 3. In this step, we show that $\|p_\epsilon\|$ is bounded as $\epsilon \to 0$. Suppose not. This means that $\lambda(y_\epsilon) \to \infty$. Then, $\|y_{A\epsilon}\| \to 0$ as $\epsilon \to 0$. Otherwise, $\lambda(y_\epsilon)$ should be bounded as we have shown in Step 1, and thus, $p_\epsilon = \lambda(y_\epsilon)y_\epsilon$ should be bounded. Therefore, $y_{A\epsilon} \to 0$.

Here, let us denote $p_\epsilon = \lambda(y_\epsilon)y_\epsilon \equiv (p_{A\epsilon}, \tilde{p}_{A\epsilon}, v_{W\epsilon}) = \lambda(y_\epsilon)(y_{A\epsilon}, \tilde{y}_{A\epsilon}, u_{W\epsilon})$. Notice,

$$p_\epsilon \Omega(r) \leq l \Leftrightarrow y_\epsilon \Omega(r) \leq \frac{l}{\lambda(y_\epsilon)} \text{ and } p_\epsilon \Omega(r)x_\epsilon = l \Leftrightarrow y_\epsilon \Omega(r)x_\epsilon = \frac{lx_\epsilon}{\lambda(y_\epsilon)}$$

holds for $\epsilon > 0$. Since $\|y_{A\epsilon}\| \to 0$ as $\epsilon \to 0$ by hypothesis, one has $y_0 \Omega(r) \leq 0$, and $y_0 \Omega(r)x_0 = 0$ which are nothing but

$$\begin{cases} [u_{W0} - \tilde{y}_{W0}] \, W_A \leq 0 \text{ and } [\tilde{y}_{W0} - u_{W0}] \, [(1 + g)E_k - W_W] \leq 0 \\ [u_{W0} - \tilde{y}_{W0}] W_A x_{A0} + [\tilde{y}_{W0} - u_{W0}] \, [(1 + g)E_k - W_W]x_{W0} = 0. \end{cases} \tag{18}$$

Clearly the following holds as $\epsilon \to 0$, due to Lemma 4:

$$z_\epsilon = \begin{pmatrix} c(p_A, \tilde{p}\,w; q) \\ -q \\ 0 \end{pmatrix} - \Omega(g)x_\epsilon \in \bigcap_{\epsilon > 0} \, (Y_{n+2k}^\epsilon)^\circ.$$

Then, one knows that the following holds by construction. (See the Remark to Lemma 4.)

$$p(y_\epsilon)z(p(y_\epsilon)) = p_{A\epsilon}c - p_{W\epsilon}q - p_\epsilon\Omega(g)x_\epsilon$$
$$= 1 + \tilde{p}_{W\epsilon} - \tilde{p}_{W\epsilon} - 1$$
$$= 0$$

where $w = 1$ and $p_\epsilon \equiv (p_{A\epsilon}, \tilde{p}_{W\epsilon}, v_{A\epsilon}) \equiv p(y_\epsilon) \equiv \lambda(y_\epsilon)y_\epsilon \equiv \lambda(y_\epsilon) \, (y_{A\epsilon}, \tilde{y}_{W\epsilon}, u_{W\epsilon})$. Calculating $p(y_\epsilon)z \, (p(y_\epsilon))$, one has

$$0 = p_\epsilon z(p_\epsilon)$$

$$= p_{A\epsilon} \left[(c(p_{A\epsilon}, \tilde{p}_{W\epsilon}; q)^T, -q^T, 0)^T - \{I - (1 + g)A\} \, x_{A\epsilon} - \{B_W - (1 + g)A_W\} \, x_{W\epsilon} \right]$$
$$+ \tilde{p}_{W\epsilon} \left[-q + W_A x_{A\epsilon} - \{(1 + g)I - W_W\} \, x_{W\epsilon} \right]$$
$$+ v_{W\epsilon} \left[-W_A x_{A\epsilon} + \{(1 + g)I - W_W\} \, x_{W\epsilon} \right].$$

Thus, one has

$$y_{A\epsilon}\left[\left(c(p_{A\epsilon}, \tilde{p}_{W\epsilon}; q)^T, -q^T, 0\right)^T - \{I - (1+g)A\}\{x_{A\epsilon} - \{B_W - (1+g)A_W\}x_{W\epsilon}\right]$$
$$+ \tilde{y}_{W\epsilon}\left[-q + W_A x_{A\epsilon} - \{(1+g)I - W_W\}x_{W\epsilon}\right]$$
$$+ u_{W\epsilon}\left[-W_A x_{A\epsilon} + \{(1+g)I - W_W\}x_{W\epsilon}\right] = 0.$$

Since, by hypothesis, we have assumed so far that $y_{A\epsilon} \to 0$ as $\epsilon \to 0$, and from the above equation and (18) we obtain $-y_{W0}q = 0$. Since $q \gg 0$ and $y_{W0} \geq 0$, we have $y_{W0} = 0$. Again from the first inequality of (18) and $u_{W0} \geq 0$, we know that $u_{W0} = 0$ must hold since each row of W_A is supposed to have at least one positive component. Consequently, $y_0 = (y_{A0}, \tilde{y}_{W0}, u_{W0}) = 0$ must hold. This, however, contradicts $y_0 e = 1$. This contradiction comes from the hypothesis that $\|p_\epsilon\|$ is not bounded. Thus, $\|p_\epsilon\|$ is bounded as $\epsilon \to 0$.

Step 4. Consequently, x_0 and p_0 are non-negative and bounded. Hence, $z(p_0, x_0)$ is well defined with $z(p_0, x_0) \leq 0$ and $p_0 z(p_0, x_0) = 0$. This completes the proof.

Appendix C

Proof of Proposition 7. Suppose the i-th component of q is zero, others being positive. (The following proof is applicable to a case where several components of q are zero.) Define q_δ as a vector whose i-th component is δ (> 0), others being the same as the corresponding components of q.

From Proposition 6, there exists a solution for any positive δ. Denote the solution as p_δ^* and x_δ^*. One has $\lambda(y_\delta^*)$ and y_δ^* such that $y_\delta^* \in Y_{n+2k}$ and $p_\delta^* = \lambda(y_\delta^*)y_\delta^*$.

Suppose $\delta \to 0$. Since

$$\frac{1 + \tilde{p}_{W\delta}^* q_\delta}{p_{A\delta}^* c(p_{A\delta}^*)} c(p_{A\delta}^*) - \{I - (1+g)A\} x_{A\delta}^* - [B_W - (1+g)A_W] x_{A\delta}^* \leq 0$$

holds for any δ, clearly $p_{A\delta}^* c(p_{A\delta}^*)$ has a lower bound, i.e. there exists $\theta > 0$ such that $\|p_{A\delta}^*\| > \theta$.

If one supposes $\|p_{A\delta}^*\|$ is unbounded as $\delta \to 0$, there should be a contradiction: for $y_\delta^* \Omega(r) \leq \frac{1}{\lambda(y_\delta^*)}l$ holds for any δ, and so $y_0^* \Omega(r) \leq 0$ holds, where y_0^* is an accumulation point of the sequence of $\{y_\delta^*\}$. But this is inconsistent with Assumption 4, since y_{A0}^* and so p_{A0}^* has at least one positive component as shown above.

Thus, considering that $p_0^* = \lambda(y_0^*)y_0^*$ holds and $(y_0^*, (x_0^*)^T)$ is an accumulation point of $\{(y_\delta^*, (x_\delta^*)^T)\}$, one knows that $(p_0^*, (x_0^*)^T)$ is a solution to (12).

Notes

* This chapter was read at the annual meeting of the Society for Environmental Economics and Policy Studies, Japan, 2008 and a seminar held at the Graz University. The author is very grateful to all the participants for their comments and criticisms. He is particularly grateful to Professors Christian Gehrke, Heinz Kurz, Christian Lager and Kimitoshi Sato.

1 We use the word "commodity" in a broad sense, allowing that it may possibly be negatively priced or a "discommodity". When we would like to be precise on this point, we use the words "commodity in a broad sense" which includes a discommodity.
2 Lager (1998) also analyzes bads, using a Sraffian model with a specific type of joint production, following the neo-Ricardian tradition.
3 For example, see Morishima (1969, Chap. IX).
4 Although a free-disposal assumption might seem to be adopted here, it is not actually, as shown soon.
5 As for vector inequalities, the following convention is adopted: Suppose $x = (x_1, ..., x_n)$ and $y = (y_1, ..., y_n)$. Then, $x \gg y$ if and only if $x_i > y_i$ for all $i = 1, ..., n$, and $x \geq y$ if and only if $x_i \geq y_i$ for all $i = 1, ..., n$. Furthermore, $x > y$ if and only if $x \geq y$ and $x \neq y$. The similar notation is applicable to matrix inequalities with slight modification.
6 Superscript T denotes transposition of a vector.
7 When we say vector q is sufficiently small, it means that each component of q is sufficiently small or equivalently $\|q\|$ is sufficiently small.
8 Refer to Hosoda (1993) and Fujimori (1982) as for the definition of F-inferiority.
9 The present model can deal with the case in which the costs of disposal of residuals are paid to capitalists themselves. Indeed, the fundamental nature of the present model would not be affected by how the value is attributed.
10 The ordinary topology of n-dimensional Euclidian space is considered here.
11 Basically, the following step is the same as the one taken in Lager (2001). Yet, since we adopt the assumption that a consumption basket depends upon prices and activities *and, moreover*, in this section, we return to the assumption that a consumption proportion vector c depends upon prices of normal goods, there is a fundamental difference in the formal procedure between his and ours.
12 See Bidard and Hosoda (1987) on this issue.
13 Clearly, x^o denotes $((x_A^o)^T, (x_W^o)^T)$, and x_i^o denotes a certain component of x^o here.
14 See Bidard and Hosoda (1987, p. 513).

References

Bergstrom, T. C. (1976) "How to Discard 'Free Disposability' – at No Cost", *Journal of Mathematical Economics*, Vol. 3, pp. 131–134.

Bidard, C. and E. Hosoda (1987) "Consumption Baskets in a Generalised von Neumann Model", *International Economic Review*, Vol. 28, No. 2, pp. 509–519.

Debreu, G. (1959) *Theory of Value*, New York, Wiley.

Debreu, G. (1962) "New Concepts and Techniques for Equilibrium Analysis", *International Economic Review*, Vol. 3, No. 3, pp. 257–273.

Debreu, G. (1982) "Existence of a Competitive Equilibrium" in Arrow, K. J. and M. D. Intriligator, eds, *Handbook of Mathematical Economics II* (Amsterdam, North Holland).

Franke, R. (1986) "Some Problems Concerning the Notion of Cost-Minimizing Systems in the Framework of Joint Production", *Manchester School*, Vol. LIV, No. 3, pp. 298–307.

Fujimori, Y. (1982) *Modern Analysis of Value Theory*, New York, Springer-Verlag.

Gale, D. (1960) *The Theory of Linear Economic Models*, New York, McGraw-Hill.

Gay, A. (1979) "A Note on Lemma 1 in Bergstrom's 'How to Discard "Free Disposability"' at No Cost" *Journal of Mathematical Economics*, Vol. 6, pp. 215–216.

Hart, O. D. and H. W. Kuhn (1975) "A Proof of the Existence of Equilibrium without the Free Disposal Assumption", *Journal of Mathematical Economics*, Vol. 2, pp. 335–343.

Hosoda, E. (1993) "Negative Surplus Value and Inferior Processes", *Metroeconomica*, Vol. 44, No. 1, pp. 29–42.

Hosoda, E. (2001) "Recycling and Landfilling in a Dynamic Sraffian Model: Application of 'The Corn–Guano Model' ", *Metroeconomica*, Vol. 52, No. 3, pp. 268–281.

Kurz, D. H. (2006) "Goods and Bads: Sundry Observations on Joint Production, Waste Disposal, and Renewable and Exhaustible Resources", *Progress in Industrial Ecology. An International Journal*, Vol. 3, No. 4, pp. 280–301.

Kurz, H. and Salvador, N. (2001) "Classical Economics and the Problem of Exhaustible Resources", *Metroeconomica*, Vol. 52, No. 3, pp. 282–296.

Lager, C. (1998) "Prices of 'Goods' and 'Bads': An Application of the Ricardian Theory of Differential Rent", *Economic Research System*, Vol. 10, No. 3, pp. 203–222.

Lager, C. (2001) "Joint Production with 'Restricted Free Disposal' ", *Metroeconomica*, Vol. 52, No. 1, pp. 49–78.

Morishima, M. (1969) *Theory of Economic Growth*, Oxford, Clarendon Press.

Sraffa, P. (1960) *Production of Commodities by Means of Commodities*, Cambridge, Cambridge University Press.

Sylos Labini, P. (ed.) (1973) *Prezzi Relativ e Distribuzione del Reddito*, Torino, Boringhieri.

2 Goods, characteristics and the shape of indifference curves

Ian Steedman

The theory of consumer behaviour has featured only marginally in the extensive writings of Sergio Parrinello – perhaps because he does not find it a very illuminating part of economic theory? Be that as it may, we shall argue here that the basis of the indifference curve version of consumer theory is even weaker than is often supposed. It is of course commonly acknowledged that the assumption that indifference curves are convex-from-above is rather poorly motivated. Plausible counter-examples are often presented; we may recall H. A. J. Green's indifference between two brown socks and two grey socks and his preference for either of those bundles over one brown sock and one grey sock. We do not propose to add to the stock of counter-examples here but to suggest a rather general consideration undermining any presumption that commodity indifference curves will be convex-from-above.

Goods and characteristics

Preferences over commodities are not foundational; they are *derived* from deeper level preferences over the characteristics (properties/qualities/attributes) of commodities. Kelvin Lancaster forcefully reminded economists of this in the 1960s but it would not of course have been news to Carl Menger, W. S. Jevons or P. H. Wicksteed (as Lancaster himself made clear in (1972)). Wicksteed indeed went so far as to insist that

> things, of which money gives us command, are, strictly speaking, never the ultimate objects of deliberate desire at all…. That is to say, there is no ultimate object of desire which itself enters into the circle of exchange and can be directly drawn thence … as soon as we deliberately desire possession of any external object, it is because of the experiences or the mental states and habits which it is expected to produce or to avert … no single thing that we ultimately desire is in the circle of exchange or can be directly drawn from it.
>
> (1933, pp. 152–153)

There is perhaps room for discussion as to whether even Lancaster's characteristics can be identified with Wicksteed's experiences or mental states but the fact remains that both authors are perfectly clear that preferences over commodities are merely derived, not fundamental preferences.

In his (re-)introduction of characteristics into consumer theory, Lancaster employed the simplest possible assumption about the relationship between characteristics quantities (z) and commodity quantities (x), the assumption of strict linearity. That was a perfectly reasonable thing to do while seeking to persuade economic theorists to think in what was (for them, at the time) a 'new' way. Yet the linearity assumption is not self-evidently correct in general. Both in terms of the objective relationship between commodity and characteristic quantities and in terms of the *perceived* relationship between them (the latter being the more directly relevant to consumer behaviour)[1] there could well be 'threshold effects' in some cases. Or, even if the relationship is already increasing for very small quantities of commodity, it could be an 'accelerating' relationship (with both (dz/dx) and (d^2z/dx^2) positive) at least to begin with. It is hardly obvious that the level of fitness resulting from the purchase of entry time at the gymnasium or the swimming pool will be strictly proportional to that time; it is quite plausible that (d^2z/dx^2) will be positive at first and then become negative for high levels of x (the time purchased). The same might be said with respect to the benefit derived from dietary supplements and the number of dietary supplements taken per day. Again, the reduction in muscle pain need not be strictly proportional to the time spent in physiotherapy; nor need the benefit derived from consultation with a lawyer be strictly proportional to the consultation time purchased. Indeed, it might perhaps be conjectured with respect to *services* that the benefit obtained will not be proportional to the service time in general, it being likely that (d^2z/dx^2) will be positive for small x and negative for large x.

Now, under Lancaster's strict linearity assumption, convexity-from-above of the indifference curves in characteristics space implies that of those in commodity space. (If we suppose, with Lancaster, that there are more commodities than characteristics, then a strictly convex-from-above 'z indifference curve' is consistent with an 'x indifference surface' ruled by straight lines – but that still leaves this latter surface weakly convex-from-above, of course.) To see what can happen when the z(x) relation is not linear, it will suffice to consider the simplest case of two commodities, each yielding only one of two characteristics.

Three examples

Suppose that, in the spirit of Lancaster, the quantity of the first characteristic, z_1, is indeed proportional to that of the first commodity, x_1, and that by choice of measurement units, we have $z_1 = x_1$. The $z_2(x_2)$ relationship is more complicated, however, being given (in inverse form) by

$$x_2 = \left(\frac{2z_2 + z_2^3}{1 + z_2^2} \right). \tag{1}$$

It will be seen from (1) that, for very small z_2 and x_2 we have *almost* $x_2 = 2z_2$, while for very large z_2 and x_2 we have *almost* $x_2 = z_2$. Relation (1) is monotonically increasing but $(d^2z_2/dx_2^2) > 0$ at first and $(d^2z_2/dx_2^2) < 0$ later. (The inflexion point is at $z_2 = \sqrt{3}$ and $x_2 = (5\sqrt{3}/4)$.)

To keep the argument as simple as possible (and we are aiming here at simplicity, not generality), we take the (z_1/z_2) indifference curve to be 'on the margin' of convexity-from-above;

$$z_1 + z_2 = u \tag{2}$$

where u is some utility index. Since $z_1 = x_1$, (1) and (2) yield

$$x_2 = \frac{2(u - x_1) + (u - x_1)^3}{1 + (u - x_1)^2} \tag{3}$$

as the indifference curve in commodity space corresponding to (2) in characteristics space. The $x_2(x_1)$ relation in (3) is always monotonically decreasing and its slope at $x_2 = 0$ is always given by $(dx_2/dx_1) = -2$, whatever the value of u. But it is *never* convex-from-above. If $u \leq \sqrt{3}$ then (3) defines an indifference curve which is convex-from-below. If $u > \sqrt{3}$ then it defines an indifference curve along which $(d^2x_2/dx_1^2) > 0$ as x_1 approaches zero but $(d^2x_2/dx_1^2) < 0$ as x_2 approaches zero. (There are inflexion points at $x_2 = 0$ and at $x_1 = (u - \sqrt{3})$.) In all cases, then, the weakly convex-from-above 'z indifference curve' corresponds to an 'x indifference curve' that is *not* convex-from-above.

In the example just considered, z_2 is always increasing with x_2, as shown by (1). Suppose now by contrast, that (dz_2/dx_2) is zero when $x_2 = 0$, as in

$$x_2 = a\sqrt{z_2} + bz_2^2 \tag{4}$$

If $z_1 = x_1$ and $z_1 + z_2 = u$, as before, then of course (dx_2/dx_1) tends to minus infinity as x_1 approaches u and z_2 approaches zero. Inevitably, then, $(d^2x_2/dx_1^2$ is *negative* for small x_2 – as will be the case in any example with (dz_2/dx_2) zero at $x_2 = 0$. (In the example (4),$(d^2x_2/dx_1^2) = 0$ when

$$4x_1 = [4u - (a/b)^{2/3}]$$

and the x_2 (x_1) indifference curve will or will not have a relevant inflexion point depending on the value of u, just as in the previous example.)

Lest the reader be made nervous by the assumption above that $z_1 + z_2 = u$, the 'z indifference curve' being only *weakly* convex-from-above, suppose now that

$$z_1^{1/2} + z_2 = 1$$

that $x_1 = z_1$ and that

$$x_2 = z_2 - z_2^2 + z_2^3$$

It follows that the 'x indifference curve' is

$$x_2 = 1 - 2x_1^{1/2} + 2x_1 - x_1^{3/2} \tag{5}$$

From (5)

$$4x_1^{3/2}\left(\frac{d^2x_2}{dx_1^2}\right) = (2 - 3x_1)$$

and there is an inflexion point at $x_1 = (2/3)$ and $x_2 = (7-8\sqrt{2/3})$ 0.47. Of course, $(d^2x_2/dx_1^2) = -(1/4)$ at $(x_1 = 1, x_2 = 0)$.

These three simple examples should suffice to make the point that *even if* good grounds could be given for assuming the conventional shape of indifference curves in characteristics space, that property cannot be 'translated' into commodity space without the assistance of quite specific assumptions about the nature of the z(x) relationships – quite specific assumptions, that is, which would *not* be obviously reasonable. The normal – and embarrassing – assumption about the curvature of indifference curves in commodity space is thus even more poorly grounded than is generally suggested.

Expenditure and prices

If the indifference curves in commodity space can fail to be convex-from-above then extra care is needed in the derivation of demand curves, whether Marshallian or Hicksian. Consider, for example, the Hicksian curve corresponding to an indifference curve that has a finite (absolute) slope at $x_1 = 0$, (d^2x_2/dx_1^2) > 0 for small x_1 and $(d^2x_2/dx_1^2) < 0$ as x_2 approaches zero. For all (p_1/p_2) greater than the slope at $x_1 = 0$, the Hicksian demand will be $x_1^H = 0$. As (p_1/p_2) gradually falls below this level, x_1^H will at first increase gradually. But at a critical value of (p_1/p_2), two alternative x_1^H will yield the same minimum expenditure (one corresponding to a positive value of x_2^H and the other to $x_2^H = 0$). As (p_1/p_2) falls still further, x_1^H will remain at the latter level. Thus the Hicksian demand curve exhibits both a stretch with $[\Delta x_1^H/\Delta (p_1/p_2)] = 0$ and a discontinuity.

The interested reader can of course consider other implications for demand curves. To this end it may be helpful to note that in some simple cases, at least, it may be interesting to focus on characteristics space, employing the more fundamental u(z) indifference curves and recognizing that non-linear z(x) relationships combine with a linear (commodity) budget constraint to yield a *non-linear budget constraint* in z space. Thus if, for example, $z_2 = x_2$ and $x_1 = 3z_1 - 3z_1^2 + 2z_1^3$ then the *budget constraint* in z space may be written as (in obvious notation)

$$p_2 z_2 = e - p_1 (3z_1 - 3z_1^2 + 2z_1^3)$$

There is an inflexion point at $2z_1 = 1$. If $e < p_1$ then this inflexion point lies below the z_2 axis and the whole *budget constraint* is convex-from-above. It naturally matters considerably, then, whether the 'z indifference curve' is or is not more sharply curved than this budget constraint. If $e > p_1$ then the *budget constraint* has an inflexion point within the positive quadrant, with (d^2z_2/dz_1^2) positive for small enough z_1 and negative for small enough z_2. Whatever the sign of $(e - p_1)$, the Marshallian 'utility maximization' problem could have a non-unique solution.

Extensions

The reader may well have already thought of ways to extend the above argument. One could write out explicitly the formal conditions under which the curve $f(x_1, x_2) = u$ is or is not convex-from-above when the curve $g[z_1(x_1), z_2(x_2)] = u$ is so. (In the simple kind of case considered above, it is readily seen that

$$\left.\frac{|dx_2|}{|dx_1|}\right|_{\bar{u}} = \left.\frac{|dz_2|}{|dz_1|}\right|_{\bar{u}} \left(\frac{dz_1/dx_1}{dz_2/dx_2}\right)$$

On increasing x_1 and z_1 (and thus decreasing x_2 and z_2) along their respective indifference curves, it is easy to see that the sign of (d^2x_2/dx_1^2) depends both on how sharply curved is the 'z indifference curve' and on the properties of $z_1(x_1)$ and $z_2(x_2)$.) One could let there be more commodities than characteristics and allow a commodity to yield more than one characteristic. One could reason in more abstract terms about quasi-concave functions of non-concave functions. And so on. Yet none of this would overturn the central points made above.

Concluding remark

The familiar assumption that commodity indifference curves are convex-from-above is even more fragile and forced than is commonly supposed. Such curves are derived from both preferences over characteristics *and* the $z(x)$ relationships. Since the nature of these latter is not self-evident, even a conventional assumption about 'z indifference curves' does *not* entail any analogous assumption about 'x indifference curves'.

Note

1 For a more general discussion of the significance of consumer misperceptions of these relationships, see Currie and Steedman (2000). It might well be thought that the more complicated are the $z(x)$ relationships, the more likely are consumers to misperceive them and hence the less well the action-guiding 'x indifference curves' (as perceived by the consumer) will reflect the fundamental 'z indifference curves'.

References

Currie, J. M. and Steedman, I. S. (2000), 'Consumer Perceptions of Commodity Characteristics: Implications for Choice and Well-being', *Manchester School*, Vol. 68, No. 5, pp. 516–538.

Lancaster, K. (1972), 'Operationally Relevant Characteristics in the Theory of Consumer Behaviour', in M. Peston and B. Corry (eds), *Essays in Honour of Lord Robbins*, London: Weidenfeld and Nicolson.

Wicksteed, P. H. (1933 [1910]), *The Common Sense of Political Economy*, London, Routledge.

3 Edgeworth without equal treatment*

Duncan K. Foley

1 The Edgeworth–Bowley box

Consider an exchange economy with two commodities, 1, 2, and $2n$ agents divided equally among *two types*, A, B, each characterized by an endowment $w^i = \{w_1^i, w_2^i\}$, $i = A, B$ and preferences represented by a continuous, monotonic, quasi-concave utility indicator $u^i[.] : R^2 \rightarrow R$, $i = A, B$. For convenience, index the agents as $A_1, \ldots, A_n, B_1, \ldots, B_n$, so that $\mathbf{x}^{Ai} = \{x_{i1}^A, x_{i2}^A\}$ is the commodity holding of agent A_i. An *allocation* is a list of commodity holdings for each agent, $X = \{\mathbf{x}_i^A, \ldots, \mathbf{x}_n^A, \mathbf{x}_i^B, \ldots, \mathbf{x}_n^B\}$. A *feasible allocation* is an allocation that satisfies the resource constraint:

$$\sum_i^n \mathbf{x}^{Ai} + \mathbf{x}^{Bi} = \sum_i^n \mathbf{w}^{Ai} + \mathbf{w}^{Bi} = n(\mathbf{w}^A + \mathbf{w}^B). \tag{1}$$

A feasible allocation is an *equal-treatment feasible allocation* if $\mathbf{x}^{Ai} = \mathbf{x}^{Aj}$ and $\mathbf{x}^{Bi} = \mathbf{x}^{Bj}$ all i, j.

The willingness of an agent to trade is represented by her *offer price*, or *marginal rate of substitution* between the two commodities, $p^i[\{x_1^i, x_2^i\}] \equiv (u_1^i [\{x_1^i, x_2^i\}] / u_2^i [\{x_1^i, x_2^i\}])$, where $u_j^i [\{x_1^i, x_2^i\}]$ is the partial derivative of $u^i[.]$ with respect to commodity j at the commodity bundle $\{x_1^i, x_2^i\}$. (In this chapter, commodity 2, plotted on the vertical axis, will always be the numeraire, so that the negative of the slope of a price line will be the price of commodity 1 in terms of commodity 2.) When two agents have an opportunity to exchange goods, they will be able to find a mutually advantageous exchange if and only if their offer prices differ. Thus a natural definition of an *equilibrium* of an exchange economy is a feasible allocation where all agents' offer prices are identical. At an equilibrium there is a well-defined *equilibrium price system, p* (without superscripts) since all the agents' offer prices are equal. At *voluntary exchange equilibria* which can be reached by voluntary exchanges of agents starting from their endowment point the agents' commodity bundles must be above the indifference curves through the endowment point. *Walrasian equilibria* are the subset of equilibria at which the value of each agent's commodity bundle is equal to the value of her endowment at the equilibrium prices.[1]

The Edgeworth–Bowley box represents allocations in two-commodity exchange economies with two types of agents by plotting the allocations of type A agents with the origin in the lower left-hand corner, and the allocations of type B agents with the origin in the upper right-hand corner. The dimensions of the box are the total economy's endowment expressed in per-agent terms, $\mathbf{w} = \mathbf{w}^A + \mathbf{w}^B$. Figure 3.1 represents a non-equal treatment feasible allocation.

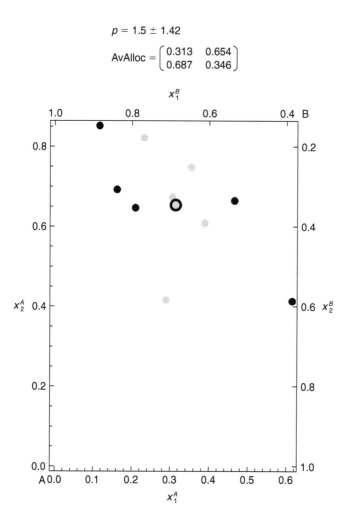

$$p = 1.5 \pm 1.42$$

$$\text{AvAlloc} = \begin{pmatrix} 0.313 & 0.654 \\ 0.687 & 0.346 \end{pmatrix}$$

Figure 3.1 The commodity bundles of agents of type A are represented by black points, and measured from the lower-left corner, and the commodity bundles of agents of type B are represented by gray points, measured from the upper-right corner, and the average of the commodity bundles of each type by a larger point of the same color. The allocation illustrated is feasible, so the two average points overlap at the same location. The average and standard deviation of the offer prices among the agents at the allocation and the average allocations are indicated in the title.

2 Equal treatment allocations

The conventional presentation of the Edgeworth–Bowley box assumes (sometimes implicitly) that the allocations presented are equal treatment allocations. In equal treatment allocations all of the agents of the same type receive the same commodity bundles.

2.1 Linear income-expansion paths

Figure 3.2 represents an equal treatment equilibrium. At any equilibrium the offer prices of all the agents are equal to the equilibrium prices, implying that the agents' commodity bundles must lie on the *income-expansion path* corresponding to the equilibrium prices, and that the equilibrium must lie at the intersection of the income-expansion paths for the two agents. In the economy pictured in Figure 3.2

$$p = 1.12 \pm (3.75 \times 10^{-8})$$

$$\text{AvAlloc} = \begin{pmatrix} 0.245 & 0.639 \\ 0.755 & 0.361 \end{pmatrix}$$

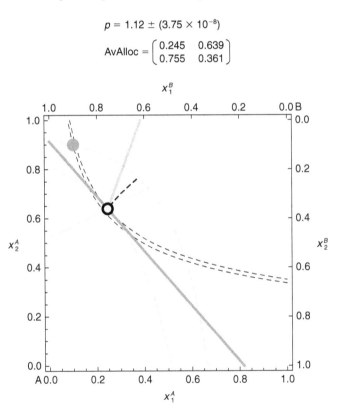

Figure 3.2 The endowment point is solid gray, and the equilibrium point (where all the agents of both types are located in an equal treatment equilibrium) is represented by overlapping black and gray points. The expansion paths of each type above their indifference curves through the endowment point are lines that intersect at the equilibrium. The set of voluntary exchange equilibria is represented by a dashed line.

the preferences are of the "Cobb–Douglas" type, which imply linear income-expansion paths.[2] The equilibrium illustrated does not, however, assume that all trades have taken place at final equilibrium prices, so the price line does not pass through the endowment point and is not a Walrasian equilibrium.

2.2 Non-linear income-expansion paths

Figure 3.3 also represents an equal treatment equilibrium, but in this case the utility functions represent non-homothetic preferences.[3] As a result the income-expansion paths are non-linear, but the assumption of equal treatment requires that the equilibrium put all the agents of each type at their intersection.

2.3 Quasi-linear economies

Quasi-linear preferences can be represented by a utility function of the form $y + \bar{u}[x]$, where $\bar{u}[.]$ is a quasi-concave function; y is the *linear commodity* and

$$p = 0.771 \pm (3.68 \times 10^{-7})$$

$$\text{AvAlloc} = \begin{pmatrix} 0.534 & 0.583 \\ 0.466 & 0.417 \end{pmatrix}$$

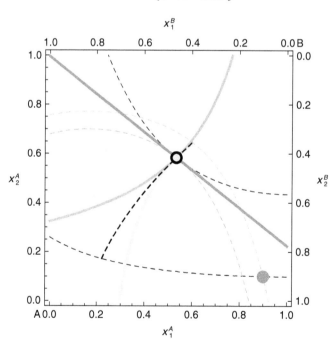

Figure 3.3 The expansion paths of each type above their indifference curves through the endowment point are non-linear curves that intersect at the equilibrium, which is in the set of voluntary exchange equilibria, represented by a dashed line.

x is the *non-linear commodity*. Economies in which all agents have the quasi-linear preferences with the same linear commodity are *quasi-linear economies*, and exhibit the same equilibrium structure as classical thermodynamic systems (Smith and Foley, 2008). Figure 3.4 illustrates equal treatment equilibrium in a quasi-linear economy.[4] The characteristic feature of quasi-linear economies is that the equilibrium set is a vertical straight line in the Edgeworth box (when the linear commodity is plotted on the vertical axis). The income-expansion paths of the two agents coincide with the equilibrium set (due to the absence of income effects with quasi-linear preferences). All equilibria have the same price for the non-linear commodity, and differ only in the distribution of the linear commodity between the agents. As Figure 3.4 illustrates, trading at non-equilibrium prices can lead the economy to a non-Walrasian equilibrium in the quasi-linear case.

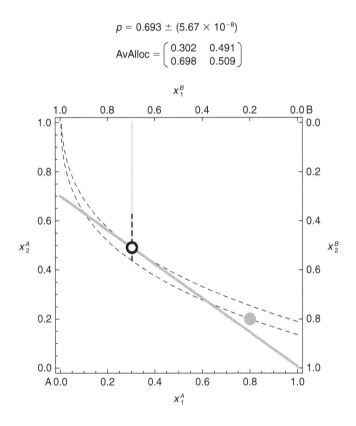

$$p = 0.693 \pm (5.67 \times 10^{-8})$$

$$\text{AvAlloc} = \begin{pmatrix} 0.302 & 0.491 \\ 0.698 & 0.509 \end{pmatrix}$$

Figure 3.4 Equal treatment equilibrium in a quasi-linear economy. The set of voluntary exchange equilibria and the income-expansion paths coincide on a vertical line in quasi-linear economies due to the absence of income effects in demands for the non-linear commodities. The indeterminacy of equilibrium due to trading at disequilibrium prices is reflected in quasi-linear economies in the indeterminate distribution of the linear commodity.

While the price and allocation of the non-linear commodity are the same in all equilibria, the allocation of the linear commodity among the agents differs among equilibria.

3 Non-equal treatment allocations

In exchange economies where there are many agents of each type it is highly restrictive to assume that all agents of each type follow exactly the same exchange path to the same final consumption bundle. In general, different agents of the same type will make exchanges at different disequilibrium prices in a decentralized market exchange, subject only to the restriction that all trades are voluntary, that is, (weakly) utility-increasing. The outcome of decentralized trading will typically be a non-equal treatment equilibrium.

In a non-equal treatment equilibrium the commodity bundles of all agents of each type have to lie on the same income-expansion path (since equilibrium requires them all to have the same offer prices). But now the commodity bundles of each agent can spread out along the income-expansion path. Feasibility still requires that the average commodity bundles of the two types of agents coincide in the Edgeworth box, but not that any *particular* pair of agents be represented by the same point. With the equal treatment assumption, the average commodity bundle for any type of agent coincides with the individual commodity bundle of any agent (since these are all identical by assumption).

3.1 Linear income-expansion paths

Figure 3.5 represents a non-equal treatment equilibrium with linear income-expansion paths.[5] Ten agents of each type wind up with commodity bundles spread out along the equilibrium income-expansion paths. (Note that while the agents' commodity bundles exhibit significant variation, their offer prices have converged, as indicated by the standard deviation.) Because the expansion paths are linear, the average commodity bundle for each agent must lie on the expansion path as well, and the average equilibrium commodity bundles of the two types lie at the intersection of the income-expansion paths, as in the equal treatment case, and hence on the locus of voluntary exchange equilibria for the equal treatment economy. Any distribution of final commodity bundles of agents of each type is consistent with equilibrium as long as the average bundles are equal. This point emphasizes the enormous multiplicity of equilibria available when equal treatment is not assumed.

3.2 Non-linear income-expansion paths

Figure 3.6 illustrates a non-equal treatment equilibrium with non-linear income-expansion paths. As a result of the non-linearity of the income-expansion paths, the average commodity bundles of the agents of each type do not lie on their income-expansion paths. At equilibrium the average commodity bundles have to coincide (to guarantee feasibility) but will generally not occupy the point at the

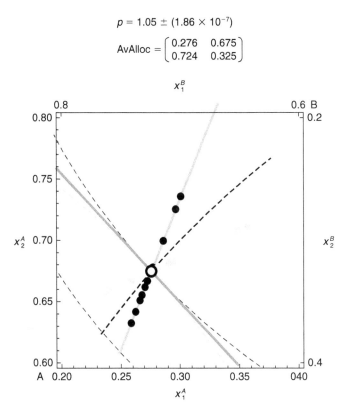

$$p = 1.05 \pm (1.86 \times 10^{-7})$$

$$\text{AvAlloc} = \begin{pmatrix} 0.276 & 0.675 \\ 0.724 & 0.325 \end{pmatrix}$$

Figure 3.5 Non-equal treatment equilibrium in an economy with linear income-expansion paths for both types of agents. While trading at disequilibrium prices spreads the agents' commodity bundles in equilibrium out on the income-expansion paths, the average bundles for the agents must lie on the linear income-expansion paths, and the average bundles coincide with an equal treatment voluntary exchange equilibrium. The equilibrium is plotted on a magnified scale to make the detailed features more legible.

intersection of the income-expansion paths, nor necessarily fall on the locus of equal treatment voluntary exchange equilibria.

3.3 Quasi-linear income-expansion paths

Finally, Figure 3.7 illustrates non-equal treatment equilibrium in a quasi-linear economy. Since the income-expansion paths are linear, the average commodity bundles lie on them, and on the equal treatment voluntary exchange equilibrium locus. Even the extreme degeneracy of the quasi-linear economy, however, is not sufficient to reduce the multiplicity of equilibrium allocations subject to these restrictions. In particular, trade at disequilibrium prices induces significant

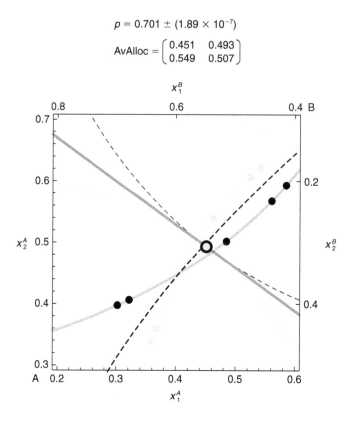

$$p = 0.701 \pm (1.89 \times 10^{-7})$$

$$\text{AvAlloc} = \begin{pmatrix} 0.451 & 0.493 \\ 0.549 & 0.507 \end{pmatrix}$$

Figure 3.6 Non-equal treatment equilibrium in an economy with non-linear income-expansion paths. The equilibrium commodity bundles of agents are spread out along their income-expansion paths at the equilibrium prices, subject to the constraint that the average commodity bundles coincide. The average bundles, however, will not generally lie on the income-expansion paths, nor on the equal treatment voluntary exchange equilibrium locus. The equilibrium is plotted on a magnified scale to make the detailed features more legible.

differences in the final holdings of the linear commodity among agents of the same type.

4 Conclusion

Equilibrium in an exchange economy places substantial restriction on equilibrium allocations in the requirement that all agents' offer prices be equal. This restriction, however, leaves an enormous multiplicity of possible outcomes available as equilibria. In general, equilibrium prices and individual commodity bundles are not determined by preferences and endowments. (In quasi-linear economies, the prices and holdings of non-linear commodities are determined by

$$p = 0.693 \pm (1.63 \times 10^{-7})$$

$$\text{AvAlloc} = \begin{pmatrix} 0.302 & 0.531 \\ 0.698 & 0.469 \end{pmatrix}$$

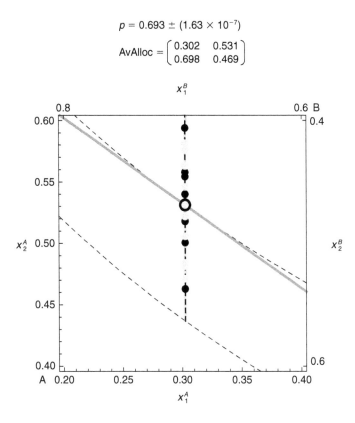

Figure 3.7 Non-equal treatment equilibrium in a quasi-linear economy. The equilibrium is plotted on a magnified scale to make the detailed features more legible.

the degeneracy of the equilibrium set, but there are many final allocations of the linear commodity consistent with equilibrium.)

One possible theoretical strategy to handle underdetermined systems with a large number of possible equilibrium states is the idea, used so successfully in statistical mechanics, of looking for the maximum entropy macro-state of the system consistent with the equilibrium restrictions. In the case of exchange economies, this approach would involve defining and calculating the appropriate entropy measures to characterize different equilibrium macro-states (Foley, 1994).

From an economic point of view the multiplicity of exchange equilibria signals an important missing dimension in conventional economic analysis, the study of the distributional impact of market exchange. The almost universally adopted equal treatment assumption does in some ways simplify the economic problem analytically, but it also suppresses this critical dimension of market economies.

Notes

* I am delighted to have the opportunity to contribute to this volume celebrating Sergio Parrinello's contributions to economic theory. My conversations with Sergio that resulted from his invitations to me to participate in the editorial board of *Metroeconomica*, and to visit the University of Rome, have helped to shape my thinking and work for many years. I am particularly grateful to Sergio for his thoughtful attention to the foundations of statistical equilibrium theory (Parrinello, 1996), a topic which underlies these notes. Parts of this paper also appear in Foley 2010.

1 The terminology here presents difficulties. The set of equilibria is often called the *Pareto set*, or *set of Pareto-optima*, but an equilibrium as defined here is Pareto-optimal only under the additional assumption that social and private marginal utilities coincide, that is, that there are no externalities present, which is an issue extraneous to the consideration of how decentralized exchange brings about an equilibrium equating private offer prices. Conventional economic theory tends to use the term "equilibrium" to refer to the narrower set of Walrasian equilibria, but this usage is unfortunate and misleading, since the concept of "equilibrium" defined here is strictly analogous to its usage in other scientific contexts such as thermodynamics, where there is no meaningful analog to Walrasian equilibria.

2 The agent utility functions are $u^A[\{x, y\}] = x^3 y^7$ and $u^B[\{x, y\}] = x^7 y^3$. Equilibria are found by iterating a simple decentralized trade algorithm adapted from Foley and Albin (1992) in which agents are randomly paired and make mutually advantageous exchanges at a random price between their offer prices until their offer prices have converged.

3 The agent utility functions are $u^A [\{x, y\}] = 1 + x - .5x^2 - (.00001 + y)^{-3}$ and $u^B [\{x, y\}] = 1 + x - .6x^2 - (.00001 + y)^{-2}$.

4 The agent utility functions are $u^A [\{x, y\}] = x^3 + y$ and $u^B[\{x, y\}] = x^6 + y$.

5 The economy is the same as the one pictured in Figure 3.2, and the equilibrium is the outcome of the same exchange algorithm.

References

Edgeworth, F. Y. (1954). *Mathematical psychics; an essay on the application of mathematics to the moral sciences*. A. M. Kelly, New York.

Foley, D. K. (1994). A statistical equilibrium theory of markets. *Journal of Economic Theory*, 62(2): 321–345.

Foley, D. K. (2010). What's wrong with the fundamental existence and welfare theorems? *Journal of Economic Behavior and Organizaton* (forthcoming).

Foley, D. K. and Albin, P. S. (1992). Decentralized, dispersed exchange without an auctioneer: a simulation study. *Journal of Economic Behavior and Organization*, 18(1): 27–52.

Walras, L. (1954). *Elements of pure economics or the theory of social wealth*. Allen and Unwin, London.

Parrinello, S. (1996). Equilibri statistici e nuovi microfondamenti della macroeconomia. In Gnesutta, C., editor, *Incertezza, Moneta, Aspettative ed Equilibrio: saggi in onore di Fausto Vicarelli*. Il Mulino, Bologna.

Smith, E. and Foley, D. K. (2008). Classical thermodynamics and economic general equilibrium theory. *Journal of Economic Dynamics and Control*, 32: 7–65.

4 Capital in the neoclassical theory

Some notes* and 'A reply to Professor Bliss's Comment'

Pierangelo Garegnani

I Two preliminary observations

1   I shall start with two preliminary observations on neoclassical theory which will form the basis of my arguments. Section II will then deal with the apparent early realization by Hicks that capital could not be consistently defined as a single magnitude, and with the way out of the problem he attempted to put forward in *Value and Capital*. These preliminary considerations will pave the way for a discussion in section III of the post-war capital controversy, taken when – in its later stages, after the recognition of phenomena like the reswitching of techniques and reverse capital deepening – the defence of neoclassical theory came to be conducted in terms, essentially, of the reformulations of the theory proposed in *Value and Capital* three decades before. Finally, in section IV, reference will be made to the argument I developed elsewhere (Garegnani 2003) according to which those reformulations also ultimately depend on the notion of capital as a single magnitude, the same which had been found indefensible, at the level of pure analysis, after the early stage of the controversy.

2   The first of my two observations is of both a historical and a logical nature. It concerns the two approaches which, at the of cost of severe simplification, can be said to have dominated the theory of distribution and relative prices in succession since its systematic inception in the eighteenth century.

The earlier approach is the classical one of the Physiocrats, Smith, Ricardo and Marx. It was founded, essentially, on the notion of the surplus which a community can dispose of, over the part of its product which must be put back into the production process to ensure its repetition on an unchanged scale. This part was taken to include, besides the consumed means of production, also the subsistence of the workers employed broadly identified with their wages: the incomes accruing to the other classes in society were then traced to the surplus. The prior, thus separately determined real wage allowed, on the other hand, for a determination of relative prices similarly separate from that of outputs, engendering a simple analytical structure deeply different from that of the later theory, and open – through the institutional determination of the wage and the flexibility of the separate determination of outputs – to an essential role for broader social, political and historical forces in the working of the economy.[1]

The later approach is instead that which after several decades of transition from classical analysis, crystallized in the last quarter of the nineteenth century around the twin concepts of marginal utility and marginal productivity and has dominated since. It is founded on the conception of a substitutability between 'factors of production', and on the demand and supply functions for factors and commodities which descend from that substitutability. It arose essentially out of the classical theory of the rent of land extended to the division between wages and profits, thereby replacing the notion of surplus by which, we saw, that division had been explained by the classics.

Now, and here we come to our first preliminary observation, one element can be argued to have been decisive in allowing for the passage from the earlier to the later approach. This element is the use in an essential role of the conception of capital as a single magnitude. We shall presently be back to clarify and justify this statement which, I know, is likely to be highly controversial, but to do so we must first proceed to our second preliminary observation.

3   This second observation concerns a basic feature of capital goods in a market economy. In the eyes of their owners physically heterogeneous capital goods are perfect substitutes in proportion to their values. As Walras had lucidly pointed out nearly a century and half ago, capital goods are demanded by savers as elements of a single commodity, 'perpetual net income'.[2] That is indeed the single commodity whose existence we imply when we assume competitive arbitrage to be sufficient to realize a uniform 'effective' rate of riskless return on the price of such goods: the reciprocal of that rate is the price of that Walrasian commodity. And little changes if, more in keeping with contemporary intertemporal general equilibrium, its finite horizon and changing prices, we refer to 'income for next year', whose gross unit[3] has the price given by the discount factor $(1 + r_t)^{-1}$, r_t being the 'effectively' uniform rate of return for the year in question[4] numerically expressed in terms of numeraire. In what follows we shall generically refer to this commodity as 'future income'.

4   We can now return to the first of our observations, and contend that it is this single commodity, or 'quantity of capital', rooted in the experience and practice of wealth owners,[5] that has suggested in the first place the idea of a generalization of the classical theory of rent to the division between wages and profits. That extension is in fact founded on assuming a variability of the proportion of capital to labour (and land), analogous to the classical one of labour (plus capital) to land. It is a variability understood to descend from either the alternative between the methods available for producing (directly or indirectly) the same consumption good, or from the methods for producing outputs of alternative consumption goods. Now, the fact is that in both cases the alternative production processes involved differ, generally, by the *kinds* of capital goods used, rather than by the *proportions* to labour in which each kind of them is employed. A variability of the 'proportion of capital to labour' in the economy could therefore have hardly been conceived for neoclassical theory, unless the heterogeneous capital goods required by the alternative methods, or by the alternative outputs, had been viewed as embodiments of quantities of the same homogeneous value commodity demanded by savers.

5   That, however, is far from being all about the role of the single savers' commodity in the origin of neoclassical theory. Another role, even more important from a strictly analytical point of view, lies in the fact that only such a commodity allowed expressing the capital endowment – a datum in marginal theory, like land or population for classical rent – in a way compatible with the homogeneity of capital goods for savers.

I am referring here to the tendency, under free competition, towards a uniform effective rate of riskless return on the capitals' supply prices – i.e. if we prefer, the tendency to an equality between the capitals' demand prices (or simply prices) and their supply prices (costs of production).[6] It is the tendency to what, following Marshall, used to be called the 'long-period equilibrium', in which 'plant' has adjusted to outputs in each industry. Indeed, that uniformity – the traditional one of the competitive 'rate of profits' – assumes the physical composition of the capital endowment to be fully adjusted to the techniques adopted and outputs produced.[7] It assumes, therefore, an *endogenous* determination of that physical composition. Now – and here we are back to the need for capital as a single magnitude in neoclassical theory – this endogenous determination is compatible with the basic neoclassical treatment of the capital endowment as a datum, only if the latter is again conceived as a fluid susceptible of taking any physical form.[8] Without this uniformity of effective returns, on the other hand, the position of the economy as determined by the theory would have been no more *persistent*,[9] under free competition, than any position of the economy with, say, different wages for labour of the same quality, or with prices of products differing from their costs of production, effects strictly analogous to those we have for capital when the above uniformity of returns does not hold.

But the question then is: why this *persistency*, leading neoclassical theory towards the troublesome notion of the given capital endowment as a single magnitude? Indeed, to such a persistency had long been attributed nothing less than the possibility of ensuring correspondence between theory and observation in economics. It was the role played – even across the deep divide between classical and neoclassical theory – by what we may indicate here as the 'normal' price or, more generally, the 'normal' position of the economy – the basis of economic analysis since Adam Smith's notion of the natural price as 'the central price, to which the prices of all commodities are *continually* gravitating' (Smith 1776, bk I, ch. VI, 51). The persistency of the normal price, as warranted under competition, by the above uniformity of the rate of return, was in fact thought to allow for a *repetition of transactions*, which by occurring on the basis of nearly unchanged data, would be generally sufficient to compensate the temporary 'accidental' deviations from it of the actual price: in that way persistency would allow for a correspondence between the theoretical variables and some average of the corresponding magnitudes in the actual economy.

6   It was thus not a matter of accident, or of mere convenience, that the capital endowment, given as a single magnitude, characterized with varying degrees of explicitness, and with the single partial exception of Walras, all mainstream expressions of neoclassical theory up to a few decades ago, and to the events we are going to discuss below. On that idea there rested in fact two key points of neoclassical theory: the plausibility of the notion of factor substitutability lying at its basis and, with the possibility to determine a 'normal position', that of a correspondence between theoretical variables and observable magnitudes – both of which are essential, it would seem, to prevent the theory from slipping into an intellectual game.[10]

It seems indeed possible to say that, *once* the neoclassical demand and supply framework is adopted, the nature of capital as the single saver's commodity carries with it the need for the treatment of capital as a single magnitude. The quantity of the commodity in terms of which savers take their demand decisions cannot, then, be absent from the system any more than the quantity of any other commodity on which individuals take their demand decisions. This need, which we have just traced with respect to the normal position goes, we submit, beyond it. We shall recall in section IV below, my contention in (2003) that such a single commodity can be retraced with its difficulties in the contemporary formulations of the theory, which have done away with it at the level of factor endowments.

As we could expect from the homogeneity of capital goods for the savers which cannot but be reflected in any theory of the market economy – the classical economists also tended to treat capital as a single magnitude. However, the essential fact in this respect is that their different 'surplus' theory of distribution and relative prices – i.e. the absence of the demand and supply framework? – exempted them from the above two needs for treating capital as a single magnitude. As shown, for example, in Sraffa's contemporary revival of classical theory, a vectorial notion of capital suffices for its determination of prices and distribution,[11] which only needs capital among the determinants for expressing the technical conditions of production.

II   The neoclassical problem and Hicks's *Value and Capital*

7   We are done with our two preliminary observations and can now get closer to the post-war capital controversy which will concern us in section III by introducing here the question central to that controversy.

The neoclassical need for capital as a single magnitude raises a problem which has been simmering since the very origin of that theory. The 'quantity' of that special factor of production had to be measured independently of the distribution and relative prices which it was brought to determine, just as the classical quantities of labour and land had to be so measured for determining rent. However, the commodity demanded by savers clearly was not *directly* measurable in any such independent terms, since its primary expression for savers lay in the *value* of the capital goods in terms of some numeraire. A basic problem of the new theory was, therefore, how to measure capital, the single magnitude in terms which would be both independent of distribution, as the value of capital goods is not, and at the same time appropriately related to the value quantity on which savers do take their decisions. The 'average period of production' over which labour and more generally non-produced factors have to remain invested under each method of production of the commodity and its direct and indirect methods of production, was the road along which a conciliation of the two requirements was attempted, from Jevons and Böhm Bawerk onwards. As is known, the attempt foundered on (1) the necessity to consider the compound rate of interest on the advances for non-produced factors; (2) on the plurality of such non-produced factors; and (3) on fixed capital.[12]

The impossibility of consistently defining a concept as basic for the intended generalization of classical rent, as we just argued the 'quantity of capital' was, might conceivably have led to the abandonment of the attempt in favour of some return to classical analysis (as had in fact happened when the 'wages fund' theories, the progenitors of neoclassical theory, were abandoned around the middle of the nineteenth century). However, the principle of factor substitution and the ensuing demand and supply explanation of distribution, had apparently taken roots too deep for them to be abandoned – while Marshall's interpretation of Ricardo and the classical economists as primitive exponents of a demand and supply theory of prices, simplified by an assumption of constant returns, had succeeded in largely cancelling the traces of the alternative analysis that had dominated economic thought for more than a century before the 'marginalist revolution'. Thus, when it began to be recognized that capital could not be ultimately treated as a single magnitude, the reaction was instead to apply the principle of substitution to each kind of capital good taken as a distinct 'factor', with little explicit consideration of the drastic difficulties such a change would raise for the theory.

8 Hicks (1939) was probably the main influence in bringing into mainstream theory this tentative way out of the difficulty. After basing his *Theory of Wages* (1932) on normal positions and therefore on the usual notion of a 'quantity of capital' as essentially the value magnitude,[13] he appears to have come to an early perception of the fact that the notion could not be made ultimately viable and had to be replaced.[14] Thus in *Value and Capital* (1939), he came to treat the given capital endowment of the theory as a vector of capital goods. It was indeed the conception that Walras had advanced as early as 1877,[15] having initially failed to realize its inconsistency with the uniformity of returns on capitals' supply prices pertaining to the 'normal position' – the position which, like all his predecessors and contemporaries, he had originally intended to determine.[16]

The necessary, if implicit, recognition of Walras's inconsistency meant, however, that Hicks had to accompany the adoption of that conception of capital with the abandonment of the normal position and hence, inevitably, with basic changes in the notions of equilibrium of the theory. The competitive tendency to a uniform rate of profits could but be powerful and quick in bringing about appreciable changes in the composition of a capital stock unadjusted to the most profitable methods and outputs, thus causing appreciable changes in the prices of productive services and commodities. The persistency which justified the determination of the normal position while abstracting from the changes the latter is undergoing, could no longer be assumed. The analysis had to attempt remedying that by considering the effect of future conditions on the markets for current commodities and productive services.

This consideration of future conditions was done in either of two ways. The first was by introducing 'price expectations' in the 'temporary equilibria' resulting from the Walrasian capital endowment. It was the way taken by Hicks himself in *Value and Capital*. Alternatively, in the search for something less volatile than expectations on which to found a theory, the analysis could be expanded to imagine present markets for future commodities and factors, so that future prices could be envisaged coming into actual existence. Taken to the limit, the assumption of future markets could be extended to all commodities and factors over the whole assumed life of the economy, as was done in the general intertemporal equilibrium of Arrow and Debreu (1954) and then Debreu (1959).

Both those drastic reformulations of neoclassical theory may in fact be seen to have been absorbed into mainstream theory, largely by *Value and Capital*, since the possibility of the second alternative – intertemporal general equilibrium – had also emerged in that book (1939, e.g. 136 ff.) and, above all, it was developed later essentially by 'dating' the commodities of the 'static general equilibria' of Parts I and II of *Value and Capital*.

These reformulations of neoclassical theory, which we may thus call 'Hicksian' for short, were, however, affected by two deficiencies which were the mirror image of the two reasons for which we contended in section I above, capital as the savers' single commodity had been at the origin of marginal theory. They were (1) the absence of substitutability between 'productive factors' when capital goods are conceived in the Walrasian way:[17] (2) the just recalled lack of persistency, and therefore lack of potential correspondence with observation. And this affected both the 'temporary equilibria', and also those equilibria of each 'date', which constitute, so to speak, the bricks of general intertemporal equilibrium.[18]

These were, presumably, the difficulties which, variously perceived and expressed, had underlain the remarkable fact that, despite the fame of its author, and the well-known difficulties of the alternative notion of a single magnitude, Walras's own conception of capital had failed to enter the mainstream during the six decades elapsing between its first 1876 formulation and its revival by Hicks in 1939. Hicks himself in 1932, not many years before *Value and Capital*, had sceptically commented

> [Walras and Pareto's theories of capital] are the last part of their work which one can consider as final or accept without the most careful consideration.
>
> (1932b, 297)

Not unlike Walras's, Hicks's notion of capital and the associated 'dynamic theory' of *Value and Capital* appear in fact to have initially had little impact on mainstream theory. The notion drew, for example, little or no attention, in what was then the centre of economic theorizing, the Cambridge of Pigou, Keynes and Robertson. It is even conceivable that its influence might have remained confined to groups of mathematical economists[19] on the margin of the mainstream, as had indeed been the case before, had it not been for the emergence of some striking results incidental to Piero Sraffa's work on the classical approach to prices and distribution over the same decades. The phenomena of the reswitching of techniques and of 'reverse capital' deepening, advanced 'in preview' in the 1950s at the hands of Joan Robinson,[20] were indeed sufficient to soon render untenable the notion of capital as a single factor at the level of pure theory. The way to dominance was then open for what was essentially the only alternative that would keep within the premises of neoclassical theory: capital on Walrasian lines, and the necessary reformulations of the conception of equilibrium on Hicksian lines – marking, so to speak, a deep 'Hicksian divide' in the evolution of neoclassical theory.

III The capital controversy and Hicks's *Value and Capital*

9 With that we have reached the heart of the post-war capital controversy, and have joined it at what we indicated above as its later stages when the defence of neoclassical theory was conducted essentially in terms of its Hicksian reformulations.

We might have therefore expected that, at such a stage, the difficulties of those reformulations would, if not take the centre of the scene, at least emerge with sufficient clarity to be debated. However, the way in which the reformulations had been introduced in *Value and Capital* nearly thirty years before made it difficult for the controversy to achieve clarity and focus on these questions. We must therefore turn back to *Value and Capital* for those aspects of Hicks's argument which are important for what, I would submit, has been the inconclusiveness of those later stages of the controversy.

10 Despite its title, what we find in the foreground of *Value and Capital* is not the problem of capital, but, rather, the claimed need for a 'dynamic theory', accompanied by a critique of what is there called the 'static theory' of 'the economists in the past' (1939, 115).[21] However, what is striking is that when we come to a description of what that 'static theory' consisted of, we do not find the normal position which was in fact the mainstay of those economists. What is attributed to them, in the forms we shall presently see, are instead two kinds of equilibria which, though showing some features in common with the normal position, are definitely not it.

The first of those two kinds is, Hicks says, what the static theory would be if stated in a 'strict', consistent way (1939, 115). It is represented by the equilibria analysed in Parts I and II of *Value and Capital*, those by which Hicks in effect replaces by a Walrasian given vector of capital goods the previous notion of the capital endowment as, essentially, a single magnitude. Hicks has, however, to admit that those equilibria cannot be taken to represent the thought of the economists of the past as it actually was.

We must therefore look for the second representation Hicks gives of those equilibria of the past (1939, 116). And here we find the stationary position: the one, that is, where the incentive to net savings has disappeared. However, this again is a notion quite different from the neoclassical normal position. It resembles it in one respect, namely the constancy of prices assumed in the definition of the equilibrium. But even in that respect the two positions radically differ. In the normal position the constancy of the capital endowment, and hence of the relative prices, is merely an abstraction from the changes which they are admitted to effectively undergo in the economy – an abstraction founded on the persistency of the position due to the comparative slowness of the changes in its data, in particular of the only endogenous such change, that in the capital endowment.[22] In the stationary position instead the same constancy of capital is the endogenous result of an equilibrium condition of zero net saving, so that the capital endowment is an *unknown* of the equations and not the *datum* it is in the normal position.[23] And the same is true for the proportion of capital to labour of the 'steady state' that since the postwar period has become the commonest form of stationary state contemplated in the analysis.

11   The paradox of *Value and Capital* is then that in its account of the 'usual course of economists in the past', we do not find the hallmark of that 'usual course' down to Hicks's own *Theory of Wages* (1932): namely the normal position.

That disappearance of the normal position entailed, then, a second and even more striking paradox: it is that we do not find in *Value and Capital* any specific criticism of the normal position of those economists – the very position which Hicks proposes there to replace by his 'dynamic theory'. The only criticism remains the generic one of the lack of realism of assuming the constancy of prices in the definition of an equilibrium (1939, 116–17) – a criticism which would have been more convincing if 'previous theory' had in fact rested, as it clearly did not, on either Hicks's 'stationary states', or on the fleeting equilibria of Parts I and II of *Value and Capital*.

As a matter of fact, the dependence of current prices on future prices was all but overlooked by those economists – starting from Adam Smith's dichotomy between 'market' and 'natural' prices, and continuing then down to Walras, Marshall, Pigou, Wicksell, etc. To the extent in which the expected prices reflected merely 'accidental' circumstances, or the undoing of those circumstances, their effects could be ignored because they would be averaged out in the normal price through the repetition of transactions allowed for by the persistency of the normal position. And to the extent in which the expected prices expressed instead changes in the *data* of the position, they would be dealt with by the comparison between the corresponding two normal positions.

The real point behind this alleged past oversight of price changes – a point which remains implicit in *Value and Capital*[24] – was, however, to be that the *persistency* allowing for the *abstraction* from those changes, had been made possible by the treatment of the given capital endowment as a single magnitude susceptible to adjusting its physical form. And this is just what the Hicks of (1939), as distinct from that of (1932), knew could *not* be done. Leaving aside the obviously unrealistic stationary states, the normal positions had therefore to be replaced by the static equilibria of *Value and Capital*, whose fleeting character made the remedy of dated prices and quantities all but inevitable. In other words the need of a dynamics was the *effect* rather than the *cause* of the change in the conception of capital, contrary to what Hicks might be taken to imply in his (1939) foreground argument.

12 The disappearance of the normal position from Hicks's (1939) argument was to weigh heavily on the controversy of thirty years later. Because of the strong direct or indirect influence of *Value and Capital* by that time, the eclipse of the normal position had a series of effects on the controversy which, I submit, converged in obscuring the basic terms of the question of capital in neoclassical theory. We may perhaps try to summarize these effects under four main points.

That disappearance meant first of all the disappearance of the most transparent form of dependence of neoclassical theory on capital as a single magnitude, namely its ultimate use as a datum for determining the position. On the one hand, that made the use of the notion in previous neoclassical theory a confused bone of contention rather than the simple historical fact it was.[25] On the other hand, it made the role of the conception of a 'quantity of capital' at the very origin of the analytical structure of the theory, much more difficult to discern and understand. As a result, and most importantly, it made it difficult to understand the continued dependence on that conception in the reformulations of neoclassical theory that were being advanced – a continuing dependence of which more will be said in the next section.

Second, the disappearance of the normal position went together with that of its key condition: the uniformity of effective returns on the capitals' supply prices or costs (i.e. the equality of their demand prices with the respective supply prices), ensuring the persistence of the position and the possibility of its correspondence with observation.[26] Thus when that condition was referred to from the critical side in order to explain the rationale of the normal position, and its neoclassical dependence on the capital endowment as a single fluid fund, that rationale was generally not understood and the condition was even confused with the altogether different condition of a uniformity in the commodity own rates of interest, a mere synonym of assuming constancy of prices in defining the equilibrium.[27]

Third and most importantly the misunderstanding of the normal position as a stationary or steady state, led many of the participants in the controversy to take for granted the Hicksian charge that 'previous theory' was inapplicable to the 'real world' (1939, 215). We have already mentioned the paradoxical character of that charge, but we may now stress how, by putting the alternative method based on normal positions out of sight, that change helped in turning a blind eye on the real undermining of the applicability of the theory, the one due to the impermanence of the new equilibria and the resulting need for a dynamic theory. It was indeed the undermining which Hicks himself had implicitly admitted when, in a little-quoted passage of *Value and Capital*, he wrote that he assumed 'the economy to be always in equilibrium' (1939, 131),[28] an assumption which should have shocked the readers of *Value and Capital*: no economist had ever before supposed the economy to actually be in an equilibrium or more generally a position of rest except by a fluke:[29] gravitation around it and not achievement of it, had always been what was thought relevant for the position of the economy object of the analysis – the only form of correspondence with observation which, it was held, economic theory could attain.[30]

And, fourth, the mist in which the discussion had been moving because of these unclarified misunderstandings, was made thicker by a tendency to see the neoclassical dependence on the notion of a 'quantity of capital' as pertaining to the empirical construct of an 'aggregate production function' purporting, that is, to represent the output of the whole economy as a single homogeneous aggregate, produced by a 'capital' homogeneous with it. Used for Solow's 1956 simplified neoclassical answer to the long-period problems raised by Keynes and aggregate demand, that notion was an initial target from part of the critics. Taken in isolation the target was, however, misleading as it risked turning an inconsistency at the foundations of the idea of a generalized 'factor substitutability' (paragraph 4 above) into difficulties pertaining only to an admittedly unrigorous approximation, and therefore presumably absent when the several productive sectors are distinguished in a general equilibrium system. It was thereby overlooked that the inconsistency is there, whichever number of sectors which we might wish to distinguish into the economy. In fact the essence of the neoclassical problem of capital is not aggregation versus general equilibrium, but, if anything, one about *two kinds of general equilibria*: the traditional one based on normal positions, exemplified by, say, Wicksell (1906), or even by Walras (as far as his original intentions went) versus the Hicksian one that renounced such positions in the attempt to avoid the single magnitude.

13   Thus, in conclusion, the later stages of the controversy appear to have been marred by multiple misunderstandings which, largely, are still waiting to be cleared. Thanks to the unambiguous phenomena of reswitching and reverse capital deepening, the first stage was conclusive in discarding from pure theory the traditional version of the theory. Subsequently, however, when the implications of those phenomena and the reformulations of the theory inevitably became the main object, those misunderstandings prevented decisive progress and led to what is in fact an inconclusive phase of the discussion. A certain unpreparedness on the critical side to extend the critique to the Hicksian reformulation of the theory advanced from the opposite side, was also relevant. Many of the critical authors had their roots in a Cambridge which, in its majority, had essentially ignored the relevant part of *Value and Capital*, judging it unnecessarily complicated and unlikely to bear serious fruit. In that, as it turned out, such a majority

had underestimated the real potential of the Hicksian proposal, which was defence and not construction. The lack of a sufficiently known and well-tested alternative like that of the classical economists[31] contributed to what I see as the halfway pause in the critical course.

It is this complex of circumstances, I submit, which has left space for the credence that, whatever its methodological deficiencies, the equilibria which became dominant with the 'Hicksian divide' are immune from the inconsistencies on capital of previous marginal theory. That in turn has left space, I believe, for a second no less unwarranted consequence: a feeling that since the 'Hicksian' reformulations and in particular general intertemporal equilibrium would confirm at the level of pure theory the essential validity of the general demand and supply framework, they would also provide some validation for the admittedly imperfect previous concepts – foremost that of a 'quantity of capital' – as workable approximation in more applied work.

IV The problem of capital is still with us

14 I think that neither of those beliefs is well founded. I have in fact argued elsewhere (2003) that intertemporal equilibrium does not avoid the dependence on the notion of the capital as a single magnitude. Though it no longer occupies its highly visible position as a *fund* among the factor endowments, the homogeneous commodity 'future income' demanded by savers, can be shown to emerge as a flow, with the respective demand and supply functions and the corresponding market. They are respectively what, after Keynes, we are used to call (gross) savings supply, (gross) investment demand, and saving-investment market. The implications of the inconsistency of that notion of capital – the same implications which enforced the abandonment of the traditional analysis in pure theory – are still there to be faced.[32]

Discussion on the matter is proceeding. The question, however, may already be asked: should we not begin to recognize that those difficulties are but the expression of a theory originally inspired by the concept of capital as an independently measurable single productive factor, which we now all agree does not exist?

Professor Bliss is, however, correct when in introducing a collection of reprints of articles on capital he writes

> ultimately, only new theory beats old theory however bad
>
> (Bliss 2008, xvi)

but he continues,

> there really is not a well worked out alternative long run capital theory to set against the various orthodox models

where we may, however, note the reference to a '*long run*' theory seems to limit the expected novelty of the alternative by implying that we already have a satisfactory short-run theory. And a similar limitation appears to underlie his reference to the alternative theory as a *capital theory* to be set against orthodox models: but the question, as I have attempted to argue in this essay, is wider than is carried by the qualification of 'capital theory'. It more properly concerns an alternative between theories of distribution and relative prices.

If we start thinking in those wider terms we must first of all set aside Marshall's interpretation of Ricardo and the classical economists as representing an early simplified version of later demand and supply theory. Demand and supply in Ricardo and the early classics had never been *determinants* of normal prices, rather than merely movers, so to speak, of 'actual' or 'market' prices (Smith 1776, 49 bk. I, ch. VI) towards a 'natural price' or 'price of production' determined independently of them, by forces governing the division of the product between wages and profits, alien to any principle of factor substitution, and, therefore, to the ultimate source of the neoclassical problem of capital.

Once that clarification is accomplished we may find there the alternative we are looking for, free from the difficulties of capital. It is a theory well tested in its long tradition. Its contemporary revival, initiated by Sraffa (1960), has involved, with a reconstruction of its analytical structure by means also of comparison with neoclassicism, the development of the theory with respect, for example, to the basic question of the stability of its normal positions. It has also involved dealing with special problems like the treatment of joint production, fixed capital or land rents. But it has above all regarded work intended to include the Keynesian analysis of aggregate demand for both the short run and, most importantly, the long run.[33]

When the vision of the forces governing the economy underlying that classical analysis will be grasped, it will be found, I believe, to be surprisingly close to that inspiring much present theorizing aiming to bring out the basic role of institutions in the economy. Classical analysis may then perhaps allow us to develop and refine that work, providing it with a solid analytical framework, free from the straitjacket of a generalized principle of factor substitution – undermined by the results of the capital controversy and, even independently of that, hollowed out by the reformulations which that controversy has brought about in neoclassical theory.

A reply to Professor Bliss's Comment

1 Professor Bliss has not responded to the arguments. Thus in the comment I find no word on the role which capital, the single magnitude, played in allowing for a neoclassical normal position and the possibility of a link between theoretical variables and observable magnitudes. Pages of equations will not remedy the need to bridge over the myriad of accidental circumstances acting on the observable magnitudes at each instant of time and making it impossible to determine them and their path in time. These are indeed the myriad circumstances which made Bliss himself refer in the past to the intractable 'Herculean programme of constructing a complete theory of the behaviour of the economy out of equilibrium' – a programme made necessary 'by the fact that, even if equilibrium were to be stable, there might not be enough time within the space of a week for prices to adjust to equilibrium' (Bliss 1975, 28).

Nor do I find any answer on how we are going to take care of substitution between productive factors within equilibria, like the initial ones of Bliss's dynamic paths, where a physically given capital endowment should provide for alternative processes of production which generally require capital goods specific to each of them. The result can only consist of rigidly determined equilibrium outputs and methods of production with abundant zero (or indeterminate) factor prices.

I do understand that these questions are not those which neoclassical scholars would generally set themselves in their routine of problem solving on bases passed down by their elders. But Bliss is one of those elders and we would like to know whether he can now vouchsafe any different answer from that he gave at the time to his doubts above, i.e. 'confine the investigations to the equilibrium state' and 'regard as the object of our investigations not the "economy" but "economic equilibrium"' (Bliss 1975) – i.e. renouncing an answer on the vital question of the relation between 'equilibrium' and the 'economy'.

Professor Bliss sees me and likeminded colleagues as taking for their criticism neoclassical theory 'on its long past ground'. As he puts it, 'a lot has happened in economics since pre-war John Hicks'. Yes, certainly a lot has happened, including the capital controversies, but where, before *Value and Capital*, did we find in mainstream theory the 'dynamical' methods of which the paths of Bliss's comment are an instance? And those paths are of today, not 'long past'. Before Hicks we had instead statements like the following

> dynamical solution in the physical sense of economic problems are unattainable ... statical solutions afford starting points for such rude and imperfect approaches to dynamical solutions as we may be able to attain to.
>
> (Marshall 1898, 38–9, PG, 21 n. 8).

It is thus to 'long past' Hicks that we have also to turn in order to criticize, for example, today's Bliss.

2   My commentator admits, however, one basic fact: that of the homogeneity of the capital goods for savers, seen by them as constituents of the single Walrasian commodity 'future income' (PG, 78),[34] and its conflict with the vectorial measurement of the given initial capital endowment of contemporary neoclassical theory. But when he envisages the conflict as a tension inherent in economic reality he overlooks two important elements.

The first is that neoclassical theory was originally conceived in a way thought to solve the problem: i.e. with capital as a fluid as much on the side of the supply (the given capital endowment), as on that of the demand.

The second is that in the alternative classical surplus theory of distribution, no such 'tension' exists between a 'fluid demand' and a vectorial 'supply' since, as we saw (PG, 90), capital as a determinant of prices and distribution emerges there only for defining the technical conditions of production. Thus, the theory of the Physiocrats, Adam Smith, Ricardo or Marx – to which Bliss fails to refer in his comment[35] – would apparently provide the 'formal ... model ... that resolves the problem' (Bliss, 1).

When we keep in mind these two elements it becomes clear that the 'tension' in question results not from economic reality, but from insisting at explaining distribution and the general functioning of a market economy in terms of a substitutability between factors of production, and resulting demand and supply forces, even in the face of the admitted failure of the basic concepts on which the theory was built.

3   Indeed, even a quick consideration of the dynamical theory Bliss outlines in his comment does, I believe, reveal the marks of the above complex origin, rather than those of a physiological advance and complement of previous analysis.

We start (Bliss, 1) from an 'idealized equilibrium', based apparently on the theory of general intertemporal equilibrium. But, to begin with, this equilibrium will be one in which, as just noted, substitution between factors is essentially absent, and when substitutability will appear at later dates it will be founded on capital, the single magnitude, in the form of the traditional 'free capital' of the investment flow. Then, in addition to the consequences of the likely, multiple zero factor prices of the early equilibria, we shall have the 'capital paradoxes' with the resulting possible multiple, unstable and zero-prices equilibria.

Bliss writes that if multiple equilibria were the end of neoclassical theory, then the theory 'is dead and buried long ago' (Bliss, 2). Certainly Marshall and the other founders of neoclassical theory worried a lot about multiple equilibria. It was, and it is, not easy to find in the centuries of history of market economies facts suggesting the possibility of multiple or unstable equilibria, validating a theory asserting such a possibility. My commentator seems in fact to mix multiple equilibria deduced from the essential assumptions of neoclassical theory – maximization of profits and utility, as is the case for reverse capital deepening and reswitching – with altogether different multiplicities resulting merely from dispensable additional hypotheses made in specific models. It is to the latter that Bliss refers, when, for instance, he mentions the possible multiplicity of steady states with proportional savings and a single capital good, and concludes that the 'aggregation of capital is not the crucial difficulty' (Bliss 2008, 21). By mixing the comparatively innocuous with the lethal, one can indeed make the lethal look less lethal.

My opponent feels, however, that he can proceed on such an insecure basis and try to demonstrate that neoclassical theory can conceivably say something on the long-run tendencies of the economy – a demonstration which he seems to think constitutes the essence of a solution to the neoclassical problem of capital.[36] Apparently basing his ideas on the obviously not very general assumption of a single 'representative agent', he utilizes the properties of a competitive equilibrium in order to identify the possible paths followed by such a representative agent, and therefore by the economy, with those developed out of Ramsey's (1928) famous article, and which are defined once the time preferences of the agent are given. That path might then bring the economy to a stationary or steady state which would give definiteness to the long-run tendencies of the economy. While trying to show that, Bliss meets the additional obstacle of the 'saddle' character attributed to that path, which should be overcome by 'transversality conditions' further restricting, apparently, the possibility that such a Ramsey path to steady states with ever be one which the economy can walk.

But the above restrictions are still far from constituting the whole of the deficiencies which Bliss himself sees in this construction, when taken as a representation of reality. At the end of his argument, he asks himself:

> how useful is it? The price dynamics [of that equilibrium] are essentially the dynamics of correctly foreseen prices [and] we do not live in a world where price movements are accurately foreseen.

He then falls back on 'non optimized dynamic equilibrium' paths of the economy of which, he states, there will be 'infinitely many'.

In fact Bliss is just experiencing here, and in the first person, some of the reasons for which, as we quoted above, Alfred Marshall had stated:

> dynamical solutions in the physical sense of economic problems are unattainable.

That firm statement by what has probably been the strongest head ever on the neoclassical side, and the main author of the original acceptance and dominance of that theory, should alone be sufficient to give Professor Bliss some doubt as to whether he really is, to use his expression, on the long-run 'plot' of science. Indeed, that plot is often very long run: my opponent mentions that, only a generation elapsed between Galileo and Newton (Bliss 2008, 24), but there were two generations between Copernicus and Galileo.

Bliss seems, however, to think that he has a way out of Marshall's denial. We might have expected that the negative answer he gives on the usefulness of his equilibrium dynamics would be followed by some recognition of shortcomings in the theory. He takes instead the *theory* as impregnable ('rock solid', Bliss, 3) and blames the failure on *reality* ('Real life capitalist economies are extremely bad at knowing where they are going in the long run and judging that destination correctly': Bliss, 3). But, knowing where the economy goes, should it not be the task of the economists, rather than that of 'the economy'?

4   Soon after that exposition of what contemporary neoclassical theory has to say for the long run of the economy – i.e. it appears that the latter can follow any of the infinitely many 'non optimized equilibrium paths' – my commentator reproaches the school of which I would be part, of a 'seeming lack of interest for the real world' (p. 3).

Certainly, after what we saw, the reflection comes naturally that if the school to which Bliss instead belongs has a strong interest for the real world, it is not served well by its own theory. As for the critics, it would certainly be odd if authors devoted to the revival and development of the theory which has been that of Adam Smith, Ricardo or Marx should have little interest for the real world – and even odder if their theory did not lend itself to serve those interests. Of course some of the authors to whom Bliss refers have contributed to the task of carrying the critique of neoclassical theory into the field of intertemporal equilibrium,[37] and it was on the other hand necessary to clarify this alternative classical theory in both its historical roots and its logical structure.[38] But certainly their ultimate purpose has never been to replace the Ramsey model by anything similar to it, but rather by, for example, a discussion of whether the fall of the rate of growth in advanced European capitalist economies from the average of 4–5 per cent of 1950–73 to an average of 2 per cent, and even lower than in later years, might not have had something to do with reactions to social movements, like those of May 1968 in France, not unconnected with a regime of full labour employment that had lasted for an entire generation, e.g. Cavalieri *et al.* (2004).

Thus if the doubt expressed by the word 'seeming' in that 'seeming lack of interest', had stimulated Bliss to research those authors' writings, he would soon have discovered that they had done much work to absorb Keynes into a classical framework where aggregate demand fits well with the characteristic broad separation between determination of outputs and determination of distribution and prices of the classical economists – and, above all, where any long-period role of Keynesian aggregate demand finds no obstacle in a theory of distribution and relative prices based on the full employment of productive resources.[39]

When combined with the Ricardian, and more generally classical, admission of long-period labour unemployment as a normal phenomenon in a market economy[40] – that analysis of aggregate demand brings to light the great potentialities of growth which exist when labour is available as it generally is. A compound rate of additional growth becomes in fact possible whenever aggregate demand allows for an initial increased use of existing capacity and then, over time, for use of the new productive capacities associated with the cumulative savings made possible by the initial increase. Though largely invisible when not utilized, this growth potential can be rapidly mobilized when conditions of aggregate demand are favourable.[41] The possible effects of that on received principles of economic policy (beginning from the idea that free competition leads to Pareto optimalities) can be imagined and have begun to be considered.[42]

It seems thus singularly odd that Professor Bliss should raise as an example of that school's lack of interest for the problems of the contemporary world,[43] the 'economic miracle' in China. Clearly, a theory which reveals the existence of such potential resources usable or wastable, would seem much more likely to explain the China 'miracle', or the Korean 'miracle', or the German post-war 'miracle', etc., than Bliss's economy analysed by means of the 'Ramsey model' and steady growth. Indeed, if I may refer to a personal experience, the development of those ideas was certainly stimulated by the Italian post-war 'miracle', and the possibility it lent to make clear that growth and the absorption of the high labour unemployment, required consumption to be encouraged, and not discouraged, contrary to the neoclassical view dominant in the Italy of the time.

5 That work, not to mention that on the stability of classical prices, which appears to have so far broadly confirmed Adam Smith's old positive conclusions,[44] or that on classical wages and their different mechanism of adjustment (cf. e.g. Garegnani 2007a, 213–15) would not seem to reflect any lack of interest in the real world – nor indeed reveal the absence of new ideas of an 'exceptionally sterile' approach (Bliss, 3).

How, then, Bliss's contrary allegations? Evidently he has not chanced to come across those works in the literature he reads. This suggests that in the future he might use his influence to facilitate access to the journals he frequents for the critics. He and likeminded colleagues might then effortlessly gain information of what goes on in that camp by direct reading, rather than by what they see as 'impact'. There, I would add, it is not common to conclude that in each given situation 'there will be infinitely many equilibrium paths' which the economy may follow.

Notes

* Thanks are due to numerous colleagues with whom parallel versions of this chapter have been discussed and, in particular, to Dr Saverio Fratini of the University of Rome 3, whose interpretations of contemporary literature have also been valuable.
1 Cf. e.g. Garegnani (2002a, 250; 2007, 186).
2 Walras (1954), 275–76, par. 242.
3 It is the price of a unit of *gross* income, because an amount $\left(\dfrac{1}{1 + r_{t+1}}\right)$ out of that unit will have to be set aside at the beginning of period $(t + 1)$, if a similar unit of gross income is to be had in $(t + 2)$.
4 The *adverb* 'effectively' is used above in order to remind the reader that this kind of uniformity of returns on capital is quite compatible with, and indeed *requires*, a 'nominal' difformity of the commodities' own rates of interest, once changes in relative prices over the period of the loan are considered in the equilibrium (see note. 7). In the latter case it is only the *numerical expression* of that uniform effective rate that will differ depending on the numeraire adopted.
5 Thus, e.g. Bliss (1975, 8) rightly notes that capital 'cries out to be aggregated'. He does not, however, notice the essential reason for that: the homogeneity of capital goods for savers.
6 Simple arbitrage, over however short a time, will be sufficient to realize a tendency to uniformity of the (riskless) effective rate on the *demand prices* of the capital goods, by lowering those prices below the respective supply prices in the case of relatively abundant capital goods. That is of course a quite different phenomenon from the tendency to the uniformity on their supply prices mentioned in the text above, which requires changes in the physical composition of the capital stock.
7 The uniformity of rate of return on capitals' supply prices of course excludes, as it is generally done at the level of abstraction of a normal price, the presence in the capital endowment of 'obsolete' capital goods – pertaining, that is, to methods of production presently dominated by other methods at all possible levels of the distributive variables. More embarrassing for a theory in which the capital endowment is a datum is the fact that the same uniformity of returns also excludes the presence in the endowment of kinds of capital goods which are not 'obsolete' in the sense above, or do pertain to methods of production other than those dominant in the equilibrium

considered. (The question does not arise in Walras, who assumes that all methods require the same kinds of capital goods though in different proportions: but it reflects the general case, and it reinforces the neoclassical need for capital as the single magnitude which can take the form of any concrete capital good.)

  8 Cf. e.g. Hicks 1932a, 20–1, on the need to refer to a marginal product of labour for which the 'quantity', but *not* the 'form', of the co-operating capital remains unchanged.

  9 'It is to this *persistence* of the influences considered, and to the time allowed for them to work out their effects that we refer when contrasting Market and Normal price' (Marshall 1898, V, III, 6; our italics). The question is discussed in Garegnani (2002b).

10 It is the risk which Malinvaud appears to detect when he writes 'the risk seriously exists that economics loses touch with real problems and develops on its own into a scholastic' (1991, 66).

11 Cf. e.g. Garegnani (1960, viii) and (e.g. 1990, 2).

12 Cf. Garegnani 1960, Part I, ch. III; and Part II, ch. IV; also 1990, 23–31 for, respectively, the notion of the average period of production, and its shortcomings from the viewpoint of marginal theory.

13 Cf. Garegnani (1976, n. 12).

14 On the effect on Hicks of Shove's remarks on capital in his review of Hicks's (1932a) cf. Garegnani 1976, n. 13.

15 *Théorie Mathématique de la Richesse Sociale*, Paris, 1877, 568–9 reproducing the paper Walras delivered in July 1876 at the Société Vaudoise des Sciences Naturelles. The year 1877 is also the one in which Walras published the second instalment of the first edition of the *Elements* (1974 and 1977) containing his theory of capital formation.

16 Garegnani (1960, Part II, chs 2 and 3, also 1990, 13–19).

17 With the factors as conceived in Walras, substitutability could be claimed to enter the system *over time* with gross investment, as new, more profitable capital goods replace the existing ones and therefore the savers' commodity (capital) can enter in its direct form of object of the saving investment flows. However, the fact remains that (1) substitution would be almost entirely absent in the initial equilibria with the existing physical capital and, in the logic of the theory, this would be bound to deeply affect all subsequent positions; and (2) the limited substitutability that would thus emerge would again appeal to capital, the single magnitude confirming its necessity for factors substitution.

18 It is interesting to note that the two difficulties of the Walrasian conception adopted are not mentioned in *Value and Capital*. This is so, despite the fact that the difficulty regarding factor substitutability had been prominent in a 1932 debate between Hicks and Robertson (cf. Hicks 1932b; Robertson 1931), when both authors stressed the necessity that the 'capital' endowment be allowed to change 'form' in order to give rise to marginal products and, more generally, sufficient substitutability between factors. The point returned with force in the *Theory of Wages* (1932a, 20) where e.g. Hicks contrasts the 'full equilibrium' marginal product of labour with a 'short-period' one, where the 'form', as well as the 'quantity', of the capital is said *not* to change: the latter is then dismissed as something which 'it is very doubtful if [it] can be given any precise meaning which is capable of useful application'. This primarily regards the difficulty of factor substitution, but the contrast drawn here between 'short-period', and 'full equilibrium' marginal product of labour appears to also imply awareness of the second deficiency of the vectorial conception of capital, i.e. the non-uniformity it entails in the effective returns on capitals' supply prices.

19 Indeed, the Walrasian conception of capital had been used long before Hicks, by mathematical economists with little notice of it being taken in the mainstream literature at the time. See e.g. Wald (1936 [1936]).

20 Cf. Robinson (1970, 144–5) about her use of the Sraffa results.

21 Cf. Garegnani 1976, 31–6 for traces of the deeper line of Hicks's (1939) criticism of previous theory, concerning capital (cf. also note 24 below).
22 As e.g. Marshall wrote 'if we are considering ... the whole of a large country as one market of capital, we cannot regard the aggregate supply of it as altered quickly and to a considerable extent by a change in the rate of interest' (Marshall 1920, VI, ii, 4).
23 Hicks's apparent replacement of the normal position by a stationary one was made easier by the frequent use of the term 'stationary' to also indicate the normal position, because of its abstraction from changes in relative prices. However, Lionel Robbins (1930) had already lucidly clarified that ambiguity by his distinction between 'static' and 'stationary' positions of the economy. Hicks's attribution of a proper stationary state, and not of a normal position, to 'the economists of the past' is on the other hand made entirely clear when he writes that, in the stationary position of those economists, the 'quantity of intermediate products – the quantity of capital – will be determined through the rate of interest ... fixed at a level which offers no incentive for net saving or dissaving' (Hicks 1939, 118).
24 Except perhaps for the indication of it which may be read in the passage quoted in Garegnani (1976, 32):

> Of course people used to be able to content themselves with the static apparatus because they were imperfectly aware of its limitations. Thus, they would often introduce in their static theory a 'factor of production' and its price interest, supposing that capital could be treated like the static factors ... That some error was involved in their procedure would not have been denied... (1939, 116 n.)

We are not, however, told by Hicks what that 'error' actually was.
25 Cf. e.g. 'It seems to me impossible (as a matter of intellectual history) to maintain that the possibility of perfect capital (or labour) aggregation is a neoclassical doctrine' (Hahn 1982, 354). It is, however, difficult to envisage an intellectual history in which, say, Böhm Bawerk, J. B. Clark, Pigou, etc., could use an 'aggregation' of capital whose possibility they did not admit.
26 It is significant and again somewhat paradoxical that Hicks's revival of Walras's theory of capital in Parts I and II of *Value and Capital* went together with the total disappearance there of Walras's own equations of 'capital formation' (Walras 1954, Lesson 23) which contained the condition of uniformity of returns, as well as the relation equalizing the demand and supply of 'net perpetual income' (par. 3 above), i.e. savings and investment, in today's terms. That disappearance left a serious gap in the 'static theory' of Parts I and II of Hicks (1939), into which we cannot, however, enter here.
27 For an example of this confusion see the discussion in Garegnani 2003, 153–4, of a passage in Hahn 1975 in which – using the above uniform rate of return (referred to by critics) in order to characterize a 'special neoclassical case' to which Sraffa would refer – he sees it as one in which

> the equilibrium price of a good for future delivery in terms of the same good for current delivery will be the same for all goods
>
> (Hahn 1975, 360)

clearly the case of uniform own commodity rates of interest, i.e. constant prices, quite compatible logically with any divergence between rates of return on capitals' supply prices, and which the effective uniformity of those rates must in fact contradict whenever price changes over time are considered in the equilibrium.
28 Samuelson appears to seriously underestimate the difficulty of tracing the actual path of the economy (as Hicks's passage reported in the text implies) when in the *Foundations* (1947) he draws the analogy of a 'cannonball [which] can be held to be in equilibrium at each point on its path'. The dominant forces acting on the cannonball at

each instant of time are in fact comparatively few in number and their effects on the position of the cannonball are accordingly calculable with a degree of approximation sufficient to establish a correspondence between the theoretical and the actual position of the ball at that instant. Given instead the numberless forces of analogous strength which affect the economy at each instant of time, the actual instantaneous position of an economy cannot even in principle be determined with any approximation: only averages of observable positions, reflecting the effects of the few most persistent among those forces, can be determined. And, the cumulation of the errors would seem to make the path of the economy even less calculable in such terms, than its instantaneous position by itself. This, it seems, is what prompted Marshall to write

> dynamical solutions in the physical sense of economic problems are unattainable. And if we are to adhere to physical analogies at all, we must say that statical solutions afford starting points for *such rude and imperfect approaches to dynamical solutions* as we may be able to attain to
>
> (1898, 38–9, my emphasis)

the 'approaches' in question being, essentially, the comparison of normal positions.
29 This assumption, to which Hicks is in effect led by the abandonment of the normal position, is similar to that we find in Bliss when he writes

> it may seem more sensible to simply assume that equilibrium will prevail and to thus confine our investigations to the equilibrium state. We could regard the object of our investigations not as 'the economy' but as 'economic equilibrium'.... This approach may seem more attractive, if only because more tractable than the Herculian programme of constructing a complete theory of the behaviour of the economy out of equilibrium.
>
> (Bliss 1975, 28)

Bliss is here, so to speak, touching with his own hand the implications of that abandonment of that normal position, where the 'Herculian task' was largely left to itself by the simple Smithian device of the 'centre of gravitation', i.e. by the concentration of the analysis on persistent forces. Those implications appear here to have in fact led to an impasse, such that the way out comes close to assuming away reality. (Cf. in this respect the passage by Malinvaud in section I, n. 10 above.)
30 As Denis Robertson wrote with admirable simplicity and lucidity:

> It seems to me that anybody who rejects these two ideas, that a system can move towards equilibrium and that it may never get into it – has made it extremely difficult for himself to interpret the course of events in the real world.
>
> (1957, 144–5)

31 Elements of an alternative theory – partly influenced by the classical theory brought again to light by Sraffa – were advanced in the initial stages of the controversy by Robinson, Kahn, Kaldor and other authors on the critical side of the controversy. The concern to rapidly fill the huge area of long-run problems which Keynes 'left covered with fragments of broken glass' (Robinson 1956, v) may, however, have prevented deriving from the revival of the classical approach all it could offer including, in my opinion, a consolidation and extension to the long period of Keynes's own achievements on aggregate demand (cf. e.g. Garegnani 1978–9 and 1992).
32 On the specific notion that the adjustment between savings and investment in an intertemporal equilibrium raises no more problems than do adjustments to relative demands for contemporary commodities, and the associated idea that the equilibrium in the markets for the future consumptions that correspond to today's saving, would take care of the equilibrium between today's saving and today's investment; cf. Garegnani (2003, 130–2, also 2005, 495–6)

33 Cf. n. 11 above.
34 References to my paper are indicated simply by the initials 'PG' and by 'Bliss' simply the references to the comment.
35 In (2008, 6) Bliss writes: 'I formed the impression that Sraffa knew that his great life's project had run into the ground: that he could not come up with a complete alternative to the classical [clearly a misprint for 'neoclassical' PG] theory he disliked.'

However, Sraffa contended in the 1960 Preface, that he was taking in his book the standpoint which is that of the old 'classical economists from Adam Smith to Ricardo … submerged and forgotten since the advent of the marginal method' (Sraffa 1960, V) and, as has been repeatedly argued in these years, that approach does provide a complete consistent alternative to neoclassical theory. Used by those economists for a century or more, completion, as distinct from rediscovery, was hardly much of a problem. The qualification of a 'prelude' in the subtitle of the 1960 book, related explicitly to the 'critique' of dominant theory, and not to the proposed underlying alternative.

36 E.g. Bliss 2008, 12–13. My commentator also implies there that the argument reported in the text answers a question I put him decades ago about the impossibility of neoclassical theory giving a long-period theory of the rate of return on capital. But what I meant was that, with the capital endowment given as a physical vector, it was impossible to determine a 'normal position' with its uniform effective rate of return on the capitals' supply prices (PG, 5–7). My question related therefore to the inability of the post-Hicksian pure theory to respect the criterion of potential correspondence with observation which had become established in economics, and not to the abstract possibility of framing an analysis of long-run tendencies of the economy by a sequence of the new equilibria. The doubt in the latter case is on the significance of the analysis (potential correspondence with observation), not its possibility.
37 Cf. e.g. Petri (2004) and a recent debate on *Metroeconomica* (2005) to which Schefold and Garegnani have contributed and which had been stimulated by a review article of works by them (Mandler 2002), or, for a more succinct précis, the general discussion at a Siena Conference of 1999 on general equilibrium, reported in Hahn and Petri (2003).
38 Cf. e.g. Bharadwaj (1989), and debates like that stimulated by Samuelson (2000), with Garegnani (2007a), Samuelson (2007), Garegnani (2007b); or that on Blaug (1999) with Kurz Salvadori (2003) and Garegnani (2002).
39 Cf. e.g. Garegnani (1978–9) and the essays in Eatwell and Milgate (1983).
40 On long-run labour unemployment in the classical economists cf. e.g. Stirati (1994); Garegnani (2007a).
41 As for aggregate demand in growth and capital accumulation cf. Ciccone (1990); Garegnani (1992); Palumbo and Trezzini (2003).
42 Cf. e.g. the Roundtable (2007) in *Review of Political Economy* with contributions by Foley, Levrero, Garegnani, Pivetti and Vianello.
43 Classical theory and the role of aggregate demand have in fact been applied to the pension crisis referred to in Bliss 3 (e.g. Cesaratto 2006), just as they have been more generally applied to problems of fiscal policy (e.g. Ciccone 2002).
44 Cf. e.g. Garegnani (1997) and the conference on the subject held in Siena in April 1990, the Acts of which are published in *Political Economy; Studies in the Surplus Approach* (1990).

References

Arrow, J.K. and Debreu, G. (1954), 'Existence of an Equilibrium for a Competitive Economy', *Econometrica*, Vol. 22, No. 3.
Bharadwaj, K. (1989), *Themes in Value and Distribution*, London, Unwin Hyman.

Blaug, M. (1999), 'Misunderstanding Classical Economics: The Sraffian Interpretation of the Surplus Approach', *History of Political Economy,* Vol. 31, No. 2.

Bliss, C.J. (1975), *Capital Theory and the Distribution of Income,* Amsterdam and New York, North-Holland/American Elsevier.

Bliss, C.J. (2005), 'Introduction', in Bliss, C.J., Cohen, A.J., and Harcourt, G.C., *Capital Theory,* 3 vols, Cheltenham and Northampton, MA, Edward Elgar.

Bliss, C.J. (2008), 'The Post-Keynesians: An Outsider's Insider View', unpublished manuscript.

Cavalieri, T., Garegnani, P. and Lucii, M. (2004), 'La sinistra e l'occupazione – Anatomia di una sconfitta', *La rivista del Manifesto,* No. 48, March, pp. 44–50.

Cesaratto, S. (2006), 'The Transition to Fully Funded Pension Schemes: A Non-Orthodox Criticism', *Cambridge Journal of Economics,* Vol. 30, No. 1.

Ciccone, R. (1990), 'Accumulation and Capacity Utilization: Some Critical Considerations on Joan Robinson's Theory of Distribution', in Bharadwaj, K. and Schefold, B. (eds) (1990), *Essays on Piero Sraffa: Critical Perspectives on the Revival of Classical Theory,* London, Unwin Hyman, pp. 417–29.

Ciccone, R. (2002), *Debito pubblico, domanda aggregata e accumulazione,* Rome, Aracne.

Debreu, G. (1959), *Theory of Value,* New Haven, CT and London, Yale University Press.

Eatwell, J. and Milgate, M. (eds) (1983), *Keynes's Economics and the Theory of Value and Distribution,* London, Duckworth.

Garegnani, P. (1958), *A Problem in the Theory of Distribution from Ricardo to Wicksell* (unpublished PhD thesis, Cambridge).

Garegnani, P. (1960), *Il capitale nelle teorie della distribuzione,* Milan, Giuffré.

Garegnani, P. (1976), 'On a Change in the Notion of Equilibrium in Recent Work on Value: A Comment on Samuelson', in Brown, M., Sato K. and Zarembka P. (eds), *Essays in Modern Capital Theory,* Amsterdam, North-Holland.

Garegnani, P. (1978–79), 'Notes on Consumption, Investment and Effective Demand', *Cambridge Journal of Economics,* Vol. 2, No 4; Vol. 3, No 1.

Garegnani, P. (1990), ' "Quantity of Capital" in *Capital Theory*', in *The New Palgrave,* London, Macmillan.

Garegnani, P. (1992), 'Some Notes for an Analysis of Accumulation', in Nell, E. (ed), *Beyond the Steady State,* London, Macmillan.

Garegnani, P. (1997), 'On Some Supposed Obstacles to the Tendency of Market Prices Towards Natural Prices', in Caravale, G. (ed.), *Equilibrium and Economic Theory,* London, Routledge.

Garegnani, P. (2002a), 'Misunderstanding Classical Economics? A Reply to Mark Blaug', *History of Political Economy,* Vol. 34, No 1.

Garegnani, P. (2002b), 'Sraffa's Price Equations: Stationary Economy or Normal Positions?', in Boehm, S., Gehrke, S.C., Kurz, H.D. and Sturm, R. (eds), *Is There Progress in Economics?,* London, Routledge.

Garegnani, P. (2003), 'Savings, Investment and Capital in a System of General Intertemporal Equilibrium', in Hahn and Petri (2003).

Garegnani, P. (2005), 'Further on Capital and Intertemporal Equilibria: A Rejoinder to Mandler', *Metroeconomica,* Vol. 56, No. 4.

Garegnani, P. (2007a), 'Professor Samuelson on Sraffa and the Classical Economists', *European Journal of the History of Economic Thought,* Vol. 14, No. 2.

Garegnani, P. (2007b), 'Samuelson's Misses: A Rejoinder', *European Journal of the History of Economic Thought,* Vol. 14, No. 3.

Garegnani, P. and Trezzini, A. (2005), 'Cycles and Growth: A Note on Development in a Market Economy', *Quaderno di Ricerca*, No. 5, Centro di Ricerche e Documentazione Piero Sraffa, Rome, Aracne (forthcoming *Review of Political Economy*).

Hahn, F. and Petri, F. (eds) (2003), *General Equilibrium – Problems and Prospects*, London, Routledge.

Hahn, F.H. (1975), 'Revival of Political Economy: The Wrong Issues and the Wrong Argument', *Economic Record*, Vol. 51.

Hahn, F.H. (1982), 'The Neo-Ricardians', *Cambridge Journal of Economics*, Vol. 6, No. 4.

Hicks, J.R. (1932a [1962]), *The Theory of Wages*, London, Macmillan.

Hicks, J.R (1932b), 'Marginal Productivity and the Lausanne School: A Reply', *Economica*, No. 37, May.

Hicks, J.R. (1939), *Value and Capital*, London, Oxford University Press.

Kurz, H.D. and Salvadori, N. (2003a), 'Understanding "Classical" Economics: A Reply to Mark Blaug', in Kurz and Salvadori (2003b).

Kurz, H.D. and Salvadori, N. (2003b), *Classical Economics and Modern Theory: Studies in Long-Period Analysis*, London, Routledge.

Malinvaud, E. (1991), 'The Next Fifty Years', *Economic Journal*, Vol. 101, No. 404.

Mandler, M. (2002), 'Classical and Neoclassical Indeterminacy in One-shot versus Ongoing Equilibria', *Metroeconomica*, Vol. 53, No. 3.

Marshall, A. (1898), 'Distribution and Exchange', *Economic Journal*, Vol. 8, No. 28.

Marshall, A. ([1920] 1962), *Principles of Economics*, Guillebaud edition, London, Macmillan.

Palumbo, A. and Trezzini, A. (2003), 'Growth without Normal Capacity Utilization', *European Journal of the History of Economic Thought*, Vol. 10, No. 1.

Petri, F. (2004), *General Equilibrium, Capital and Macroeconomics*, Cheltenham, Edward Elgar.

Pivetti, M. (1991), *An Essay on Money and Distribution*, London, Macmillan.

Political Economy; Studies in the Surplus Approach (1990), special issue on 'Convergence to Long-Period Positions', Vol. 6, Nos 1–2.

Ramsey, F. (1928), 'A Mathematical Theory of Saving', *Economic Journal*, Vol. 38, No. 152.

Robbins, L. (1930), 'On a Certain Ambiguity on the Notion of Stationary State', *Economic Journal*, Vol. 40, No. 158.

Robertson, A. (1957), *Lectures on Economic Principles*, London, Fontana.

Robertson, D.H. (1931), 'Wage-Grumbles', in *Economic Fragments*, London, King & Son.

Robinson, J. (1956), *The Accumulation of Capital*, London, Macmillan.

Robinson, J. (1970), 'Capital Theory Up to Date', *Canadian Journal of Economics*, Vol. 3, No. 2.

Roundtable (2007), 'Classical Theory and Policy Analysis: A Roundtable Discussion', *Review of Political Economy*, Vol. 19, No. 2 (contributions by D. Foley, P. Garegnani, E.S. Levrero, F. Vianello).

Samuelson, P.A. ([1947] 1983), *Foundations of Economic Analysis*, Cambridge, Harvard University Press.

Samuelson, P. (2000), 'Sraffa's Hits and Misses', in Kurz, H.D. (ed) (2000), *Critical Essays on Piero Sraffa's Legacy in Economics*, Cambridge, Cambridge University Press.

Samuelson, P. (2007), 'Classical and Neoclassical Harmonies and Dissonances', *European Journal of the History of Economic Thought*, Vol. 14, No. 2.

Smith, A. ([1776] 1950), *The Wealth of Nations*, 2 vols, London, Dent and Sons.

Solow, R. (1956), 'A Contribution to the Theory of Economic Growth', *Quarterly Journal of Economics*, Vol. 70, No. 1.

Sraffa, P. (1960), *Production of Commodities by Means of Commodities*, Cambridge, Cambridge University Press.

Stirati, A. (1994), *The Theory of Wages in Classical Economics – A Study of Adam Smith, David Ricardo and Their Contemporaries*, Aldershot, Edward Elgar.

Wald, A. (1936 [1951]), 'Über einige Gleichungssysteme der mathematischen Okonomie', *Zeitschrift für Nationalökonomie*, Vol. 7, No. 5. English translation [1951]: 'On Some Systems of Equations in Mathematical Economics', *Econometrica*, Vol. 19, No. 3.

Walras, L. (1877), *Théorie Mathématique de la Richesse Sociale*, Paris, Guillaumin.

Walras, L. (1954), *Elements of Pure Economics or The Theory of Social Wealth*, London, George Allen & Unwin.

Wicksell, K. ([1906] 1962), *Lectures in Political Economy*, Vol. I, London, Routledge and Kegan Paul.

5   Spurious 'margins' versus the genuine article[*]

Heinz D. Kurz and Neri Salvadori

1 Introduction

In the preface to his book, Piero Sraffa expressed a warning concerning the use of the concept of 'margin' in economic theory. He wrote:

> Caution is necessary … to avoid mistaking spurious 'margins' for the genuine article. Instances will be met in these pages which at first sight may seem indistinguishable from examples of marginal production; but the sure sign of their spuriousness is the absence of the requisite kind of change. The most familiar case is that of the product of the 'marginal land' in agriculture, when lands of different qualities are cultivated side by side: on this, one need only refer to P. H. Wicksteed, the purist of marginal theory, who condemns such a use of the term 'marginal' as a source of 'dire confusion'.
> (Sraffa, 1960, pp. v–vi; the reference is to Wicksteed, 1914)

As the debate after the publication of Sraffa's book showed, this warning was appropriate, but unfortunately has not always been respected. The result is that the debate would have provided Wicksteed with additional cases to chastise because the term 'marginal' is used in a way that is anew the source of 'dire confusion'.

In this chapter we deal with one such case. For reasons that become clear in the sequel, the starting point of our reasoning is chapter 21, 'The marginal equalities', of Christian Bidard's book *Prices, Reproduction, Scarcity* (Bidard, 2004). Indeed, the present essay is essentially a comment on it. We proceed in the following way. We begin with a discussion of a famous numerical example provided by Garegnani (1970). Bidard has criticized the example as not dealing with heterogeneous capital at all. In our view this criticism is unfounded. In order to show this the salient features of Garegnani's example are emphasized by means of counterposing it with another example taken from Kurz and Salvadori (1995) (Section 2). We then turn to a brief critical account of a contribution by Sato (1974), who argued that reswitching is unimportant because it can be ruled out by assumptions that in Sato's judgement are 'weak' in some sense (Section 3). It is then argued that Bidard in chapter 21 of his book based his argument as to the absence of reswitching on what he calls 'differentiability hypothesis'. While he does not clearly define the concept, it appears to be clear that his reasoning is similar to Sato's (Section 4). Next we deal with a proposition by Bidard concerning the concept of the 'marginal productivity of capital'. We stress in particular that the finding of an equality between the rate of profits and the marginal productivity of capital, appropriately defined, implies nothing whatsoever as regards the determination of the level of the rate of profits. 'Marginal equalities' must not be mistaken for substantive explanations of economic phenomena, that is, they must not be taken for the 'genuine article', as Sraffa said (Section 5). Section 6 concludes.

Before we enter into our argument, the following remark is apposite. The problem of discriminating between spurious margins and the genuine article was present throughout the years of existence of the Trieste Summer School, organized by Sergio Parrinello in cooperation with Pierangelo Garegnani and Jan Kregel. The School was of great importance to many of those who participated in it. It provided a stimulating environment and led to fruitful discussions and it brought people together. As a matter of fact, the two authors of this chapter met for the first time in the summer of 1981 on the occasion of the annual Summer School. It was shortly afterwards that we began our collaboration, which has continued up until today. Sergio Parrinello in his capacity as main organizer of the meetings served not only as the medium that brought us together, he and other friends were also involved in many of the discussions we had over the years. If our approach to and understanding of economic problems happens to have improved over time, then this is partly due to the exchanges we had with him together with his support for what we were doing. Parrinello's contribution to our intellectual development could hardly be called 'marginal'.

2 In defence of Garegnani (1970)

In section 5 of Chapter 21 Bidard (2004, pp. 244–8) investigates a famous example by Garegnani (1970) and criticizes it on the basis of what he calls a 'WS analysis', where W stands for Walras or Wicksell and S for Sraffa (see Bidard, 2004, p. 240). Alas, Bidard's analysis is difficult to sustain. This can be clarified with reference to some problems posed in Kurz and Salvadori (1995, pp. 160–2). These problems, couched in the form of exercises, were constructed in order to alert the reader of our book to the kind of difficulties that concern us here.

For the reader's convenience the appendix of this chapter reprints the three related exercises. Here is a summary account of their rationale. The first exercise presents Garegnani's numerical example. The second gives an example which might at first sight appear to be similar to it, but which is actually totally different. In fact, in the former exercise there is an infinite number of commodities, one of which is a consumption good and all the others are capital goods. However, in the latter there are just two commodities: a consumption good and a capital good. In the former exercise for each capital good there is only one process to produce that capital good (by labour and itself) and only one process to produce the consumption good by using that capital good (and labour). Since there is an infinite number of capital goods this means that there is also an infinite number of processes to produce the consumption good (each by means of a different capital good) and an infinite number of processes producing capital goods, one for each of them. In the latter exercise there is an infinite number of processes to produce the consumption good using the same capital good and an infinite number of processes producing that capital good by labour and itself. Further, the two examples are built in such a way that the technology appears to be the same, but the symbols used carry a different meaning. The difference consists in the fact that in the former example there is only one index, whereas in the latter there are two indexes. This is so because in the former example a process producing the consumption good by means of a specific capital good can be operated if and only if the unique process producing that capital good by the capital good itself and labour is also operated, whereas in the latter example a process producing the consumption good can be operated if and only if any process producing the unique capital good by itself and labour is also operated. The third exercise consists just in asking the reader to compare the two previous exercises and thus to develop the argument summarized here, stressing the fact that whereas in the second exercise there is a single capital good, in the first there are many capital goods, indeed an infinite number of them. Therefore 'capital' is heterogeneous in the first exercise and homogeneous in the second.

It appears to have escaped Bidard's attention that the examples of the two exercises contain valid descriptions of possible technologies (which, however, are not identical). Instead he thinks that only the second one (i.e. the one using two indexes) contains such a description. This becomes clear when he writes:[1]

> Garegnani is not a faithful Sraffian: in his numerical example, the methods used in both industries depend on one parameter only ($u = v$ by *definition*), therefore the choices of methods are not independent and there is no basis for the wage-maximization property. Nor is he a faithful Walrasian, for the same reason: the differentiability hypothesis presumes a sufficient number of degrees of freedom on the isoquant, not only a 'derivative'; this is why an apparent reswitching is found in his calculations.
>
> (Bidard, 2004, p. 247)

As against this it has to be stressed that Garegnani uses a single index in his calculations, because he deliberately and explicitly chose to rest his argument on an assumption regarding technology that allows for an infinite number of capital goods. As a consequence, the reswitching he found is not at all 'apparent'. The title of Garegnani's essay 'Heterogeneous Capital ...' already draws the attention to a fact which Bidard appears to have overlooked. In his version of Garegnani's example 'capital' is *not* heterogeneous. This is all the more surprising because Garegnani left no doubt that his example started *explicitly* from the kind of technology introduced by Samuelson (1962), who had analysed an 'economy' in which for each method to produce the 'single consumption good A' there is 'a capital good $C^{(\alpha)}$ specific to the method', as the following quotation shows:

> The economy Samuelson assumes in his article is one where production takes place in yearly cycles and where a *single* consumption good A exists, obtainable by a number of alternative 'systems of production', α, β, γ, etc. Each 'system', e.g., consists of two 'methods of production': a method for the direct production of A by means of fixed quantities $l_a^{(\alpha)}$ of labour, and $C_a^{(\alpha)}$ of a capital good $C^{(\alpha)}$ *specific to the method*; and the method for pro-ducing $C^{(\alpha)}$ by $l_c^{(\alpha)}$ of labour and $C_c^{(\alpha)}$ of itself.
>
> (Garegnani, 1970, p. 408, emphasis added)[2]

The idea of introducing two indexes in order to eliminate reswitching is not new: it had already been used by Sato (1974) a few years after the publication of Garegnani's essay in a paper mentioned in the References of Bidard's book.[3] It is perhaps useful to scrutinize in some detail Sato's approach to the problem under consideration and then assess Bidard's argument against this background.

3 Why Sato's assumptions cannot be considered weak

Sato (1974) introduced a 'Technology Frontier' (TF), which is the set of all efficient techniques available in a given state of technical knowledge. The TF represents a functional relationship among the production coefficients. Sato argued that reswitching can occur only if not many techniques are available from which cost-minimizing producers can choose and that 'when techniques are available more abundantly than assumed in the usual discussion of this phe-nomenon, we are not likely to observe the strict coming back of any particular technique' (Sato, 1974, p. 365). From this Sato concluded that with a suffiently large number of technical alternatives we may ignore the phenomenon of reswitching.

   Throughout his analysis Sato explicitly assumed that the TF is continuous and twice differentiable. He contended that this assumption 'is made only for mathe-matical convenience' (Sato, 1974, p. 364) and thus does not in the least preju-dice the results obtained. Yet this is not the case. As Salvadori (1979) has shown, because of this assumption Sato's results amount to a restatement of results already known at the time when he published his paper concerning technological assumptions which suffice to rule out reswitching. Sato's claim that if there are sufficient technical alternatives, then we can ignore reswitching, is just an unproven contention. As a matter of fact, it would not even suffice to have an infinite number of technical alternatives: these must rather be arranged in a very special way in order to obtain continuous differentiability and strict convexity. Let us briefly clarify the issue at hand.[4]

   Sato assumed a state of technical knowledge analogous to the one studied by Samuelson (1962) and Garegnani (1970): for every technique T, there is one capital good (which can be different for different techniques) and a consumption good (which is the same for all techniques), so that each technique T is defined by its input matrix:

$$T = \begin{bmatrix} \alpha & \beta \\ a & b \end{bmatrix}$$

where α (capital) and β (labour) are the unit production coefficients of the consumption good and a (capital) and b (labour) are the unit production coefficients of the capital good. He then normalized the physical magnitude of capital by putting $b = 1$. This allowed him to define a technique by the vector $T = (a, \beta, \alpha)$ so that the whole technology can be represented by the function

$$\alpha = \psi(a, \beta).$$

This function Sato called the 'Technology Frontier' (TF). The description of technology through a 'Technology Frontier' is in itself not restrictive. In particular, if the domain of TF is finite or countable, it represents the usual case of a finite or countable set of techniques (once dominated techniques have been eliminated); if it is a curve on the plane (a, β), it represents the case of the continuous set of techniques as studied, for example, by Garegnani (1970); if it is a portion of the plane (a, β), it represents the case studied by Sato, which requires two indexes instead of just one. What is restrictive is the assumption entertained by Sato (1974, pp. 362–4) that

> $\psi(a, \beta)$ is everywhere continuously differentiable with respect to both a and β and strictly convex.[5]

In fact, if this is so, for each $\bar{a}$ – which means for each process to produce a capital good, since b has been normalized and equals 1 – the function $\alpha = \psi(\bar{a}, \beta)$ can be interpreted as the unit isoquant of a production function, which, because of the assumptions employed by Sato, is also convex and continuously differentiable. As a consequence, it is possible to apply the proof used by Burmeister and Dobell (1970, p. 273) to demonstrate that reswitching cannot occur. This is not what Sato does, since he arrives at his non-reswitching theorem directly, without recognizing that the assumptions he had adopted 'only for mathematical convenience' had effectively transformed the problem into a different and already known one in which reswitching was successfully ruled out.

Consider the wage frontier as the envelope of partial wage frontiers, each of which is defined by a given $\bar{a}$ and an infinite number of processes defined by the unit isoquant $\alpha = \psi(\bar{a}, \beta)$. If the technique $\bar{T} = (\bar{a}, \bar{\beta}, \bar{\alpha})$ pays the largest wage rate at a given rate of profits r^* among all techniques such that $a = \bar{a}$, then

$$\frac{w_T(r^*)}{p_T(r^*)} = -(1 + r^*)\frac{\partial\psi}{\partial\beta}\bigg|_{a=\bar{a},\, \beta=\bar{\beta}}$$

where $w_{\bar{T}}(r)/p_{\bar{T}}(r)$ is the wage rate in terms of the price of the capital good for technique $\bar{T} = (\bar{a}, \bar{\beta}, \bar{\alpha})$. If the same technique is on the same partial wage frontier at $r = r^{**} \neq r^*$, then it is also true that

$$\frac{w_{\bar{T}}(r^{**})}{p_{\bar{T}}(r^{**})} = -(1 + r^*)\frac{\partial\psi}{\partial\beta}\bigg|_{a=\bar{a},\,\beta=\bar{\beta}}$$

which is impossible since $w_{\bar{T}}(r)/p_{\bar{T}}(r)$ is a decreasing function of r and $\partial\psi/\partial\beta$ for $a = \bar{a}$, and $\beta = \bar{\beta}$ is a negative constant (with respect to r). Hence on the wage frontier we can have a reswitching of a partial wage frontier, but not the reswitching of a technique.

It is immediately checked that if the function $\psi(a, \beta)$ is convex, but not strictly convex, then the same technique can contribute to a partial wage frontier over a whole range, and, as a consequence, reswitching of partial wage frontiers allows for a reswitching of techniques. Therefore it is by no means sufficient to assume that 'techniques are available more abundantly than assumed in the usual discussion of this phenomenon'![6] We are now in a position to scrutinize Bidard's view against the background of Sato's argument and in full recognition of the latter's deficiencies.

4 Bidard's view and his 'differentiability hypothesis'

In his book Bidard stresses variously that it is important for an author to be as clear and rigorous as possible in order to avoid ambiguity of expression, which is a source of misunderstanding and misinterpreting. Happily, in his book he mostly succeeds in following this laudable (and highly demanding!) principle. But there are exceptions to this. Chapter 21 carries several statements that are rather vague; in particular, Bidard nowhere defines in a clear-cut way what exactly he means by the 'differentiability hypothesis' which plays an important role in the chapter. We tried hard to understand his reasoning and have arrived at the following conclusion: His contention that reswitching is excluded when the differentiability hypothesis holds amounts essentially to a restatement of Sato's argument. In case our interpretation happens to hold true, and we found nothing in Bidard's book that contradicts it, then his contention suffers from the same shortcoming as Sato's: if only one of the assumptions of strict convexity and continuous differentiability is not met, then the contention cannot be sustained.

Let us have a closer look at Bidard's reasoning. He writes:

> The reswitching phenomenon ... has been at the centre of the Cambridge debates, because it clearly undermines the logical foundations of the neo-classical aggregate production function. It may occur in the presence of finitely many methods or a continuum of methods. Why not under the *differentiability hypothesis* (note that differentiability requires a high enough dimension of the space of methods, in order to allow a marginal change of

one input without changing the other inputs)? A simple economic argument is: given a technique within the family of available techniques, the marginal productivity of labour is well defined by local comparisons. So is the associated wage.... The use of the same technique at two levels of the rate of profit would imply that the wage would be the same, which contradicts the *w–r* trade-off.

(Bidard, 2004, p. 240; emphasis added)

This formulation directs us to Bidard's differentiability hypothesis. Alas, no definition of it is provided in chapter 21 (or, as far as we can tell, in the rest of the book). Yet there is reason to think that what he intended with the hypothesis is this. For each commodity i any input vector $(l_i, a_{i1}, a_{i2}, ..., a_{in})$ satisfying a smooth and convex isoquant

$$1 = F^i(l_i, a_{i1}, a_{i2}, ..., a_{in}) \tag{1}$$

is technically feasible and the smoothness and convexity properties imply that there is an infinite number of such vectors.

In terms of this assumption it is immediately shown that the technique (necessarily unique) which can pay the largest wage rate for a given rate of profits r^*, $(\mathbf{A}^*, \mathbf{I}^*)$, whatever is the numeraire, is also the technique which satisfies the condition

$$w \, dl_i + (1 + r^*) \sum_k^n da_{ik} \, p_k = 0 \tag{2}$$

where $dl_i, da_{i1}, da_{i2}, ..., da_{in}$ are any scalars such that

$$\frac{\partial F^i}{\partial l_i}\bigg|_{\mathbf{A} = \mathbf{A}^*, \, \mathbf{I} = \mathbf{I}^*} dl_i + \sum_k^n \frac{\partial F^i}{\partial a_{ik}}\bigg|_{\mathbf{A} = \mathbf{A}^*, \, \mathbf{I} = \mathbf{I}^*} da_{ik} = 0 \tag{3}$$

and $(p_1, p_2, ..., p_n)^T = \mathbf{p} = w \left[\mathbf{I} - (1 + r^*)\mathbf{A}^* \right]^{-1} \mathbf{I}^*$. As a consequence

$$(1 + r^*)\frac{\partial F^i}{\partial l_i}\bigg|_{\mathbf{A} = \mathbf{A}^*, \, \mathbf{I} = \mathbf{I}^*} = \frac{\partial F^i}{\partial a_{i1}}\bigg|_{\mathbf{A} = \mathbf{A}^*, \, \mathbf{I} = \mathbf{I}^*} \frac{w}{p_1} = \frac{\partial F^i}{\partial a_{i2}}\bigg|_{\mathbf{A} = \mathbf{A}^*, \, \mathbf{I} = \mathbf{I}^*} \frac{w}{p_2} = \cdots$$

$$= \frac{\partial F^i}{\partial a_{in}}\bigg|_{\mathbf{A} = \mathbf{A}^*, \, \mathbf{I} = \mathbf{I}^*} \frac{w}{p_n} . \tag{4}$$

In order to obtain equation (2) we start from equation

$$\frac{p_i}{w} = (1 + r^*) \sum_k^n a_{ik} \frac{p_k}{w} + l_i \tag{5}$$

and obtain

$$d\frac{p_i}{w} = (1 + r^*) \sum_k^n a_{ik} d\frac{p_k}{w} + (1 + r^*) \sum_k^n da_{ik} \frac{p_k}{w} + dl_i$$

and since $(\mathbf{A}^*, \mathbf{l}^*)$ is the technique which can pay the largest wage rate at the rate of profits r^* whatever is the numeraire, $d(p_i/w) = d(p_k/w) = 0$. Hence equation (2) is obtained. Equation (4) can also be written as

$$\frac{\dfrac{\partial F^i}{\partial l_i}}{\dfrac{\partial F^i}{\partial a_{ih}}}\Bigg|_{\mathbf{A}=\mathbf{A}^*,\,\mathbf{I}=\mathbf{l}^*} = \frac{w}{(1+r^*)p_h} \qquad \forall h \tag{6a}$$

$$\frac{\dfrac{\partial F^i}{\partial a_{ih}}}{\dfrac{\partial F^i}{\partial a_{ik}}}\Bigg|_{\mathbf{A}=\mathbf{A}^*,\,\mathbf{II}=\mathbf{l}^*} = \frac{p_h}{p_k} \qquad \forall h,\, k \tag{6b}$$

which can be interpreted as the usual relationship which in equilibrium must hold between the slope of the isoquant and the relative prices of the inputs.

Since function $F^i(l_i, a_{i1}, a_{i2}, \ldots, a_{in})$ in (1) is homogeneous of degree one, we have

$$1 = \frac{\partial F^i}{\partial l_i} l_i + \sum_k^n \frac{\partial F^i}{\partial a_{ik}} a_{ik}$$

which, because of equation (6a), becomes

$$\frac{w}{\dfrac{\partial F^i}{\partial l_i}\Big|_{\mathbf{A}=\mathbf{A}^*,\,\mathbf{I}=\mathbf{l}^*}} = wl_i^* + (1+r^*)\sum_k^n a_{ik}^* p_k$$

and because of (5)

$$\frac{\partial F^i}{\partial l_i}\Bigg|_{\mathbf{A}=\mathbf{A}^*,\,\mathbf{I}=\mathbf{l}^*} = \frac{w}{p_i}. \tag{7}$$

Finally, from (6a) for $h = i$ and (7) we obtain

$$\frac{\partial F^i}{\partial a_{ii}}\Bigg|_{\mathbf{A}=\mathbf{A}^*,\,\mathbf{I}=\mathbf{l}^*} = 1 + r^* \tag{8}$$

and from (8) and (6b) for $k = i$ we obtain

$$\frac{\partial F^i}{\partial a_{ih}}\Bigg|_{\mathbf{A}=\mathbf{A}^*,\,\mathbf{I}=\mathbf{l}^*} = \frac{(1+r^*)p_h}{p_i} \qquad \forall h$$

which can be interpreted as the equilibrium condition stating the equality between the marginal productivity of an input and the price of that input in terms of the output.

These are well-known facts which, to the best of our knowledge, no 'Sraffian', 'Post-Sraffian' or 'Neo-Sraffian' has ever contested (or should contest), and in fact Bidard provides no evidence to the contrary. Bidard does not claim that his differentiability hypothesis is new; it has, in fact, been exhaustively explored and used by Burmeister and Dobell in chapter 9 of their book (Burmeister and Dobell, 1970, especially p. 273)[7]. We have argued in the above that Sato's Non-reswitching theorem amounts to a theorem by Burmeister and Dobell. The same applies to Bidard's Non-reswitching theorem.

The above procedure exposes a number of properties of the cost-minimizing techniques in the case in which the special assumption holds which Bidard (supposedly) wishes to express with his differentiability hypothesis. It can also be used to determine the cost-minimizing techniques for a *given* rate of profit in the same conditions. In this context it has to be stressed that these equilibrium properties or equalities provide no support whatsoever to the received marginalist attempt to *explain* the rate of profits in terms of the 'marginal productivity' or 'relative scarcity' of a factor called 'capital'.[8] We shall come back to this fact below in Section 6.

Now, in chapter 21 Bidard is not on the look-out for an explanation of the rate of profit. His observation concerning the circumstances in which reswitching can be ruled out is not accompanied by any doubts as to the possibility of a rising 'demand for labour curve', which contradicts conventional theory. In fact, in section 3 of the chapter Bidard shows by means of a neat numerical example that a rising demand for labour schedule can obtain; he also stresses that an example is all that is needed in order to rebut the conventional view that the demand for labour is inversely related to the real wage rate. Of course, more could be said in this regard. Mas-Colell (1989), for example, showed that given any set of pairs of consumption levels per capita and levels of the rate of profits satisfying a simple restriction Mas-Colell calls 'Golden Rule Restriction', a 'well-behaved' technology with two capital goods can be found having precisely this set as 'the steady-state comparative static locus', that is as the relationship between consumption per unit of labour and the rate of profits.

Since we agree with what is stated in section 3 of chapter 21 we turn immediately to section 4, which is devoted to the concept of the marginal productivity of capital.

5 The marginal productivity of capital

Section 4 of chapter 21 concludes with the statement of a theorem:

> *Theorem 2.* When adequately measured, the marginal productivity of capital is equal to the rate of interest. (p. 243)

The meaning of the statement is not clear and may give rise to misunderstandings and thus confusion. Substantially it says that we can define the concept of 'marginal productivity of capital' in such a way that it equals the rate of profits. This is not a new finding. Indeed, what Bidard proves in the section is well known. The problem is that it may be read as meaning something totally different. Therefore, as we learned already, 'caution is necessary ... to avoid mistaking spurious "margins" for the genuine article'. In the case under consideration we are indeed facing the case of a spurious margin.

The readers will remember that the so-called Cambridge debate about the marginal productivity of capital started in 1956 with a paper by Joan Robinson, that is, four years before the publication of Sraffa's book (Robinson, 1956). The argument developed by Joan Robinson, while obviously and admittedly inspired by Sraffa, was not based on Sraffa's own construction, but on something else. The description of the technology advocated by Joan Robinson was in terms of what she called 'productivity curve' and 'pseudo-production function'.[9] A productivity curve is a sort of production function but presupposes a *given* rate of profits. This allows one to measure capital in terms of the product where for each technique the relative prices specific to that technique are used. (For a recent formalization of the argument, see Salvadori, 1996.) Once this is done, the cost-minimizing techniques at the given rate of profits turn out to be those (possibly only one) which satisfy the condition that the derivative of the productivity curve with respect to capital is equal to the given rate of profits. Of course, for each level of the rate of profits we can carry out the same exercise and arrive at a 'family of productivity curves', which can be represented by the function

$$y = F(k, r) \tag{9}$$

while the cost-minimizing techniques are characterized by the condition

$$\frac{\partial F(k, r)}{\partial k} = r \tag{10}$$

and the relationship between k and y implicitly defined by equations (9) and (10) is what Joan Robinson called 'pseudo-production function'.

Therefore, the controversy is not about whether the marginal rule plays, or does not play, a role, but rather whether the derivative of the pseudo-production function is, or is not, equal to r. In fact, what Bidard calls 'marginal productivity of capital' is the derivative of income with respect to capital when not only the rate of profit, but also the prices are taken as *given* and are equal to those of the cost-minimizing technique at the given rate of profit. What Bidard has proved is well known and to the best of our knowledge has never been disputed.

The so-called pseudo-production function, that is, the locus of k and y for which there is an r satisfying both equations (9) and (10), is in fact not a function as Joan Robinson also recognized: it is a correspondence. However, if (k^*, y^*) is a point of this locus, and if at this point $\partial^2 F/\partial k \partial r \neq 1$, then a segment of this locus including point (k^*, y^*) can be represented as a differentiable function. Moreover

$$\frac{dy}{dk} = r + \frac{\partial F}{\partial r} \cdot \frac{\dfrac{\partial^2 F}{\partial k^2}}{1 - \dfrac{\partial^2 F}{\partial k \partial r}}.$$

Obviously $dy/dk = r$ if either

$$\frac{\partial F}{\partial r} = 0 \tag{11}$$

or

$$\frac{\partial^2 F}{\partial k^2} = 0 \tag{12}$$

(or both). It is possible to prove (see Salvadori, 1996) that equation (11) holds in the following cases: (i) the capital and the product consist of the same commodity; (ii) the derivative of the function of the value of capital in terms of r for the technique used in that point equals zero in that point, even if not in general; (iii) the rate of profits equals the growth rate. Equation (12) holds (iv) when two techniques are cost-minimizing at that r. These four cases are well known to those who have studied the reswitching debate. Case (i) has been investigated by Samuelson (1962), Bhaduri (1969) and mainly Garegnani (1970). Case (ii) is Ng's counter example (see Harcourt, 1972, pp. 149–50). Case (iii) is related to the 'golden rule of accumulation': Bhaduri (1966) maintained that it was proved by von Weizsäcker (with no reference); Harcourt (1972, p. 149) referred to Koopmans (1965), Pearce (1962), Bhaduri (1966), Nell (1970) and Harcourt (1970) and maintained that the formulation presented by himself is due to Laing (with no reference). Case (iii) has also been investigated by Garegnani (1984). Case (iv) has been investigated by Solow (1967, 1970), whose interpretation of the result under consideration has been criticized by Pasinetti (1969, 1970).

The debate between Solow and Pasinetti just mentioned is also relevant in the present context. At the time Robert Solow thought he could escape the criticism levelled at the marginalist theory of capital and distribution by adopting Irving Fisher's concept of 'rate of return' and by replacing the stock concept of capital by the flow concept of investment. However, as Luigi Pasinetti succeeded in demonstrating, Solow was mistaken: the concept showed no way out of the impasse in which marginalist long-period theory found itself. In his paper 'Switches of Technique and the "Rate of Return" in Capital Theory', published in 1969, Pasinetti stated the fact of the equality of the marginal product of capital, measured in value terms at given prices, and the rate of profits, but added that this must not be misunderstood as providing any support whatsoever for the marginalist theory. A finding such as the one presented in equation (10) or, in Solow's case, the use of 'rate of return' as a synonym for 'rate of profits' apparently contribute nothing to an explanation of the rate of profits. Pasinetti added:

> The idea which had been basic to marginal capital theory was another and deeper one. The idea was that, even at the simplest stage of a stationary economic system, there exists something – to be called the 'rate of return' – *which can be defined autonomously and independently of the rate of profit*; something which is higher or lower according to whether the existing 'quantity of capital' is lower or higher, and as such represents a general technical property of the existing 'quantity of capital.' Such a thing would justify and *explain* the rate of profit. It is this idea which has been shown to be an illusion; for, in general, such a thing does not exist.
>
> (Pasinetti, 1969, p. 529; second emphasis in the original)

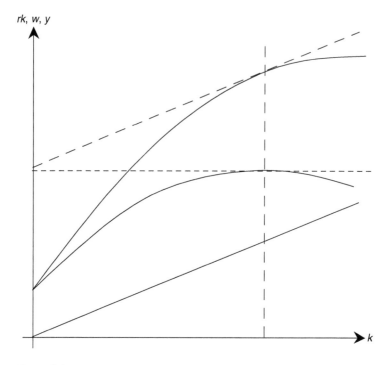

Figure 5.1

We conclude this section by making use of a diagram for illustrative purposes. In Figure 5.1 we put rk, w, and y as functions of k. Since $y = w + rk$, the value of k where w assumes its maximum level coincides with the value of k where $y = w + rk$ has the slope r. How are these curves built? Consider a given growth rate g, a given consumption basket **c**, and a given rate of profits r^*, then for each technique α we can determine the wage rate w_α and the capital per head k_α. We insert into the $w - k$ plane all these points, and the frontier of the convex hull of all these points is the w function plotted in the diagram. Since $r = r^*$ is given, the other two curves are immediately obtained. The fact that

$$\frac{\partial y}{\partial k} = r$$

is equivalent to

$$\frac{\partial w}{\partial k} = 0$$

is an obvious fact, but it does not add anything to the determination of r, which in this construction is, and has to be, given from the outside.

6 Concluding remarks

This chapter scrutinizes some of the propositions contained in chapter 21, 'The marginal equalities', of Bidard (2004, pp. 237–52). In it Bidard maintains that 'the debates about marginal equalities and capital theory have an ideological emphasis which, on the whole, has been detrimental to the post-Sraffian stream of thought' (pp. 237–8). He exemplifies his contention as follows:

> A typical unfortunate argument is: 'A comparison between the Euler identity $Q = F(K, L) = F'_K K + F'_L L$ and the accounting equality $Q = rK + wL$ shows the logical equivalence between the two relations $F'_K = r$ and $F'_L = w$. Since the theory of capital proves that the first equality is wrong, the real wage rate is not equal to the marginal productivity of labour.' We stress, on the contrary, that under a differentiability hypothesis, the Sraffa models imply the equality between the wage and the marginal productivity of labour. Though we do not claim that this is Sraffa's own position, we consider that it would be inconsistent to study the model and not to mention one of its necessary consequences (Bellino 1993 is an exception).
>
> (Bidard, 2004, p. 238)

This passage and Bidard's subsequent argument elicit the following remarks. First, unfortunately Bidard does not tell the reader who, if anyone, has put forward the statement in quotation marks. (We are not aware of anyone who has expressed such an opinion.) Second, there is reason to assume that Bidard has misinterpreted Garegnani's famous numerical example (Garegnani, 1970). The example was explicitly designed to discuss the case with heterogeneous capital goods. We conclude that Bidard's criticism of Garegnani is unwarranted. Third, Bidard refers to a differentiability hypothesis (pp. 238 and 240) but does not define it. However, the hypothesis is designed to clarify an important theoretical problem. As Bidard stresses:

> note that differentiability requires a high enough dimension of the space of methods, in order to allow a marginal change of one input without changing the other inputs.
>
> (p. 240)

This remark is added in parentheses to the contention that by means of the differentiability hypothesis the reswitching of techniques can effectively be ruled out (p. 240).

It is our contention that Bidard's argument is very similar to an argument put forward by Sato in 1974. Sato contended that 'when techniques are available more abundantly than assumed in the usual discussion of this phenomenon, we are not likely to observe the strict coming back of any particular technique' (Sato, 1974, p. 365). We think that it is safe to assume that Bidard's notion of 'a high enough dimension of the space of methods' is designed to express essentially the same thing.

Does this mean that in order to rule our reswitching the 'Technology Frontier', to use Sato's term, has to be strictly convex, or continuously differentiable, or both? Sato apparently thought that he could do without the assumption that the Technology Frontier is continuous and twice differentiable. In fact he insisted that this assumption 'is made only for mathematical convenience' (Sato, 1974, p. 364). However, his contention cannot be sustained. The unobtrusive assumption does the job, a result well known at the time, since it had been established as early as 1970 in a widely read textbook on economic growth by Burmeister and Dobell (1970, p. 273). Sato's argument and *a fortiori* Bidard's suffer from the same shortcoming: reswitching is effectively ruled out only by the twin assumptions of strict convexity and continuous differentiability. If one of them is not met, then the no-reswitching contention falls to the ground.

Whether economic theory is well advised to rest its case entirely on the twin assumptions of strict convexity and continuous differentiability is, of course, another matter. Bidard does not appear to think that it should. At any rate, an economic theory based on these two assumptions can hardly be called general. We are also not aware of empirical evidence according to which economists are well advised to adopt the two assumptions. It follows that reswitching cannot be ruled out in general. However, if one adopts the two assumptions for whichever purpose, then certain implications follow, whether these are mentioned or not. Why 'it would be inconsistent to study the model and not to mention one of its necessary consequences', as Bidard stresses, is not clear to us.

The real issue is whether the fact that there are 'marginal equalities' provides any support for the marginalist explanation of the real wage rate or the rate of profits. This is definitely not so, and Bidard in some passages makes it very clear that it is not. The fact that the rate of profits equals the marginal productivity of capital, *appropriately defined*, should not come as a surprise. It should especially not be mistaken to mean that the rate of profits *is determined* by the marginal productivity of capital. If the latter is ascertained in terms of a given and known rate of profits, the marginal equality under consideration cannot be taken to involve a causal relation leading from the marginal productivity to the rate of profits. (The contrary direction would be more correct.) As Pasinetti had pointed out a long time ago, the idea underlying marginal productivity theory, that one could 'justify and *explain* the rate of profit' in terms of the marginal productivity of 'capital' 'has been shown to be an illusion; for, in general, such a thing does not exist'.

Beware of spurious 'margins'!

Appendix

8.23. (Calculus) (Garegnani, 1970) Let $U = \{u \in \Re \mid 0 \leq u \leq 1.505\}$ be a set of indices. Let us assume that for each $u \in U$ there is a commodity, called u-commodity, which can be utilized either to produce itself or to produce a further commodity called corn. Corn is the only commodity required for consumption. Finally, for each u there exist the processes defined by Table 5.1, where $x = 27e^{-2u}$, $y = \sqrt[10]{u^{11}}$, and e is the base of natural logarithms.

Explore this technology and show that

i   this economy can be analysed within the framework of Subsection 3.3, but it cannot be analysed within the frameworks of Subsections 3.2 and 3.4;

ii   as r rises from 0 to 0.13 the u-commodity which is utilized to produce corn will vary continuously from the 0-commodity to the 1.505-commodity;

iii as r rises from 0.13 to the maximum admissible level in the economy, 0.2, the u-commodity which is utilized to produce corn will vary continuously from the 1.505-commodity to the 0-commodity;

iv   there is no switch point in the sense that for no level of the rate of profits two distinct techniques are cost-minimizing.

[Hint: for each u the w-r relationship is

$$w = \frac{1 - (5 + y)r}{(5 + y) + [x - (5 + y)2]r}$$

the envelope is found by setting the derivative with respect to u equal to zero; in doing this it is convenient to recall that $x' = -2x$ and $y' = (11y/10u)$, where x' and y' are the derivatives of x and y with respect to u.]

8.24. (Calculus) There exist two commodities, corn and iron. Only corn is required for consumption. Let $U = \{u \in \Re \mid 0 \leq u \leq 1.505\}$ and $Z = \{z \in \Re \mid 0 \leq z \leq 2\}$ be two sets of indices. Let us assume that for each $u \in U$ there is a process producing corn and for each $z \in Z$ there is a process producing iron defined in Table 5.2 where $x = 27e^{-2u}, y = \sqrt[10]{u^{11}}$.

Table 5.1

	Material inputs				Outputs	
	Corn	u-commodity	Labour		Corn	u-commodity
(u)	0	$\dfrac{x}{6+y}$	$5+y-\dfrac{x}{6+y}$	$\rightarrow$	1	0
(2u)	0	$\dfrac{5+y}{6+y}$	$\dfrac{1}{6+y}$	$\rightarrow$	0	1

Table 5.2

	Material inputs				Outputs	
	Corn	Iron	Labour		Corn	Iron
(u)	0	$\dfrac{x}{6+y}$	$5+y-\dfrac{x}{6+y}$	$\rightarrow$	1	0
(z)	0	$\dfrac{5+z}{6+z}$	$\dfrac{1}{6+z}$	$\rightarrow$	0	1

Explore this technology and show that

i   this economy can be analysed within the framework of Subsections 3.3 and 3.4, but it cannot be analysed within the framework of Subsection 3.2;

ii whatever value r takes in the interval $[0, 0.2]$, where $r = 0.2$ is the maximum admissible r, iron is produced with the process corresponding to $z = 0$;

iii there is r^*, $0.15 < r^* < 0.16$, such that as r rises from 0 to r^* the process operated to produce corn will vary continuously from that corresponding to $u = 0$ to that corresponding to $u = 1.505$;

iv whatever value r takes in the interval $[r^*, 0.2]$, corn is produced with the process corresponding to $u = 1.505$;

v   there is no switch point, in the sense that for no rate of profits are two distinct techniques cost-minimizing.

[Hint: since iron is the unique basic in all techniques prove point (ii) by taking iron as the numeraire. The wage frontier is then

$$w = 1 - 5r.$$

Prove that the cost-minimizing technique is that which minimizes the price of corn in terms of iron. Show that the relation between u and r for $0 \geq r \geq r^*$ is the locus

$$r = \frac{11y(6 + y)^2}{55y(6 + y)^2 + 6(120u + 20uy + 11y)x}$$

which is increasing in the relevant range and such that when $u = 1.505$, $r = r^*$.]

8.25. Compare the results of exercises 8.23 and 8.24.

Notes

* An earlier version of this essay was presented at a roundtable entitled 'Prices, Reproduction, Scarcity' held on 11 March 2005 at the Università Cattolica del Sacro Cuore, Milan. We are grateful to the participants of the roundtable and especially to Enrico Bellino, Christian Bidard and Sergio Parrinello for valuable comments on the earlier version.

1 Instead of index z as in the appendix below he uses index v, where $z = \sqrt[10]{v^{11}}$.

2 In his article Garegnani sometimes refers to a single technique of this example as a 'two commodity system', which in itself is not wrong because in a single technique only two commodities are involved. It would be unfortunate if an inaccurate reading were to prompt the reader to interpret the example as if there were just two commodities not in a single technique only (or what Garegnani calls a 'system'), but in the technical alternative available to the economy as a whole.

3 We were unable to locate any reference to Sato's paper in Bidard (2004); at any rate neither Sato's name nor his concept of 'Technology Frontier' are to be found in the book's author or subject index.

4 For a more detailed discussion, see Salvadori (1979).

5 Sato (1974, pp. 362–3) shows that if the function is concave somewhere only the convex parts are relevant, and this seems to justify at least partially his assumptions,

but what he needs in order to avoid reswitching is not just convexity, but *strict convexity*, and not differentiability almost everywhere, but *differentiability everywhere*.

6 It goes without saying that Sato's above formulation is surprisingly unrigorous.

7 The book is, however, not contained in the References of Bidard (2004).

8 It has also been argued that such an assumption is dangerous because it prompts one to think that two techniques that are close to one another as regards small variations in the rate of profits are also similar with respect to the kinds and quantities of capital goods they employ. Yet there is no reason for this supposition.

9 Initially she called this curve 'real-capital-ratio curve', but then she changed to the other name which she borrowed from Solow.

References

Bhaduri, A. (1966), 'The Concept of the Marginal Productivity of Capital and the Wicksell Effect', *Oxford Economic Papers*, Vol. 18, No. 3.

Bhaduri, A. (1969), 'On the Significance of Recent Controversies on Capital Theory: A Marxian View', *Economic Journal*, Vol. 79, No. 314.

Bidard, Ch. (2004), *Prices, Reproduction, Scarcity*, Cambridge, CUP.

Burmeister, E. and Dobell, A. R. (1970), *Mathematical Theories of Economic Growth*, London, Macmillan.

Garegnani, P. (1970), 'Heterogeneous Capital, the Production Function and the Theory of Distribution', *Review of Economic Studies*, Vol. 37, No. 2.

Garegnani, P. (1984), 'On Some Illusory Instances of "Marginal Products" ', *Metroeconomica*, Vol. 36, Nos 2–3.

Harcourt, C. G. (1970), 'G. C. Harcourt's Reply to Nell', Journal of Economic Literatures, Vol. 8, No. 1.

Harcourt, G. C. (1972), *Some Cambridge Controversies in the Theory of Capital*, Cambridge, Cambridge University Press.

Kurz, H. D. and Salvadori, N. (1995), *Theory of Production*, Cambridge, Cambridge University Press.

Kurz, H. D. and Salvadori, N. (2001), 'Classical Economics and the Problem of Exhaustible Resources', *Metroeconomica*, Vol. 52, No. 3.

Mas-Colell, A. (1989), 'Capital Theory Paradoxes: Anything Goes', in Feiwel, G. R. (ed.) *Joan Robinson and Modern Economic Theory*, London, Macmillan, pp. 505–20

Nell, E. J. (1970), 'A Note on Cambridge Controversies in Capital Theory', *Journal of Economic Literature*, Vol. 8, No. 1.

Pasinetti, L. L. (1969), 'Switches of Techniques and the "Rate of Return" in Capital Theory', *Economic Journal*, Vol. 79, No. 314.

Pasinetti, L. L. (1970), 'Again on Capital Theory and Solow's "Rate of Return" ', *Economic Journal*, Vol. 80, No. 317.

Pearce, I. F. (1962), 'The End of the Golden Age in Solovia: A Further Fable for Growthmen Hoping to Be "One Up" on Oiko', *American Economic Review*, Vol. 52, No. 4.

Robinson, J. V. (1956), *The Accumulation of Capital*, London, Macmillan.

Salvadori, N. (1979), 'The Technological Frontier in Capital Theory: A Comment', *Economic Notes*, Vol. 8, No. 1.

Salvadori, N. (1996), ' "Productivity Curves" in *The Accumulation of Capital*', in Marcuzzo, M. C., Pasinetti L. L. and Roncaglia, A. (eds), *The Economics of Joan Robinson*, London and New York, Routledge, pp. 232–48.

Samuelson, P. A. (1962), 'Parable and Realism in Capital Theory: The Surrogate Production Function', *Review of Economic Studies*, Vol. 29, No. 3.

Sato, R. (1974), 'The Neo-Classical Postulate and the Technological Frontier in Capital Theory', *Quarterly Journal of Economics*, Vol. 88, No. 3.

Solow, R. (1967), 'The Interest Rate and Transition between Techniques', in Feinstein, C. H. (ed.), *Socialism, Capitalism and Economic Growth, Essays Presented to Maurice Dobb*, Cambridge, Cambridge University Press, pp. 30–9.

Solow, R. (1970), 'On the Rate of Return: Reply to Pasinetti', *Economic Journal*, Vol. 80, No. 317.

Sraffa, P. (1960), *Production of Commodities by Means of Commodities*, Cambridge, Cambridge University Press.

Wicksteed, P. H. (1914), 'The Scope and Method of Political Economy', *Economic Journal*, Vol. 24, No. 93. Presidential Address to Section F of British Association, Birmingham, 1913.

6 Can Sraffa point us to a better future?

Lynn Mainwaring

Introduction

In his review of *Piero Sraffa's Legacy in Economics* (Kurz 2000), Sergio Parrinello (2002) noted that forty years of development of Sraffian theory had resulted in "losers" (wounded neoclassicals) and "non-winners" – Sraffians who had little constructive to offer in place of neoclassical theory. The following passage (Parrinello 2002, p. 258) is, I believe, a remarkably frank assessment of the state of modern Sraffian theory and serves admirably as a text for this essay:

> The contributions to *Sraffa's Legacy* on the Sraffian side continue to develop the criticism of marginalism or they pertain to the history of economic thought. This attitude contrasts with the works of the Classics [who] were actively concerned with applying their theories to the important economic problems of their own time. Ricardo and Marx, in particular, did not wait until the defects of the theory of value (of which they were indeed aware) were overcome before dealing with the problems of growth, innovation and distribution in the nineteenth century.

The question I should like to explore, albeit at a rather informal level, is whether Sraffian theory is capable of providing distinctive guidance (by which I mean guidance rooted clearly and to some degree uniquely in Sraffian theory) to policy makers confronted with today's most pressing economic problems.

Consideration of the policy relevance of Sraffian economics is not new. Thirty years after *Production of Commodities* (Sraffa 1960), Roncaglia (1990) struggled to find much in this approach that could yield insights into problems of applied economics. But Roncaglia was at least consoled that Sraffa's work had brought about "a shift in the research programme from the marginalist approach to the classical one ... offering new foundations for a fruitful reappraisal of lines of enquiry stemming from the classical vision of the economy" (p. 476). On my reading of the economics literature over the last two decades, there is scant evidence of any real shift in research programmes; rather it appears that lines of enquiry stemming from the classical vision have themselves become marginalised (no pun intended). Moreover, the modern classical vision, although broader than Sraffian price theory, is arguably inseparable from it. After all, Garegnani (1984) considers Sraffian theory to be the "core" of this vision, in which case that theory must, somehow, be capable of incorporation into any classical line of enquiry.

Marginalised it may be but the Sraffian programme continues. Have mainstream economists, rightly or wrongly, failed to accept the Sraffian critique? Or is it that they believe that Sraffians have little to offer in terms of practical prescriptions? A little of both, I think. I suggest that though the critique succeeded in wounding neoclassicals, the wounds are not necessarily fatal: a flawed theory may still, under certain circumstances, be a useful theory – as, according to Parrinello, Ricardo and Marx well understood. At the same time, I can find little in Sraffian writings that can be described as useful, in the practical, policy-oriented sense. Nor am I sanguine about the possibility that a great deal remains to be drawn out of it.[1] The real problem is the "objective" nature of the classical vision, which sits happily with long-period analysis but is at odds with any substantive treatment of behaviour. Since so many contemporary policy problems exist because of the peculiarities of individual and social behaviour, it is not surprising that Sraffians have little to say about them.

Sraffian theory as critique

It would be right to acknowledge the possibility that Sraffa never intended *Production of Commodities* to be anything other than what he implied in the subtitle: the first steps in a critique of (neoclassical) theory. That is to say, its purpose was the negative, but none the less valuable, even essential, one of identifying the flaws in the prevailing orthodoxy. If that critique were broadly accepted, it would then be necessary to rebuild economics on foundations that were not neoclassical – but not necessarily Sraffian either. If Sraffa, or more relevantly, Sraffians, had only aspired to a critical role, the only interesting question would be whether, or to what extent, the critique had succeeded. My assumption is that most practising Sraffians would not wish to operate entirely within the constraints of criticism but are convinced that Sraffa provided the prelude not merely for an assault on neoclassical theory but for the creation of an alternative to that theory. In that case it will be necessary to move on to a more interesting question: whether, and to what extent, that constructive project has succeeded or is likely to succeed.

First, has the Sraffian critique been successful? On its own terms, it seems to me to be undeniable that it has. By "on its own terms", I mean those set out by Sraffa himself in the 1958 Corfu Conference on Capital (Lutz and Hague 1961, pp. 305–306). In the context of a discussion of statistical measures of capital, Sraffa drew a distinction between statistical and theoretical measures. The latter "required absolute precision. Any imperfections in these theoretical measures were not merely upsetting, but knocked down the whole theoretical basis."

Responding to some doubts of Hicks, Sraffa opined: "Surely the usefulness of any theory lay in its explanatory value. Was one only interested in a theory if one could fit actual figures into it; or was one interested independently of that?" When Hicks replied "that if a theory was to explain the workings of the social mechanism, it ought to be capable of having measurable concepts fitted into it",

> *Mr. Sraffa* took the view that if one could not get the measures required by the theorists' definitions, this was a criticism of the theory, which the theorists could not escape by saying that they hoped their theory would not often fail. If a theory failed to explain a situation, it was unsatisfactory.

In the light of the *Production of Commodities*, the insistence on absolute precision in theoretical measures has been interpreted as a reference to the inadequacies of neoclassical aggregate capital embodying well-behaved properties. If that aggregate is of heterogeneous capital goods, then Sraffa and his followers have successfully demonstrated the imperfections. More interesting is the intertwining of measurement precision and explanatory value, suggesting that Sraffa believed that a theory could have no explanatory value if it embodied concepts that were not precisely measurable. What is crystal clear is what his conception of explanatory value implies: "If a theory failed to explain *a* situation, it was unsatisfactory."

These oft-quoted statements have been cited by Sraffians (see, for example, Kurz and Salvadori 1995, p. 450) in an attempt to undermine one neoclassical justification for ignoring the Sraffian critique: empirical significance. A typical neoclassical position would be to accept that capital-related irregularities may occur in a model which explicitly incorporates multiple, heterogeneous capital goods and whose measurement is subject to "absolute precision", i.e., independently, in terms of their own units, or as a value aggregate in terms of prevailing prices. But if, in practice, such irregularities do not occur too often, then models which ignore them – say, models with a single capital good – will yield explanations or predictions which will not be wrong too often (at least, on that account). Sraffians may well respond that we have no good reason to believe that capital irregularities rarely occur (see below); but even if they were convinced otherwise they would not, if they follow Sraffa, concede the general principle. The usefulness of a theory may well lie in its explanatory value, but Sraffa has laid down the criterion by which we must judge usefulness. A theory that explains only 99 situations in 100 or, for that matter, 999 in 1,000, is, it seems, unsatisfactory. Neoclassical theories in which heterogeneous capital is represented by a single value clearly fall foul of this criterion – as do the theories of Ricardo and Marx.

Such demanding theoretical exactitude may seem appropriate in the natural sciences. But even there, its rigorous application is to ensure scientific progress rather than to determine whether a particular theory is useful or not. We know that General Relativity explains every situation that Newtonian theory explains and many that it does not. In that respect, the development of General Relativity represented scientific progress, but that does not mean that Newtonian physics is, in any absolute sense, unsatisfactory. For almost all practical purposes – that is, purposes which, for good or ill, impact on human welfare – Newtonian calculations are quite sufficient.[2]

Of course, it is helpful to know when one can reasonably appeal to a simpler theory and when one should not, and our understanding of the more complete theory may be able to tell us what the conditions are. But while that seems relatively straightforward in physics, in the messy world of human interaction and social relationships it may prove well beyond our reasonable aspirations. In the case of Sraffian theory it would require that we identify those problems – objects of prediction, explanation or policy formation – where the complications arising from many capital goods and sectoral interdependencies can safely be ignored and those where they cannot. Unlike physics, theories in the social sciences involve such a degree of simplification and abstraction that we cannot rely on the theory itself to determine its boundaries of relevance and we must turn instead to other criteria. The usual approach, of course, is to test the theory empirically.

The Popperian criterion of falsification is not readily applicable to a science in which it is not possible to control for every conceivable parameter in the testing of a theory. Thus, it is rarely the case in the social sciences (or even the biological sciences) that a theory is abandoned because of a single apparent refutation.[3] A theory that works well most of the time, or within vaguely understood limits, is far too valuable to jettison. If we have reason to believe that a theory works most of the time, it is better to use it to make "probably right" decisions than to rely on hunch or inspiration. None of this is to say that neoclassicals (themselves a fairly disparate and heterogeneous bunch) get things right most of the time. But neither is it possible to say if Sraffians do. Where is the Sraffian empirical literature?

So far as I can tell, robust empirical tests of Sraffian theory are pretty thin on the ground. Early attempts to construct empirical w-r curves (e.g., Ochoa 1989; Petrovic 1991) were dismissed by Kurz and Salavadori (1995, p. 450) on the grounds that the observed relations are historical whereas the theoretical relation "refers to technical knowledge *at a given moment of time*" (authors' italics). This may well be correct but, given the compromise that is typically required in social sciences to reconcile theoretical and measurable concepts, this appears like an attempt to protect the main pillar of Sraffian theory from empirical scrutiny. Han and Schefold (2006), on the other hand, are content to test for paradoxes on the basis that "what [technique] is used today, can be used tomorrow, and what was used yesterday might be used again" but dismiss the earlier attempts on the more compelling grounds that they failed to investigate the complete w-r envelope. In that case, theirs is, so far as I am aware, the only contender for a robust empirical examination of a central Sraffian proposition. What do they find? Out of 496 envelopes, one involves reswitching while reverse capital deepening is involved in about 3.65 per cent of cases.

As an alternative to empirical testing, some have attempted analytical assessments of the likelihood of capital irregularities. Mainwaring and Steedman (2000) confirmed earlier findings (e.g., D'Ippolito 1989) that the probabilities of reswitching and capital reversing were rather small, consistent with the empirical results of Han and Schefold. Both their methodology and results have been challenged and at least one subsequent attempt (Zambelli 2004) has yielded much higher probabilities. It may be some time before any consensus emerges on the question. The higher the probabilities that are established, the stronger the grounds for questioning the reliability of predictions and explanations of models built on simple concepts of capital. But suppose that any convergence were to rather low probabilities, like the one or two per cent reported in Mainwaring and Steedman. What then, we asked? Would the pragmatic view prevail or, recalling Sraffa's Corfu contributions, would Sraffians still take refuge in the need for absolute precision and explanation without exception?[4] We did not answer this question ourselves but, without implicating Ian Steedman in any way, my own position is for pragmatism.

Parrinello's (1999) interpretation of the w-r relationship is even more nihilistic, in respect of empirical testability, than the conventional "moment in time" view. He argues that the technology matrix is not one of observable quantities (at a moment of time) but merely a "normal construction", like the normal values it supports, a concept related to understanding rather than prediction and which, in general, cannot be used to predict. Understanding, even without explicit prediction, can be of great value in the formulation of policy. I think it likely that when Sraffa talked of the importance of "explanation" he was referring to understanding rather than prediction. The danger with all theory is that understanding becomes an intellectually satisfying but ultimately introverted puzzle-solving exercise rather than the truly valuable identification of actions that promote the general good, however defined. I shall shortly consider some examples of Sraffian explanation to see how far they have got in terms of shaping policy.

Sraffa's views on imperfect and precise measures of capital parallel his thoughts on partial and general methodologies. His early papers were essentially a critique of Marshallian partial equilibrium theories while the later *Production of Commodities* was a theory of multi-sectoral interaction. There can be few economists of any persuasion who are unaware of the theoretical limitations of partial methods and it is clearly advisable to subject a partial theory to both analytical and empirical scrutiny before applying it to a particular circumstance. But if a partial theory got things tolerably right (according to some criterion) most of the time, should we nevertheless deny its explanatory or predictive value on account of an occasional failure? Should we not contemplate tax/subsidy instruments based on the assumption of downward-sloping demand curves and upward-sloping supply curves – or, indeed, any tax/subsidy regime that has not been tested in a computable Sraffian model (if such a thing exists, or could exist in the short-period context of much of tax policy)?

All this raises intriguing questions, not least the perennial one of the relative merits of Sraffian and neoclassical theory. In the opening quotation, Sergio Parrinello appears to condone (contra-Sraffa) the practice of applying theory to policy even when the theory is flawed. That the early classical theorists (unlike some modern neoclassicals) were aware of the flaws may be a virtue, but it doesn't make their theory any less flawed as a consequence. Compared to Sraffians, neo-classical theorists appear willing to offer policy guidance on just about anything. Are the (undoubted) flaws in their theories so grave as to render such advice worthless or even dangerous?

The constructive contributions of Sraffian theory – and their limitations

What are the constructive contributions of Sraffian theory? Kurz (2006) helpfully supplies a list of applications[5] to date: "exhaustible resources, costly disposal of dis-commodities, capital utilization, the treatment of services, and capital accumulation and growth". Even if I may be permitted to add international trade and investment to this list, it does not strike me as particularly impressive, not so much because of the breadth of these subject headings but rather the extent of the Sraffian contribu-tion within each. To illustrate the point, consider three[6] of the headings: exhaustible resources, international trade and growth. Under each, one can list a number of pressing problems, locally and/or globally, where informed policy insight would be of great value. In each case we can ask what is the Sraffian prescription (if any), what is the neoclassical and, where there is no explicit Sraffian answer, whether Sraffians would deny the essential validity of the neoclassical solutions.

1 Exhaustible resources

In addition to exhaustible resources proper (resources with strictly finite reserves), I include under this heading depletable resources, i.e., resources which though renewable may be renewed at a rate insufficient to prevent their elimina-tion. This is partly to be fair to Sraffians, who have made some attempt to deal with depletable resources (e.g., Kurz and Salvadori 1995, ch. 12) and partly to prevent them from getting off the hook, in that global warming, the main issue I wish to consider, really falls into this category.

There have been notable attempts to incorporate exhaustible resources such as fossil fuels and minerals into the Sraffian framework. (For a convenient over-view of different approaches and disagreements, see papers in the 2001(1) issue of *Metroeconomica* by Bidard and Erreygers (2001a, 2001b); Hosoda (2001); Kurz and Salvadori (2001); Lager (2001); Parrinello (2001); and Schefold (2001). The question that has been addressed by these writers is how the inter-temporal price changes needed to sustain the exploitation of a basic (in the Sraffian sense) privately owned natural resource can be accommodated in a long-period theory. Getting to grips with this problem is not easy and, in many respects, the progress made and the controversies engendered suggest that there is plenty of life yet within this paradigm. What worries me, however, is that by being bound to a long-period approach in which prices are determined by the traditional Sraffian data (outputs, technology coefficients, initial natural resource stocks and a distributive datum), many of the critically important aspects of the problems we face are being ignored altogether.

Consider a specific example. Hosoda (2001) has modelled the choice of technique between waste disposal (whose means are exhaustible) and recycling, by building on the "corn-guano" approach of Bidard and Erreygers (2001a). This is a very welcome attempt to direct the theory to a well-defined and pressing problem and it deals explicitly with the problem of costly disposal. Even so, the real achievement of Hosoda is not his actual solution (which is that the cheaper disposal option is used first and then, when it becomes sufficiently expensive, gradually gives way to the backstop recycling process) but that he demonstrates that the solution is consistent with the underlying long-period framework. Putting aside the criticisms of the corn-guano model (Schefold 2001; Kurz and Salvadori 2001), this is a fine intellectual achievement, but how far does it get us in terms of understanding specific waste-related problems?

At the time of writing, the city of Naples was undergoing a crisis related to waste disposal. Criminal gangs have, among other things, imported toxic waste from northern Italy where enforcement of regulations is stricter and dumped it in an unregulated manner in the vicinity of the city. There it is believed to have got into watercourses and entered the human food chain. There are several economic elements to this story: the scarcity of appropriate means of disposal of wastes; the roles of waste taxes and regulation; the inducements to criminals to acquire scarcity rents; the inducements to corruptible politicians and bureaucrats to share those rents; and, of course, the negative external effects of unregulated waste disposal. While the Naples case is an extreme one, the result of historical-cultural factors which economists must take as givens, both littering and organised illegal dumping are widespread. Each of the elements of this story is amenable to orthodox economic analysis (which is not to say such analyses are wholly without flaws). For example, it would be perfectly sensible to ask whether, given the *social* costs of illegally dumped imported toxic waste, additional public funds should be used to expand the means of regulated disposal in the north of the country. Neoclassicals would have no methodological difficulty in this respect. What would be the Sraffian approach? Let us again turn to Hosoda to find a genuine chink of light.

In a recent paper, Hosoda (2009) begins by briefly reviewing the existing (mainstream) literature advocating the upstream treatment of waste (such as Extended Producer Responsibility) rather than leaving the onus on the final consumer. This literature focuses on avoiding inefficient market signals (such as the incentive to carry out illegal dumping when disposal is costly to the consumer and the incentive not to minimise waste when disposal is subsidised). What is interesting is that Hosoda does not deny or minimise the relevance of these and other market distortion arguments for upstream treatment. Instead, he shows that even when these distortions are fully corrected for there are other reasons, inherent in the interdependency of production, that favour upstream treatment. An upstream policy is consistent with competitive equilibrium whereas a downstream policy is not. As this hinges on the fact that the upstream waste process is basic, in the sense of Sraffa, whereas the end-of-stream process is non-basic, this is an unambiguous practical insight using explicit Sraffian concepts. But the important lesson is that this insight is *additional* to those of the market-failure approach rather than an alternative. This suggests a constructive role for Sraffian theory, but one altogether more modest than is implied by "a *complete* alternative paradigm" (Chiodi and Ditta 2008) (italics added).

If an increasingly scarce resource is a non-basic then the theoretical problems of accommodating price changes are less severe. This is how Kurz and Salvadori (1995) deal with depletable resources such as a fish stock. But this simply won't work with the most serious depletable-resource problem we face: global warming. Though natural systems may well be self-correcting given sufficient time, the atmosphere's capacity to absorb greenhouse gases without significant climate impacts is limited and the loss of such capacity may prove irreversible over time-scales relevant to human concerns (which brings to mind Keynes's observation on the long run). It is likely that climate change will impact, directly or indirectly, on every aspect of economic activity. In that sense, the atmosphere is "basic"; but the key characteristic of global warming is that it is a global externality. Whether or not it is possible to develop a comprehensive model of externalities and public goods within the Sraffian approach, it is difficult to envisage how such a theory can offer credible insights, let alone specific policy guidance, without taking account of the implications of the structure (or lack) of property rights, of strategic behaviour (particularly free-riding consumers, suppliers and governments), and of how expectations are formed and acted on.

Consider a somewhat stylised neoclassical policy package that does take these issues on board: (1) Press for a (near-)global agreement on a carbon trading scheme, supplemented by credits for carbon offsets on projects in countries outside the scheme. (2) Within tax jurisdictions: introduce carbon emissions taxes and/or internal trading schemes. (3) Give individuals, households and firms tax/subsidy incentives to innovate and invest in low-carbon technologies. Though higher prices from (1) and (2) will help in that respect, specific instruments such as feed-in tariffs for micro-generators might also be adopted. (4) Give incentives to researchers (public and private), through shares in intellectual property rights, to pursue low-carbon R&D that is commercially effective (at prices influenced by (1) – (3)).

This is not to say that neoclassicals are unanimous in advocating such a package. There are, for example, disputes about the desirability and design of Kyoto-2 and arguments for emphasising adjustment to change rather than avoidance or mitigation. Nevertheless, these are debates taking place within the broad neoclassical framework.

It would be a challenge to formulate an equally comprehensive package with a distinctively Sraffian flavour and, to be frank, I am not aware of *any* specifically Sraffian contribution to the debate. My instinct (no more than that) is that many Sraffians would see some merit in some or all of (1) – (4), despite the fact that the intellectual roots of these policies are to be found in Pigou's treatment of externalities and Coase's ideas on property rights, both extensions of the partial-equilibrium theory of supply and demand or their notional counterparts (marginal damage and marginal social benefit). And underlying much of the mainstream debate is an acute awareness of the significance of Prisoners' Dilemma-type behaviour on the part of the relevant agents. If there is (to be) a Sraffian contribution, my guess is that its emphasis would be on identifying appropriate technologies. But what it would say about the innovation and selection of such technologies in the context of global externalities, I do not know.

Perhaps this should come as no surprise when one considers Sraffa's own thoughts on the matter. Kurz (1998) quotes from Sraffa's unpublished notes relating to his development of a "physical real cost" theory which, unlike the labour cost theory of Ricardo and Marx, includes

> natural resources that are used up in the course of production (such as coal, iron, exhaustion of land) – [Air, water etc. are not used up: as there is an unlimited supply, no subtraction can be made from ∞].
>
> (D3/12/42:33)

It is certainly not fair to criticise Sraffa for not foreseeing that (unpolluted) air and fresh water would one day become severely depleted. What is more interesting is his attitude to those resources that cannot either be reproduced or substituted for. Such resources

> cannot find a place in a theory of *continuous* production and consumption: they are dynamical facts, i.e., a stock that is being gradually exhausted and cannot be renewed, and must ultimately lead to the destruction of the society. But this case does not satisfy our conditions of a society that just manages to keep continuously alive.

Not only were these "dynamical facts" incapable of incorporation within the theory, but Sraffa had no interest in extending the theory by introducing dynamical assumptions, saying:

a that the system is much more statical than we believe, and its "short periods" are very long,

b that the assumptions being too complicated it becomes impossible for the mind to grasp and dominate them – and thus fails to realise the absurdity of the conclusions.

> (D3/12/11:33)

Sraffa here seems to be drawing a distinction between resources which are replaceable and amenable to theorising, and those which are not and whose exhaustion must lead to the collapse of society and about which only absurd conclusions may be reached. Following his lead, modern Sraffians have shown how, for the first kind of resource, cost-minimising technical choices of private capitalists will bring about the necessary replacements to some backstop technology. This misses the essential point about global warming, freshwater reserves, soil fertility, food-crop gene pools, biodiversity, etc., which is not that these resources are necessarily exhaustible but rather that they are being exhausted, and they are being exhausted as a consequence of these very same private cost-minimising choices. What we want to know is how best to *change* those choices in way that will make the future a little more comfortable.

2 International trade

As Steedman (1999) points out, *The Production of Commodities* contains no reference to international trade. The fundamental concepts appear to have been worked out entirely in a closed-economy context. Consequently, its extension to include international trade and investment is by no means trivial. Early attempts by Parrinello, Steedman and Metcalfe and Mainwaring (see Steedman 1979) succeeded in showing that the choice between autarky and free trade could be characterised as a choice of technique. By exploiting the w-r/c-g duality, it was also possible to say something about the gains from trade. In the purely comparative sense inherent in the long-period method, it turned out that the gains from trade could be negative. This immediately struck at the central policy conclusion of international trade theory going back to Ricardo but wholly embraced by neo-classical theorists: free trade is good, protectionism bad. Neoclassicals retorted that if the rate of profit were taken to be equal to the rate of time preference (itself equal to the rate of discount), any comparative losses would be more than offset by gains accruing along the transitional path between the two regimes. Our response was that, from a classical perspective, the rate of profit was a measure of surplus and bore no necessary relationship to the rate of time preference.

Though I continue to endorse that classical position, I doubt that I could any longer (cf. Mainwaring 1991, p. 61) be persuaded to advocate – on these grounds – that any nation under any (realistic) circumstances pursue a policy of trade restraint. The neo-Ricardian analysis is far too abstract. It misses out entirely the economies-of-scale benefits of specialisation and the role of trade and investment as conduits for technology transfer. So did the 1950s proponents of import-substituting development strategies – which is why those strategies failed.

But if the big question evades the grasp of Sraffians, what about the standard fare of trade policy? Consider the problems and what they involve (all involve price–quantity interdependence): comparison of the merits of export subsidies, tariffs, quotas and voluntary export restraints (uncertainty, rent-seeking behaviour); dumping (predatory behaviour); infant-industry protection (learning by doing, dynamic externalities); retaliation (strategic behaviour); strategic trade policy (imperfect competition, strategic behaviour); globalisation failures (social and environmental externalities, monopoly abuses). Given that governments need to consider these issues in the context of fluctuations in the terms of trade and of surprisingly rapid shifts in international competitiveness (witness China and India), I doubt that many could be comfortably incorporated into an approach based on the presumption "that the system is much more 'statical' than we believe". It is no surprise that Sraffians appear to have little to say about them, except perhaps that the Sraffian critique applies to the neoclassical theory of international trade, even in the case of the small open (i.e., price-taking) economy (Steedman 1999), and that neoclassical policy recommendations must, therefore, be suspect. Even if that is so, would they think it better, nevertheless, to endorse such recommendations (for example, that tariffs are generally preferable to quotas) or say nothing?

More pointedly, Steedman shows that many Sraffian concepts are also inapplicable (at least in their familiar guises) to the small open economy. These include: basics; the proportionality of relative prices to labour costs when r = 0; the standard commodity's non-dependence on relative prices; and the notion of outputs as data. Worse, Steedman notes that an economy need only be "small" in relation to one or more goods that it trades for these conclusions to follow:

> By definition, the analysis of such an economy must recognise that, for one or more commodities ... the relation between price and quantity is crucially important. Now the discussion of such a relation is entirely outside the formal framework of *The Production of Commodities by Means of Commodities*, so that there is little or no scope for making straightforward comparisons of its closed economy theory and large, open economy theory.

The implications of this statement are far-reaching; yet I am not aware of any response to Steedman's analysis. That economies contain heterogeneous capital goods is manifestly obvious; that almost any economy of interest in the modern world is an open economy (price-taking in respect of at least one good) ought also to go without saying. Can Sraffian theory be said successfully to explain the open economy? And if a theory fails to explain a situation is it satisfactory?

3 Growth

Sraffian analysis sits comfortably in a steady-growth framework (though at the cost of abandoning the cherished "non-assumption" of constant returns). What policy conclusions this generates is another matter.

Even today, growth remains a largely unquestioned objective of most governments, regional and national. But there has been a change: a shift in emphasis from quantity to quality. On the side of growth generation, the stress is less on traditional "factor" accumulation and more on technological progress and knowledge creation. And on the "output" side, there is a realisation that broader welfare measures, and sometimes happiness, are more important than GNP gains.

The importance of R&D, innovation and of skill acquisition is consistent not only with neoclassical endogenous growth theory but also, as Kurz and Salvadori (1998) reminds us, with the classical tradition. But to what extent have Sraffians engaged with these matters at a policy level? Entire journals are now dedicated to issues such as research policy and technology transfer. Important debates concern: the extent and form of government support for R&D (How should universities be funded? Should private R&D be subsidised? Should governments attempt to create research networks?); and the design and reach of intellectual property rights (Should universities be allowed/encouraged to register rights on publicly funded research? Should software be protected by patents as well as copyright? Should governments promote the involvement of small enterprises with intellectual property?) These questions are mainly concerned with balancing incentives against the potential for monopoly abuses and rent-seeking in the context of knowledge as a public good. Is there, in the Sraffian tradition, any apparatus for addressing these questions?

As for what growth is for, the Sraffian answer is, presumably, to increase consumption, or consumption per capita, taken to be a basket of privately producible goods and services. I don't think that Sraffians would have any aversion to quality-of-life measures, in principle, but it would be difficult to credit Sraffian theory as contributing to the debate. That debate itself is partly related to the question of whether growth is sustainable in the face of environmental constraints. The tricky issues there, involving the treatment of "natural capital", are similar to those relating to depletable resources and do not need repeating.

Looking for relevance in the classical "mantle"

Could the reason for the meagre policy pickings from the Sraffian approach be because this is the wrong place to look? Roncaglia (1990), who also found little of direct relevance, nevertheless remained positive about Sraffa's role as a catalyst in bringing about a shift towards classical thinking. Garegnani (1984) suggests that price determination subject to given data be regarded as the "core" of classical theory, while relationships between data, and the reverse effects of prices and distribution on the data, be analysed separately, outside of the core – what I shall call the "mantle".[7] These separate fields of analysis need, of course, to be connected and Garegnani suggests that this is done in an iterative manner. The mantle could be the place to look for a treatment of many of the issues we have failed to find in the core: dynamic processes, externalities, strategic behaviour, the public sector and government and, of course, demand.

In a later paper, Garegnani (1998) himself points to work on two issues. One is to resolve the tension between the potentially exogenous determinants of the rate of profit and the real wage rate, the first via the banking sector, and the second via historical and cultural factors. This may be a necessary part of the classical programme, but I don't think it will contribute much to arguments about a minimum wage, or why activity rates in Wales are so low, or what should be the response of a central bank be to a rapid fall in house prices (not to mention a sudden collapse in the global financial system). The second issue concerns the possibility of a deficiency of aggregate demand in the long period. It remains to be seen whether work on the first issue results in a monetary theory that is fully integrated into the core (by iteration or any other means). Until such time, it seems difficult to escape Minsky's (1990) assessment that "At the arid level of Sraffa, the Keynesian view that effective demand reflects financial and monetary variables has no meaning, for there is no monetary system in Sraffa."

It is certainly possible to find a great deal of non-neoclassical work on relevant policy issues coming from post-Keynesian, institutional, evolutionary and other economists. Some have been tempted to regard these contributions as part of a "connected" classical vision; as such, Roncaglia (1990) cites the work of Biasco, Hirsch, Hirshman, Kaldor and, ironically given his views, Minsky. I suggest that these contributions are connected more by what they are not (neoclassical) than by what they are (potentially integrable elements of a modern classical approach). And even if they are claimed to be part of the classical mantle, the two-way relationship between them and the core has yet, so far as I am aware, to be demonstrated.

The limited policy relevance of modern classical theory may be because of an explicitly anti-subjectivist outlook deriving from an understandable mistrust of the exogenous fixed preferences of neoclassical demand theory. The result, in Sraffa at least, is a theory of relative (normal) prices in objective terms, the only concession to behaviour being that is implicit in the competitive tendency to uniform distributive returns. The absence of any explicit and substantive (i.e., subtle and sophisticated) behaviour in a theory in the social sciences is remarkable. This is something which, to his credit, Schefold (1990) has attempted to remedy (see also, Parrinello 1982). He points to the limiting assumption of gross substitutability as a condition for the stability of neoclassical general equilibrium. In classical thinking, he argues, "goods that are gross substitutes fulfil the same need and are, for the purposes of classical theory, conveniently treated as one and the same good". His distaste for substitutability in consumption draws him to the opposite extreme of perfect complementarity. This, in effect, boils down to a vertical social demand curve, allowing prices to be wholly determined by the Sraffian price equations. The lead that Schefold gives is not to reject demand as an issue of economic significance but to reformulate it in terms that reflect a socio-psychological understanding of individual behaviour. He nevertheless seems eager to pick those concepts, notably Maslow's (1970) hierarchy of needs, that support social complementarity while neglecting others of equal importance.

The treatment of demand in neoclassical theory is, I believe, a major weakness; but not because of substitutability. That people make substitutions in response to price changes seems to me undeniable and should be part of any theory of prices and outputs. Cars and buses may fulfil essentially the same need, but if a theory is required to consider them as the same good, then that theory will have very limited insights into transport policy. The problem of neoclassical theory is the assumed *fixity* of preferences, in the face of psychological evidence that preferences are "positional" (Hirsch 1976), that is, conditioned by the individual's "frame of reference" (Kahneman and Tversky 1982; Frank 1985). Welfare depends on one's own accustomed level and pattern of consumption and on those of one's peer group (the "Joneses"). As the reference frame changes, so do consumption aspirations and welfare. An urban congestion charge may cause an initial drop in the welfare of some commuters, as they switch from cars to public transport, but once they have adjusted to the new situation, welfare levels are to some degree restored. As a description of people's *actions*, the conventional utility function is a tolerable simplification; as an indicator of the direction of short-lived changes in welfare it is useful; as an index of enduring welfare changes (and policy costs and benefits) it is highly misleading (Mainwaring, 2001). Neoclassical theory has difficulty digesting the normative implications of positional preferences. Sraffian theory appears unable even to accommodate the positive.

Conclusion

There is no denying what Sraffian theory has achieved: a modern reformulation of Ricardian value theory; identifying the flaws in neoclassical conceptions of capital and in the Marxian theory of value; proper schemata for fixed capital and rent; and a number of extensions like those considered above. This amounts, I believe, to a series of valuable insights into the functioning of the economy. But they do not constitute a monopoly of insight. Most well-considered paradigms yield insights, despite their flaws; they add something to our understanding of complex phenomena. Having achieved its initial goals, I am not sure how much Sraffian theory has left to offer. I doubt that it can become a primary source for policy formulation because of its inability to incorporate the types of complex behaviour (i.e., beyond full-information cost minimisation) inherent in so many policy issues and because the world is actually a good less "statical" than Sraffa claimed. What it may be able to do is offer some additional illumination. Hosoda (2009) is an example, and there may be others; but the list is hardly impressive.

One possible riposte to this is to say that it misses the point; that it criticises Sraffian theory for not doing what it was never intended to do. In that case, it is incumbent on its practitioners to spell out the boundaries of their project, to say whether what lies outside those boundaries has relevance to economics and, if it has, what school or schools of thought have legitimacy in dealing with it.

Acknowledgement

I should like to thank Adriano Birolo for encouraging me, against my initial inclinations, to tackle this subject and Ian Steedman for his helpful comments of the first draft. Given the nature of the chapter, the usual caveats are more than usually important.

Notes

1 The editors of a recent volume share my view that the Sraffian project "seems to have lost much of its initial strength and persuasion" (Chiodi and Ditta, 2008, backcover notes), while claiming that their collection "suggests how [Sraffa's] ideas can provide a complete alternative paradigm.... and challenge the persistent dominance of the widespread postclassical culture". Yet, even the most policy-relevant paper in Chiodi and Ditta (by Cesaratto on pensions) is really a restatement of the classical vision rather than of practical policy. History of thought, mathematical introspection, and refined criticism make up the rest. I concede that an alternative view of how the economy func-

tions may well imply an alternative, and probably revolutionary, view of how it ought to function (a planned economy?) rather than yield specific policy instruments for the existing system. But if that is what its advocates believe, they should spell it out.

2 There may be some merit in economists adopting Penrose's (1989, ch.5) fourfold classification of theories: Superb; Useful; Tentative; and Misguided. To qualify as Superb, a theory need not apply without refutation. In physics, such theories include (among others) Euclidean geometry, Newtonian mechanics, Maxwell's theory of electromagnetism, and Special Relativity. In Penrose's view, the only non-physics theory that comes close to being Superb is the Darwin–Wallace theory of evolution. The arguments set out in this chapter are consistent with placing neoclassical theory in the Useful category and Sraffian in the Tentative.

3 And it is not always the case in the physical sciences, if Feyeraband (1975) is to be believed; see also Penrose (1989).

4 Han and Schefold (2006), while conceding that paradoxes are infrequent, argue that "they seem to suffice to undermine the neoclassical production and distribution theory, both in a stochastical and falsificatorial sense". I do not understand their bullishness. The infrequency hardly amounts to a stochastical refutation; and while a reference is made to Popper, there is no discussion of the relevance of the falsification criterion in this context.

5 "Extensions" may be a better word since Kurz does not claim that the work is necessarily of an applied nature. On the other hand, he does refer in the same paragraph to joint production and fixed capital as "empirical problems", though I should have thought they, too, were (theoretical) extensions.

6 I have chosen those with which I have most familiarity; but I should also acknowledge here, Parrinello's (2004) contribution to the treatment of services. This shows how time-phased production systems allow for a proper distinction between goods and services. In that respect, greater clarity of thought should lead to improved policy formulation.

7 I prefer this (geologically inspired) term to "periphery" (cf. Chiodi and Ditta 2008) which seems to imply that the issues treated there are of a peripheral nature.

References

Bharadwaj, K. and Schefold, B. (eds) (1990), *Essays on Piero Sraffa: Critical Perspectives on the Revival of Classical Theory*, London, Unwin Hyman.

Bidard, C. and Erreygers, G. (2001a), "The Corn-Guano Model", *Metroeconomica*, 52, No. 3, 243–253.

Bidard, C. and Erreygers, G. (2001b), "Further Reflections on the Corn-Guano Model", *Metroeconomica*, 52, No. 3, 254–267.

Cesaratto, S. (2008), "The Classical 'Surplus' Approach and the Theory of the Welfare State and public pensions", in Chiodi and Ditta (2008), 93–113.

Chiodi, D. and Ditta, L. (eds) (2008), *Sraffa or an Alternative Economics*, Basingstoke, Palgrave Macmillan.

D'Ippolito, G. (1989), "Delimitazione dell'area dei casi di comportamento perverso del capitale in un punto di mutamento della tecnica", in Pasinetti, L. L. (a cura di), *Aspetti controversi della teoria del valore*, Bologna, Il Mulino.

Feyeraband, P. (1975), *Against Method*, London, Verso.

Frank, R.H. (1985), *Choosing the Right Pond: Human Behavior and the Quest for Status*, New York, Oxford University Press.

Garegnani, P. (1984), "Value and Distribution in the Classical Economists and Marx", *Oxford Economic Papers*, Vol. 36, No. 2, pp. 292–325.

Garegnani, P. (1990), "Sraffa: Classical versus Marginalist Analysis", in Bharadwaj and Schefold (1990), 112–141.

Garegnani, P. (1998), "Sraffa: The Theoretical World of the 'Old Classical Economists' ", *European Journal of the History of Economic Thought*, 5, No. 3, 415–429.

Han, Z. and Schefold, B. (2006), "An Empirical Investigation of Paradoxes: Reswitching and Reverse Capital Deepening in Capital Theory", *Cambridge Journal of Economics*, 30, No. 5, 737–765.

Hirsch, F. (1976), *Social Limits to Growth*, Cambridge, MA, Harvard University Press.

Hosoda, E. (2001), "Recycling and Landfilling in a Dynamic Sraffian Model: Application of the Corn-Guano Model to a Waste Treatment Problem", *Metroeconomica*, 52, No. 3, 268–281.

Hosoda, E. (2009), "Malfunction of a Market in a Transaction of Waste: A Reason for the Necessity of an Upstream Policy in Waste Management", in Vint, J., Metcalfe, S.J., Kurz, H.D. and Samuelson, P. (eds) (2009), *Economic Theory and Economic Thought*, Abingdon, Oxford, Routledge.

Kahneman, D. and Tversky, A. (1982), "The Psychology of Preferences", *Scientific American*, 246, 160–173.

Kurz, H.D. (1998), "Against the Current: Sraffa's Unpublished Manuscripts and the History of Economic Thought", *European Journal of the History of Economic Thought*, 5, No. 3, 437–451.

Kurz, H.D. (ed) (2000), *Critical Essays on Piero Sraffa's Legacy in Economics*, Cambridge, Cambridge University Press.

Kurz, H.D. (2006), "The Agents of Production Are the Commodities Themselves: On the Classical Theory of Production, Distribution and Value", *Structural Change and Economic Dynamics*, 17, No. 1, 1–26.

Kurz, H.D. and Salvadori, N. (1995), *Theory of Production: A Long-Period Analysis*, Cambridge, Cambridge University Press.

Kurz, H.D. and Salvadori, N. (1998), "The 'New' Growth Theory: Old Wine in New Goatskins", in Coricelli, F., Di Matteo, M. and Hahn, F.H. (eds), *New Theories in Growth and Development*, London, Macmillan.

Kurz, H.D. and Salvadori, N. (2001), "Classical Economics and the Problem of Exhaustible Resources", *Metroeconomica*, 52, No. 3, 282–296.

Lager, C. (2001), "A Note on Non-stationary Prices", *Metroeconomica*, 52, No. 3, 297–300.

Lutz, F.A. and Hague, D.C. (eds) (1961), *The Theory of Capital*, London, Macmillan.

Mainwaring, L. (1991), *Dynamics of Uneven Development*, Aldershot, Edward Elgar.

Mainwaring, L. (2001), "Environmental Values and the Frame of Reference", *Ecological Economics*, 38, No. 3, 391–402.

Mainwaring, L. and Steedman, I. (2000), "On the Probability of Reswitching and Capital Reversing in a Two-sector Sraffian Model", in Kurz (2000), 323–353.

Maslow, A. (1970), *Motivation and Personality*, New York, Harper and Row.

Minsky, H.P. (1990), "Sraffa and Keynes: Effective Demand in the Long Run", in Bharadwaj and Schefold (1990), 362–369.

Ochoa, E.M. (1989), "Values, Prices and Wage Profit Curves in the US Economy", *Cambridge Journal of Economics*, 13, No. 3, 413–429.

Parrinello, S. (1982), "Flexibility of Choice and the Theory of Consumption", *Metroeconomica*, 34, Nos 1–3, 1–10.

Parrinello, S. (1999), "Explaining and Understanding Economic Events by Contrasting Alternatives", *Metroeconomica*, 50, No. 3, 325–350.

Parrinello, S. (2001), "The Price of Exhaustible Resources", *Metroeconomica*, 52, No. 3, 301–315.

Parrinello, S. (2002), "Sraffa's Legacy in Economics: Some Critical Notes", *Metroeconomica*, 53, No. 3, 242–260.

Parrinello, S. (2004), "The Service Economy Revisited", *Structural Change and Economic Dynamics*, 15, No. 4, 381–400.

Penrose, R. (1989), *The Emperor's New Mind*, Oxford, Oxford University Press.

Petrovic, P. (1991), "Shape of a Wage–Profit Curve: Some Methodology and Empirical Evidence", *Metroeconomica*, 42, No. 2, 93–112.

Roncaglia, A. (1990), "Some Remarks on the Relevance of Sraffa's Analysis for Economic Policy", Bharadwaj and Schefold (1990), 467–478.

Schefold, B. (1990), "On Changes in the Composition of Output", in Bharadwaj and Schefold (1990), 178–203.

Schefold, B. (2001), "Critique of the Corn-Guano Model", *Metroeconomica*, 52, No. 3, 316–328.

Sraffa, P. (1960), *Production of Commodities by Means of Commodities*, Cambridge, Cambridge University Press.

Steedman, I. (ed) (1979), *Fundamental Issues in Trade Theory*, London, Macmillan.

Steedman, I. (1999), "*Production of Commodities by Means of Commodities* and the Open Economy", *Metroeconomica*, 50, No. 3, 260–276.

Zambelli, S. (2004), "The 40 Per Cent Neoclassical Aggregate Theory of Production", *Cambridge Journal of Economics*, 28, No. 1, 99–120.

7 Can Sraffa point us to a better future?

A comment on Mainwaring

Guglielmo Chiodi and Leonardo Ditta

In his stimulating and, in some respect, provocative essay, Lynn Mainwaring posits interesting questions on whether Sraffa's theory (i) "is capable of providing distinctive guidance [...] to policy makers" (p. 119]); (ii) " [it] provided the prelude not merely for an assault on neoclassical theory but for the creation of an alternative to that theory" (p. [120]). The author is ultimately inclined to answer those questions in the negative "because of its [Sraffa's theory] *inability* to incorporate the types of complex behavior [...] inherent in so many policy issues" (p. [132]), italics added.

As the writers of the present comment have recently edited a book on Sraffa, Chiodi and Ditta (2008), whose purpose was essentially to argue in the opposite direction, we feel obliged to make some critical remarks on some of the crucial statements in Mainwaring's chapter. Before doing this, however, we have to recognize the correctness of other statements therein – as will be evident in the course of the present comment.

1   The widespread and consolidated view is that Sraffa's book rescued from oblivion the old classical economists' approach. The greatest part of the literature stemming from Sraffa's book, however, has mainly directed its efforts to emphasizing the impossibility of treating "capital" as a value independently of distribution and, as a consequence, the impossibility of considering both the rate of wage and the rate of profits as scarcity indexes.

The deep and controversial debates on capital theory, which took place over the 1960s and in the beginning of the 1970s, were essential for the initial frontal attack to the then dominant post-classical economic theory. Afterwards, however, they revealed themselves excessively pedantic, for their concentration and monotonous insistence on *one* aspect only of the critique. The capital controversy became perhaps even a hindrance, in so far as it impeded a full-fledged bringing to the fore of the far more general *new paradigm* proposed by Sraffa.

Some constructive contributions based on Sraffa's theory have been published in recent years; but these works do not strike Mainwaring "as particularly impressive, not much because of the breadth of these subjects headings but rather the *extent* of the Sraffian contribution within each" (p. [124], italics added).

In this respect, we firmly share Parrinello's view on Sraffianism – on which Mainwaring himself explicitly agrees – according to which the contributions on Sraffa's theory "continue to develop the criticism of marginalism or they pertain to the history of economic thought" (Parrinello 2002, p. 258). In contrast to Mainwaring, however, we believe that there are alternative explanations for the present condition of Sraffianism, as succinctly expressed by Parrinello in the above quoted sentence. These explanations can be seen from two different perspectives: (a) the historical; (b) the analytical.

2   From the former perspective, it should be noted that it took more than 100 years before the post-classical theory was accepted as a new paradigm in economics between the 1870s and 1890s and, in particular, as *the* alternative paradigm to the old classical political economy one. It suffices here to remember the very first contributions on utilitarianism before and after Adam Smith's *The Wealth of Nations*, such as those of Beccaria, Verri, and Bentham, let alone that of J.B. Say, published after Adam Smith's *The Wealth of Nations* but *before* Ricardo's *Principles*. Say's contribution centered on individualism, utility, and market exchanges – for this characterization of the economy, he can legitimately be considered one of the precursors of Walras. All these contributions notwithstanding, the old classical political economy paradigm was still maintaining its own hegemony on the theoretical ground as well as on the practical policy-oriented one, over the years preceding the so-called "marginalist revolution". The opinion according to which that "revolution" was mainly based on the refutation of the faulty labor theory of value characterizing the old classical approach has, in our view, a very feeble and weak basis. In this connection, the Pareto–Robbins line of thought – culminating in the well-known methodological essay by Robbins (1932) on the very *nature* of economics – suggests a deeper and more radical explanation of that "revolution": a strong aversion to the old classical political economy "core" (to use Garegnani's terminology), as contrasted against the strict *logical* reasoning supposed to be at the basis of any scientific theory. Thus economics must be concerned just with the relevant rational choices of the agents, with the market mechanism making any single choice consistent with any other.

The main characterizations of the old classical political economy "core", namely, (i) the central role attributed to the *social product*; (ii) the *distribution* of the latter regulated by forces and elements operating outside the actual processes of production and *before* any market exchange would have taken place (for which the labor services were *not* considered a *commodity*), were canceled out altogether by the newly established post-classical paradigm, as Robbins made clearly evident, by negating relevance to the social product and by considering income distribution among the "factors of production" as regulated by the same set of market forces regulating any other commodity. The Paretian criterion of economic "efficiency" coupled with the two Fundamental Theorems on Welfare Economics closed up the boundaries within which the post-classical economic theory had erected its own "autarchic" system.

It should not be considered a failure, therefore, that *only* 50 years having elapsed since the publication of Sraffa's seminal book, Sraffianism – according to the opinion of Mainwaring – "contains little that can be described as useful in the practical, policy-oriented sense" (p. [120]).

To complete our alternative explanation of the present state of the art we now refer to the second perspective, the analytical one, indicated above.

3   The capital theory debates, which took place soon after Sraffa's book was published, were essentially conducted from a *logical* consistency point of view, with the bona fide expectation that undermining a theory from *that* point of view was sufficient for "substituting" the alternative Sraffian paradigm for the traditional post-classical one.

Unconsciously hidden in this very attitude was the mistaken view of economics as a natural *science* rather than a *social* discipline, with the obvious expectation that the post-classical theory was to be discarded simply because it proved *logically wrong*. This was patently a big mistake, since the debates were centered, as a consequence, on the well-known "paradoxes" in capital theory, neglecting the vital parts of the classical approach.

The "sacrificed" vital parts basically pertain to what has been called the "periphery" of the "core" – the "mantle", as Mainwaring prefers to term it – or, more precisely the *interaction* between the "core" and the "periphery" of the theory. To this, scanty reflection has been devoted and very little has been produced, both theoretically as well as on the policy-oriented ground. Working on *that* intersection, however, requires a perspective which is, by its own nature, *ideological*, simply because it cannot be otherwise. Compare, for instance, the ultimate goal the economy should pursue, from the post-classical and from the Sraffa viewpoint, respectively.

From the former viewpoint, the ultimate goal of the economy rests on making consistent and realizable through the market mechanism each and every consumption and production plan *individually* designed by the agents; by contrast, the analogous ultimate goal of the economy according to the Sraffian perspective is that of making possible the *reproduction* of the economy as a whole – "reproduction" meaning, first and foremost, assurance that the laborers, *as human beings*, can at least receive the necessaries for life. This viewpoint necessarily implies, and not only for the specific case now under consideration, a strong *value judgment*, which in turn implies that the notion of a "surplus", for example, is not at all a technical or a natural notion, but *a historical, political and a social one* – on this specific point cf. Pearson (1957), Chiodi (2008), and Chiodi (2009).

Sraffa's "prelude to a critique of economic theory" should be basically viewed as an *alternative paradigm* to the post-classical one, the latter centered exclusively on market mechanisms, the former on a more articulated framework, whose individual objectives and corresponding behaviors, not obeying any "natural" and universal law whatsoever, cannot be analyzed independently of the specific historical contexts in which they arise and are shaped.

In this respect, an example of particular relevance can be found in the post-classical growth theory (Ditta 2008). The underlying assumptions of that theory make it independent from any historical and institutional context. Growth is deemed as determined by universal laws operating across countries and time, independently of any specific geographic, historic or institutional context. Thus the policy implications are identical for each country and the policy prescriptions universally valid. Classical and Sraffian perspective on this issue is completely different: if the claimed universal validity of the post-classical approach was abandoned, alternative answers along classical and Sraffian lines could be provided trespassing the narrow boundaries of economics.

4 The paradoxes arising by considering "capital" as a value not given independently of distribution do not belong exclusively to the Sraffian framework as such. They simply arise because they are *inherent* to that very notion of "capital". Reswitching of techniques and capital reversal, for example, can also be found in a flow-input/flow-output neo-Austrian model of production (Nuti 1970) – not to mention the critiques of the notion of "capital" expressed first by Wicksell (1901) and subsequently by Cassel (1923) (cf. Chiodi 2004, 2008). The paradigm conveyed by Sraffa's theory was not so *essential* for that purpose. But the insistence on this point made it more difficult to appreciate the far more general novelty contained in Sraffa's theory, as the focus was forcibly directed only towards *logical* issues, rather than on the *intersection* between the "core" and the "periphery", and thus on the *ideological* side involved in the theory.

An example of this can easily be seen by looking at distribution theory: the post-classical theory of distribution received a complete formulation after 20 years' delay following the marginalist revolution that took place in the early 1870s. It is our contention that this lag was due to the difficulties of dealing with the evident ethical aspects of the theory (Chiodi and Ditta 2009). As is well known, the marginal theory of distribution postulates that each productive factor is rewarded according to its contribution. In this formulation distribution appears to be *objective* and *just*, avoiding in this way any value or ethical aspect of the problem. Now Sraffa's analysis undermines the foundational link between capitalist profits and productivity of capital, and this is a far-reaching conclusion that goes beyond any logic-based critique. If this line of reasoning stemming from classical and Sraffian approaches were to be pursued, post-classical theory could be contrasted also on the grounds of its ethical and political premises.

5 A similar destiny to that of Sraffa's book can be said to have befallen Keynes's *General Theory* (1936). Although Keynes, for his own admission, was working *within* the same theoretical framework of the post-classical theory, in the shape left over by the Marshallian tradition, nevertheless his contribution was seen as an "inadmissible" attack on the *ideology* of the market – a fundamental and an indissolubly linked aspect of the traditional theory. This prompted an almost immediate and long-lasting "counter-revolution" which, starting from the neoclassical synthesis and then passing through monetarism, ultimately devolved into rational expectation models first, and then into the maze of neo-Keynesian literature.

The main intention behind the book on Sraffa edited by the authors of the present comment was to stimulate research in the positive direction outlined above. In this respect, we would like to draw Mainwaring's attention again to the *Introduction* and essays in that book, particularly those by Peter Edwards and Kumaraswamy Velupillai. This could help, perhaps, to present a different perspective on Sraffa's contribution from that expressed by Mainwaring.

References

Cassel, G. (1923), *The Theory of Social Economy*, London, Ernest Benn Limited.

Chiodi, G. (2004), "Sraffa e le premesse a una critica della teoria economica", *Quaderni di Teoria Sociale*, pp. 247–64.

Chiodi, G. (2008), "A Wicksellian Monetary Theory of Production and Distribution", mimeo.

Chiodi, G. (2008) "Beyond Capitalism: Sraffa's Economic Theory", in Chiodi, G. and Ditta, L. (eds) (2008), *Sraffa or An Alternative Economics*, Basingstoke, Palgrave Macmillan, pp. 187–98.

Chiodi, G. (2009), "The Means of Subsistence and the Notion of 'Viability' in Sraffa's Surplus Approach", in Zambelli, S. (ed), *Computable, Constructive and Behavioural Economics Dynamics*, Abingdon, Routledge.

Chiodi, G. and Ditta, L. (eds) (2008), *Sraffa or An Alternative Economics*, Basingstoke, Palgrave Macmillan.

Chiodi, G. and Ditta, L. (2009) "Una ricostruzione storico-analitica del legame tra salari e produttività", mimeo.

Ditta, L. (2008), "Notes on Early Development Economics' Story and Its Relation to Sraffa's Contribution", in Chiodi, G. and Ditta, L. (eds) (2008), *Sraffa or An Alternative Economics*, Basingstoke, Palgrave Macmillan, pp. 199–208.

Garegnani, P. (2004), "Professor Foley and Classical Political Economy", Centro di Ricerche e Documentazione "Piero Sraffa", *Classical Theory and Political Analysis: A Round Table*, Materiali di Discussione n. 1.

Keynes, J.M. (1936), *The General Theory of Employment, Interest and Money*, London, Macmillan and Co. Ltd.

Mainwaring, L. (2009), "Can Sraffa Point Us to a Better Future?", this volume.

Nuti, D.M. (1970), "Capitalism, Socialism and Steady Growth", *Economic Journal*, Vol. 80, No. 317, March, pp. 32–57.

Parrinello, S. (2002), "Sraffa's Legacy in Economics: Some Critical Notes", *Metroeconomica*, Vol. 53, No. 3, pp. 242–60.

Pearson, H.W. (1957), "The Economy Has No Surplus: A Critique of A Theory of Development", in Polanyi, K., Arensberg, C.M., Pearson, H.W. (eds) (1971), *Trade and Market in the Early Empire. Economies in History and Theory*, Gateway Edition, Henry Regnery Company, Chicago (originally published in 1957), pp. 320–41.

Robbins, L. (1932), *Essay on the Nature and Significance of Economic Science*, London, Macmillan and Co. Limited.

Sraffa, P. (1960), *Production of Commodities by Means of Commodities: Prelude to a Critique of Economic Theory*, Cambridge, Cambridge University Press.

Wicksell, K. (1901), *Föreläsningar i Nationalekonomi*, Första delen: Teoritisk Nationalekonomi, Lund. English edition: *Lectures on Political Economy*, translated from the Swedish by E. Classen and edited with an Introduction by Lionel Robbins, vol. I, New York, Macmillan Company.

8 Competitiveness and comparative advantage

Towards an evolutionary approach to growth and foreign trade

Stan Metcalfe

Introduction

This chapter offers some preliminary ideas in relation to an evolutionary theory of foreign trade. Capitalist economies are never in equilibrium, there are always powerful incentives to seek new profit opportunities, to attack the established market positions of incumbent firms and this Schumpeterian competitive process of mutation and flux holds inevitable consequences for the international distribution of different economic activities. The changing structure of world production is reflected directly in the changing pattern of world trade. In assessing Schumpeterian competition in international terms, an equilibrium theory of comparative advantage is of limited help, for it takes as given the very facts which need explanation, but this does not mean that the concept can be dispensed with altogether. What is needed is an appropriate dynamic concept since patterns of comparative advantage can change dramatically over time, with formerly profitable industries passing into irreversible decline and new industries and locations rising to dominate world production. This is not only a question of the differential growth of different national industries; it is also a question of the entry and exit of different countries in specific lines of production. Industries experiencing the transfer of production capabilities and foreign investment include the cotton textile industry, the television industry, the automotive industry, the steel industry, the natural rubber industry, for example, which all speak in their own historically distinctive ways to this general theme of differential growth, technology transfer and innovation and imitation on an international scale. If we need a theory of comparative advantage we equally need a theory of the competitive, creative firm, because it is innovation and growth at the level of firms which is the direct causal factor behind changes in trade patterns. In turn, this implies that serious attention must also be given to the national institutional context in which firms innovate and grow. In this emphasis Porter is surely right when he argues that we need to go behind comparative advantage to the competitive advantage of the nation. His fundamental point is that "National prosperity is created, not inherited. It does not grow out of a country's natural enhancements, its labour pool, its interest rate, or its currency value as classic economics insists" (Porter 1998, p. 155). However, one cannot in this way ignore relative costs and exchange rates; we need a nuanced concept of competitive advantage that connects with the idea of comparative advantage and yet allows for the adaptive consequences of innovation. Krugman's (1994) critique of the idea of national competitive advantage is well aimed. It turns out that the competitiveness of firms and industries and comparative advantage are complementary notions. This is the theme that we now develop. Before doing so, one or two brief remarks on the literature are appropriate.

Trade and innovation

There can be no doubt that one of the great achievements of economic analysis has been the formulation of rigorous and coherent theories of international trade and investment. The two major trade theories differ only in their emphasis as to the origin of autarky price differences.[1] The Ricardian theory stresses international differences in technology in conjunction with international differences in real wage levels, while the Heckscher–Ohlin theory assumes the international identity of national tastes and technology, tracing the origins of trade to *given* differences in endowments of the primary productive agencies. In either case, illuminating propositions may then be derived concerning the determinants of the terms of trade (i.e. the price structure in a trading world), the distribution of the gain from trade, and the costs and benefits of policies to restrict trade. Moreover, effects of hypothetical changes in tastes, technology and resources on these dimensions of an equilibrium trading world are readily deduced from the comparison of long-period positions. These theories are extremely powerful and of considerable practical significance but for our purpose a critical deficiency of both is their failure to treat how economies adapt to opportunities for foreign trade. For example, the question, "What is the process by which an autarky equilibrium is transformed into a free trade equilibrium?" is not addressed, and nor can it be addressed by a method of comparison of equilibrium positions. Similarly, the process by which an innovation in one country modifies the pattern of trade and thus production in other countries is not explained. Important contributions to this latter problem were made by Posner (1961), Hufbauer (1966), Hirsch (1967) and Vernon (1966) who demonstrated how sequences of innovation and international imitation, combined with the differential growth of national production and consumption patterns, generated shifting trade patterns. These approaches provided important insights into two important phenomena shaping the evolution of the world economy, namely the international imitation of technology and accumulation of capabilities by low-wage economies (often aided by foreign investment from firms in advanced economies), and the need for high-wage economies to innovate continually if they are to maintain their relative standard of living. However, these are old themes. Marshall (1919), in his *Industry and Trade* devoted a great deal of attention to national differences in the competitiveness of firms and the consequent shifting balance of international leadership across different industries. Reflecting on the threats to England's competitive position in many industries he drew attention to German characteristics in relation to the application of science to industry and to the natural inventiveness of American firms. Ultimately, in Marshall, these differences are traceable to varying styles of management practice, one of the central but largely ignored themes in the *Principles* (1920). The crucial point to understand in Marshall is that firms in any industry are different and that these differences are changing continually due to differential attempts at innovation both nationally and internationally. In a world of changing knowledge there is not the slightest reason to expect the emergence of a long-run position, with technological information diffused equally across all economic agents. This means that there is no scope for innovative, entrepreneurial activity, which can find no place in the long-period equilibrium framework. Indeed we normally mean by innovation the application of privileged information to economic activity as reflected in the differentiation of firms in the same industry. The uneven distribution of knowledge is clearly a fundamental determinant of patterns of international trade. Moreover, knowledge is not static and we must expect patterns of trade to change over time in a way which reflects different national capabilities in the production of new knowledge.

One economist who understood this Marshallian perspective was Ely Devons (1961), who, in his inaugural lecture at the LSE, sketched out his misgivings in relation to orthodox trade theory. He argued that the most important elements determining trade flows are the result of purposive accumulation processes in relation to knowledge, skills and capacity. Thus factors of production are "firm specific" and are certainly not homogeneous across countries. Neither the quantities nor the quality of the relevant inputs are independent of the competitive process. As he put it,

> The explanation of a country's export trade, and especially of its export trade in manufactures, with other industrial countries has to be sought at least as much, if not more, in the energies, capacities, initiative and enterprise of individual businesses, as in the availability of general factors of production which are at everyone's disposal.
>
> (Devons 1961, pp. 353–354)

To do full justice to this perspective is well beyond the scope of this chapter. Consequently it will focus on one aspect only of international economic evolution, the differential growth of different national industries according to their competitive advantages. Questions of the entry of a country into the production of a particular commodity are set aside and with them all the matters related to the international transfer of technology and the processes of learning and capability accumulation. Innovation is suppressed except in so far as prior differential innovation has generated the particular distributions of firm efficiencies that underpin the evolution of trade.

Firm variety and the competitive process

A crucial assumption in standard trade theory is that all firms operating in a particular industry have full access to the most efficient of all the possible production methods, that is to say, their knowledge is the same. Of course, this assumption does not cohere with the world as we know it. Managers may well be rational but their deliberations are necessarily constrained by bounded knowledge sets, limited with respect to contemporaneous and future information. Consequently, the population of firms defining any particular industry is differentiated in multiple dimensions, each of which has implications for its competitive performance. From an evolutionary viewpoint a firm is more competitive than a rival in the same industry if it is growing faster than that rival and increasing its share of the total market as a consequence. An important element in determining this ability to grow faster is the superior profitability of a firm premised on its having developed a superior technology or superior organisation. The dimension of cost differentiation is perhaps the most powerful of sources of competitive advantage but it is not the only relevant dimension of evolutionary differentiation. Since our approach is focused on the long-period process it is concerned with the different rates at which firms invest in capacity expansion and this depends not only on their differential profitability but on what we shall call their differential propensities to accumulate. Neither the willingness and ambition to grow, nor the capability to manage growth, nor the access to external capital resources will be the same across firms so even firms with identical profitability may expand capacity at different rates. If we then add to these two dimensions the possibility of firms innovating at different rates we have a rich source of evolutionary development to apply to international trade.[2] Throughout most of this essay we will only allow variation with respect to the determinants of efficiencies and thus unit costs; we will provide some discussion of national differences in propensity to accumulate and no discussion at all of differential rates of innovation. These important aspects remain for further development.

The second major difference with orthodox trade theory lies in what is meant by the idea of competition. In both Ricardian theory and Hecksher–Ohlin–Samuelson theory, competition is a state of equilibrium, characterised as a long-period position. In the evolutionary approach, by contrast, we have a process view of competition in which the measure of the intensity of competition is not the number of firms but rather the rate of change in the structure of the industry as measured by the output shares of the different firms. Competition here entails rivalry and a struggle for market share; it is a perpetual condition of disequilibrium and change, not a state of balance between forces of equal marginal significance. Even in perfect markets, which we assume, differential profits are not then explained by differential market power but rather by the differential productive superiority of rival firms. This concept of competition as a process is what we find in Smith and Marshall and it also owes a great deal to Austrian theoretical perspectives, to Hayek and, in particular, to Schumpeter with his emphasis on change from within the capitalist system and the competition which is fostered by innovation. Of all the different sources of competitive advantage it is undoubtedly those based on superior product and process technology which are of dominant long-run importance since they underpin superior profitability and thus the resource base to enhance further competitive advantage. So how does an industry evolve when it is engaged in an international competitive process?

The evolutionary dynamics of international competition: a single industry

We begin by considering trade and production in a single industry, and how the international distribution of production changes over time according to the differential competitiveness of the rival national industries. Following from our definition of competitiveness, a national firm (industry) is competitive relative to any rival national firm (industry) if its share of world production is increasing relative to that of the rival in question.

Consider a particular industry located in two countries A and B. This industry produces an internationally homogeneous commodity, and in each country the industry is composed of a given number of firms each producing the commodity with different degrees of efficiency. There is a distribution of firm performance within each industry, ranging from a best practice firm with the lowest costs and at the other extreme a worst practice firm, which we take to be a firm that is just covering its normal, long-period costs of production. Each firm produces subject to constant returns to scale, so there are no limits on its absolute size, only limits on its rate of investment in capacity expansion, as in Penrose (1959). Somewhere in this range lies average practice unit cost but what this is depends not only on the efficiencies of the population of active firms but also on their relative size as measured by their shares in the output of each national industry. Because the firms operate with different efficiencies they are differentially profitable: the worst practice firm just breaks even, covering all its long-run costs including the cost of capital, and all other firms earn superior profits or quasi-rents. What these profits are also depends on the relation between input costs and prices for a given distribution of efficiencies. If unit costs are expressed in terms of labour equivalent units, h, we can denote the industry average, real unit cost level in A by h_A and in B by h_B. If s_i denotes the share of output of firm i in A and s_j denotes the corresponding share of firm j in B, then, $h_A = \sum s_i h_{iA}$, and $h_B \sum s_j h_{jB}$. Let w_A and w_B be the wage rates in national currency units and let e be the exchange rate defined as the number of units of A currency to a unit of B currency.

Because this is a long-period process we must consider the rate at which firms invest, or disinvest, in production capacity. In order to focus entirely on the traditional questions concerning the effect on trade of costs of production, we will assume that all firms in each national industry invest in the same proportion to their profitability, such that two firms with the same profitability have the same rate of growth of capacity. Let f denote this propensity to grow, then industry A grows at the average rate $g_A = \sum s_i g_{iA}$ and industry B at the average rate $g_B = \sum s_j g_{jB}$. It follows that these average growth rates, within which there is intra-industry variation are given by

$$g_A = f_A(p_A - w_A h_A) \quad \text{and} \quad g_B = f_B(p_B - w_B h_B) \tag{1}$$

where p_A and p_B are the industry prices expressed in national currencies. Under the assumption of perfect markets in each economy, prices are the same for all firms within the industry as are money wage rates.[3]

In a trading world the growth rates of the two industries are not interdependent but reflect two coordinating rules. First, that the growth rate of the "world" industry equals the given growth of world demand, g_w, so that capacity and demand grow in a balanced long-period manner,

$$s_A g_A + s_B g_B = g_w \tag{2}$$

where s_A and s_B are the respective shares of the national industries in total "world" output. Second, that the national prices are linked by the exchange rate such that

$$R p_A = e p_B \tag{3}$$

when R reflects influences such as transport costs, tariffs and other barriers which stand in the way of the "law of one-price". Without serious loss, we set $R = 1$. It is also convenient to define, $z = e w_B / w_A$, the ratio of national wage rates expressed in terms of the currency of A.

Since our concern is with the relation between cost differences and the evolution of this world industry it is necessary to begin by setting $f_A = f_B = f$ so that we isolate the effect of cost differences on competitiveness. On combining (1), (2) and (3), it follows immediately that the normal price which equates the rate of growth of world capacity and demand is

$$p_A = \frac{g_w}{f} + (s_A h_A + z s_B h_B) = \frac{g_w}{f} + h_w \tag{4a}$$

where h_w is the world average unit cost level expressed in A currency.

The growth rates of the national industries follow directly and we have for country A

$$g_A = g_w + f(1 - s_A)(z h_B - h_A), \tag{5a}$$

so that A's industry grows at a rate above or below the world average in proportion to its absolute cost advantage over the industry in B. In country B, the same logic holds, and

$$g_B = g_w = f(1 - s_B)(h_A - z h_B). \tag{5b}$$

Consequently, the difference in the national growth rates is

$$g_A - g_B = f(z h_B - h_A), \tag{5c}$$

a direct relation between comparative rates of expansion and absolute cost differences. The industry that has the competitive advantage is the industry that has the real cost advantage.

Now consider some implications of the world industry being coordinated in this way such that the prices in each country satisfy the law of one price and simultaneously maintain equality between the growth in world capacity and the growth in world demand.

Any increase in the relative wage ratio, e.g., that associated with a depreciation of A's currency, will increase A's absolute competitive advantage and so increase the growth rate of A's industry at the expense of B's industry and increase A's growth rate relative to the world average rate. The magnitudes of the changes relative to the world average depend on the prevailing structure of world output. The increase in A's growth rate is smaller the greater is A's share of world output, which means that the decrease in B's growth rate must be correspondingly greater to maintain balanced world conditions. When the wage ratio is equal to the real cost ratio, h_A/h_B, the differences in competitive advantage are nullified but there is no reason to expect that this ratio will hold in general. There are many determinants of exchange rates that are independent of the many other determinants of national wage levels and relative real costs in any one industry. Consequently, at any given wage ratio the two industries are normally growing at different rates and the structure of world output is shifting in favour of the country with the absolute competitive advantage. Thus, for example, the world market share of country A increases at the rate

$$\frac{ds_A}{dt} = s_A(g_A - g_W) = fs_A(h_W - h_A) = fs_A s_B(zh_B - h_A) \tag{6}$$

with a similar expression holding in country B. Equation (6) is a particular instantiation of the general rule that countries increase their share of world production, industry by industry in accordance with their absolute competitive advantages. This is based in turn on one of the central principles of evolutionary dynamics that the movement of the relative positions of the two industries depends on how their efficiencies compare with the average efficiency for the world population of firms in this industry. As long as A has a competitive advantage, its share grows according to (6) as a logistic process that asymptotically accounts for the entire market in relative terms. The industry in B may continue to survive and grow but in relative terms it is of no economic consequence, its effective weight is zero.

Trade balances

If the structure of world production is changing, it follows directly that the balance of payments for the industry is also changing. However, trade flows depend on patterns of demand as well as on patterns of production, and to be a net exporter of the commodity a country must have a greater share in world production than it has in world consumption. To see this more explicitly, let, c_A, c_B, respectively denote the shares of countries A and B in the total world consumption of the industry's output. Define b_A as the trade balance for the industry in A, expressed as a fraction of national production in A, then

$$b_A = 1 - \frac{c_A}{s_A}$$

and, for country B, the corresponding ratio of trade to national production is

$$b_B = 1 - \frac{c_B}{s_B}$$

from which it follows that $b_A = -(s_B/s_A) \cdot b_B$. While it is perfectly possible that changes in the pattern of world consumption contribute more to the change in trade flows than do changes in world production, we shall follow a rather traditional trade theory approach and eliminate consumption-related effects by holding the consumption shares constant, thus isolating the effect of changes in production structure.[4] In this case, it follows that

$$\frac{db_A}{dt} = \left(\frac{c_A}{s_A}\right)(g_A - g_w) \tag{7a}$$

which is equivalent to

$$\frac{db_A}{dt} = f\left(\frac{s_B}{s_A}\right)c_A(zh_B - h_A), \tag{7b}$$

so that A is improving its net trade position whenever it has an absolute competitive advantage over the industry in country B and this is true whenever the wage ratio exceeds the real cost ratio. The change in the absolute volume of A's net trade, T_A is given by,

$$\frac{dT_A}{dt} = s_A(g_A - \left(\frac{c_A}{s_A}\right)g_w) X \tag{7c}$$

where X is the aggregate volume of world production.

It is clear that the mere fact of A having a competitive advantage in this industry does not imply that A is a net exporter of the commodity, that depends on the comparison of the production and consumption shares.

What we can say is that if A is the more competitive, then either its net imports are falling or its net exports are increasing. Suppose, for the sake of illustration, that $g_A > c_A/s_A \cdot g_W$. If the share of A's industry is sufficiently low relative to A's share of world consumption, A will have a deficit but its imports will be falling and so the absolute volume of trade is declining. Conversely, if $c_A < s_A$, then the volume of its exports and its total volume of trade will be increasing.

Some evolutionary dynamics

The dynamics of differential growth and trade sketched above is based upon a standard method of evolutionary analysis, the principles of variation and selection. The variation is provided by the real cost differences within and across national industries, and the forces of selection are provided by the competition for customers in the world market. Can we say anything more about the rate at which the structure of world production is evolving? The affirmative answer to this question rests on the so-called Fisher/Price Principles of evolutionary dynamics: principles that capture the idea that change is distributed according to how the costs in the different countries are distributed around the world average, a particular instantiation of the idea of a replicator dynamic process. When the structure of the industry is changing, and even if the average cost levels in countries A and B are taken as given, it nonetheless follows that the world average unit cost level is changing, in fact it is converging on the cost level in the more competitive of the two countries at the ruling wage ratio. In turn this means that the national average cost differences are also evolving. All is flux in an evolving world economy, and it is not unreasonable to ask "How does this process of change operate?"

Consider first the evolution of the world average unit cost level, on the provisional assumption that the national average cost levels are given. Then

$$\frac{dh_W}{dt} = \frac{ds_A}{dt}h_A + \frac{ds_B}{dt}h_B = f[s_A(g_A - g_W) + s_B(g_B - g_W)]$$

$$\frac{dh_W}{dt} = f[s_A(h_W - h_A)h_A - s_B(h_W - zh_B)zh_B] = f \cdot V_s(h) \qquad (8)$$

where $V_s(h)$ is the world variance in the national average, real unit cost levels.[5] This is the famous Fisher Principle, the idea that evolutionary change is driven by evolutionary variety. The change in the world average naturally means that the national competitive advantages are continually being revised as the world average converges to the cost level in the more competitive of the two countries.

The logic that governs the evolution of the world production structure also applies within the two countries, so that the national cost averages cannot be constant even if the costs in the individual firms are constant. Thus average unit costs in both countries decline in proportion to their respective internal variances in unit costs, so that, for example, A's cost advantage evolves according to the relation,

$$\frac{dh_W}{dt} - \frac{dh_A}{dt} = -f\left[V_s(h) + (1 - s_A)\left(\frac{dh_B}{dt} - \frac{dh_A}{dt}\right)\right]$$

$$\ldots \ldots \ldots \ldots \ldots = -f[V_s(h) + (1 - s_A)(V_A(h) - V_B(h)]. \qquad (9)$$

The second and third variances in this expression are the internal cost variances in country A and B respectively. Suppose we want to illustrate that A has the competitive advantage. Then the operation of the Fisher Principle between countries naturally works to reduce A's competitive advantage by increasing A's share of world output, bringing world average unit costs closer to A's unit costs. The operation of the Principle within countries reduces unit costs in both but which cost level falls more quickly depends on a comparison of the national variances in costs. If the cost variance in B is greater than the cost variance in A then this reduces the rate of decline in A's competitive advantage.

This simple account of the dynamics of the world production structure and its effects on the volume of trade are capable of two immediate generalisations, one to cover many industries and two countries and the other to cover many countries and the one industry. Let us consider them *seriatim*.

Two countries and many industries

If there are many industries engaged in foreign trade then for each one the analysis above applies, and taking any industry the criterion for it to grow faster in A than in B is simply that

$$z > \frac{h_A}{h_B}$$

that is to say, that the wage ratio exceeds the real cost ratio. If we now arrange a list of industries in descending order of their real cost ratios, then we can draw Figure 8.1 and notionally cut the real cost chain, C_1, at the ruling particular value of the wage ratio, say, z^0. Industry m is the industry for which neither country has a competitive advantage, so that for this industry both countries are expanding their production capacity at the same rate and their respective trade balance ratios are constant. All the industries to the right of m are industries where country A has an absolute competitive advantage so that $g_A > g_B$ and country A is becoming relatively more important in total world production of these industries. For the industries to the left of m the converse is true, country A has an absolute competitive disadvantage and is declining in relative importance as a world producer. If we now compare any two industries either side of industry m, say industry i and industry r, then it will naturally follow that $(h_A/h_B)_i > (h_A/h_B)_r$ so that we have a dynamic form of the traditional chain of comparative advantage theorem. A has a comparative cost advantage in any industry in which it is gaining world market share compared to any industry in which it is losing world market share.

If A's currency should be devalued, given the money wage levels in A and B, it would be greater and it would follow that A had a competitive advantage in a greater number of industries. Consequently A would be increasing its exports faster or reducing its imports faster in a greater number of industries, so improving its overall balance of trade more quickly, not in a one-off fashion but continuously.

Many countries, one industry

With many countries, k in number, sharing a common propensity to grow but with different real costs and different wage ratios, exactly the same considerations apply as in the two-country case. We continue to express prices in A's currency so each country has its own value of z, measuring its wage relative to the wage in country A. If we take country Q, for example, then,

$$g_Q - g_W = f(h_W - z_Q h_Q).$$

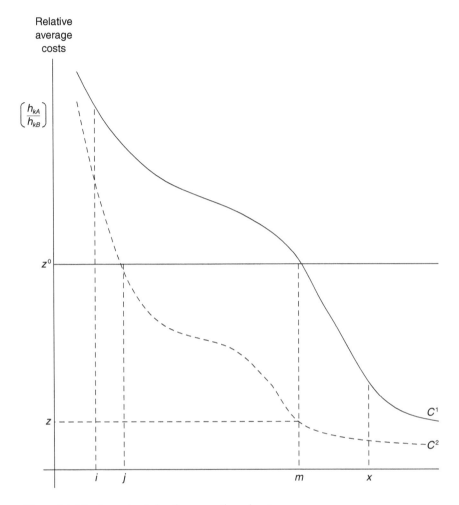

Figure 8.1 The dynamic chain of comparative advantage.

Country Q has a competitive advantage, which depends on the absolute difference between its real costs and world average real costs for this industry, where $h_W = \sum s_k h_k$.

As in the two-country case, the Fisher/Price dynamics continue to operate so that each country's real cost value and the world average cost value evolve over time according to the respective cost variances at national and world level. Thus, world average real costs change according to the relation,

$$\frac{dh_w}{dt} = \sum \frac{ds_k}{dt} h_k + \sum s_k \frac{dh_k}{dt} = -f \left[V_s(h) + \sum s_k V_k(h_k) \right]. \tag{10}$$

In this expression, the first term is the variance in the average unit costs across the countries and the second term is the weighted sum of the variances of the unit costs within the countries.

Differential propensities to accumulate

We began by assuming that the propensities to grow are the same in each country, a device that had the merit of focusing our attention on the differences in real cost of production across the two countries. Competitive advantage then translates directly into real cost advantage as demonstrated above. But the limitations of this one-dimensional view of the competitive process will be obvious when we consider the possibility that different firms and industries also differ in their propensities to expand capacity. Not all firms in any given industry are willing or able to grow at the same rate as rivals even if they are equally profitable, and these differences will apply across countries too. If so, it is no longer the case that real cost advantage and competitive advantage are the same.

To sketch the essentials we continue to assume that firms in a national industry have a common propensity to accumulate but that these propensities differ between countries A and B. Specifically, let $f_A > f_B$. By adding a second dimension to the international selection process we open up a new set of considerations that alter the process of international competition. If it so happened that neither industry had an absolute cost advantage it would still be the case that industry A expanded relative to industry B, even though the two industries are equiprofitable, A is more competitive. Even if A's industry started as a net importer of the commodity it would at some point become a long-term exporter of this commodity even though costs are the same in the two countries. The source of its trade advantage would not be in its comparative costs but in its comparatively greater propensity to grow, a difference that might be influenced by many factors but would certainly be dependent on dynamic, managerial capabilities.

The steps in the argument are straightforward but are worth spelling out in a little detail. Define $f_S = s_A f_A + s_B f_B$ as the world average propensity to accumulate, and define the weights $u_A = s_A f_A/f_S$ and $u_B = s_B f_B/f_S$, to measure the proportionate contribution that each country makes to the world average propensity to accumulate. Then in place of (4a) we have,

$$p_A = \frac{g_W}{f_s} + (u_A h_A + z u_B h_B). \tag{4b}$$

It then follows that the relation between A's industry growth rate and the world growth rate is given by

$$g_A - g_W = \left(\frac{f_A - f_s}{f_s}\right) g_W + f_A(1 - u_A)(z h_B - h_A). \tag{11}$$

Two immediate consequences follow. First, a competitive advantage for B's industry does not necessarily mean that it will be the faster-growing industry now that B has the smaller propensity to grow. It will be more profitable than the A industry but the correlation between profitability and growth may now be negative, if A's growth propensity is sufficiently greater than B's. Second, the excess of A's growth rate over the world growth rate, the proportionate rate of increase in A's market share, is no longer independent of the world growth rate, even though we are assuming constant returns to scale in both industries. The higher the world growth rate is the greater is the competitive advantage of A's industry, precisely because the higher unit profit margins associated with a higher world market growth rate have a proportionately greater effect on A's rate of expansion.

In the case of many industries common national propensities to grow across national industries the same considerations hold. We find the industry that has no competitive advantage by finding a value of the wage ratio that equalises the growth rates in the two countries. This is now given by

$$z^* = \left[\frac{h_A}{h_B} - \left(\frac{1}{h_B} \right) \left(\frac{f_A - f_B}{f_A f_B} \right) g_W \right].$$

The condition for A to have an absolute competitive advantage now becomes $z > z^*$. If we refer to Figure 8.1 we find that the new chain of comparative advantage is given by curve C_2, which lies below C_1 but not uniformly. Consider industry m, the industry which previously was competitively neutral at the ruling wage ratio, we find now that country A has a competitive advantage in m at the original wage ratio by virtue of its higher propensity to grow. It would require a wage ratio z^1 to remove the competitive advantage given to m by its higher propensity to grow. The new marginal industry is industry j, and so, at the given value of the wage ratio and by virtue of its superior accumulation capabilities, country A has a greater number of industries in which it is increasing its share of world markets relative to country B.

Trade and comparative advantage: a conundrum

The most important premise of this evolutionary account of trade is that each country has a distribution of firms in each industry, each firm having different real production costs. We trace these differences to different firm characteristics and capabilities, which as we have seen, influence not only real costs but also the ability of the different firms to grow. This is why competitive advantage involves more than matters of cost advantage. However, as soon as we allow, in Marshallian style, a distribution of costs we must face a conundrum.

The traditional argument involves taking two economies and two industries in conditions of autarky and comparing their price structures. If they are "opened up" to trade and trade is at a wage ratio that supports balanced trade, it would follow that the direction of trade is predicted by a comparison of autarky prices. However, autarky prices would not be equal to costs in the average firm but to costs of production in the marginal firms in each industry, that is to say, those firms that are just breaking even. All the other firms will be making positive profits on the lines discussed above. Suppose that it is commodity two that is produced more cheaply at the margin in A then it would follow that the costs of the marginal firms (h') would be ranked as follows:

$$\frac{h'_{1A}}{h'_{1B}} > z > \frac{h'_{2A}}{h'_{2B}}.$$

The correct prediction would be that A will export commodity two and B will export commodity one.

Now suppose that the best practice firms in each country generate a different cost ranking (h'') such that in these terms A has a comparative advantage in industry one. Then,

$$\frac{h^f_{1A}}{h^f_{1B}} > z > \frac{h^f_{2A}}{h^f_{2B}}.$$

The immediate pattern of trade will be determined by the marginal firms but the long-run pattern of trade will be determined by the best practice firms which, on the lines sketched above, are the fastest-growing firms and thus come to dominate average practice in each industry. Thus, at some point the trade pattern will be reversed and A will export commodity one and B will export commodity two. Autarky prices are in this case not a guide to the future pattern of comparative advantage.

What is the source of the conundrum, which would be no surprise to an evolutionist? It is the assumption in traditional theory that within any industry all firms are producing with identical technologies and forms of organisation so that within industries there are no absolute cost advantages. However, trade depends on national differences in costs between economies. It seems unduly restrictive to allow cost differences between countries but not to allow them within industries. Once we take the later step then the entire evolutionary nature of trade dynamics becomes clear. To return to the autarky example, autarky costs determine the initial pattern of trade but this will only be reinforced if average cost conditions are ranked in the same order as costs in the marginal firms, and ultimately costs in the best-practice firms. Since inter-industry cost differences appear as one of the most persistent of stylised facts these considerations are not irrelevant to the understanding of real world trade dynamics.

However, our main concern has not been with the traditional question of the relation between comparative advantage and autarky prices but on the evolution of an ongoing trading world, the development of which is guided by average cost conditions in the various national industries. The relative national growth rates of a given industry depend as we have shown on its absolute cost advantage, yet the concept of comparative advantage in relation to average cost levels of the industries still indicates how the world production pattern will evolve.

Suppose that the average costs are such that $h_{1A}/h_{1B} < h_{2A}/h_{2B}$ so, in this sense, the dynamic comparative advantage of A is in industry 1. The evolution of the world production structure then depends on the ruling value of the wage ratio. If

$$h_{1A}/h_{1B} < z < h_{2A}/h_{2B}$$

the industry growth rates will be ranked such that $g_{1A} > g_{1B}$ and $g_{2A} < g_{2B}$, so that A is increasing its world market share in industry 1 and B is increasing its world market share in industry 2. However, for example, if z is such that

$$z < h_{1A}/h_{1B} < h_{2A}/h_{2B}$$

then both B's industries will be growing faster than A's industries. This is not sustainable, for it would imply at some point that A imports both commodities. Consequently, evolution with balanced trade requires that the wage ratio lie between the two cost ratios, in traditional fashion. It is not possible for a country to have a sustainable dynamic competitive advantage in all commodities. However, and as we have already pointed out, the fact that A has a competitive advantage in industry 1 does not mean that it is exporting commodity one. We might have caught the system at a point in which $s_{1A} < c_{1A}$ so that A is importing commodity one. What we can say in this situation is that A is reducing its imports relative to its production of commodity one. This is the sense in which the comparative cost principle applies to the dynamic evolution of trade patterns when it does not apply to the pattern of trade, a possibility that the conventional theory avoids by focusing on long-period positions in which all firms in a given "world" industry produce with the same costs.

Coordination of the world economy

We turn finally to the question of how this evolutionary process is coordinated. Given the money wage levels in each country this cannot be separated from the question of the determination of the exchange rate and thus the determination of the terms of trade between the two countries. These are rather more complex questions than we have space to do justice to but we can pursue them a little further here. Define the terms of trade as $\rho = p_2 / p_1$ and we can write the condition for balanced trade between A and B as follows:

$$(s_{1A} - c_{1A})x_1 - \rho(s_{2B} - c_{2B})x_2 = 0$$

where x_1 and x_2 are the levels of world production (consumption) of the two commodities. Then we can express the familiar condition for payments equilibrium in this long-period process, in an unconventional way, namely as

$$\frac{s_{1A} - c_{1A}}{s_{2B} - c_{2B}} = \rho \cdot \gamma$$

where $\gamma = x_2 / x_1$ is the world production ratio. Clearly $s_{1A} > c_{1A}$ implies $s_{2B} > c_{2B}$ and conversely. If the money wage rates are given in each country, this implies a corresponding exchange rate at which trade is balanced and thus a particular value of the wage ratio which must lie between the limits set by average comparative costs. The balanced exchange rate must not only be consistent with balanced trade it must also ensure that industry by industry the rate of growth of world capacity is equal to the rate of growth of world demand. That is to say, given the money wage levels in each country, the balanced exchange rate supports a pattern of industry profit margins between and within countries consistent with this requirement. It follows from the argument leading to (4a) that this balanced exchange rate, e^*, is given by,

$$e^* = \frac{1}{\gamma} \left[\left(\frac{g_{1W} + fh_{1W}}{g_{2W} + fh_{2W}} \right) \left(\frac{s_{1A} - c_{1A}}{s_{2B} - c_{2B}} \right) \right].$$

Suppose the actual exchange rate was greater than the balanced value (a notional depreciation of A's currency) then the effect will be to raise prices and profit margins in all firms in A relative to firms in B, and thus cause s_{1A} to increase more rapidly and s_{1B} to increase less rapidly, so opening up a trade surplus for A. A stable foreign exchange market then implies that the exchange rate appreciates until the new balanced exchange rate is established, one that will be higher than originally because of the induced changes in the structure of world production caused by the temporary undervaluation of A's currency. How the exchange rate and country A's terms of trade evolve within a balanced evolutionary process depends on the differences in real costs and on how the world growth rates of the two industries compare. Even given the world market growth rates and average world unit costs, this balanced exchange rate will be changing in general as the production shares change. To this must be added the further changes induced by the operation of the Fisher Principle on the world unit cost values, as well as changes in the relative world size of the two industries. It is scarcely surprising that a restless, evolving world economy implies an ever-changing balanced exchange rate. Unless it is contended that money wage rates can adjust easily this is surely part of the powerful reasoning behind the arguments in favour of flexible exchange rates.

Conclusion

By way of a summary, our purpose in these brief notes has been to begin the exploration of some implications of an evolutionary approach to international trade, a picture which emphasises the forces making for changes in the flow and direction of trade and which allowed us to formulate a dynamic analogue to the traditional concept of comparative advantage. Within this variation-cum-selection framework, national differences in average costs are the driving force behind the evolution of trade patterns. In this rather limited way we can connect to the effects of the new international competition following from the entry of China and India, for example, into world markets in many industries and the importance of exchange rates for the dynamic evolution of the resulting trade patterns. The traditional questions are not lost in the evolutionary approach but the answers are different. In particular, in an ever-changing world of innovation and international technology transfer, the role of comparative costs is primarily in relation to the change in world production structures and the implied trade patterns, rather than to which countries export which commodities. The movements of the production structure will, if sufficient time is allowed and other things remain equal, generate trade according to the traditional criterion but only if the influences on the propensities to accumulate are sufficiently common across countries. Evolutionary selection is not always in favour of firms with low costs, except in the one-dimensional process discussed above. Evolution is a complex matter but it is always with us.

Notes

1 Bhagwati and Srinivasan (1983) provide an excellent account of the nature of current trade theory. Kemp (1969) is also a comprehensive treatment of the main elements of neoclassical trade theory.
2 There is an important connection here with the very rich literature on the capabilities theory of the firm. See Nelson and Winter (1982), Winter (1967), Nelson (1991), and related literature by Barney (1991), Castanias and Helfat (1991) and Teece *et al.* (1997). The origins of much of this literature is to be found in Penrose (1959).
3 The propensities to accumulate are equal to the ratio of investment rate to profit margin, divided by the ratio of the value of capital to the rate of physical output. An equal proportionate change in all prices increases the value to capital ratio in proportion to the increase in profit margin per unit of output, so leaving the growth rate unchanged.
4 I do not hold that the evolution of demand and consumption is irrelevant to international trade, quite the contrary. But with important exceptions (e.g., Burenstam Linder 1961) trade theory does not give serious attention to the demand side, partly a product of the HOS assumption that the only differences between national economies relate to their resource endowments of primary factors. Evolutionists have important but as yet unrealised contributions to make here.
5 Note that $V_s(h) = s_A(1 - s_A)(zh_B - h_A)^2$. A notional increase in z increases this variance if $zh_B \phi h_A$, and conversely.

References

Barney, J. (1991), "Firm Resources and Sustained Competitive Advantage", *Journal of Management*, Vol. 17, No. 1.
Bhagwati, J. and Srinivasan, T. (1983), *Lectures on International Trade*, Cambridge, MA, MIT Press.
Burenstam Linder, S. (1961), *An Essay on Trade and Transformation*, Stockholm, Almqvist & Wicksell.
Castanias, R.A. and Helfat, C. (1991), "Management Resources and Rents", *Journal of Management*, Vol. 17.
Devons, E. (1961), "Understanding International Trade", *Economica*, Vol. 28, No. 112.
Hirsch, S. (1967), *Location of Industry and International Competitiveness*, Oxford, Clarendon Press.
Hufbauer, G.C. (1966), *Synthetic Materials and the Theory of International Trade*, London, G. Duckworth.

Kemp, M.C. (1969), *The Pure Theory of International Trade and Investment*, London, Prentice Hall.

Krugman, P. (1994), *Pop Internationalism*, Boston, MA, MIT Press.

Marshall, A. (1919), *Industry and Trade*, London, Macmillan.

Marshall, A. (1920) *Principles of Economics (8th edition)*, London, Macmillan.

Metcalfe, J.S. (1998), *Evolutionary Economics and Creative Destruction*, London, Routledge.

Nelson, R.R. (1991), "Why Do Firms Differ; And How Does It Matter", *Strategic Journal of Management*, Vol. 12, No. S2, pp. 61–74.

Nelson, R.R and Winter, S. (1982), *An Evolutionary Theory of Economic Change*, Harvard, MA, Belknap Press.

Penrose, E.T. (1959), *The Theory of the Growth of the Firm*, Oxford, Basil Blackwell.

Porter, M. (1998), *On Competition*, Cambridge, MA, Harvard Business School Press.

Posner, M. (1961), "International Trade and Technical Change", *Oxford Economic Papers*, Vol. 13, No. 3.

Teece, D.J, Pisano, G. and Shuen, A. (1997), "Dynamic Capabilities and Strategic Management", *Strategic Management Journal*, Vol. 18, No. 7.

Vernon, R. (1966), "International Investment and International Trade in the Product Cycle", *Quarterly Journal of Economics*, Vol. 80, No. 2.

Winter, S. (2006 [1967]), "Towards a Neo-Schumpeterian Theory of the Firm", *Industry and Corporate Change*, Vol. 15, No. 1.

9 Labour values in linear models with international trade

Takao Fujimoto *

1 Introduction

As we proceed along the approach adopted by the classical economists, that is, to determine the values of various commodities before their prices come on to the stage without resorting to supply and demand, there arise difficulties brought in by joint production, heterogeneous labour, international trade, exhaustible resources, etc. Morishima (1964, 1973) proposed a solution against the existence of joint production, using a linear programming problem. Bowles and Gintis (1977) offered a definition in a model with heterogeneous labour but without joint production. On the other hand, several authors considered how to grasp the amount of a particular commodity contained in various products directly and indirectly: see Jeong (1982, 1984); Fujita (1991); and Manresa *et al.* (1998). These contributions are all for models with single production and homogeneous labour without international trade.

In this chapter, we present new definitions of labour values in models with joint production, heterogeneous labour, and international trade, using the method in Fujimoto and Opocher (2007). In section 2, a simple Leontief model without international trade is used so that the reader can grasp our approach in an easy way. In section 3, we describe our definition in a modified von Neumann–Morishima model. Section 4 is devoted to models with international trade. The final section 5 contains several remarks.

2 A Leontief model

Let us consider a Leontief-type simple input–output model without joint production and with homogeneous labour. There are n kinds of commodities, and corresponding to these, we have n industries. The symbols are:

A : a given $n \times n$ matrix of material input coefficients,
ℓ : a given row n-vector of labour input coefficients,
c : a given column n-vector of consumption basket to reproduce one unit of labour force,
I : the identity $n \times n$ matrix,

λ : the row n vector of labour values, and

λ_ℓ : the labour value of one unit of labour force.

As explained in Okishio (1977) and Morishima (1973), the labour value vector λ is defined by

$$\lambda = \lambda A + \ell,$$

and the labour value of labour is computed by

$$\lambda_\ell = \lambda \cdot c.$$

Now we define an $(n + 1) \times (n + 1)$ matrix $\mathbb{A}$ as[1]

$$\mathbb{A} \equiv \begin{pmatrix} A & c \\ \ell & 0 \end{pmatrix}.$$

Then the above two equations can be combined into one, leading to

$$(\lambda, \lambda_\ell) = (\lambda, 1) \, \mathbb{A}. \tag{1}$$

It is important to note here that in eq.(1), the *direct* input of labour is given unity as its value on the RHS, while the value of one unit of labour is calculated as λ_ℓ on the LHS. Then eq.(1) is rewritten as

$$(\lambda, 1) = (\lambda, 1) \, \mathbb{A} + (0'_n, 1 - \lambda_\ell), \tag{2}$$

where 0_n is the column n-vector whose elements are all zero with a prime indicating transposition. This leads to

$$(\upsilon\lambda, \upsilon) = (\upsilon\lambda, \upsilon) \, \mathbb{A} + (0'_n, \upsilon(1 - \lambda_\ell)),$$

where υ is a positive scalar. Supposing $(1 - \lambda_\ell) > 0$, we normalize υ so that $\upsilon(1 - \lambda_\ell) = 1$. By putting $q \equiv (\upsilon\lambda, \upsilon)$, we finally obtain the equation

$$q = q \cdot \mathbb{A} + (0'_n, 1). \tag{3}$$

We make the following assumption.

Assumption AP (Productiveness assumption): There exists a nonnegative column $(n + 1)$-vector x such that $x \gg \mathbb{A} x$. Thus, $(I - \mathbb{A})^{-1} > 0$.[2]

Now eq.(3) is solved for q as

$$q = (0'_n, 1) \, (I - \mathbb{A})^{-1}. \tag{4}$$

On the other hand, from eq.(2) we get

$$(\lambda, 1) = (\mathbf{0}'_n, 1 - \lambda_\ell)(I - \mathbb{A})^{-1}.$$

It is evident from eq.(4) that q is the last row of the inverse $(I - \mathbb{A})^{-1}$, thus the above equation gives

$$1 = q_{n+1}(1 - \lambda_\ell), \text{ that is, } \lambda_\ell = \frac{q_{n+1} - 1}{q_{n+1}}, \text{ and} \tag{5}$$

$$\lambda_j = \frac{q_j}{q_{n+1}} \quad \text{for} \quad j = 1, \ldots, n. \tag{6}$$

It naturally follows that $0 \leq \lambda_\ell < 1$ and $\lambda_j \geq 0$ for $j = 1, \ldots, n$, i.e., the labour value of one unit of labour is less than one.[3] When labour is indispensable to produce a basket c, we have $0 < \lambda_\ell$. Therefore, when the productiveness assumption AP is given, all we have to do is to solve eq.(4) first, and then calculate labour values using eqs (5) and (6).

Through the studies on nonsubstitution theorems, we know the solution q can be obtained by solving the following linear programming problem.[4]

$$\max q_{n+1} \text{ subject to } q \leq q \cdot \mathbb{A} + (\mathbf{0}'_n, 1) \text{ and } q \geq \mathbf{0}'_n. \tag{7}$$

The dual problem to the above is

$$\min x_{n+1} \text{ subject to } x \geq \mathbb{A} \cdot x + \begin{pmatrix} \mathbf{0}_n \\ 1 \end{pmatrix} \text{ and } x \geq \mathbf{0}_n.$$

In fact these linear programming problems have the optimal solutions by which the constraints are all satisfied with strict equality. The meaning of the constraints in the primal problem is that in each process the value of output cannot exceed the total value of inputs, and in the dual problem the constraints require that the gross output vector x should produce one unit of labour force as the net output.

3 A generalized von Neumann–Morishima model

Now we are ready to jump at a general von Neumann model with heterogeneous labour, in which there can be alternative household activities to reproduce each type of labour. Besides, there can be durable consumption goods as well. In more detail, our model is a generalization of Morishima model (Morishima 1964). That is, different from the original model in von Neumann (1945–46), we explicitly deal with labour input coefficients, and moreover we allow for the existence of joint production as well as heterogeneous labour. Thus, we are able to deal with durable capital goods. Various types of labour are treated exactly like normal commodities, and so we use the symbols $\mathbb{B}$ and $\mathbb{A}$ as the output and input coefficient matrices, both of which now have n rows and m columns. There are altogether n kinds of goods, services, and various types of labour. On the other hand, there exist m production processes or household activities. This way of formulation enables us to take into consideration durable consumption commodities in household activities: a durable consumption commodity in a column of household activity of $\mathbb{A}$ will appear in the corresponding column of $\mathbb{B}$ as one period, say one year, older commodity. For each type of labour, there can be more than one household activity to reproduce that labour. Workers may save a part of their incomes, and may have properties. These complicating elements from the real world do not disturb our study while we deal with values and exploitation: this should be true in any linear model including Leontief models.

Now we choose a type of labour as the standard and let it be the i-th labour commodity. We give our definition of labour values as follows.

Definition of values for our general model: Values in a general input–output model are nonnegative magnitudes assigned to commodities (including services and various types of labour) such that the value of the numeraire commodity be maximized under the condition that the total value of the output of each possible process should not exceed that of the input. When calculating the total value of the input of a process, unity is assigned to the direct input of the numeraire commodity.[5]

The economic meaning of our definition is almost the same as classical economists had in mind: the value of a commodity is the necessary amount of the numeraire commodity required directly or indirectly to produce one unit of that commodity. Because of joint production, we have to admit of inequalities. The supposed maximization is not arbitrary because its dual side of minimization carries a concept of efficiency, which is implicit even among classical definitions as explained in the previous section.

Our productiveness assumption here is:

Assumption APG: There exists an $x \geq 0_m$ such that

$$(\mathbb{B} - \mathbb{A})x \gg 0_n.$$

Having defined values as above, we can now explain how to compute values in a way similar to the problem (7) in section 2. Let us first define the following vectors:

$$\Lambda^{[i]} \equiv (\lambda_1^{[i]}, \lambda_2^{[i]}, \ldots, \lambda_{i-1}^{[i]}, \lambda_i^{[i]}, \lambda_{i+1}^{[i]}, \ldots, \lambda_n^{[i]}), \text{ and}$$

$$\Lambda_{[i]}^{[i]} \equiv (\lambda_1^{[i]}, \lambda_2^{[i]}, \ldots, \lambda_{i-1}^{[i]}, 1, \lambda_{i+1}^{[i]}, \ldots, \lambda_n^{[i]}).$$

The vector $\Lambda^{[i]}$ is the vector of values with i-th labour being the standard of value, and the element $\lambda_j^{[i]}$ stands for the value of commodity j with i-commodity as the standard of value. Our definition above is rewritten like this:

Find out $\Lambda^{[i]} \geq 0$ such that $\lambda_i^{[i]}$ should be maximized

subject to $\Lambda^{[i]} \cdot \mathbb{B} \leq \Lambda_{[i]}^{[i]} \cdot \mathbb{A}.$ $\qquad\qquad(8)$

We can proceed as we have done for a Leontief model in section 2. That is, the constraint in this problem can be transformed first through adding $(1 - \lambda_i^{[i]}) \cdot b^{(i)}$ to both sides, then multiplying both sides by a positive scalar v, yielding

$$v \cdot \Lambda_{[i]}^{[i]} \cdot \mathbb{B} \leq v \cdot \Lambda_{[i]}^{[i]} \cdot \mathbb{A} + v \cdot (1 - \lambda_i^{[i]}) \cdot b^{(i)},$$

where $b^{(i)}$ is the i-th row of $\mathbb{B}$. Then, we set

$$v \cdot (1 - \lambda_i^{[i]}) = 1 \quad \text{or} \quad \lambda_i^{[i]} = 1 - \frac{1}{v},$$

assuming that $(1 - \lambda_i^{[i]}) > 0$ or $\lambda_i^{[i]} < 1$, which should be confirmed below as a proposition under the assumption (APG). Now, this normalization yields as our constraint

$$v \cdot \Lambda_{[i]}^{[i]} \cdot \mathbb{B} \leq v \cdot \Lambda_{[i]}^{[i]} \cdot \mathbb{A} + b^{(i)}. \qquad\qquad(9)$$

Since we have $\lambda_i^{[i]} = 1 - 1/v$ from our normalization, maximizing v is equivalent to maximizing $\lambda_i^{[i]}$. Writing $v \cdot \Lambda_{[i]}^{[i]}$ simply as a variable vector q, thus $q_i \equiv v$, we have the linear programming problem (DG) analogous to (7):

(DG) max q_i subject to $q'\mathbb{B} \leq q' \mathbb{A} + b^{(i)}$ and $q' \geq \mathbf{0}_n'.$

We first solve this linear programming problem. Next, the values can be calculated exactly as in eqs (5) and (6), i.e.,

$$\lambda_i^{[i]} = \frac{q_i^* - 1}{q_i^*} \quad \text{and} \quad \lambda_j^{[i]} = q_j^*/q_i^* \text{ for } j = 1, \ldots, n, j \neq i. \qquad(10)$$

It is not difficult to establish

Proposition. Given the productiveness assumption (APG), the i-th labour value of i-th labour is less than unity, i.e., $\lambda_i^{[i]} < 1$.

Proof. Consider the linear programming problem dual to the above problem (DG):

(PG) min $b^{(i)} x$ subject to $\mathbb{B}x \geq \mathbb{A}x + e_{[i]}$ and $x \geq \mathbf{0}_m,$

where $e_{[i]}$ is the *n*-column vector whose *i*-th entry is unity with all the remaining elements being zero. By the duality theorem, we know that the optimal values satisfy $q_i^* = b^{(i)}x^*$. On the other hand, it is clear from the constraint in (PG) that $b^{(i)}x^* \geq 1$. Thus we get $q_i^* \geq 1$, which gives $0 \leq \lambda_i^{[i]} < 1$ because of eq.(10).

Thanks to this proposition, the reader can now trace from the problem (DG) back to the definition of value (8).

4 Models with international trade

Now, as in the real world, we have to introduce international trade to our model. First of all, we assume that while goods and services are transported among countries, people in general are not allowed to migrate among countries. In this section, we employ concrete numerical examples to explain our method, and the country names used, England and Portugal, have nothing to do with the real world: we simply follow the notable classical economists.

To incorporate international trade, many methods are surely conceivable, and one of the easiest is to include, as production processes, possible vectors of imports (positive entries) and exports (negative entries), or just the statistical average of the past few years' imports and exports. Let us consider a small country with two commodities, corn and wine, both produced by homogeneous labour, here called unskilled labour or simply labour. The technical data without international trade are as follows:

$$\mathbb{B} - \mathbb{A} \equiv \begin{pmatrix} 4 & 0 & -1 \\ 0 & 3 & -1 \\ -1 & -1 & 1 \end{pmatrix}.$$

The first row represents corn, the second wine, and the last simple labour. The last column describes the only household activity to produce labour. The solutions of (PG) and (DG) are

$$x^* = (0.6, 0.8, 2.4)',$$

$$q^{*\prime} = (0.6, 0.8, 2.4), \text{ and so}$$

$$\lambda \doteqdot (0.25, 0.333, 0.58333).$$

When we add a process of import and export, $(-1, 1, 0)'$, that is, exporting one unit of corn in exchange for one unit of wine imported, the technical data become

$$\mathbb{B} - \mathbb{A} \equiv \begin{pmatrix} 4 & 0 & -1 & -1 \\ 0 & 3 & -1 & 1 \\ -1 & -1 & 1 & 0 \end{pmatrix}.$$

The solutions are now

$$x^* = (1.0, 0.0, 2.0, 2.0)',$$

$$q^{*\prime} = (0.5, 0.5, 2.0), \text{ and so}$$

$$\lambda \doteqdot (0.25, 0.25, 0.5).$$

These results show that by international trade, one unit of corn for one unit of wine, this economy specializes in the production of corn, and through trade, the labour values decrease or remain unchanged. One can add another process, $(1, -1, 0)'$, that is, exporting one unit of wine in exchange for one unit of corn, but this causes no change to the above results because the process is not used by the economy. In this model of a small open economy, the terms of trade, expressed here in vector form, $(1, 4/3)$, are the switch point, across which what is exported is interchanged for what is imported. (Here, in short, 4/3 is the price of wine in terms of corn.)

Likewise, a two-country model can be constructed. For example, consider two countries, England and Portugal, two commodities, again corn and wine, and homogeneous unskilled labour in each country. The technical data are:

$$\mathbb{B} - \mathbb{A} \equiv \begin{pmatrix} 4 & 0 & 0 & 0 & -1 & 0 & -1 & 1 \\ 0 & 3 & 0 & 0 & -1 & 0 & 1 & -1 \\ 0 & 0 & 2 & 0 & 0 & -1 & 1 & -1 \\ 0 & 0 & 0 & 3 & 0 & -1 & -1 & 1 \\ -1 & -1 & 0 & 0 & 1 & 0 & 0 & 0 \\ 0 & 0 & -1 & -1 & 0 & 1 & 0 & 0 \end{pmatrix}. \tag{11}$$

The first two rows are corn and wine for England, the next two rows are for Portugal, the fifth row shows the labour force of England, and the last row that of Portugal. The last two columns represent possible international trade vectors with the price ratio being unity. We have exactly the same solutions as in the above when we solve labour values in terms of English labour units. In this case there is, for Portugal, another switch point of terms of trade, again expressed in vector form, $(1, 2/3)$. Between the two switch points, the interests of the two countries may coincide.

The foregoing ways to incorporate international trade need price ratios among commodities. Thus one can insist values depend on prices. Or when we apply these methods to the days of imperialism, we may admit colonial exploitation as a part of "technical data" in order to calculate labour values. We have to avoid such distortions. One intuitive way is to regard the unskilled labour of each country as homogeneous, and consider a joint optimization problem in a symmetrical way.[6] In so doing, processes expressing international trade do not need price ratios, but simply show that the export of a commodity is to bring that commodity to the international market, and the import is a reverse operation. That is, export and import are regarded as separate processes. Look at the following matrix.

$$\mathbb{B} - \mathbb{A} \equiv \begin{pmatrix} 4 & 0 & 0 & 0 & -1 & 0 & -1 & 0 & 0 & 0 & 0 & 1 & 0 & 0 \\ 0 & 3 & 0 & 0 & -1 & 0 & 0 & 0 & -1 & 0 & 0 & 0 & 0 & 1 \\ 0 & 0 & 2 & 0 & 0 & -1 & 0 & 1 & 0 & 0 & -1 & 0 & 0 & 0 \\ 0 & 0 & 0 & 3 & 0 & -1 & 0 & 0 & 0 & 1 & 0 & 0 & -1 & 0 \\ -1 & -1 & 0 & 0 & 1 & 0 & 0 & 0 & 0 & 0 & 0 & 0 & 0 & 0 \\ 0 & 0 & -1 & -1 & 0 & 1 & 0 & 0 & 0 & 0 & 0 & 0 & 0 & 0 \\ 0 & 0 & 0 & 0 & 0 & 0 & 1 & -1 & 0 & 0 & 1 & -1 & 0 & 0 \\ 0 & 0 & 0 & 0 & 0 & 0 & 0 & 1 & -1 & 0 & 0 & 1 & -1 \end{pmatrix}.$$

The upper-left 6×6 matrix is the same as in (11), and the added last two rows mean corn and wine in the international market respectively. The added 8 columns represent the transportation of one unit of commodities from a country to/from one of the international markets.[7] No ratio between two commodities is involved here. We make

Definition. Values in our model with international trade are nonnegative magnitudes assigned to commodities (including services and various types of labour) such that the sum of the values of the numeraire commodity in each country be maximized under the condition that the total value of the output of each possible process should not exceed that of the input. When calculating the total value of the input of a process, unity is assigned to the direct input of the numeraire commodity in each country.

We adopt the sum of the values as the objective function to be maximized because of symmetry for all the countries. Thus, when the input–output coefficients are completely the same among countries, the same values obtain as in the case of isolation. On the other hand, we require that the input of the numeraire commodity should be assigned unity in each country because otherwise, i.e., zero is assigned in one or more countries, the constraint would be so severe that an optimal value cannot go beyond unity. When looked at from the quantity side, if the vector b below contains only one unity, the country corresponding to this sole unity may feed upon the other countries by producing less and by importing more unilaterally.

Then, the linear programming problem to be solved is a variant of (DG), i.e.,

(DG) max $q' \cdot c$ subject to $q' \mathbb{B} \leq q' \mathbb{A} + b'$ and $q' \in R^8_{++}$,

where $b' \equiv (0, 0, 0, 0, 1, 1, 0, 0, 0, 0, 0, 0, 0, 0)$, and

$c \equiv (0, 0, 0, 0, 1, 1, 0, 0)'$.

Here, b' is actually $b^{(5)} + b^{(6)}$. The dual to the above is

(PG) min $b' \cdot x$ subject to $\mathbb{B}x \geq \mathbb{A}x + c$ and $x \in R^{14}_+$.

In sum, in defining labour values, we do not discriminate English labour from Portuguese, and try to minimize the total labour necessary to produce one unit of labour in both countries. Values can be calculated by the same eq. (10) for a similar reason in section 4, because we identify English simple labour with Portuguese.[8] It should be noted again that the problems are set for two countries in a symmetric way.

The solutions of these problems are

$$x^* = (1.2, 1.6, 0, 0, 3.8, 1.0, 1.0, 1.0, 1.0, 1.0, 0, 0, 0, 0)',$$

$$q^{*\prime} = (0.6, 0.8, 0.6, 0.8, 2.4, 2.4, 0.6, 0.8), \text{ and}$$

$$\lambda \doteq (0.25, 0.333, 0.25, 0.333, 0.58333, 0.58333, 0.25, 0.333).$$

It seems awkward that values, for England, show no change from the model without international trade, no normal production processes are used in Portugal, Portugal imports corn and wine while exporting nothing, hence there is no gain for England in this virtual minimization problem. On reflection, however, this result is not so strange when the world economy is to be organized with efficiency as is defined above.[9] When given data allows the nonsubstitution theorem to hold, values will not change even if c assumes whatever nonnegative nonzero vector. Thus, values remain unchanged when we make c as

$$c \equiv (0, 0, 0, 0, 1, 0, 0, 0)' \text{ or } (0, 0, 0, 0, 0, 0, 1, 0, 0)'.$$

That is, the net output labour vector is one unit of English labour or one of Portuguese. Indeed, when unskilled labour in each country is not jointly produced by normal production processes, which is likely, we can prove a sort of nonsubstitution theorem under which our values do not change, even if the above vector c takes on any positive values among unskilled labour of various countries with the remaining entries being zero. (See Fujimoto *et al.* 2003.)

The above sort of awkwardness does not appear when one country is not absolutely superior to the other in both industries. For example, when the coefficient $(\mathbb{B} - \mathbb{A})_{44}$, for Portuguese wine production, increases from 3 to 3.01, we have

$$x^* \doteq (1.197, 0, 0, 1.590, 2.197, 2.590, 2.590, 2.590, 0, 0, 0, 0, 2.197, 2.197)',$$

$$q^{*\prime} \doteq (0.598, 0.795, 0.598, 0.795, 2.394, 2.394, 0.598, 0.795), \text{ and}$$

$$\lambda \doteq (0.25, 0.332, 0.25, 0.332, 0.582, 0.582, 0.25, 0.332).$$

showing complete specialization in each country and proper exchange in international markets. We can thus say that comparative or absolute advantage of one country over another in the production of a certain commodity is made clear after calculating values. When an awkward result comes out on the quantity side, i.e., in the principal problem (PG), it shows absolute advantage of one country over another.

At this point, the reader may wonder if the ratio of workers employed in two countries, here in this model 3.8 to 1.0, may not coincide with the actual ratio between two countries' working populations, thus causing unemployment of simple labour in a country *if* we carry out the optimal solutions to the problem (PG) above. So, it seems we had better add one more constraint of a strict equality that the ratio of workers employed in two countries should be that of two countries' working populations. When we add this constraint as 3 to 1 to the preceding numerical example, we get the following solutions.

$$x^* = (1.2, 1.4, 0, 0.2, 3.6, 1.2, 1.2, 1.2, 0.6, 0.6, 0, 0, 0, 0)',$$

$$q^{*\prime} = (0.6, 0.8, 0.6, 0.8, 2.4, 2.4, 0.6, 0.8), \text{ and}$$

$$\lambda \doteqdot (0.25, 0.333, 0.25, 0.333, 0.58333, 0.58333, 0.25, 0.333).$$

In this case, the values need not change, and can be obtained through the same problem (DG), with the shadow values to the added constraints set to zero. In general, the values change as the real ratio is far from that obtained through the problem (PG) without the constraint.

This additional equality constraint is, however, unnecessary simply because the problem (PG) has nothing to do with an efficiency-seeking problem in the the real world, as is noted in section 2. The problem (PL) is just auxiliary and virtual, and is useful only to understand the dual side better. When prices are dealt with, the discrepancy from the actual working population ratio can mean uneven distribution of unemployment between two countries through international trade.

Now then, the problem is how to define prices for models with international trade. England will not be interested in international trade unless it brings forth profits calculated in terms of prices. And this task we wish to perform with no resort to demand theory. Our method is to introduce instrumental efficiency conversion rates among the unskilled labour of various countries. Thus, in the above model, we regard one unit of Portuguese labour as e $(e < 1)$ unit of English labour based on Portuguese inferiority in technical level of production. Again to make our story simpler, we assume the profit rate is zero, and $e = 0.5$.[10] The programming problem is now

(DG) max $q' \cdot c$ subject to $q' \, \mathbb{B} \leq q' \mathbb{A} + b'$ and $q' \in R^8_{++}$,

where $b' \equiv (0, 0, 0, 0, 1, e, 0, 0, 0, 0, 0, 0, 0, 0)$, and

$c \equiv (0, 0, 0, 0, 1, 1, 0, 0)'$ or

$(0, 0, 0, 0, 1, 0, 0, 0)'$ or

$(0, 0, 0, 0, 0, 1, 0, 0)'$.

(PG) min $b' \cdot x$ subject to $\mathbb{B}x \geq \mathbb{A}x + c$ and $x \in R^{14}_+$.

When c is assigned to the first one, the solutions of these problems turn out to be

$$x^* = (1.2, 0.0, 0.0, 1.6, 2.2, 2.6, 2.6, 2.6, 0, 0, 0, 0, 2.2, 2.2)',$$

$$q^{*\prime} = (0.5, 0.5, 0.5, 0.5, 2.0, 1.5, 0.5, 0.5), \text{ and}$$

$$p \doteqdot (0.25, 0.25, 0.25, 0.25, 0.5, 0.25, 0.25, 0.25).$$

The optimal solution vector q^* does not change when c shifts among the above three vectors. Now, the necessary labour amount has decreased from 2.4 without trade to 2.2 with trade for England, and from 6.0 to 2.6 for Portugal, with each country perfectly specialized in one commodity. And the price ratio 1 to 1 is inductive for would-be traders of both countries. As one revises the efficiency conversion rate e, in general different prices come out, and yield an alternative equilibrium price vector, which may lead to international trade or not. Thus, there exist in general multiple equilibrium price vectors depending on efficiency rates among countries. We may think that this efficiency rate represents a sort of ratio between the purchasing powers of the two countries, and it is a more convenient tool to calculate equilibrium prices in linear models with international trade than taking into consideration all too many price ratios among commodities when one considers a substantial number of goods and services. Moreover, these efficiency rates in turn may be thought of as parameters reflecting the relative political as well as military strengths of nations. When $e = 0$ or sufficiently small, Portugal becomes a perfect colony of England.

As the reader has noticed, our method can allow for any finite number of countries and of commodities. Besides, one can easily introduce transportation processes necessary to carry out international trade.

5 Remarks

5.1 Smith (1776) emphasized the importance of division of labour, which, in an advanced capitalist economy can be a synonym of heterogeneity of labour. Abstract labour by Marx (1867) seems to be a teleological concept to construct a two-class model, and then a theory of exploitation. See Steedman (1977) and Fujimoto (1978).

5.2 As our formulation in section 3 is symmetrical between labour types and commodities, we can easily define the values in terms of a commodity chosen as the numeraire. Thus, our definition so modified is more general than those in Fujita (1991) and Manresa *et al.* (1998). Certainly the reader may not be interested in the pencil-value or the iron-value of bread, but many people today are eager to know the petroleum-value of bread, electricity, etc. (Here another difficult problem arises of how to deal with exhaustible resources. For the moment, however, we assume that petroleum is produced by using normal input–output processes as observed 'on the surface'.)

5.3 It is easy to notice that our definition includes the definition by Morishima (1974) as a special case. For example, in Morishima's model, our complete matrices are:

$$\mathbb{B} \equiv \begin{pmatrix} B & \mathbf{0}_{n-1} \\ \mathbf{0}'_{m-1} & 1 \end{pmatrix}, \text{ and } \mathbb{A} \equiv \begin{pmatrix} A & c \\ \ell & 0 \end{pmatrix},$$

where B and A are normal von Neumann material output and input coefficient matrices, and the final n-th row stands for the homogeneous labour. Then, the constraints in our linear programming problem (DG), after dividing both sides by q_n, become

$$\Lambda B \leq \Lambda A + \ell, \text{ and}$$

$$1 \leq \Lambda c + \frac{1}{q_n}.$$

Here Λ is $\Lambda^{[n]}$ in the previous section, i.e., the labour value vector. Maximizing q_n is equivalent to maximizing Λc. Thus, we reach the same definition as in Morishima (1974). In his model, there are no durable consumption goods or alternative household activities to reproduce the homogeneous labour. These restrictions are removed in our formulation.

5.4   Krause (1981) and Fujimori (1982) considered the models with heterogeneous labour. They, however, adopted a method of reducing various types of labour to a particular labour, which is unnecessary in our definition.

5.5   In section 4, we employed concrete numerical examples for models without joint production and heterogeneous labour. The reader can, however, recognize abstract models with many countries, joint production, and heterogeneous labour.

5.6   For difficulties in treating direct or instantaneous services in input–output models, the reader is referred to Parrinello (2007).

Notes

*   Faculty of Economics, Fukuoka University. Thanks are due to Professor Sergio Parrinello for his comments on earlier versions written in Padua with Professor Arrigo Opocher.
1   This enlarged matrix is called the "complete matrix" in Brody (1970).
2   See Hawkins and Simon (1949) for their conditions concerning A.
3   This has nothing to do with exploitation. See Fujimoto and Fujita (2008). See also Okishio (1963), Roemer (1981, 1982, 1986) and Bowles and Gintis (1981).
4   For nonsubstitution theorems, see, e.g., Fujimoto *et al.* (2003).
5   Among a plural number of solutions, we adopt those which realize the maximum number of equalities in the constraints. And yet, a solution may not be unique.
6   We assume that there exists a common type of labour in each country one unit of which is produced by the same set of household activities.
7   We here find it easy to allow for non-tradable goods and services, especially services rendered by direct human labour.
8   Consider $\Lambda^{[i,j,\ldots]}_{[i,j,\ldots]}$, where unity is set at all the entries for simple labour of each country, and apply the argument leading to eq. (9).
9   In different contexts, we have criticisms against the theory of comparative advantage. See Bhagwati *et al.* (1998) and Parrinello (2009).
10   We may also think that profits are already included as the rewards on various services: managerial, banking, and other services. When there is only one homogeneous labour, this does not seem to cause any problem.

References

Bhagwati J.N., A. Panagariya and T. N. Srinivasan (1998), *Lectures on International Trade*, 2nd ed., Cambridge, MIT Press.

Bowles S. and H. Gintis (1977), "The Marxian Theory of Value and Heterogeneous Labour: A Critique and Reformulation", *Cambridge Journal of Economics*, Vol. 2, pp. 173–92.

Bowles S. and H. Gintis (1981), "Structure and Practice in the Labor Theory of Value", *Review of Radical Political Economy*, Vol. 12, pp. 1–26.

Bródy, A. (1970), *Proportions, Prices and Planning: A Mathematical Restatement of the Labor Theory of Value*, Budapest, Akadémiai Kiadó.

Fujimori, Y. (1982), *Modern Analysis of Value Theory*, Berlin, Springer-Verlag.

Fujimoto, T. (1978), "Exploitation, Profits, and Growth: A Disequilibrium Analysis", *Economic Studies Quarterly*, Vol. 29, pp. 268–75.

Fujimoto, T. and Y. Fujita (2008), "A Refutation of Commodity Exploitation Theorem", *Metroeconomica*, Vol. 59, pp. 530–40.

Fujimoto, T. and A. Opocher (2007), "Commodity Contents in a General Input–Output Model", mimeo, University of Padova, to appear in *Metroeconomica*.

Fujimoto, T., C. Herrero, R. R. Ranade, J. A. Silva and A. Villar (2003), "A Complete Characterization of Economies with the Nonsubstitution Property", *Economic Issues*, Vol. 8, pp. 63–70.

Fujita, Y. (1991), "A Further Note on a Correct Economic Interpretation of the Hawkins–Simon Conditions", *Journal of Macroeconomics*, Vol. 13, pp. 381–4.

Hawkins, D. and H. A. Simon (1949), "Note: Some Conditions of Macroeconomic Stability", *Econometrica*, Vol. 17, pp. 245–8.

Jeong, K. (1982), "Direct and Indirect Requirements: A Correct Economic Interpretation of the Hawkins–Simon Conditions", *Journal of Macroeconomics*, Vol. 4, pp. 349–56.

Jeong, K. (1984), "The Relation between Two Different Notions of Direct and Indirect Input Requirements", *Journal of Macroeconomics*, Vol. 6, pp. 473–6.

Krause, U. (1981), "Heterogeneous Labour and the Fundamental Marxian Theorem", *Review of Economic Studies*, Vol. 48, pp. 173–8.

Manresa, A., F. Sancho and J. M. Vegara (1998), "Measuring Commodities' Commodity Content", *Economic Systems Research*, Vol. 10, pp. 357–65.

Marx, K. (1867), *Capital I*, available on the Internet at http://www.marxists.org/archive/marx/works/download/capital.zip. The original German edition was published in 1867.

Morishima, M. (1964), *Equilibrium, Stability and Growth: A Multi-Sectoral Analysis*, London, Oxford University Press.

Morishima, M. (1973), *Marx's Economics: A Dual Theory of Value and Growth*, Cambridge, Cambridge University Press.

Morishima, M. (1974), "Marx in the Light of Modern Economics", *Econometrica*, Vol. 42, pp. 611–32.

Okishio, N. (1963), "Mathematical Note on Marxian Theorems", *Weltwirtschaftliches Archiv*, Vol. 91, pp. 287–99.

Okishio, N. (1977), *Marx's Economics: Values and Prices* (in Japanese), Tokyo, Chikuma-Shobou.

Parrinello, S. (2007), "Introduction: A Note on Goods and Services and Input–Output Analysis", *Metroeconomica*, Vol. 58, pp. 361–7.

Parrinello, S. (2009), "The Notion of National Competitiveness in a Global Economy", in Vint, J. Metcalfe, J.S., Kurz, H.D., Salvadori, N. and Samuelson, P. (eds) (2009), *Economic Theory and Economic Thought, Essays in Honour of Ian Steedman*, London, Routledge.

Roemer, J.E. (1981), *Analytical Foundations of Marxian Economic Theory*, Cambridge, MA, Harvard University Press.

Roemer, J.E. (1982), *A General Theory of Exploitation and Class*, Cambridge, MA, Harvard University Press.

Roemer, J.E. (1986), "Should Marxists Be Interested in Exploitation?" in Roemer, J.E. (ed.) *Analytical Marxism*, Cambridge, Cambridge University Press, pp. 260–82.

Smith, A. (1776), *An Inquiry into the Nature and Cause of the Wealth of Nations*, http://www.gutenberg.net/.

Steedman, I. (1977), *Marx after Sraffa*, London, New Left Books.

von Neumann, J. (1945–46), "A Model of Economic Equilibrium", *Review of Economic Studies*, Vol. 3, pp. 1–9.

Part II

Post-Keynesian macroeconomics

10 The interlocked crisis of the real and the financial sector

Amit Bhaduri

How money, and more generally the financial arrangements affect the level of production of goods and services in the real economy has long been a matter of controversy among economists. One could easily trace it back at least to David Hume, but a more convenient recent landmark would be the so-called Keynesian–Monetarist controversy, which was influenced by Friedman and Schwartz's (1963) account of the monetary history of the United States. They attributed the Great Depression almost exclusively to monetary causes and over-regulation by the Federal Reserve System (Fed) at the critical juncture.[1] Ironically we seem to have completed the full circle in so far as economists and policy makers seem to hold overwhelmingly the opinion that under-regulation of the financial sector by the Fed was responsible for the current crisis.

Assigning pre-eminence to monetary factors in the working of the economy is hardly new. Before the Second World War, a similar debate took place about the relative importance of 'industry' and 'finance' in Britain, and the official doctrine favoured maintaining a high international credit rating for British sterling at the cost of substantial unemployment as home. The official doctrine of 'sound finance' claimed that government deficit spending to fight unemployment would only result in a corresponding deficit in the balance of payments without improving the employment situation. This led Winston Churchill to observe,

> The Governor [of the Bank of England] shows himself perfectly happy in the spectacle of Britain possessing the finest credit rating in the world simultaneously with a million and a quarter unemployed … I would rather see Finance less proud and Industry more content.[2]

Kalecki, who independently discovered the main principles of effective demand (Kalecki 1971), apparently used to say that the acceptance of Keynesian demand management became politically acceptable only when the prestige of 'high finance' and the City of London was in ruins following Britain's humiliating exit from the Gold Standard in 1931 (Bhaduri and Steindl 1985). With the current financial crisis spreading rapidly in the global economy, the intellectual history of this debate might once again be repeating itself, as captured by a currently circulating joke, 'We are all Keynesians in times of crisis, but become Monetarists in interpreting the crisis as soon as it is over.'[3]

The comfort of returning repeatedly to Monetarism is understandable. Monetarism provides ideological support to free market capitalism by denying the need for intervention by the state to maintain high employment and growth. This is based on the assumption that markets are self-regulating with the real economy mimicking the Walrasian market story. The message has been extended even to the financial markets by claiming that financial markets are efficient, because asset prices always fully reflect available information, which cannot be improved upon by other private agents or the state (Fox 2009). Reiterated in different ways, the message is clear: the real economy along with the financial sector is best left to the supposedly self-regulating market mechanism.[4]

The Monetarist ideology of relying as far as possible on the free market system provided the intellectual background to the current crisis. The general mood of deregulating finance as far as possible from control and supervision by public agencies resulted in massive financial innovations and the creation of new credit institutions and instruments. What might best be described as a 'shadow banking system' steadily expanded its reach with three main characteristics. (a) It had no lender of last resort and operated on the one hand without the guarantee of the central bank, but on the other escaped its regulations. Thus, between 1970 and 2007 just before the onslaught of the present crisis in the US, the assets of the financial system held by the more traditional financial institutions like the depository commercial and savings banks had dropped from 54 to 23 per cent, insurance companies had reduced their share from 17 to 11 per cent, pension funds had gained only marginally from 15 to 17 per cent, but the assets of the less traditional financial institutions like mutual funds had soared from 4 to 18 per cent, that of security brokers from 1 to 5 per cent, that of mortgage banks from 4 to 13 per cent, and a residual category of 'others' from 0 to 10 percent (Wray 2008). (b) In the absence of a monetary authority at the top, the shadow financial system resembled a circular rather than a vertical structure of mutual guarantees of insurance and credit and debt swaps. In consequence, the effects of default could get magnified through exceeding correlation among credit instruments. (c) This also paved the way for converting each other's debt into asset through securitization, and the lending base, although more fragile, was augmented. At the same time the capacity to lend increased vastly through high leverage. Profit from lending operations soared on the principle, 'Low margin, high volume' by typically leveraging around 30 times on a shaky capital base, and earning enormous fees rather than interest income on each credit transaction.

With enormous possibilities for credit expansion the system tended to become increasingly credit driven in maintaining effective demand. It is a matter of speculation whether this was a conscious pro-rich demand management policy, or simply an unintended outcome of adhering to the free market ideology.[5] Be that as it may, a simple extension of the consumption function captures the impact of financial expansion on demand. Consumption (C) is postulated as a linear function, positively influenced by both income (Y) and the increase in notional wealth (dW/dt) but negatively influenced by repayment obligation on the stock of debt (R).

$$C = cY + j(dW/dt) - uR, \ 1 > c > 0, \ 1 > j > 0, \ 1 > h > 0. \tag{1}$$

The increase in wealth cannot, however, directly support consumption through realised capital gains. Macroeconomically speaking, if many participants in the market try to realise their individual capital gains simultaneously, asset prices would collapse and the notional or virtual capital gains would evaporate. This problem of fallacy of composition inherent in realising virtual into realised wealth is solved through financial institutions, as they treat the increased virtual wealth as a mark of greater creditworthiness (a kind of 'mark to market' procedure) of the wealth holder, advancing on that basis greater credit. The seed of the problem also lies here, because in case of a sudden drop in the value of virtual wealth, the borrower becomes less creditworthy, but the commitment to repay on the higher stock of inherited debt remains the same (Bhaduri *et al.* 2006).

Assuming simple proportionality between increase in wealth and increase in debt, we may thus rewrite a modified consumption function as,

$$C = cY + [jk(dR / dt)] - uR \tag{2}$$

where k > 0 is the factor of proportionality between wealth and debt.

From the expenditure side of national income accounting,

$$GNP = Y = C + I + [\text{current account balance}] = C + I + (dR_F/dt) \tag{3}$$

where (in the case of the US) the current account deficit is covered by increased foreign debt (R_F) liabilities denominated mostly in dollars. Using (2) and (3) and simplifying,

$$(1-c)Y = [I + (dR_F/dt)] + jk(dR/dt) - uR. \tag{4}$$

Written in the notationally simpler form, it is

$$Y = a(dR/dt) - bR + F \tag{5}$$

where a = jk/(1 – c), b = u/(1 – c), and F = (1/1 – c)(investment + current account balance). Although F would be a function of time, for simplicity of exposition we treat it as a constant to highlight the basic mechanism of the domestic debt problem.

Again focusing on the simplest case to highlight the mechanism involved, we assume that there is an arbitrarily given ceiling to the debt stock, E, such that

$$\text{for } R < E, \ (dR/dt) = A > 0, \ \text{and, for } R = E, \ (dR/dt) = 0. \tag{6}$$

On these assumptions, for non-negative debt flows, $(dR/dt) \geq 0$, Y reaches its maximum value at $R = 0$ to yield $Y_{max} = aA + F$. And its minimum value at $R = E$ to yield $Y_{min} = aA + F - bE$.

Note, however, this is the normal range of maximum and minimum values of Y so long as debt flow is non-negative, but the economy can plunge into even lower values of Y if net debt retirement is forced and $(dR/dt) < 0$.

The economy would normally fluctuate between this maximum and minimum value of Y in the two-dimensional plane of the stock of debt (R) and income (Y). The sequence can be summarised this way. Initially, with the stock of debt near zero, Y is near its normal maximum Y_{max}. However, with a positive flow of debt at the rate A, the stock of debt accumulates gradually over time until it reaches the ceiling to reduce Y to its normal minimum value Y_{min}. Since lending stops at $R = E$, but the obligation on repayment of past debt remains, the obligation has to be met largely through reduction of debt by selling assets. This turns (dR/dt) negative, Y falls even below its normal minimum level (Y_{min}), and the stock of debt R begins to decrease. At the same time, however, attempts to sell assets on a large scale leads to falling asset prices leading to a classic debt deflation (Fisher 1933). The process may continue until debt reaches a sufficiently low value for lending to start again and recovery begins with a positive flow of debt. Thus the economy typically oscillates.

The ceiling to the stock of debt might be set by the conditions of Ponzi finance when the flow of debt freezes due to financial institutions' fear of getting caught into a sort of 'lenders' trap' with huge non-performing assets. This means they have to go on lending on an increasing scale simply to be repaid their debt with their own money! At the other extreme the floor might be reached as borrowers, without access to credit, get caught in the debt trap of having to sell assets causing a deflationary spiral of falling asset prices. Thus Ponzi finance and debt deflation set the upper and lower limits to fluctuations.

The starkly schematised model outlined in Figure 10.1 intends to highlight the basic mechanism of fluctuation in debt and income based on the contradictory pulls on demand generated by the stimulating influence of the flow of credit for financing consumption, and the depressive effect of servicing the accumulated stock of debt. This stock–flow mechanism (of investment flow and capital stock) causing sustained oscillations would be familiar from several endogenous business cycle models (e.g. Kalecki 1971; Kaldor 1960; Goodwin 1951).[6] However, the present model is different in its emphasis. In keeping with recent experiences, in the present model fluctuations are generated by debt-financed consumption originating in the virtual economy, rather than fluctuations in real investment or in the changing expectations and financing conditions of investment (Keynes 1936; Minsky 1986).

The simplifications introduced to focus on the basic mechanism of fluctuations caused by debt-financing does violence to reality in many ways, some of which can be addressed at least partly, while others would require further research. For instance, the evidently extreme assumption of a constant flow of debt (A) until the debt ceiling (E) is reached when it drops suddenly to zero makes the

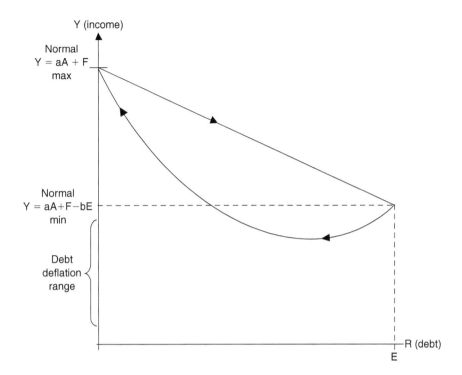

Figure 10.1

fluctuations unrealistically abrupt. The sharp edges of fluctuations could be partially smoothed by introducing a suitable time structure of lagged adjustments in
the model (Arrowsmith and Place 1982). In particular, in so far as the wealth and
debt dynamics are driven purely by asset price rise, capital gains from asset price
rise which eases the debt servicing problem might introduce lagged adjustments
(as in the case of lending for the housing bubble in the recent US episode).

The problem of defining a ceiling through Ponzi finance is less straightforward, but a simple one-period (not intertemporal) specification would be to postulate that income must not be less than the debt-servicing obligation in any period,
$Y - rR > 0$, r = repayment obligation per unit of debt this would set the ceiling in
terms of the income to debt ratio, instead of the threshold level of debt (E).

The final, and perhaps the most important and difficult task, would be inte-
grating into the analysis asset price movements as the driving force of virtual
wealth. Mainstream 'rational market' theories find it difficult to come to terms
even with the existence of financial bubbles either because market prices are presumed to reflect all available information efficiently, or because profitable speculation is considered to have a stabilising influence on price (Friedman 1953). An
alternative analytically tractable approach in the context of the present model
would be to assume that the change in asset prices depends on the state of excess

demand or supply in that market. However, they have a speculative element in so far as (say) demand for assets are influenced not only by the price level but also the expected change in prices. Assuming static expectations (or any extrapolation into the future in the same direction as the current direction of change in prices) the demand for assets is represented by a linear function,

$$D = vP + z(dP/dt), v < 0; z > 0 \tag{7}$$

The supply of assets is presumed to depend positively on price level, and also the layers of leverage (x) on the credit base. As x increases, the quantity rationing on credit supply is eased, and credit is more easily available; but higher leverage also entails the probability of higher defaults on loans, and thus makes the capital base for lending more fragile. Credit supply S is represented as

$$S = S(x, P) \tag{8}$$

The adjustment equation for asset price is given as,

$$(dP/dt) = b[vP + z(dP/dt) - S(x, P), b > 0] \tag{9}$$

which can be rewritten as,

$$(dP/dt) = [b/(1 - bz)][vP - S(P, x)] \tag{10}$$

Note if $(1 - bz) > 0$, i.e. $z < (1/b)$, the system is stable for $S_P > v$, $\qquad$ (11)

as is normally the case.

But for $z > (1/b)$ the opposite holds, and demand has to be more responsive than supply for the stability of the system.

Interpreted economically this means, when the speculative element is relatively weak and z is sufficiently small, the usual stability condition of greater supply having a stronger response than demand holds, but when the speculative element in the credit market becomes relatively strong at sufficiently large values of z, the stability condition is reversed. This suggests a way of looking at asset price driven credit fluctuations through the virtual wealth effect. Suppose, with continuous financial innovations under weak supervision, the financial system maintains a high supply response, and the speculative element on the demand side is moderate (i.e. z is sufficiently small). This renders the credit system stable, while high supply response and easy availability of finance induces asset prices to rise gradually. In the course of rising prices confidence builds up, and the speculative element gets stronger (z becomes larger) tending to destabilise the system, and the direction of price change might get reversed to cause a negative wealth effect (see eq. 11). Asset price movement changing direction due to speculation remains one of the least understood areas of macroeconomics, but it is badly needed to complete the story satisfactorily.

Notes

1 The current chairman of the FED, Ben Bernanke (2000), as a faithful follower of this tradition, had approved strongly of that diagnosis. Highlighting the pre-eminence of money, finance and monetary policy, the Monetarist doctrine downplayed, and in extreme cases denied altogether any useful role for fiscal intervention by the state to fight unemployment or counter a cyclical downturn.

2 Minutes of the Parliament in Britain of 22 February 1925.

3 When the financial sector is on the defensive in times of a financial crisis, the chorus is loud and clear among academic economists for state intervention. Yet, as soon as the financial sector becomes stronger, its tendency to dominate and shape the real economy to its advantage surfaces again. Theories are put forward accordingly to justify minimal state action. Recall, for example, the doctrine of the 'natural rate of unemployment', 'non-accelerating inflation rate of unemployment' or NAIRU, the ineffectiveness of fiscal policy under capital mobility, the public choice theory of the selfish government incurring public debt or the importance of the independence of the central bank for maintaining currency value by targeting inflation and not unemployment and many similar theoretical pronouncements that ruled academic orthodoxy until the crisis hit us.

4 Some recent incidents in the United States are instructive in showing how this ideology ruled. Just before the bursting of the high-tech (dot.com) bubble of 2000–1, it was officially held that the financial sector was not keeping up with the dynamism of the new economy. The commercial banks were considered not high-risk dynamic ventures, as they were used to managing other people's money conservatively under government guarantee of the Glass–Stegall Act. Accordingly, that Act was repealed, and high-risk-taking investment banks operating on high leverage were merged with commercial banks under the Gramm–Leach–Bliley 'financial services modernisation act' in 1999. Again, in 2004 a decision of the Securities and Exchange Commission allowed in one stroke investment banks to raise their debt capital ratio from 12:1 to 30:1 or even higher. Interestingly, economist Larry Summers, one of the key economic players in President Obama's administration, is reported to have also been a key supporter of both these Acts.

5 Foster and Magdoff (2008) argue forcefully that this was intended to avoid stagnationist tendencies arising from worsening income distribution, and weakness of manufacturing profit.

6 For a mathematically more sophisticated and interesting extension by introducing money into the analysis along similar lines, see Chiarella and Flaschel (2000).

References

Arrowsmith, D.K and Place, C.M. (1982), *Ordinary Differential Equations*, ch. 5, London, Chapman and Hall.

Bernanke, B.S. (2000), *Essays on the Great Depression*, Princeton, NJ, Princeton University Press.

Bhaduri, A. and Steindl, J. (1985), 'The Rise of Monetarism as a Social Doctrine', in Arestis, P. and Skouras, T. (eds), *Post Keynesian Economic Theory*, New York, M.E. Sharpe.

Bhaduri, A., Laski, K. and Riese, M. (2006), 'A Model of the Interaction between the Real and the Virtual Economy', *Metroeconomica*, No. 3.

Chiarella, C. and Flaschel, P. (2000), *The Dynamics of Keynesian Monetary Growth*, Cambridge, Cambridge University Press.

Fisher, I. (1933), 'The Debt Deflation Theory of Great Depressions', *Econometrica*, No. 4, October.

Foster, J.M. and Magdoff, F. (2008), 'Financial Implosion and Stagnation', *Monthly Review*, Vol. 60, No. 7, December.

Fox, J. (2009), *The Myth of the Rational Market*, New York, Harper.

Friedman, M. (1953), *Essays in Positive Economics*, Chicago, University of Chicago Press.

Friedman, M. and Schwartz, A. (1963), *A Monetary History of the United States, 1867–1960*, National Bureau of Economic Research, Princeton, NJ, Princeton University Press.

Goodwin, R.M. (1951), 'Non-linear Accelerator and the Persistence of the Business Cycle', *Econometrica*, No. 1, January.

Kaldor, N. (1960), 'A Model of the Trade Cycle', in Kaldor, N., *Essays on Economic Stability and Growth*, London, Duckworth.

Kalecki, M. (1971), *Selected Essays on the Dynamics of the Capitalist Economy*, Cambridge, Cambridge University Press.

Keynes, J.M. (1936), *The General Theory of Employment, Interest and Money*, London, Macmillan.

Minsky, H.P. (1986), *Stabilising an Unstable Economy*, New Haven, CT, Yale University Press.

Wray, L.R. (2008), *Financial Markets Meltdown*, Public Policy Brief No. 94, Annandale-on-Hudson, NY, Levy Economics Institute.

11 Financial risk redistribution and income fluctuations*

Claudio Gnesutta

"Danger? What danger do you foresee?"

"It would cease to be a danger, if you could define it."

Arthur Conan Doyle

1 Risk management in the present economic situation♦

The recent decades have been characterised by a financial revolution in rapid growth and radical transformation. It is commonly held that the process of financial innovation was of decisive importance in fostering the long-lasting growth witnessed in all countries over this period, but particularly in the economy of the United States. In the course of time, however, some concern has been shown over the excessive weight of financial activities in the economic system due to a spree of innovative finance.[1] Given this background, the issue of risk management has again been brought to the attention of economic agents, monetary authorities and the more aware researchers in economics. However, the search for ways to redistribute the debtor's risk in the direction of other institutions and individuals ready to take it on with due compensation seems to be more the necessary result of the financial institutions' modes of operation than a matter of economic theory and policy. The greater profitability of the *originate to distribute* model has been seen as a sign of greater efficiency, increasing confidence in the solidity of the financial institutions' budgets, rewarded by the market with ever higher quotations.[2] Their growing market value boosted the capital backing their investments and, by enabling further expansion of their activity (leveraging), intensified the innovative process on ever wider markets. This led to enhancement of the risk transfer-transformation function, structurally associated with the fundamental function of transfer-transformation of funds.

Looking back to another episode of financial crisis – the crisis of the 1970s – I felt that, evaluating the processes that lead to restructure of the financial institutions, it was necessary to distinguish the "financial risk" from the "real risk", meaning by the latter term "the expected variability, *at the aggregate level*, of capital income to be drawn from the productive process; in other words ... the risk that the *aggregate* future returns on capital depart from the expectations that prompted ... its formation" (Gnesutta 1983, 81; author's translation, italics added). The reference to the aggregate level of capital income is an important distinction since it brings the risk dimension back to the dynamics of the entire productive system and the trends in social relationships that determine the coordinates within which the flow of future incomes is brought about.

Given that it is the complex of financial activities that generates the process by which the owners of productive capital assign its use to those who take on its management, then, as is classically recognised by the true bankers, the financial risk turns out to be a changed form of the risk on productive capital; it is the entrepreneurial risk on the future profitability of capital which is transferred to the holders of the financial assets. The (macroeconomic) efficiency of the system is therefore to be gauged on its capacity to trigger processes of redistribution of the risk on productive capital able to support and stabilise the future productive processes: the microeconomic viewpoint cannot suffice to govern a process whose roots are macroeconomics.

The variability of the perception of macroeconomic risk is a characteristic of Keynes's thought, seeing the interest he took in the degree of confidence fluctuations both of the financial institutions (the *state of credit*) and the firms regarding future productive conditions (the *marginal efficiency of capital*).[3] It can reasonably be argued that the behaviour of economic agents coping with the risk inherent in financial relations is a decisive element in the Keynesian monetary *theory of production* (Keynes 1973, 408), or in other words that the dynamics of an economy cannot be understood without full awareness of how the financial risk is distributed at every point in time.

Risk evaluation depends on the expectations regarding the variability of future incomes and thus on the capacity of the financial system to provide complete and accurate information on the current productive situation and its future trends. The need is for two different orders of information, one of an intersectorial nature regarding the current conditions offered by the various financial activities and the other of an intertemporal nature regarding future prospects for the economy;[4] it is the latter that sounds out the real risk. If, as is the case in this chapter, I assume a non-ergodic economic process (Davidson 2003, 50–9), the promises of future yield incorporated in the stock of existing activities at a given moment are essentially uncertain, and there can therefore be no assuming sufficient information on the flow of capital incomes able to satisfy the overall requirement of returns on their assets on the part of wealth-owners. The fact that individual expectations find no "objective" point of convergence implies that the decisions of single agents (with different ways, opportunities and skills in gathering and processing the information available to them) do not necessarily tally. The gap between real risk and financial risk reflects the contrast between autonomous economic agents who, operating on different real and financial markets, are characterised by their own distinct information structures regarding specific parts of the macroeconomic process.

With this chapter I wish to verify whether, and if so how, interpretation of the way a financial system operates is modified under the action of the behaviour of agents in risk management, both real and financial. The starting point of my analysis (section 2) is a model that considers only two distinct and autonomous agents (entrepreneurs and rentiers), in the absence of any credit or monetary intermediary, thereby pointing out that the fundamental financial relationship lies in the structural link between the productive capital of the entrepreneurs and the wealth of the rentiers. This "substance" of the financial relationships takes on manifold "forms", according to the particular contractual procedures adopted, of importance for the macroeconomic equilibria. In the following sections I will examine how the various conclusions emerge when I consider the operation of "outside" monetary (and financial) activities (section 3), and "inside" monetary (and financial) activities (section 4). By bringing money into the picture I can delineate its role and financial (and thus real) risk management, and the role of monetary policy vis-à-vis real accumulation. On the evidence of the picture that emerges I can interpret (section 5) some significant aspects of the present financial crisis which cast doubt on the idea that advanced financial systems are in themselves a guarantee of efficient allocation of financial funds in support of stable growth for productive capital.

2 Fund allocation and risk redistribution in the finance–credit relationship

2.1. Ownership titles as the fundamental relationship in a financial economy

Here I consider a simplified economy in which there are two classes of agents, the aggregate sector of entrepreneurs and the aggregate sector of rentiers, linked by one and the same financial asset, business ownership titles (henceforth, ownership titles) V, representing the underlying real asset, the productive capital of firms. The rentiers possess the entire stock of these titles. There are no other assets, nor any tool performing the function of money as liquid asset, and so for the rentiers the alternative to holding titles (serving for greater future consumption) is to increase current consumption. The ownership titles are indicative of the rentiers' power to identify the entrepreneurs to be entrusted with management of the capital goods, the productive uses of which will yield the income to remunerate the titles themselves.

The rentiers trade on the (secondary) financial market whose exchange at current market prices results in the redistribution of the stock of titles within. With their demand for productive capital, the entrepreneurs influence the (primary) financial market, determining the expediency for the rentiers to invest in new capital goods. For their financing new ownership titles are issued and absorbed by the saving of the rentiers themselves. On this latter market, the equilibrium position corresponds to equality between saving and investment and so to equilibrium income. In a purely financial economy, the price of the titles (indicative of the rentier return required) determines the greater amount of capital that the entrepreneurs are prepared to manage in the period and the rentiers' decision to invest takes on the form of their demand for credit on the market, satisfied by the other rentiers' saving: all the saving is invested, all the investment is financed, and all the titles are absorbed. By representing it thus, it will be seen that in analysis in terms of "loanable funds market" there is no sense in distinguishing whether the macroeconomic implications are the result of equilibrium of stock on the "financial" market or equilibrium of flow on the "credit" market.

2.2. Entrepreneurs' and rentiers' decisions and temporary loanable fund market equilibrium

The rentiers are prepared to hold stocks of ownership titles if they expect to draw a sufficient flow of net return in the future. More specifically, individual rentier h is prepared to hold the volume of title equal to his/her own wealth only if the value v_V^h that he/she attributes to the title is superior, or at worst equal, to the current market price v_V. Evaluation of v_V^h depends on expectations of future net return (inclusive of appreciation) per unit of title $\mathcal{R}_V^h$ and the rate of return required r_V^h consisting of the net rate of returns ρ_V^h and the risk premium σ_V^h run in holding it, if the rentier decides to hold/acquire the title; in the contrary case he/she will prefer to get rid of it (and increase own consumption).

$$\mathcal{R}_V^h/r_V^h = \mathcal{R}_V^h/(\rho_V^h + \sigma_V^h) = v_V^h \geq v_V. \qquad [1]$$

Taking the rentiers en masse, each shows different evaluations for $\mathcal{R}_V$, ρ_V e σ_V and thus a different v_V^h. As market price v_V grows, fewer will be prepared to hold the titles: their market demand $V^d(v_V)$ is decreasing with the increasing market price. Given the stock of existing titles V, there will be a rentier d to whom applies the condition $V^d(v_V^*) = V$. This condition identifies the price v_V^* for which the entire stock is willingly held by some of them; at this price, the possibility for some rentiers to invest their wealth in titles arises from the decision of others to get rid of them. Given the market evaluation $\mathcal{R}_V$ of the future expected return, market price v_V determines the market rate of return required r_V:

$$r_V(V) = \mathcal{R}_V/v_V(V). \qquad [2]$$

The rate [2] with deduction of market evaluation of risk premium σ_V can be interpreted as the market rate of interest $\rho(= r_V - \sigma_V)$; it indicates the minimum net return that, at a given moment, the rentiers in general require to hold the entire stock of existing titles in portfolio. It is determined by the opportunity cost in terms of future consumption, the cost influenced by various factors including the degree of uncertainty about the future, which affects precautionary saving.

As for the entrepreneurs, they take over management of the capital stock K with the commitment to derive a flow of capital incomes sufficient to repay the rentiers on the basis of return required r_V. Thus the individual entrepreneur e is prepared to take on a volume of productive capital K^e only if, given the price of capital goods p_K, the flow of future net income $\mathcal{R}_K^e(K^e)$ which he/she expects to obtain per capital goods unit yield not only the return required r_V but also promises to cover the risk σ_K^e of expectations being belied; the entrepreneur's evaluation of capital v_K^e must satisfy the relation:

$$\mathcal{R}_K^e(K^e)/r_V + \sigma_K^e = v_K^e \geq p_K. \qquad [3]$$

Taking the entrepreneurs as a whole, each will exhibit a different evaluation $\mathcal{R}_K$, e σ_K so that, as the market price of capital goods p_K grows, fewer will be prepared to manage the productive capital.[5] Entrepreneur s to whom condition [3] applies at the level of equality discriminates between those who are ready to involve themselves in the productive process and those who are not, determining the overall demand for capital on the part of the potential entrepreneurs. Given the market evaluations of the entrepreneurs' expectations of future capital incomes $\mathcal{R}_K$, of the market risk premium regarding the volatility of the expected capital incomes σ_K and the current price of capital goods p_K, as the price grows of ownership titles v_V (with diminishing rate of return required r_V), there will be an increase in these titles supplied on the primary market and in the overall stock V supplied on the secondary market. Productive capital K is therefore determined by the relation:

$$r_V(V) = \mathcal{R}_K(K)/p_K - \sigma_K. \qquad [4]$$

Establishing, for the sake of simplicity, conditions $V = K$ and $p_K = 1$, the system is in equilibrium if the stock of ownership titles V guarantees equality between the rate of return required by the rentiers $r_V^d(V)$ and the rate of return offered by the entrepreneurs $r_V^s(K)$:

$$r_V^d(V) = \mathcal{R}_V/v_V(V) = \mathcal{R}_K(V) - \sigma_K = r_V^s(V). \qquad [5]$$

Any disequilibria between the two rates are absorbed by a variation in the stock of titles V, the intensity of which will depend on the flexibility of its price and the elasticity of expenditure for investments relative to the cost of capital. With [5] I can obtain the equilibrium rate of interest ρ as:

$$\rho(V) = \mathcal{R}_K(V) - \sigma_V - \sigma_K \qquad [6]$$

and the ratio between current evaluation of the capital representative titles v_V and evaluation of the stock of productive capital p_K as:

$$v_V/p_K = [\mathcal{R}_V(V)/\mathcal{R}_K(V)] \, (1 + \sigma_K/r_V). \qquad [7]$$

With [6] I have the market rate of interest (risk-free) in terms of the entrepreneurs' expectations of future capital return net of the risk evaluation of both rentiers and entrepreneurs, highlighting the "subjective" nature of the market factors underlying financial equilibrium.[6] On the other hand, [7] illustrates how evaluation of ownership titles diverges progressively from the price of capital goods the more the entrepreneurs' expectations of incomes $\mathcal{R}_K$ differ from those of the rentiers $\mathcal{R}_V$ and the greater proves the risk premium required by entrepreneurs to take on the task of managing the physical capital. Thus, the diverging evaluation of the stock of wealth and of the stock of capital reflects the different views held on future productive conditions on either side.[7]

The financial mechanism described above highlights the important role that the two different sets of information play in short-period macroeconomic equilibrium, in the sense of that "temporary" equilibrium which guarantees consistency in the ex-ante plans of the various operators drawn up on the basis of expectations deriving from the information available at the particular historical time.[8] On the basis of these expectations the financial system redistributes the titles among the rentiers, and the productive capital among the entrepreneurs, towards those who, all other things being equal, are most inclined to take on the relative risk. Of importance for financial equilibrium is the evaluation rentiers make of their *financial risk* (i.e. the possibility that the return from the ownership titles does not correspond to expectations); of importance for the aggregate product is the evaluation the entrepreneurs make of their *enterprise risk* (i.e. the possibility that the use of capital does not yield capital incomes corresponding to expectations); the sum of the two risk premiums (σ_V and σ_K) is indicative of the market evaluation of the "real risk".

2.3 The stability of (temporary) financial equilibrium

As evidenced by [7], evaluation of financial wealth differs from that of productive capital although their compensation consists in the same financial asset, the capital representative title. Fluctuations in the expectations of the rentiers and entrepreneurs influence the dynamics of the aggregate product which, as pointed out analysing [5], depends on the elasticity of investment expenditure and of the demand for ownership titles; to use Keynes's expression, it depends on the "market sentiments" (factors $\mathcal{R}_V$, ρ_V, σ_V regarding the current expectations of future flows of yields expected by the rentiers) and on the entrepreneurs' "animal spirits" (factors $\mathcal{R}_K$, σ_K regarding current expectations of future flows of yields expected by the entrepreneurs). Being independent of one another, the decisions of the rentiers and entrepreneurs can combine in various ways, generating a range of temporarily stable, even if not optimal, potential macroeconomic equilibria.

Let us, for example, take the case of a contraction in the rentiers' risk premium due to higher expectations of future financial incomes or reduced risk aversion. At the same price, v_V, more people are interested in investing their wealth in ownership titles; if the elasticity of their demand is very marked, there will be limited variation in their price. The limited fall in the rate of return required on these titles stimulates expansion of investments (and product) only if they show marked elasticity to the financial conditions, otherwise the effect remains essentially confined to the secondary market with no great incidence on price. A rather different picture emerges if the entrepreneurs, infected by the behaviour of the rentiers, revise their expectations in a more optimistic direction (with increases of R_K or reductions of σ_K); the greater propensity to invest heightens the stimulus deriving from the improved financial conditions. Perception of approaching improvement in the economic conditions may be on the part of finance[9] with the entrepreneurs taking longer to recognise it, but the contrary case is also possible, entrepreneurs perceiving improvement in the outlook before the rentiers. Improving prospects for firms entail a greater demand for investments (a greater supply of titles), which, rentiers' expectations being equal, is satisfied only as long as the financial conditions do not become restrictive as a result of reduced elasticity in the rentiers' demand for titles. In this case, too, if the expectations of wealth-owners respond to the more optimistic expectations on the part of the firms, the increased demand for titles supports the expansive phase opened up by investments.

The possibility of manifold equilibria emerges from the differences in information available to firms and rentiers, summed up in the divergence in value between capital and wealth in the equilibrium position. As it is a matter of the information supplied to economic agents by the market, this divergence can persist over time on account of obstacles obstructing the circulation of information between the two groups of agents as well as a structural difference in their risk aversion due to the different horizons within which they evaluate the flow of future yield (on account of the greater or lesser short-termism characterising their roles). It can reasonably be argued that with a greater and better circulation of information and closer identification between wealth-owners and entrepreneurs the evaluation of wealth and capital will prove more even; in fact, I observe with [7] that if market relations are eventually able to bring all the relevant information into full and symmetrical circulation, $R_K/R_V = 1$ and $\sigma_K = 0$, so that equality in the evaluations of wealth and capital implies that, all autonomy being eliminated from the decision-making, there will be identity between entrepreneurs and rentiers in their way both of evaluating their future yield and in their readiness to take on the associated risks: essentially, the economy would be represented by a single agent. However, even admitting this *reductio omnium ad unum*, complete and symmetrical information does not suffice for long-period stability. For this to come about, information on the consequences of the current decisions regarding future economic trends must be such as to generate evaluation of the "real risk" $(\sigma_V + \sigma_K)$ which reflects the "true" consequences of the current choices. To arrive at this it would be necessary for the market to function as an efficient mechanism transmitting *information on the future* so as to provide all agents with that one unambiguous point of convergence compatible with "*the*" long-period position.

3 The production of liquidity and the outside money

3.1 *Stores of value in extension of the rentiers' portfolio*

The credit–finance relation analysed in the previous section is a drastic simplification of the real situation given that the capital representative titles are not the only property assets that rentiers can invest their wealth in. In every economy there are assets desired by the wealth-owners as "stores of value" due to the fact that they guarantee their purchasing power over time through exchange on the market with other rentiers. Such, for example, is the wide range of real assets that has developed in the course of time constituted by shelter goods (jewellery and works of art, but also real estate in the form of housing, land that can be built on, etc.) which form part of the rentiers' wealth without, even indirectly, being capital representative titles. As Gurley and Shaw put it, they are "outside" financial assets, alternative to ownership titles in the allocation of the rentiers' wealth, being characterised by entirely different expected returns and risk premiums. Moreover, their supply is characterised by a very low, if not zero, production elasticity since it does not depend on variations in its rate of return.

"Outside money" also belongs to this class of stores of value. On the basis of historical experience, this money is assumed to be the debt of an institution (identified as the central bank) issued solely as offset for the purchase of public bonds. This implies the presence of a public sector whose decisions are independent of the decisions of firms; of a sector that has accumulated an interest-bearing debt for having in the past financed its excesses of expenditure resorting to the saving of the rentiers. With the guarantee of a (normally certain) flow of interest over time, the risk involved in public bonds is usually less than that of other stores of value and ownership titles, in comparison with which they therefore appear more "liquid". These are the true outside assets alternative to ownership titles; the action of the central bank in converting public bonds into monetary assets is simply a qualitative transformation (in terms of greater liquidity) of the stock of outside assets.

The wide range of alternative property instruments (stores of value, money, public bonds and ownership titles), each with different characteristics in terms of risk and returns, affects the financial process described in the previous section only through the possibility open to the wealth-owners to diversify their portfolio. On the other hand, it entails no change in the behaviour of the entrepreneurs since investment expenditure is still financed entirely with the issue of ownership titles, absorbed into the saving of rentiers not serving to finance public deficit. Nevertheless, the presence of a public sector and of a monetary institution extends (through monetary and fiscal policies) the range of assets available to the rentiers, affecting its quality. Thus, the financial and macroeconomic equilibrium is influenced.

3.2 Stores of value and ownership titles: their complementarity or substitutability in the rentiers' portfolio

The rentiers' portfolio choice lies between capital representative titles and stores of value representative titles, whose quality (in terms of liquidity) can vary according to the decisions of the monetary authorities. First, I will examine the financial equilibrium in the alternative between ownership titles V and stores of value U with the qualification that the last consist of public bonds. I will then go on to consider the consequences of transforming the latter into money.

If $\mathcal{R}_U^h$ is the expected flow of yields by rentier h on the stores of value and r_U^h the rate of return required on such assets (consisting of the net rate of returns ρ_U^h and risk premium σ_U^h), he/she will be prepared to hold them in his/her portfolio if, as I have seen in the case of ownership titles, his/her evaluation v_U^h is more favourable than market evaluations v_U:

$$\mathcal{R}_U^h/r_U^h = \mathcal{R}_U^h/(\rho_U^h + \sigma_U^h) = v_U^h \geq v_U. \qquad [8]$$

The rentier chooses the combination of ownership titles and stores of value that will guarantee, given their current prices v_U and v_V, that the two rates of return be equal (net of risk) ρ_U^h and ρ_V^h:

$$\rho_U^h = \mathcal{R}_U^h/v_U - \sigma_U^h = \mathcal{R}_V^h/v_V - \sigma_V^h = \rho_V^h. \qquad [9]$$

If the evaluation of expected returns and risk are, for both forms of wealth, an item independent of the portfolio composition, the rentier's choice will normally fall on only one of the two assets, namely the one for which the current prices determine the higher net return. If, on the other hand, the overall portfolio risk is affected by its composition ($\sigma_U^h = \sigma_U^h (V, U); \sigma_V^h = \sigma_V^h (V, U)$), equality between the two rates of return will depend upon the (desired) portfolio composition.

Taking the rentiers as a whole, with different evaluations for $\mathcal{R}, \rho$ and σ for the two forms of wealth, a demand will be determined for each of them – $V^d(v_V, v_U)$ for the ownership titles and $U^d(v_V, v_U)$ for the stores of value – that will prove decreasing with increase in its price and increasing with increase in the price of the alternative asset. Given the comprehensive stock of existing V and stock of U, the pair of prices (v_V^*, v_U^*) to which apply at the same time the two conditions $V^d(v_V^*, v_U^*) = V$ and $U^d(v_V^*, v_U^*) = U$ will identify the situation in which the stocks of the two wealth representative titles are held entirely and willingly by the rentiers. Equality between the two net market rates of return

$$\rho_U(V, U) = \mathcal{R}_U/v_U(V, U) - \sigma_U(V, U) = \mathcal{R}_V/v_V(V, U) - \sigma_V (V, U)$$
$$= \rho_V (V, U) = \rho(V, U) \qquad [10]$$

indicates that the market rate of interest ρ depends on the stock of both assets $\rho(V, U)$, only that of the ownership titles being determined endogenously. The presence of stores of value influences the rate of return required on ownership titles and, along this channel, the entrepreneurs' decisions and the macroeconomic equilibrium.

The rentiers' expectations being equal, a greater stock of stores of value influences the prices (and the rate of return required) of the ownership titles. Greater wealth on the part of the rentiers leads to an increase in the demand for both assets; as a result of excess in demand for ownership titles the relative price will increase, while the price of the stores of value will show a contraction due to the excess of supply. However, the wealth-effect is offset by the substitution-effect due to the opportunity of arbitrage in favour of these, which offer higher returns;

the gap between the two rates narrows and the entire rate structure shifts upwards favouring absorption of the greater stock of assets. The increase in the rate of return required on ownership titles reduces the entrepreneurs' demand for productive capital: an increase in the (exogenous) stock of stores of value entails a reduction in the (endogenous) stock of ownership titles. This conclusion is based on the assumption that their expansion generates a wealth-effect lower than the substitution-effect; if, on the other hand, their greater availability should determine a significant reduction in portfolio risk, increase in the price of ownership titles would indicate that the stores of value were, in this case, more complementary than alternative in the rentiers' portfolio.

I may arrive at somewhat different considerations if I take the case of an increase in expected return on stores of value (and/or a reduction in their risk premium), the corresponding expectations for ownership titles remaining, of course, the same. On the evidence of [10] I see that an increase in $\mathcal{R}_U$ (and/or a reduction in σ_U) entails an increase in the rate of return required on stores of value, and consequently on ownership titles; demand shifts from the less profitable ownership titles to the more remunerative stores of value: the greater desirability of these on the secondary market produces less favourable conditions on the primary market. However, if elasticity in the production of the funds is, as may be supposed, very low, the consequent increase in their price will at length bring their rate of return required back into equilibrium with that on the other title. This conclusion rests, moreover, on the assumption that $\mathcal{R}_U$ undergoes no change during the process; however, the returns on the stores of value, lying essentially in expectation of their being revalued, can be influenced by the current revaluation so that the increase in $\mathcal{R}_U$ can set their rate of return at a level below which the rate of return required on the ownership titles cannot drop: yield constrains profits, stock decisions take the lead over flow decisions.

As I have seen, public bonds have the characteristics of stores of value entailing returns and risk normally below those of ownership titles, and having them available means enjoying a higher degree of portfolio liquidity. It is not surprising, therefore, that their inclusion in the portfolio represents an encouragement to hold a larger share of riskier assets (ownership titles) if the complementarity effect offsets the substitution-effect so that reduction in the overall risk of individual portfolios will tend towards a reduction in the rates of return required on both assets. On the basis of the above considerations on stores of value with respect to increase in their stock of public bonds and the variations in the evaluation of their returns and risk, it is possible to delineate the area of potential and conditioning of public debt policy.[10]

3.3 Outside money and macroeconomic equilibrium: the role of monetary policy

In order to support the process of accumulation, the financial institutions intervene to enhance the conditions of liquidity for the rentiers' portfolio. If public bonds meet the liquidity needs of the rentiers, these needs are even more satisfied by (outside) money, offering the advantage that it can readily be exchanged for other property assets with virtually zero risk since it can be done without costs and without incurring loss in its capital value.

Since (outside) money is considered as a financial instrument issued by a central bank subsequent to the acquisition of (public) bonds, the decision as to how many securities to acquire and how much money to issue is an autonomous decision of monetary policy. A greater supply of money, increasing the assets deemed risk-free in the rentiers' portfolio, essentially has the effect of modifying the "quality" (in terms of degree of liquidity) of the stock of public bonds.

Now [10], adjusted to take into account the fact that the stores of value U consist of money M and public bonds available on the market $(B - M)$, shows that, for a stock of public bonds given externally, the central bank has the possibility – as monopolist – to determine the quantity M of money or, alternatively, its rate of returns ρ_M:

$$\rho_V(V, B{-}M, M) = R_V/v_V(V, B{-}M, M) - \sigma_V(V, B{-}M, M) =$$

$$= \rho_B(V, B{-}M, M) = R/v_B(V, B{-}M, M) - \sigma_B(V, B{-}M, M) =$$

$$= \rho_M(V, B{-}M, M) + \lambda_M(V, B{-}M, M) = \rho(V, B{-}M, M). \qquad [11]$$

Given the rentiers' expectations and stock of wealth, increased liquidity conditions in the economy imply a reduction in the supply of public bonds on the market with a consequent increase in their price; the reduced market rate of interest also drives the price of ownership titles upwards, reinforced by the reduction of risk in a more liquid portfolio. Also in this case, the structure [11] of market prices of the three property assets guarantees that their existing stock (exogenous for public bonds and money, endogenous for ownership titles) be entirely and willingly held by the rentiers. Given that ρ stands for the market rate of interest as opportunity cost of future consumption, the rate of returns of money ρ_M will prove lesser with lesser readiness of the market to forego the ready availability of liquid means (as the premium λ_M proves greater).

Should such fluctuations in the expectations of the rentiers unfavourably affect evaluation of the risk of the various property assets, monetary policy may take it upon itself to intervene to moderate such movements. The central bank, then, on the basis of an information structure thanks to which it can interpret them correctly, and having its own appraisal of the financial equilibrium to be achieved, establishes the quantity of money that the rentiers must hold; if the view taken by the monetary authorities corresponds to the real and financial conditions perceived by rentiers and entrepreneurs, then, and only then, will the structure of rates of return and macroeconomic dynamics be stabilised. In situations (fairly frequent in recent monetary experience) where the central bank attributes informational value to the rentiers' and firms' market behaviours as better placed to interpret current productive potentialities, its intervention will consist in supply of the liquidity required by the financial system at the monetary rate of the market. When this kind of "accommodating" attitude obtains, the stocks of all three assets are determined endogenously and, therefore, the composition of the aggregate portfolio reflects the needs of the wealth-owners and the entrepreneurs: the quantity of money, the monetary policy, is (largely) decided by the rentiers.[11]

The real effects of the monetary policy depend upon the reaction of the rate of return required on ownership titles to the increased degree of liquidity. Whatever form intervention by the monetary authorities may take, there will be a positive effect on accumulation only if overall evaluation of the real risk $(\sigma_V + \sigma_K)$ is reappraised. Considering that when outside assets are involved (stores of value, public bonds and money) the risk of negative future results in production falls entirely upon the rentiers, the relation obtained from [11]:

$$r_V = r_B + (\sigma_V - \sigma_B) = (\sigma_V - \sigma_B) + (\sigma_B + \lambda_M) + \rho_M, \qquad [12]$$

evidences the fact that a reduction both in the rate of return on public bonds r_B and in the gap between risk premiums $(\sigma_V - \sigma_B)$ leads to a reduction in the rate of return required on ownership titles r_V: the possibility of "mixing" ownership titles with other property assets acts as an incentive to hold a greater quantity of capital representative titles in the portfolio, but the increase in demand on the part of the rentiers characterised by a reduced propensity to take on risky positions may prove insufficient if the gap between risk premiums increases $(\sigma_V - \sigma_B)$, in which case the effects of monetary policy remain largely confined to public bonds-money substitution, with no effective incidence on the real macroeconomic conditions.

4 Finance autonomy: inside money

4.1 Credit intermediation in the rentiers–entrepreneurs relation

So far I have conducted my analysis of the functioning of the financial system within a highly simplified context, with no involvement of credit intermediaries ("banks" or "bankers"), whose function in transferring funds sees transformation of the funds themselves: the forms of contracts with which they collect the funds do not correspond, in terms of income and risk, to the forms of contract with which they lend them. If both final debtor and creditor belong to the private sector, the intervention of the banks consists in production of "inside assets", particularly in high liquidity liabilities or "inside money".

The greater number of agents (rentiers, entrepreneurs and bankers) and assets traded (ownership titles, financial credit, financial securities, money) involved in the production of inside indirect securities makes the financial process more complex and more interesting. The assets of varying degrees of liquidity issued by the credit intermediaries are an alternative to ownership titles for the rentiers, the liabilities an alternative to ownership titles for firms. The money and securities issued by the intermediaries and held by the rentiers are capital (indirectly) representative titles inasmuch as they are compensation for the financial credit granted by the intermediaries to firms to finance the accumulation of capital; thus the sum of the indirect assets held by the rentiers corresponds to the sum of the indirect liabilities of the firms, whatever the financial form taken on.

With their action, the credit intermediaries slacken the constraints acting on portfolio restructure with the varying expectations of the rentiers. In order to achieve the asset composition desired, the rentiers are no longer constrained to seek out another rentier with contrary preferences, but can now resort to the banks to transform titles into money and vice versa; the total stock of assets available on the market finds a limit only in the willingness of the banks to grant credit (to transform illiquid assets into liquid assets). The financial structure shows even more flexibility if the activity of credit intermediation also extends, as indeed is the case, to relations between one bank and another and consequent growth at the same time of their assets and liabilities (*leverage*). Yet further extension of the financial intermediation activities is called for with the additional financial activities in addressing the bank debt of firms and families (Gambino 1969).

The "autonomous" decisions of the rentiers in selecting the best composition of their assets and of firms in determining the most appropriate combination of their liabilities are conditioned by the decisions of the bankers, who also have their own "autonomous" information structure and their own objectives, in determining the level and composition of their assets and liabilities. This is achieved on the basis of expediency, in terms of returns and risk, of transforming risky credit to firms into assets involving reduced risk for the rentiers. In this transformation, the risk of indirect liabilities on the part of the entrepreneurs is not entirely transferred into the indirect assets of the rentiers; the part that is not transferred is absorbed by the banks, resulting in more indirect management of the financial risk covering the real risk.

4.2 Complementarity and substitutability between the financial institutions' assets and liabilities

Let us take a simplified case in which the credit of the intermediaries to the firms L corresponds exactly to the total sum of titles F and money M issued by them and held by the rentiers.[12] Although taken with reference to different financial instruments, the rentiers' portfolio decisions are made as customary; for given prices of assets, they equalise the rates of return (net of the risk premium) of all three forms of assets; in aggregate, equilibrium is determined by the structure of the stock of ownership titles V, financial securities F and money M which respect the condition:

$$\rho_V(V, F, M) = \mathcal{R}_V/v_V(V, F, M) - \sigma_V(V, F, M) =$$
$$= \rho_F^R(V, F, M) = \mathcal{R}_F^R/v_F(V, F, M) - \sigma_F^R(V, F, M) =$$
$$= \rho_M(V, F, M) + \lambda_M^R(V, F, M) = \rho^R(V, F, M) \qquad [13]$$

where the net rate of return ρ^R of the rentiers' portfolio, corresponding to evaluation of their opportunity cost of future consumption, determines – taking into account the liquidity premium λ_M^R – evaluation of the net return ρ_M which the rentiers obtain from the availability of a monetary unit.

Having access to the banks, many entrepreneurs are able to leverage not only by issuing ownership titles but also by borrowing from the banks. Should they hold no financial assets, the individual entrepreneurs will determine, on the basis of their own expectations and for given prices of the two forms of liabilities, the composition of their debt which equals the respective costs of the capital (χ_V, χ_L):

$$\chi_v = \mathcal{R}_K(K)/v_V(V, F, M) - \sigma_V^E(V,L)$$
$$= \mathcal{R}_K(K)/v_L(L, F, M) - \sigma_L^E(V,L) = \chi_L = \chi^E(V, L, F, M). \qquad [14]$$

Extending [3] to the case at hand, the cost of debt is a (weighted) average of the rates of return required respectively by the rentiers r_V and the banks r_L ($\theta_V r_V + \theta_L r_L$, where θ_V e θ_L, with $\theta_V + \theta_L = 1$, are the shares respectively of ownership titles and financial credit in the total debt of the firms, to which is added the risk premium required by the firms $\sigma_K(V,L)$:

$$\mathcal{R}_K(K)/\{(\theta_V \chi_V + \theta_L \chi_L) + (\theta_V \sigma_V + \theta_L \sigma_L) + \sigma_K(V,L)\}$$
$$= \mathcal{R}_K(K)/(\chi^E + \sigma_D(V,L) + \sigma_K(V,L)) = p_K \qquad [15]$$

where $\sigma_D(V,L)$ is the weighted average of the risk premiums and $\sigma_K(V,L)$ depends not only on the level of their debt but also on its composition.[13]

The intermediation activity of the individual bank is set at the level at which the net rate of return on the assets corresponds to the rate of return on the liabilities, while equality between the net rates of return on the various assets and liabilities determines the composition of its balance sheet. At the aggregate level, the (endogenous) stocks of the intermediaries' assets and liabilities must respect the condition:

$$\phi_L(L, F, M) = \mathcal{R}_L/v_L(L, F, M) - \sigma_L(L, F, M) =$$
$$= \phi_F(L, F, M) = \mathcal{R}_F^F/v_F(L, F, M) - \sigma_F^F(L, F, M) =$$
$$= \phi_M(L, F, M) + \sigma_M^F(L, F, M) = \phi^F(L, F, M) \qquad [16]$$

where the net rate of returns ϕ^F required by the bankers corresponds to the opportunity cost of expanding intermediation activities. Given the balance constraint of the intermediaries ($L = F + M$) and given the desired stocks of credit and financial instruments, the condition of equilibrium determines unequivocally the supply of money M and, given the bank risk σ_M^F regarding liabilities characterised by liquid assets, also determined is the opportunity cost of money ϕ_M (the monetary rate of interest).

Should the firms hold no financial assets nor the families be indebted, then the rentiers' demand for ownership titles is met only by the supply of the firms.

As for the other assets, the demand of the rentiers and the demand of the entrepreneurs are for assets of a different nature: in contrast with the firms' demand for bank credit, the rentiers' demand is for financial instruments and monetary assets. The discrepancy is smoothed out through intermediation activity, since the supply of credit to the firms is, on account of the budget constraint, matched by supply to the rentiers of an equivalent sum of financial and monetary assets; the rentier–entrepreneur equilibrium – and thus also the volume of new capital – is arrived at through the decisions of the bankers.

In the absence of outside assets, the financial structure of the economy is entirely endogenous, depending solely on the expectations of private agents (rentiers, entrepreneurs and bankers); it is their autonomous choices, in response to variations in their expectation of profitability and in their risk premiums, that determine fluctuations in the financial and real equilibria. Take, for example, the case of an improvement in the prospects for firms (an increase in $R_K(K)$ or a contraction in σ_K). The greater supply of ownership titles and the greater demand for credit on the part of the entrepreneurs generate pressure on the prices of ownership titles and bank credit lending; on the one hand, the rentiers to shift their demand to the more profitable ownership titles (reducing the demand on financial instruments and monetary assets) and, on the other hand, the banks to increase not only the supply of credit, but also the supply of financial instruments and money. All four markets are characterised by an excess of supply, with the effect of a generalised reduction in prices and increase in the rates of return. The more elastic financial intermediation is to the interest rates, the greater will be the response of the banks in supplying the sums of credit desired by the firms and the sums of financial instruments and monetary assets desired by the rentiers.

The outcome is different if it is the prospects of the rentiers vis-à-vis ownership titles that improve. The increase in their demand and consequent increase in their price can drive the firms to borrow in this form at the expense of their bank exposure. Since the increase in demand for ownership titles entails a reduction in the demand for more liquid assets, there will be an excess in supply both of financial instruments and of money at the same time. The fall in the prices of financial instruments (and reduced demand for money) curbs financial intermediation, the bankers' expectations being equal, with the effect of containing both bank assets and bank liabilities. The rentiers, being more inclined to take on direct titles, will replace the intermediaries' titles with ownership titles in their portfolio.

With an improvement in the expectations of the bankers the outcome is different. With a greater supply of credit conditions for the financing of firms are eased, the rentiers' and entrepreneurs' expectations being equal, and the supply of financial instruments is encouraged; the firms are induced to replace direct debts with indirect debts and the rentiers to shift shares of their portfolio towards financial instruments at the expense of ownership titles. While demand and supply tend to balance out on the market for these titles, the other three markets see an excess of supply; the improvement in the bankers' expectations has positive effects on the accumulation of new capital. In any case the consideration always applies that the possible configurations of demand and supply elasticities on the various financial instrument markets, in determining the intensity of the effects on the cost of capital and expenditure for investments, bring about such multiple equilibria as the economy may show. It should also be noted that with changes in the ratio between direct and indirect titles and increase in the share of less risky assets in the rentiers' portfolio, the distribution of the firms' risk between banks and rentiers will also be changed.

4.3 Inside money and macroeconomic equilibrium: the financial structure endogeneity

Where there are only inside financial assets, their stock (and the stock of productive capital) must be modified to ensure consistency in the – non-homogeneous – expectations of the various agents; their portfolio structures, like the structure of prices and expected returns on the various financial assets, thus reflect the particular configuration of information available to the individual agents. Multiple equilibria are clearly possible given that the net rate of return ρ^R of [13] (opportunity cost of the rentiers' future consumption) does not necessarily coincide with the net rate of returns ϕ^F of [16] (opportunity cost of funds through bank intermediation). Applying the financial equilibrium condition to F, it is found that the various expectations of future returns or the various risk premiums required by rentiers and bankers result in the two sectors showing different propensities to expand their financial accumulation:

$$\rho^R/\phi^F = (R_F^R/R_F^F) \{1 + \sigma_F^F [1 - (\sigma_F^R/R_F^R)/(\sigma_F^F/R_F^F)]/\phi^F\}. \qquad [17]$$

A high ratio value indicates that the readiness of the banks to intensify the intermediation process is curbed by the reduced propensity of the rentiers to expand their portfolios. If this ratio is considered indicative of bank support for the financial process, I must not lose sight of the fact that greater credit intermediation is to be evaluated positively only on certain conditions. The main condition is that bankers have a more "correct" picture of the situation and prospects for firms than the rentiers are able to obtain from the market in order to be able to arrive at a more "correct" evaluation of the risk premiums required on the various assets they deal with. The effectiveness of their action is gauged on the basis of capacity to lighten the financing cost for the entrepreneur, cutting down to size the overvaluation of risk premiums on the funds granted them. This is achieved through the action of agents specialised in selecting and monitoring the capacity of borrowers to realise incomes in the future, all the more important in so far as the productive process is shrouded in uncertainty. With access to better information on the risk faced by firms the bankers are able to compete with the rentiers in management of the risk, taking on part of it themselves. Given the overall debt of the firms, the risk premium σ_D required of them by the rentiers and bankers does not correspond to the share of risk σ_W that the rentiers are prepared to take on; the two (weighted) averages are:

$$\sigma_D = \theta_V \, \sigma_V^R + \theta_L \, \sigma_L^F \tag{18}$$

$$\sigma_W = \theta_V \, \sigma_V^R + \theta_F \, \sigma_F^R \tag{19}$$

and the gap between the risk insured by the firms and the risk taken on by the rentiers

$$\sigma_D - \sigma_W = \theta_L \, \sigma_L^F - \theta_F \, \sigma_F^R \tag{20}$$

is that part of risk that "apparently" does not befall the rentiers by virtue of having substituted financial assets deemed safer than ownership titles in their portfolio. Coverage of the risk on the credit of the banks σ_L^F is secured only partly by its transference into financial instruments

$$\theta_L \, \sigma_V^F = \theta_L \, \sigma_L^F - \theta_F \, \sigma_F^F \tag{21}$$

so that the residual risk σ_V^F falls formally on the intermediaries, whose owner-ship titles are, however, held by the rentiers. Combining the risk taken on directly by the rentiers with the risk implicit in the titles of the banks,[14] I obtain the effective risk weighing on the rentiers σ_W^*, which will prove less than the risk insured by the firms only if the risk premium required by the banks on their financial instruments is less than that required by the rentiers on the same instruments:

$$\sigma_W^* = \sigma_W + \theta_L \, \sigma_V^F = \theta_V \, \sigma_V^R + \theta_L \, \sigma_L^F - \theta_F \, (\sigma_F^F - \sigma_F^R) = \sigma_D - \theta_F (\sigma_F^F - \sigma_F^R). \tag{22}$$

The risk management performed by the credit intermediaries is thus of a strate-gic nature. Through the intermediation process, the banks can reduce the overall risk premium (direct and indirect) chargeable to the rentiers in so far as the premium required by the banks comes below that of a corresponding issue of ownership titles. With [21] I have an indication of how management of the finan-cial risk by the banks can be finalised to taking it upon themselves (collateral guarantees, portfolio compositions minimising the correlated risks, monitoring of risky positions, provision of reserve funds, etc.) but also to transferring it to other agents ready to take it on for a consideration, as it sees with recent experi-ence of *originate to distribute* and in the growth of markets dedicated to risk-covering operations (regarding derivatives, credit default swap, etc.).

The scope open to intermediaries to reduce the financial risk means a competi-tive advantage for them in providing funds to firms in a form that the rentiers are not able to guarantee. The pressure to exploit this advantage induces the banks to extend their intermediation activities to involve both other credit intermediaries and firms and families. Should the titles issued by the banks be absorbed by other banks, then the aggregate sector balance will show a rise both in assets $(L + F_A^F)$ and in liabilities $(F_P^F + M)$. The amount of funds coming to the firms and rentiers $(L = [F_P^F - F_A^F] + M)$ remains unchanged, but the greater gross size of the bank balance will not be without consequences for the financial process. The occurrence of double (triple, …) intermediation of funds reflects the non-homogeneity of issuer and financial instruments holder in terms of respective risk evaluation and aversion. The means intermediated expand beyond the need for productive capital financing, finding a limit only in the reciprocal expedience for the bankers to share among themselves the part of the firms' yield and risk not absorbed by the rentiers. This should result in a greater gap θ_F $(\sigma_F^F - \sigma_F^R)$ of [22], duly redefined to take into account the distribution of risk premiums within the financial institutions; moreover, the greater complexity encountered in redefining this gap reflects the greater difficulty in understanding, with this institutional system, who has taken on the financial risk and to what extent. If, to come yet closer to the realities, I admit the fact that firms hold financial assets[15] and families borrow from banks, then the leverage potential of the credit intermediaries is considerably enhanced. All the points made above are amply borne out, including the greater "opacity" shown in this broader (more realistic) complex by the risk-redistributing mechanism, and all the more so because growth in financial leverage is attended by growth in the monetisation of the economy with the consequent effect that a growing share of the overall financial risk of the rentiers remains implicit.

An important point to bear in mind here, however, is that in all these considerations the "financial" efficiency of the risk management is evaluated in terms of the capacity to constrict assessment of the "real risk" borne by the firms $(\sigma_D + \sigma_K)$. But the big issue here is that such management can conflict with its "real" efficiency if, instead of downsizing a "real" risk overrated by the rentiers and firms, it leads to or aggravates undervaluation of the risk. And yet, to size up the situation emerging, it would take someone commanding an overall view of the macroeconomic dynamics. The financial efficiency that brings about leverage is inevitably accompanied by a fragmentation of the realities involved, which means that there is no guarantee that the financial and monetary dimension of the economy, determined endogenously, be consistent with evolution of all its productive potentialities. Like the case of an outside money system with an "accommodating" central bank, the lack of an adequate filter in terms of monitoring and control of the indications offered by the "financial market" on the effective conditions of production in the future entails yet greater risk that financial behaviours may not act in such a way as to keep the economy running steadily along the road of sustainable growth: the financial system, and the economy, are seen to be inherently unstable.[16]

5 Between real growth and financial stability

With this chapter I set out to provide a picture of financial realities suited to analysis of risk management at the macroeconomic level through a conceptual structure based on the fundamental financial relationship between the ownership of wealth and productive capital. With this representation my aim was to point out that behaviours associated with evaluation and redistribution of financial risk are to be considered among the factors which, characterising a concrete financial system, determine the equilibria between finance, credit and money which influence the real macroeconomic equilibrium.

The connection between wealth and capital is contemplated within a mechanism of Keynesian tradition, taking into account – as was the practice of Keynes – the "state of credit", or in other words the confidence the intermediaries have in those who apply for loans. Reference to confidence, and the degree of trustworthiness thereby accorded, attributes expectations, and the risk of their being disappointed, with a primary analytic role in explaining how the financial process works. The various aspects of the risk – its pervasiveness, the differences it shows with the different agents, its subjectivity and the inherent instability of evaluations of it – all make it eloquently clear why Keynesian interpretations of the macroeconomic process cannot neglect to take it explicitly into consideration (Keynes 1936, 202–4). Moreover, by addressing a system made up of autonomous agents who, acting in a situation of uncertainty, have inadequate knowledge of the evolution of the economy,[17] I have been able to see how the equilibrium rates of return structure is entirely accounted for in the structure of the various agents' expectations. Admittedly, given the limited aims of this chapter, expectations are not explained endogenously; obviously, greater insight into the macroeconomic process would require an understanding of the mechanisms, governed by the market or other institutions, by means of which the information determining the level and interdependence of the various agents' expectations is generated and transferred.[18] However, even limiting analysis, as is the case here, to simple considerations of comparative statics, it seems to me to emerge quite clearly that without adequate mechanisms to eliminate differences in information among the various agents the economy is open to a multiplicity of potential equilibria depending on the particular combination of the various agents' different evaluations of prospective yield.[19]

This multiplicity of equilibria leads, in terms of accounting, to a difference between the rentiers' evaluations of wealth and the entrepreneurs' evaluations of productive capital. It is a divergence that recalls the gap, expressed with Tobin's q, between the cost of reproduction of productive capital and evaluation of its representative titles, although Tobin's disequilibrium is short period since it is, apparently, eventually rebalanced with spending on the investments thereby induced.[20] In the context of this chapter, there is no inevitable convergence to the long-period position due to the lack of a cogent mechanism able to even out all the agents' evaluations of the risk premiums, which is an essential condition for the value of the firms' capital stock to correspond systematically to the value of the families' wealth.

Another implication to be noted at the level of accounting has to do with the evaluation of the incomes (both sectoral and aggregate) generated by financial equilibrium. The returns on financial assets are broken down into the net returns and the sum of the risk premiums that the entrepreneurs, bankers and rentiers charge on the rates of return of the various titles. Now, given that risk premiums represent insurance against possible future surprises, the *current* income is an *advance on future* income to be allocated to covering the reduced incomes should the undesirable events take place. If the gross returns on property assets were to be considered available current income – as is glaringly the case of that part of the remunerations of the (financial or industrial) managers associated with values that anticipate expected future profits (stock options) – then the corresponding consumption would be financed by the stock of wealth and not the flow of income; the agents' behaviour is influenced by a "false" wealth-effect.

These distorted wealth-effects and income-effects are obstacles in the way of a possible process of convergence towards a univocal long-period position, to arrive at which the need is for an effective mechanism to circulate information among the financial agents both to iron out the imperfections and distortions of information and to provide reliable indication of developments in the economy. Any such convergence to a predetermined equilibrium (natural or potential as it may be) would call for that *reductio omnium ad unum* mentioned above, or in other words identity between the sets of information of the various agents. Only if the entrepreneurs and rentiers (and, indeed, bankers) were in possession of the same knowledge of both the present situation and the "real" future productive conditions would they lose their decision-making autonomy and the economy run as if there were one single agent endowed with perfect knowledge for the short and long period. In this case the financial system would be able to elicit that (natural) market rate of interest that corresponds to the (natural) rate of growth of the economy. The crucial point here is anchorage of current expectations to the feasibility of productive results in the future, since the ability to achieve correct evaluation of the real risk of accumulation and compare it with the financial risk ensures that the economy will continue to develop without straying from the path leading eventually to the expected increase in capital incomes. If the hypothesis of an efficient and "prophetic" financial system is abandoned, then the need arises to formulate an interpretation – that will prove useful at the operational level – of how the complex money–credit–finance relationship translates into manifold configurations of macroeconomic equilibrium, among which economic policy has the responsibility of making the choice.[21]

Introducing this chapter I mentioned that the major stimulus prompting the reflections set out here was the outbreak of the 2007–8 financial crisis. Actually, a number of aspects of this upheaval in the global economy seem to bear out the usefulness of the scheme proposed.

According to Minsky (1975, 129), when financial relations become self-referential in a Wall Street-type economy and lose sight of the real risk trend, then the economic system is characterised by potential instability. However, the present crisis does not show the typically Minskian characteristics of excessive exposure in the formation of capital by firms, as might have been the case if the crisis had broken out at the end of the previous cycle of dot.com investments; it does, however, show marked characteristics of financial disequilibrium due to the erroneous evaluations of the financial institutions which led them to take a few steps too far in the direction of consumer credit and mortgages. As a consequence of underestimation of the consumers' excessive financial liabilities, financial support for demand in the short period eventually came into conflict with income growth over the longer period; the financial risk premium underestimated the real risk. The conditions for a distribution of income such as would corroborate the current financial decisions[22] are clearly violated when, on the outbreak of crisis, the incomes perceived in the past (and used as "real" incomes) are not available to cope with the emerging losses, and the savings of third parties (the taxpayers) have to be drawn upon to bail out the banks.

The point I have stressed here is that the extension of financial relations with final debtors and creditors and, indeed, the intensification of relations among the financial operators render the relationship between financial risk and real risk somewhat murky. Such was the state of affairs shown lately by the American financial system when the matching of loaners and debtors was carried out by a widening range of financial institutes (investment banks, hedge funds, investment management companies, insurance companies, etc.) characterised by very different regulatory constraints and operational procedures from those of the banks. That the information regarding risk be provided correctly and transparently may be seen as an essential condition for the financial risk to be redistributed efficiently through the market towards those who opt to take it on, but experience of the recent crisis has shown that even in the context of highly sophisticated financial markets the condition may not be satisfied. On the contrary, the greater complexity of the financial process seems to have reduced market transparency. Increasing leverage together with contraction of the risk premium on financial instruments has, despite all the forms of coverage adopted at the micro level, had the effect of sedimenting a considerable part of the financial risk among the credit intermediaries. If I also take into account the fact that the extension and greater complexity of the risk premium structure has made the market more "opaque", it is hardly surprising that the "implicit" rentier risk has increased out of all proportion. The powerful stimulus for the banks to exploit financial opportunities has met with no counterbalance to make their decisions compatible with productive potentialities.

Monetary policy itself, relying on market information as indicator of the "naturalness" of the current equilibria, has inflated the financial dimension of the economy with the justification that the effects of "great moderation" confirmed the correctness of the policies adopted. This infectiously optimistic position also affected firms and rentiers with the result that the new, more sophisticated titles were attributed with rather more safety than they warranted, leading to a lowering of risk premiums that drove the entire interest-rate structure downwards. With the decision to play along with the expectations – and thus the risk premiums – of the bankers and rentiers, the central bank took upon itself the responsibility of underpinning the persisting financial equilibria that favoured the short-period "financial" dimension rather than the longer-period "productive" dimension. Eventually this became an instability factor, and the more effective it had proved in the short period, the more worrying it appeared now.[23] The perils of financial instability went on growing until 9 August 2007, when the doubts about the sustainability of the dynamics that had characterised the growth of the American economy proved all too well grounded.

The question that the recent crisis poses for economists, then, is how the financial system, in its composition of markets and institutions, can serve as a means of macroeconomic stability and growth. Past experience has shown the capacity of the system to function as a shock absorber for relatively long periods of time, but recent events have demonstrated – not without theoretical foundations – that it has acted as a shock magnifier. If these considerations are indeed borne out by the facts, which of the two ways of functioning will characterise a concrete financial economy at a given time will depend on how the financial risk is managed consistently with future productive developments. Nowadays it is hardly necessary to urge the need to pay due attention to these aspects of (macroeconomic) risk management. The international and national institutions have given ample support for examination of this aspect, and are now proposing ways to enhance monitoring and control of the financial risk. Meeting with rather less response, however, is the need to understand how to link the trend in the financial risk with the trend in productive accumulation in such a way as to ensure that short-period equilibria will not generate instability over the longer period. It is essential to get to grips with this issue before the (costly) re-establishment of conditions of stability in the global financial system fosters a new edition of the financial growth model already tried and found wanting, albeit adapted to a more rigorous regulatory framework. The fact that an accommodating monetary policy has ambiguous effects on the stability of the system depending on the capacity of the market to grasp the real prospects for future productive activity has yet to be recognised in economic research and monetary management as *the* problem of monetary policy or, to be more precise, the problem of economic policy.

If one denies, as indeed is my position, that it is possible to rely on predefined long-period positions (natural or potential as they may be), then all the greater is the need for comprehensive, flexible terms of reference to understand the concrete processes underway in the critical situation we are going through. The danger that stock needs (of wealth, of the rentiers on the secondary market) may jeopardise flow needs (of accumulation, firms on the primary market)[24] with fallout on the economy spelling instability or decline signals the importance of a perspective, not only monetary but also in economic policy, that does not focus on the market alone as a source of information about the future. The economist's task cannot be limited to supplying general schemes of reference, necessary as they are, but, bringing forth that "dentist" role that Keynes wished to see economists playing, should contribute to an understanding of those concrete aggregates behaviours that govern our future.

Notes

* To Sergio, my professor, colleague and friend, with the admiration, appreciation and affection of half a century of valued dialogue.
♦ I wish to thank Riccardo De Bonis and an anonymous referee for valuable comments. Any remaining errors are my own.
1 Bordo *et al.* (2001) point out that, as from the financial liberalisation launched in the 1980s, bank crises have been, even in the developed countries, as numerous as they were in the 20-year period ending in 1914.

2 Fischer (2008, 18) sets Greenspan's (2005) assertion "that the growing array of derivatives and the related application of more sophisticated methods for measuring and managing risks had been key factors underlying the remarkable resilience of the banking system", against Warren Buffett's colourful remark that the "derivatives [are] financial weapons of mass destruction, carrying dangers that, while now latent, are potentially lethal".

3 "The three fundamental factors of market psychology of the prevailing attitude to the future, as expressed in the state of liquidity preference, in the expectation of quasi-rent, and in the rate of time preference" (Keynes 1973, 404).

4 Bernand and Bisignano (2003, 25) observes that the recent financial innovations have shown greater efficiency in the intersectoral redistribution of (financial) risk and then in its intertemporal redistribution. See also Allen and Gale (2001, 153–7)

5 Given the limits to the scope of this chapter, I have assumed only the expected flow of net future yields $\mathcal{R}_p^h$, and not also the risk premium required by the entrepreneurs σ_K, as a function of the stock of capital. This does not affect the considerations set out in the text, although adopting a Kaleckian hypothesis of increasing risk (Kalecki 1937) would indeed enhance the account of the macroeconomic dynamics (not performed here) (Dimsky 1996).

6 The two risk premiums show strong analogies with the lender's risk and the borrower's risk described by Minsky (1975, 140–9), both functions of the level of debt.

7 Although the relationship shows the same construction as the q of Tobin (1969), even though the elements that define it allow for a different interpretation (see note 20, below).

8 Parrinello (1998) and Birolo (in this volume, "The Path of a Scholar", paragraphs 4.1 and 4.3) for a thorough analysis of Parrinello's view of the equilibrium concept. I deem this conclusion is consistent with Parrinello's view of the effective demand principle (1976, 92–3). In his opinion, the Keynesian model can be usefully integrated with the stock market, as long as there are [a monetary economy,] uncertainty, separation between investment decisions and saving decisions and the role of income as adjustment variable; and this is exactly my model.

9 I use the term "finance" to refer to the financial asset stock and its movements in a given period.

10 Interesting as it is, I do not examine here the effect of an increase in public debt due to the formation of financial public deficits on the market. Associated with the financial effect, of course, is that of the aggregate demand whose consequences are of particular importance for the expectations of the entrepreneurs, rentiers and bankers, as indeed emerges from the debate on the management of the present crisis.

11 For discussion of the post-Keynesian interpretations of the behaviour of monetary policy, see Lavoie (1996).

12 It is to be noted that this hypothesis neglects the fact that the banks obtain profits upon which depends the value of their possessory titles held by the rentiers, who finance not only the entrepreneurs' business but also that of the bankers. I return to consider the importance of this aspect in the comment on relation [21].

13 The explanation reflects the packing order theory of the firms debt hypotheses (Myers and Majluf 1984).

14 The productive risk of firms financed with bank credit is not reflected explicitly in the deposits, in the depositors' conviction that the net capital of the banks (as well as the bank deposit insurance funds) is a sufficient guarantee against any mishap, and yet it is neither improbable nor infrequent for banks to get into financial trouble (see note 1).

15 The need for firms to have liquid assets available to launch the productive process is an important aspect for macroeconomic equilibrium in the "circuitist approach" (Graziani 2003).

16 See Vercelli (2001) for the stress placed on the structural instability of a sophisticated monetary economy.

17 The analytic approach is as proposed in Vicarelli (1974).
18 Expectations and conventions are taken by Ciocca and Nardozzi (1993) to account for the trend in the rate of interest in the 1980s.
19 In his explanation of the present crisis, Visco points out that the non-emerging risks reinforce the distorted expectations (Visco 2009).
20 The analytic hiatus between short and long period in Tobin's analysis (Gnesutta 1992, 291n) is examined by Panico (1992, 347–50).
21 On the need for an analytic approach that considers the behaviours of the economic agents in conditions of essential uncertainty, see Vicarelli (1983).
22 Nardozzi (2002, 56–64) considers the market pressures driving firms to adapt their productive apparatus, technology and internal organisation to achieve those increases in productivity essential to attain the higher rate of returns on capital required by the rentiers to guarantee in consequence the stability of the system.
23 Kregel (2007) formulates a thesis of inherent instability in the financial system, with reference to the specific conditions that characterised it in the first half of 2007.
24 Vicarelli (1987, 243). It is, however, to be borne in mind that for this author the accumulation of capital is not limited solely to the production of commodities, and economic policy cannot therefore seek pointers solely in market indications (Garofalo and Gnesutta 2009, 24–6)

References

Allen, F. and Gale, D. (2001), *Comparing Financial Systems*, Cambridge, MA, MIT Press.

Bernand, H. and Bisignano, J. (2003), *Financial Intermediary Transformation: Risk Absorption, Transfer and Trading in the U.S. Financial System*, Ente per gli studi monetari, bancari e finanziari "Luigi Einaudi", Quaderni di ricerche, No. 54.

Bordo, M., Eichengreen, B., Klingebiel, D. and Martinez-Peria, M. S. (2001), "Is the Crisis Problem Growing More Severe?", *Economic Policy*, Vol. 16, No. 32.

Ciocca, P. and Nardozzi, G. (1993), *L'alto prezzo del denaro. Un'interpretazione dei tassi d'interesse internazionali*, Bari-Roma, Laterza.

Davidson, P. (2003), "The Terminology of Uncertainty in Economics and the Philosophy of an Active Role for Government Policies", in Runde, J. and Mizuhare, S. (eds), *The Philosophy of Keynes's Economics: Probability, Uncertainty and Convention*, London, Routledge.

Dimsky, G. A. (1996), "Kalecki's Monetary Economics", in King, J. E. (ed.), *An Alternative Macroeconomic Theory: The Kaleckian Model and Post-Keynesian Economics*, Boston/Dordrecht/London, Kluwer Academic Publisher.

Fischer, S. (2008), "Concluding Panel Comments", in BIS, *Financial System and Macroeconomic Resilience*, Sixth BIS Annual Conference, 18–19 June, BIS Papers, 41.

Gambino, A. (1969), *Introduzione alla economica creditizia*, Turin, Boringhieri.

Garofalo, G. and Gnesutta, C. (2010), "A Return to Fundamentals: Fausto Vicarelli's Thought on Finance v. Growth and Efficiency v. Stability in the Financial System", *Rivista italiana delgi economisti*, Vol. 15, n.1.

Gnesutta, C. (1983), "Il rapporto tra dinamica dell'accumulazione ed evoluzione dei sistemi finanziari: alcune riflessioni sul caso italiano", *Note economiche*, Vol. 16, No. 3.

Gnesutta, C. (1992), "Il rapporto flussi-stock nei modelli macroeconomici di derivazione keynesiana", in Jossa, B. and Nardi, A. (eds), *Lezioni di macroeconomia*, Bologna, Il Mulino.

Graziani, A. (2003), *The Monetary Theory of Production*, Cambridge, Cambridge University Press.

Greenspan, A. (2005), *Risk Transfer and Financial Stability*, Federal Reserve of Chicago, 41st Annual Conference on Bank Structure, 5 May.

Kalecki, M. (1937), "The Principle of Increasing Risk", *Economica*, Vol. 4, No. 16 (reproduced in Osiatysky, J. (1990), *Collected Works of Michal Kalecki, Vol. I: Capitalism. Business Cycles and Full Employment*, Oxford, Clarendon Press).

Keynes, J. M. (1936), *The General Theory of Money, Interest, Employment*, London, Macmillan.

Keynes, J. M. (1973), *The Collected Writings. XIII: The General Theory and After. Part I Preparation* (edited by Moggridge, D.), London, Macmillan.

King, J. E. (ed.) (2003), *The Elgar Companion to Post Keynesian Economics*, Cheltenham/Northampton, Edward Elgar.

Kregel, J. (2007), *The Natural Instability of Financial Markets*, Levy Economic Institute WP No. 523.

Lavoie, M. (1996), "Horizontalism, Structuralism, Liquidity Preference and the Principle of Increasing Risk", *Scottish Journal of Political Economy*, Vol. 43, No. 3.

Minsky, H. P. (1975), *John Maynard Keynes*, New York, Columbia University Press.

Minsky, H. P. (1982), *Can "It" Happen Again: Essays on Instability and Finance*, Armonk, NY, Sharpe.

Myers, S. C. and Majluf, N. J. (1984), "Corporate Financing and Investment Decision When Firms Have Information That Investors Do Not Have." *Journal of Financial Economics*, Vol. 13, No. 2.

Nardozzi, G. (2002), *Interesse, profitto e borsa negli anni Ottanta e Novanta*, in Nardozzi, G. (a cura), *I rapporti tra finanza e distribuzione del reddito: un'interpretazione dell'economia di fine secolo*, Rome, LUISS Edizioni.

Panico, C. (1992), *Un confronto tra i modelli macroeconomici finanziari di Tobin e quelli di derivazione kaldoriana*, in Jossa, B. and Nardi, A. (eds), *Lezioni di macroeconomia*, Bologna, Il Mulino.

Parrinello, S. (1976), "Aspetti controversi del modello keynesiano", *Politica ed Economia*, No. 6.

Parrinello, S. (1998), "Equilibrium", entry in Kurz, H. and Salvadori, N. (eds), *The Elgar Companion to Classical Economics*, Cheltenham, Edward Elgar.

Sawyer, M. C. (1996), *Money, Finance and Interest Rates*, in Arestis, P. (ed.) (1996), *Keynes, Money and the Open Economy: Essays in Honour of Paul Davidson*, Aldershot, Edward Elgar.

Tobin, J. (1969), "A General Equilibrium Approach to Monetary Theory", *Journal of Money, Credit, and Banking*, Vol. 1, No. 1.

Vercelli, A. (2001), *Minsky, Keynes and the Structural Instability of a Sophisticated Monetary Economy*, in Bellofiore, R. and Ferri, P. (eds), *Financial Fragility and Investment in the Capital Economy*, Vol. II, Cheltenham, Edward Elgar.

Vicarelli, F. (1974), *Introduzione*, in Vicarelli, F. (a cura di), *La controversia keynesiana*, Bologna, Il Mulino.

Vicarelli, F. (1983), *From Equilibrium to Probability: A Reinterpretation of the Method of the General Theory*, in Vicarelli, F. (ed.), *Keynes's Relevance Today*, London, Macmillan.

Vicarelli, F. (1987), *La questione economica nella società italiana. Analisi e proposte*, Bologna, Il Mulino.

Visco, I. (2009), "La crisi finanziaria e le previsioni degli economisti", *Bancaria*, No. 3 (also "The Financial Crisis and Economists' Forecasts", *BIS Review*, No. 49).

12 A new Triffin paradox for the global economy?[1]

Jan A. Kregel[2]

In the 1950s Robert Triffin warned of the breakdown of the Bretton Woods international monetary system.[3] Economists are not well known for the accuracy of their predictions. Triffin is one of the few economists to have made a correct prediction. Yet, no one took any heed of his predictions, even when it was clear that they were coming true. His analysis produced what has come to be known as the "Triffin paradox" or the Triffin dilemma. I am going to suggest that there is a similar "paradox" inherent in the globalisation of the international trading and financial system, and that it threatens the breakdown of the system.

I The original Triffin paradox

Under the Bretton Woods Agreement, countries were given the choice of setting the par value of their currencies for current account transactions in terms of gold or dollars. Since virtually all belligerent countries finished the war in debt to the US for emergency aid or war supplies, the US held virtually all the gold or a claim on it. Thus, the US was the only country able to fix the par value of its currency in terms of gold, while all other countries set their par values in terms of the dollar. The dollar thus effectively replaced gold in the Bretton Woods system and the value of the dollar was determined by the holdings of US gold reserves. Since all other countries had set par values against the dollar, they required dollar reserves to ensure current account convertibility. This meant that the stability of exchange rates was dependent on the intervention by all central banks, except the US, to support the dollar. It made the US dollar the only intervention currency and placed the stability of exchange rates on the willingness and ability of non-US central banks to intervene in foreign exchange markets to defend the value of the dollar. (It also meant that the US dollar enjoyed an intervention band that was double that of the other currencies since all cross rates were traded and calculated by trading against the dollar.) As a result the US dollar became the source of international liquidity and the basis for the reserves of the international monetary system. It thus effectively replaced gold. However, under the Bretton Woods system, unlike the operation of the gold standard, where the supply of gold was determined by mining and the dishoarding of jewellery, the supply of dollars was determined by the balance of payments position of the US.

Immediately following the war, nearly all of the world's monetary gold was in the US, most of the signatories of the Bretton Woods treaties owed money to the US. Further, their reconstruction depended on imports from the US, the only economy not damaged by war, so the US was in balance of payments surplus. Thus, not only was gold scarce outside the US, the dollar was also scarce. Although "dollar scarcity" was thought by some economists to be a permanent condition, the US external position soon reversed and the US was creating the dollar liquidity that the international system so badly needed to allow central banks to build the dollar reserves necessary to preserve exchange rate stability. However, the amount of dollars held outside the US eventually surpassed the gold reserves held by the US evaluated at the official Bretton Woods parity. Thus the Triffin paradox: the successful operation of the international financial system depended on an expansion of dollar reserves to keep international liquidity growing in step with rapidly expanding world trade. But this could only be achieved by a US payments deficit that continually increased foreign claims on the fixed US gold supply. Once these claims exceeded the dollar value of the gold supply at the $35 parity, the convertibility of the dollar into gold at the official parity depended on the willingness of foreigners to refrain from converting dollars into gold. This created a dilemma for foreign holders of dollars, in particular foreign central banks that were responsible for stabilising the dollar and thus had to accumulate ever-larger dollar balances as non-official holders converted dollars to other currencies, in particular DM. A recognition of the appreciation of the dollar value of gold – a depreciation of the dollar relative to the other currencies – would mean capital losses on the dollar reserves. Thus foreign holders of the dollar faced a catch-22 situation reflected in the Triffin paradox. If they converted the dollars into gold at the US Treasury (they could not sell the dollars for other currencies since they were responsible for fixing the rates of their currencies relative to the dollar, which was already in chronic excess supply in foreign exchange markets) this would further reduce the gold backing the outstanding dollar balances and make it more likely that the dollar would be devalued, depreciating all of their dollar reserve holdings and producing large foreign exchange losses on their balance sheets. If they converted excess dollar balances they risked precipitating a devaluation, and if they did not they risked even larger losses if the devaluation occurred in any case.

Many countries (especially France) argued that the problem of excess dollar balances could be resolved if the US tightened its domestic policies and ran balance of payments surpluses, but this remedy for the dollar surplus would simply have reduced the growth of international liquidity and created the risk of global recession – it was just such a case that Keynes had warned against when he pointed out the necessity of avoiding "asymmetric balance of payments adjustments" in the new Bretton Woods system.

The result was a series of ad hoc measures to prevent dollar conversion into gold and to increase foreign demand for dollars, while at the same time countries put pressure on the US to absorb some of the outstanding dollars by reducing growth in order to produce a balance of payments surplus. The US resisted, mainly because John Kennedy had already pledged to close the ICBM missile gap, and most importantly the GNP gap through expansionary fiscal policy, both of which were incompatible with the domestic policies required to stabilise the value of the dollar, which he had also pledged to defend in the closing days of his campaign. Most of the subsequent difficulties of the Bretton Woods system were due to the attempts by the US to preserve the gold value of the dollar in the presence of a US expansion that continued to produce US deficits and expanding foreign claims on the US. The result was a menagerie of ad hoc policy measures including two-tier gold markets, interest equalisation taxes, operation twists, liquidity balances of payments and the birth of the policy of benign neglect that eventually showed that the internal contradictions elucidated in the Triffin paradox could not be resolved. The problem, as Triffin had pointed out, was the use of a national currency as the international means of payment and liquidity. To be an international currency it had to meet the needs of international trade financing, but as a national currency its international supply was determined by domestic demand conditions that would not necessarily produce changes in supply in step with world demand. Since the issuing country would be unwilling to subordinate its domestic economic policy to the needs of the international economy, the currency would be inherently unstable.

There were three ways out of the Triffin dilemma, a truly international currency issued by a global central bank to replace the dollar at the centre of the international system, a global deflation produced by an attempt to reduce the supply of dollars to the US gold supply, or the default by the US on its foreign debts through the elimination of the convertibility of the dollar, devaluation of the dollar and the introduction of flexible exchange rates. The last remedy was chosen (note that the US had never allowed residents to own gold for monetary purposes, so that there was no domestic indebtedness in either gold or other foreign currencies and the devaluation thus had no direct impact on domestic balance sheets).

The introduction of flexible exchange rates did not prove to be a solution, for it did not remove the basic paradox, the use of a single national currency as the international reserve and vehicle currency. It also produced a profound change in the international system. The Bretton Woods system was founded on recognition of the incompatibility of a system of fixed exchange rates and free international capital flows. Although the gold standard had survived what were extremely free and integrated international capital flows to the end of the century, the experience of hot money flows in the interwar period and the difficulties encountered by the major economies had convinced most economists that free capital flows and fixed rates were incompatible. With the introduction of flexible rates there was no longer any theoretical impediment to allowing capital flows, and the most vocal adherents of the floating rate system argued that international speculation would in fact make the floating rate system behave as if it were stable.

There are a large number of factors that accompanied the liberalisation of international capital markets, such as the oil crisis, the declining profitability of banks in the segmented US system, the creation of financial futures and options to hedge the fluctuations in flexible exchange rates, the growth of the Eurodollar market in response to the restrictions introduced in the US in the 1960s, financial deregulation, the Volcker revolution in monetary policy and the increasing globalisation of the economy. They are all directly or indirectly the result of the attempts to escape from the horns of the Triffin dilemma.

II The twenty-first-century Triffin paradox

The proposition advanced in this chapter is that the current globalised international financial system has produced a new strain of the Triffin paradox in which developing countries have replaced the US, but since they do not issue an international currency they are forced to undergo the solution to the Triffin paradox that the US avoided: deflation and recession to ensure that the international supply of their currencies does not exceed global investment demand. The rest of this chapter will attempt to give a brief outline of this twenty-first-century Triffin paradox.

Let us start by recalling that one of the objectives for the reform of the international monetary system raised by Lord Keynes, the representative of the British Treasury, was that the new system should not jeopardise domestic policy objectives. Keynes was in particular concerned to defend the right of countries to full employment. As noted above, the breakdown of the gold standard system, indeed of the entire political system in Europe was due to the high levels of unemployment that were generated by what were judged to be excessively mobile international capital flows under the gold standard. In order to protect national policy autonomy Keynes's proposals for reform argued that the design of the international system should produce

> the least possible interference with internal national policies ... [and] operate not only to the general advantage but also to the individual advantage of each of the participants.... No participant must be asked to do or offer anything which is not in his own true long-term interest.
>
> (Keynes 1943, pp. 19–20)

Indeed, Keynes went further and insisted that the plan "must be capable of application, irrespective of the type and principle of government and economic policy existing in the prospective member states" (Keynes 1943, p. 19).

In addition, Keynes argued that fixed exchange rate systems, such as the gold standard, produced what he called an "asymmetric" international adjustment burden that penalised countries in balance of payments deficit. Since a deficit eventually depletes foreign reserves, an adjustment policy would be required if the country were to remain on the gold standard. Because a deficit country usually had a public or private sector deficit, the elimination of the foreign imbalance meant reducing current public or private spending, thereby reducing total demand, and income and employment. It was usually argued that such countries were "living beyond their means" and thus the "belt tightening" was also morally justified.

But the international economy is a zero sum game; for every country with a balance of payments deficit there is a balance of payments surplus in some other country or group of countries. By analogy with the deficit countries, these countries may be classified as having excess savings. However, these countries are seldom accused of living *below* their means. Saving is morally justified, promoting growth and employment is not.

Since the international economic system is simultaneously determined it is impossible to determine whether balance of payments disequilibria are caused by the excess saving or the excess spending countries – one could not exist without the other. However, in a fixed exchange rate system the fact that the country with the balance of payments deficit eventually runs out of foreign exchange reserves means that it is forced to adjust its internal policies to accommodate the policy of the excess saving countries. Since this can only be done by reducing imports (increasing exports would require the rest of the world to spend more, which it is unwilling to do) it involves reducing income and employment. Since the excess savers are never forced to reduce their saving due to an excess accumulation of international reserves, only one group of countries, those in deficit, has to adjust – thus the adjustment is asymmetrical. And since the adjustment always requires lower employment, it not only jeopardises national employment policy, it also produces a reduction in employment and unemployment for the global economy. Under asymmetric adjustment the global economy could never reach full employment of labour and would suffer from excess saving. But, for Keynes, this was not morally justified since unemployed labour was just as inefficient a use of resources as the misallocation of capital.

In the present international economic environment the differences go beyond different national employment policies and extend to growth rates. Developed countries, with relatively high levels of per capita income and wealth are more interested in ensuring the economic efficiency of the international economic system; this is expressed as policies designed to preserve their capital and maximising the rate of return on capital. Thus, exchange rate and asset price stability and allocative efficiency of financial markets carry a high priority. This is achieved by ensuring that prices are stable – and the only successful inflation-fighting policies that developed countries appear to have discovered is to keep growth below potential, i.e. conditions of excess supply.

Developing countries, on the other hand, with much lower per capita income and wealth levels, might be more interested in increasing their income and wealth levels as rapidly as possible. Here the goal is more appropriately the highest achievable rate of growth of per capita incomes. But, not only is there a difference in growth policies, there are substantial natural differences in potential growth rates. Not only do developed countries operate policies to keep growth below potential, the potential growth rates are themselves lower than in developing countries. These differences complement the differences in employment policies observed in the Bretton Woods discussions.

Now, there is no reason why these diverse objectives should not be compatible, indeed theory argues that the free flow of capital around the globe in search of the most remunerative uses should maximise global growth (although it says little about how these benefits are distributed across countries). However, the recent experience of increasingly frequent and intense financial crises suggests that this is not the case.

Further, the experience of the response to the recent financial crises suggests that protecting the interests of those seeking to preserve their capital and to maximise their rates of return on the investment of capital has tended to dominate the objectives of those countries seeking to maximise growth of per capita incomes. The provision of emergency funding in support of exchange rate convertibility and stability has served primarily to provide the means of repaying international creditors without loss and has clearly been at the expense of the borrowing countries seeking higher income levels. The introduction of austerity policies in the name of reducing the inflationary potential of the bailout of failed domestic banking systems, but which simply curtail growth in order to provide balance of payments surpluses capable of generating foreign exchange to repay foreign creditors is an even more direct example of sacrificing income growth in developing countries for the preservation of capital values in developed countries.

It was to be the role of the new international monetary system created at Bretton Woods to provide the means of making domestic full employment policies compatible with fixed exchange rates. In the post-Bretton Woods world the developing countries, with high potential growth rates relative to the developed countries with lower potential growth rates, have both the tendency and the necessity of running balance of payments deficits. This tendency is linked to the generally accepted existence of a resource gap or savings gap that has to be filled by imports of instrumental goods and can only be paid for by borrowing from foreign suppliers, i.e. financed with foreign capital inflows. This is buttressed by the idea that developing countries with high growth potential also have high relative real rates of return on investment and thus are ideal investment targets for developed countries with excess savings and few attractive domestic outlets for investment. But, the larger the differential in relative growth rates and the larger the resource gaps, the larger the required capital inflows and associated balance of payments deficits. But, the larger the deficit, the higher the likelihood of an exchange rate adjustment or depreciation, creating higher volatility in returns and greater risks to developed country investors, leading to reductions in capital inflows and demands for higher risk-adjusted rates of return. Thus, the more successful the system is in allowing developing countries to achieve their potential growth rates, the less willing will developed country investors be to lend to them to permit it.

Thus, the Triffin paradox of the twenty-first century implies that the more successful developing countries are in achieving their potential growth rates by borrowing in international capital markets to fill their resources gaps, the larger will be their foreign imbalances and the less likely they will be to retain the capital inflows required to support the growth rate. Just as large US deficits increased the risk of holding dollars, larger developing country deficits increase the risk of investing in them. In the case of the dollar, dollar balances were held because central banks had to support their Bretton Woods parity and the dollar retained international value that was in excess of its gold backing. In the case of developing countries, exchange rates are held up by the force of capital flows themselves, which in most cases exceed the funds needed to meet balance of payments shortfalls and produce a continuous upward pressure on the currency. Also, because of their higher potential growth rates, most developing countries' monetary policies produce interest rates that are higher than those abroad, providing an additional attraction for foreign investors. This produces a condition for foreign investors that is much like the "catch 22" faced by central banks under Bretton Woods. As the balance of payments deteriorates the risk-adjusted rate of return on investment declines, but withdrawing capital will inevitably produce exchange rate instability that erodes or eliminates the nominal excess returns expected to be earned in developing countries. Eventually, the balance tips towards increased risk and the result is that the dilemma is resolved by an exchange rate crisis that requires an adjustment policy that generates a decline in income growth and employment, in many cases wiping out the accumulated benefits of the period of high growth.

Thus, the same asymmetric adjustment that made deficit countries adjust their policies to those of surplus countries also forces developing countries to adjust their policies to make them compatible with the policy objectives of the developed countries. But, in a difference from the Bretton Woods regime, it is now the reversal of international capital flows that produces the adjustment. A country that grows too rapidly, and produces a large balance of payments deficit that threatens exchange rate stability and thus its excess rate of return finds that foreign capital reverses and a financial crisis forces adjustment. It is somewhat ironical that when these crises occur, or appear to be impending, it is the IMF that enforces adjustment in the form of stabilisation policies and letters of intent that reduce income growth and employment, without any recognition that the difficulties faced by developing countries might be at least in part caused by the slow growth and insufficient imports of the developed countries. Thus, the current system suffers from the same defects as that prior to Bretton Woods, a tendency to converge towards the (lower) growth rate of the developed countries and the tendency to accept their policy objectives of financial asset and goods prices stability and efficiency to preserve capital and maximise rates of return.

Notes

1 This chapter represents an elaboration of a presentation to the 13th meeting of the Brazilian Congress of Economists and the 7th Congress of the Association of Economists from Latin-America and the Caribbean, 15 September 1999.
2 Levy Economics Institute of Bard College and Center for Full Employment and Price Stability, Kansas City.
3 In a series of articles that originally appeared in the Banca Nazionale del Lavoro Quarterly Review and were republished as Triffin (1960)

References

Keynes, J. M. (1943). Proposals for an International Clearing Union, British Government Publication, Cmd. 6437, London (April). Reprinted in J. Keith Horsefield (ed.) (1969), *International Monetary Fund, 1945–65: Twenty Years of International Monetary Cooperation*, vol. III: *Documents*, Washington, DC, International Monetary Fund, pp. 19–36.

Triffin, R. (1960). *Gold and the Dollar Crisis*, New Haven, CT, Yale University Press.

13 Interest and the general price level

Some critical notes on 'The new consensus monetary policy model'

Massimo Pivetti[*]

1 This contribution aims to compare the relationships between the money rate of interest, the mark-up and the general price level one finds in the inflation targeting framework, known also as the new IS-LM model, with those one finds in the explanation of the price level based on the so-called monetary theory of distribution. The two approaches have a few features in common, which I think make such a comparison an interesting undertaking.

Both approaches view the rate of interest as the monetary policy instrument. By directly controlling nominal short-term rates, monetary authorities are believed to be generally capable of also governing the course of long-term rates.[1] In both approaches money is regarded as demand determined, and, given the course of labour productivity and the external price of imports, a country's inflation performance is seen as ultimately reflecting the behaviour of the following three nominal variables: the money rate of interest, the exchange rate and money wages. However, as we shall see in what follows, the connection between these variables – notably between the rate of interest and money wages – is altogether different in the two approaches.

The inflation targeting (IT) framework is permeated by the neoclassical notion of a long-run equilibrium real interest rate – Wicksell's 'natural' rate of interest – to which the interest rate policy instrument must be adjusted in order to check fluctuations in inflation and keep output at potential. The 'natural' rate notion accounts for two essential features of the IT framework.

The first is that money is neutral, at least in the long run. It is perhaps worth pointing out that, with respect to the simultaneous presence of money endogeneity and monetary neutrality, there is actually nothing new in the 'new consensus model'. As I have argued elsewhere (see Pivetti 2001), in any approach in which the existence of some mechanism is postulated by which the money rate of interest adjusts, or is adjusted, to a 'natural' rate, money will be ultimately regarded as neutral, independently of whether it is treated as exogenous or endogenous.

The second feature of the IT framework which is strictly linked to the 'natural' rate notion is the distinction one finds in that framework between a 'headline' or actual rate of inflation and an 'underlying' or core rate of inflation (see e.g. Debelle 1997; Goodfriend 2007, and Wynne 2008 on estimation problems). The latter is the inflation rate that would just reflect any discrepancy that may from time to time arise between the 'natural' rate of interest and the actual or money rate; it is the inflation rate on which central banks should focus their attention and to which they should respond through their interest rate policy. The 'headline' inflation rate would instead be acted upon also by 'non-monetary' determinants of inflation – i.e. by circumstances which have nothing to do with those changes in money wages and prices that are believed to reflect the balance of demand and supply factors in the economy. For example, rises in food and energy prices, as well as in indirect taxes and other government-set prices, would be included in the 'headline' inflation rate but excluded from the measurement of the 'underlying' rate.

Central banks should therefore not respond to such 'non-monetary' price rises by increasing their interest rate policy instrument, unless they were expected to have 'second round effects' on inflation – i.e. unless they were expected to act in due course upon the behaviour of money wages. In the latter case, however, by trying to check the future course of money wages through the contraction of activity levels, interest rate policy would in fact aim, by a sort of pre-emptive action, at offsetting cost-push pressures on inflation: the 'natural' rate/policy rate antinomy – the very core of the entire IT framework – would just disappear from the picture (more on this below).

In the IT literature it is generally assumed that the 'natural' rate of interest is known by the monetary authorities, in the sense that, though central banks cannot directly observe its level, they are, however, believed to be capable of tracking the natural equilibrium of the economy and the corresponding equilibrium real rate of interest. It is, however, rather immaterial whether, within the IT framework, one assumes that the bank can actually measure through time the level of the 'natural' rate, or that its course is *inferred* from that of inflation. (The former of these two views may be simply regarded as a vulgar or 'rational expectations' version of the latter, which is actually Wicksell's theory.[2]) What really matters for IT is the tenet that, if inflation rises, a raising of nominal interest rates by the bank, provided it is sufficiently large as to raise real rates also, will succeed in lowering inflation, while keeping output at potential.

2 In actual fact, however, a dearer money policy is, by itself, directly inflationary. In the words of a former chairman of the US Joint Economic Committee, raising interest rates to fight inflation is like 'throwing gasoline on fire' (Patman, quoted in Seelig 1974, p. 1049). Empirical work on firms' pricing behaviour has given robust evidence of the fact that interest rates are regarded as a cost, with the corollary that they look to establish a price rise in response to increased interest costs (cf. on this also Gaiotti and Secchi 2004).[3] Evidence has also been produced showing that the price/wage ratio tends to increase following increases in interest rates, i.e. that real wages tend to fall as a consequence of dearer money policies (see e.g. Barth and Ramey 2001, pp. 17–18). That policy rate increases may cause prices to rise, rather than to fall, has been acknowledged even within the IT literature, in which references can occasionally be found to mortgage interest payments and their impact on the consumer price index (CPI) or 'headline' inflation rate (see e.g. Debelle 1997; Ball 2005, p. 136n; Wynne 2008, pp. 211–12). But the inflationary effect of a dearer money policy, due to the passing over of increasing interest costs to prices, is generally viewed as a short-run phenomenon. With respect to the longer run, the general conviction remains that the demand channel is bound to dominate, more than counterbalancing, through lower money wages, the inflationary effect of higher interest rates.

Thus, according to the 'new monetary policy consensus model', in which conditions of monopolistic competition are assumed within a 'real business cycle' framework, given the price p of a unit of consumption goods and labour productivity a in units of consumption goods, a raising of the rate of interest by the central bank will reduce aggregate consumption by increasing the opportunity cost of current consumption in terms of future consumption – interest as the opportunity cost of capital may be disregarded, since capital and capitalists are generally absent in the model under consideration, where positive mark-ups simply mean that firm profits are positive and constitute a component part of total household income: see Appendix 1.[4] In the face of the reduced consumption demand, firms will offer a lower nominal wage w, thereby inducing households to supply a smaller quantity of labour: the smaller quantity of labour required to satisfy, given a, the reduced consumption demand. Both w and total labour input n will thus fall (the fall in n being viewed as merely amounting to a reduction in hours per worker), with a causal relation going from w to n. Since perfect price flexibility is ruled out, i.e. p is not adjusted downward in the short run, the real wage w_r also falls and the mark-up μ rises above its profit maximizing level μ^*. In the longer run, however, firms would tend to adjust p so as to keep μ constant at μ^*: p will therefore eventually be reduced to restore μ to its profit-maximizing level.

So, in this vision, the rise of the ratio of prices to money wages consequent upon a dearer money policy is only a short-run phenomenon. The mark-up is *not* directly connected to the rate of interest. Indeed, the rate of interest is not seen as a distributive variable in the long run: its role is merely that of ensuring that consumption moves over time in line with labour productivity, so as to clear the economy-wide goods market by inducing households to keep spending neither more nor less than their whole current income. A raising of the rate of interest lowers money wages and eventually also prices by directly bringing about a contraction of aggregate spending. The opposite occurs in the case of a lowering of interest by the central bank. Dearer or cheaper money policies do not affect the price/wage ratio in the long run.

If the central bank knew the level of the 'natural' rate of interest, then the best monetary policy would be one which kept through time the actual real rate at its 'natural' level, so as to keep output at its potential while at the same time ensuring price stability. The main challenge for those in charge of monetary policy would be that of not yielding to the political temptation of keeping the real rate below its 'natural' level, with a view of bringing output and employment above their 'natural' levels. Thus, to the extent that monetary policy was performed at its best, money would be neutral in the short as well as in the long run. In any case, according to the new consensus theory, even if monetary policy could not be performed at its best, possibly due to an 'imperfect estimate' of the 'unobservable' equilibrium real rate by the bank, it would have only short-run effects on real activity, and, provided that it targeted inflation at a low level, would keep economic activity near capacity. In sum, the new consensus theory of monetary policy shares with the whole neoclassical tradition the conviction that monetary policy can affect only nominal variables in the longer term.[5]

3 There is, however, little evidence that the real world works in the way postulated by the new consensus model, which encourages central banks to focus single-mindedly on fighting inflation. While several central banks have actually followed some sort of IT strategy, their interest rate policies appear to have produced long periods of high unemployment. Empirical evidence seems in fact to show that when central banks have succeeded in lowering inflation – no matter whether they were explicit inflation targeters or not[6] – they have also brought about slower growth and higher unemployment.[7]

An outstanding example of a central bank which has focused single-mindedly on fighting inflation is that represented by the European Central Bank (ECB), the world's most independent central bank (on this see Buiter 2006, pp. 20ff.). If the relevant criteria are the long-run neutrality of monetary policy as being among the central banker's firmest beliefs and the inflation rate as the bank's overriding policy objective, then the ECB is indeed an inflation targeter. However, this central bank tends to present its monetary strategy as somewhat more traditional, with respect to the strategy supported by the current consensus (see e.g. European Central Bank 2008). Its published materials keep emphasizing the role of the money supply as a determinant of inflation, as well as the tenet that money is the variable that the monetary authority can actually directly control. Monitoring some measure of the money supply, together with the conditions of supply and demand in the goods and factor markets, is the declared ECB's monetary policy strategy. Although how this so-called 'dual pillar approach' works in practice is not very clear, it would seem that it ultimately boils down to the Governing Council of the ECB taking into account deviations of M3 growth from some reference or 'benchmark' value when making decisions about the policy rates.[8]

In any case, ever since its conception in 1992 (the statute of the ECB is part of the Treaty of Maastricht), and even more from its birth as a monetary authority in 1999, the average rate of growth of real GDP in the Euro area has been very low by historical standards, contributing to the area's persistently high levels of unemployment, largely as a result of the inflation rate having been the bank's overriding policy objective.[9] Outside the Euro area, the United Kingdom is the largest European country whose central bank is generally regarded as having pursued through the 1990s an IT strategy (cf. Stiehler 1995; Debelle 1997), and one could hardly speak of a long-run vertical Phillips curve with respect to that experience.[10]

4 The fact that IT policies have on the whole resulted in slower growth and higher unemployment hardly supports the notion of a long-run neutrality for monetary policy, by far the most significant theoretical tenet of the IT framework. This fact seems rather to support an analysis of the relationships between interest rates and the general price level significantly different from that put forward by the new consensus theory.

Outside the neoclassical analytical framework, one would normally acknowledge that output is demand constrained both in the short and the long run, and that the level and composition of effective demand through time largely depend on the behaviour of income distribution. Hence the overall relevance of a 'monetary' explanation of distribution to the question of the real effects of monetary policy: if monetary policy does play a significant role in the determination of normal distribution, it will also exert a key influence on the level and composition of output. Indeed, as we shall see presently, no monetary neutrality can possibly be postulated on the basis of the relationships between interest rates and prices one can arrive at within the framework of the monetary explanation of distribution (on which see especially Pivetti 1991, 1998a and 1999).

In this framework, the mark-up and the long-term rate of interest are closely related, in the sense that, *ceteris paribus*, the course of the former through time is governed by that of the latter. As in the IT framework, monetary policy exerts itself over interest rates (both short- and long-term rates), and money is endogenous. But, differently from the IT framework, here there is no 'natural' or equilibrium real rate of interest. The rate of interest is just a policy variable, determined from outside the system of production, ultimately by class relations (cf. Pivetti 1999, pp. 292–4), which governs the ratio of prices to money wages. Given w and a, a raising of interest rates by the central bank raises p, the price level, because it increases the mark-ups, lowering w_r at the same time: see Appendix 2.

The rate of interest is thus regarded as an autonomous determinant of normal prices: a dearer money policy is by itself inflationary, through its direct impact on mark-ups. The overall net impact on the price level essentially depends on the effects that the policy determined interest rates will eventually exert on aggregate demand and employment, through their impact on income distribution and the other channels by which changes in interest rates are bound to affect activity levels,[11] starting from the leverage they exert on net exports through the exchange rate (more on this below). Should the net impact of a dearer money policy on aggregate demand and employment be negative, then the *higher* price/wage ratios brought about by it might eventually be accompanied by *lower* inflation if the repercussions of a weakening workers' bargaining power on the dynamic of money wages were sufficiently robust.

While what has just been said makes the direction of the long-run effects of a country's interest rate policy on the rate at which its price level increases highly problematic – both the impact of changes in distribution on aggregate demand and the responsiveness of money wages to changes in employment will be different in each different concrete situation – things are decidedly more clear-cut with respect to the inflation effects exerted by interest rate policy through the exchange rate channel. Let us now briefly comment on this aspect of the interest–inflation transmission.

5   A fixed exchange rate regime is not consistent with the IT framework, since the former, in association with freedom of capital movements, makes interest rate policy substantially endogenous. IT policies therefore *imply* flexible exchange rates, and it appears most likely that the exchange rate channel has actually played a decisive role in those cases in which dear money policies have succeeded in checking inflation (cf. Serrano 2008, on the Brazilian case; see also Ball 1999, pp. 136n and 155; Bodkin and Neder 2003). It is hardly necessary to point out that, to the extent to which a raising of interest rates by the central bank lowers inflation through a stronger domestic currency and lower import prices, we are completely outside the scope of the IT theoretical framework.

As to the alternative view of the relationships between interest rates and prices, one can say, once all the transmission channels referred to in the previous section are taken into account, that higher interest rates may succeed in checking inflation only if the higher ratio of prices to money wages they bring about, through their direct impact on mark-ups, is more than counterbalanced by: 1) the lowering of prices of imported inputs, expressed in domestic currency, through the exchange rate channel; 2) a reduction or slower rise of money wages as a result of the likely negative impact on employment brought about both by the change in normal income distribution and by the change in the exchange rate – i.e. by the contractionary effects on consumption spending and net exports caused by higher interest rates. This overall picture appears to be supported by the already mentioned circumstance that IT policies have on the whole resulted in higher unemployment and slower growth.

In the light of the monetary explanation of distribution, it is rather a *cheap money policy*, in the context of a fixed exchange rate regime, that should be regarded as the most promising policy to ensure low and stable inflation, without at the same time negatively impinging upon real activity levels. Capital control would of course have to become again a component part of the picture, in order to make cheap money consistent with the fixed exchange rate regime. As to the dynamic of money wages, it would have to be kept under control by means other than increases in unemployment – essentially by income policies, i.e. through the expansion of the welfare state, which in turn would be rendered financially easier by cheap money and the consequent lesser weight of interest payments in the public budget. Back to Bretton Woods, then? Yes, in a sense. But without the weakest component part of its theoretical underpinnings – without the 'marginal efficiency of capital' schedule, that is to say, and the connected Keynesian notion that all the shortcomings of capitalism would ultimately boil down to an insufficient downward flexibility of the rate of interest, which would make it difficult to bring it – and keep it – at its 'natural' or full-employment level.

6   The final question I should like to touch upon concerns the cultural derivation of the IT framework from the 'rules rather than discretion' framework, i.e. from the analyses of Kydland and Prescott (1977), Barro and Gordon (1983) and others. The notion that committing the central bank to a monetary policy rule is

necessary to avoid the inefficiency that arises when policy is formulated in a discretionary manner, thereby improving overall economic stability and welfare, has clearly inspired several specific monetary policy rules, such as the Taylor rule in its various formulations,[12] and may be regarded as a distinctive feature of the IT framework. As is well known, the theoretical considerations that monetary policy can affect only nominal variables and that rules are to be preferred to discretion, to resolve a time-inconsistency problem, eventually brought about the conviction that delegating monetary policy to individuals insulated from the rest of government was the best solution to achieve lower inflation. Central bank independence thus gradually emerged from those theoretical developments, buttressed through the 1990s and the current decade by the IT framework's insistence on the necessity for the central bank to pursue the inflation target without any constraints on its ability to set the instrument of monetary policy.

Supporters of the new consensus model of monetary policy are prone to believe that budgetary policies should also be supportive of the inflation target. This is because they believe that the central bankers' counter-inflationary credibility ultimately depends on inflation expectations remaining 'anchored', and they tend to regard a large and rising stock of public debt as a source of inflationary expectations, which may make it more difficult for the central bank to stabilize actual inflation. It is therefore important, in this view, for inflation targeting to succeed, that dearer money policies are *counterbalanced* by the formation of primary surpluses, so as to avoid the outcome of higher interest rates, by increasing the debt servicing burden for the government, adding to the stock of debt and to inflationary expectations, resulting in a vicious circle of higher interest rates and higher debt. It is also very likely that inflation targets, as they are pursued in actual fact – notably by the ECB – need to be supported by primary surpluses with a view to checking the possible sensitivity of money wages to movements in the 'headline' or consumer price index inflation rate.[13] So, in the face of rising food and energy prices, or of higher indirect taxes and other government-set prices, as well as higher mortgage interest charges, the formation of primary surpluses will be deemed necessary in order to 'pre-empt', through its contractionary impact on economic activity and employment, cost-push pressures on inflation.

In the light of all this, it can be said that not only has the IT framework helped to buttress central bank independence; it has also contributed to the gradual diffusion of the idea that overall policy-making – that is, both monetary and budgetary policy – in the hands of independent technocrats, rather than politicians, would be the most appropriate solution to bring about the best possible outcome in terms of economic stability and long-run welfare.

7   While the theoretical developments mentioned in the previous section have all had their origin in American academic circles, it is in the European context especially that they have exerted a significant leverage on actual policy-making. As to US overall policy-making, it can be affirmed that the influence of the theoretical developments under consideration on this has been close to zero – as if

the Fed and the other US policy-makers had 'not learned modern theory too well' (Ball 2005, p. 268)[14] – so that the inflation rate has never become, in the US context, the overriding policy objective.

I think that this interesting difference between the European and the American case can be accounted for by three sets of factors. First, account must be taken of the Treaty of Maastricht and the Stability Pact, and the consequent renunciation of national sovereignty in the monetary and fiscal fields by each EU member country. For each national government, this has brought about a situation of 'political irresponsibility', which has greatly facilitated in Europe a declining policy commitment to low unemployment (see on this Pivetti 1998b and 2004). In the case of the United States, a situation of substantially unlimited national sovereignty deprives policy-makers of any pretext: employment and growth must be sustained almost at any cost, if the certain loss of domestic consensus is to be avoided. Second, owing to an older and much more marked declining influence of the unions, relatively high levels of unemployment have long ceased to be necessary, in the US case, to check the dynamic of wages and allow significant changes in distribution in favour of the wealthiest sections of the population. Finally, the change in class relations and overall distributive conditions aimed at over the last thirty years within the two social contexts was undoubtedly much more radical for Europe than for the United States – think of the privatization drive and the process of gradual dismantling of the powerful European welfare state. Actual policy-making in Europe could hardly have been capable of focusing single-mindedly on fighting inflation, if the conviction had not been pervasively spread that this focus would have benefited the real economy as well, and was in any case ineluctable.

As far as the European context is concerned, therefore, it seems reasonable to regard the theoretical developments under consideration and their chief more direct underpinnings – the notions of credibility and commitment to policy rules born out of the rational expectations 'revolution' – as a thick theoretical make-up that has exerted a significant influence in playing down the attraction of a return to the full-employment and growth policies of the first three post-war decades, and especially a return to the class relations those policies had helped to bring about in a substantial part of Europe. In other important social contexts, the role actually played by the new consensus model of monetary policy may be altogether different, and perhaps more pre-emptive in character.

Consider for example the outstanding case of Brazil, whose '*governo popular*' might eventually decide that the time is ripe to pass from an alms policy aimed at the most miserable part of the population, to substantial and lasting improvements in the living standard of its great majority – through agrarian reform, higher real wages and overall income redistribution, with the consequent more rapid expansion of a potentially enormous domestic market. It seems to me that an independent central banker, possibly of American academic formation, in any case fiercely addicted to fighting inflation by the dearest possible money policy, is the surest antidote against all this.

Appendix 1

Interest and prices: an IT framework

The following outline of the IT approach is essentially derived from Goodfriend (see Goodfriend 2002, 2005 and 2007), one of the chief exponents of the new consensus theory of monetary policy and perhaps its most convinced supporter. In stating the theoretical underpinnings of the consensus to analyse and discuss monetary policy as explicit interest rate policy, he underlines the fact that, besides rational expectations and a real business cycle setting, 'the consensus theory of monetary policy has at its core monopolistically competitive firms that set product prices at a mark-up on the marginal cost of production. Because price adjustment is costly, firms consider changing their product prices only if demand and cost conditions threaten to compress or elevate actual mark-ups significantly and persistently relative to flexible-price profit-maximizing levels. An excessively high mark-up yields too much market share to competitors, and a mark-up that is too low fails to exploit market power enough to maximize profits' (Goodfriend 2007, pp. 24–5).

So let us see how by manipulating the short-term rate of interest central banks are believed to be capable of acting upon the price level and the behaviour of actual ouput. Following Goodfriend, we can write for aggregate output

$$C = a \cdot n$$

where C is the quantity produced of a single composite consumption good, a is labour productivity in units of consumption goods and n is overall labour input. There are neither means of production (i.e. capital) nor capitalists. Households own the firms, so that total household income can be written

$$w_r \cdot n + (a \cdot n - w_r \cdot n) = a \cdot n$$

where w_r is the real wage rate. Firm profits $(a \cdot n - w_r \cdot n)$ are positive because, as we shall see in a moment, $w_r < a$ and hence there is a positive mark-up. Output is not limited by demand – by consumption expenditure, that is to say – thanks to the existence of a 'natural' rate of interest, whose role is that to clear the economy-wide market by inducing households to keep spending their whole current income. If a is expected to rise, then the equilibrium real interest rate will also rise so as to keep equating aggregate supply and demand.

Finally, the rate of interest and the mark-up are not closely connected. Substantially, the rate of interest is not a distributive variable, its role being merely that of ensuring that consumption moves over time in line with a, thereby clearing the market. As already mentioned, however, there is here a positive mark-up because conditions of monopolistic competition are assumed. Let us write for the mark-up

$$\mu = \frac{p}{\frac{w}{a}} = \frac{a}{\frac{w}{p}} = \frac{a}{w_r}$$

The real wage will therefore be the higher the higher labour productivity is and the lower the mark-up is

$$w_r = \frac{a}{\mu}$$

In the model under consideration the mark-up which maximizes profits is constant, since the monopolistically competitive firms are assumed to face a constant elastic demand for their products. For any value of a, the equilibrium real wage therefore is

$$w_r^* = \frac{a}{\mu^*}$$

where μ^* is the profit-maximizing level of μ.

Now, short-term interest policy, through its leverage over long-term interest rates, is believed to act upon aggregate current spending. So what happens if, given p and a, the central bank decides to lower the short-term rate of interest? Consumption spending rises, because the opportunity cost of current consumption in terms of future consumption is reduced. Firms offer a higher nominal wage so as to induce households to supply the larger quantity of labour necessary to satisfy the increased consumption demand: both w and n therefore rise. As a result w_r also rises and μ falls below μ^*. In the long run, however, firms will raise their product prices so as to keep exploiting their market power enough to restore μ to its profit-maximizing level, and w_r will thus return to its equilibrium level w_r^*.

In this vision, in conclusion, a lowering (raising) of the policy rate instrument below (above) the level of the 'natural' rate raises (lowers) w and eventually p, by causing an expansion (a contraction) of aggregate spending, together with a temporary rise (fall) of actual output above (below) its 'natural' level.

Appendix 2

Interest and prices: an alternative framework

The price level can be determined in a system of price equations *à la* Sraffa (cf. Sraffa 1960), in which, however, both the wage rate and the prices of the k goods produced in the economy are expressed in money proper (i.e. there is no produced money-commodity: see Pivetti 1998a, p. 45)

$$(A_a p_a + B_a p_b + \ldots + K_a p_k)(1 + r_a) + L_a w = A p_a$$
$$(A_b p_a + B_b p_b + \ldots + K_b p_k)(1 + r_b) + L_b w = B p_b$$
$$\vdots$$
$$(A_k p_a + B_k p_b + \ldots + K_k p_k)(1 + r_k) + L_k w = K p_k$$
$$r_a = i + \rho_a i$$
$$r_b = i + \rho_b i$$

$$\dot{r}_k = i + \rho_k i$$

$$(A_w p_a + B_w p_b + \ldots + K_w p_k) = p_w$$

$$w_r = w/p_w.$$

Together with the policy-determined rate of interest i – the rate to be earned on long-term riskless financial assets – and the normal profits of enterprise of the different industries, expressed in terms of given ratios ρ_a, ρ_b, ..., ρ_k to the rate of interest, the money wage rate w in this system of equations is taken as given. The money wage is the direct outcome of wage bargaining and depends on economic as well as institutional conditions, such as the levels of employment and the forms of organizations of the workers. Given w, for any value of p_w there will be a corresponding real wage w_r. The system thus determines the normal distribution of income between profits and wages, together with normal product prices. In a closed economy and for any given situation of technique, the price level depends on w and i, with the latter acting as the regulator of the ratio of the price level to the money wage.

The normal rate of profit of each sphere of production $(r_a, r_b \ldots, r_k)$ is arrived at by adding up two autonomous components: the long-term rate of interest or 'pure' remuneration of capital, plus the normal profit of enterprise or the remuneration for the risk of productively employing capital in that sphere of production. Provided this latter remuneration is a sufficiently stable magnitude, by the competition among firms within each industry lasting changes in i will cause corresponding changes in profit rates, and inverse changes in w_r. Monetary policy and wage bargaining come out of this analysis as the main channels through which class relations act in determining distribution, and the level of the real wage prevailing in any given situation is viewed as the *final result* of the whole process by which distribution of income between workers and capitalists is actually derived.

In the face of increases in the general price level, competition among firms within each industry causes profit rates to adapt not to the nominal but to the real rate of interest (the interest rate net of inflation), as it is the latter that represents the real opportunity cost of any capital (be it borrowed or not) invested in production. Thus, with a constant nominal interest rate, the higher the rate of inflation the lower the real rate both of interest and of profit. Assuming therefore an increase in money wages, in order for the real profitability of capital to remain unaffected, nominal interest must be adjusted upward – taking, however, into account that any such adjustment in the nominal rates of interest affects in its turn prices and hence real interest. It can be shown that, in the face of any change in money wages, a nominal interest always exists such that the prices resulting from the calculation at that nominal rate would keep the real rate at a desired or target level (see Pivetti 1991, ch. 6). Hence, to the extent to which monetary policy-makers possess the power to establish the level of the nominal rates of interest, it is for them possible in principle – albeit at the cost of an accelerating inflation process – to leave distribution unaffected in the face of any increase in money wages or of any other initial agent of price increases.

Finally, it is worth stressing that the normal margin for profit considered appropriate to each sphere of production will also be based upon the same two magnitudes to which attention has been directed above: the long-term rate of interest and the remuneration for the risk attached to each different productive undertaking. Indeed, in computing the profit margin as a percentage of the estimated prime cost, firms must take into account the amount of capital invested – the object of 'full-cost' or mark-up pricing obviously being to arrive at a final price figure high enough to return a 'fair' yield on the investment. And in the long run, for a firm to be willing to continue in the business, the yield will have to exceed the income which the capital might be expected to earn if invested conservatively in high-grade securities, where there is less illiquidity risk and no manufacturing or trading risks are taken. So the normal profit rate is actually the relevant reference magnitude when reasoning in terms of mark-up pricing. It can be said that it is the *rate* of profit which logically comes first, and regulates the profit *margin*.

Let us then proceed to consider the relationships between the different notions of profit, starting from a formula for the gross mark-up, here defined as the ratio of value added per unit of labour to the money wage rate

$$1 + \mu = \frac{p \cdot a}{w} \tag{1}$$

where p is the unit price of output (a composite commodity representative of the gross product of a closed economy), a is output per unit of labour and w is the money wage rate. We may then write the following expression for the rate of profit r:

$$r = \frac{r_l}{k} = \frac{p \cdot a - w}{k} = \frac{p \cdot a}{k}\left(1 - \frac{w}{p \cdot a}\right) = \frac{p \cdot a}{k} \cdot \frac{r_l}{p \cdot a}$$

where r_l and k are profits and capital per unit of labour, and from which we get the following relationship between the share of profits in value added and the rate of profit

$$\frac{r_l}{p \cdot a} = r \cdot \frac{k}{p \cdot a} \tag{2}$$

The share of profits in value added is thus an increasing function of both r and the capital/output ratio k/pa. Finally from (2), taking into account (1), we get

$$1 + \mu = \frac{1}{1 - r\frac{k}{pa}} \tag{3}$$

and

$$\mu = \frac{r}{\frac{pa}{k} - r} \tag{4}$$

which also tell us that the mark-up $(1+\mu)$ and the ratio of profits to wages (μ) are increasing functions of r and k/pa.

All the notions of profit appearing in the above expressions refer to gross profits, so that rate margin and share of profits increase if, all the rest remaining unchanged, the average life of producers' equipment becomes shorter, thereby raising the normal allowances for average indirect costs per unit of output and reducing the share of wages in value added through the rise of p in (1).

Notes

* University of Rome "La Sapienza". A preliminary version of this essay was presented at the International Symposium on 'Perspectivas de Desenvolvimento para o Século XXI' organized by the Celso Furtado Center for Development Policies, Rio de Janeiro, 6–7 November 2008. I wish to thank Gilberto Tadeu Lima and Franklin Serrano for valuable comments.

1 The connection between short-term interest rates and long-term rates may be variously accounted for conceptually: arbitrage and competition in the capital market; the influence that the present course of short-term rates, which are under direct official control, exerts on the market opinion about the future course of long-term rates; or 'the expectations theory of the term structure', according to which longer-term interest rates move with an average of expected future short-term rates. But independently of how it is conceptually accounted for, the connection between the policy-determined short-term rates and long-term interest rates is strongly supported by the mere evidence that, through time, short and long-term rates behave consistently with each other.

2 Starting from Wicksell, the so-called 'price puzzle' (the old 'Gibson Paradox'), i.e. the positive correlation between interest rates and the price level, has been acutely accounted for within the neoclassical approach. Wicksell pointed out that, since in actual fact the movements of prices and the interest rate tend to occur in the same direction, then variations in the price level must ultimately be the effect of changes in the 'natural' rate, to which actual money rates are only tardily adapted by the bank (cf. Wicksell 1906, pp. 204–5; see on this also Pivetti 1991, pp. 98–102).

3 As a matter of fact, the notion of interest as a cost, independently of who furnishes capital, has long been acknowledged in the literature on cost accounting: see e.g. the 1924 book by Clinton H. Scovell, certified public accountant (New York and Massachusetts), in which it is thoroughly argued that the inclusion of interest in cost is 'not only theoretically proper but practically necessary' (Scovell 1924, p. 21).

4 In the words of an exponent of the consensus theory of monetary policy: 'The New IS-LM model abstracts from investment and capital ... my suspicion is that the omission of investment and capital from the New IS-LM model may be an important, if not fatal, flaw' (King 2000, pp. 88–9). With the inclusion of investment and capital into the model, one would essentially have to go back to Wicksell's 'real equilibrium capital rate'. Woodford, however, another outstanding exponent of the new consensus theory, who regards his main work as an attempt to conform Wicksell's 'insights' into the monetary transmission mechanism to 'modern standards of conceptual rigor ... with clear foundations in individual optimization' (see Woodford 2003, pp. 5, 6 and 10), does not appear to be very familiar with the real foundations of Wicksell's theory of money, as developed in Vol. I of his *Lectures* (1901, *General Theory*).

5 This is somewhat at odds with the idea one can occasionally find in the IT literature that increases in interest rates to safeguard price stability are also the best way to sustain long-run growth and avoid long-run real distortions in the sectoral composition of output. There is a certain tendency, in that literature, to shift from the convic-

tion that stabilizing inflation contributes to stabilizing employment and output at their 'natural' levels – i.e. that inflation targeting yields the best cyclical behaviour of the economy – to the suggestion that high inflation lowers economic activity and household welfare in the long run, while low inflation helps increase the rate of economic growth (see e.g. Mishkin 2008; see also Woodford 2003, p. 5). The point here perhaps is that if inflation was actually neutral with respect to the level and composition of output in the long run, then such an overriding importance attached to price stability or low and stable inflation would be somewhat difficult to swallow. As has been recently pointed out,

> After all, if all the central bank controls is the price level in the long run, and if the rate at which the price level increases has no implications for the level of real economic activity, then one inflation rate is just as good in welfare terms as another. There is no reason to prefer a steady-state inflation rate of 2 percent over one of, say, 20 percent.
>
> (Wynne 2008, p. 222)

6 The evidence that adopting IT leads to lower or less variable inflation does not appear very compelling, and there appears to be no systematic difference in the inflation outcomes of low-inflation countries with and without explicit inflation targets (cf. Blinder *et al.* 2008, pp. 937ff.).

7 For empirical evidence on some IT-adopting countries, see Laidler and Robson 1993; Fortin 1996; Debelle 1997; Akerlof *et al.* 2002; Bodkin and Neder 2003; Ball 2005.

8 Consider for example the following statement by the President of the Bank:

> [in 2005] the signals coming from the economic analysis [i.e. from the analysis of the conditions of supply and demand in the goods and factor markets] were not yet so clear and strong. But the continued strong expansion of money and credit in the course of 2005 gave an intensifying indication of increasing risks to medium term price stability which played a decisive role in our decision to start increasing policy rates in late 2005.
>
> (Trichet 2008, p. 334)

On the 'journalistic' origin of the 'dual pillar' definition of the ECB's strategy, see Issing 2008, p. 260. Cf. Papademos 2008, p. 198, on what is perhaps the most solid argument in favour of regarding money and credit as relevant aggregates for the conduct of monetary policy: the existence of liquidity and credit constraints which do affect the behaviour of economic agents and economic activity.

9 Thus in Italy the average CPI rate of inflation did fall from 9.7 in 1981–90 to 3.8 in 1991–2000 and 2.4 in 2001–7, but also the average rate of growth of real GDP fell from 2.2 to 1.6 and 1.1, respectively. Data for France over the same three decades are 6.4, 1.7 and 1.9 for the average rate of inflation, and 2.4, 2.0 and 1.8 for the average growth rates of real GDP. For Germany, the other major Eurozone member, the whole picture is much too blurred by the unification of the country in 1991.

10 In the face of a fall of the average rate of inflation (CPI excluding mortgage interest payments) from 6.6 per cent in the 1980–90 decade to 3 percent in 1990–2000, the average rate of growth of employment also fell in the UK from 0.7 percent in the first of those two decades to only just 0.1 percent in the second.

11 Persistent interest rate changes are bound to affect the economy's propensity to consume, not only through their impact on normal income distribution, but also through their impact on the aggregate value of households' assets and their debt service burden (as measured by debt service as a share of disposable personal income). As to the influence of lasting changes in interest rates on private investment, it cannot be predicted on the basis of some a priori functional link essentially because the impact of changes in normal distribution on the inducement to invest is bound to

be different in each different concrete situation, and may go either way (see on this Pivetti 1991, pp. 43–6).

12 Taylor rules are monetary policy rules that prescribe how a central bank should adjust the interest rate in response to developments in inflation. Basically, the prescription is that if inflation rises the central bank should raise the nominal interest by more, so that the real interest rises (see Orphanides 2007; see Taylor 1999 for a wide variety of models).

13 Thus the ECB tends systematically to broaden the scope of its power and influence to areas beyond monetary policy. As has been pointed out, '[r]ight from its birth as a monetary authority in 1999, the ECB has adopted advocacy roles in areas such as budgetary policy and structural reform, that are beyond its mandate and competence' (Buiter 2006, p. 16).

14 Think of the long Greenspan years, when flexibility and discretion, rather than commitment to some sort of policy rule, were the characteristic features of the monetary policy actually followed by the Fed (see on this also Mankiw 2006). Also Greenspan's successor, though an outstanding academic supporter of inflation targeting, once Chairman of the Federal Reserve, was quickly called to his institutional duty to sustain employment, so that over the six months following September 2007, expectations of a dramatic fall of 'core' inflation being totally absent, he hastily reduced six times the federal funds rate, bringing it in March 2008 to less than half its September 2007 level. As to US budgetary policy, just think of the huge deficits of the last eight years, in response to the weakening of the incentives to invest throughout the economy and the fear of a fall in household spending.

References

Akerlof, G.A., Dickens, W.T., Fortin, P. and Perry, G.L. (2002), 'Inflation and unemployment in the US and Canada: A common framework', Département des sciences économiques, UQAM, Cahier de recherche Nos. 20–16, July.

Ball, L. (1999), 'Policy rules for open economies', in Taylor, J.B (ed.), *Monetary Policy Rules*, Chicago and London, The University of Chicago Press.

Ball, L. (2005), 'Commentary on M. Goodfriend, "The monetary policy debate since October 1979: lessons for theory and practice"', *Federal Reserve Bank of St. Louis Review*, Vol. 87, No. 2, Part 2.

Barro, R.J. and Gordon, D.B. (1983), 'A positive theory of monetary policy in a natural rate model', *Journal of Political Economy*, Vol. 91, No. 4.

Barth, M. and Ramey, V. (2001), *The cost channel of monetary transmission, NBER Working Paper Series*, No. 7675, Cambridge, MA, National Bureau of Economic Research.

Blinder, A.S., Ehrmann, M., Fratzscher, M., De Haan, J. and Jansen, D.J. (2008), 'Central bank communication and monetary policy: a survey of theory and evidence', *Journal of Economic Literature*, Vol. 46, No. 4.

Bodkin, R.G. and Neder, A.E. (2003), 'Monetary policy targeting in Argentina and Canada in the 1990s: a comparison, some contrasts, and a tentative evaluation', *Eastern Economic Journal*, Vol. 29, No. 3.

Buiter, W.H. (2006), 'Rethinking inflation targeting and central bank independence', European Institute, London School of Economics and Political Science, Inaugural Lecture given on the 26 October.

Debelle, G. (1997), *Inflation targeting in practice, IMF Working Paper* 97/35, March.

European Central Bank (2008), *The Role of Money – Money and Monetary Policy in the Twenty-First Century*, Fourth ECB Conference, 9–10 November 2006, Beyer, A. and Reichlin, L. (eds), Frankfurt am Main, ECB.

Fortin, P. (1996), 'Presidential address: the great Canadian slump', *Canadian Journal of Economics*, Vol. 29, No. 4.

Gaiotti, E. and Secchi, A. (2004), *Is there a cost channel of monetary policy transmission? An investigation into the pricing behaviour of 2,000 firms*, Temi di Discussione, No. 525, Rome, Banca d'Italia.

Goodfriend, M. (2002), 'Monetary policy in the new neoclassical synthesis: a primer', *International Finance*, Vol. 5, No. 2.

Goodfriend, M. (2005), 'The monetary policy debates since 1979: lessons for theory and practice', *Federal Reserve Bank of St. Louis Review*, Vol. 87, No. 2, Part 2.

Goodfriend, M. (2007), 'How the world achieved consensus on monetary policy', *NBER Working Paper Series*, No. 13580, Cambridge, MA, National Bureau of Economic Research.

Issing, O. (2008), 'The ECB's monetary policy strategy: why did we choose a two pillar approach?', in European Central Bank (2008).

King, R.G. (2000), 'The IS-LM model: language, logic, and limits', *Federal Reserve Bank of Richmond Economic Quarterly*, Vol. 86, No. 3.

Kydland, F. and Prescott, E.C. (1977), 'Rules rather than discretion: the inconsistency of optimal plans', *Journal of Political Economy*, Vol. 85, No. 3.

Laidler, D.E.W. and Robson, W.B.P. (1993), *The Great Canadian Disinflation: The Economics and Politics of Monetary Policy in Canada, 1988–93*, Toronto, C.D. Howe Institute.

Mankiw, N.G. (2006), 'A letter to Ben Bernanke', *American Economic Review, Papers and Proceedings*, Vol. 96, No. 2.

Mishkin, F.S. (2008), *Does stabilizing inflation contribute to stabilizing economic activity?*, *NBER Working Paper Series*, No. 13970, Cambridge, MA, National Bureau of Economic Research.

Orphanides, A. (2007), 'Taylor rules', entry for the second edition of *The New Palgrave: A Dictionary of Economics*, January.

Papademos, L. (2008), 'The role of money in the conduct of monetary policy', in European Central Bank (2008).

Pivetti, M. (1991), *An Essay on Money and Distribution*, London, Macmillan.

Pivetti, M. (1998a), 'Thomas Tooke and the influence of the rate of interest on prices: implications for distribution theory', *Contributions to Political Economy*, Vol. 17.

Pivetti, M. (1998b), 'Monetary versus political unification in Europe. On Maastricht as an exercise in "vulgar" political economy', *Review of Political Economy*, Vol. 10, No. 1.

Pivetti, M. (1999), 'On Sraffa's "cost & surplus" concept of wages and its policy implications', *Rivista Italiana degli Economisti*, Vol. IV, No. 2.

Pivetti, M. (2001), 'Money endogeneity and monetary non-neutrality: a Sraffian perspective', in Rochon, L.P. and Vernengo, M. (eds), *Credit, Interest and the Open Economy: Essays in Horizontalism*, Cheltenham and Northampton, Edward Elgar.

Pivetti, M. (2004), "La teoria monetaria della distribuzione e il caso americano", *Rivista Italiana degli Economisti*, Vol. IX, No. 2.

Scovell, C.H. (1924), *Interest as a Cost*, New York, Ronald Press Company.

Seelig, S. (1974), 'Rising interest rates and cost push inflation', *Journal of Finance*, Vol. 29, No. 4.

Serrano, F. (2008), 'Juros, câmbio e o sistema de metas de inflação no Brasil', Universidade Federal do Rio de Janeiro, Instituto de Economia, mimeo.

Sraffa, P. (1960), *Production of Commodities by Means of Commodities*, Cambridge, Cambridge University Press.

Stiehler, U. (1995), 'The new monetary policy framework of the United Kingdom', IMF PPAA No 95/1, Washington, International Monetary Fund.

Taylor, J.B. (ed.) (1999), *Monetary Policy Rules*, Chicago and London, The University of Chicago Press.

Trichet, J.C. (2008), 'The role of money: money and monetary policy at the ECB', in European Central Bank (2008).

Wicksell, K. (1901 [1934]), *Lectures on Political Economy*, Volume I: *General Theory*, London, Routledge & Kegan Paul.

Wicksell, K. (1906 [1935]), *Lectures on Political Economy*, Volume II: *Money*, London, Routledge & Kegan Paul.

Woodford, M. (2003), *Interest and Prices: Foundations of a Theory of Monetary Policy*, Princeton, NJ, Princeton University Press.

Wynne, M.A. (2008), 'Core inflation: a review of some conceptual issues', *Federal Reserve Bank of St. Louis Review*, No. 3, Part 2.

14 Equilibrium, stability and path dependence in post-Keynesian models of economic growth

Amitava Krishna Dutt *

1 Introduction

This chapter examines why it may be desirable to incorporate two features into post-Keynesian models of economic growth: first, the existence of bands within which economic actors do not change their behavior, and second, the fact that economic actors may adjust in more than one way in reacting to a particular disequilibrium situation. For this purpose the chapter considers two post-Keynesian growth models, one based on the work of Roy Harrod (1939) and the other on that of Michal Kalecki (1971) and Josef Steindl (1952).

It argues that introducing these features into these models is desirable because they formalize plausible behavioral characteristics of economic decision-makers in uncertain environments. These characteristics draw on the writings of economists such as G. L. S. Shackle and others. It also argues that incorporating them has useful and interesting consequences for these models.

First, it presents two possible ways of introducing path dependency into these models. It is increasingly being recognized by economists in what can be called the post-Keynesian tradition that models of growth should reflect path dependency, given that economic decisions are actually made in environments in which the future is uncertain and the past is irreversible.[1] The ideas of the band and multiple responses to disequilibria provide two of several alternative ways of introducing path dependence into these models.

Second, doing so has implications for some controversies surrounding the Harrodian model and the Kalecki–Steindl model, involving the characterization of long-run equilibrium in the Kalecki–Steindl model as one in which the equilibrium rate of capacity utilization need not be equal to some desired level of it, and the problem of knife-edge instability in the Harrodian model.

The rest of this chapter proceeds as follows. Section 2 briefly reviews the two basic Harrodian and Kalecki–Steindl growth models and discusses some alleged weaknesses in them that will be addressed later. The next two sections examine, in turn, the two routes, explaining their behavioral foundations, justifying their use, incorporating them into the growth models, and examining their implications for the models, including how they address the criticisms of the models. Section 3 pursues the idea of the band based on, among others, Shackle's analysis of decision-making under uncertainty involving the notion of potential surprise. Section 4 explores the route of allowing decision-makers more than one way of responding to a particular disequilibrium situation that they may face. Section 5 summarizes and makes some concluding comments.

2 Post-Keynesian growth models

This section reviews two basic post-Keynesian models of growth into which the subsequent two sections will introduce path dependence.

The two models have some features in common. They consider a closed economy with no government fiscal activity which produces one good with two inputs, homogeneous labor and non-depreciating homogeneous capital, the latter being the same good as the produced good. Firms hire workers (equal to one unit of labor) in proportion to the output they produce, with the labor–output ratio given by *a*. Labor employed in the economy is therefore given by

$$L = a\,Y, \tag{1}$$

where *Y* is the level of real output and income. Firms set their price level as a markup on their wage cost per unit of output, and adjust output to meet aggregate demand. It is assumed that unemployed workers are always available and that firms hold enough capital to make these output adjustments possible. The price equation is given by

$$P = (1 + z)\,W\,a, \tag{2}$$

where *P* is the price level, *W* is the money wage, and *z* is the markup rate which, following Kalecki (1971), is given by the degree of monopoly power (that is, by factors such as the degree of industrial concentration, and the bargaining power of workers relative to firms). Since aggregate demand in the economy consists of consumption and investment demand, *C* and *I*, for equilibrium in the goods market we have

$$Y = C + I. \tag{3}$$

There are two classes in the economy, workers who receive wage income, and capitalists who receive all of the non-wage income, which we will call profit income. Workers consume their entire income, while capitalists are assumed to save a constant fraction, s_c, of their income, so that

$$C = (W/P)\,L + (1 - s_c)\,rK, \tag{4}$$

where *K* is the stock of capital and *r* the rate of profit on capital valued at the price of the good.

The two models part ways in how they treat investment.

2.1 The Harrodian model

The Harrodian model assumes that investment demand as a ratio of capital stock is given in the short run, which we write as

$$I/K = g, \tag{5}$$

where g is the short-run investment parameter which, since we abstract from depreciation, also denotes the rate of growth of capital. In the long run, following Flaschel et al. (1997), the model assumes that g adjusts according to the equation

$$dg/dt = \xi\,[u^e - u_d], \tag{6}$$

where $u = Y/K$ is a measure of capacity utilization, u^e its expected value, u_d its value desired or planned by firms, taken to be exogenously given, and $\xi > 0$ a speed of adjustment parameter which represents the rate at which firms adjust their investment plans in response to deviations of expected capacity utilization from their desired level. Expected capacity utilization, again following Flaschel et al. (1997) is assumed to change adaptively according to the dynamic equation

$$du^e/dt = \beta[u - u^e], \tag{7}$$

where $\beta > 0$ is an adjustment parameter representing the rate at which firms adjust their expected utilization rate due to deviations from the actual utilization rate.

In the short run we assume that K, g and u^e are given, and that the goods market clears through variations in output and hence, the capacity utilization rate. The short-run equilibrium level of capacity utilization, using equations (1) through (5), is given by

$$u = \frac{g}{s_c\sigma}, \tag{8}$$

where ($\sigma = z/(1 + z)$, the share of profits in income. An increase in g increases the short-run equilibrium level of capacity utilization through the standard multiplier mechanism, the multiplier being $1/s$ where the economy's overall saving propensity, $s = s_c\sigma$.

In the long run g and u^e change according to equations (6) and (7), and the dynamics can be shown in the phase diagram in Figure 14.1. The su^e line shows combinations of g and u^e at which $du^e/dt = 0$ and its equation is obtained by substituting equation (8) into equation (7) and setting its right-hand side equal to zero. The vertical line at u_d shows combinations of g and u^e at which $dg/dt = 0$, as can be seen from equation (6). The vertical and horizontal arrows show the directions of change for g and u^e, as can be verified from equations (6) through (8). The long-run equilibrium where both g and u^e are stationary, that is where the two lines $g = su^e$ and $u^e = u_d$ intersect at E, is found to be saddle-point

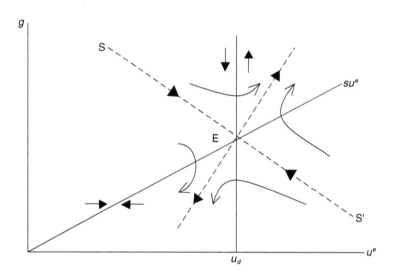

Figure 14.1 Long-run dynamics in the Harrodian model.

unstable. If g happens to be slightly above (below) the separatrix SS', g will eventually increase (decrease), moving further away from the long-run equilibrium value, su_d.

The saddle-point result formalizes Harrod's notion of knife-edge instability. The long-run equilibrium rate of capital accumulation in this model is given by su_d which can be written as Harrod's s/v, since su_d is the firms' desired output–capital ratio, the reciprocal of the desired capital–output ratio, v. The model shows that if g is greater (less) than the warranted rate of growth, $g_w/s/v$, g will eventually move further away from it. The actual rate of investment, g, may seem to move towards g_w for a while (if it starts with $g > g_w$ and $u^e < u_d$ or with $g < g_w$ and $u^e > u_d$) but (upon crossing the u_d line) it will eventually move further away. When g moves further away from g_w it is easy to see that the actual rate of growth of output eventually will move away from the warranted rate of growth of output. The rate of growth of output in the model is given by $g + \hat{u}$ where the overhat denotes the rate of growth of a variable, which implies, from equation (8), that it is equal to $g + \hat{g}$. Since at long-run equilibrium $\hat{g} = 0$, the rate of growth of output is equal to g, so that s/v is also the warranted rate of growth of output. Since g moves further away from g_w when it is above (below) it when $u^e > u_d$ ($u^e < u_d$), it follows from equation (6) that the movement of g away from g_w implies a movement of the actual rate of growth of output away from the warranted rate of growth of output.

The specific assumption about expectations formation may be modified without changing the instability result. Suppose, for instance, that β in equation (7) approaches infinity, so that $u^e = u$ always holds, that is, there is perfect foresight on the part of firms. In this case equation (6) gets replaced by

$$dg/dt = \xi\,[u - u_d].\tag{9}$$

Substituting equation (8) into it we find that long-run equilibrium for this model again occurs at the warranted rate of growth, but that an increase (decrease) in g above it implies that g rises (falls) monotonically, implying knife-edge instability.

This Harrodian model has the obvious problem that it portrays the capitalist economy as being too unstable, poised on a sharp knife edge, from which the slightest departure would result in explosive growth or unstoppable stagnation. Harrod himself did not believe that the knife edge was so sharp. Although his presentation in Harrod (1939) and Harrod (1948) suggests a high degree of insta-bility, as Neville (2003, 104) points out, Harrod objected strongly to the knife-edge terminology and said that "I hope that we shall hear no more of the 'Harrod knife-edge'" (Harrod 1970, 741). Harrod (1973, 32–3) stated that actual econo-mies did not exhibit such extreme instability. He wrote:

> I have argued that an equilibrium growth path is normally unstable. A body is said to be in unstable equilibrium if, when pushed away from its position, it does not tend to return to it but to move further from it. If it is on a knife-edge a very tiny push would serve to push it away; but it would also be in unstable equilibrium if it were at the top of a shallow dome. Then a much larger push would be needed to set it moving. All depends on: (i) the gradi-ent of declivity around it, about which, I think, I have not pronounced, and (ii) friction. In the economic case the amount of friction depends on built-in procedures, degree of conservatism, sensitivity to changes, changes in expectations, the kind of phenomena that affect expectations, etc. It needs empirical study, rather than theory, to evaluate the amount of friction.
>
> (Harrod 1970, 740)

There have been numerous attempts to "stabilize" the Harrodian system by introducing the dynamics of additional long-run variables, involving labor market issues (see Skott 1989, 2008) and monetary factors (see Flaschel *et al.* 1997). But the investment-saving adjustment has itself been taken to be unstable which seems to be contrary to Harrod's own view.

2.2 The Kalecki–Steindl model

The Kalecki–Steindl model assumes that investment as a ratio of capital stock is a positive function of the rate of capacity utilization. Adopting a simple linear form for the investment function, we have

$$I/K = \gamma_0 + \gamma_1 u,\tag{10}$$

where $\gamma_i > 0$ are fixed investment parameters.

In the short run we take K as given and solve for the equilibrium rate of capacity utilization using equations (1) through (4) and (10), which is given by

$$u = \frac{\gamma_0}{s_c\sigma - \gamma_1}. \tag{11}$$

For a meaningful equilibrium value of capacity utilization we require that $s_c\,\sigma > \gamma_1$. The condition also implies that the adjustment of capacity utilization to excess demand and supply in the goods market is a stable one, which is the familiar condition of macroeconomic stability in Keynes–Kalecki models, that is, the responsiveness of saving to changes in output and capacity utilization exceeds that of investment.[2] The short-run equilibrium rate of investment is obtained by substituting equation (11) into equation (10) and denoting I/K by g, we have

$$g = \frac{s_c\sigma\gamma_0}{s_c\sigma - \gamma_1}. \tag{12}$$

The determination of the short-run equilibrium level of capacity utilization is shown in Figure 14.2 to be determined at the intersection of the S/K and I/K curves. Capacity utilization and the rate of capital accumulation (abstracting from depreciation as noted earlier) increase with the investment parameters γ_i (since increases in investment propensities increase effective demand and output, and consequently, investment), fall with s_c (the paradox of thrift), and fall with the profit share, σ, more on which later.

In the long run K increases due to investment. With the growth rate of capital given by g, we find from equation (12) that the rate of growth of the capital is, in

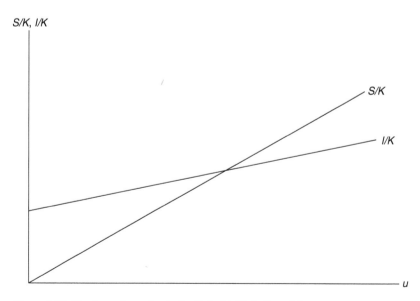

Figure 14.2 Short-run dynamics in the Kalecki–Steindl model.

the long run, the same as it is in the short run, since K does not affect g. In other words, when the economy is in short-run equilibrium, it is also in long-run equilibrium: there is no off-equilibrium long-run dynamic path for g and u and other relevant variables which are determined in the short run. Thus, the effects of changes in the parameters are the same in the long run as in the short run. In particular, it remains true that an increase in the profit share reduces the rate of capacity utilization and the rate of growth of capital (and hence output). As discussed by Dutt (1984) and Rowthorn (1982) and others, the increase in the profit share increases the overall propensity of the economy to save, reduces aggregate demand, which reduces capacity utilization and investment. This property of a positive relationship between the wage share and the rate of growth of the economy is sensitive to specifications of the investment function. For instance, if investment depends positively on both the profit *rate* and the rate of capacity utilization, the result continues to hold (as in Dutt 1984, and Rowthorn 1982) but if investment depends positively on the profit *share* and the rate of capacity utilization, it is possible for a rise in the profit share to result in an increase in the rate of growth (since the direct positive effect of the increase in the profit share on investment may outweigh the negative effect through reduced consumption demand, as shown in Bhaduri and Marglin 1990). However, this class of models brings up the interesting possibility of a positive relation between income distribution (in the sense of an increase in the wage share) and the rates of accumulation and growth, in contradiction to the classical–Marxian presumption that greater inequality, by increasing overall saving, increases growth.

The model has been subjected to a number of criticisms, a persistent one being that it allows the rate of capacity utilization to be endogenously determined in the long run. It is asked why firms continue to invest if the level of capacity utilization is persistently below what they plan or desire, and therefore, whether any deviation of actual and planned or desired capacity utilization is consistent with the notion of long-run equilibrium. This type of growth model has been criticized by a number of writers, including Auerbach and Skott (1988) and Committeri (1986) as being internally inconsistent because it implies that the long-run equilibrium u will not, in general, be equal to u_d. There have been some attempts to defend the model against such charges (see Lavoie 1995 and Dutt 1997), but the debate continues (see Skott 2008).

3 Potential surprise and desired bands

Several major criticisms of both growth models relate to the notion of some unique desired or planned level of capacity utilization.[3] The knife-edge instability property of the Harrodian model emerges from the fact that whenever the expected or actual level of capacity utilization deviates from its unique planned level firms will adjust their investment levels (either directly or in response to expectational changes). The long-run problem of the Kalecki–Steindl model occurs from the fact that in long-run equilibrium the actual degree of capacity utilization is not generally equal to the unique planned level of capacity utilization. The first solution to these problems and route to path dependence we consider takes the view that under conditions of uncertainty, economic decision-makers may not have a unique level of planned or desired level of some target variable, like the level of capacity utilization

A useful way to motivate the notion of the band is with Shackle's concept of potential surprise. Shackle argues that the standard concept of probability may be fine for analyzing situations in which events recur under similar circumstances, but it is not appropriate for analyzing situations in which decision-makers make decisions in situations in which circumstances differ in unknowable ways, and in fact in situations in which the actions of these decision-makers can affect the circumstances in new and unknowable ways. In these situations of true uncertainty (following the use of the term by Frank Knight and John Maynard Keynes) decision-makers act using their subjective opinions and Shackle proposes the concept potential surprise.

Shackle considers the possible outcome (say profits) of an action (say investment) which can be measured according to its desirability to the decision-maker and suggests that some outcomes would not surprise the decision-maker at all, some would result in some degree of surprise, and others would be considered virtually impossible. The relation between the outcome and the degree of potential surprise which the decision-maker subjectively associates with it can be shown by the heavier bowl-shaped curve with a flat bottom in Figure 14.3. The realization of the value of x in the interval between x_l and x_h would come as no surprise to the decision-maker and therefore yield potential surprise, measured by z of zero; values below x_{min} and above x_{max} are considered impossible, so that $z = \bar{z}$ where $\bar{z}$ is the maximum value of potential surprise; and values between x_{min} and x_l and between x_h and x_{max} would yield intermediate degrees of surprise. The level x_n Shackle calls the neutral value of x, which may be the pre-existing level, or the level the decision-maker considers to be neither good nor bad, so that in the intermediate ranges of x, greater deviations from it are considered

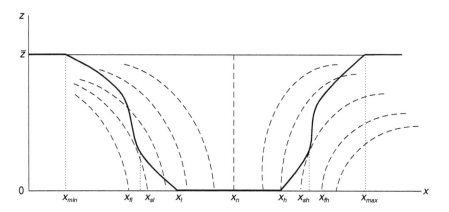

Figure 14.3 Potential surprise and focal points.

more surprising. The decision-maker's attention is attracted more by values of x which are more desirable (as they attract attention because they are highly favorable) at values of x higher than x_n or less desirable (as they attract attention because they are highly unfavorable) at values of x lower than x_n, and by lower values of z, that is, outcomes which are less surprising (since less surprising outcomes draw greater attention and remotely possible outcomes are uninteresting). Thus, in the region $x > x_n$, starting from any iso-stimulation curve a rise in x will attract more attention and increase the degree of stimulation, so that the level of surprise needs to be increased to make it less interesting. The figure shows as dashed lines iso-stimulation curves, which are curves yielding the same level of stimulation or attract the attention of the decision-maker to the same extent. The level of stimulus increases (decreases) as we move to curves further to the right (left) and lower at $x > x_n$ ($x < x_n$).

Shackle argues that decision-makers evaluate, and choose between, activities on the basis of what he calls focus points, that is, by focusing on the two most attention-attracting levels of outcomes, one high and one low. These levels are found from the points of tangency between the iso-stimulation curves and the potential surprise function, and are seen to be at levels x_{fl} (for low-level focal point) and x_{fh} (for high-level focal point), since these points show the most attention-attracting levels of x among the combinations of outcomes and their degree of potential surprise, as shown by the potential surprise function. Shackle states that the decision-maker's decision about a project will be affected by these focal points or their standardized focal points, that is, levels of x which attract the same degree of attention as these focus points but with zero potential surprise. Shackle's decision-maker chooses activities using these two focal points. Shackle suggests that the decision-maker has indifference curves which make utility depend positively on the high focal point and negatively on the low focal point, and chooses projects or activities over others when they yield higher utility.

Although Shackle's concern is with how decision-makers choose activities based on their potential surprise functions for activities and other subjective characteristics, the approach has implications for how decision-makers revise their potential surprise functions for a particular activity depending on actual outcomes, once the outcome of the activity is known. One can argue that if the actual outcome falls within a range of values, decision-makers will not revise their potential surprise functions and therefore not change their judgment about an activity and thereby not change their behavior. It is plausible that the actual range of such outcomes is the no-surprise range, in the interval between x_l and x_h, since if the decision-maker is not surprised by the outcome, he or she will continue to believe that his or her reasoning which led to the choice is fine. Or it may even extend beyond that to the range between x_{cl} and x_{ch}, if the decision-maker believes that if the outcome falls within the range his or her judgment is not incorrect to warrant a change. It is even possible that the potential surprise function can change, at least to some extent, to make the realized value closer to the new neutral value, a procedure which will make the behavior of the decision-maker less prone to changes despite the neutral value not being realized.

All of this is not to argue that Shackle would have endorsed the use of his potential surprise approach to show that decision-makers may not change their behavior if outcomes occur within a range, and not at some specific predetermined value. He seems to be somewhat critical of Hicks's suggestion that people may refrain from revising their expectations because they define them for a particular range of outcomes rather than with a particular value (Shackle 1988, 198–9). Earl (1993, 254) points out, however, that to accept this range view of expectations is

> by no means ... inconsistent with his own view that it is surprise that makes a person think that a fresh start may be necessary – though it would reduce considerably the number of occasions on which changes in the state of new produced kaleidic shifts of strategy.

Shackle, of course, did stress the kaleidic nature of the economy as seen from a Keynesian perspective (Shackle 1974). However, two features of this metaphor may be noted. One, small movements in a kaleidoscope need not bring about dramatic shifts in its images. Two, the band view does not imply the absence of kaleidic changes, since once we leave the band such changes may well occur.

It should also be pointed out that Shackle's theory of potential surprise is not the only way to motivate the idea of a band of outcomes within which decision-makers may not revise their expectations. First, even the standard probability approach does not imply that an outcome different from the expected value of that outcome necessarily warrants a revision of the expected outcome, since an error of this form may well be within a specified confidence interval. However, the use of probability distributions may result in an overemphasis on the expected value, and therefore to changes in expectations and hence behavior when actual outcomes differ from their expected value. Second, it is plausible that when new information becomes available to decision-makers who have cognitive limitations on calculating optimal outcomes, they may not change their behavior, unless the new information drastically changes their environment (Heiner 1983). The Shacklean perspective confirms this point without committing itself to whether or not the decision-makers' problem is due to cognitive limitations or due to the unknowability of the future, and provides a method of identifying bounds within which decision-makers will not alter their behavior. Third, the idea of a range emerges from Hicks's ideas on attempts to seek liquidity in an uncertain environment.

The variable for which we will introduce the band notion is the rate of capacity utilization. This is not a variable regarding which the firm may intrinsically prefer high values over low values but, with other considerations given, firms will prefer higher values because they imply higher rates of profit. If firms make decisions regarding investment, but find that a decision they make, in conjunction with the decisions of other consumers and firms, does not lead to an actual rate of capacity utilization equivalent to their planned range of capacity utilization, if the actual rate is still within the planned band, firms may not alter their investment behavior (in the sense of altering their investment function). To use

Shackle's approach we could assume that firms have a band of values within which they expect capacity utilization to be, and if actual capacity utilization falls within that expected band they will not change their plans. What is important for equilibrium is that the planned level (if it is unique) also lies within this expected band. To express this briefly we may say that firms have a desired band of capacity utilization rates, and if actual capacity utilization falls within this band they will not change their behavior. This interpretation of the planned level of capacity utilization as a band leads to the following changes in how we think of the Harrodian and Kalecki–Steindl models.

For the Harrodian model we consider the simpler version in which $u^e = u$ always holds. Now suppose that firms do not have a unique u_d, but instead have a band of values within which actual realizations of u will not induce them to change their investment plans (as a ratio of capital stock). This band is shown by the range u_- to u_+ in Figure 14.4. For any given g, the short-run equilibrium level of u is found from line $g = s_c \sigma u$. For any short-run realization of u within the range u_- to u_+ there will be no induced change in g, but when u exceeds (is less than) u_+ (u_-), g will tend to increase (decrease). Thus, if there is any autonomous change in g which keeps g in the range between g_- and g_+ or, alternatively, changes in σ and s_c which keep the $g = s_c \sigma u$ such that it does not intersect the vertical lines at u_- (or u_+) above (or below) g_+ (or g_-), there will be no further changes in g. The Harrodian knife edge has been blunted by a corridor of stability. This corridor seems to capture Harrod's zone of inertia which prevents there from being a blunt knife edge. However, sufficiently large parametric shifts can take u out of this corridor, and result in explosive growth or implosive decline.

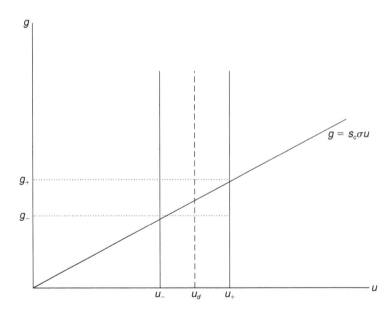

Figure 14.4 The Harrodian model with a band.

This model results in path dependence in the sense that within the zone of stability shocks to the growth rate will not make the economy return to its equilibrium level before the shock, but instead stay on at the new equilibrium, which is neutral.

For the Kalecki–Steindl model, the implication is obvious. If the equilibrium capacity utilization determined by equation (11) is within the range given by u_- to u_+, then the equilibrium can legitimately qualify as a long-run equilibrium if we insist that at that equilibrium actual capacity utilization should be within a planned band. If the equilibrium does not lie within that range, we would need to specify what firms will do when in such a disequilibrium situation. One possibility is that they will change the "autonomous" component of investment, that is, γ_0. If the level of capacity utilization happens to be below (above) the desired range, firms can be assumed to reduce (increase) γ_0. But since an increase in γ_0 has the effect of increasing equilibrium u, this change would push the economy further away from the band, so that the situation would become unstable, as in the case of the Harrodian model. However, within the desired range the model would behave just like the standard Kalecki–Steindl model and growth can be wage-led and will be wage-led if the saving and investment equations are as described in our model.

So far we have assumed that firms will not change their investment behavior in the sense that they will follow their behavioral rule as given by the investment function of equation (10). Specifically, within the band we assumed that they will not change the "autonomous" component of investment, given by γ_0. Given this assumption the model does not imply path dependence in the sense of neutral equilibria, as in the Harrodian model. We may, however, interpret "no change in investment behavior" in the sense of the Harrodian model, that is, within some band of values of capacity utilization they may not change their investment–capital ratio. Let us suppose, then, that there is a band in which this is the case, and there is a somewhat wider band in which firms follow the investment function given by equation (10) while leaving γ_0 unchanged. Then, in the narrower band exogenous shocks to γ_0 will result in a move to a new neutral equilibrium, so that we will have path dependence in this sense. However, in this band an increase in the wage share will have no effect on the investment–capital rate, although it will have a positive effect on capacity utilization. Thus we will have only a level effect on capacity utilization, but not a growth effect on output growth (since the growth rate of capital will not change). It is when we are no longer in the narrower band but in the broader one that wage-led growth in the normal sense will occur, but there will be no path dependence in our sense.

4 Multiple responses to disequilibria

Economic analysis which examines how disequilibria in a part of the economy affect the behavior of individual decision-makers or groups typically associates one disequilibrium with one responding variable. Consider an economy with a single firm or with many identical firms with differentiated products which take other firms' prices to be given parametrically. Suppose that the firm(s) are not currently in a profit-maximizing situation, which means that there is a disequilibrium in the economy. The firms are then usually modeled *either* as choosing their price, in which case the price is the responding variable, *or* their quantity produced, in which case the quantity is the responding variable. The reason for this is that firms take as given their (perceived) demand curve which relates their price to the quantity, so that they cannot choose the two independently.[4] Optimizing firms cannot ignore their demand curves since, if they did so, they would not be optimizers. It may be noted that this procedure also solves two other problems which would occur if the model did not specify one of the price or the quantity as the adjusting variable. First, if the firms were to choose both price and quantity independently, rather than taking the demand curve into consideration and choosing one, there is no guarantee that the chosen variables would actually respect the market demand curve, so that the situation would not be an equilibrium at all. If the firms are allowed to hold stocks of inventories, their inventories would change. Second, choosing one variable as the adjusting variable allows the model to come to a unique equilibrium. If both variables adjusted independently to the disequilibrium, there would be no unique equilibrium.

This procedure of linking one responding variable to one situation of disequilibrium is also found in post-Keynesian growth models. We start with an examination of the Harrodian model. Assume that the investment–capital ratio be exogenously given in the short run so that capacity utilization adjusts to clear the goods market, and we have, as in the dynamic model of section 3, u determined by equation (8). Assume also, as in the previous models, that firms have a desired rate of capacity utilization, u_d. When firms find that the actual rate of capacity utilization departs from this desired level, they adjust their behavior. Two types of adjustment for this general model are usually discussed in the literature.

One is that if firms have higher (lower) capacity utilization than they desire, they increase (reduce) their investment levels in an attempt to restore capacity utilization to their desired level. This adjustment can be formalized with equation (9). Having only this adjustment mechanism and keeping all other parameters constant implies that the long-run adjustment, in which the dynamics of g are given by equation (9), implies an unstable adjustment process: substitution of equation (8) into (9) shows that an increase in g increases u, which leads to an increase in the rate of change of g. This is precisely the Harrodian model with knife-edge instability in which we assume that $u = u^e$ always holds.

Another adjustment mechanism is that firms, finding they have excess capacity, reduce their markup, z, to increase their sales and hence, capacity utilization. Assuming an adjustment which increases the markup when they have a degree of capacity utilization greater than they desire, and noting that $\sigma = z/(1 + z)$, we can depict the adjustment with the equation

$$\frac{d\sigma}{dt} = \eta\,[u - u_d], \tag{13}$$

where $\eta > 0$ is a positive. If we assume that g is a constant, this adjustment implies a stable dynamic adjustment process since, substituting equation (8) into (13) we find that a rise in σ reduces u and leads to a fall in the rate of change of σ. The long-run equilibrium rate of capacity utilization is given by u_d, and the growth rate of the stock of capital and output are given exogenously by g.

Although the two adjustment mechanisms are usually taken to be mutually exclusive, there are no overriding reasons to insist upon it. First, firms are not being treated here as profit-maximizers in the usual sense. In an uncertain environment firms do not know or even care about their demand curve, but instead do whatever they find plausible to react to a particular situation. If they find that their actual capacity utilization is not equal to their desired level, they may change a number of things in their power to attempt to bring the actual closer to their desired level. If they believe that they can increase their capacity utilization by lowering their markup and their price, this is one thing they will do. If they believe that they can increase their capacity utilization by reducing their investment, they will do that as well. Second, in this model there will be no unintended changes in inventories: output always adjusts to clear the market in the short run. The disequilibrium occurs only in the long run. Third, there is nothing sacrosanct about having a unique equilibrium. If the model implies that it is not unique, or it does not exist, and the model's assumptions are plausible, so be it.

Thus, instead of having these two adjustment mechanisms as alternatives, assume that firms actually change *both* g and σ when they are not at their desired rate of capacity utilization. In this case the dynamics of the economy can be shown by Figure 14.5. The model turns out to be a zero-root model with a continuum of equilibria.

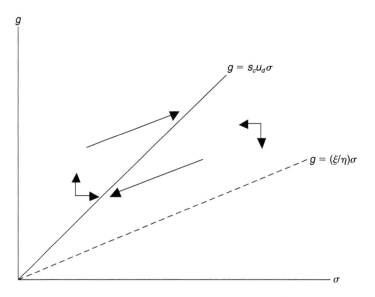

Figure 14.5 Harrodian model with endogenous profit share.

Since the dynamics of the model involve two processes, one unstable (the adjustment in g) and one stable (the adjustment in σ), the overall stability of the model depends on which is stronger. This can be shown by considering the function

$$V = \frac{1}{2}[u - u_d]^2 \tag{14}$$

In the neighborhood domain of the equilibria, assuming all partial derivates exist and are continuous, and V is positive definite, stability is ensured by the second method of Liapunov if $dV/dt < 0$. Differentiating equation (14) with respect to t and substituting from equations (9) and (13), we obtain

$$\frac{dV}{dt} = (u - u_d)^2 \, u[(\xi/g) - (\eta/\sigma)]$$

which implies that stability is ensured if $g > (\xi/\eta)\sigma$. This condition is more likely to be satisfied the larger is η (the speed of adjustment of the profit share) relative to ξ (the speed of adjustment of investment).

The stable case is shown in Figure 14.5. Depending on where the economy starts from, it will end up at particular levels of g and σ. In this sense the model is path dependent: its long-run equilibrium will depend on its initial position (and shocks along its path).

It may be noted that higher equilibrium levels of g are associated with higher equilibrium profit shares and the same is true along disequilibrium paths. In these senses growth is profit-led. However, if starting from a long-run equilibrium there is a shock which increases (reduces) the profit share, the equilibrium growth rate will fall (rise) and if there is a shock which increases (reduces) the growth rate, the equilibrium growth rate will rise (fall) and eventually the equilibrium profit rate will be lower (higher) than the initial one. Thus, policies which reduce the profit rate at a point in time will have the effect of increasing the growth rate, but also eventually increasing the profit rate. However, it is possible to keep reducing the profit share when it increases, thereby increasing the rate of growth. The reason why the growth rate becomes endogenous in this manner in the model is that investment and the profit share are competing as adjusting variables along the dynamic path. If the profit share is initially lower, it will have a longer road to travel to attain long-run equilibrium, and with this longer time for adjustment, investment will have more time to increase aggregate demand and expand the economy's growth rate.

The model developed here has some similarities with two earlier Keynesian and post-Keynesian models, that is, those of Van de Klundert and Van Schaik (1990) and Bhaduri (2008). Both of these models imply path dependence in the sense of zero-root models involving the dynamics of income distribution and quantities in response to the same disequilibrium. The model of this section shares several features with the Van de Klundert and Van Schaik model: the determination of output at any point in time by aggregate demand, and the response of both the price level and investment to deviations of capacity utilization from desired capacity utilization. However, our model differs from that model because the latter employs a stationary state framework in which the stock of capital becomes constant in long-run equilibrium, with investment depending on the gap between capacity utilization and "full" or desired capacity, rather than changes in investment depending on capacity utilization (since the chapter aims to explain path dependence in the unemployment rate). It is also different in assuming a conventional consumption function with a real balance effect rather than differential saving propensities between wage and profit income which make consumption depend on the real wage, in introducing real wage dynamics that depend on labor market conditions, and in allowing capital–labor substitution in production. It also has no clear discussion of short-run market-clearing equilibrium, and seems to conflate "full" capacity output with aggregate supply, therefore making the price adjustment story somewhat unclear. The long-run version of the model involves three state variables – capital, the price level and the real wage – making the algebraic analysis more complicated than that of our model.

Our model shares several features with the Bhaduri model: it is a steady state model, and there are different saving rates out of wages and profits so that saving depends on the profit share and capacity utilization and the profit share are both adjusting variables. However, there are important differences: capacity utilization and the profit share both adjust to excess demand in the goods market, so that only one "run" is considered, in which capacity utilization and the profit share both adjust to clear the goods market. The model does not imply that actual and desired capacity utilization rates are equal in equilibrium (and therefore does not address the alleged problem of the failure of actual capacity utilization to reach its desired value in equilibrium), and does not explain what happens to bring saving and investment to ex post equality at an instant (a problem that is swept aside in our model by allowing instantaneous or short-run adjustment in capacity utilization). The model also allows investment to depend on capacity utilization and the profit share, which raises all kinds of possibilities about wage-led and profit-led growth, which are not addressed in our model, but which could be introduced into it, as we shall see later.

Our model shows that stability can be obtained in the Harrodian model by adding the dynamics of the markup and the profit share to that of investment. This is not to say that Harrod would necessarily have approved of this method. Harrod (1970, 738) wrote that "if there is more than one possible equilibrium profit share in dynamic equilibrium, consistent with other dynamic determinants, there must be more than one equilibrium growth rate. I would not deny that a multiplicity of equilibrium profit shares and profit rates is a possibility; but it seems to be unlikely." The reason that Harrod gives for this last comment is that the profit share depends on the degree of monopoly, and that he believes that it is "unlikely for the degree of monopoly to have great influence" because it is unlikely for the markup to rise substantially higher than what provides a minimum acceptable rate of return on capital (Harrod, 1970, 738). However, Harrod (1936, 92) clearly recognizes that there is a higher propensity to save out of profits than out of wages, so that a rise in the profit share will reduce aggregate demand, and gives changes in the profit share prominence as a stabilizing influence on the economy during the trade cycle.

Turning to the Kalecki–Steindl model, we assume that in the short run K, γ_0 and σ are given, and equations (1) through (4) and (10) hold. Hence, we determine the short-run equilibrium levels of u and g from equations (11) and (12). In the long run we assume that K changes according to investment, that σ changes according to equation (13) and exactly for the same reason as in the Harrodian model with endogenous σ, and that γ_0 changes according to the equation

$$\frac{d\gamma_0}{dt} = \xi[u - u_d],\qquad\qquad(15)$$

where $\xi > 0$ is a speed-of-adjustment constant, that is, the "autonomous" term in the investment function increases when actual capacity utilization exceeds desired capacity utilization.

The long-run dynamics of this model can be analyzed by substituting equation (11) into equations (15) and (13) to examine the dynamics of γ_0 and σ. The dynamics are very similar to those of the Harrodian model just discussed and can be analyzed using a phase diagram with γ_0 replacing g, as shown in Figure 14.6. The main difference between Figures 14.6 and 14.5 is that the line on which the two state variables are stationary has a negative vertical intersect in the former case (but went through the origin in the latter case). The $d\gamma_0/dt = d\sigma/dt = 0$ locus in this case is shown as the line marked $\gamma_0 = s_c u_d \sigma - \gamma_0 u_d$. As in

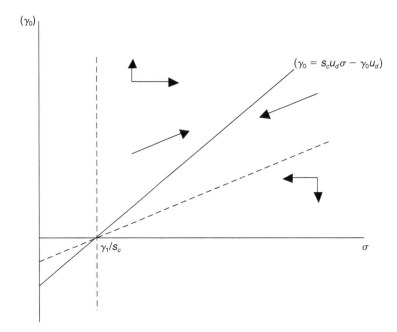

Figure 14.6 Kalecki–Steindl model with endogenous profit share.

Figure 14.5, the arrows point to the northeast above the line and southwest below it. Using the second method of Lyapunov, and again using equation (14) we get

$$\frac{dV}{dt} = (u - u_d)^2 u \left[\left(\frac{\xi}{\gamma_0} \right) - \left(\frac{s_c \eta}{s_c \sigma - \gamma_1} \right) \right].$$

The sufficient condition for stability is $dV/dt < 0$. This will be satisfied if

$$\gamma_0 > \frac{\xi}{\eta} \sigma - \frac{\xi \gamma_1}{s_c \eta}$$

and $\sigma > s_c/\gamma_1$. The first condition is satisfied if, for given ξ, η, s_c and γ_1, the economy is above the positively sloped dashed line with slope ξ/η and horizontal intercept s_c/γ_1, and the second condition is satisfied if the economy is to the right of the dashed vertical line at s_c/γ_1. The zone of stability will be larger, as in the Harrodian model, if ξ is small relative to η.

In the stable case, depending on where we start from, the economy will converge to a long-run equilibrium in which γ_0 and σ attain their stationary values. Since we have a zero-root model with a continuum of equilibria, the model again exhibits path dependence. Moreover, it "solves" the problem of the Kalecki–Steindl model of capacity utilization not generally being equal to its desired level in long-run equilibrium, by ensuring that $u = u_d$. But it does so by making growth profit-led (given other parameters) in terms of long-run equilibria since in such equilibria we have $g = s_c u_d \sigma$, so that g and σ change in the same direction. However, a short-run shock which increases the wage share, reducing σ, will increase the growth rate of the economy and improve distribution, but will then lead to a rise in σ and an increase in growth thereafter. As in the case of the Harrodian model, the government can repeat distributional shocks which shift income distribution towards labor, thereby increasing the growth rate of the economy

5 Conclusion

This chapter has examined the desirability and consequences of introducing "bands" and multiple responses to individual disequilibria in two post-Keynesian models of growth, that is, the Harrodian model and the Kalecki–Steindl model.

It has argued that in an uncertain environment it is plausible to model decision-makers as not changing their behavior if actual outcomes fall within a band of their expected or desired outcomes. To do so it has drawn especially on Shackle's analysis of potential surprise which uses the concept of attention-attracting focus points, although Shackle himself did not draw such conclusions from it. It has applied this idea to the analysis of investment responses to the level of capacity utilization. It has also argued that under uncertainty it is likely that decision-makers will seek to react to disequilibrium situations in multiple ways, for instance, by changing both the price level and their investment plans.

To do so it has drawn on earlier analysis in which excess demand leads firms to adjust their price as well as their output and capital stock.

The introduction of these features into the post-Keynesian models has weakened the force of some of the alleged criticisms of these models. The introduction of the band has made the knife edge in Harrod's model less sharp, thereby deflecting the criticism – and indeed, making it closer to Harrod's own views – of the knife-edge instability property. The introduction of the band has also defended the Kalecki–Steindl model with endogenous capacity utilization from the criticism that in long-run equilibrium actual and desired capacity utilization rates are not necessarily equal, by arguing that having the actual capacity utilization falling within a desired band is a plausible characterization of long-run equilibrium.

Allowing the price as well as the rate of investment to respond to changes in the deviation of actual capacity utilization from a unique desired rate of capacity utilization has raised the possibility that the instability created by knife-edge response of investment can be stabilized through distributional changes in the Harrodian model, and that the actual and desired rates of capacity utilization are equalized in long-run equilibrium. While the resultant models change some of the implications of standard post-Keynesian models, such as the possibility of wage-led growth, these models still leave room for policy-induced improvements in income distribution to have positive effects on economic growth.

While in these ways our analysis has relevance for debates within post-Keynesian growth theory, the arguably more important implications of our analysis are what they imply for the path dependence in post-Keynesian dynamic models. Our analysis of bands in Harrodian and some interpretations of Kalecki–Steindl models implies that exogenous shocks to growth may have permanent effects because of the existence of neutral equilibria within the bands. Our analysis of multiple responses to disequilibria implies that the models have zero roots and a continuum of equilibria, such that initial conditions and shocks along the growth path will have permanent long-run effects. While not the only ways of producing path dependence, our formulations provide potentially useful ways of allowing history to have a more important role in the analysis of economic growth.

Notes

* I am grateful to Marc Lavoie for his comments on an earlier draft.
1 See, for instance, Arestis and Sawyer (2009).
2 The condition is satisfied in the short run for the Harrodian model, since investment (as a ratio of capital), which is given at the level g, does not adjust to changes in capacity utilization, but saving, which is given by $s_c \sigma u$, does. However, it is violated in the long run, since the only adjustment in the long run is in investment, not in saving.
3 Here I focus on the uniqueness of the planned or desired level at a point in time. There is also the issue that the planned level (which may be unique at a point in time) adjusts endogenously over time. I have discussed this second issue elsewhere (Dutt 1997, 2009) and pointed out that this may also provide a route to path dependence, and will not discuss it here.
4 A similar property holds in a model of perfect competition, although the adjustment

could feature the response of "markets" and not just of firms. In this case, firms are sometimes modeled as choosing to produce profit-maximizing quantities, based on an expected price, and the market price is assumed to clear the market at that given output (with quantities demanded by consumers responding to the price). Then, firms are taken to revise their price expectations by responding to the gap between their original expected price and the equilibrium market price and thereby change their output levels: this is a quantity adjustment story along Marshallian lines. Alternatively, firms are modeled as price takers who choose output levels at the going market price to maximize their profits. The "market" determines whether there is excess demand or supply (with quantity demanded by consumers depending on the price), and accordingly adjusts the price level: this is a price adjustment story along Walrasian lines.

References

Arestis, P. and Sawyer, M. (eds) (2009), *Path Dependency and Macroeconomics*, New York, Palgrave.

Auerbach, P. and Skott, P. (1988), "Concentration, competition and distribution – a critique of theories of monopoly capital", *International Review of Applied Economics*, 2, No. 1, 44–61.

Bhaduri, A. (2008), "On the dynamics of different regimes of demand-led expansion", *Cambridge Journal of Economics*, 32, No. 1, 147–60

Bhaduri, A. and Marglin, S. A. (1990), "Unemployment and the real wage: the economic basis of contesting political ideologies", *Cambridge Journal of Economics*, 14, No. 4, 375–93.

Committeri, M. (1986), "Some comments on recent contributions on capital accumulation, income distribution and capacity utilization", *Political Economy*, 2, No. 2, 161–86.

Dutt, A. K. (1984), "Stagnation, income distribution and monopoly power", *Cambridge Journal of Economics*, 8, No. 1, 25–40.

Dutt, A. K. (1990), *Growth, Distribution and Uneven Development*, Cambridge, Cambridge University Press.

Dutt, A. K. (1997), "Equilibrium, path dependence and hysteresis in post-Keynesian models", in Arestis, P. and Sawyer, M. (eds), *Essays in Honour of G. C. Harcourt, Vol 2: Markets, Unemployment and Economic Policy*, London, Routledge, 238–53.

Dutt, A. K. (2009), "Path dependence, equilibrium and economic growth", in Arestis, P. and Sawyer, M. (eds), *Path Dependency and Macroeconomics*, New York, Palgrave.

Earl, P. E. (1993), "The economics of G. L. S. Shackle in retrospect and prospect", *Review of Political Economy*, 5, No. 2, 245–61.

Flaschel, P., Franke, R. and Semmler, W. (1997), *Dynamic Macroeconomics: Instability, Fluctuations, and Growth in Monetary Economics*, Cambridge, MA, MIT Press.

Harrod, R. F. (1936), *The Trade Cycle: An Essay*, Oxford, Clarendon Press.

Harrod, R. F. (1939), "An essay on dynamic theory", *Economic Journal*, 49, No. 157, March, 14–33.

Harrod, R. F. (1948), *Towards a Dynamic Economics*, London, Macmillan.

Harrod, R. F. (1970), "Harrod after twenty-one years: a comment", *Economic Journal*, 80, No. 319, September, 737–41.

Harrod, R. F. (1973), *Economic Dynamics*, London, Macmillan.

Heiner, R. A. (1983), "The origin of predictable behavior", *American Economic Review*, 73, No. 4, September, 560–95.

Kalecki, M. (1971), *Selected Essays on the Dynamics of the Capitalist Economy*, Cambridge, Cambridge University Press.

Lavoie, M. (1995), "The Kaleckian model of growth and distribution and its neo-Ricardian and neo-Marxian critiques", *Cambridge Journal of Economics*, 19, No. 6, 789–818.

Neville, J. W. (2003), "Expectations, lags and particular parameter values in Harrod's dynamics", *History of Economics Review*, 37, Winter, 100–8.

Rowthorn, R. (1982), "Demand, real wages and growth", *Studi Economici*, 18, No. 1, 3–54.

Shackle, G. L. S. (1955), *Uncertainty in Economics and Other Reflections*, Cambridge, Cambridge University Press.

Shackle, G. L. S. (1961), *Decision, Order and Time in Human Affairs*, Cambridge, Cambridge University Press.

Shackle, G. L. S. (1974), *Keynesian Kaleidics: The Evolution of a General Political Economy*, Edinburgh, Edinburgh University Press.

Shackle, G. L. S. (1988), Business, time and thought: selected papers of G. L. S. Shackle, Frowen, S. (ed.), New York, New York University Press.

Skott, P. (1989), *Conflict and Effective Demand in Economic Growth*, Cambridge, Cambridge University Press.

Skott, P. (2008), "Growth, instability and cycle: Harrodian and Kaleckian models of accumulation and income distribution", unpublished, Amherst, University of Massachusetts.

Steindl, J. (1952), *Maturity and Stagnation in American Capitalism*, Oxford, Blackwell.

Van de Klundert, T. C. M. J. and Van Schaik, A. B. T. M. (1990), "Unemployment persistence and loss of productive capacity: a Keynesian approach", *Journal of Macroeconomics*, 12, No. 3, 363–80.

15 On the circulation of real and fiat money in fix-price and flex-price economies

Edward J. Nell

The chapter begins by setting out a framework of production and distribution enabling the economy to be maintained and supported; then goes on to show how that framework can be "monetized", i.e. showing that a unique definite sum of money can "circulate", so that all transactions are carried out by means of money, ending up ready to circulate again in the next round.

Two different kinds of money can be identified, "real" money and "credit" money, issued by banks and government, but ultimately resting on government fiat. Bank money circulates along the same path as real money. But government money has a separate circuit, which normally will not cover the whole economy; so government money must be supplemented or extended.

Money enters circulation through spending or lending. Two different patterns of demand and response to demand can be identified: demand can primarily affect prices, or it can primarily impact quantities. In the first case we have flexible-price adjustments, in the second fix-price multiplier adjustments; the different responses are based on different production technologies and cost structures. Government and real money will function differently in relation to these two patterns of adjustment. It will be shown that real money supports the flex-price system, whereas fiat money would destabilize it, tending to inflation, while real money would lead to recession in fix-price systems, where fiat money is more appropriate.

I Production and distribution: the two-sector model

The two-sector model of production and distribution can be taken as a framework for studying the circulation of money and fluctuations in aggregate demand.[1] The model abstracts from many important actual features of an economy, and shows how the economy *ought* to work, if everyone did what they are supposed to do. But it does not *idealize* agents, institutions, or relationships, in the sense of attributing powers or knowledge to agents which they could not possibly have.

The coefficients for the two sectors will be fixed in the short run. Each sector's output should be thought of as a composite commodity (and, for some purposes, as we shall see, production in each sector can be understood as the outcome of a modified *vertically integrated process*; each sector produces, as its unit net output, the composite commodity the other needs, while replacing the amount it consumes of its own product). The "consumer good" is produced by labor and capital goods, including unfinished goods-in-process, which in turn have been produced by an even "earlier" stage, using labor and capital goods to work on even more rudimentary goods-in-process. The same holds for capital goods. The final goods are the results of stages of intermediate processing. This will prove to be important in understanding circulation. Wages will therefore be figured as a ratio of payment in consumption goods to labor, measured in consumption goods – analogous to the rate of profits on capital. *Both* elements entering into production, capital and labor, are *produced*. Neither is "scarce"; neither is "given".

The capital goods sector is on the RHS, consumer goods on the left. Output of each good in value terms (price $\times$ quantity), Y_k and Y_c respectively, is measured vertically, and employment in each sector, N_k and N_c, horizontally. Output is shown by a steep line rising from the origin. The real wage bill in each sector, W_k and W_c, is given by a shallower straight line rising from the origin. Profits, P_k and P_c, equal to investment, are shown by the difference between output and wages. The given capital stock of each sector, K_k and K_c, is measured horizontally in the opposite direction, allowing for the display of profit rates. See Figure 15.1.

Although the model makes strong simplifying assumptions, all variables are observables. Note that the basic observables are "revenue" variables, except for N and w. That is, income/output Y, consumption C, investment I, the wage bill W, profits P, the money supply M, government spending G, taxes T, and K are all "revenue" in form: products of prices times quantities. The empirical versions of the relationships between r, w, and prices, on the one hand, and g, c, and quantities, on the other, are, as noted before, "constructed". The primitive observations are not of, e.g., varying prices and correlated changes in quantities, but of relationships between variables representing changing revenue flows.

All aggregates are expressed in relative prices, convertible to an arbitrary unit of account. The rate of profit is the same in both sectors, as is the wage rate: $P_k/K_k = P_c/K_c$, and $W_k/N_k = W_c/N_c$. (The net rate of profit is r, the gross rate $1 + r$.) The diagram on the left shows output of capital goods on the vertical axis, and

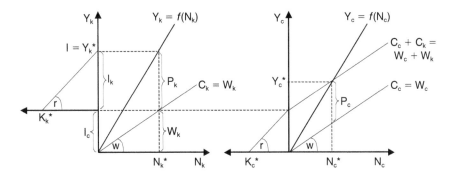

Figure 15.1 The two-sector model of production and distribution.

measuring to the right, capital goods employment, N_k, on the horizontal. The steeper line is the output function, the shallower the wage bill, assumed equal to consumption by capital goods workers, C_k. Investment demand $I = I_k + I_c$ is marked off on the vertical axis; this determines output and employment in the sector, and so its wage bill. This wage bill represents demand for consumer goods, and so is mapped onto the diagram on the right, showing output of consumer goods as a function of employment in the consumer goods sector. It is clear that the wage bill of the capital goods sector equals the gross profit of the consumer goods sector, $W_k = P_c$.[2] Also $P = 1$. These two will figure in the account of the circulation of money to follow.

We can easily see how this model could be used to study variations in effective demand in a *flexible* employment system. Investment spending may be assumed to fall in the "normal" range of capacity utilization; that is, in the range in which constant returns to utilization prevail, as indicated by the straight lines in the diagram. When investment demand is higher or lower, the level of employment in capital goods will be higher or lower in proportion. If I changes from I_0 to I_1, W_k will go from W_{k0} to W_{k1}, and $I_0/I_1 = W_{k0}/W_{k1}$. Therefore profits in the consumer goods sector will vary in proportion to the overall change in investment; profits in the two sectors will be affected in the same proportion. So the uniformity (or divergence) of the rate of profit will be unaffected, whatever the level of investment, as long as it falls in this range. Indeed, when investment changes, everything changes in proportion, as a result of the multiplier – outputs, profits, employment, and the wage bills in the two sectors, all change but stay in the same ratios to each other. No valuation problems are created by such changes, and when studying them, the sectors can be aggregated – as we do later (note that the multiplier here rests on the "balancing condition", $W_k = P_c$; cf. Nell 1977, 1992).

Later (p. 259) it will be shown that a flexible employment system calls for a flexible monetary system in which bank advances adjust promptly to changes in demand, so that M will be endogenous in the short run.

Total output during a period of production is

$$Y = Y_k + Y_c = W_k + W_c + P_c + P_k,$$

and total expenditure

$$E = C_k + C_c + I_c + I_k,$$

where all profits are saved and all wages consumed, so that $P = I$.

These terms all represent transactions, which must be conducted in money. The first problem then, is to explain how a given amount of money, circulating, can enable all of these to be carried out, with the money returning to its starting point, ready to circulate the next round of production. This approach goes back to the early Keynesians: Joan Robinson is very clear that capitalist activity is always fully monetized; indeed, she argues that money is necessary both for the division of labor, and, even more importantly, for the system of wage labor, which is the basis of capitalism.

> it is a necessary condition for the operation of a capitalist economy ... that its members should think in terms of money ... We can imagine an artisan economy in which trade takes place by direct barter, or in which simple triangular transactions are made in kind ... the basket-maker may sell his wares to the blacksmith for nails which he does not propose to use but to exchange ... the degree of specialization and trade that would be possible in these conditions would be very limited. ... In particular, a wage economy requires money ... it would be most inefficient to pay the workers with their own product ... a society which had not succeeded in inventing money could not develop a capitalist economy.
>
> (Robinson 1956, pp. 25–7)

II Circulation and monetization

The expressions for Y, output, and E, expenditure therefore present the variables that have to be monetized; the Classical Savings function greatly simplifies the argument, since if a component of either Y or E is monetized, the corresponding component of the other is also.

Profits are retained and used to finance investment purchases. Managerial consumption is subsumed in household consumption, underwritten by wages and salaries. Initially the Golden Rule is assumed; saving out of wages and consumption out of profits can easily be considered.

Production times in the two sectors are coordinated, and all firms act in concert. If production times were not coordinated, some firms would have a competitive advantage. Here it will be assumed that production, rather than running continuously, can be broken into distinct periods, each with a definite beginning and ending. Within each period inputs are used up, incomes are paid and outputs produced. Growth takes place from period to period, as new capital goods are put in place, enabling production to take place on a larger scale.[3]

Circulation is a repeated process. We can choose to break into the cycle at any point, but it will be convenient to start with inventories of consumer goods assumed to be on hand, the result of production in the previous period. New capital goods and replacements, however, have been sold and are in place. This, then, will be the starting point, and also must be the end-point.[4]

Let's develop this. We will start with firms in the capital goods sector having possession of their wage funds (or of receivables that will be paid shortly). These funds will total W_k. This sum will be advanced to workers in the sector as they work; they will spend it on consumer goods, generating receipts in the consumer goods sector, and leading to production there. In the end, the funds have to return to the firms of the capital goods sector, and they have to be in a position to start the cycle again. (An alternative, also based on cash, would begin with merchants buying the net output of consumer goods, equal to the profit of the consumer sector. But the same circuit also holds for bank money. We could have banks advancing funds to the capital goods sector as needed.[5] Or, banks could advance funds to firms in the consumer sector equal to the cost of their proposed purchases of capital equipment for replacement and new investment. These possibilities have been explored elsewhere; it should be noted, however, that these are not just "alternatives" – each is an institutional setup that reflects particular historical, social, regulatory, and technological conditions. The monetary system evolves.)

Drawing on wage funds, capital goods firms begin production, paying wages to households,[6] who begin purchasing consumer goods, running down inventory, but building up the receipts of consumer sector firms, so that their capital remains intact. As soon as these balances begin to accumulate[7] consumer goods firms can draw on them to pay wages, which promptly return to them as consumer goods workers buy consumer goods.[8]

The circulation of wages as consumer spending needs to be traced out carefully. First, the consumer sector receives revenue from sales to the workers of the capital sector; it delivers its net product to these workers, and as it does so, it sets aside part of that revenue as profits, and pays the rest as wages to workers who are directly employed in the subsector that produces those goods (the net product). These workers then spend their wages on consumer goods; the receipts again are divided and profits set aside, while wages are paid to the workers who produce the consumer goods for the workers and it takes place again. At each stage the wage bill of the *previous* stage constitutes the revenue of *that* subsector, and will equal the combined profits of that and all subsequent subsectors.[9] The wage-bill profit relation thus holds at every stage in the circulation of money through the consumer sector.

When production is complete in both sectors, the consumer sector will have received the entire wage fund as revenue, and its inventories will be wholly depleted. At each stage it will have set aside profits and then passed along a smaller amount as wages. In the end – the limit – the sum of the amounts set aside will add up to the entire revenue the sector initially received, while all the workers in the consumer sector will have received and spent their wages. So the sector's profits, P_c, will be available to spend on its desired gross investment, I_c, returning the wage fund to the capital goods sector.

At this stage W_k has been spent on C_k, and has provided the funds for W_c, which has been spent on C_c, while W_k has re-emerged as P_c, which has been spent on I_c. All have been monetized by the circulation of wage funds equal to W_k. To complete the circulation I_k must be sold for money, realizing profits P_k, and enabling the advances to be repaid, closing the circuit.

The capital goods sector may be divided into two subsectors, one of which sells to the consumer goods sector, the other being the rest of the firms.[10] Then the first subsector receives the whole revenue, I_c; it replenishes its wage fund and spends its gross profit purchasing its desired investment goods. The second subsector receives the gross profits of the first as its revenue; it replenishes its wage funds, and spends its gross profits on its desired investment goods. This process will be repeated until a subsector is reached – the "machine tool" sector – which makes its own capital goods. In each step, a subsector sells its output to a "later" subsector, which pays a revenue consisting of the later subsector's profits (equal to its investment), and then pays its wages and buys the output of an "earlier" subsector. At each stage of the circulation in the capital goods sector, therefore, profits equal investment.[11] At each stage, the loan for wages will be repaid, so that overall, when output at every stage has been sold, the total borrowing for wages will be repaid: spending the profits of the consumer sector will have generated repayments equal to the wage bill of the capital goods sector, while at the same time accomplishing the sale of the full output of the capital goods sector.

More precisely, the consumer goods sector spends $P_c = I_c$, which will be the initial revenue of the capital goods sector, received by the first subsector. Call this I_{k0}, and from it will be subtracted the wage bill of the first subsector, W_{k1}, which will be used to reestablish the wage fund, leaving P_{k1} as profits. Hence,

$$I_{k0} - W_{k1} = P_{k1} \Rightarrow$$
$$I_{k1} - W_{k2} = P_{k2} \Rightarrow$$
$$I_{k2} - W_{k3} = P_{k3} \Rightarrow$$
$$\Rightarrow$$
$$\overline{\phantom{I_{kn-1} - W_{kn} = P_{kn} = }}$$
$$I_{kn-1} - W_{kn} = P_{kn} =$$
$$I_{kn}$$

where $\Sigma_{i=1}^{n} W_{ki} = W_k$, and

$$\Sigma_{i=1}^{n} P_{ki} = P_k,$$

$$\Sigma_{i=1}^{n} I_{ki} = I_k, \text{ and } \Sigma_{i=0}^{n} I_{ki} = I$$

It is easily seen that the repayments of the wage bills sum to P_c.[12]

The nth sector is the "machine tool" sector, which makes its own capital goods. However, the firms in this sector may have preferences for each other's goods, or may prefer to contract out with each other. Firm A may use funds in a "short circuit" to buy from B which in turn buys from C, who buys from A.[13]

At this point the sale for money of I_k will be complete, P_k will have been realized, and all the advanced wage funds replenished. Wage funds equal to W_k will have circulated the entire output Y. In each sector the circulation of funds will trace out the pattern of that sector's *vertical integration*. In the consumer sector, at each stage profits will be set aside until, in the limit, P_c is accumulated, whereas in the capital goods sector at each stage, wage loans will be repaid, until, in the limit, the entire wage bill, W_k, will have been returned to the banks. In each sector the funds will travel "backwards" through the successive stages that directly and indirectly produce the final product of that sector, where that product consists of the goods required by the other sector for replacement, plus the goods required for net expansion.[14]

Income can be paid in money and shown to equal the value of output in circulation, then:

$$Y = W + P = W_k + W_c + P_c + P_k = Y_c + Y_k$$

Now let us assume that the labor coefficient will be the same for every sub-sector in consumer goods. Then $W_c = Y_c - P_c = W_k [(1/(1 - wn_c) - 1]$, a simple multiplier relationship. Since $W_k = P_c$, $Y_c = W_k[1/(1 - wn_c)]$. Next assume that the labor coefficient will be the same in all subsectors in capital goods, and further assume that the machine tool subsector is vanishingly small. Then the first subsector receives P_c ($=W_k$) in revenue from its sales of capital goods to the consumer sector. It withdraws $wn_k P_c$ to repay its loans, and spends $(1 - wn_k)P_c$ purchasing its replacements and new capital goods from the second subsector. This second subsector will withdraw $wn_k(1 - wn_k)P_c$ and spend $(1 - wn_k)$ $(1 - wn_k)P_c$. The resulting sequence, taken to infinity, will sum to $(1/wn_k)P_c$. But this is Y_k, since $wn_k Y_k = W_k = P_c$.

So we have

$$Y = W_k[1/(1 - wn_c) + 1/\{wn_k\}] = W_k [\{wn_k + (1 - wn_c)\}/ wn_k(1 - wn_c)]^{15}$$

Y is income expressed in real terms; the RHS shows the sum required for cir-culation, in units of account, multiplied by the sum of the multipliers for the two sectors, showing how that sum circulates. This expression may be considered the "velocity of circulation".[16]

Velocity, then, consists of a sum of two multiplier expressions, each of which is based on distribution – the real wage and productivity. Hence velocity will reflect the average mark-up, as has been noted before (Nell 1989, 1991, 1998a).[17]

Each of the multipliers in the expression for velocity sums up a process of respending that traces out the pattern of vertical integration for a sector. And the process of circulation as whole depends on the condition that $W_k = P_c$. But that condition also underlies each step of the circulation in the consumer goods sector. In the same way the condition $P = I$ underlies the vertically integrated circulation in the capital goods sector.

So this explains how, when we have a given amount of money, equal in value to W_k, so that,

$$M/\Pi = W_k$$

(where M is the amount of the money article, and $1/\Pi$ is its value) the circulation will monetize all transactions in the economy, and return to its starting point, ready for the next round. It explains "where the money to pay profits comes from", a question posed by Marx, Wicksell, many Keynesians, some Monetar-ists, and the French "Circuit School" (Nell 1967, 1998a; Arena and Salvadori 2004). It provides the foundation for a precise account of the Quantity Equation, giving a mathematical foundation to the idea of endogenous money.[18] When there is a supply function for the money article, M, giving the unit costs at varying levels of output, when an amount of money equals W_k, we can derive the Quantity Equation by substitution:

$$MV = \Pi Y.$$

But the same equation will hold even if the money is pure fiat money, so long as it is introduced with a pre-determined value. Clearly, the quantity of M adjusts to the conditions of circulation.

III Real money, fiat money and confidence

So far the argument has run in terms of money issued by banks; but we have not said whether that money is real – backed by assets – or fiat – backed by government. What matters for circulation is that the public should accept and use the money, *not whether that money is a net asset*. But whether money is backed by assets or by government is important for many other issues.

Being a net asset, like gold, will help to make a potential money-article acceptable; if such an asset is acceptable, but inconvenient (like heavy metal coins), paper or deposits slips can be issued against it. Banks issue against reserves. But governments do not; tax-based money is issued against the tax liabilities of the public.

Convertible paper depends on confidence that the banks will be able and willing to redeem their paper in gold or silver. This can be a serious issue; to ensure confidence, banks must hold adequate reserves, and the banking system as a whole must be prepared to lend to banks that are fundamentally solvent, but temporarily short. Coins are gold or silver, so redeeming is not an issue. But they do give rise to a small fiduciary problem: they may be worn or damaged, so below weight. To continue to circulate at par, the public must have confidence that the issuing mint will redeem them for full-weight coins.

If there are appropriate institutions to guarantee that the banks are holding the necessary level of reserves, and these institutional arrangements also ensure that lending will be available to sound banks that find themselves in short-term need, the public can be expected to view the system with confidence. (In practice, the real reserves are held by a central bank, which issues convertible paper; this paper is held by the ordinary banks as reserve against deposits, which are convertible into paper.) The same holds for worn coins and the mint; there has to be a well-publicized system for easily converting worn coins for new ones. If so the public will gladly circulate the coinage at par. In other words, if the public has confidence that convertibility will be possible, it will readily accept the currency. And the ability of the banking system to meet the demands for conversion is a matter that the financial community has the expertise to judge.

A metallic currency has the advantage that if price level rises above or falls below the level corresponding to the value of the metal, coins will be melted down or bullion will be coined. The mint in short acts as a stabilizer, adjusting the quantity of metal in circulation to the correct level. However, when institutions of credit are well developed variations in the price level are not principally due to fluctuations in the amount of the circulating medium; they are due to expansions and contractions of credit, and these are not necessarily well or directly controlled by adjusting the amount of metal. A great deal of the disagreement over monetary issues in the nineteenth and early twentieth centuries concerned how best to manage reserves so as to limit or expand credit most effectively and at the right points in the cycle.[19] In general, convertible paper currencies were supposed to mimic the behavior of a metallic system (although Mill persuasively argued that this was not the best approach, precisely because credit was not adequately controlled by manipulating reserves (Mill 1848, Book III, ch. 24)).

By contrast in the case of fiat money the government issues money in order to be able to spend without having first to raise money. To ensure the public's acceptance of the money it issues it levies taxes payable only in that money. The public not only accepts the money, it sells goods and services in order to get it, so that it will have what it needs to pay taxes. For a government to issue fiat money it must be stable and legitimate, *and* it must have a large budget. If a government is seen as precarious, its money will always trade at a disadvantage to money with "sound backing" – gold or silver, usually. If it is very precarious or unable to enforce collection of taxes, no one will accept its issue. If the government budget is small once taxpayers have the money they need for taxes they will not need to accept further government money. Some taxpayers may never accept it, but as tax time nears, will buy it with real money, hoping to get it at a discount. At worst they can buy it at par from the government.

The question of confidence in fiat money is problematical, and depends on many factors. First, unlike real money, fiat money has no built-in stabilizing mechanism. The government can set the value, by setting the wage level at which it will hire labor or the price at which it will make its purchases. But there are no market mechanisms to automatically defend or support those prices. Confidence in the value of the currency has to rest on confidence in the ability of the government to manage it.

Second, a fiat currency should be backed by a strong legitimate state with a sizable budget, but this may not be enough to ensure acceptance. To begin with, of course, we cannot always suppose that states that seem well established will remain strong. Civil wars do break out, conflicts over borders are widespread, and even limited wars can have a drastic impact on the ability of a government to manage its currency. Fear of such problems will undermine confidence in fiat money. By contrast none of these factors will cause gold or silver to lose value; quite the contrary – an impending crisis will generally lead prudent wealth-owners to stock up on gold and silver, driving up their value in terms of paper currencies.

However, even supposing that the state is well established (not likely to split in civil war, or be conquered by another state), there could be a change of government, such that the new government

- might devalue the currency, or introduce a new currency
- might over-issue and flood the economy with money
- might repudiate the debts of the previous government
- might temporarily or permanently suspend debt servicing (or change the terms) because of political disputes.

The possibility of any of these will erode confidence.

In other words, real money (money backed by metal) will be accepted if the public feels convertibility is assured;[20] but fiat money depends on a variety of political factors which are hard to judge and may fluctuate suddenly with the state of politics. As a result it is generally the case that real money will be preferred whenever a choice is possible. Fiat money will be spent as quickly as possible; real money will be hoarded.

A special case

Consider a special (quite implausible) case, in which the government issues enough money to circulate the *entire* aggregate output, and in the process takes that money back in taxes, so that the budget is in balance.

In this case the government will purchase the entire net national income, i.e. there are no profits, and no rents, and profits of unincorporated enterprise are reduced to the level of managerial salaries. Consumption supporting labor will be included in the means of production – we ignore luxury consumption and assume all private consumption supports wage earners or managers. Only the consumption of government employees and pensioners will be part of the net product.

Government issues money and purchases capital equipment, and also issues money to pay wages to its employees and pensions to veterans. So government purchases the "final outputs" of capital goods producers and government employees and pensioners purchase with their wages and pensions the final output of the consumer goods sector. In each case the "final output" is produced by labor and means of production, which in turn are produced by labor and means of production. This of course is "vertically integrated" production. Each of these government actions sets up rounds of secondary spending, which in turn set up still further rounds of respending. Producers of final capital goods pay wages, buy unfinished goods, and pay taxes. Sellers of unfinished capital goods pay wages, buy even earlier-stage goods – or raw materials, and pay taxes. Even earlier stages of production do the same – all down the line. Wages from each stage are spent on final consumer goods, along with the wages of government employees, and pensioners. Sellers of final consumer goods pay wages, buy unfinished consumer goods, and pay taxes. Sellers of unfinished consumer goods, in turn, pay wages, buy still fewer finished goods or raw materials, and pay taxes, likewise all down the line.

The "final outputs" purchased by the government set in motion a sequence of transactions in which goods are purchased as inputs and labor is paid. Since the government is buying the *entire net output* all the rest of the economy must be employed directly or indirectly in producing it. The vertically integrated transactions will include all of the rest of the economy – since government is buying *all* the final goods, all other goods are inputs, direct or indirect. So, in this special case, all goods and services will be "monetized" by the government's actions. And at each step of the way taxes will be collected, at a rate such that the sum of the taxes collected through all the rounds, will equal the value of the initial expenditure.[21]

But governments, in fact, do *not* purchase the entire net output; in general in developing countries, only a small fraction, in advanced countries a substantial fraction, but far less than half (not counting transfers). The amount of money issued will be equal to the level of government purchases, but it will circulate that amount of output times the multiplier. From the theory of circulation it is easy then to calculate the amount of money that banks must advance to circulate the remainder of output. So, in general, money issued by governments cannot by itself circulate the aggregate output of the economy. Bank money (or some alternative) will be required. This means that in general there are (at least) *two* issuers of money in the system.

Of course, the state could nationalize the banks; then government spending plus government lending could combine to circulate the entire output. But there would still be two different sources of issue and two different patterns of circulation: the government would issue money for its purchases, and the government banks would create credit money to lend for working capital. Alternatively, even if the government did not own the banks, it could regulate them, accept their notes in payment of taxes, and back them as Lender of Last Resort. In this case the banks could issue credit money that would be, for all practical purposes, the same as money issued by nationalized banks. In either case if the government is sound and able to collect taxes the bank money will be readily accepted at par with the government issue.

Two issuers of money, government and the banking system, would seem to imply two kinds of money, presumably real and fiat. But there could be – and in practice in the advanced world has been – only one form of backing – the full faith and credit of the government. If gold and silver are "demonetized", as they have been since 1933, the only backing for currency is the government, and the fact that it accepts the currency for payment of taxes. But if gold and silver are *also* in circulation there will be two kinds of money, real and fiat, distinguishing by their backing. And they will be in competition.

Yet if there are two issuers of money, should we not look for two basic rates of interest, one for government money, the other for bank money? Consider the example again: the government issued money, and purchased the system's net product (including support for its own employees). The money then circulated through the system, so that all other goods and services, and all labor, exchanged for money. And the money advanced was taxed back. At no point is there any need for interest. Or, it could be said: the rate of interest is zero (Forstater and Mosler 2005). Only when the government runs a deficit does a rate of interest come into play, and then it is the rate the government *pays*.

By contrast, when banks issue money by granting credit, they must have a corresponding asset for anything issued. They issue by lending. Their expenses must be covered by earnings from the issue – so they have to charge an interest rate that will cover those expenses. (Moreover, next period output will have grown, so their lending ability must also grow; their net profit must allow them to expand their capital at the same pace as their demand – similar to any other business.[22]) So the two issuers of money are in very different positions; government has no need for interest, but the banks require it.

Which kind of money can we expect to circulate and why? Before we can address this question we have to consider how the system reacts to demand shocks, particularly fluctuations in investment.

IV Two ways of responding to demand shocks

The two-sector framework shows the coefficients for the normal position of the economy. But the level of demand will fluctuate above and below this position. There are two kinds of responses, one operating through price adjustments, the other through quantity. In the first case the economy is assumed to be characterized by a conventional Marshallian production function, with returns to additional employment first increasing then decreasing. The "normal" or best-practice point will be where a ray from the origin is just tangent to the function. At this point average product equals marginal; this is the point the coefficients represent. In the second case the economy is characterized by constant returns to employment, and the output–employment function will be a straight line rising from the origin, running from left to right.

• The flex-price economy: the price mechanism and Marshallian technology[23]

The flex-price economy centers on the employment–output relationship.[24] In an economy based on "craft technology" (Nell 1998a, 1998c), we can reasonably assume diminishing returns to the employment of labor, in relation to a normal position. Adding extra workers to work teams operating given equipment brings progressively lower rewards, while removing workers leads to progressively larger losses of output. In general, it will be difficult to adjust levels of employment. Workers cooperate in teams that cannot be lightly broken apart or added to; all workers have to be present and working for a process to be operated at all; processes cannot easily be started up and shut down. So the craft economy not only has diminishing returns, it also has inflexible employment (Nell 1998a, ch. 9).[25]

The model is based on an aggregate utilization function, which has a conventional shape and properties. The craft economy[26] will be represented by a curved line that rises from the origin with a diminishing slope (by contrast, mass production – examined in the next section – will be characterized by a straight line rising from the origin).[27] As a first approximation consumption can be identified with wages and salaries,[28] while investment can be taken as exogenous. As employment rises, the wage bill – and so consumption spending – will rise at a constant rate, namely the normal wage rate. Total expenditure will then be shown by adding investment to the wage–consumption line.

The diagram presents an aggregate utilization function, with output on the vertical axis and labor employed on the horizontal. The function of the craft economy is curved, its slope falling as N increases (the mass production line would rise to the right with a constant slope). The wage bill (including salaries) will be assumed to be equal to consumption spending (see Figure 15.2 below for the inclusion of transfer payments). No household saving and no consumption out of profits – but both assumptions are easily modified.[29] So the wage bill, also representing consumption spending, is shown by a straight line rising to the right from the origin; its angle is the wage rate. Investment spending will be treated as exogenous in the short run, so will be marked off on the vertical axis. Aggregate demand will then be the line C + I, rising to the right from the I point on the vertical axis; its slope is the wage rate.

Flex-price adjustment to demand fluctuations

Suppose investment is unusually low, below normal, so that this line cuts the utilization function at a point below the normal level of output and employment. Since it is difficult to adjust employment and output, there will tend to be overproduction, and prices will fall. Since it is even harder to adjust employment than output, prices will fall more readily than money wages. Hence the real wage will rise. As a result the C + I line will swing upwards, until it is *tangent* to the utilization function.[30] Notice that this point of tangency will tend to be close to the normal level of employment and output, and will be closer the more concave the function. In short, when investment is abnormally low, consumption will increase.

Conversely, suppose investment was exceptionally high, or that the C + I line had too steep a slope, indicating too high a real wage. In either case, expenditure

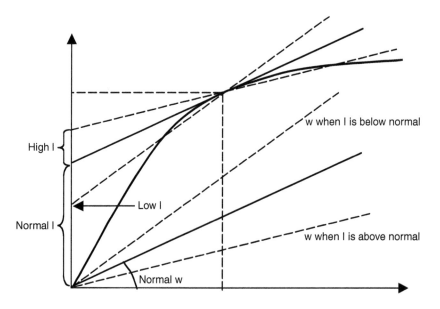

Figure 15.2 Adjustment in the flex-price economy.

would lie above output at any feasible level of employment. Under these conditions prices would be bid up relative to money wages, and the C + I line would swing down, until it came to rest on the utilization function in a point of tangency (Nell 1998a, pp. 455–7). Again this point would tend to lie close to the normal level, being closer the more concave the function. When investment is unusually high, consumption will adjust downwards, and vice versa.

That price flexibility dampens fluctuations by partially offsetting them, in conditions of strongly diminishing returns, can be shown very simply. Recalling our equations: Y is real output, N employment, w/π the real wage, and I investment. All wages are consumed. As above,

$$Y = Y(N), \ Y' > 0, \ Y'' < 0$$

$$Y = C + I$$

$$w/\pi = Y'(N)$$

$$C = (w/\pi)N.$$

Clearly

$$Y = I + (w/\pi)N, \ \text{so}$$

$$dY/dI = \delta I/\delta I + N[\delta(w/\pi)/\delta I] + (w/\pi)[\delta N/\delta I] = 1 + N[\delta(w/\pi)/\delta I] + (w/\pi)[\delta N/\delta I]$$

where $N[\delta(w/\pi)/\delta I] < 0$ and $(w/\pi)[\delta N/\delta I] > 0$. So $dY/dI >$ or < 1 according to whether $N[\delta(w/\pi)/\delta I] >$ or $< (w/\pi)[\delta N/\delta I]$.[31] So long as returns diminish sufficiently $dY/dI < 1$; price changes due to variations in investment demand will lead to a partial offset.[32]

This form of adjustment brings to mind the doctrine of "forced saving" (Thornton 1802; Hayek 1932; Robertson 1926). Here, however, the price changes are assumed to reflect changes in demand pressure – not necessarily connected to changes in the quantity of money – and are shown to result in a Marshallian "marginal productivity" equilibrium.[33] The traditional "forced saving" discussion usually started from an assumed increase in the money issue or in an exceptional extension of credit, and, indeed, a rise in demand of the kind considered here would require just such additional finance – which the resulting rise in prices relative to money wages would tend to support. (The higher profits will allow banks to charge higher interest rates, enabling them to attract additional reserves. The higher interest rates, however, should tend to dampen further expansion.[34])

The multiplier replaces the price mechanism

Fluctuations in I will normally have some impact on N even in a craft economy. But there will be an offsetting movement in C so long as the curvature of the employment function is large. The price mechanism is stabilizing for the system as a whole, but the effect is that profits fluctuate sharply for individual businesses. So firms will be motivated to redesign their production systems to allow greater flexibility in adapting to demand fluctuations. This means being able to add on or lay off workers, without greatly disturbing unit costs. As such redesigning takes place, it will reduce the curvature of the employment function; that is, diminishing returns will be lessened. We can think of this as a progressive "flattening" of the employment function. When this has reached the point where the marginal product curve has unitary elasticity, so that the proportional change in the real wage is just matched by that in employment, then the total wage bill is unaffected by the price changes following the change in I. If the total wage bill is unaffected, then, on the assumptions made earlier, total C will be unchanged.

This will be the case, for example, when the employment function takes the form: $Y = A(\ln N)$. Hence I may fall, for example, but C will not change. There will be no offset. So $dY/dI = 1$. Any *further* reduction in the rate at which returns diminish will mean that the *change in employment will outweigh the change in the wage bill*, so that C will move in the same direction as I. In this event $dY/dI > 1$ will always hold (Nell 1998a, 1992a, 1992b).[35]

• The fix-price economy: demand fluctuations in mass production

In mass production economies (Nell 1998a), constant returns appear to prevail in the short run; to put it differently, unit costs are broadly constant. Workers need only be semi-skilled and teams can easily be broken up and reformed; processes can be operated at varying levels of intensity in response to variations in demand, and they can easily be shut down and started up. It is likewise easy to lay off and recall workers. Investment is driven by the desire for power and wealth, and there is no definable "optimum". It expands productive power, but does not move the economy towards any definite destination. Given a general (competitively driven) motivation to expand and the important role of technological innovation, the urge to invest will sometimes be strong and widespread, but at other times weak and uncertain.

As before we have an aggregate utilization function: here the mass production economy will be characterized by a straight line rising from the origin. As a first approximation consumption can be identified with wages and salaries, while investment can be taken as exogenous. As employment rises, the wage bill – and so consumption spending – will rise at a constant rate, namely the normal wage rate. The wage bill – assumed equal to consumption spending – is represented by a straight line rising to the right from the origin; its angle is the wage rate. Investment spending will be treated as exogenous in the short run, so will be marked off on the vertical axis. Aggregate demand will then be the line $C + I$, rising to the right from the I point on the vertical axis; its slope is the wage rate. See Figure 15.3.

The origin, here and in later diagrams, is the point at which labor cost absorbs all output. Employment in such an economy will depend only on effective

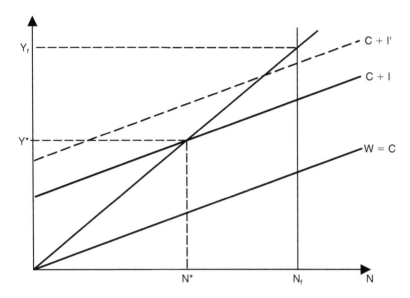

Figure 15.3 Adjustment in the fix-price economy.

demand; there is no marginal productivity adjustment.[36] Output will increase with the amount of labor employed (capacity utilized); all and only wages will be spent on consumption, and all profits will be saved as retained earnings. Investment can be taken as exogenous as a first approximation.[37] Expenditure is given by the C + I line. (This ignores G, government spending, for the moment, although in the modern world it will be much greater than in the earlier forms of the capitalist economy.) But the output function will be a straight line rising from the origin with a slope equal to the average productivity of labor. Suppose investment is exceptionally high; then employment will be increased, and consumption will also be exceptionally high. Conversely, if investment is low, employment will be low, and thus so will consumption. Consumption adjusts in the same direction that investment moves.[38] When investment rises, consumption, output and employment also increase in a definite proportion.[39]

The government budget

The model must include government spending and taxation. Taxes may be levied at a fixed rate on wages, t, and government spending, G, added on to investment. For given t and G and a given output function, whether the government is in deficit or surplus will depend on investment and the real wage. Unemployment can be reduced or eliminated by increasing G or lowering t.

Government may be considered to be largely welfare payments to the unemployed. When employment is minimal, welfare payments will be maximal; at full employment they will drop to zero.

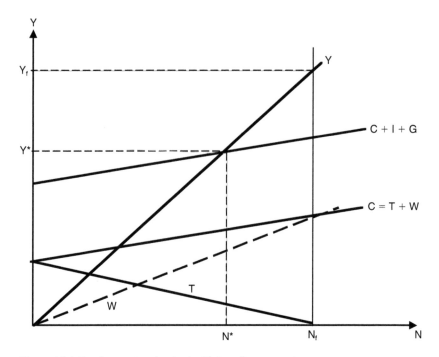

Figure 15.4 Employment and output with transfer payments.

Introducing such welfare payments creates an automatic stabilizer that changes the way the mass production economy adjusts; it raises consumption at every level short of full employment, while reducing its range of variation. This can be seen in Figure 15.4, which plots income on the vertical axis and employment on the horizontal. Private employment runs from the origin to N_f here (and in subsequent diagrams.) At full employment, N_f, transfers will be zero; as employment falls, transfers rise, until at zero employment transfers reach their maximum at the intercept of the line T. The aggregate household income function will be the sum of wages plus transfers, and by assumption, this will equal household consumption, $C = T + W$. When investment (and government spending on goods and services) are added, the result is aggregate demand, which intersects the utilization function to determine employment and output.

The budget itself can be illustrated (Figure 15.5): tax revenues rise with N, and welfare spending falls. Rates are adjusted so the budget balances at full employment. If investment spending falls below the level required for full employment, tax revenues decline and welfare spending rises, providing a stimulus. If investment booms, taxes rise and spending falls, and the resulting surplus acts as a drag on the economy.

In the earlier craft economy, a stabilizing price mechanism ensured that investment and consumption tended to move inversely to one another. This

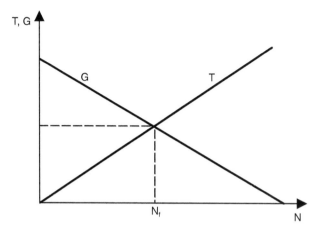

Figure 15.5 Government stabilization in the fix-price economy.

provided an automatic stabilizing adjustment. By contrast, in modern economies investment and consumption tend to move in the same direction, so that fluctuations are enhanced, rather than dampened. The system is volatile, and will be even more so if investment responds to changes in output through an accelerator. But the government budget automatically moves countercyclically.

V Alternative currencies – real (metal-backed) vs nominal (fiat money)

The theory of circulation allows us to determine the amount of money needed for completing all transactions; it also enables us to determine the exact impact of a government issue of fiat money. So we can contrast the working of the two kinds of money in flex-price and fix-price economic systems, knowing that in the analysis we are always working with the correct amounts of money and a precisely determined velocity. None of the results depend on overissue or underissue.

In an economy operating with real money, there is a monetary constraint. The amount of money depends on the amount of backing – the stocks of gold and silver – and on the reserve ratio, which is fixed institutionally, but reflects the market's perception of the risk of a liquidity shortfall. But the amount is fixed in the short run. If activity in one area of the economy needs more money, other areas must make do with less. Or there will have to be an increase in the reserve stocks, which will be costly. Real money stocks can be increased, but the marginal cost is positive. There is, in principle, a well-defined supply function.

By contrast, in the case of fiat money, there is no monetary constraint. There cannot be any shortage of money since the government can create any amount it likes. There is no marginal cost to creating money. So there is no supply function.

This has a special significance when we consider the impact of the government budget. When the government budget is balanced, money issued and tax obligations just balance. In the case of real money, what is spent is equal to what has been taken out in taxes. But when there is a deficit, more is being spent, so the difference must be borrowed. In the case of fiat money, when the budget is balanced, taxes draw out what government pending puts in – there is no net government money left in the system. But with fiat money when the government runs a deficit there will be *excess* reserves, regardless of how reserves are defined, and these will have to be sterilized somehow. Otherwise the excess will push down the interbank lending rate, since any bank would rather have some interest than none. When the government runs a surplus it will absorb reserves – and if this is to continue indefinitely, the government will ultimately have to lend to the banks (if the banks create money to finance the surplus, there has to be an offset on their balance sheets).

We will first explore the operation of real and fiat monetary systems in both flex- and fix-price economies, and then turn to the question of what happens when these two kinds of currencies "compete", that is, both circulate at the same time, in flex- and fix-price economies. Throughout we will assume a developed economy presided over by an established state. The economy is assumed to be operating at a normal level at the outset.

The "real" currency consists of coins of precious metal, and paper or deposits redeemable in that precious metal; the fiat currency consists of paper issued by the government of the state, and this paper money, or cheques denominated in it, is the only means of payment the government will accept in settlement of taxes. There are two cases, then. A flex-price economy will operate craft-based industry; a fix-price economy will operate a mass production system. In either case the two currencies will exchange at par when the government's budget is in balance, and the interest rate will also be the same for bonds denominated in either currency. But when the government budget is in deficit the currencies may not exchange at par, and the interest rates may diverge; however, the way divergences develop will be different in the two different systems of production.

Analysis of money in the flex-price economy

Suppose the economy is based on craft production. In such an economy, real reserves are supplied by mining and minting, and money for circulation – daily use – is issued by banks against their reserves. Such money will be convertible paper. The rate of interest will be determined by supply and demand for reserves (Nell 2004). Government taxation will draw money out of circulation, and reduce spending; government spending then reintroduces the money into circulation and replaces the spending. Goods and services are thereby diverted from the private sector to the public. When the government's budget is balanced, there will be no effect (provided the taxes are properly allocated). But if the government were to run a deficit, it would no longer reduce spending (by taxes) as much as it added to it. This would imply a net increase in demand pressure, which would tend to drive up prices relative to wages (since output is relatively inflexible). The lower real wage will tend to reduce household spending, releasing goods to shift to the government. The higher prices and the deficit require additional money to fuel the circulation – the government will have to borrow from the banks. Hence more reserves will be needed to cover the additional issue. And this can be expected to drive up the interest rate. But the higher interest rate would lead businesses to cut back on investment, releasing resources which can then be diverted to producing the goods the government wants. Both the lower real wage and the higher interest rate tend to bring about adjustment.

If fiat money were to replace real money completely, in such a system, there would be a danger of instability. The money required to circulate the entire output cannot all be government issue; the government will issue only what it needs for its spending. But the banking system could issue fiat money based on government-issued reserves, provided the government central bank agreed to act as Lender of Last Resort. Or if the banking system were nationalized. If the government budget is balanced, it would seem that such a system could work; taxes reduce demand and draw money out of the system, while government spending raises demand and pumps money back into the system.

Now consider the government budget, in a simple case. Assume that the government taxes wages, but spends on both wage-earning employees and on goods and services, in about equal measure. (Taxes on profits or capital gains – withdrawals from circulation – would modify our conclusions.) Then suppose there is a demand shock – private investment booms unexpectedly; prices rise, but wages remain unaffected in the short run. So now the government runs a deficit. This, however, is a net addition to demand pressure, so drives up prices further, since output cannot easily by increased. In a fiat money system the government does not have to borrow in order to spend, so there is no pressure to drive up the interest rate. The government spends the newly issued money; this money will now appear in the banking system as excess reserves. To support the pegged interbank rate the government (or the central bank) will have to reabsorb it by issuing bonds. These will typically be short bonds; banks will then want to readjust their portfolios, to reestablish their desired ratios of short to long (and government to private). They will therefore sell the government short bonds, and buy long bonds. But the government – or the central bank – is pegging the short rate, so short bonds cannot fall. Hence the adjustment will mean that *long bonds will rise*. Thus the long rate will fall – the yield curve will flatten.[40] And this will tend to stimulate investment, especially given the higher profit margins and the fact that the market already faces exceptionally strong demand. Further, the rise in prices will mean that both tax revenues and government spending will increase in nominal terms; in other words, the initial nominal deficit will not cover the desired spending. So government monetary issue will increase, setting off another round of adjustment that will result in a further flattening of the yield curve – further encouraging investment, and so bidding up prices even more.

So far the story is only concerned with the "t" – or lack of fit – between the price mechanism (reflecting the technology) and the monetary/banking system.

A system of real reserves "fits" with flex-price system; but fiat money tends to encourage inflation. Once this begins, labor is likely to demand cost-of-living adjustments in wages and salaries; when such increases are granted, business, in turn, will want to adjust prices to the higher level of costs, and at this point a wage–price spiral will become established. This, in turn, could easily interact with the exchange rate – domestic inflation will lead to a fall in the exchange rate, implying higher prices for imports, and thus a rise in the cost of living, which further drives up domestic inflation, and so on.

Real money checks inflation; fiat money supports inflation

In a real system if money falls in value (prices rise) gold and silver production will slow down or be halted, so the supply of reserves will be constrained automatically – but in a fiat system there are no automatic checks on the supply of reserves, and failure on the part of the government to supply reserves would make the government a contributing cause of the resulting financial failures, when parts of the banking system come up short of reserves. In a fiat system there is nothing to check the fall in the value of money, once it has begun, as it must in a flex-price economy. (Think of Germany and Central Europe after World War I (Ferguson 2001).

As inflation moves into a wage–price spiral, interest rates as a whole will come under pressure to rise since lenders will want to be repaid in full real value. As prices rise, lenders will demand higher interest rates, but they will typically lag behind. The banking system will provide advances to cover the higher wages and prices, demanding additional reserves and backing in turn. The reserves will be supplied, as part of the central bank's obligation to maintain orderly markets. Bank capital, of course, provides a constraint – banks cannot make more loans than their capital warrants.[41] But this will not provide a countercyclical constraint: higher interest rates and increased activity will give banks and financial institutions higher profits in money terms, so *bank capital* can grow in tandem with inflation. Bank capital moves pro-cyclically.

Analysis of money in the fix-price economy

A mass production economy is the relevant example of a fix-price system. Prices are set in the light of long-run expectations of market growth and the evolution of costs.[42] Because output and employment are flexible, when a government deficit leads to an increased demand, the result is higher output and employment, but not higher prices. Reserves will be increased to accommodate the increased level of activity; but there need be no pressure on prices.

Under mass production fiat money comes into its own. Reserves no longer constrain and the monetary authority has to accommodate. If it does not, there will be either excess or shortage of funds in the interbank system, which will drive the overnight rate of interest rapidly to zero or to infinity (in practice, indefinitely large rises). To avoid this instability, the monetary authority has to buy and sell bonds, stabilizing the interest rate, by ensuring that the system has the correct level of reserves. It has to do this whatever the level of activity; hence the rate of interest cannot be set by interaction between the level of activity and the level of reserves. So a deficit will affect neither prices nor the interest rate; instead, it will lead to an expansion.

Now suppose we have a fix-price economy, with a monetary system based on real reserves. Suppose initially the economy is operating at a healthy level, and the government budget is in balance. Then private investment takes a nosedive, and the government comes up with a deficit.[43] Because it is a real monetary system, the government will have to borrow to spend; it cannot create money. So it will have to attract the funds, which means bidding up the interest rate – even though there is available capacity. By attracting the funds, and raising interest, the government will crowd out private investment. This reduction in investment will tend to be offset by the government's deficit spending; but the rise in interest rates has other effects. It raises the costs of working capital and inventory for normal production for all businesses; such higher costs will reduce profit margins, and thus increase risk. This higher risk will act as an *additional* disincentive to investment. Higher interest rates will increase the costs to households of installment buying, thereby reducing household demand for consumer durables. Both of these effects will tend to reduce output and employment. But this means that tax revenues will decline – so the deficit will widen even more. In short, a deficit in a fix-price economy with real money will tend to drive the system into a downswing – or intensify a downswing if one begins for other reasons.

	Real	Fiat
Flex-price	Support	Inflation
Fix-price	Recession	Support

A real reserve monetary system supports the stability and working of a flex-price economy; a fiat monetary system with nominal reserves supports the working of a fix-price economy. But fiat money will tend to generate inflation in a flex-price economy, while real reserves will tend to bring about recession in a fix-price system.

"Competing currencies" – flex-price and fix-price economies with both kinds of money

When the government budget is balanced the two currencies will exchange at par in both kinds of production systems. But when the government runs a deficit in either system, pressures will mount against one of the currencies. In a flex-price economy difficulties will develop for fiat money; in a fix-price economy, real money will tend to be phased out.

In a craft system of production with two currencies, the government issues fiat money, while the banks issue convertible paper. In the case of a deficit, the government will not have reduced private sector activity enough, through taxation, to provide the resources it needs. So it has to bid for resources, to attract them away from private business; this will drive up their prices in fiat money. Fiat money, however, will tend to be spent more quickly than real money, which will be held in reserve by both households and businesses. So the rise in prices will tend to open a gap between fiat and real money. But as the inflation develops, the nominal deficit will widen, so that the government will have to issue more and more fiat money. Not only will fiat fall in value relative to real money, but this will also lead to a rise in the rate of interest on fiat-denominated bonds relative to real bonds. This will require additional government issue, tending to a cumulative decline in fiat money relative to real. Gresham's Law tells us that real money will be held, ceasing to circulate, while fiat money steadily declines in value. At some point it will no longer be a convenience to the government, which will begin to demand payment of taxes in real money (as the Confederacy did).

There is a practical message here. Traditional agriculture and small-scale craft-based industry still predominate in many Latin American and African economies; they are essentially flex-price systems (Delamonica (1998) finds this to be true even of Argentina). But these flex-price economies have often tried to run fiat monetary systems, issuing inconvertible paper, or mixed systems. A fiat money system does not work well in a flex-price economy. Such an economy calls for money with sound backing (although, as the economy develops, the banking system must become more flexible).

In a mass production fix-price system, when demand increases, output and employment will rise instead of prices. A higher level of activity requires a higher level of active money. If the increase in demand comes from government, then the money will be available automatically. The supply of fiat money will be given by government spending, and demand will be taxes plus government borrowing. The increase in government spending will put the additional money into circulation, and it will cover the additional activity generated by the multiplier. Supply and demand for fiat money balance, so there will be no pressure from the government side for fiat money to change in value relative to real, nor for the real interest rate to change.

But suppose the increase in demand comes from the private sector? Then there will have to be an increase in private sector deposits or bank notes to meet transaction needs. An increase in activity requires an increase in working capital; banks will have to make additional loans. Banks will have set their reserve levels for the "normal" level of activity; when activity rises above that level they will have to raise additional real reserves, which will drive up interest rates. When activity is below normal, banks will find themselves with excess real reserves, and interest rates will fall (Currie 1934). So we should see a schedule of interest rates and bank advances (loans creating deposits) that slopes upwards, but centers on a normal rate appropriate to a normal level of activity. (This normal rate would presumably reflect long-term expectations.) Such a schedule might be one way to understand the traditional LM curve; the "vertical" supply curve drawn in textbooks would then represent the "money multiplier" times the fixed level of reserves.

Yet in the long term this is an untenable system. Money issued by the two sources – banks and government – is indistinguishable. Its acceptability is therefore adequately guaranteed by the fact that it is what is used to pay taxes. Convertibility is not necessary to make money acceptable; so real reserves – as opposed to clearing balances – are not needed. Yet as long as the real money system is in place, the private sector cannot meet higher demand without a rise in reserves, and is stuck with non-earning assets when demand is low. Additional reserves can be had, but only at a higher price in interest; while excess reserves act as a drag. *Banks therefore have an incentive to move away from the system of real reserves* (Minsky 1986). Given that they compete for business, any bank that can "stretch" its reserves, through liability management or other innovations, will earn a premium and very likely improve its market share. Moreover, reserves increasingly take on the character of deposits at the Fed – deposits of any kind. Calculating the reserves of an individual bank becomes a matter of "reserve accounting", which typically has a significant lag (Meulendyke 1990). Given such a lag, reserves cannot function as an effective constraint. And banks will seek to dispose of real assets by lending them to governments, in effect, swapping them for government paper. There will therefore be competition to find the best ways to lift the constraint imposed by reserves. The real money system will be phased out.

In a flex-price system, then, real money will tend to act to stabilize the economy, but fiat money will tend to lead to inflation. If the two kinds of currency compete, fiat money will decline in value relative to real money. In a fix-price economy, fiat money will neither stabilize nor destabilize, but will adapt; real money, however, will tend to lead to recession. If they compete, real money will lose out.

Circulation theory shows us exactly how money circulates, tracing out the path, which, in turn, has been laid out by the system of production and distribution. Money is not a veil; it is a mirror – but we have to know how to hold it correctly! Then we can see that an amount of money equal to the wage bill in the capital goods sector will monetize all transactions, and circulate with a velocity equal to the sum of the "multipliers" defined for the vertically integrated sectors of consumption and investment, returning to the starting point. We can also see that under normal conditions government-issued fiat money will not be sufficient to circulate the whole of output; some kind of banking advances will be needed. But whether bank money is based on real reserves or is a form of fiat money it is *endogenous in the short run*; that is, it responds to demand. But then it matters what kind of demand system characterizes the economy.

Notes

1 The production and distribution model may be thought of as a "long-period" framework, in which case the circulation analysis should be understood in the same way.

But then it is difficult to adapt the model to study adjustments to varying levels of aggregate demand, since the long-period position is one towards which the economy gravitates, implying stability. A better approach understands the model as a "true abstraction", one with no idealization, and which shows how essential features of the system work to ensure its continued existence. "True" here is judged in terms both of the model's internal coherence and the way it connects to other parts of the system (Nell 1998a; Nell *et al.* forthcoming).

2 Joan Robinson (1956) makes this point, *AC*, p. 75: "quasi-rent [profit] obtained from the sale of consumption goods is equal to the wages bill for capital goods". On p. 76 she argues the case for P = I.

> The relation between profits and accumulation is two sided. For profits to be obtainable there must be a surplus of output per worker over the consumption per worker's family necessary to keep the labour force in being. But the existence of a potential technical surplus is not a sufficient condition for profits to be realized. It is also necessary that entrepreneurs should be carrying out investment. The proposition that the rate of profit is equal to the rate of accumulation ... (when no profit is consumed) cuts both ways. If they have no profit, the entrepreneurs cannot accumulate, and if they do not accumulate they have no profit. (We just saw that both these expressions are equivalent to bq = tAp.)

3 These assumptions are convenient but not necessary; even continuous production has a beginning and ending and lasts for a definite time. Continuous production can be modeled as a case of overlapping periods.

4 Joan Robinson suggested an account of circulation (Robinson 1960, vol. 2, p. 255):

> We may now ... inquire what has happened to the increment of money which has been created. At any moment some money is in course of traveling round the active circulation – from income earner to shop-keeper, from shop-keeper to producer, from producer to income earner and so back again. Some is in the financial circuit, passing between buyers and sellers of paper assets ....

5 Such advances are drawn on open lines of credit negotiated by the firms as part of their operating capital, and backed by collateral as required by banks, based on the firms' balance sheets.

6 Note that *last* period's output of consumer goods must support *this* period's household consumption, and will be purchased with this period's wage bill. This requires an adjustment to the production equations. Since there is growth from period to period, last period's output must exceed last period's total wage bill by gC. This inventory must be carried over from period to period, as part of the capital of the consumer goods sector. But in the current period of circulation total wages paid and spent will equal total consumption.

7 Notice that the wage bill of the capital goods sector *gradually* accumulates in the hands of the firms of the consumer goods sector. It isn't spent until the production process in capital goods is complete, at which point the entire wage bill will have been paid out and spent. Part of it will be used to circulate the wage bill of the consumer goods sector itself, but a good part will be idle while production is still being carried out in the capital goods sector. These temporarily idle funds can be used for clearing purposes.

8 It might be thought that some of the funds spent on consumer goods and redeposited in the accounts of consumer goods firms, could be returned to be reloaned by the banks to the capital goods sector. In the case of purely nominal money this would not matter; the loans by banks to the capital goods sector create deposit money. The banks have the capital necessary to justify these loans, so they do not need loans from other banks. In the case of real money – metal coins – at first glance this would appear to

save on coins; but it would be dangerous, since the consumer goods firms might call on their deposits before the wage-earners in the capital goods sector had completed their spending of the recirculated coins, which would return those coins to the banks.

9 Thus, the wage bill of capital goods constitutes the revenue of the first subsector in consumer goods, but is equal to the profits of the entire consumer sector. The wage bill of the first subsector will be the revenue of the second subsector, but will equal the profits of that subsector plus all the remaining ones, and so on.

10 Joan Robinson (1956) repeatedly notes that the output of the investment goods sector consists of two kinds of goods (also cf. A. Lowe 1976). For example, on p. 145, she writes, "[As a result of certain changes] the output of the investment sector now consists of a smaller proportion of capital goods required to produce capital goods and a larger proportion of capital goods to produce commodities."

11 Each stage may be considered what Sraffa termed a "subsystem"; taken together they form a vertically integrated system, as Pasinetti has shown. The "final" stage shows the economy so arranged as to produce consumer goods to support labor and the capital for expansion. The next "earlier" stage produces the capital goods for consumer goods, and for the expansion of capital goods. The stage before that produces the capital goods needed for that next-to-final stage, and so on. At each stage the investment spending by that stage provides the revenue for the next stage, and equals the combined profit of that next stage plus all subsequent stages. So the profit equals investment relationship holds throughout.

12 The initial expenditure is $I_c = P_c$. This is spent on the output of the first subsector of the capital goods sector; the profits of that subsector then are spent on the output of the next, and so on, for each further subsector. Thus

$$P_c = P_{k-1} + W_{k-1}$$
$$P_{c-1} = P_{k-2} + W_{k-2}$$
$$P_{c-2} = P_{k-3} + W_{k-3}, \text{ so that, substituting}$$
$$P_c = W_{k-1} + W_{k-2} + \ldots + W_{k-n} + P_{k-n},$$

where this can be extended indefinitely so that P_{c-n} can be made indefinitely small. Thus the sequence converges to the sum of all the wages paid in the capital goods sector, W_k.

13 *Payments* in the capital goods sector take place in succession, but production is simultaneous. A clearing system would simplify the process. There is no implication that firms must wait for an "earlier" stage to be complete. "Earlier" and "later" stages refer to a logical ordering, not a temporal one.

14 This suggests that vertical integration is not just an algebraic rearrangement of industries for the convenience of model-builders. It has an *actual* significance in that it provides the path which monetary circulation follows.

15 If the two sectors were to have the same capital–labor ratios, then this expression would simplify to: $Y = W_k[1/\{wn(01 - wn)\}]$. The multiplier can be expressed in terms of the wage and the productivity of labor because *profits* are saved, and thus are the "withdrawal". This accords with the stylized facts for the US, in which gross business savings have long been far larger than household savings.

16 Lautzenheiser and Yasar (2006), correct a small slip in Nell (2004) and develop the argument nicely.

17 It has been found empirically that when the mark-up has changed, as with the oil shocks of the 1970s, the "transactions demand for money" has shifted accordingly.

18 And it shows the impossibility of such perennial gems of the introductory course, as "a single dollar could exchange against all the goods and services produced, if it could just circulate fast enough", a claim which the author remembers from his course at Princeton, and is apparently still taught there, to judge from the recent novel, *The Rule of Four*, published in 2004.

19 Ricardo (1810) proposed an alternative: paper should be issued by the government, tied to a standard, so that a pound note is worth so much gold. Mill (1848) comments, Book III, ch. 13, sect. 2:

> If, therefore, the issue of inconvertible paper were subjected to strict rules, one rule being that whenever bullion rose above the Mint price, the issues should he contracted until the market price of bullion and the Mint price were again in accordance, such a currency would not be subject to any of the evils usually deemed inherent in an inconvertible paper.

But Mill goes on to comment that the only advantage to this would be that reserves would no longer be needed, this being more than offset in his view, by a great temptation to overissue. He might have added, in view of his analysis of credit or his later discussion of banking practices when markets are in a "speculative state" (ch. 24), that control over the issue of notes, and even more of deposits created by loans, would not be practicable. Even in the nineteenth century the government/bank would be very hard put to manage the issue so that the value would remain stable. However, if the treasury or the bank were to buy and sell bullion at the desired price, it would work. If there were too much paper in circulation paper would fall, making it profitable to turn in paper for bullion. If there were too little paper, it would rise, making it profitable to sell bullion to the state. Since bullion is bulky and inconvenient it does not circulate; thus this scheme would provide for an automatic expansion and contraction of the quantity of paper notes, keeping their value stable. However, the scheme requires a large stockpile of a useless commodity – gold. Later writers, notably B. Graham and N. Kaldor, have advocated similar schemes for buffer stocks of useful commodities.

20 Different banking systems may assemble different kinds of "reserves" (to be distinguished from clearing balances) – they may be real monetary assets, gold or silver, into which notes and deposits may be converted, or they may be stocks of commodities or claims to commodities (as in the proposals by B. Graham (1944) and N. Kaldor (1964)), which are illiquid, so that paper issued by the system would be only indirectly convertible. Or – more problematically – the banking system may be issuing largely against its own capital; but if this capital is illiquid, it will not have much protection in the case of a run – even if an effective clearing system has been established. Convertibility means that mere tokens can be converted on demand into items of real value which are also liquid.

21 The tax rate required must absorb all profits, bonuses, and net income of any kind. Vertical integration is explained in Pasinetti 1973. See also Pasinetti 1977, 1981; Nell 1998a, Ch.7; Sraffa 1960, Appendix on Sub-Systems.

22 Individual banks can increase their capital by raising it on the market; but the banking system as a whole could face difficulties precisely when it needs additional capital. Suppose the economy is growing at rate g, and that stocks as a consequence are appreciating at g (or in proportion to g). But let us suppose that bank earnings are lower than those on other capital so that reinvestment of bank profits produces capital growth at less than g. The demand for money for transactions will grow at g; but the fact that bank capital is growing more slowly means that *the ability to lend* will grow more slowly than g (Nell 2000). But precisely because they are less profitable, banks cannot raise additional capital from outside the banking community.

23 Early capitalism, through the nineteenth century, appears to have had a weak built-in automatic stabilizer in a "price mechanism", which depended on technological inflexibility, and moved countercyclically, in tandem with the monetary system. This was swept away with the advent of mass production, and replaced by a volatile pattern of adjustment, in the multiplier augmented by the accelerator (or capital-stock adjustment process), so that the system came to rely on government for stabilization. This has been explored for six countries, the US, the UK, Canada, Germany, Japan, and Argentina, in which adjustment during the period 1870–1914 is contrasted with that

in 1950–90. Evidence of a weakly stabilizing price mechanism is found in all six in the early period; the transition to a multiplier-based adjustment is apparent in all but Argentina, which did not seem to fully accomplish the transition to a modern economy during the period studied (Nell 1998b).

24 This is a short-run relationship in which given plant and equipment is operated with more or less labor. Marshall and Pigou arguably operated with such a conception (Hicks 1989). A "true" production function (Hicks 1963) would require changing the technique when the amount of labor per unit capital varied. This is not a viable conception, as the "capital controversies" showed (Kurz and Salvadori 1995; Laibman and Nell 1977).

25 In post-war mass production (Nell 1998a), by contrast, constant returns prevail in the short run; to put it differently, unit costs are broadly constant. Workers need only be semi-skilled and teams can easily be broken up and reformed; processes can be operated at varying levels of intensity in response to variations in demand, and they can easily be shut down and started up. It is likewise easy to lay off and recall workers. The widespread existence of constant unit costs came to light beginning with the debate on prices and pricing in the 1930s and 1940s; cf. Hall and Hitch (1939) and Andrews (1949). The suggestion here is that constant costs were the result of technological developments in manufacturing processes. The evidence for constant costs is summarized and discussed in Lavoie (1994, ch. 3).

26 To move from individual firms to the aggregate it is not necessary to hold the composition of output constant, so long as the movements are small. In both craft and mass production the adjustment is better shown in two sectors. The aggregate function oversimplifies. When proportions of capital to consumer goods change in the craft world, prices change; when they change in mass production the degree of utilization changes, but unit costs and prices are not affected.

27 The Penn World Tables provide data making it possible to plot output per head against capital per head with a large number of observations. When this is done for the advanced OECD economies, the scatter diagram shows no evidence of curvature. The same plot for the backward economies exhibits pronounced curvature, for middle-range economies moderate curvature. Of course this can be considered no more than suggestive.

28 Wages and salaries in the aggregate are closely correlated with consumption spending, but do not fully explain it. Some obvious adjustments are easily made. Consumer spending also depends on the terms and availability of consumer credit. In addition it reflects transfer payments. Wealth and profitability are significant variables. But for the present purposes, which are purely illustrative, a simple "absolute income" theory will suffice.

29 This, of course, directly contradicts one of Modigliani's most celebrated contributions, the life cycle hypothesis. But half a century of empirical evidence has shown that in the US (and other advanced countries) household consumption spending tracks wage and salary income "too closely" for any simple version of the life cycle hypothesis to be correct (Deaton 1992).

30 So the real wage equals the marginal product of labor, just as Keynes insisted. Modigliani interpreted Keynes to mean that employment would therefore be determined in the labor market, unless that market were prevented from working by some kind of "imperfection". But Keynes could be understood quite differently, as implying that prices would adjust relative to money wages, in order to bring the real wage into alignment with productivity at the margin. In this case there is no "labor market" of the traditional type, but the system of price adjustment will tend to provide stabilization. However, as we shall see, this tendency to stabilize will be eroded as technology develops – the production function "flattens" – so that business comes to have a greater ability to adjust employment and output to the variations in demand.

31 It is tempting to set the model out in the form $Y = AN^\alpha$, so that $w/p = \alpha AN^{\alpha-1}$. Then α becomes the parameter governing the rate at which returns diminish. However, the

power function is only one of several forms that the relationship between Y and N might take. In particular the log form will be important.

32 Rymes 1989, pp. 37–8 suggests that the real argument of the "Manifesto" by Robinson and Kahn concerned this effect. Rymes argues:

> If the increase in investment … results in a sufficient increase in demand, not only a higher price but also an increase in the costs of production facing the entrepreneur in the consumption goods sector, such that the new equilibrium … entails a higher outlay on consumption goods, then it is possible the decline in the *output* of consumption goods could, in terms of effects on the volume of employment, more than offset the increase in the output of capital goods.

33 "Forced saving" was traditionally ascribed to the effects of an exceptional increase in the quantity of money, leading to a bidding up of prices, lowering consumption and so making an expansion of investment possible. One issue was whether the resulting increase in capital was permanent or temporary; another concerned the effect of the higher prices on rentiers. How the money supply was increased also became an issue, as did the relationship to interest rates. (See also Ricardo 1810, Malthus 1811 and Keynes 1940, as well as those cited above.)

34 But the process cannot continue for too long, for with I rising and C falling, the ratio of capital goods to consumer goods will be moving further and further from its normal level (Nell 1998a, pp. 458–9). However, the monetary/credit system may support prices for too long – "overshooting" – provoking a sharp crash.

35 In his Second Lecture in the Easter Term, 1932, Keynes reached "the remarkable generalization that, in all ordinary circumstances, the volume of employment depends on the volume of investment, and that anything which increases or decreases the latter will increase or decrease the former" (Keynes 1987, Vol. XXIX, p. 40. See also Rymes 1989, pp. 30–44). The "Manifesto" written by Joan Robinson and Richard Kahn, with the concurrence of Austin Robinson, challenged not the result, but the reasoning used in reaching it. As noted above, part of their discussion concerned the effects of price changes. Rymes notes, "The 'manifesto' claimed that the case of no increase in the demand for consumption goods [following an increase in investment spending] was the one exceptional case Keynes had dealt with…. It is … an obviously special case." On the assumptions here it is the case where the elasticity of the marginal product curve is unitary. Both Keynes and the "Manifesto" authors considered the "elasticity of supply" to be a determining factor, but neither presents a precise analysis.

36 That is, employment is *not* determined in the labor market. It follows directly from the demand for output, given the output–employment function – as in Kalecki. Hicks, following Keynes, initially modeled effective demand by setting up the IS-LM system together with a labor market and a conventional production function. Later he came to feel that this was a mistake (Hicks 1977, 1989).

37 On these assumptions investment determines – and equals – realized profits. When households save a certain percentage out of wages and salaries the consumption line will swing below the wages line – profits will be reduced. When wealth-owning households (or businesses subsidizing top managers) add to their consumption spending in proportion to the level of activity, this swings the C + I line upwards, increasing profits.

38 The output multiplier in this simple example will be $1/(1 - wn)$, where w is the real wage and n is labor per unit of output.

39 And money? Let household saving increase with the rate of interest (as consumer durable spending declines), while business investment declines as the rate of interest rises. (Neither influence is likely to be very great.) We can then construct a downward-sloping function (an analog to the traditional IS) relating the rate of interest, i, to employment, N. It will intersect a horizontal line representing the level of the rate of interest as pegged by the central bank; this will determine the level of employment.

40 If part of tax revenues come from profits or capital gains, those funds will have been withdrawn from financial markets, so will have to be subtracted from the funds created by deficit spending, to get the net inflow into financial markets.
41 Individual banks, of course, can raise capital. But the system as a whole is constrained by the level of investment, and the competition for investible funds from corporate business and government bonds.
42 When demand fluctuates strongly, there will normally be some price-cutting or price-gouging, but it will be limited; long-term, large-scale contracts will usually not be affected. The proportional variations in output and employment will be larger than the proportional changes in prices.
43 This is not fanciful. In the early 1930s the US economy had already moved into mass production, but its monetary system was based on gold and silver. Following the collapse of Wall Street, the economy moved into a serious downswing, so that a deficit emerged.

References

Andrews, P. (1949), *Manufacturing Business*, London, Macmillan.
Arena, R. and Salvadori, N. (2004), *Money, Credit and the Role of the State*, Aldershot, and Burlington, VT, Ashgate.
Currie, L. (1934), *The Supply and Control of Money in the United States*, Harvard, MA, Harvard University Press. Reprinted 1968, New York, Russell and Russell.
Deaton, A. (1992), *Understanding Consumption*, New York, Oxford University Press.
Delamonica, E. (1998), "Transformational Growth in the Absence of New Cycle", in Nell, E. J. (ed.), *Transformational Growth and the Business Cycle*, London and New York, Routledge.
Ferguson, N. (2001), *The Cash Nexus: Money and Power in the Modern World, 1700–2000*, London, Allen Lane.
Forstater, M. and Mosler, W. (2005), "The Natural Rate of Interest Is Zero", *Journal of Economic Issues*, Vol. 39, No. 2.
Graham, B. (1944), *World Commodities and World Currency*, New York and London, McGraw-Hill.
Hall, R. L. and Hitch, C. J. (1939), "Price Theory and Business Behaviour", *Oxford Economic Papers,* Vol. os-2, No. 1.
Hayek, F. A. (1932 [1999]), "The Fate of the Gold Standard." Reprinted in Kresge, S. (ed.), *The Collected Works of F. A. Hayek. Good Money, Part I: The New World*, 153–68, Chicago, University of Chicago Press.
Hicks, J. R. (1963), *The Theory of Wages*, 2nd edn, London, Macmillan.
Hicks, J. R. (1977), *Economic Perspectives*, Oxford, Clarendon Press.
Hicks, J. R. (1989), *A Market Theory of Money*, Oxford, Clarendon Press.
Kaldor, N. (1964), "The Problem of International Liquidity", *Oxford Bulletin of Economics and Statistics*, Vol. 26, No. 3.
Keynes, J. M. (1940), *How to Pay for the War: A Radical Plan for the Chancellor of the Exchequer*, London, Macmillan.
Keynes, J. M. (1987), *Collected Writings: General Theory and After – Suppt v. 29 (Collected Works of Keynes)*, London, Palgrave Macmillan.
Kurz, H. D. and Salvadori, N. (1995), *Theory of Production. A Long-Period Analysis*, Cambridge, Melbourne and New York, Cambridge University Press.
Laibman, D. and Nell, E. J. (1977), "Reswitching, Wicksell Effects and the Neo-Classical Production Function", *American Economic Review*, Vol. 67, No. 5.

Lautzenheiser, M. and Yasar, Y. (2006), "Circulation and Effective Demand: A Comment on Nell", *Cambridge Journal of Economics*, Vol. 30, No. 4.

Lavoie, M. (1994), *Foundations of Post-Keynesian Economic Analysis*, Aldershot, Edward Elgar.

Lowe, A. (1976), *The Path of Economic Growth*, Cambridge, Cambridge University Press.

Malthus, R. T. (1811), "Depreciation of Paper Currency", *Edinburgh Review*, Vol. 17, February.

Meulendyke, A. (1990), *U.S. Monetary Policy and Financial Markets*, New York, Federal Reserve Bank of New York.

Mill, J. S. (1848 [1987]), *Principles of Political Economy*, ed. Sir William Ashley, reprinted New York, Augustus M. Kelley

Minsky, H. (1986), *Stabilizing an Unstable Economy*, New Haven, CT, Yale University Press.

Nell, E. J. (1967), "Wicksell's Theory of Circulation", *Journal of Political Economy*, Vol. 75, No. 4, 386–94.

Nell, E. J. (1977), "Population, the Price Revolution and Primitive Accumulation", *Peasant Studies*, Vol. 6, No. 1 (January), 32–40.

Nell, E. J. (1989), "The Rate of Profit in Kalecki's Theory", in Sebastiani, M. (ed.), *Kalecki's Relevance Today*, London, Palgrave Macmillan.

Nell, E. J. (1991), *Transformational Growth and Effective Demand: Economics after the Capital Critique*, New York, New York Press.

Nell, E. J. (1992a), "Demand, Pricing, and Investment", in Millberg, W. (ed.), *The Megacorp and Macrodynamics: Essays in Memory of Alfred Eichner*, Armonk, NY and London, Sharpe.

Nell, E. J. (1992b), "Transformational Growth: Mass Production and the Multiplier", in Halevi, J., Laibman, D. and Nell, E. (eds), *Beyond the Steady State: Essays in the Revival of Growth Theory*, London, Macmillan.

Nell, E. J. (1998a), *The General Theory of Transformational Growth: Keynes after Sraffa*, Cambridge, Cambridge University Press

Nell, E. J. (ed.) (1998b), *Transformational Growth and the Business Cycle*, London and New York, Routledge.

Nell, E. J. (1998c), "From Craft to Mass Production: The Changing Character of Market Adjustment", in Nell, E. J. (ed.), *Transformational Growth and the Business Cycle*, London and New York, Routledge.

Nell, E. J. (2000), "Full Employment and the Value of Money: The Implications of 'Exogenous Pricing' for an ELR Program", *Economic and Labour Relations Review*, Vol. 11, Supplement.

Nell, E. J. (2004), "Monetizing the Classical Equations", *Cambridge Journal of Economics*, Vol. 28, No. 2, 173–203.

Nell, E. J., Mayor, F. and Errouaki, K. (2010), *Humanizing Globalization*, forthcoming.

Pasinetti, L. L. (1973), "The Notion of Vertical Integration in Economic Analysis", *Metroeconomica*, Vol. 25, No. 1, 1–29.

Pasinetti, L. L. (1977), *Lectures on the Theory of Production*, New York, Colombia University Press and London, Macmillan Press Ltd.

Pasinetti, L. L. (1981), *Structural Change and Economic Growth – A Theoretical Essay on the Dynamics of the Wealth of Nation*, Cambridge, Cambridge University Press.

Ricardo, D. (1810), *The High Price of Bullion: A Proof of the Depreciation of Bank Notes*, London, John Murray.

Robertson, D. H. (1926), *Banking Policy and the Price Level: An Essay in the Theory of the Trade Cycle*, London, P. S. King and Son.

Robinson, J. (1956), *The Accumulation of Capital*, London, Macmillan.

Robinson, J. (1960), *Collected Economic Papers, vol. II*, Oxford, Basil Blackwell.

Rymes, T. K. (1989), *Keynes's Lectures. 1932–35. Notes of a Representative Student* (transcribed, edited and constructed by Thomas K. Rymes), Ann Arbor, University of Michigan Press.

Sraffa, P. (1960), *Production of Commodities by Means of Commodities*, Cambridge, Cambridge University Press.

Thornton, H. (1802 [1939]), *An Enquiry into the Nature and Effects of the Paper Credit of Great Britain* (ed. with an Introduction by F. A. von Hayek), London, George Allen and Unwin.

Part III

History of economic thought and methodology

16 The origins of social inequality

Beavers for women, deer for men

Alessandro Roncaglia[1]

1 The issue

The issue of power and power inequalities and their basic importance in social stratification is nowadays relegated to an incidental role within the realm of economic theorising, more or less held to pertain to some different and separate field – sociology, for instance. Recalling Lionel Robbins's (1932, 16) definition of economics as 'the science which studies human behaviour as a relationship between ends and scarce means which have alternative uses', mainstream economists tend to attribute the differences between individual agents in the social arena to their resource endowments. These include a part (the original endowment) considered a datum external to the economists' proper field of analysis, and a part for which the individual agent concerned is directly responsible, stemming as it does from the agent's own saving and investment decisions. Resource endowments consist both in wealth external to the person of the agent (commodities and financial assets) and in the personal abilities of the agents themselves. In a competitive environment, the latter account for earning differentials, and are considered to be partly innate, and partly acquired through investment in education.

The classical economists took quite a different view of the economy and society, seeing social stratification as a central part of their subject matter (up to the point of identifying political economy with the study of income distribution between the social classes of landlords, capitalists and workers, as Ricardo stated at the very beginning of his *Principles*). Also, as we shall see, they – and in particular Adam Smith – took a different view of the economic agents' 'innate' abilities.

This chapter focuses on the latter issue. The main question is whether social stratification is a natural phenomenon or, rather, is bound up with society's past history. In discussing this issue, we shall draw on what Adam Smith and other authors, from Plato and Aristotle on to Paul Samuelson, have to say on the origins of the division of labour. As we shall see, we can identify (at least) two very different, indeed opposite, views on this issue: the approach proposed by Smith is in contrast with the tradition of classical antiquity, which in turn reappears once again in the very foundations of the marginalist (scarcity) approach.

This comparison should help us appreciate the possibilities of different inter-pretations of the same phenomenon based on underlying differences in world views – what Schumpeter calls *Weltanschauung* – an aspect often overlooked in contemporary economic debate. One of the very few instances in which direct comparison between different approaches was at the centre of the stage was in the course of the Trieste Summer School on International Economic Studies, organised by Sergio Parrinello, in collaboration with Pierangelo Garegnani and Jan Kregel, from 1979 to 1990.[2] The revival of the classical–Keynesian approach represented the driving force behind organisation of the School, and thus the confrontation between it and the marginalist–neoclassical mainstream; but at the same time the main element of interest which attracted scholars from all over the world to the Trieste School was the fact that, thanks to Parrinello, the School organisers and teaching staff included representatives from all the varieties of non-mainstream economics, from neo-Ricardian and post-Keynesian to evolu-tionary or institutionalist economists. And, although the focus of the School was mainly on theory and policy, the history of economic thought was systematically utilised as a tool for investigation into the different natures of the various approaches. Thus, I would like to see this essay considered as belonging to the Trieste School tradition.

First of all (in section 2) I shall consider Smith's views on the origins of the division of labour, traced to the human propensity for social life. The second step (in section 3) consists in illustrating the criticisms Smith's views came in for immediately after publication of the *Wealth of Nations* from Thomas Pownall, a respected Member of Parliament, who recalled the long tradition focused on innate differences in abilities. We shall then discuss (in section 4) Paul Samuelson's modern reformulation of the traditional view, presented in terms of the gender division of labour and Smith's example of deer and beaver hunting. Finally (in section 5) I will endeavour to vindicate Smith's original views against Samuelson's subtle reformulation, while also commenting on the differences between the classical and marginalist approaches to economics.

2 Adam Smith

Smith tackles the issue of the origin of the division of labour in chapter 2 of book I of the *Wealth of Nations*. In Smith's words (1776, 25):

> This division of labour, from which so many advantages are derived, is not originally the effect of any human wisdom, which foresees and intends that general opulence to which it gives occasion. It is the necessary, though very slow and gradual consequence of a certain propensity in human nature which has in view no such extensive utility; the propensity to truck, barter, and exchange one thing for another.
>
> Whether this propensity be one of those original principles in human nature, of which no further account can be given; or whether, as seems more probable, it be the necessary consequence of the faculties of reason and

speech, it belongs not to our present subject to enquire. It is common to all men, and to be found in no other race of animals, which seem to know neither this nor any other species of contracts.

Smith's thesis is, then, that the division of labour originates in the tendency of men to enter into relations of reciprocal exchange, or in other words – we might say – in human sociability. This is a thesis that constitutes a fixed point in Smith's thought. In fact, he had already stated it, in virtually the same terms, in his university lectures on jurisprudence and in the so-called *Early Draft* of the *Wealth of Nations*.[3] It is an important instance of the typical Enlightenment doctrine of the unintended consequences of human actions in a social context. To the same characteristic Smith (1776, 26) also attributes the origin of language; moreover, it distinguishes men from animals:

> No one ever saw a dog make a fair and deliberate exchange of one bone for another with another dog [...]. When an animal wants to obtain something either of a man or of another animal, it has no other means of persuasion but to gain the favour of those whose service it requires. [...] Man sometimes uses the same arts with his brethren [...]. He has not time, however, to do this upon every occasion. In civilised society he stands at all times in need of the cooperation and assistance of great multitudes, while his whole life is scarce sufficient to gain the friendship of a few persons. In almost every other race of animals each individual, when it is grown to maturity, is intirely independent, and in its natural state has occasion for the assistance of no other living creature. But man has almost constant occasion for the help of his brethren, and it is in vain for him to expect it from their benevolence only. He will be more likely to prevail if he can interest their self-love in his favour, and shew them that it is for their own advantage to do for him what he requires of them.

This long quotation is useful because it brings to the fore an important logical step that Smith takes – a little too rapidly, perhaps – from the propensity to barter as the basis for the division of labour to the role of self-interest for the sound functioning of a system founded on the division of labour.[4] This nexus implies that the propensity to barter may be interpreted as a manifestation of sociability only if we do not confuse the latter concept with the idea of altruism. Let us recall that before writing the *Wealth of Nations* Smith had published an important book on *The Theory of Moral Sentiments* (Smith 1759); if we take this work into account as well, we can appreciate the complexity of Smith's views on the passions and interests motivating human actions – a complexity of views typical of his times. In particular, Smith considers the market economy as predominantly grounded on self-interest rather than mere selfishness. In short, self-interest is compatible with, indeed relies on, attributing a central role to moral rules for the sound functioning of common life in society.[5] It is this specification of the two terms – propensity to barter as sociability, and self-interest as respectful of the basic rights of other human beings – that allows for their immediate connection.

Thus, while the division of labour implies the necessity of exchanges, according to Smith it is in fact the propensity to exchange as a manifestation of sociability which opens the way to the division of labour. This means, *inter alia*, that the market economy is seen not (at least not only, and possibly not mainly) as a solution for coordinating activity in the different sectors of the economy and for regulating the inter-industry flows of means of production and consumption, but more fundamentally as corresponding to the basic human characteristic of sociability.[6]

Far from being at the origin of the division of labour, differences in individual abilities are rather – mainly, though not solely – its consequence; occasional factors, but especially the initial position in society, determine each individual's employment path and through this the very development of her/his abilities:

> The difference of natural talents in different men is, in reality, much less than we are aware of; and the very different genius which appears to distinguish men of different professions, when grown up to maturity, is not upon many occasions so much the cause, as the effect of the division of labour. The difference between the most dissimilar characters, between a philosopher and a common street porter, for example, seems to arise not so much from nature, as from habit, custom, and education. When they came into the world, and for the first six or eight years of their existence, they were, perhaps, very much alike, and neither their parents nor play-fellows could perceive any remarkable difference. About that age, or soon after, they come to be employed in very different occupations. The difference of talents comes then to be taken notice of, and widens by degrees, till at last the vanity of the philosopher is willing to acknowledge scarce any resemblance.[7]
>
> (Smith 1776, 28–9)

An important instance of this view is to be seen in Smith's notion of the entrepreneur as a normal person, with at most the characteristics of a good paterfamilias. This is quite different from the heroic view of the entrepreneur that would subsequently be proposed, most notably by Schumpeter (1912), and which also extends in general to the idea of 'entrepreneurship' as a fourth factor of production, together with labour, land and capital.

Actually Smith, with characteristic prudence, does not deny the existence of original individual differences or, as we would say today, genetic differences. What he maintains is the dominant importance of the elements of differentiation acquired through the vicissitudes of life, and in particular through working experience, but also through education. Indeed, he attributes great importance to education, also as an antidote to the negative consequences of the division of labour.[8] Thus work acquires an additional dimension, as a formative factor, be it positive or negative.

3 Thomas Pownall

The propensity to barter is conceived of by Smith as the mere desire to get in touch with our fellow creatures, independently of the ensuing advantages or disadvantages. Advantages dominate, through the division of labour and its consequences for the wealth of nations, but this is a typical instance of unintended consequences of human actions.

At first sight this idea might seem not to differ greatly from the thesis according to which the division of labour originates in the desire to exploit the innate differences in labour abilities of the different individuals. However, the latter thesis holds very different implications for the origins of social stratification. In fact, it was advanced in direct opposition to Smith's views by Thomas Pownall (1722–1805), who had been governor of the Massachusetts colony (1757–9) and who was at the time a Member of the British Parliament (from 1767 to 1780). Pownall reacted to the publication of Smith's magnum opus with a pamphlet (Pownall 1776), which appears to represent his only claim to a place (a rather minor one at that) in the history of economic thought. The pamphlet criticises the *Wealth of Nations* over a wide range of issues; however, the very first topic Pownall takes up for criticism concerns Smith's views on the origins (or, as he says, the 'springs') of the division of labour.

At first sight Pownall's criticism (1776, 338–9) of Smith seems quite bland, aimed not at errors in his observations, but at his failure to carry his analysis further, without arriving at the first principles:

> I think you have stopped short in your analysis before you have arrived at the first natural cause and principle of the division of labour. [...] Before a man can have the propensity to barter, he must have acquired somewhat, which he does not want himself, and must feel, that there is something which he does want, that another person has in his way acquired [...]. Nature has so formed us, as that the labour of each must take one special direction, in preference to, and to the exclusion of some other equally necessary line of labour [...]. Man's wants and desires require to be supplied through many channels; his labour will more than supply him in some one or more; but through the limitation and the defined direction of his capacities he cannot actuate them all. This limitation, however, of his capacities, and the extent of his wants, necessarily creates to each man an accumulation of some articles of supply, and a defect of others, and is the original principle of his nature, which creates, by a reciprocation of wants, the necessity of an intercommunion of mutual supplies; this is the forming cause, not only of the division of labour, but the efficient cause of that community, which is the basis and origin of civil government.

Pownall's thesis is, however, in clear-cut opposition to Smith's. What he maintains is that there are natural differences between (groups of) human beings, so that – in modern terminology – each agent, or group of agents, is naturally led to produce only part of the bundle of commodities required for use, and needs to enter into relations of exchange with other agents in order to get what is wanting to him/her, in exchange for what is in excess of his/her needs or desires. Society (and civil government) was born because of the reciprocal needs of agents.[9]

As far as the latter aspect is concerned, the view of the individual as a logical *prius* with respect to society is opposed to the Smithian idea, typical of the whole tradition of the Scottish Enlightenment, of the individual as an intrinsically social being.[10] As for the former aspect, namely the existence of natural roots for economic and social differentiations, it is explicitly rejected by Smith, who, as we saw above, considers the different working abilities as mostly acquired as a consequence of the division of labour.

The contrast between the democratic content of the Smithian thesis (with its roots in Locke and Hume) and the conservative element in Pownall's thesis (with its roots, as we shall see, in the ancient classical tradition of Plato and Aristotle) is evident. It is a contrast worth stressing, both because it helps us appreciate the innovative and progressive nature of Smith's social philosophy, and because the contrast between the two views repeatedly manifests itself in the course of time.

4 The 'natural scarcity' tradition, from Aristotle (and Pownall) to Samuelson

The doctrine of the intrinsic – natural and original – differences of abilities was already present (and dominant) in the Greek tradition, and subsequently in the Scholastic period. Suffice it here to recall a few well-known facts.

In Plato's *Republic*, three social classes are recognised: peasants, soldiers and philosophers; the origin of the state is located in the division of labour between specific roles such as peasant, mason and textile worker; in turn, the division of labour originates from the fact that 'our several natures are not all alike but different. One man is naturally fitted for one task, and another for another.'[11] Aristotle follows Plato, notably in specific assertion of the differences in roles between man, woman and slave: 'Thus the female and the slave are by nature distinct [from the male citizen] (for nature makes [...] one thing for one purpose [...]').[12] Plato and Aristotle thus characterise social (and gender) stratification as a fact of nature, stemming from intrinsic differences between human beings.

This thesis was to remain dominant for centuries, its authoritarian connotations fitting in well with the hierarchical social and political structure of the times. Thus, for instance, Thomas Aquinas – and behind him the Scholastic tradition – spoke of an equitable distribution of talents among men on the part of Providence and accepted as just a distribution of incomes and wealth based on the inequalities of rank, merit, abilities, craft and condition from one individual to another.[13]

The traditional doctrine was still alive in Smith's times. What is more, being embedded in a centuries-long tradition, it had acquired the force of an obvious truth, as can be seen in Pownall's confident reaction to Smith, who is in fact treated as a heterodox – quite curiously, to our eyes, but correctly with respect to the mainstream culture of eighteenth-century Europe. The traditional doctrine was in fact a recurrent theme around the mid-eighteenth century, cropping up, for instance, in the framework of a subjective theory of value as exemplified by Galiani (1751, 49): 'By providence men are born to various crafts, but in unequal proportions of rarity, corresponding with wondrous sagacity to human needs.' This passage is noteworthy because it also points to a difficulty in the traditional view: if we admit that the distribution of abilities among the individuals is innate, only a *deus ex machina* – represented here by the 'invisible hand' of Providence – can guarantee that the overall availability of the different abilities corresponds to the requirements of society, since any social mechanism of adjustment is ruled out by definition. (Only later, with general equilibrium theory, would substitution in consumption in response to price differentials consequent to market-determined wage differentials provide the required adjustment mechanism; but at the time, and indeed long after, the structure of consumption was considered – for various plausible reasons – as mainly determined by habits.) Galiani (1751, 50) is also aware of the implications of the doctrine of the innate differences in abilities for income distribution: 'It will be seen that wealth does not go to any person otherwise than in payment for the just value of his works.'

In the nineteenth century, the traditional doctrine reappeared in the context of the debate on slavery – for instance, in the writings of Carlyle and Ruskin, representatives of the anti-abolitionist position.[14] On the opposite side we may recall John Stuart Mill, who advocated the abolition of slavery.[15]

At the end of the nineteenth century there was, then, Pareto's (1896) law concerning personal income distribution, summarised in a famous formula:

$$\log N = \log A - \alpha \log x$$

where N is the number of families with an income at least equal to x, A is a parameter indicating the size of the population, and α is an estimated parameter, generally standing at 1.5. The apparent applicability of this formula to different populations and different epochs is interpreted as demonstrating that income distribution is independent of historical and social vicissitudes. According to Pareto, his 'law' mirrors innate differences in personal abilities, distributed randomly among the population, and is therefore a law of nature.

Thus, in our summary overview, we arrive at contemporary mainstream theory. In maintaining the superiority of the mainstream marginalist theory to the classical approach, Paul Samuelson (1971, 404–5) recalls the issue of income distribution between agents with different natural endowments:

Natural differences show a Gaussian-like spread. 'A man's a man, for all of that' is a proper legal dictum. But a woman is not a man, and men are not at any age homozygous twins. Thus, let women be three times as efficient in beaver production and two times as efficient in deer production. [...] what predictions about exchange ratios can we now obtain from the labour theory of value? [...] Without the Walrasian conditions of full demand equilibrium, which Ricardo wished to avoid in dealing with income distribution, little progress is possible. The beaver–deer exchange ratio can range anywhere from 4/3 to 2/1 depending upon whether tastes are strong for deer or for beaver.[16] Attempting to apply a simple labour theory would result in wasteful neglect of comparative advantage (in which no woman should be producing deer while any man is producing beaver, etc.). Indeed, to understand the statics and dynamics of men–women distributive shares requires use rather than neglect of the tools of bourgeois economics (i.e. of simple general equilibrium pricing).

According to Samuelson, thus, job specialisation between men and women is determined with a reasoning analogous to that concerning specialisation in international trade and based on Ricardian comparative advantages. As a matter of fact, Samuelson is so kind as to attribute superiority to women in both the deer and the beaver sectors; however, since their superiority is greater in dealing with beaver (women, we are told, are better with traps than with open-ground hunting ...), then it is to this sector that women should be confined.

This thesis calls for a number of comments. The first and most relevant point to make is that Samuelson assumes as given (and unchangeable!) the different original endowments of abilities of men and women.[17] The second point concerns a side issue: Samuelson's idea that the labour theory of value implies neglect of comparative advantage is clearly wrong. As a matter of fact, Ricardo illustrated his theory of comparative advantage in international trade precisely with an example framed in terms of labour values; insufficient in itself to determine international terms of trade, it is, however, sufficient to determine the convenience of specialisation for both countries (or, in the case discussed by Samuelson, for both groups, men and women). This brings us to our third comment: the assumption of given original endowments of abilities enjoyed by the different (groups of) individuals in society is by itself insufficient to 'understand the statics and dynamics of men–women distributive shares'; knowledge of individual preference maps and application of the tools of general equilibrium analysis, and hence a subjective approach, are also necessary. It is along these lines that the modern marginalist theory of wage differentials, and of income distribution in general, is constructed.[18]

5 Classical and marginalist approaches compared

The modern marginalist theory of wage differentials may thus be traced back to Pownall's position (innate differences in personal abilities), to which contemporary economists add investment in 'personal capital'. On the other hand, the classical political economists tended to stress the importance of circumstances that determine the work role of each individual, largely connected to the pre-existing social placement, so that social stratification emerges as a mechanism endowed with self-reproducing capacity. Thus, the issue of the origins of the division of labour takes on the dimensions of something rather more than a minor episode in the history of economic thought – an exchange of views that took place over two centuries ago, in 1776. It is, indeed, an important instance of the general opposition between two basically different views of the economy and society, the classical approach and the marginalist one, with its roots in classical antiquity.

Let us recall, albeit very schematically, the nature of this opposition.[19]

On the one hand, the classical economists saw the economy as characterised by the division of labour. This implies not only the separation of tasks within each individual production process, but also the fact that different productive units attend to the various production processes leading to different (bundles of) commodities. Thus, at the end of each productive process, each productive unit (and each sector, or in other words each set of productive units utilising similar production processes and producing similar commodities) needs to recover its means of production in exchange for at least part of its products. This gives rise to a web of exchanges which are necessary for the economy to continue functioning. In a market economy, the exchange ratio between commodities must be such as to allow each sector to recover physical production costs and obtain profits representing sufficient incentive to continue activity. Thus, in the light of technology and the distributive rule of a uniform profit rate – corresponding to the assumption of free competition, or in other words of the absence of obstacles to capital movements from one sector to another – we are able to determine production prices: those prices, that is, which are compatible with continuation of economic activity. Here income distribution between profits and wages is not determined by technical givens, and is commonly treated as an open social issue.

On the other side, according to the marginalist (or scarcity) approach, economic agents have at their disposal given amounts of scarce resources (or original endowments), and these are utilised (directly, through exchange and consumption, and indirectly, through production processes in which productive resources are transformed into consumption goods and services) to satisfy their needs and desires. The market here is a point in time and space where demand and supply meet: its archetype is the market fair, and in more recent times the stock exchange (while within the classical approach the market is a web of commodity flows, recurring period after period, which link up all sectors of the economy). Within the marginalist approach, prices are indicators of the relative scarcity of goods and services available to satisfy the needs and desires of economic agents, which implies a quantitative (utilitarian) assessment of the intensity of needs and desires. In the classical approach, on the other hand, prices are indicators of relative difficulty of production; the problem here is how to express in value terms, that is, in terms of a single magnitude, all the different physical costs while at the same time respecting the distributive rules of a capitalist economy.

We thus have two different representations of the economy: as a circular flow of production and consumption (or better as a spiral, as Sylos Labini 1985 suggested, since the economy develops over time) for the classical approach; as a one-way avenue connecting resources on the one hand, and the needs and desires of economic agents on the other, for the marginalist–subjective approach.[20] In the latter representation, the notion of equilibrium is taken up from physics (or, more precisely, from static mechanics), in the sense of the balancing of opposite forces. To use a metaphor, equilibrium is a sort of spark originating from the two opposite poles of an electric arc – available resources on one side, human needs and desires on the other – or in other words supply and demand. It is clear that the notion of equilibrium concerns prices and quantities simultaneously: prices are equilibrium prices precisely because they equalise the quantities demanded and supplied of the various commodities. It is also clear that this applies to the equilibrium prices of original resources, labour included, which are therefore fully utilised in competitive equilibrium, so that income distribution (including wage differentials) is determined by original resource endowments and their scarcity relative to the needs and desires of economic agents.

The 'one-way avenue' view is thus led by its very internal logic to assume as naturally given the different endowments of qualities and skills of the individuals. It is precisely this assumption that, through specialisation motivated by comparative advantages and the supply–demand equilibrating market mechanisms, determines the (groups of) individuals' distribution among jobs and income levels. Of course, all this presupposes perfect competition – in other words, a society perfectly driven by meritocracy. However, this is not an insurmountable difficulty:[21] other elements, interpreted as frictions or rigidities in the working of the market adjustment mechanism, may be brought into the picture as further approximations to reality, complicating but not changing the substance of the theory. The major limitations, on which we briefly focus attention here, are three in number: the static nature of this approach; the one-dimensional view of the economic agent (the so-called *homo oeconomicus*); and the idea that the economy is driven by a demand–supply equilibrating mechanism.

i) Original endowments of skills are assumed to be given. Let us recall, in this context, that the critiques (for instance, by List 1841) of the Ricardian theory of international trade based on comparative advantage concerned precisely this assumption. The first country to develop a manufacturing industry based on machinery, England, had a comparative advantage in this sector, as compared to the more backward countries: hence, according to the theory of international specialisation based on comparative advantages, the countries left behind had to retain their agricultural orientation, and refrain from developing their own manufacturing sectors. The possibility of exploiting dynamic increasing returns to scale was then, in turn, invoked, thereby stressing that technological relativities were not to be considered as given once and for all by Nature, but – above all – a product of past history, and subject to change over time. Smith's idea that work experience modifies the worker's skills implies cumulative mechanisms analogous in their effects to strong increasing dynamic returns to scale. (The opposition between static and dynamic views here may well reflect a contraposition between a generally static view of society and of the nature of human beings, implicit in pre-modern culture, and the stress on progress which characterised Enlightenment culture.)[22]

As a specific instance of the opposition between a static and a dynamic–evolutionary approach, we may recall Pareto's law of income distribution. As pointed out above, Pareto's law can be interpreted in static terms, as the consequence of a given, Gaussian-like, distribution of abilities between different individuals. However, as subsequent researches have shown,[23] not only are the empirical foundations of the 'law' far from having the consistency of solid rock, but in particular the 'law' itself can be derived as the result of stochastic processes (Markov chains). Such is the case with Gibrat's law, in which the income of each individual depends on his/her income in the previous year plus or minus a casual change, where the probability of a given percentage change remains constant over time.

ii) Since the marginalist counter-revolution, mainstream economic theory has been characterised by a mono-dimensional view of the economic agent, derived – albeit with important changes[24] – from Bentham's utilitarianism. This view is also implicit in the 'human capital' theory, where the individual decides on investments in education motivated by the possibility of obtaining increases in income (or, more generally speaking, utility) due to the newly acquired skills. It is quite different from the more complex view of individuals motivated by passions and interests that prevailed in the seventeenth and eighteenth centuries.

iii) The idea that the economy is driven by a demand–supply equilibrating mechanism is so dominant nowadays as to appear obvious. And yet it implies specific assumptions that are, at least, debatable, such as a notion of the market derived from the Greek agora, the medieval fairs and the modern stock exchanges (a point in time and space where demand and supply converge) rather than from the experience of modern trade in manufactures and services (a web of relations connecting the different sectors of the economy, such as to allow for reproduction of economic activity over time). Moreover, not only original endowments, but also preferences for final consumption goods and services must be considered as given data for the problem (an assumption which reinforces the static nature of the approach). A more modest idea of what economic theory can effectively determine (limited, as in classical theory, to the conditions of reproduction of the economy), on the contrary, opens the way to the possibility of taking into account social, political and historical elements in an evolutionary view of the economy and society.[25] This is, quite clearly, of the utmost relevance to a topic like social stratification, where economic aspects intermingle with issues of power, custom and culture.

In this context, public interventions in the field of education, such as those suggested by Smith in the fifth book of *The Wealth of Nations*, have the function both of a remedy to the perverse effects that the division of labour has on human nature, and of a democratic mechanism fluidifying social stratification.

Admittedly, the brief observations offered here fall far short of full-scale illustration and evaluation of the two theses contrasted here – the thesis of the natural origins of social inequality, and the thesis of evolutionary–cumulative origins of social stratification. However, this story may hopefully represent an example of the ways in which the history of economic thought can help to illuminate understanding and critical evaluation of current views on important aspects of the economy and society.

Notes

1 Department of Economics, University of Rome 'La Sapienza'. In parts of what follows I have utilised material drawn from my books *The Wealth of Ideas* (Roncaglia 2005a) and *Il mito della mano invisibile* (Roncaglia 2005b). A different version of this essay was presented at the 5th Conference of the Iberian Association of the History of Economic Thought, Madrid, 12–15 December 2007. The topic has been chosen so as to be a homage not only to Sergio, recalling his strongly progressive political motivations and some after-dinner talks in Trieste and elsewhere, but also to Giuli, his companion.

2 For an illustration of the Trieste School's cultural project, cf. Parrinello 1988.

3 Smith 1978, 347 (LJ-A, vi.44), 492–3 (LJ-B, 219), 570–1 (*Early Draft*, 20–1).

4 We can perceive here an echo of Mandeville's *Fable of the bees* (1714). There he criticises traditional moral views (as represented for instance by Shaftesbury) as only adequate for a small-scale society, where everyone can be directly in touch with everyone else. A mercantile society, based on the division of labour, necessarily acquires a broader scale; in it, behaviour is driven by individualistic motivations. It is richer than a traditional, small-scale society; hence it also fosters arts and sciences.

5 For an illustration of this point and further bibliographical references, cf. Roncaglia 2005a: 121–6.

6 In so far as it is a response to the social nature of humans, the market economy needs to be organised in such a way as not to contradict its primary origin. Thus, for instance, differences in income, wealth and power so wide as to create fractures in the texture of society should be contrasted. This point deserves a separate treatment; it allows us to hypothesise a Smithian root for contemporary liberal socialism: cf. Roncaglia 2005b.

7 Smith 1776, 28–9. Once again this is a fixed point in Smith's thought. Cf. Smith 1978, 348 (LJ-A, vi.48: 'The difference of employment occasions the difference of genius'), 493 (LJ-B, 220–1), 572–3 (*Early Draft*, 26–8). While the ancient tradition of inborn differences was at the time strong, possibly still dominant, as Pownall's reaction shows, we can find views similar to Smith's, though less clearly enunciated, in authors such as David Hume (see the passage quoted in note 9 below).

8 These aspects are discussed in book 5 of the *Wealth of Nations*, and constitute in the negative a confirmation of the dominant role Smith attributes to work for the formation of the worker's abilities. The passage is well known, but worth recalling here:

> In the progress of the division of labour, the employment of the far greater part of those who live by labour, that is, of the great body of the people, comes to be confined to a few very simple operations; frequently to one or two. But the understanding of the greater part of men are necessarily formed by their ordinary employments. The man whose whole life is spent in performing a few simple operations, of which the effects too are, perhaps, always the same, or very nearly the same, has no occasion to exert his understanding, or to exercise his invention in finding out expedients for removing difficulties which never occur. He naturally loses, therefore, the habit of such exertion, and generally becomes as stupid and ignorant as it is possible for a human creature to become. The torpor of his mind renders him, not only incapable of relishing or bearing a part in any rational conversation, but of conceiving any generous, noble, or tender sentiment, and consequently of forming any just judgement concerning many even of the ordinary duties of private life. Of the great and extensive interests of his country, he is altogether incapable of judging.
>
> (Smith 1776, 781–2)

9 This is also in clear-cut opposition to the (contractualist) idea illustrated for instance by Adam Smith's great friend, David Hume (1752, 467–8): 'When we consider how nearly equal all men are in their bodily force, and even in their mental powers and

faculties, till cultivated by education, we must necessarily allow, that nothing but their own consent could, at first, associate them together, and subject them to any authority.' This thesis is quite important, for it is the basis for maintaining (Hume 1752, 486–7, italics in the original, and echoing Locke) 'that absolute monarchy is inconsistent with civil society'.

10 The issue of logical priority should not be confused with that of political or ethical priority. Cf. Roncaglia 2005a, 421–2.

11 Plato 1930, 151–3 (*Republic*, II.11).

12 Aristotle 1977, 5 (*Politics*, I.2, 1252b).

13 Cf. De Roover 1971, 43–4, also for references to Thomas's writings.

14 Illustration of these debates is provided, for example, by Levy (2001) and Canfora (2004). Thus, for instance, Ruskin (quoted by Levy 2001, 22) maintains 'the impossibility of Equality. My continual aim has been to show the eternal superiority of some men to others.'

15 Mill also criticises Carlyle's thesis that Ireland's backwardness is due 'to a peculiar indolence and *insouciance* of the Celtic race' (quoted by Levy 2001, 95n). Amusingly, the right-wing Lega Nord party in Italy maintains the superiority of the Po Valley populations on the ground of their presumed Celtic origins!

16 Samuelson assumed that the labour time required to men for getting a beaver is twice that required for getting a deer.

17 Analogously, in his contribution to international trade theory (the so-called Heckscher–Ohlin–Samuelson theorem), Samuelson assumes as given the endowments of resources of the different countries. This theory too has been criticised both for its static nature, which is contradicted inter alia by such widespread phenomena as (static and especially dynamic) increasing returns in production, stressed in the so-called 'new economic geography', and because (as first shown by Parrinello) it implicitly relies on the assumption of a one-(basic) commodity world: cf. Parrinello 1970, 1973.

18 Human capital theories, where wage differentials are the consequence of investment in acquiring skills valued by the market, constitute an addition to the scheme outlined here but do not change its basic analytic structure whenever they rely on the assumption of scarce and given resource endowments, precisely as adding a production stage to the pure exchange model does not modify the structure of general equilibrium theory. In itself, obviously, the idea that time and money expended in the acquisition of skills account for part of wage differentials is compatible with both the classical and the marginalist approaches. Adam Smith, for instance, expresses it quite clearly: 'The wages of labour vary with the easiness and cheapness, or the difficulty and expence of learning the business' (Smith 1776, 118).

19 For fuller discussion, including the cautions needed because of the differences internal to the two approaches, see Roncaglia 2005a.

20 The counter-position of the 'circular approach' and the 'one-way avenue' representations is set out by Sraffa (1960, 93).

21 Although it is an important limit, since it implies the assumption that phenomena like family or group power and recommendations (the so-called amoral familism), together with spillover effects in education internal to the family, and similar elements, are wholly absent.

22 Cf. Pollard 1968; Im Hof 1993.

23 For a survey cf. Corsi 1995.

24 For this story, cf. Roncaglia 2005a, chs 8 and 10.

25 On this cf. Roncaglia 1975, 117–30.

References

Aristotle (1977), *Politics*, with an English transl. by H. Rackham, Loeb Classic Library, vol. 21, Cambridge, MA, Harvard University Press.

Canfora, L. (2004), *La democrazia. Storia di un'ideologia*, Rome-Bari, Laterza.

Corsi, M. (ed) (1995), *Le diseguaglianze economiche*, Turin, Giappichelli.

De Roover, R. (1971), *La pensée économique des scholastiques: Doctrines et méthodes*, Montréal, Institut d'études médiévales.

Galiani, F. (1751), *Della moneta*, Naples, Giuseppe Raimondi; 2nd edn, Naples, Stamperia simoniana, 1780; repr. Milan, Feltrinelli, 1963. (English transl., *On Money*, ed. Toscano, P.R., Ann Arbor, MI, University Microfilm International, 1977.)

Hume, D. (1752), *Political Discourses*, Edinburgh, A. Kincaid and A. Donaldson; repr. in *Essays: Moral, Political, and Literary*, ed. Miller, E.F., Indianapolis, IA, Liberty Press, 1987.

Im Hof, U. (1993), *L'Europa dell'illuminismo*, Rome-Bari, Laterza.

Levy, D.M. (2001), *How the Dismal Science Got Its Name*, Ann Arbor, University of Michigan Press.

List, F. (1841), *Das nationale System der politischen Oekonomie*, Stuttgart: J.G. Cotta. English transl., *The National System of Political Economy*, ed. Lloyd, S.S., London, Longmans, Greene and Co., 1909.

Mandeville, B. (1714), *The Fable of the Bees, or Private Vices, Public Benefits*, London, J. Roberts. Critical edn, ed. Haye, F.B., Oxford, Clarendon Press, 1924; repr. Indianapolis, IA, Liberty Press 1988.

Pareto, V. (1896), 'La courbe de la répartition de la richesse', in *Recueil publié par la Faculté de Droit de l'Université de Lausanne à l'occasion de l'Exposition nationale de 1896*, pp. 373–87. Italian transl., *La curva di ripartizione della ricchezza*, in Corsi, M. (ed.) 1995, pp. 51–70.

Parrinello, S. (1970), 'Introduzione ad una teoria neoricardiana del commercio internazionale', *Studi economici*, Vol. 25, No. 2.

Parrinello, S. (1973), 'Distribuzione, sviluppo e commercio internazionale', *Economia internazionale*, Vol. 26, No. 2.

Parrinello, S. (1988), 'Il ruolo di una scuola estiva di economia', *Economia Politica*, Vol. 5, No. 3.

Plato (1930), *The Republic*, Books 1–5 (vol. 1), with an English transl. by P. Shorey, Loeb Classic Library, London, Heinemann and Cambridge, MA, Harvard University Press.

Pollard, S. (1968), *The Idea of Progress*, London, C.A. Watts; repr. Harmondsworth, Penguin Books, 1971.

Pownall, T. (1776), *A letter from Governor Pownall to Adam Smith, L.L.D. F.R.S., being an examination of several points of doctrine, laid down in his 'Inquiry into the Nature and Causes of the Wealth of Nations'*, London, repr. New York, Augustus M. Kelley, 1967; repr. in Smith 1977, pp. 337–76.

Robbins, L. (1932), *An Essay on the Nature and Significance of Economic Science*, London, Macmillan, 2nd edn, 1935.

Roncaglia, A. (1975), *Sraffa e la teoria dei prezzi*, Rome-Bari: Laterza. English transl., *Sraffa and the Theory of Prices*, New York, Wiley, 1978.

Roncaglia, A. (2005a), *The Wealth of Ideas*, Cambridge, Cambridge University Press.

Roncaglia A. (2005b), *Il mito della mano invisibile*, Rome-Bari, Laterza.

Samuelson, P.A. (1971), 'Understanding the Marxian notion of exploitation: a summary of the so-called transformation problem between Marxian values and competitive prices', *Journal of Economic Literature*, Vol. 9, No. 2.

Schumpeter, J. (1912), *Theorie der wirtschaftlichen Entwicklung*, Munich-Leipzig, Duncker & Humblot; 2nd edn, 1926; 3rd edn, 1931; 4th edn, 1935. English edn, *The Theory of Economic Development*, Cambridge, MA, Harvard University Press, 1934; repr. New York, Oxford University Press, 1961.

Schumpeter, J. (1954), *History of Economic Analysis*, ed. Boody Schumpeter, E. New York, Oxford University Press.

Smith, A. (1759), *The Theory of Moral Sentiments*, London, A. Millar; critical edn, ed. Raphael, D.D. and Macfie, A.L., Oxford, Oxford University Press, 1976.

Smith, A. (1776), *An Inquiry into the Nature and Causes of the Wealth of Nations*, London, Strahan, W. and Cadell, T.; critical edn, ed. Campbell, R.H. and Skinner, A.S., Oxford, Oxford University Press, 1976.

Smith, A. (1977), *Correspondence*, ed. Mossner, E.C. and Ross, I.S., Oxford, Oxford University Press.

Smith, A. (1978), *Lectures on Jurisprudence*, ed. Meek, R.L., Raphael, D.D. and Stein, P.G., Oxford, Oxford University Press.

Sraffa, P. (1960), *Production of Commodities by Means of Commodities*, Cambridge, Cambridge University Press.

Sylos Labini, P. (1985), 'La spirale e l'arco', *Economia politica*, No. 2, pp. 3–11.

17 Johann Heinrich von Thünen and the history of economic thought

Context and theory[1]

Bertram Schefold

1 Appreciations of Thünen

Thünen was one of the great economists – there is no controversy about that. Eugen Dühring regarded him as the first German economist of international significance (Dühring 1900 [1871], p. 322). The actual debate on the importance of various aspects of his work was launched by Samuelson in 1983 with his article "Thünen at Two Hundred" (Samuelson 1983). He is not much read, however, and the literature about him is not very large, at least not outside Germany. I see three main reasons for this. The first is a shameful one for German economists: Plans to provide a comprehensive edition of his works, to be based on the Thünen Archive in Rostock, were discussed at the beginning of the twentieth century and on later occasions (Buchsteiner and Viereck 2000) and had come to no fruition at its end (for a bibliography see Lehmann 1990). Second, little apart from the second edition of his main book has been translated into English and some other languages (see also Lehmann 1990). The third reason does not concern a deficiency of reception of Thünen's work but one of its main merits: Thünen's work is of amazing diversity. There are many different aspects of his one book, and it is quite difficult, even for a modern reader, standing on the shoulders of giants, to do justice to each of them. As Samuelson put it:

> The economist who met a payroll and, in recording and analysing his Junker estate accounts, not only created *marginalism* and *managerial economics*, but also elaborated one of the first models of *general equilibrium* and did so in terms of realistic *econometric* parameters.
>
> (Samuelson 1983, p. 575)

One might add that Thünen contributed to location theory – indeed, he founded it – to agricultural economics and to methodology (for bibliographic references see Lehmann 1990; van Suntum 1988; and Baloglou 1995).

Thünen regarded Smith and Thaer as his masters. Smith was the comprehensive economist whose classical traits seemed attractive to Thünen when he was young, but he was mainly to develop the Smithian theory of capital in the neoclassical direction. In Thaer's case, the influence worked both ways. Solid empirical work was at the root of Thünen's synthesis of theoretical and agricultural economics. The accounts of his estate concern not only an analysis of the economic costs and benefits of the different activities undertaken but also a scientific analysis of the effects of fertilisers and of different systems of field rotation on the growth of plants, with anticipations of results of Liebig's agricultural chemistry.

He kept three kinds of accounts (Ehrenberg 1909): a monetary account of income and expenditure, an account of agricultural goods, as they were bought and sold, used, stored or produced, and a diary of the activities undertaken, as described in his "Isolierter Staat" (Thünen 1990, p. 27).

He does not seem to have had much natural inclination to this painstaking work. His brother saw in Thünen primarily a theoretical mind, creating ideas which thoughts were to justify and prove. Ehrenberg (1909) provides evidence of how Thünen formed such theoretical ideas in his work on agriculture, postulating a certain theory of fertilisation and humus formation, and how his experience forced him to modify those ideas. Ehrenberg links this empiricism with observations of Thünen's character which apparently changed in the middle of his life as he became more of a realist.

The management of the estate was not an easy task. It took Thünen about thirty-five years to pay off the initial debts. Prices fluctuated a great deal due to the effects of the Napoleonic Wars and the considerable impact of the British Corn Laws. The actual effects of the changing economic environment on the production conditions of his estate were similar to what happened in his thought experiments in the "Isolierter Staat" where he asked how the activity of a farm had to be modified when it was placed in a different ring. Stable relationships were found by comparing different situations with regard to the determining circumstances, isolating the primary differences and abstracting from others which were set equal; this method could only be followed in a pure form as a mental experiment but it was to be approximated in practical experience.

Ehrenberg (1909, p. 553) regards this method as Thünen's most important achievement. It seems familiar to the modern economist. Niehans thus believes that Thünen used empirical evidence in the same way as the econometrician (Niehans 1987, see also 1990). However, Thünen was not so much concerned with the testing of models; rather, he was interested in stylised facts. Thünen's "Isolated State" contains a sequence of agricultural systems employed in different rings which is demonstrated to be dependent on prices, therefore of being susceptible to change with changing prices. This could be said to represent a test of the theory of rent. But the main results are presented like general truths. For instance, to have milk production in the first, forestry in the second, corn production in rings farther away is presented like a generic result; the figures are not arbitrary data which happen to be available for the test but are regarded as typical for his time and his country.

It is therefore no surprise that Thünen, although the most theoretical of the early German economists, was treated with sympathy by the adherents of the Historical School with their emphasis on induction and their endeavour to uncover characteristic traits of the economies of nations or periods. Schmoller said cautiously: "Er hat … einen Kausalzusammenhang, auf den ihn die Beobachtung führte, erst isoliert, für sich untersucht und dann wieder mit den realen Zuständen verglichen. Die Anwendung solch schematischer, isolierter Beobachtung ist eines der wichtigsten Hilfsmittel wissenschaftlichen Fortschrittes"[2] [1] (Schmoller 1923, p. 118). Salin's interpretation of Thünen's method in his history of economic thought of 1923 was a little more explicit than Schmoller's. Thünen's method involved abstraction but he avoided the "mistake" (*Fehler*) of the classical economists of using unreal working hypotheses (Salin 1923).

What was meant only really becomes clear in Roscher's appreciation, according to which Thünen's most important discovery was his doctrine of the relative usefulness of different agricultural systems (Roscher 1992 [1874], p. 889), each of which presented a functional whole. The historical economist felt attracted not by the abstract theory of rent, be it based on differences in transport cost or of fertility, but by an ordering of different forms of agricultural production which were described in concrete terms: the properties of the soil, the techniques of cultivation (using some system of rotation of plants, of applying manure, of using cattle), together with the economic and social forms of organisation. Roscher also appreciated Thünen's remarks on the education of labourers (Roscher 1992 [1874], p. 894), because it was supposed to imply a qualitative change of the character of the people. Schumpeter, by contrast, regarded Thünen already in his first book on the history of economic thought as an analytical economist ("every inch a thinker" – Schumpeter 1912, p. 55), and ranked Thünen as an equal to the best English classical economists. Later, Schumpeter considered that Roscher had not even understood Thünen (Schumpeter 1954, p. 465).

The most obvious distinguishing feature of the Historical School was its emphasis on the differences between the forms of economic life among peoples and, especially, in different phases of development (Schefold 1996). Thünen occasionally stresses such contrasts, for instance, that between the Old and the New World. Why do the high wages paid in the United States not set a floor for wages in Mecklenburg? There are differences of language, of customs, of laws, of climate, and there are the costs of migration to distant lands. It turns out to have been one of Thünen's most central ideas that wages must rise if workers have the possibility to colonise free lands, for the incomes they produce for themselves act like a reservation wage for the remainder of the economy. The Malthusian theory of population applies if labourers have no access to new territories. The growth of population then causes wages to fall to the subsistence level. One of Thünen's major concerns was to find ways to change this state of affairs.

Marx denies the possibility of such change, except by means of a revolution. He described the emigration of a rich man to Australia who took several hundred poor people with him in order to found an estate on which they would work for him. But when the ship arrived, they all ran away in order to be independent settlers (Marx 1969, pp. 793f.). Marx remarked ironically that the rich man carried everything with him but had failed to export the capitalist relations of production to Australia. Improvement in Europe was possible only by abolishing these capitalist relations.

The liberal socialist Openheimer wished to change capitalism (Caspari and Schefold (Hg.) 1996). He spoke of the "land barrier" (*Bodensperre*). He thought that land for new cultivation existed even in Central Europe but that the monopoly of landowners prevented the workers from taking it under cultivation, and thus wages remained depressed.

As we shall see in more detail, Thünen can be seen as a theorist and reformer along similar lines. He did not organise agricultural communities on new land, as Oppenheimer did in order to circumvent the "land barrier" (see the contributions in Caspari and Schefold (Hg.) 1996) but tried to show what free access to land would mean by modelling the process of colonisation in his "Isolated State". This clearly was, contrary to Salin, an "unreal abstraction", but there was one important element of historical thought in it: he stressed the institutional differences between his model and the actual world surrounding him. He discussed the institutions underlying the formation of agricultural wages, and the variants of the theory depended on the institutional setup.

Although he was not widely read in classical German literature, he was acquainted with some of it, and he was thus exposed to the idea of cultural history. He chose not to introduce it in his economic work. By contrast, the "Isolated State" abounds with references to the natural sciences – indeed, it contains a theory of the fertility of the soil which was speculative in his conception but which he tried to buttress by means of empirical data. This aspect has been emphasised by Heinz Kurz (1995). Thünen resembled Ricardo in his scientific interests, and, like Ricardo, he does not seem to have been tempted to introduce subjective utility into his theory, although he lived at a time when utilitarian philosophy developed, and long after the introduction of subjective utility in Scholastic economic thought. *Utilità* and *rarità* explained prices in Galiani, not to speak of Bernoulli's formalisation of marginal utility. Thünen was not a subjectivist, on the contrary, he was always intent to provide objective measures. This endeavour is obvious in his theory of fertilisation, but also in his economic conceptions. For instance, the costs of transportation are first measured in monetary terms, then expressed in real terms and at last reduced to one common denominator. The cost of transporting rye consists in feeding the horses and the driver so that there is a maximum distance beyond which rye cannot be carried over land because the load will have been eaten up. This "rye model of transportation" is similar to the famous Ricardian corn model of production. It yields a determination of transport costs which is independent of subjective valuations if wages are regarded as subsistence wages and as such are an objective datum. The extent of Thünen's direct involvement with the natural sciences can be assessed, if one reads Thünen's references to different agricultural systems in conjunction with a commentary which provides information both on the agricultural practices of his time and on Thünen's own experiments (Lehmann 1990, e.g. pp. 551f., 570f.). Comparisons with scientific achievements further underline this scientific bent of von Thünen (for instance, his enthusiasm about Herschel's telescope; Thünen 1990, p. 323).

Thünen himself characterised his method of isolating the causal factors one by one and of making abstraction from the influence of others as a "Form der Anschauung" (Thünen 1990, p. 12), a form of visual theorising, which he regarded as the most important element of his book. According to Salin, however, isolation and abstraction were only the first steps. As Thünen went on, his interest in problems of development grew, under the influence of Hegel (Salin 1963, p. 118), and he asked whether institutions were rational within their social context. He was not a half-socialist as Schmoller put it (Schmoller 1923, Bd. 2, p. 344), but, according to Salin, a "patriarchal conservative" (Salin 1963, p. 104). He initiated the discourse on what Alfred Weber called social and cultural factors of location, to be contrasted with those given by nature and technique. In this view, the step which remained to be taken from Thünen's "intuitive" theorising (Salin's "anschauliche Theorie", see Schefold 2004) to the embedding of economics in cultural history (as in the Historical School) was not so large.

"Nobody, before or after, ever understood so profoundly the true relation between 'theory' and 'fact' " (Schumpeter 1954, p. 466) said Schumpeter, unfortunately without explaining what this "true relation" consists of. As we saw, the "Isolated State" resembles more a scenario than an econometric analysis. Plausible empirical figures are used in order to present a typical image of reality. It does not apply to any particular city with the surrounding countryside, but it is not a purely theoretical construction in which arbitrary figures are used for illustration either, but something in between, in that the values chosen for the parameters correspond to the experience drawn from his time and his country.

There is also a normative aspect to the order thus described. Thünen's ethical beliefs have, like his method, been the object of some controversy. Helmstädter (1995) emphasises that Thünen's theory of the natural wage and of marginal productivity – the relationship between both will be discussed below – is based on an equilibrium condition which results from optimisation; Binswanger (1995) points to the fact that the natural wage may not be reached without policy endeavours to change institutions. An effort, motivated by ethical considerations, is necessary to arrive at the natural wage. A motive for analysing the natural wage undoubtedly is ethical; Thünen writes "Friede erzeugt Wohlstand, Wohlstand Überbevölkerung, Überbevölkerung Elend" [2] (Thünen 1990, S. 405). With the idealism characteristic of the first third of the nineteenth century, Thünen strove for the constitutional monarchy and the understanding between the different classes and layers of society which was pragmatically reached in the last third of that century. He wrote in 1848: "Eine wunderbare Umwälzung hat stattgefunden. Rang, Stand, Geburt, Reichtum, selbst das Wissen – Alles hat seine Bedeutung, seine Herrschaft verloren, statt dessen hat die *Gesinnung* den Thron eingenommen, nur sie gibt noch, nur sie hat noch Einfluß, nur sie kann noch herrschen" [3] (Letter from Thünen to his daughter of 1 April 1848, quoted in Buchsteiner 1999, p. 178). That ethical ideals had become – or seemed to have become – the primary driving force in 1848 was what drew Thünen towards the revolutionary movement.

The ambivalence of Thünen's stance as a theorist is perhaps not so difficult to explain in broad terms, although the details of his position with respect to Smithian and Ricardian theory and of his early contribution to marginal productivity theory are intricate and have been subject to often inaccurate interpretations which differ as widely as those of his methodology. An exhaustive treatment of this topic would require a prior study of Thünen's notes on the classical economists of which only excerpts are published; some can be found in Lehmann's edition of "Der isolierte Staat". Thünen used the first edition of Ricardo's "Principles" by C. A. Schmidt (Weimar 1821, see Lehmann 1990, p. 535). These notes contain the confession of how much Thünen felt attracted by typical traits of the classical methodology, such as the gravitation of market prices to natural prices, the objectivity of the latter, the – in the absence of supply and demand curves at any rate – vagueness of the determination of the former, the sharp distinction between value in exchange and value in use, between values and riches (on this point in particular see the excerpts in Thünen 1990, p. 535–537). These positions, taken together, seem to establish that Thünen's economics were firmly rooted in the English classical tradition. However, there were other voices. Salin (1963, p. 91) regarded it as a rumour that Thünen had used and amplified Ricardian theory. Kurz accepts only two elements as particularly "classical" in Thünen: the theory of production leading to the Ricardian theory of rent, and the asymmetrical treatment of the distributional variables (the real wage being primarily a subsistence wage) (Kurz 1995). It is clear that Thünen's position shifted over time. Among the stable elements, one might add that he was particularly careful in distinguishing between short-run and long-run effects, his essential analytical concern being the latter, as in Smith and Ricardo.

Thünen's move towards what we call marginal productivity theory was slow and cautious. He felt that it would have to be based on an empirical analysis of production functions. He was not able to isolate them in his data, although he had been looking for evidence of them for more than twenty years, as he confessed in 1845 to his half-brother:

> Zwar sind schon aus der Kenntnis, daß der Arbeitslohn = $\sqrt{ap}$ ist, für mich die wichtigsten Resultate hervorgegangen, aber soll ich mit wahrer Freudigkeit fortarbeiten, muß ich die Verbindung zwischen q (dem zur Produktion verwandten Kapital) und p (dem Producte) kennen. Die Erforschung dieses Gesetzes hat mich seit zwanzig Jahren beschäftigt, aber, da die Wirklichkeit gar keine Daten dazu liefert, leider immer vergebens. [4]
>
> (quoted in Roscher 1992 [1874], p. 897)

The acceptance of this part of his work by his contemporaries was at best lukewarm; Schumpeter wrote about the early reactions: "For though he continued to be quoted, the marginal productivity theory of distribution was independently rediscovered later, and his message was fully understood only at a time when all that would strike the reader was its short-comings" (Schumpeter 1954, p. 466). It seemed possible to play down its importance, as economists of the

German Democratic Republic in its later years tried to do, preferring to see Thünen as an advocate of the labour theory of value (Lehmann 1990), while his earlier work was simply denounced as bourgeois and apologetic (Töpel 1964). Streissler (1995) regards marginal productivity theory as an outgrowth of German economics in the early nineteenth century, elaborated by Rau, Schütz, Roscher, Hermann, Thünen and, of course, Gossen. What Menger and the Viennese School added was utility theory, but this was also present in Gossen.

The use Thünen made of marginal productivity is illustrated by his analysis of the wage at full employment. If wages have been pushed up too high, rents are said to turn negative on marginal land, and marginal farms will go out of business. The displaced workers migrate to the city, but they will be employed only if "Kulturmethoden angewandt werden, die weniger einträglich sind und sich beim bisherigen Arbeitslohn nicht bezahlt machen" [5] (Thünen 1990, p. 324). Full employment is thus reached only through a process of substitution of methods of production in the long run. The rate of interest is then determined by the profit earned on the last dose of capital invested, and Thünen insists on the change of distribution engendered by the process of accumulation of capital: the rate of interest will fall and wages rise. More capital does not mean more exploitation, he insists, but higher wages. Thünen often reckons in terms of an agricultural commodity so that the problem of distribution is presented in terms similar to those of Ricardo's corn model, but his equilibrium normally includes a full employment condition which was absent in the classical scheme. The wage is essentially uniform and regulated at the margin of cultivation (Thünen 1990, p. 372). His theory of value (to be analysed in part 2 of this chapter) is based on that of the natural price, but, with distribution determined by marginal productivity, closer to that of Adam Smith than to that of Ricardo; marginal productivity explains what in Smith are the natural rates of wages, profits and rent, and given these, natural prices are determined by adding up the costs – Ricardo's criticism of "adding up" notwithstanding (Sraffa, Introduction to Ricardo 1951–1973; here 1951). Moreover, value in use is no longer, as in the classical authors, a category describing the socially relevant physical characteristics of a commodity, it is not a quality of the commodity as opposed to value in exchange and price, which are quantitative characteristics (Schefold 1999), but it becomes the price people are prepared to pay. Value in exchange then is a cost price, value in use a demand price. The most advanced of Thünen's theoretical constructions is that for the value of capital, as applied to the theory of forest values in the posthumous edition of his book, but this will not be discussed here (see van Suntum 1995, p. 104).

One may ask why neoclassical theory did not emerge in Germany around 1850, if so many important elements had been developed by then. Schumpeter provides the following answer:

> jene Richtung, deren Höhepunkt Hermann und Thünen waren, hat um jene Zeit ihre Stellung eingebüßt unter dem Eindruck der Werke von Rodbertus und Marx, der auch eine Renaissance Ricardos zufolge hatte. Es entwickelte

sich schnell eine orthodoxe Marx-Schule unter der Führung von Engels und Kautsky, und auch die ihr nicht angehörigen, sich für Theorie interessierenden Geister wandten sich wesentlich an Rodbertus und die englischen Klassiker, vor allem an Ricardo. Sie erblickten in der Grenznutzentheorie eine Entdeckung zweifelhaften Wertes und nahmen einen prinzipiellen Kampf gegen sie auf. [6]

(Schumpeter 1912, p. 114)

The counteraction took place in England, led by Jevons, and Marshall stated about Thünen that he was the one whom he "loved above all my other masters" (quoted in Schumpeter 1954, p. 465).

Thünen must be reckoned among the early mathematical economists, and he was better equipped in this regard than all English economists of comparable importance prior to Jevons. But he was not the first German economist to use calculus for optimisation, having been preceded in particular by Graf Buquoy (Baloglou 1995).

2 Value, growth and distribution

We shall now focus on Thünen's theoretical contribution in part II of "Der isolierte Staat" without trying to do justice to the other parts of his work. He is one of the earliest authors whose theoretical conceptions are sufficiently definite for an unambiguous translation of some core passages into modern theory, and the essential steps towards formalisation were taken by Thünen himself.

Such formalisation is hardly ever complete, however. Even the modern economist invariably has an intuitive view of the functioning of the economy which is richer than what can be expressed in precise mathematical terms. The intuitive notions may lead in different theoretical directions and often appear contradictory. The modern translator is at a dead end, for instance, if a mercantilist author like Serra seems to combine competitive markets with a discussion of what we call increasing returns to scale; these two traits cannot be reconciled within the neoclassical theory of perfect competition. One then discovers that more modern theories of industrial organisation are better able to express what Serra meant (Schefold 1994). Since they do not exhaust the vision either, the task of reinterpreting old authors can be taken up by every new generation of economists in this as in other cases; the young will always find something new in the heritage of the past.

This has happened repeatedly with Thünen's theory of rent and location. The comparison with Ricardo revealed the importance of transport in the determination of rents. The consideration of different forms of transport, the inclusion of mining and of manufacturing and of the centres of production and consumption led to the theory of location. Samuelson has drawn attention to the fact that Thünen's model itself, if formalised by means of production functions, with location taken into account, leads to the discovery of intricacies which had escaped the attention of earlier readers. What does it mean to have a uniform wage in the

"Isolated State" if the transport of wage goods like bread, timber, milk, cloth, is costly? Can one expect that the intensity of labour diminishes monotonically from the outskirts of the city to the outer rings? Samuelson (1983) shows that this is not necessarily the case. One such refinement leads to the next: once it is understood that a uniform subsistence wage defined in real terms is not compatible with a cost of this basket of goods uniform in space, one may turn to the landowners and ask where they, with their different consumption patterns, are to be located.

Thünen himself makes it very clear that the agricultural systems to be employed are different in different rings because prices change. Yet he does not go as far as Sraffa did in 1925 when he denied that the notion of fertility had any meaning independently of prices. This radical critique (Sraffa 1925) was represented in purely formal terms: the fertility of a certain type of soil was defined in terms of the maximum value of output per man which could be reached. A change of prices, for whatever reason, could in principle upset the order of fertility completely, and concrete examples could be found to justify the consideration of the thought experiment. The possibilities of applying fertilisers or of improving the land by means of drainage or irrigation depend on incomes and prices, and cases of more drastic changes in land use are imaginable if non-agricultural uses are also taken into account.

The critique was radicalised in Sraffa's book of 1960 in which processes of production were represented by linear activities. As I have shown on various occasions elsewhere (Schefold 1989 [1971]), a theory of the specialisation of land results, if one counts the equations. Using Thünen's image of concentric rings, we could visualise this specialisation as follows: Wheat is grown in every ring up to the most distant land which is still cultivated. With distribution and the prices of other commodities regarded as given (but they have really to be determined in an interdependent system of equations), the cost of production and of the transport of wheat to the centre can be determined. The cost is highest on the most distant land which determines the price of wheat; rents rise, as one gets to the inner rings. To the extent that costs are influenced by transport and not by fertility, the rents rise monotonically as one approaches the city. Hence rents and the prices of non-agricultural commodities and of corn are determined. Other agricultural crops will then be grown on various rings, but each on at most one ring (supposing that no more of this commodity is needed) since the cost of production of any other commodity like milk will be different on different rings, and a uniform price for this commodity, say milk, is only possible if it is produced on only one land.

A change of prices, engendered for instance by a change in distribution, will alter the pattern of specialisation of the lands. This argument for specialisation does not apply, however, if the production of different agricultural commodities is linked by joint production or joint costs. Field rotation leads to an economic link between different plants grown successively on the same land, like clover and wheat (Schefold 1989 [1971]). Although it was clear to Thünen that economic considerations, i.e. prices, determine the use of land, he was far from limiting his analysis to this formal consideration. On the contrary, he aspired to show that certain spatial arrangements of agricultural production were more appropriate than others. Hence he made an exemplary use of concrete figures to show which order was natural, taking into account not only physical, but also social and economic conditions of his time.

Most modern economists find it difficult to understand Thünen's concrete assumptions, being separated from his world by a century and a half. The most abstract form of his theory is his rye model which resembles Ricardo's corn model in that not only is everything expressed in terms of rye; as we have seen, even transport is in terms of rye since the rye which is being transported serves also to feed those who transport it. Distribution of the surplus between profit and wages is determined at the margin of cultivation, in order to get rid of rent. He wants to make a point which is different from that usually made in the Ricardian tradition, however. The surplus found on the marginal land, above the subsistence level of workers, is not simply appropriated by capitalists, determining the rate of profit over capital advanced, with the gloomy perspective that with the extension of cultivation this rate of profit must fall and the rents on better lands rise. Rather, this surplus is to be divided between workers and capitalists in a fair manner. The conception of fairness is influenced by the possibility for workers to settle on free marginal land, as we had already hinted at and as we shall have to show in greater detail, for this peculiar construction does not make sense outside the social universe which Thünen had in mind.

He took much care to explain and justify his assumptions. Like later German authors such as Mangoldt (1855), he regarded the profit of the entrepreneur as an important variable and the function of the entrepreneur as crucial for the economic process. He thought that the essential function of the entrepreneur could not be delegated. When business is bad, good employees will try to improve matters, but only the entrepreneur will sacrifice his sleep in order to find new solutions. The theory of distribution regards this profit of the entrepreneur as given and is concerned with the trade-off between the rate of interests and the wage rate.

The analysis is based on a two-sector model; consumption goods are produced by means of capital goods and labour, while capital goods are produced by labour alone, to simplify the analysis. Capital goods embody technical progress. A production of consumption goods is not possible in northern latitudes, if labour is not assisted by capital. Thünen uses a speculative historical reconstruction to establish this point. It demonstrates that he thought that his fundamental economic categories applied to all periods. Human society must have its origins in tropical attitudes, for it is possible to live off the fruits of trees, i.e. by labour alone, only there. The construction of nets for fishing and of bows and arrows for hunting then allows, like in Austrian capital theory, a society to reach a higher productivity in the production of consumption goods, and it is progress in this production of capital goods which eventually enables man to live in the temperate and northern zones.

Different strata of people are involved in the investment process. On the one hand, progress presupposes schooling and scientific activities, hence intellectuals. On the other hand, the investment must be undertaken, and here the entrepreneur plays the crucial role in reality. However, Thünen is interested in the emancipation of the workers, and they also invest to the extent that they can. For the agricultural labourers are not entirely without property. They have their cottages, perhaps a cow, perhaps a small plot of land on which they farm part-time by themselves, but their main income derives from working on the estate of the landowner. Their income is above the subsistence level, but not by much. In an example, Thünen presents such a labourer with an annual income of 100 monetary units, who owns one cow of the value of 20. Suppose that this cow dies (Thünen 1990, p. 343). To lose one-fifth of one's annual income is unpleasant but not a great calamity, one should think. But if the subsistence level of this person (including the family) is 90, the entire annual disposable surplus of 10 is required for two years to make good for the loss. How can accumulation proceed if the disposable surplus is so small?

Thünen now constructs a two-sector model of the Austrian type which was liked and well summarised by Böhm-Bawerk (1991 [1989], vol. 1, p. 146). Böhm-Bawerk begins his rendering of Thünen's theory of capital with such a worker who needs an annual subsistence of $a = 100$, has a surplus $y = 10$ and therefore an income of $w = 110$. After ten years, the worker will therefore be capable of abandoning the production of consumption goods for one year in order to produce capital goods – bows and arrows or whatever. Efficiency rises so that $a = 100$, $y = 50$. The worker will now be able to suspend the production of consumption goods and to produce capital goods after two years, but he can also lend to another worker who so far has worked without capital. The borrower can thus produce 150 instead of 110; he then has 40 more than he would have had without capital, and he will have to pay interest out of these 40 to the lender. It is assumed that he will return the capital intact. Thünen knows that this is not strictly possible in the transfer of individual capital goods, but a balanced stock of capital may exist in society as a whole in which the capital worn down in every year is exactly compensated by new capital produced during the same period.

Böhm-Bawerk concludes his summary with the following question: "Für den Wert dieser Lehre kommt nun alles darauf an, in welcher Art die Verknüpfung zwischen der größeren Ergiebigkeit der durch Kapital unterstützten Arbeit und dem Bezug eines Wertüberschusses durch den Kapitaleigentümer hergestellt wird" [7] (Böhm-Bawerk 1991 [1989], vol. 1, p. 148). Böhm-Bawerk recognises that von Thünen does not fall into the trap of ascribing the surplus value generated by the use of the capital good to its physical productivity but he criticises him for assuming that the capital good is rendered intact. For this assumption begs the question of what the capital is worth and of why the price of the capital good does not rise to the point where this surplus value vanishes. What he misses in von Thünen is the insight that borrowing and lending involves an intertemporal exchange of goods which differ at least insofar as they are available at different dates.

Thünen, who did not argue in terms of subjective utility theory, does not in fact use time preference to discuss accumulation. But what else can govern this process? One knows the Aristotelian answer: production is for use, and what the household needs is defined by cultural limits. Wealth is not an end in itself but a mean to pursue higher goals in life, and these are jeopardised if the getting of wealth is pursued excessively. This happens if wealth is looked at in monetary terms, for there is no visible limit to the accumulation of money (Schefold 1989a). The classical authors, Ricardo in particular, saw no limit to the process of accumulation except through a fall of the rate of profit which would reduce the inducement to invest. It seems surprisingly difficult to locate Thünen's position in this triangle of the cultural or ethical, of the formal neoclassical and of the classical view.

The difficulties start with Thünen's theory of value on which any formal theory of accumulation must be based.

Thünen made it clear that he regarded supply and demand as not sufficient to determine prices (Thünen 1990, p. 326). It is necessary to explain why supply and demand are what they are. Supply will be high today, for instance, because the price was high yesterday. A durable equilibrium can exist only when the price corresponds to the natural price (Thünen 1990, p. 329). This Smithian confession was based on the hope that prices could be reduced to "objective" data, but Thünen observes that Smith himself limited the domain of the application of the labour theory of value to simple states of society prior to the accumulation of capital (Thünen 1990, p. 364). Ricardo wanted to use the labour theory for advanced states, also but he was unable to integrate interest into this analysis. Thünen was therefore prevented from fully accepting the classical theory of value because he thought that Ricardo had not solved the problem of relating values into natural prices or, as Marx put it, of transforming labour values into prices of production. I have seen no evidence that Thünen understood how Ricardo used the "invariable standard of value" in order to obtain an approximate solution (Schefold 1989 [1971], part III, chs 2 and 6).

Moreover, von Thünen did not distinguish adequately between the labour time historically embodied in a commodity and the socially necessary time for its production. He was aware that the socially necessary labour time to produce a commodity falls with technical progress; for this he provides impressive examples. A watermill allows one person to produce as much flour in a given time as twenty people manually. One labourer ploughs more land with two horses and a plough than thirty people can dig up by means of spades (Thünen 1990, p. 344). In this context it is not always clear when accumulation means more capital goods of a type which had been known or new kinds of capital goods.

We now approach Thünen's model of accumulation, bearing in mind his social concerns, his institutional framework, his method and his tools of analysis. The amount of capital used is measured by the number of years needed to produce it, if one unit of labour is expended on capital production every year. Here he abstracts from inputs other than direct labour (Thünen 1990, p. 351). The value produced is then expressed not in money, but in real terms, such as rye (Thünen 1990, p. 330).

He also uses labour commanded when he writes: "Ist das Kapital Q in Silber angegeben, so muß, um dasselbe in Jahresarbeit auszudrücken, Q ebenfalls mit $\frac{p}{1+qz}$ dividiert werden ..." [8] (Thünen 1990, p. 364; $\frac{p}{1+qz}$ is an expression for the wage, as we shall see immediately). Of course, since capital is thought to be produced by direct labour only and since the wage is paid *ex post*, the difference between labour commanded and labour embodied disappears.

The value p of the consumption good, expressed in rye, is the sum of the labour used in the consumption good industry plus the interest on the cost of the use of capital (which represents the labour of several years). Capital is here assumed to be everlasting, hence this interest cost amounts to Qz, where z is the rate of interest. Thünen assumes that one unit of labour produces an amount of the good with value p at a wage rate w. The equation for the equality of the price of the consumption good and its cost of production is

$$w + Qz = p. \tag{1}$$

Capital in terms of labour commanded Q/w is in Thünen's special case equal to the direct labour embodied in capital q (per man employed in the consumption good industry), since capital is produced by unassisted labour. This yields the formula for the wage quoted above:

$$w + wqz = p, \tag{2}$$

hence

$$w = p/(1 + qz) \cdot \tag{3}$$

This theory of price formation is highly simplified by comparison with Ricardo, and there is a neoclassical aspect to it because it is assumed that value in use "exceeds" value in exchange or is at least equal to it (otherwise the commodity could not be sold), instead of saying that value in use is a qualitative prerequisite for the production of commodities (Thünen 1990, p. 370).

Thünen has yet another way of reducing the value of production to labour time by looking at marginal productivity. The intensity of capital q (the amount of labour used in capital production per unit of labour used in consumption goods production), is called by Thünen "relatives Kapital", and he writes: "Der Unternehmer, sein Interesse kennend und verfolgend, wird das relative Kapital q gerade soweit erhöhen, bis die Kosten der Arbeit des Kapitals und der des Menschen im direkten Verhältnis mit der Wirksamkeit beider bei der Produktion stehen" [9] (Thünen 1990, p. 363). This means that the relative factor price is equal to the ratio of the marginal productivities of the factors. He continues: "Dadurch sind wir nun in den Stand gesetzt, die Mitwirkung des Kapitals bei der Produktion eines Tauschguts auf Arbeit zu reduzieren" [10] (Thünen 1990, p. 363).

Thünen's statements about the theory of value are not wrong. They are consistent if applied to the simple model of accumulation which we shall look at. But it is less clear what theory of value Thünen would defend in more complex cases, in particular, if commodities are produced by means of commodities and if the production processes of capital goods are interdependent (in the language of Sraffa: if there is a basic commodity in the system). One is tempted to speculate that Thünen stuck to his "Austrian" model of capital formation (in which capital is produced by means of direct labour alone) because he did not know how to extend the classical theory of natural prices.

Thünen's distinction between the necessary and the surplus wage is questioned by most modern commentators. The necessary wage is presented in terms which anticipate Marx. This necessary or subsistence wage is what the family of the labourer needs for its maintenance. "Die Arbeitskraft erscheint dadurch als eine sich nicht abnutzende, unveränderliche Größe" [11] (Thünen 1990, p. 331). But the subsistence level was a grim reality, even if most labourers had some income in excess of subsistence:

> Der freie Arbeiter besitzt in der Regel als Eigentum einiges Vieh – eine Kuh, Schweine und Federvieh –, das nötige Hausgerät und einen Teil der Werkzeuge ..., womit er arbeitet. Der Lohn, den er erhält, ist also nicht bloß Belohnung seiner Arbeit, sondern ist zugleich Vergütung für den Gebrauch des Kapitals, was er besitzt, und umfaßt also den Lohn für die Arbeit an sich und die Zinsen des Kapitals. [12]
>
> (Thünen 1990, p. 331)

The conditions were specific for the region. Roscher said: "Sein vielbesprochener Sozialismus mag sich zum Theil aus der hoffnungslosen Abhängigkeit des mecklenburgischen Landproletariats erklären, die Thünen desto mehr betrübte, je minder ihm von seiner oldenburgischen Heimat her solche Zustände gewohnt waren" [13] (Roscher 1992 [1874], p. 892).

Hence the importance of considerations of justice in Thünen's work. The marginal land in the "Isolated State" is by assumption physically not inferior to land closer to the city in the "Isolated State". The workers who colonise it therefore have a fair chance of producing for a fair wage, of accumulating capital and of obtaining a fair return on the capital accumulated through saving (Ferrero and Gilibert 1984, p. 5). These conditions did not obtain in Thünen's contemporary Europe, because workers did not have access to good lands where they might produce under average conditions. Colonisation in the "Isolated State" will allow the workers to reach the corresponding average product, with the marginal product of labour being reckoned as the wage and the difference between the marginal product and the average product of labour being regarded as a return on capital accumulated, while land is free.

The average product therefore is reached only if the workers become farmers. But even to obtain the marginal product is a significant advance in Thünen's scheme, relative to the conditions which prevail, because actual workers do not get much more than what corresponds to the subsistence level, and conditions according to his description are often such that wages fall below that threshold, which means hunger. In the theory of the "Isolated State", by contrast, it is not even necessary that workers realise their plans to colonise free land; the threat that they might do so will raise the wage to the level where it is equal to the marginal product if there is full employment (Ferrero and Gilibert 1984, p. 21).

It is a unique feature in Thünen's theory that he envisages an accumulation of capital up to a point which he regards as optimal from the point of view of workers who set up a scheme of colonisation. The optimality condition leads to a formula for the fair or "natural" wage which is in between the subsistence wage and the average product, and this wage turns out to be equal to the marginal product in the optimum. The subsistence wage is denoted by a, the surplus wage by y, so that $w = a + y$. We attempt a first formulation of the model which is a little simpler and closer to modern conceptions than Thünen's own.[3]

He works with a two-sector model, since there is production of consumption goods and capital formation. Let us visualise it as follows:

ploughs $\oplus$ farming $\rightarrow$ rye

forging $\rightarrow$ ploughs

Units are chosen in such a way that the annual labour performed in each sector is equal to one.[4] The annual wage for farming and forging is the same. (Capital formation for Thünen is something more complicated than the production of a specific capital good like a plough: it is the building up of an estate, and the same type of agricultural workers who build the estate later use it to produce agricultural goods. But he does not formalise the complexity of estate building.) The wage is measured in amounts of rye per year, like output. Wages are paid *ex post*. Abstraction is made from capital needed to produce ploughs; the amount of capital (number of ploughs available in a given year) is q, and the price of new ploughs (they do not deteriorate) is, in our notation, π (Thünen does not introduce a price of capital goods explicitly). Hence we now have, with z and p defined as above in equation (2):

$$zq\pi + w = p \tag{4}$$

$$w = \pi. \tag{5}$$

The amount of capital q increases over time up to the optimum to be determined, but it is given in any given period. Since profit has been reduced to interest, the rate of interest is equal to net profit, divided by capital:

$$z = \frac{p - w}{q\pi}.$$

Since capital is produced by direct labour alone, we have $\pi = w$ and

$$z = \frac{p - w}{qw}, \tag{6}$$

where the wage rate in the nominator refers to the wage paid in the consumption goods industry, that in the denominator to the wage paid in the capital goods industry; in both cases $w = a + y$.

Colonisation means that workers become independent. They do not all act as borrowers but some can act as lenders, by saving the surplus wage. For instance – Thünen's somewhat different story will be told below – the surplus wage is one-tenth of the annual wage and ten agricultural colonisers decide to invest their surplus wage jointly in capital production so that they can employ one additional worker in the capital goods industry, with $10y = w$, hence they have one additional plough at price π and they will have an additional interest income of $z\pi$ ever after.

These workers are free to set the wage on their estate as they please; the higher the wage rate, the lower the rate of interest, given the amount of their capital. Output per head p corresponds to what can be produced by means of the capital and labour available to them. There is a trade-off between the rate of interest and the wage rate, characterised by equation (6)

$$z(w) = \frac{p - w}{qw},$$

which is monotonically falling and zero at $w = p$. This function corresponds to the wage curve encountered in classical economics (Schefold 1989 [1971], part III, ch. 6).

If the colonisers continue to invest on their estate, without increasing the number of participants in their enterprise, q will rise and also their output $p = p(q)$. But there will be diminishing returns with

$$p'(q) > 0, p''(q) < 0,$$

since the most productive techniques are used first. The workers could keep investing their surplus wage (or part of it, since it can rise), but diminishing returns imply that it may sooner or later be better for them to cultivate another estate rather than to keep investing on the same estate. Thünen therefore does not look for a "Golden Rule" to determine the point at which accumulation will end but he is looking for a criterion which will determine at which point accumulation will change its form, from intensive growth by deepening the capital on the same estate to extensive growth by widening capital and acquiring new estates.

The criterion proposed is controversial, but logical within the chosen framework. The investment of each worker is y, the return on it is

$$zy, \tag{7}$$

hence zy is the function to be maximised, both in the short run (q given) and in the long run (q variable).

The long-run optimum must be regarded as an equilibrium condition both for the wage and for the intensity of capital which is relevant for the economy as a whole, i.e. also for the inner rings of the "Isolated State", since if the wage is below what corresponds to the optimum, workers will begin to colonise free land. The individual decision of the colonisers regarding the trade-off between interest and wages therefore turns out to determine the equilibrium distribution for the economy as a whole.

Thünen himself describes the setting up of the colony in greater detail which helps to motivate the criterion for optimisation. The workers who colonise are divided into two:

> Abteilungen ... wovon die eine sich mit der Urbarmachung des Feldes, der Errichtung der Gebäude, der Verfertigung der Gerätschaften ... beschäftigt, die andere aber einstweilen bei der Arbeit für Lohn verbleibt und durch ihren in Roggen sich aussprechenden Überschuß die Subsistenz mitliefert, welche die mit der Anlegung des Guts beschäftigten Arbeiter konsumieren. [14]
>
> (Thünen 1990, p. 379)

Our equation (4) describes what the second "Abteilung" does and (5) the activity of the first "Abteilung".

"Zu der Schaffung eines neuen Guts gehört unstreitig nicht bloß Arbeit, sondern auch Anwendung von Kapital. Nach §13 können wir aber die Mitwirkung des Kapitals auf Arbeit reduzieren und somit die Anlagekosten ganz in Arbeit angeben" [15] (Thünen 1990, p. 380). This is not correct. Either the value of the capital used in capital production is expressed in terms of labour commanded, then this value varies with distribution, or it is expressed in terms of labour embodied, then changes in distribution are not adequately reflected in the costs so calculated. This is why we preferred to say that the capital good is produced by means of direct labour alone.

Thünen assumes that n workers will eventually be working on the new estate; they need an equipment of capital nq. If this equipment is to be produced in one year, nq workers will be needed for that, while anq units of rye will be necessary for their subsistence. This subsistence will in this same year have to be provided by $(anq)/y$ workers out of their surplus wage y. Each of the workers producing consumption goods in this colony therefore sacrifices y, supporting capital production, but each of the workers producing capital goods also sacrifices y since their wage is reduced to a. The number of workers who each sacrifice y now therefore is

$$nq + \frac{anq}{y} = nq\,\frac{a+y}{y} = nq\,\frac{w}{y}. \tag{8}$$

The estate will later be cultivated by n workers with capital nq. The interest on capital will then be equal to capital $n(p - w)$. The total interest which will annually be obtained in the future, divided by the total number of workers directly or indirectly involved in setting up this estate now (8) equals

$$\frac{n(p-w)}{nq\,\dfrac{w}{y}} = \frac{p-w}{qw}\,y = zy; \tag{9}$$

we obtain (9): the same function to be maximised as above for a "closed" group of colonisers, (6) and (7), while above we were looking at individual colonising workers.

The maximisation of zy in the short run (q and p given) yields

$$zy = \frac{p-w}{qw}y = \frac{p-w}{qw}(w-a) = \frac{p}{q} - \frac{pq}{qw} - \frac{w}{q} + \frac{a}{q}.$$

Setting the derivative with respect to w equal zero yields the well-known necessary condition

$$w = \sqrt{ap}. \tag{10}$$

Several interpreters confined their renderings of Thünen's formula for the natural wage to inadequate summaries of this short-period situation (Samuelson 1983, p. 1483).

Thünen's treatment of the maximisation in the long run – which is the more important case – is lengthy, but in my view, essentially correct.[5] I here propose a more direct analysis. Clearly, we have for the marginal product

$$\frac{dp}{dq} = p' = \pi z, \tag{11}$$

since the interest on an additional plough is equal to the increase in a production obtained by an increase of one unit of capital, with labour kept constant. This, with (4) and (5), yields a new expression for the function to be maximised by varying q

$$zy = \frac{p'}{\pi}y = \frac{p'}{w}(w-a) = \frac{p'}{p-qp'}(p-qp'-a) = p' - \frac{ap'}{p-qp'}, \tag{12}$$

hence we obtain the derivative, to be set equal to zero:

$$(zy)' = p'' - \frac{ap''(p-qp') + ap'qp''}{(p-qp')^2} = p'' - \frac{app''}{(p-qp)^2} = 0,$$

which, using (4), (5) and (11) to take account again of

$$w = p - qp',$$

yields the necessary condition

$$w = \sqrt{ap}; \tag{10}$$

the same as (10). We have here assumed that the rate of return on capital is equal to its marginal product which implies, with constant returns to scale, that the wage is equal to the marginal product of labour.

Thünen interpreted his natural wage as a fair distribution between capital and labour by establishing a geometric mean between the average product and the necessary wage. He claimed that the possibility of colonisation would cause this condition to prevail in the short run where the wage is not necessarily equal to the marginal product of labour (Keynes postulated that equality, but he did not assume full employment and the uncertainty of investment prevented the adaptation of capital). Thünen's long-run condition implies an equilibrium in which capital has been accumulated to the point where the wage is not only fair according to Thünen's criterion but labour gets its full contribution. What could be more neoclassical than this preneoclassical construction?

There is a formal problem. The maximum does not necessarily exist; the second derivative of zy (12) is not necessarily negative. In the Cobb–Douglas case, with $p = q^\beta$, one can calculate the equilibrium intensity of capital q^* for which zy is a maximum. One obtains

$$q^* = \left(\frac{a}{(1-\beta)^2}\right)^{1/\beta}. \tag{13}$$

The maximum here exists for $0 < \beta < 1$.

But the optimum reached is not an equilibrium for which the accumulation of the individual comes to a halt, at least in Thünen's own eyes. He wrote:

> Nun ist es ganz und gar in die Willkür der kapitalerzeugenden Arbeiter gestellt, ob sie nach der Vollendung des Guts ein zweites Gut anlegen oder ob sie auf dem ersten Gut das Kapital vermehren wollen. Ihr eigenes Interesse wird sie hierin leiten; und so kommt es zur Frage, was am vorteilhaftesten für sie ist. [16]

(Thünen 1990, p. 364)

He also says: "Die Kapitalerzeugung müßte … unbegrenzt fortgehen, wenn nicht mit der Vermehrung des Kapitals die Nutzung desselben gleichzeitig abnähme" [17] (Thünen 1990, p. 410). What limits accumulation? We pursue the interpretation and critique of his model in a more modern variant of the same.

3   Simple formalisations in the context of more modern models

Thünen's thought experiment can also be carried out in the context described by the neoclassical one-sector model, with a production function

$$y = f(k),$$

where y is output per head, k capital per head and the production function exhibits diminishing returns. We may imagine a farm labourer who is also a peasant. His subsistence wage is a, k his petty property, he invests $w - a$, obtains a profit $f - w$ so that the rate of profit is $(f - w)/k$ and

$$\frac{f-w}{k}(w - a)$$

is to be maximised. In the short run, k is given and w the independent variable. The necessary condition for the maximum yields

$$w = \frac{a+f}{2}; \tag{14}$$

the "natural wage" is an arithmetic mean of the subsistence wage and average output, both per unit of labour.

To take the arithmetic mean is a rule for dividing a contested property which Aristotle proposes as a symbol for commutative justice (Schefold 1989a). Niehans (1987) remarks that this rule is obtained in one-sector models; the point was already made by Knapp in his dissertation in 1865 (Niehans 1987).

The dynamic problem again concerns the question of how much capital is to be accumulated on the same estate. We first show that if the wage rate and the rate of profit are equal to the corresponding marginal products, an equilibrium intensity of capital $k*$ exists for suitable production functions such that the profit earned on the investment of $w - a$ is maximised. For the marginal productivity condition implies for our maximand

$$(w-a)\frac{f-w}{k} = (f-kf'-a)\frac{f'k}{k} = ff' - kf'^2 - af'$$

which yields the necessary condition

$$f - 2f'\,k - a = 0. \tag{15}$$

In the special case of the Cobb–Douglas production function $f = k^\beta$, the necessary condition is $k^\beta - 2\beta k k^{\beta-1} - a = 0$, and this is fulfilled for

$$k* = \left(\frac{a}{1-2\beta}\right)^{1/\beta}. \tag{16}$$

A meaningful solution exists for $0 < \beta < \frac{1}{2}$. (One can easily show that the second derivative then is negative so that we have a true maximum. It may be noted that, as in (13), the equilibrium intensity of capital here is the higher, the higher is the subsistence wage.) If the production function is such that the maximum exists, we have from the condition (15) for maximisation $f - f'k = a + f'k$; the marginal productivity wage turns out to be equal to the subsistence wage plus profits per head, hence

$$f + a = f - f'k + f'k + a = 2(f - f'k) = 2w$$

so that the "natural wage" condition (14) is confirmed for the long run:

$$w = \frac{a+f}{2}.$$

Conversely, assume that the natural wage is being paid and $w = (f + a)/2$; we demonstrate that the same $k*$ will be determined (if it exists) and that the marginal productivity theory holds. Here we have to maximise

$$\left(\frac{f+a}{2}-a\right)\frac{f-(f+a)/2}{k}=\frac{1}{4k}\left(f^2-2fa+a^2\right).$$

The necessary condition can be expressed as

$$2ff'k-2af'k=f^2-2fa+a^2$$

$$2f'k(f-a)=(f-a)^2$$

$$2f'k=f-a;$$

the equilibrium value for k^* is the same as in the previous case (15). It follows

$$\frac{f-a}{2}=f'k$$

$$f-f'k=f-\frac{f-a}{2}=\frac{f+a}{2}=w$$

and the marginal productivity condition has been proved.

An individual estate owner will accumulate capital up to the equilibrium value of k^*; then he may continue to accumulate capital without increasing k^* further by saving his surplus wage – and possibly also his interest income – and by supplying capital to others or by buying estates as long as labour and land are still available. Such a propensity to accumulate will drive up estate values in conditions of full employment; the determination of the full employment equilibrium therefore is not complete, and precisely for the reason advanced by Böhm-Bawerk against von Thünen: Thünen lacks a theory of the supply of capital. It may have been unimportant to him, given his social concerns. He wanted to improve the lot of the agricultural labourers by encouraging them to save. We therefore do not find a "Golden Rule" condition, as Samuelson and others have ascribed to him. Böhm-Bawerk's idea, in its simplest form, is this: in a world in which capital does not deteriorate, I may go on accumulating and output and income will always rise, but more and more slowly because of diminishing returns. Because of my impatience, I shall sooner or later prefer not to accumulate any more, or, beyond that point, to consume some of my capital rather than save it and to wait for a small additional return. If consumers are heterogeneous in their (recursive) preferences, as in Epstein's model (discussed in Schefold 1997, ch. 18.1), a certain rate of interest will eventually prevail at which all individuals have found a balance between saving and consuming, but the wealth they will have reached in the stationary state will be different according to their degree of impatience.

A different critique could be advanced against Thünen from a classical point of view. The inadequacy of his two-sector model and of his use of the Ricardian theory of value could be overcome by adopting Sraffa's theory of long-run prices, determined by

$$(1+r)Ap+wl=p, \tag{17}$$

where A is an indecomposable input-output matrix, p the vector of prices, r the rate of profit and w the wage rate. For a given standard of prices, the distributional variables are inversely related. A particularly simple relationship is obtained if Sraffa's standard commodity is chosen as the standard for prices; the relationship between the rate of profit and the wage rate then is

$$w = 1 - \frac{r}{R}, \tag{18}$$

where R is the maximum rate of profit of the system. Prices and the wage rate are determined at each level of the rate of profit which may be exogenously given.

Let us try to carry out Thünen's thought experiment in this classical world. The equations can easily be complemented by introducing fixed capital and rent; Sraffa's linear wage curve will then still hold (except for certain cases of intensive rent, see Schefold 1989 [1971], p. 234). There is again a subsistence wage a, workers can invest $w - a$ so that they now maximise, using (18),

$$(w - a)r = (w - a)R(1 - w) \cdot$$

The necessary condition for a maximum is $0 = R[1 + a - 2w]$, therefore $w = (1 + a)/2$. This is better written as

$$w = \frac{a + s}{2}, \tag{19}$$

where s is the value of the standard net product which has been chosen as the standard of prices and which is therefore equal to unity in equation (18), as it is usually written.

We thus get the same equation (19) for Thünen's "natural wage" as in the one-sector model (14). The "natural wage" is an arithmetic mean of the subsistence wage and the standard net product. This is not surprising since it is well known from the Sraffa literature that the use of the standard commodity establishes an analogy between a multisectoral classical model and a one-sector corn model. It is natural for our case to assume $a < s$.

If a different standard of prices is chosen, a more complicated wage curve results, and an explicit formula for the "natural wage" is more difficult to obtain. But it is clear that the function $(w - a)r$ has a maximum, since $(w - a)r$ is zero where w is at its maximum (because r is zero), since the function is zero at the minimum wage (subsistence wage) $w = a$ and since it is continuous and positive in between. But the wage at which the maximum is obtained will not be an arithmetic mean if the numéraire is not the standard commodity.

The maximisation which we have carried out here corresponds to the short run maximisation of the neoclassical case; the technique and all quantities have been kept constant. But we have not explained the quantities, while the point of this peculiar theory of distribution is that the wage is determined through the investment behaviour of workers. Are they going to accumulate capital on the same estate up to some equilibrium value for the intensity of capital? The modern criticism against neoclassical theory may here be advanced against Thünen.

Different levels of capital per head mean different techniques of production. The equilibrium value of capital per head is the most efficient one because it yields the highest return according to Thünen's criterion. Why is this technique not chosen from the beginning? Thünen assumes that the amount of labour (the workers who want to set up an estate) is given, but the co-operative does not have enough "capital" at its disposal. We should not object, as we would have to in modern theory, that the co-operative could borrow in a capital market because that was not accessible to the poor in von Thünen's world. To found agricultural savings banks for poor farmers was part of a social movement which set in precisely as a result of the political movement represented by authors like von Thünen. Hildebrand, a founding member of the Historical School, was to proclaim the advantages of the new "stage" of a "credit economy" for the setting up of small-scale business by able workers a few years later (Schefold 1998). Thünen's assumptions about the production function imply that a group of workers with little capital will produce more, if they employ all workers using that capital and a labour-intensive technique than if they use the more capital-intensive long-run optimum technique, the use of which would compel part of the workforce to remain idle. The long-run optimum technique therefore would be used only as soon as the capital shortage had been overcome. The co-operative in Thünen's world is in the same position as a closed country in the modern theory of growth.

The full employment within the co-operative thus is based on the assumption of a continuous substitutability of capital and labour. If there is a spectrum of linear techniques, as in the modern version of classical theory, the substitution will, if possible at all, not be smooth, and the shortage of capital can only mean a limited availability to finance the purchase of inputs. Our short-run maximisation of $(w - a)r$ did not take this into account explicitly but assumed a co-operative in a given state of reproduction, attained after having acquired the inputs necessary to start the processes.

The application of Thünen's theory of distribution to the long run in this classical framework, with constant returns to scale, would then have to take an enlarged choice of techniques into account. We shall not work out here in detail how this might be done, since we should be led away rather far both from Thünen's own formulations and from modern theories of distribution which one would regard as more plausible than Thünen's. Let us be content with a loose formulation: that technique might be regarded as most efficient and be adopted which yielded the highest return on the surplus wage, i.e. the highest $(w - a)r$, and the technique thus chosen in the short run might not be the technique chosen in the long run, because "expensive" inputs for the start-up could not be bought with "little" "capital".

Thünen's vision that capital must be accumulated relative to labour up to the point where the rate of interest has fallen to a critical value is common to many economists, Wicksell being a famous example. Thünen determined the critical value by maximising the return on the surplus wage; such a maximum seemed to exist because the wage rose and the rate of interest fell with an increasing intensity of capital. However, the critique of the neoclassical theory of capital which originated with the debate on reswitching demonstrated that the inverse relationship between the intensity of capital and the rate of interests need not exist. This modern criticism can be applied against Thünen, but the elimination of the marginal productivity theory of distribution from his scheme does not invalidate his theory of the natural wage. We have seen that it is formally possible to determine distribution according to Thünen's rule of the return on the investment of the surplus wage within the classical system. The classical approach does not rely on the existence of an inverse relation between the rate of profit and the intensity of capital.

One will not regard Thünen's wage formula as appropriate for a theory of distribution which would be applicable to the modern world, but the broad idea that distribution must be determined by looking at the conditions of accumulation is topical and alive in the post-Keynesian theory of distribution. Thünen is also close to modern approaches in that he held more than one theory of distribution. Their application depended on circumstances. His "natural wage"-theory of distribution may have been privileged by him for theoretical and normative reasons, but he also envisages at least one other state of the economy in which another distribution will result: unemployment, leading to wages at the subsistence level.

We thus find that Thünen was not only an abstract theorist, even as far as his model of accumulation and his views of distribution are concerned. His theory appears strange to the point of being incomprehensible, if one does not take into account his intermediate position between classical and neoclassical economics, his social and political views, the historical universe in which he lived and even his expertise in farming. His work is also topical because he emphasises the conditions under which the poor can help themselves if they are ready to work and to save. His particular solution, farming the land, indeed colonisation, would not seem palatable to most of the poor in advanced countries who prefer easier work or to live on the dole.

Few economists were ever as versatile and as interested in many fields as Thünen was, and if they were, they wrote different books on different subjects. He was unique in focusing his many interests in one book, and it is therefore not surprising that his interpreters differed so much in their appreciations of him.

Appendix: Translations of German quotations

[1]　He would first isolate a causal connection which he observed, he would analyse it in itself and then compare it again with the actual facts. The application of such schematic, isolated observation is one of the main vehicles of scientific progress.

[2]　Peace engenders welfare, welfare surplus population, surplus population misery.

[3]   A wonderful revolution has taken place. Rank, station, birth, riches, even knowledge: everything has lost its significance, its dominance. Instead, character has ascended to the throne, it alone remains and has influence, it alone dominates.

[4]   Already to have found that the wage of labour = $\sqrt{ap}$ led me to the most important results, but if I am to continue working in true happiness, I must know the connection between q (the capital employed for production) and p (the product). The investigation into this law has kept me busy for twenty years; however, since reality does not furnish any data for this, always in vain.

[5]   (only if) methods of cultivation are applied which are less remunerative and not worthwhile at the wages paid hitherto.

[6]   that direction, which culminated in Hermann and Thünen, lost its position around that time under the impression of the works by Rodbertus and Marx, which also entailed a renaissance of Ricardo. There rapidly developed an orthodox Marx-school guided by Engels and Kautsky, and also those not belonging to it – intellectuals not interested in theory – turned essentially to Rodbertus and to the English classics, mainly to Ricardo. They saw in marginal utility theory a discovery of dubious value and undertook to fight it in principle.

[7]   The value of this doctrine will now wholly depend on the manner in which the relationship is established between the increased productivity of labour, supported by capital, and the attainment of an increase in value by the owner of the capital.

[8]   If capital Q is given in silver terms, it is necessary, in order to express it in annual labour, to divide Q also by $\frac{p}{1+qz}$.

[9]   The entrepreneur, knowing and pursuing his interest, will increase relative capital q exactly to the point where the cost of the working of capital and that of the working of the man will be in a direct relationship with the efficiency of both in production.

[10]   By this we have now been enabled to reduce the assistance of capital in the production of an exchangeable good to labour.

[11]   The labour power thereby appears as a magnitude not subject to wear and tear and as unchangeable.

[12]   The free labourer possesses in general as his property some cattle – a cow, pigs and poultry –, the necessary home equipment and some tools ... by means of which he works. The wage, which he obtains, therefore is not only a recompense for his work, but is at the same time a compensation for the use of the capital which he owns, and it therefore contains the wage for the labour as such and the interest on the capital.

[13]   His much discussed socialism may in part be explained by the hopeless dependence of the country proletariat of Mecklenburg which saddened

Thünen all the more, the less he was used to such a state of affairs from the conditions in his home region of Oldenburg.

[14]   ... (divided into two) departments, ... one of which is busy with clearing the fields, erecting the buildings, making the implements ..., while the other first continues to work for wages, procuring the subsistence by means of the surplus in terms of rye which is consumed by the workers occupied to establish the estate.

[15]   For the establishment of a new estate unquestionably not only labour, but also the application of capital is needed. According to §13, we can reduce the assistance of capital to labour and we therefore can express the whole cost of construction in labour terms.

[16]   Now it is entirely up to the workers engaged in capital production whether they want to build a second estate after having completed the first or whether they want to increase capital on the first. Their own interest will guide them in this, and hence the question arises as to what is more profitable for them.

[17]   The production of capital would have to proceed ... indefinitely, if, with the increase of capital, the use of the same would not diminish.

Notes

1 This paper was presented as an invited paper to the International Thünen conference at Rostock (September 2000) and to the ESHET conference at Darmstadt (February 2001). The title has been changed and the text revised.
2 The numbers in [...] refer to my translations of German quotations in the Appendix.
3 Readers who are interested in a mathematically faithful rendering of Thünen's four variants of his model should consult the rich essay by Paola Tubaro (2006). Her treatment of capital is different from ours.
4 Suppose we have the following data: ten men produce three ploughs per year, twenty men, using twelve ploughs, produce 100 tons of rye per year. The labourer unit then is ten men, and the plough unit three ploughs. One labour unit, using six ploughs or two plough units, produces fifty tons of rye per year, and this will be the rye unit.
5 According to my interpretation, capital (ploughs) here is like the perennial machines in Schefold (1989 [1971], p. 147).

References

Baloglou, C. (1995), *Die Vertreter der mathematischen Nationalökonomie in Deutschland zwischen 1838 und 1871*, Marburg, Metropolis.
Binswanger, H. C. (1995), 'Der "natürliche Lohn" als Gleichgewichtspreis oderals ethische Forderung? Bemerkungen zum Referat von Ernst Helmstädter "Wiekünstlich ist von Thünens natürlicher Lohn?"', in Rieter, (1995), pp. 83–86.
Böhm-Bawerk, E. von (1991 [1989]), *Positive Theorie des Kapitales*, Düsseldorf, Verlag Wirtschaft und Finanzen. Klassiker der Nationalökonomie. Published together with *Vademecum zu einem Klassiker der Kapitaltheorie*. Kommentar zur Faksimile-Ausgabe der 1889 erschienenen Erstausgabe von Böhm-Bawerk, E. von, *Positive Theorie des Kapitales*, Düsseldorf, Verlag Wirtschaft und Finanzen 1991, Klassiker der Nationalökonomie.

Buchsteiner, I. (1999), *Thünen und das Jahr 1848*, Rostock, Historisches Institut der Universität.

Buchsteiner, I. and Viereck, G. (2000), *Heinrich von Thünen. Schriften – Literatur – Nachlaß*, Rostock, Historisches Institut der Universität.

Caspari, V. and Schefold, B. (eds) (1996), *Franz Oppenheimer und Adolph Lowe: Zwei Wirtschaftswissenschaftler der Frankfurter Universität*, Marburg, Metropolis.

Dühring, E. (1900 [1871]), *Kritische Geschichte der Nationalökonomie und des Socialismus von ihren Anfängen bis zur Gegenwart*, 4th edn, Leipzig, C. G. Naumann.

Ehrenberg, R. (1909), "Entstehung und Wesen der wissenschaftlichen Methode Johann Heinrich von Thünens", *Thünenarchiv Jena*, No. 2, pp. 511–553.

Ferrero, M. and Gilibert G. (1984),"Von Thünen's Theory of the Natural Wage and the Free Land Hypothesis. A Comment on Samuelson". Working Paper, Department of Economics, Turin University.

Helmstädter, E. (1995), "Wie künstlich ist von Thünens natürlicher Lohn?", in Rieter (1995), pp. 43–81.

Kurz, H. D. (1995), "Über die Knappheit und eine mißglückte Analogie zwischen Arbeit, Boden und Kapital: Thünens Theorie der Produktion und Verteilung", in Rieter, pp. 115–151.

Lehmann, H. (1990), " 'Vorrede' and Other Materials and Comments" in Thünen pp. 11–12, p. 483 sq.

Mangoldt, H. C. E. von (1855), *Die Lehre vom Unternehmergewinn. Ein Beitrag zur Volkswirthschaftslehre*, Leipzig, Teubner.

Marx, K. (1969), *Das Kapital. Kritik der politischen Ökonomie. 1. Band*, Berlin, Dietz, p. 793 sq. *MEW* 23.

Niehans, J. (1987), "Thünen, Johann Heinrich von", entry in *The New Palgrave: A Dictionary of Economics*, Eatwell, J., Milgate, M. and Newman, P. (eds), London, Macmillan, vol. IV, pp. 636–639.

Niehans, J. (1990), *A History of Economic Theory: Classic Contributions, 1720–1980*, Baltimore, MD, Johns Hopkins University Press.

Ricardo, D. (1951–1973), *The Works and Correspondence*, 11 vols, Sraffa, P. (ed.) with the collaboration of Dobb, M.-H. Cambridge, University Press for the Royal Economic Society, 1951–1973. Vol. 1: *On the Principles of Political Economy and Taxation.*

Rieter, H. (ed) (1995), *Johann Heinrich von Thünen als Wirtschaftstheoretiker*, Berlin, Duncker & Humblot. (Studien zur Entwicklung der ökonomischen Theorie 14), (Schriften des Vereins für Socialpolitik, Gesellschaft für Wirtschafts- und Sozialwissenschaften, N.F. Bd. 115/XIV).

Roscher, W. (1992 [1874]), *Geschichte der National-Oekonomik in Deutschland*, Düsseldorf, Verlag Wirtschaft und Finanzen. Klassiker der Nationalökonomie. Published together with *Vademecum zu einem Klassiker der deutschen Dogmengeschichte*, Kommentar zur Faksimile-Ausgabe der 1874 erschienenen Erstausgabe von Roscher, W., *Geschichte der National-Oekonomik in Deutschland*, Düsseldorf, Verlag Wirtschaft und Finanzen, Klassiker der Nationalökonomie.

Salin, E. (1923), "Geschichte der Volkswirtschaftslehre", in *Enzyklopädie der Rechts- und Staatswissenschaft* 34, Berlin, J. Springer.

Salin, E. (1963), *Lynkeus. Gestalten und Probleme aus Wirtschaft und Politik*, Tübingen, Mohr.

Samuelson, P. A. (1983), "Thünen at Two Hundred", *Journal of Economic Literature*, Vol. 21, No. 4, pp. 1468–1488.

Schefold, B. (1989 [1971]), *Mr. Sraffa on Joint Production and Other Essays*, London, Unwin & Hyman [now: London, Routledge], enlarged edn of *Piero Sraffas Theorie der Kuppelproduktion, des Kapitals und der Rente*, Dissertation, Basel, Privatdruck, 1971.

Schefold, B. (1989a), "Platon und Aristoteles", in Starbatty, J. (ed.), *Klassiker des ökonomischen*, Munich, Beck, pp. 15–55.

Schefold, B. (1994), "Antonia Serra: der Stifter der Wirtschaftslehre?", in *Vademecum zu éinem unbekannten Klassiker*, Kommentar zur Faksimile-Ausgabe der 1613 erschienenen Erstausgabe von Serra, A., *Breve Trattato delle cause, che possono far abbondare li regni d'oro, & argento*, Düsseldorf, Verlag Wirtschaft und Finanzen, pp. 5–27, Klassiker der Nationalökonomie.

Schefold, B. (1996), "The German Historical School and the Belief in Ethical Progress", in Brady, F. N. (ed.), *Ethical Universals in International Business*, Berlin etc., Springer, pp. 173–196.

Schefold, B. (1997), *Normal Prices, Technical Change and Accumulation*, London, Macmillan.

Schefold, B. (1998), "Bruno Hildebrand: Die historische Perspektive eines liberalen Ökonomen", in *Vademecum zu einem Klassiker der Stufenlehre*. Kommentarband zum Faksimile-Nachdruck der 1848 erschienenen Erstausgabe von Hildebrand, B., *Die Nationalökonomie der Gegenwart und Zukunft*, Düsseldorf, Verlag Wirtschaft und Finanzen, pp. 5–53, Klassiker der Nationalökonomie.

Schefold, B. (1999), "Use Value and the 'Commercial Knowledge of Commodities': Reflections on Aristotle, Savary and the Classics", in Mongiovi, G. and Petri, F. (eds), *Value, Distribution and Capital: Essays in Honour of Pierangelo Garegnani*, London, Routledge, pp. 122–144.

Schefold, B. (2004), "Edgar Salin and His Concept of 'Anschauliche Theorie' ('Intuitive Theory') during the Interwar Period", *Annals of the Society for the History of Economic Thought*, No. 46, pp. 1–16.

Schmoller, G. F. von (1923), *Grundriß der allgemeinen Volkswirtschaftslehre*, Munich, Duncker & Humblot.

Schumpeter, J. A. (1912), *Epochen der Dogmen- und Methodengeschichte*, Tübingen, Mohr, p. 55.

Schumpeter, J. A. (1954), *History of Economic Analysis*, London, Allen & Unwin and New York, Oxford University Press.

Sraffa, P. (1925), "Sulle relazioni fra costo e quantità prodotta", *Annali di economia*, vol. 2, pp. 277–328.

Sraffa, P. (1951–1973), s. Ricardo.

Sraffa, P. (1960), *Production of Commodities by Means of Commodities. Prelude to a Critique of Economic Theory*, Cambridge, Cambridge University Press.

Streissler, E. W. (1995), "Die Grenzproduktivitätstheorie der deutschen Protoneoklassik unter besonderer Berücksichtigung von Johann Heinrich von Thünen", in Rieter (1995), pp. 17–41.

Suntum, U. van (1988), "Vindicating Thünen's Tombstone Formula $\sqrt{ap}$", *Jahrbücher für Nationalökonomie und Statistik*, Band 204/5, pp. 393–405.

Suntum, U. van (1995) *The Invisible Hand*, New York, Springer Verlag.

Thünen, J. H. von (1990), *Der isolierte Staat in Beziehung auf Landwirtschaft und*

Nationalökonomie, herausgegeben und unter Benutzung unveröffentlichter Manuskripte kommentiert von Hermann Lehmann in Zusammenarbeit mit Lutz Weber, Berlin, Akademie Verlag.

Töpel, A. (1964), "Johann Heinrich von Thünen – Ein Vorläufer der apologetischen bürgerlichen Grenzproduktivitätstheorie", *Wirtschaftswissenschaft*, Band 12, pp. 1282–1299.

Tubaro, P. (2006), "Mathématiques et économie dans le détermination du 'salaire naturel' de J. H. von Thünen", *Cahier d'économie politique*, No. 50, pp. 59–85.

Werner, L. (ed) (1990), s. Thünen.

18 A twenty-first-century alternative to twentieth-century Peer Review

Grazia Ietto-Gillies[1]

1 Introduction

The last two decades have seen an increasing number of academic works on the issue of research evaluation systems and specifically on Peer Review (PR): this is a system by which academic works are evaluated prior to being put in the public domain through publication. The evaluation is done by experts in the subject/field and thus by peers. The evaluation by PR may relate to a variety of means of dissemination: from book proposals to chapters in edited books, to papers submitted for presentation at conferences or for domain publication in academic journals. It is on the last one that most of the writings on PR concentrate and so will this chapter.

Though the main issue which authors have considered in writing about PR is indeed evaluation of academic works, the PR system has wide implications also for the dissemination of such works and indeed for the way academics communicate their results. The PR system, in fact, affects whether a work is published or not and, if so, in which journal. Moreover, the process leading to the final evaluation affects the speed with which an academic work is put into the public domain.

The PR system has been in operation for a long time and it is therefore legitimate to ask why it has come in for increasing criticism in the last few years. I suggest that this is for the following reasons. First, the fact that there has been an increase in evaluations in general: we seem to be living in an audit and control culture and this may be inducing people to start asking whether it is all necessary and indeed whether this type of culture encourages academic endeavours. Second, the proliferation of papers and journals is leading to increasing work to meet the demands of the PR process and, indeed, to overload for many reviewers[2] of submitted papers. A third – and in my view the most relevant – factor is that changes in the information and communication technologies (ICTs) are making the old system redundant. Essentially, what I am saying is that – whether the commentators realize it or not – our critical attitude to PR is emerging because there is a way out. It is on this last point – on the way out – that this chapter focuses and makes suggestions.

The next two sections consider issues of efficiency and effectiveness in the PR system; section four analyses the role of PR and section five proposes a different system of interaction and evaluation. The last section summarizes and concludes.

2 Efficiency issues

Most authors who have written on PR accept that we need a system for evaluating the worth of a work and for assessing whether it is good enough to be put into the public domain. While some academics have written in favour of retaining the system (Lederberg 1978; Garfield 1986; Legendre 1995), many question it and propose improvements.

There are two broad lines of criticism; the first relates to issues of efficiency: how good the PR system is in relation to its costs. The second line relates to effectiveness: how good is the system at doing what it is supposed to do; this latter issue will be discussed in the next section.

As regards costs, Campanario (1998a and b) gives an excellent review of various studies relating evidence from several disciplines and showing that – in addition to the paid administrative and editorial time – the editors and referees invest in the PR system a very large number of uncompensated hours. Ginsparg (2002) also tackles the issue of costs. He starts by noting that revenues per published article vary considerably from circa $1,000 to 10,000. What is revenue for journal publishers is a cost for libraries and journals buyers in general. The lower figure pertains to journals edited and published by not-for-profit organizations such as academic and professional associations, rather than by commercial publishers. However, not many journals are run on a not-for-profit basis because, in the last two decades, commercial publishers have gradually taken over most of the scholarly publications.

There are two main issues connected with costs: (1) costs in relation to the type of provider of editing and publishing services, i.e. not-for-profit versus commercial providers; (2) costs built into the system of selection of papers to be published: this is largely independent of the type of providers as in (1).

Regarding (2) we should note that the monetary costs of getting a paper published grossly underestimate the actual social costs for the research community and society as a whole. This is because a considerable amount of the work which goes into journals publication – over and above the actual development of research and production of papers by the authors – is done on a voluntary basis by academics as part of their professional activities. This includes, in particular, the activities of referees and in many cases those of the editors themselves. This is what is discussed by Campanario, who, however, also notes that most academics consider these jobs as part of their professional duties and that the jobs are – indirectly – compensated because they count towards career advancement.[3]

Neither Campanario nor Ginsparg consider the opportunity costs of the PR activities. This is time that the academics might have been spending on their own research/scholarly or didactic activities: thus there is a heavy opportunity cost for each published article under the current PR system – whether run under a for-profit or not-for-profit regime – and therefore a heavy social cost for the research community.[4]

It could be claimed that the review process and its many rounds help to improve the paper. This may indeed happen in many cases. However, the situation may also be problematic in many others. As anyone who has received two or three referee reports knows, they are often ambiguous and inconsistent: Ref A may like the parts that Ref B dismisses; Ref C misunderstands a whole section of the paper. These are not problems specific to one or two referees: they are faults of the system. Any of us who has been a referee is bound to have fallen into one of these problems which, moreover, we have all experienced at some point in our career from the other side, i.e. when submitting papers or, for some of us, as editors.[5] The problem is endemic to the system: as referees, we all read a paper with our own preconceptions and frameworks in mind; often we read it very quickly as the number of requests from journal editors increases. In extreme cases the paper may be damaged by the author's attempts to fit in comments by successive referees and indeed by adding bogus references in the attempt to ingratiate editors and reviewers; a practice that, incidentally, also distorts citations indices.

Ginsparg (2002) notes that editorial and administrative costs are escalating under the pressure of increasing number of submissions. Some editors are calling for systems in which the authors and/or their institutions pay for each submitted or accepted paper: a practice already operated by some journals. While this move may help publishers and editors in meeting their costs, it does not deal with the social costs issue because it ignores who the ultimate payer is. The truth is that, whether the costs are borne by libraries or by authors/institutions, the ultimate payer is the taxpayer. Most libraries are publicly funded and thus, if the library bears the cost, it is the public that pays and the opportunity cost of excessive payments is the fact that higher library expenditure leaves fewer financial resources for the funding of research or the employment of extra lecturers. However, the situation is no different if the authors/institutions were to pay: the burden is likely to fall on the department/institution and thus, ultimately, on the taxpayer: in this case also there would be an opportunity cost of excessive departmental or library outlays in terms of forgone academic services to which the extra outlays could have been allocated.

These considerations point to two sets of conclusions. First, that – unless there are clear quality gains by having commercial publishers as providers – a not-for-profit system of production and dissemination of journals is in the overall interest of the scholarly community and of society. Second, that it is in the interest of the research community and society as a whole to minimize the amount of resources involved in the process leading to publication.

3 Effectiveness issues: what is Peer Review for?

Let us now turn to the other issue, the one which has been the subject of most critiques of the Peer Review system: effectiveness. This immediately begs the question: effectiveness in relation to what? Therefore the questions arise what is Peer Review for and what role is it supposed to play in academic works? Before we attempt to answer these questions let us analyse more closely the characteristics of Peer Review, a system which I would like to call *ex-ante top-down PR system* (abbreviated to PR) because it is characterized by the following: (1) It a system of *ex-ante* review because the Peer Review process intervenes prior to publication and is, indeed, instrumental to it. (2) It is also a *top-down* system because the Peer Review is set in motion and applied by the editors who together with the referees have power over the decision to publish or not to publish.

Peer Review is not the only possible ex-ante top-down system of validation: in the past the decision to publish or not was taken mainly by the editors without the refereeing process; a few journals still apply this system. An alternative system of validation – one which is not ex-ante and top-down but ex-post and bottom-up – will be introduced in section five.

Peer Review is supposed to perform the following roles.

1   Weeding out papers which are very obviously not up to standard; this is usually done by the editors on the basis of a first quick read and prior to any review process by outside referees.
2   Guidance to readers as regard fields of specialization which tend to vary from journal to journal. The editors and the referees assess whether the paper falls within the sphere of interest of the journals and its readership.
3   Guidance to editors in the allocation of limited journal space. This is probably the most important function of the PR system. Most journals – particularly the prestigious ones – receive far too many applications for the available journal space and they need an allocation mechanism that scales down the supply of papers to the demand by editors (constrained by the journal's space). The reports from reviewers are the filtering mechanism for such allocation.
4   The system is also used as a guidance tool for allocating jobs and grants in the academic community. Such allocation is strongly influenced by the type of journal in which the research is published.

Points (1) and (2) are considered fairly unproblematic and most criticisms concentrate on (3) and related (4). Campanario (1998a) and Bedeian (2004) report a number of criticisms which include the following issues.

* credentials of participants in the system and specifically how referees are chosen;[6]
* reliability and accuracy of reviews and inconsistency among reviewers;
* inability to spot ground-breaking works (Horrobin 1990; Gans and Shepherd 1994; Campanario 1995);
* inability to weed out very poor works;[7]
* bias in favour of statistically significant results and thus denial of publication of results that though non-significant may be relevant;
* bias against research that replicates existing results.

Obscurity of the text seems to correlate highly and positively with acceptance into highly rated journals (Campanario 1998a: 195). There are also reports of unethical behaviour in the process (Campanario 1998b). Many authors seem to conclude that whether a work is accepted by a journal or not may be accidental, depending on who reviews it (Bedeian 2004; Campanario 1998a). Indeed, some argued that there does not exist a universal standard of 'what is fit for publication' within which referees can work and against which they can make their assessment. Ginsparg is quite explicit on what we should not expect from the PR system; he writes:

> peer-reviewed journals do not certify correctness of research results. Their somewhat weaker evaluation is that an article is a) not obviously wrong or incomplete, and b) is potentially of interest to readers in the field. The peer review process is also not designed to detect fraud, or plagiarism, nor a number of associated problems – those are left to posterity to correct.
>
> (p. 2)

Braben (2008: 250) reports that Richard Horton, the editor of *The Lancet*, expresses the following critical view on PR:

> The mistake, of course, is to have thought that peer review was any more than a crude means of discovering the acceptability – not the validity – of a new finding. Editors and scientists alike insist on the pivotal importance of peer review. We portray peer review to the public as a quasi-sacred process that helps to make science our most objective truth teller. But we know that the system of peer review is biased, unjust, unaccountable, incomplete, easily fixed, often insulting, usually ignorant, occasionally foolish and frequently wrong.

Sir James Black, the 1988 Nobel Prizewinner for Medicine, expresses similar critical views on the impact of the PR system on innovative research in a *Financial Times* (2009) interview where the following is attributed to him:

> The anonymous peer review process is the enemy of scientific creativity. ... Peer reviewers go for orthodoxy....

In spite of the acknowledged difficulties and known criticisms, the PR system is seen as the 'gold standard' in quality assurance for academic works. The PR process is widely used not only for space allocation in journals but also as a filtering system for jobs and grants applications (see (4) above): if an article has been published in a prestigious journal it gives the author a strong basis for jobs and grants applications. Moreover, in the UK the process is used in the so-called Research Assessment Exercise (RAE) in which the government – through its higher education funding body – decides on the allocation of research funds to universities according to periodic rating of departments' research output. The latter are assessed – to a large extent – on the rating and prestige of the journals in which staff have published over the assessment period. It is known that –

within the RAE process – a journal article is, in most subjects, rated higher than a chapter in a book or a research monograph on the basis that the journal article has undergone a stricter PR process.

Though many academics would acknowledge the problems of PR in relation to publication, some of these problems seem to be forgotten when it comes to the impact on jobs and research funding allocation. It is as if, though we know that the metal we are dealing with is not pure gold, when it reaches its final destination, the 'jobs and research funding allocation desk' we treat it as pure gold. Yet, it is at this second level that the impact on individual academics' lives,[8] on the research community and on the direction of research, is most felt.

4 Scholarly activities and the management of gates

Points (3) and (4) above mean that the most important function of the *ex-ante top-down PR* process is its gate-keeping role giving or denying access to journal space and – indirectly – to academic jobs and research funds. The process leads to a decision to open or shut the entry gate for publication into a particular journal. In effect, in most cases, the management process results in the shutting of the gate: the most prestigious journals may have a 90 per cent rejection rate. This leads the author whose paper has been rejected to try another journal. To continue with the 'gates' analogy it is as if the authors, finding the first gate shut to their papers, go along the path to the next gate and then the next till they may manage to find one that opens for them.

Once the authors find themselves in the field of published works, their pieces are available to readers and thus the PR system performs its dissemination function: readers are, partly, guided in their choice of which works to consider by the prestige of the journal in which papers have been published, as well as, of course, by the field of specialization of the journal.

To continue with the analogy of gates, our authors now find themselves in the green field of published authors; they have left behind, outside the gates, the miserable authors whose works have not been accepted for publication. However, the field of publication is not the point of destination but only a necessary staging post.

Here comes the impact of the process on point (4), i.e the effects on jobs and grants allocation. It is well known that people and institutions with the responsibility and power to allocate academic posts and/or research funds, in assessing the quality of candidates or of applications are, to a large extent, guided by the worth of their publications as indicated by the quality of the journal in which they have been published. The British RAE – mentioned in section three – is also based on a second stage PR system.

All our authors need to use their reputation as published authors to access the next even greener field: the luscious field of academic jobs, promotions, grants allocation. To have access to these, a further selection process will be in operation depending on the reputation of the journal in which the works have been published. So, from our green field where the published authors are assembled they will all try to move on and pass through further gates, and here comes selection again. There are several gates leading to different shades of green in the grass: from the very deep green of top jobs in top institutions to the paler green of less prestigious jobs. Whether our authors get in to the very deep, brilliant green field of most prestigious jobs or in one of the progressively paler green fields depends on the reputation of the journal in which they have published. Some authors who have published in less prestigious journals may never progress towards this second set of gates.

The gates analogy is here kept deliberately simple and schematic. In practice, other elements affect the passage into the second set of gates: book publication and the reputation of the publisher is taken into consideration in the social sciences and the humanities; conferences seem to count more in the physical or engineering sciences; the reputation of one's institution counts towards grants allocation; in the social science and humanities, the ideological perspective of the research may affect the ability of its authors to proceed through the first set of gates (to the field of published works) and to the second set, to the field of jobs and grants.

Thus PR is very influential on two levels: in the dissemination process (i.e in which journals the paper is published, if any) and in the assessment of performance of individuals and institutions. These two levels affect both the allocation of academic jobs and of research funds. Moreover, when PR is applied also to the assessment of institutions (as in the RAE), the two levels of assessment result in cumulative costs; to those costs of the PR system highlighted in section two must be added the costs of the RAE for the British academic community. The latter are enormous as the evaluation system requires a large central administration system as well as administrators at each university and of, course, the investment of considerable time by academics themselves to prepare their own and their institution's cases.

The PR system may serve editors and publisher reasonably well in their main problem of space allocation; but how well does it serve the research community and society? Not very well I would say for the following reasons, some of which emerge from the critical literature cited above. First, the introduction of long delays between completion of a paper and its publication. The review process in each journal takes months; as most papers are sent to several journals consecutively, the lag between completion of a paper and its publication may be counted in years. This is a problem for the authors but also for the research community as further developments in an area in which an author has made a contribution are delayed.

Second, the very high private and social costs of the system as argued in section two. Third, the possible distortion of research paths introduced by the authors' race to get into the more prestigious journals: authors, under pressure to get into top journals, may incline to work in areas, paradigms, ideological frameworks acceptable to specific journals. Authors may adjust their behaviour and work to meet targets – including the target of making it into a specific journal – rather than to advance research and science (Frey and Osterloh 2007).[9] This is a trend which would not matter if it applied to only a few cases, but can be serious as the practice becomes widespread under the pressure from institutions such as the British RAE.[10]

Fourth, a built-in bias against papers that are very innovative and outside the established paradigm. The reason for this is that most referees and editors work within well-established paradigms, while ground-breaking research by its own nature and definition is something outside the standard paradigm. When refereeing, the reviewers will read a paper with the mind frame of the paradigm they are working under. What is presented to them may appear as strange, unusual, not properly researched; it may be something presented in a new and untried language or framework.

If the readers of this chapter think that all this is nonsense and that any researcher competent in the field is able to spot 'the great work', they should consider evidence from the history of science as in Gillies (2008). Researchers of the past who are now acknowledged as having made ground-breaking contributions saw their efforts rejected by their peers working under different paradigms. Gillies concludes that, had an RAE-type of system been in operation during the lifetime of these great researchers, they would not have been supported by the system.

It could be argued that the latter problem does not matter that much because many works will reach the public domain eventually. However, when a piece of research is ground-breaking and very important, an urgency is also required in publishing and in wide dissemination for the following reasons: (1) the author may want to establish intellectual priority; (2) the research community would benefit from early release of results and from potential further developments following interaction between readers and authors; moreover, some research may be very relevant for human life[11] or for business and the economy; (3) for some academics delays may lead to loss of tenure with long-term effects on individuals, families and research communities. Highly innovative work may go unrecognized for decades. It may also need years of quiet, unglamorous, undisturbed, hard work to lead to the relevant results.[12] The PR system and the highly control-based RAE system stifle such research and indeed may lead to cuts in its funding.

Most academics would agree that a system of evaluation and dissemination of academic works is needed, though many would also agree that the current PR system is imperfect. Some have proposed amendments mostly at the margin, that is the type of amendments that leave the basic tenets of the system in place: the conclusion seems to be that imperfect though the system is, it may be the best available on offer. The next section challenges the last statement in the light of alternative systems made possible by new technology.

5 An *ex-post* bottom-up Peer Comment system

As mentioned above, it could be argued that – constraints on journal space – the current PR system is the best available. This may have been the case till a decade or so ago. However, with the new technology at our disposal alternatives are possible and must be considered.

Let us start from first principles. What do we want from an evaluation and dissemination system? We may not all agree on the details, but in reality most academics aspire to a system with the following characteristics.

1   an efficient system that absorbs less compensated and uncompensated time, i.e. less private and social resources than the present one;
2   a system that cuts the length of time between the completion of a paper and its appearance in the public domain and thus its availability to the potential readership;
3   a system that substantially reduces the probability of shutting the publication gate to ground-breaking research works;
4   a system that weeds out the very poor papers;
5   a system that alongside the evaluation function performs an interaction function within the community of researchers.

Regarding points (3) and (4), I would like to make the following comments. Gillies (2008: ch. 4) notes that most people in charge of resources allocation and selection are obsessed with avoidance of type I error that is with avoiding letting poor papers through the gates. However, type II error – not letting through ground-breaking research results – has much more serious consequences for the research community and society in general.

Regarding point (5), Bedeian (2004) stresses that the interaction between author, editor and referee makes the end product – the published paper – the result of a social interaction; in effect the published work becomes a social product often different from the original product sent to the journal. Frey (2003) comes down strongly against one aspect of this type of socialization of the academic work because he feels that the anonymous referees have excessive power to impose their views on the author and that the work may end up not reflecting the original views. He concludes in favour of laying the decision power entirely in the hands of editors who have more invested interests in the success of the journal than anonymous referees.

I see social interaction as a very important part in the development of research; however, it does not have to be the specific power-based social interaction built into the current PR system as discussed by Bedeian and by Frey. Information and communication technologies offer us the potential for a new system of evaluation, dissemination and indeed interaction within the research community. Open Access (OA) systems – in which research papers are placed in the public domain with some preselection by the site editors – are already in existence in many subjects. For example, in economics RePEc and NEP perform this function; Ginsparg (2002) mentions arXiv in relation to physics. He is concerned with the efficiency of the scholarly communication infrastructure and favours the use of Open Access in order to achieve speedy and low-cost dissemination; however, he thinks that a form of PR is still necessary in order to validate the worth of research works and to aid selection for jobs and grants allocation. Therefore, he favours a double system in which Open Access in internet sites secures fast and low-cost dissemination while later publication with a prior PR process supplies a mechanism for selection in jobs and grants applications.[13]

However, I feel that we could go a step further and develop a system that takes full advantage of ICTs. I therefore propose the following *ex-post bottom-up Peer Comment system* (henceforth abbreviated as PC).

- Use of Open Access sites categorized by fields of specialization for each subject. Research papers to undergo a first selection designed to (1) weed out the crankish papers and (2) make sure that – as far as possible – they pertain to the right field of specialization. The latter point is designed to help readers as well as authors.

- For each paper published on Open Access the editor should open an electronic 'Comments Link' inviting readers to send comments which – following a vetting to weed out crank or offensive contributions – will then be placed on the Link site. These open debates should be positively encouraged as a way of developing research; they are a way of recognizing that research is a social activity and the interaction of various researchers can aid progress. As already noted Bedeian (2004) stresses that papers published in journals are the result of social interaction between author, editor and referees. The type of social interaction proposed here differs from the one discussed in Bedeian because: (1) it is based on a potentially much larger number of commentators; (2) it is not power-based in the sense that the commentators do not have the power to stop the paper being put into the public domain: it is already there; and (3) the comments are signed unlike the anonymous referee reports.

- Academic associations could encourage the publication – in books or in dedicated e-journals – of selected 'Readers', i.e. collections of papers and their critiques – mostly already available on Open Access sites – with a specific focus in order to give further guidance to readers.[14] Ginsparg (2002: 7) cites the case of successful Mathematical Reviews, published by the American Mathematical Society.

- The publication of articles on 'Literature Surveys' should be encouraged in order to help readers sift through the large amount of literature now available. In fact doctoral students worldwide engage in this useful activity. Papers from this part of their effort are usually not published. We should encourage their publication because it may provide helpful feedback for authors and other interested researchers. It could be argued that good literature reviews are not easy and they need considerably more experience than that of the average research student. I tend to agree with this and I suggest that experienced people should also get involved in this.

- Reviews of web articles as well as of books should be encouraged as they perform a very valuable service; this would reverse a trend of the last couple of decades which have seen the downgrading of book reviews for the purpose of the RAE or jobs and grants applications. This downgrading discourages authors from employing their time in reviewing activities and deprives the community of a valuable tool in the selection and discrimination of which papers/books to read.

The above system I call *ex-post bottom-up Peer Comment* for the following reasons. First, to stress that the comments occur after the paper has been put into the public domain. Moreover, it is bottom-up because the comments and reviews are not power-based: the commentators do not have the power to stop the paper going into the public domain.

Among the advantages of this system are the following. First, it secures quick dissemination of research ideas and results. Second, it is very cost-efficient because both private and social costs are very low. Third, the bottom-up approach is likely to give better assessment because of the large number of potential contributors against the few referees in the *ex-ante top-down PR* system. Fourth, a further advantage of the PC system is that those who are prepared to read the relevant papers and write criticisms are likely to be people interested in the specific topic and thus their criticisms are likely to be relevant. Fifth, the wider dissemination of papers on e-sites has a major advantage: within a large readership of potential commentators we are more likely to have a few who can spot the occasional ground-breaking research than if we confine such a task to a small number of referees as in the present PR system.

Sixth, from the reader's perspective, there is evidence that the opportunity to read comments and debates is viewed positively: Bedeian reports that 'Subscribers either to the *American Psychologist* or the *American Sociological Review* often find that the sometimes-heated interchanges appearing in the Comment and Reply sections can be more intellectually stimulating than the original works being disputed' (Bedeian 2004: 211). Seventh, as regards jobs and grants/funds allocation, the proposed system has the following advantages over the PR system: the allocators of grants and jobs can rely on a wider number of potential commentators than in the current system and thus will be better able to assess the impact of the paper. Eighth, the development of 'Readers', literature surveys and review articles will support the system and may help readers as well as jobs and grants allocators to find their way through the large amount of papers and comments.

Lastly, the Link site for comments invites people to participate disclosing their identity rather than anonymously. This lack of anonymity has the advantage that, if someone has a brilliant idea following the reading of the original paper, s/he will not be tempted to hold it back for fear of losing attribution – as may happen under the current system of anonymous refereeing. They know that whatever comments they place on the site will be attributed to them. Moreover, openness is likely to lead to more positive developments and the process would strengthen the social character of research: further progress along the line of specific papers would emerge from critiques and discussions. It could, however, be claimed that the lack of anonymity discourages academics from making negative comments. This is possible; however, we should not forget that the Internet interaction spans the whole globe; while someone in Britain may not want to offend co-researchers whom they are likely to meet often and/or who may have power over jobs allocation, they may be less worried about academics further afield. Moreover, as academics are well prepared to stick the knife in when writing signed reviews of books, why should they not do it when writing comments on other papers? It is partly a matter of culture. Once a culture of signed comments develops, then most academics will be prepared to write sober, reasonable comments.

This conclusion is borne out by a micro test regarding the content of this very chapter. A previous version published on an Open Access journal (Ietto-Gillies 2008a) was followed by an opening of a Comments Link by the editor. There were many comments, most of which were edited and published by the editor (2008b). Many comments were critical and I was able to answer these in a rejoinder published alongside the comments.

One further objection to the PC system proposed here is that it would put into the public domain a considerable number of worthless papers and/or comments. I agree with this but would suggest that it is something that already happens in published form. At least in the Open Access system costs would be kept very low unlike under the current PR system. Moreover, the encouraged comments in the PC system and the proposed increase in Readers would flush out the poverty of content in papers and/or some comments.

Excessive worries about poor papers getting through – what Gillies (2008) calls type I error – are misplaced. Our main concern should be with systems that do not allow ground-breaking research to be speedily placed in the public domain (type II error): they are the ones with the most serious consequences for the research community and society. I would like to bring to the attention of readers a striking example from the history of physics:[15] a case in which a policy of support for (and trust in) authors rather than hindrance through excessive scrutiny and controls led to the quick dissemination of ground-breaking research work. Miller (1981: 2) argues that Einstein's famous 1905 relativity paper had all the characteristics of papers that are rejected by referees. It was by a young, unknown author who had neither academic post nor doctorate. The paper contained 'no citations to current literature'; was 'unorthodox in style and format'; it contradicted the main paradigms in the discipline; and the title had 'little to do with most of its content'. It might not have been put in the public domain quickly had *Annalen der Physik* not followed – at the time – a policy of trust in the author rather than one of assessment and control. Miller writes on this point:

> As far as we know the editorial policy of the *Annalen* was that an author's initial contributions were scrutinized by either the editor or a member of the Curatorium; subsequent papers may have been published with no refereeing. [...] Einstein's ... paper was probably accepted on receipt.
>
> (p. 2)

It should be stressed that a new Open Access system for putting papers into the public domain is already with us or underway. Most researchers now post their papers on their own websites prior to publication in journals. Moreover, the move towards assessment of research output via metrics is having an effect on this process. Some very prestigious universities – including Harvard and University College London – are organizing websites featuring all the research papers – published, unpublished, current and past – by their staff. The aim is to have an institutional e-archive in which their academics' works become easily accessible to other researchers throughout the world can consult and cite them. The reasoning and purpose behind this initiative are obvious: if what matters is citation, then let us make citation easier and this means making works more accessible.[16] So the move towards an Open Access system is well underway. It could, indeed, be claimed that what I propose is too conservative and that people see no need for any overseeing editorial process at all: they can just put their papers on the web and it is for others to decide which to read and cite. It is already happening: many of us cite papers published on the web rather than in journals. Whether we like it or not, the process is unstoppable.

My proposal is for a more managed process, one in which there are light-touch editors in charge; editors who would also encourage and channel comments and debates which I consider essential to the process. Why do I want an OA system for putting research results into the public domain? The answer in one word is: *efficiency.* There are several respects in which the proposed system is more efficient than the current PR system. It would mean that ground-breaking, unusual works would face fewer obstacles when seeking rapid entry into the public domain. It would also greatly lower the costs involved in this process: here the savings are seen both in terms of financial costs and in terms of the opportunity costs of all the time that editors, administrators and referees of journals put into the process. It would ensure a speedier system for getting papers into the public domain. It would encourage a culture of open debate in which the community of researchers will not shy away from making critical comments or adding new points to somebody else's paper because they know they will get attribution. It would create sites of specialized research contributions similar to the current system in journals. A further advantage of my proposal is that it would make access to research works more democratic because it would be equally accessible by researchers in rich as well as in poor countries: all the researcher needs is a computer. Currently many researchers in developing countries are cut off by the high costs of journals in relation to the resources of their libraries.

The research community and society would get the maximum benefit – while bearing the lowest cost – from this proposed system if the providers of services on these websites were not-for-profit organizations such as academic and professional associations. The editing of Open Access and related 'Comments Link' sites should be supported by public funds to encourage competent and keen people to engage in the task.

The transition towards the *ex-post bottom-up PC* system may have to be gradual to avoid excessive disruption to ongoing processes.[17] It would be facilitated by the fact that the system is changing anyway under the effect of the establishment of many Open Access publication sites. It is a matter of seizing the initiative and moving towards an interaction and evaluation infrastructure for research appropriate to the twenty-first century.

6 Summary and conclusions

The chapter first presents a summary of critiques of the current system for evaluating research papers: the Peer Review system which is labelled as *ex-ante top-down Peer Review*. Two sets of criteria are considered in the critiques: efficiency and effectiveness; that is how good the PR system is in relation to private and social costs and how good it is in fulfilling its roles. A discussion of the roles and functions of the PR system leads to an analysis of its problems.

The last section proposes an alternative system – an Open Access system characterized by *ex-post bottom-up Peer Comment* – one that is more appropriate to the twenty-first century because it utilizes new technologies to achieve the following.

- low cost and speedy dissemination of research papers;
- encouragement of comments and discussions on papers, these to be put in the public domain under the name of the commentator;
- strong and open interaction between authors and commentators thus emphasizing the perspective of research as a social process.

Notes

1 Emeritus Professor of Applied Economics and Director, Centre for International Business Studies, London South Bank University (iettogg@lsbu.ac.uk). I am grateful to the following academics for useful comments on earlier drafts of this paper: N. Acocella, B. S. Frey, D. A. Gillies, M. Gillies, M. Rigby, A. Rosselli, A. Sparkes and M. Tiberi. A version of the chapter first appeared in Ietto-Gillies (2008a).
2 In relation to the PR process I am using the terms reviewer and referee interchangeably.
3 A. Sparkes has pointed out to me, in correspondence, that refereeing is now such a widespread activity that it no longer counts for career advancement.
4 A perceptive analysis of the problems and costs of evaluation systems applied to research can be found in Frey and Osterloh (2007).
5 The author has been Associate Editor of *Transnational Corporations*.
6 Campanario reports that some studies show evidence that appointed referees pass the job on to more junior colleagues. In a conversation with a colleague on this issue she mentioned to me that the practice was well known in her department and that – when working for her doctorate – she used to be asked by her supervisor to write reports on papers he had been asked to referee.
7 Campanario cites research reporting that the editors of a specific journal 'tend to accept about 10 percent of manuscripts they should have rejected, and rejected about 10 percent of manuscripts that should have been accepted' (1995: 194).
8 A poignant fictional story of the impact of the RAE on individual academics is told in Sparkes (2007). In a written exchange, Sparkes has pointed out to me how 'bluntly negative and destructive' reports can crush a young academic.

9 The introduction of targets has also become very widespread in the British National Health Service (NHS) and this is leading to behaviour distortions on the part of health workers under pressure from their managers to perform well. The devastating effects of all this have been highlighted by some high-profile failures in hospitals (Carvel 2006: 9 and 2007: 14).

10 Here is an example of undergoing adaptation of behaviour. The PR part of the RAE system has now been officially dropped by the British higher education funding body in favour of REF (Research Excellence Framework), a system based on metrics including citation indices. Changes in behaviour are already occurring and there is talk of establishing 'citation clubs' (Corbyn 2007) and of pressure on authors by journals editors for more citations of their own journals' works.

11 Gillies (2008: 2.3) cites the case of medical research by Semmelweis in 1840s and 1950s Vienna into puerperal fever. His statistical observations led him to recommend that doctors wash their hands, prior to examination of patients in maternity wards. The research community rejected the publication of his research.

12 See Sir James Black's view on this in the *Financial Times* (2009).

13 This approach is curious in view of Ginsparg's critical attitude towards the quality assurance of the PR process cited in section three.

14 In the 1950s and 1960s the American Economic Association – through the publisher Allen & Unwin – issued a series of 'Readers in Economics' collecting major published articles in a specific field. They were – at the time – very useful reference texts particularly for researchers working in institutions/countries not well endowed with library resources. As I write I can look on my shelves at Readers in 'Business Cycles', in 'Price Theory', in the 'Theory of Income Distribution' and in the 'Theory of International Trade'. The aim and format of twenty-first century Readers would differ by taking account of the opportunities offered by new technologies as well as of the scholarly infrastructure proposed here.

15 I am grateful to my husband Donald Gillies for bringing this example to my attention. In Gillies (2008: ch. 9) he develops the Einstein case further.

16 A long-term effect of the spread of e-archives will be savings on journal subscriptions by libraries. This, of course, will undermine the viability of many publishers.

17 I owe this point to Mario Tiberi.

References

Bedeian, A. G. (2004), 'Peer Review and the Social Construction of Knowledge in the Management Discipline', *Academy of Management Learning and Education*, 3(2), 198–216.

Braben, D. W. (2008), 'Comment on A XXI-century alternative to XX-century peer review" *real-world economics review*, 47, 250–1, October, available at www.paecon.net/PAEReview/issue47/CommentslettoGillies47.

Campanario, J. M. (1995), 'Commentary: On Influential Books and Journal Articles Initially Rejected because of Negative Referees' Evaluations', *Science Communication*, 16, 304–25.

Campanario, J. M. (1998a), 'Peer Review for Journals as It Stands Today – Part 1', *Science Communication*, 19(3), 181–211.

Campanario, J. M. (1998b), 'Peer Review for Journals as It Stands Today – Part 2'. *Science Communication*, 19(4), 277–306.

Carvel, J. (2006), 'Hospital's Focus on Waiting Time Targets Led to 41 Superbug Deaths', *Guardian*, 25 July, 9.

Carvel, J. (2007), 'Trust Failed to Warn of Outbreak or Improve Hygiene', *Guardian*, 11, 14 October.

Corbyn, Z. (2007), 'Tough New Hurdle for Top Researchers', *Times Higher Education Supplement*, 23, 1 November, 8

Financial Times (2009), 'An Acute Talent for Innovation. The Monday Interview: Sir James Black', 2 February.

Frey, B. S. (2003), 'Publishing as Prostitution? Choosing between One's Own Ideas and Academic Failure', *Public Choice*, 116, 205–23.

Frey, B. S. and Osterloh, M. (2007), 'Evaluations: Hidden Costs, Questionable Benefits, and Superior Alternatives', IEW Working Paper Series No. 302, February.

Gans, J. S. and Shepherd, G. B. (1994), 'How the Mighty Have Fallen: Rejected Classic Articles by Leading Economists', *Journal of Economic Perspectives*, 8, 165–79.

Garfield, E. (1986), 'Refereeing and Peer Review. Part 2. The Research on Refereeing and Alternatives to the Present System', *Current Contents*, 11 August, 3–12.

Gillies, D. (2008), *How Should Research Be Organized?* London, College Publications.

Ginsparg, P. (2002), 'Can Peer Review Be Better Focused?', available at http://people. ccmr.cornell.edu/ginsparg.

Horrobin, D. F. (1990), 'The Philosophical Basis of Peer Review and the Suppression of Innovation', *Journal of the American Medical Association*, 263, 1438–41

Ietto-Gillies, G. (2008a), 'A XXI-century alternative to XX-century peer review', *real-world economics review*, 45, 10–22, March, www.paecon.net/PAEReview/issue45/IettoGillies45.

Ietto-Gillies, G. (2008b), 'Six Comments and Rejoinder', *real-world economics review*, 47, 259–60, October, available at www.paecon.net/PAEReview/issue47/CommentsIettoGillies47.

Lederberg, J. (1978), 'Digital Communication and the Conduct of Science: The New Literacy', *Proceedings of the IEEE*, 66, 1314–19.

Legendre, A. M. (1995), 'Peer Review of Manuscripts for Biomedical Journals', *Journal of the American Veterinary Medical Association*, 207, 36–8.

Miller, A. I. (1981), *Albert Einstein's Special Theory of Relativity. Emergence (1905) and Early Interpretation (1905–1911)*, Reading, MA: Addison-Wesley Publishing Company, Inc.

Sparkes, A. C. (2007), 'Embodiment, Academics and the Audit Culture: A Story Seeking Consideration', *Qualitative Research*, 7(4), 521–50.

19 Research standards for young Italian academics

What has changed over the last 30 years?

*Adriano Birolo and Annalisa Rosselli**

1 Introduction

Taking as good the famous definition of economics attributed to Viner, "Economics is what economists do", it is surprising to see how little the history of economics has addressed the matter of what economists actually do, above all outside the US. The vast mass of data on research output which has recently become readily accessible has found little use other than in compilation of classifications of excellence in the field of scientific journals or departments, and rather more rarely with respect to individuals (Backhouse *et al.* 1997). On the other hand, precious little study has been dedicated to the "representative" economist, who represents the backbone of the profession and who, if research is performed mainly in the universities, also moulds the future followers of the discipline.

The aim of this chapter is to fill in some pieces that are missing from the picture, taking the case of Italy and concentrating on the economist at the first level of the academic career, the "Researcher" (*ricercatore*).[1]

Actually, our study – which entailed construction of an extensive database on the publications of young economists – serves a twofold purpose. The first is to trace out the scientific profile of the university Researcher at the beginning of the 1980s, and the change this has undergone over the last 30 years[2] as a result both of the broad developments that have affected the professional figure of the economist, and of the specific conditions of the Italian academic market. In particular, we will seek to define how and in what direction scientific standards have changed (number and typology of publications) for access to the first rung of the academic ladder[3] (section 2). The second aim is to see whether the progressive internationalisation of the profession, the increasing influence of the Anglo-Saxon way of organising research and the introduction of evaluation criteria taking into account the prominence achieved by publications have effectively modified the subjects and methods of research. Therefore, we will go on to a qualitative analysis of developments in the contents of the publications using as control models the classification of papers published in the *American Economic Review* and the *Economic Journal* (section 3). In this respect the case of Italy may prove emblematic of the situation of countries that already had a well-developed university system and national traditions when they began opening up to international competition.

2 How many publications and where?

2.1 Who are the university Researchers in the field of economics

The figure of the Researcher was instituted in Italy in 1980, and has since seen hardly any change. In 1983 selection procedures were launched on the basis of a "competitive examination". The selection committee, consisting of three members, is chaired by a full professor, designated by the university for which the post has been announced and almost always belonging to the same faculty. The other committee members, who come from other universities formerly appointed by the Minister, are now elected by all the Italian academics in the same field. Over the last ten years information regarding the availability of new posts has become widely accessible thanks to the Internet; at the same time the number of posts announced in the field of economics has been rising, mitigating competition. In fact, the yearly average number of Researchers appointed came to 21.9 in the period 1983–90, 33.5 in the period 1991–8, and 49.0 in the period 1999–2007.[4] And yet the flow has never been uniform: indeed, the distribution of posts up for competition has been very uneven, as can be seen in Figure 19.1. The discontinuity in the flow of posts, which were decided upon by the Ministry of Education in the 1980s, has remained such even after a new law granted individual universities the faculty to manage and control the entire competitive procedure, from announcement to appointment, at the end of the 1990s.

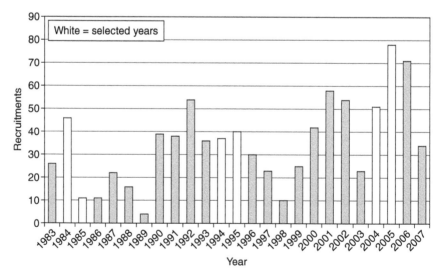

Figure 19.1 Recruitments by year.

In order to reconstruct the Researcher profile, we analysed the relevant competitive examinations held in three two-year periods at intervals of ten years: 1984–5; 1994–5; and 2004–5.[5] The years chosen were characterised by a considerable concentration of posts relative to the period, so that by analysing only six years out of 24 we were able to cover 30 per cent of the total of the 884 Researchers recruited up to 2007.

The data on the winners were provided to us by the Ministry for the University as far as the period 1980–99 was concerned; for the following period we gleaned our data from the information available online in the official university recruitment site.[6] The list provided by the Ministry for the first years shows certain rather odd gaps,[7] but it is evidently the most reliable source available. A previous study (Corsi 1999) based on information obtained laboriously from the personnel offices of the individual universities inevitably has rather more limited data to show. In order to determine which competitive examinations concerned the field of economics, we made use of the official descriptor which must be indicated when a post is announced. We selected the descriptors – which have over time seen various changes – so as to include the whole range of economics in the strict sense, excluding the management sectors.[8] We grouped the competition sites into the three broad geographical areas into which Italy is customarily divided : North, Centre, and South and Islands.

The three cohorts of the winners show many points in common, although they vary somewhat in numerical terms, as shown in Table 19.1.

To begin with, the average age remains around 33 years, with slight signs of rising. In the 1984–5 cohort it was 32.7 years, while by the latest it had risen to 33.3.[9] Second, the percentage of successful women remains higher in the South than in the North, where it has remained steady throughout the period at around 30 per cent. In the South, however, while remaining higher than elsewhere, the women's share shows a drop, so that at the national level it falls from the 36 per cent of 1984–5 to a little over 29 per cent in the youngest cohort. With no data on the geographical origin of the successful candidates, we cannot tell whether the better chances of success for women in the South depend on the practice, widely followed by Southern families until relatively recently, of sending the ablest sons to the North to study, reserving the universities nearer by for the daughters.

On the other hand, there are striking signs of change in the geographical distribution of posts subsequent to the extended autonomy of the universities, favouring the possibility to open positions of Researcher in the South (Table 19.2). At the historical level, the imbalance noted in comparison with the

Table 19.1 New recruitments

	M	F	F/T (%)	Total
1984–5	37	21	36	58
1994–5	58	22	27	80
2004–5	93	39	29	132

Table 19.2 Vacancies by geographical area and resident population (%)

	Vacancies 1984–5	Population 1982	Vacancies 1994–5	Population 1991	Vacancies 2004–5	Population 2001
South and Islands	17	35	11	36	29	36
Centre	31	19	33	19	28	19
North	52	46	56	45	43	45
	100	100	100	100	100	100

resident population can be put down to the different distribution and scale of the universities in the various parts of Italy – few and relatively small in the South, many, and some very large, in the Centre.

Career prospects are also decidedly better for the younger cohorts. Of the Researchers appointed in 1984–5, only 33 had arrived at the position of full professor 20 years later, while 10 per cent had completely abandoned the academic career. Of the Researchers appointed in 1994–5, on the other hand, only 10 per cent had continued in the role, while 46.3 per cent had been promoted to associate and 40 per cent to full professorships. Again, of those appointed in 2004–5, nearly 10 per cent had already become associate professors by 2007. Thus the choices made in earlier periods do not appear to have found confirmation in the successive stages of the academic career. This can be interpreted in various ways: discouragement due to the scant chances of promotion marking the 1980s and 1990s; local preferences rewarding people with little motivation or aptitude; greater eccentricity in the 1980s as compared with the model subsequently prevalent. On the other hand, improved career prospects in recent years may possibly have encouraged many younger Researchers, already closer at the outset to the model of scholar prevalent at the international level, to take a truly committed approach to the academic career.

2.2 Scientific publications

We can obtain further information by reviewing the scientific publications of the successful candidates at the time of the competition. In order to construct the publication database, lacking the successful candidates' "curricula vitae" we resorted to various bibliographic sources to track down their possible publications, divided into the categories of books, chapters in books, articles in scientific journals and working papers. The sources drawn upon were:

1   *Econlit*, the well-known electronic bibliography of the American Economic Association.
2   Essper (http://www.biblio.liuc.it/essper/default.htm), which came into operation in 1996[10] and sifts the Italian journals (i.e. those published in Italy, regardless of language) excluding only book reviews and working papers.

3   The OPAC catalogue (http://www.internetculturale.it/moduli/opac/opac.
jsp), with which we were able to extend research to books and even small
monographs (it gives the number of pages of each publication). OPAC
covers all the publications appearing in the catalogue of the Servizio Bibli-
otecario Nazionale (SBN – National Library Service), the Italian library
network including over 2,900 libraries of the State, local bodies, universities and public and private institutions working in various fields of learning. In the SBN catalogue we find descriptions of documents acquired by
the network libraries as from the 1990s or from the entry of individual
libraries into the SBN, and descriptions drawn from the printed catalogues
anterior to the 1990s. It is also to be borne in mind that according to Italian
press law, a copy of every publication must be consigned to a National
Library.

4   British Library catalogue, available online.

In view of the fact that selection committees may take into account, even if
not officially, work presented in manuscript form but in press, we extended our
research to the first year subsequent to the appointment. Given that one year
usually elapses between the announcement of the vacancy, when publications
must be submitted to the selecting committee, and the appointment of the successful candidate, we can reasonably assume that few publications can have
escaped our attention. These are:

1   working papers which do not appear in our sources;
2   journal articles published two years or more after the announcement;
3   books and chapters in books brought out by small, non-Italian publishers;
4   works in languages other than Italian or English and published in foreign
journals not included in *Econlit*.

The situation thus emerging is summarised in Table 19.3.

From the point of view of productivity, taking into consideration all the publications and all the successful candidates we find a distinct increase in the number
of publications in the two younger cohorts. The difference may in part be due to

Table 19.3 Productivity of successful candidates

	1984–5	*1994–5*	*2004–5*
Total number of publications	111	305	567
Successful candidates	58	80	132
Publications per successful candidate, average	1.9	3.9	4.3
Successful candidates with at least 1 publication	41	69	122
Number of publications per successful candidate with at least 1 publication, average	2.7	4.4	4.6
As above, weighted average	2.5	4.0	3.9
As above, weighted average and working papers excluded	2.1	2.9	2.2

the fact that both *Econlit* and OPAC are rather less reliable sources for the 1980s, when *Econlit* took a smaller number of journals into account, while in the case of OPAC some items may have been lost in transference from printed to electronic catalogues. Even confining the field solely to "active" Researchers, i.e. with at least one publication, there is still an appreciable increase in the number of works between the first and second cohorts, but hardly any difference between the second and third. We might therefore be inclined to conclude that selection has become more meritocratic over time, with an – at least quantitative – rise in benchmark.

However, this difference is greatly reduced, almost to disappearing point, if we take two further factors into account. The first is a greater propensity for working in collaboration among the younger generations, who produce more co-authored works than the previous generations. Thus we found it appropriate to weight the publications by number of authors, assigning 0.7 when there are two authors and 0.4 for three or more. These weights were chosen with the consideration that collective work by its very nature calls for an additional activity of coordination, although the returns to scale may be increasing in qualitative terms. In other words, co-authored works may turn out better, but they take only a little less time than individual efforts.[11] Thus the difference in number of publications for Researchers who have at least one proves somewhat less. The second factor is the inclusion of working papers. As we have extended research to cover publications over the entire calendar year after year, the working papers submitted as such at the time of the competitive exam will almost certainly have become publications and are therefore taken into account. By including the working papers we run the risk of duplication and taking into account publications of little worth or those written after the term for submission of applications had expired.[12] With weighting and exclusion of working papers the differences are appreciably reduced, with the result that no great difference in productivity is to be seen among the cohorts, apart from a slight increase in the 1994–5 cohort.

The difference between the averages calculated for all the successful candidates and for only those who have at least one publication is greater for the earlier cohorts, which include a number of Researchers without publications. An apparent lack of publications may simply be due to deficiencies in the present online bibliographic databases. In any case, passing the competitive exam without any publications seems to have become more difficult, although not impossible. As Table 19.4 demonstrates, nearly 8 per cent of the successful candidates still make it, but with a large drop between 1984–5, when there was still no possibility of gaining a doctorate unless abroad, and 2004–5.

2.3 The numerical distribution of publications

How do the Researchers fall into classes in terms of number of publications? For each cohort, how many of the Researchers publish little, and how many a lot?

The Researchers were grouped on the basis of having the same number of publications.[13] None of the Researchers of the first cohort has more than 11 publications, the majority falling into the 0 or 1 publication class. The situation appears very different

Table 19.4 Successful candidates with 0 publications

Cohort	North	Centre	South & Is.	Total
1984–5	5	9	3	17
	16.7%	50.0%	30.0%	29.0%
1994–5	5	5	1	11
	11.1%	19.2%	11.1%	14.0%
2004–5	2	3	5	10
	3.5%	8.1%	13.1%	7.6%

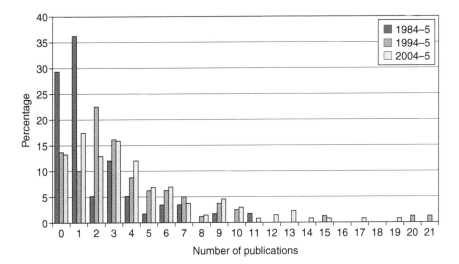

Figure 19.2 Successful candidates by number of publications.

for the following cohorts, the distribution curve peaking at around two publications to make a fairly steady descent to the threshold of 20 publications (Figure 19.2)

The change in distribution of Researchers by number of publications between one cohort and another can better be appreciated by grouping the Researchers into four broad numerical classes of publication, 0–3, 4–7, 8–11, 12–21. The results are set out in Table 19.5.

In the first cohort 82 per cent of the Researchers fall into the class of 0–3 publications. Ten years later the percentage had dropped to 62 per cent, and after another ten years to 53 per cent, thus with a reduction of 35 per cent. Consequently the 1994–5 and 2004–5 cohorts come above the original cohort, for all the classes exceeding the first, following very similar trends markedly distinct from the first.

2.4 *"Prominence" achieved*

While the average productivity, albeit "adjusted", seems to have changed little over the years, if we go on to look at the publications listed by *Econlit*, the

Table 19.5 Successful candidates by number of publications

Number of publications	1984–5	1994–5	2004–5
0–3	82.8	62.5	53.8
4–7	13.8	26.3	29.6
8–11	3.4	7.5	9.8
12–21	0.0	3.8	6.8
Concentration index	0.9	0.6	0.5

Notes
Concentration index: ratio between successful candidates in the largest group and total. Maximum value = 1, minimum = 0.25.

Table 19.6 Successful candidates with at least 1 publication appearing in *Econlit*, absolute values and percentages

	M	F	Total	Gender gap
1984–5	10	6	16	
	27.0%	28.6%	27.6%	−1.5%
1994–5	30	12	42	
	51.7%	54.5%	52.5%	−2.8%
2004–5	71	22	93.0	
	76.3%	56.4%	70.5%	19.9%

change from one cohort to another is quite evident in terms of prominence achieved. As can be seen in Table 19.6, the percentage of successful candidates with at least one publication appearing in *Econlit* nearly doubles between the 1980s and the 1990s (but we must also bear in mind that the *Econlit* coverage was extended in those years), increasing even more for the youngest generation.

An interesting difference is to be seen between the second and third cohort. While no significant difference appeared in the behaviour of men and women up to 1994–5, the last cohort shows a striking gender gap. The men seem to develop a flair for grasping the rules of the game, and by now three out of four enter into the fray with at least one publication in *Econlit*. In fact, the percentage of those with a book among their publications drops sharply: if papers had always represented the bulk of the publications, the books plunge to 8.1 per cent (see Table 19.7), replaced by contributions to collected volumes (classified as "other"). The percentage with at least one book behind them, even though only as co-author, went from the 26 per cent of the successful candidates in 1984–5, when in Italy doctorates had yet to be brought in, to 29 per cent in 1994–5, when the doctorate thesis still took the form of a monographic research, and then to the 17 per cent of the last generation, for which the doctorate thesis is conceived as a collection of papers.

Table 19.7 Typology of publications

Cohort	Books (%)	Journal articles (%)	Other (%)
1984–5	21.8	74.1	4.1
1994–5	11.4	80.3	8.3
2004–5	8.1	79.1	12.8

3 The scientific profile of the Italian Researcher

3.1 Comparison with the American Economic Review model

An even more interesting problem, still harder to solve, is to trace out the cultural profile of the Researcher. As they are young economists, supposing that Keynes was right in asserting that "in the field of economic and political philosophy there are not many who are influenced by new theories after they are twenty-five or thirty years of age" (Keynes 1936, 383–4), then investigation into the Researcher's cultural profile should cast light on future trends in the field. Each will be wanting to reap the fruits of their investment in human capital, and will hardly be likely to abandon research methodologies, if not areas of investigation, cultivated in their youth.

We have concentrated on a concern raised above all recently in the course of discussion on the criteria to evaluate economic research according to "objective" parameters, as required by an increasing number of agencies supplying funds, and the public ones in particular. One cannot help wondering whether a "monistic" view of economics is being emphatically imposed, to the effect that the way to funding and career progress is only through recognition of one established research model. Pluralism in the methods, subjects and results of research would thus be sacrificed, and with them the chances for the discipline to embrace real innovations (Artoni 2004, 2007; Bardhan 2003; Gillies 2006, 2008; Hodgson and Rothman 1999; Lee 2007; Lee and Harley 1997, 1998; Oswald 2007; Sen 2002; van Dalen 2007).

The question we set ourselves, therefore, is whether the Researchers of the youngest cohort answer more than those of the earlier ones to the need to conform to a model of economist such as emerges from the syllabuses of the major US universities, and whether the range of subjects and methods has effectively been reduced.

Arriving at an answer is no easy task. The first stumbling block is that any attempt at classification – whether of contents or methods – is inevitably dated, reflecting the approach to economics at that particular time. Earlier attempts to identify the "fads in economic writing" (Stigler 1965; Bronfenbrenner 1966) had already come to this conclusion, which is borne out by any, even superficial, examination of the items appearing in the classifications historically adopted by the profession. As for the subjects of research, the American Economic Association, for example, published from 1886 to the 1960s an *Index of Economic Journals* with over 20 headings, also including "War and defense economics" and "Consumer economics" – areas which no economist would now consider worth headings of their own – while on the other hand we also find subjects that have now become disciplines in their own right, like "Population". In the 1970s the editors of the *Economic Journal* offered in their annual report a table in which the articles published were grouped according to the subjects addressed.[14] Among the classification headings there appeared "Distribution" and "Theory of the rate of interest" set at the same level as "Money and banking" and "Economic development". The *Journal of Economic Literature* itself, which provides the now dominant classification also adopted in this paper, felt the need to change the number of headings, raising it from 10 to 20 in 1991, in response to the changes that had come about in the discipline. To this is to be added the consideration that, under the same heading, what had been classified 25 years ago as microeconomics would not necessarily be placed as such today.

No less challenging are attempts to classify the method of research. The very division of papers between "theoretical" and "empirical" itself clashes with variable opinions as to what effectively constitutes a theoretical or empirical paper. Would an "analysis without any mathematical formulation and without data", 12 examples of which the *AER* published between 1977 and 1981 (Morgan 1988, 160), find room in any journal of economics today? And does the paper model defined PME (Holub 1989), i.e. Problem–Model–Empirical-statistical support, prevalent by far in the 1990s, still represent the classical typology of empirical analysis?

For this reason we have not attempted diachronic classification, which would inevitably have led us to view the past through today's lenses, but preferred to make comparison for each period with a model *of the same period*. Thus we compare the scientific profile of the Italian Researcher with two standard models, one drawn from the papers published *in the same years* in the *American Economic Review (AER)*, in this section, and one from those published in the *Economic Journal (EJ)*, in the following section.

The choice of the *American Economic Review (AER)* as the container of research subjects from which to draw the standard profile of the economist of the period was made for fairly obvious reasons. *AER* is the generalist economic journal with the widest circulation in the world; it is the official organ of the American Economic Association, the leading US "learned society" in the field of economics – it is not a mouthpiece for a school of thought but embraces orthodox economic research, albeit conducted according to the prevalent US standards, in its various forms. Hence the *AER* shows reliable performance over time in attesting to the evolution of themes and methods prevalent in economic research. Finally, it is also sufficiently international in its approach, receiving contributions by authors from various parts of the world outside the US, although they tend to be authors with "US based" grounding in any case.[15]

For the purpose of comparison use was made of nine years of the *American Economic Review*,[16] distributed in three-year periods: 1983–5, 1993–5 and

2003–5. A database was constructed containing the articles of each year ordered on the basis of the *JEL* descriptor with which each article appeared in *Econlit*.[17] Included in the same database are the publications of Italian authors of the 1984–5, 1994–5 and 2004–5 cohorts listed in *Econlit* on the basis of the first respective *JEL* descriptors, chosen by the authors.[18]. The first descriptor reflects, if not the effective content of the article, at any rate the category the authors wish to see them accorded. For the sake of completeness, although it means introducing a somewhat arbitrary element, we have also included in the database the publications of each Researcher that do not appear in *Econlit* – mainly articles in Italian, monographs, contributions to volumes and working papers. Each publication is provided with a descriptor on the evidence of the title and abstract or, in doubtful cases, determined by examining the publication.[19]

In the first overview table (Table 19.8) we indicate for each cohort the composition of papers appearing in the *AER* sorted on the basis of their first *JEL* descriptor, and with the same criterion the composition of the Researchers' publications found in *Econlit*. We then added a column with the composition of all the Researchers' publications, those in *Econlit* being added to the others – the majority – identified in the remaining bibliographic sources indicated in the previous section.[20]

The data emerging from the *AER* columns of Table 19.8 are the areas of economic research prevailing in the three-year period 1983–5 and the evolution this model showed in the following two decades.

In the three-year period 1983–5 the descriptor of most weight (28 per cent) is "D", microeconomics, followed by "E", macroeconomics (21 per cent). Together they cover half the papers appearing in the *AER* in the three-year period. The other descriptors of some weight are "J", labour economics (12 per cent) and "L", industrial organisation (7 per cent). Other descriptors later to become "weighty", like "F" (international economics) and "G" (financial economics) show very low figures. In the three-year period 1993–5 microeconomics, while remaining the area with the relatively greater weight (20 per cent), shows rather less importance. Such is also the case of macroeconomics, which slips down to 15 per cent. These two descriptors together add up to 35 per cent of the papers published. Of growing importance are international economics (from 4 per cent to 10 per cent) and the financial economics (from 0.25 per cent to 7 per cent). Both labour economics and industrial organisation maintain the weight of the previous decade. The last three-year period shows sharp growth in microeconomics (from 20 per cent to 33 per cent) while macroeconomics declines, losing half the weight of the previous 20-year period (from 21 per cent to 10 per cent), possibly as a consequence of the decline of economic policies using the traditional tools of monetary and fiscal measures in the agendas of academic economists. Microeconomics and macroeconomics together cover 43 per cent of the papers published, an increase over the previous decade accounted for, however, by the performance of microeconomics alone. International economics (10 per cent) and the financial economics (from 7 per cent to 8 per cent) confirmed the level of importance already achieved in the previous decade. Sharp drops are shown by labour economics and industrial organisation, losing half their weight

Table 19.8 Subjects of the *AER* articles and of the Italian Researchers' publications by *JEL* descriptor

JEL descriptor	% AER 1983–5	R. pub *Econlit 1984–5	R. pub All** 1984–5	% AER 1993–5	R. pub Econlit 1994–5	R. pub All 1994–5	% AER 2003–5	R. pub Econlit 2004–5	R. pub All 2004–5
A General and teaching	2.2	0.0	1.8	0.7	0.0	0.5	1.3	0.4	0.4
B History of economic thought and methodolgy	2.2	15.4	11.7	1.1	5.0	5.4	0.3	8.2	6.7
C Mathematical and quantitative methods	5.0	7.7	3.6	4.3	6.9	8.3	7.6	5.7	2.5
D Microeconomics	28.6	0.0	3.6	20.6	13.9	8.3	33.6	14.8	9.0
E Macro- and monetary economics	21.4	30.8	19.8	15.7	19.8	8.8	11.0	19.7	11.5
F International economics	4.2	23.1	7.2	10.0	6.9	2.5	11.0	5.7	3.5
G Financial economics	0.3	3.9	4.5	7.5	10.9	18.6	8.3	10.7	7.8
H Public economics	3.2	3.9	18.9	4.3	9.9	14.7	3.7	7.4	7.1
I Health, education and welfare	0.3	0.0	0.9	3.2	1.0	0.0	6.3	2.1	5.8
J Labour economics	11.9	7.7	3.6	12.8	5.9	4.4	6.6	4.5	7.9
K Law and economics	1.2	0.0	0.9	0.4	0.0	0.5	1.0	1.2	0.7
L Industrial organisation	7.5	0.0	16.2	7.1	5.9	3.9	3.0	4.5	12.5
M Business	3.5	0.0	0.0	0.4	4.0	0.0	0.0	0.8	0.4
N Economic history	3.7	0.0	0.9	2.1	0.0	0.0	1.7	0.8	0.4
O Economic development	3.0	3.9	2.7	5.3	4.0	11.8	2.3	4.1	4.2
P Economic systems	0.5	0.0	0.9	1.1	3.0	0.0	0.0	0.4	0.2
Q Agriculture, natural resources, environment	0.3	3.9	0.9	2.1	0.0	2.0	1.3	1.2	7.9
R Urban, rural, regional	1.0	0.0	1.8	0.7	3.0	9.8	0.7	2.5	7.1
Y Miscellaneous	0.0	0.0	0.0	0.0	0.0	0.5	0.3	3.7	1.6
Z Other special topics	0.0	0.0	0.0	0.7	0.0	0.0	0.0	1.6	3.0
100	100	100	100	100	100	100	100	100	
Total journal articles	402	26	111	281	101	305	301	244	567

Notes

* publications listed in *Econlit*.

** all publications, listed and not listed in *Econlit*.

(respectively from 13 per cent to 6 per cent and from 7 per cent to 3 per cent). A reasonably likely explanation could be that in both these areas the ever wider adoption of Game theory took the upper hand over content, and that an appreciable portion of works in these areas fell into microeconomics pure and simple, and into the area of mathematical methods (descriptor "C"). As interpreted by the *AER* over a 20-year span, economics seems largely to be the discipline of individual choices and optimisation methods.[21]

How much of this model is reflected in the publications of the Italian Researchers? The figures in Table 19.8 appearing in the second and third columns of each cohort offer initial indication.

The last row in Table 19.8 indicates the number of publications examined, papers in the case of the *AER* and publications in the broad sense in the case of the Researchers. We observe that the total publications of the Researchers grow over fivefold between the first and third cohort, but almost ten times those included in *Econlit*, a point already discussed in the previous section but worth recalling to underline the growing external visibility achieved by the average Researcher, and, with it, the soundness of the comparisons we develop.

It is, however, Table 19.9 that offers an unequivocal measure of the degree to which the Italian model differs from the *AER* model. In this table, the differences are calculated between the composition of the Researchers' publications, distinguishing those appearing in *Econlit* from the total, and the composition of the *AER* papers. The values in the table limit the dimension effect in the differences between the compositions of the Researchers' publications and the *AER* papers through normalisation by standard deviation.[22] Thus can be seen the weight of Italian specialisation (positive values and equal to, or greater than one) or despecialisation (negative values and equal to, or less than one) as compared with the *AER* model. The Italian Researchers' publications diverge sharply for descriptor "B" (history of thought and methodology), above all in the first cohort. In the second cohort specialisation is less pronounced, but again looms large in the third. Thus we see an evident specificity in Italian economic research into the

Table 19.9 "Specialisation" and "despecialisation" of the Italian Researchers' publications relatively to the *American Economic Review* by *JEL* descriptor

JEL descriptor	(%R. 1984–5 – % AER 1983–5)/SD		(%R. 1994–5 – % AER 1993–5)/SD		(%R. 2004–5 – % AER 2003–5)/SD	
	Econlit pub.	All pub.	Econlit pub.	All pub	Econlit pub.	All pub.
A General and teaching	−0.2	−0.1	−0.2	0.0	−0.2	−0.1
B History of economic thought and methodology	1.4	1.2	1.1	0.7	1.4	0.9
C Mathematical and quantitative methods	0.3	−0.2	0.8	0.7	−0.3	−0.7
D Microeconomics	−3.1	−3.2	−2.0	−2.0	−3.4	−3.5
E Macro- and monetary economics	1.0	−0.2	1.2	−1.1	1.6	0.1
F International economics	2.1	0.4	−0.9	−1.2	−0.9	−1.1
G Financial economics	0.4	0.5	1.0	1.8	0.4	−0.1
H Public economics	0.1	2.0	1.6	1.7	0.7	0.5
I Health, education and welfare	0.0	0.1	−0.6	−0.5	−0.8	−0.1
J Labour economics	−0.5	−1.1	−2.0	−1.3	−0.4	0.2
K Law and economics	−0.1	0.0	−0.1	0.0	0.0	0.0
L Industrial organisation	−0.8	1.1	−0.3	−0.5	0.3	1.4
M Business	−0.4	−0.4	1.1	−0.1	0.2	0.1
N Economic history	−0.4	−0.4	−0.6	−0.3	−0.2	−0.2
O Economic development	0.1	0.0	−0.4	1.0	0.3	0.3
P Economic systems	−0.1	0.1	0.6	−0.2	0.1	0.0
Q Agriculture, natural resources environment	0.4	0.1	−0.6	0.0	0.0	0.9
R Urban, rural, regional	−0.1	0.1	0.7	1.5	0.3	0.9
Y Miscellaneous	0.0	0.0	0.0	0.1	0.6	0.2
Z Other special topics	0.0	0.0	−0.2	−0.1	0.3	0.4

history of thought. An interesting point is that the widest divergence appears with the more prominent publications, those in *Econlit*, evidencing the recognisability from outside of this Italian specificity and the capacity to take a commanding position in the international debate in this field.

Particularly glaring is the despecialisation for descriptor "D", microeconomics, tempered only by the figure for the second cohort. In Table 19.9 the highest absolute values are seen in the row corresponding to descriptor "D". This despecialisation increases over time, the values of the last cohort exceeding those of the first, blithely challenging academic fashions. It may be the result of a tradition in Italian economic culture, developed in the 1960s and 1970s with the emphasis on matters of macroeconomics and development economics, reflected and persisting – unconsciously even – in the younger generations despite the "American lessons" many apprentice Researchers were immersed in.

Descriptor "E", macroeconomics, shows results for the publications included in *Econlit* diverging from the others. For the former, specialisation is seen to be positive and growing over time; it is negative for the other publications, with less international prominence.

For international economics, descriptor "F", specialisation is very pronounced for the *Econlit* publications of the first cohort, probably reflecting the Italian and European debate of those years on exchange rates, balance of payments adjustments, devaluation and so forth. In the following two cohorts the sign changes from plus to minus and despecialisation emerges, accentuated by the non-*Econlit* component of the publications.

Specialisation in industrial organisation, descriptor "L", appears for the non-*Econlit* publications in the first and third cohort, but not in the second. This is the result of publications tending largely to domestic themes finding reception above all in national containers.

In the two most recent cohorts there emerges an Italian specialisation in regional economics, descriptor "R", generated by the non-*Econlit* component of the publications.

Table 19.10 offers a qualitative overview of the results. The positive or negative sign indicates specialisation or despecialisation if the corresponding values fall outside the interval $(-1,1)$. The number of superscript stars shows the degree of specialisation (despecialisation). This is "high" if specialisation holds for both *Econlit* and non-*Econlit* publications and for the publications added Econlit publications and for the publications added together, "medium" if it holds for either the *Econlit* or the non-*Econlit* publications in such a degree that also the publications added together appear specialised, "low" in the opposite case.

Ultimately, the two lines of strong continuity are specialisation in the history of thought and in methodology, and the particularly pronounced despecialisation in microeconomics, the latter calling for further investigation if it is to be accounted for.

Over and above the differences by descriptor of the Italian and *AER* models, can we arrive at a general measure of the distance between the two models? To this end we compared for each cohort the vectors of publication composition

Table 19.10 Specialisation and despecialisation of Italian Researchers relatively to *AER*

JEL descriptor	1984–5	1994–5	2004–5
B History of economic thought and methodology	+***	+*	+*
D Microeconomics	_***	_***	_***
E Macro- and monetary economics	_*	_*	+*
F International economics	+*	_**	_**
G Financial economics	...	+***	...
H Public economics	+**	+***	...
I Health, education and welfare	...	...	...
J Labour economics	_**	_***	...
L Industrial organisation	+**	...	+**
M Business	...	_*	...
O Economic development	...	+**	...
Q Agriculture, natural resources, environment	...	...	+*
R Urban, rural, regional	...	+**	+**

Notes
+ = specialisation.
– = despecialisation.
number of stars = high, medium, low level.

Table 19.11 Indicators of similarity between Italian Researchers and *AER*

	1984		1994		2004	
	Econlit pub.	*All pub.*	*Econlit pub.*	*All pub.*	*Econlit pub.*	*All pub.*
Correlation coefficient	0.4	0.4	0.8	0.4	0.7	04
Standard deviation	9.1	7.8	3.4	6.3	5.6	7.0

with the vector of the composition of *AER* articles and formulated two indexes, summarised in Table 19.11.

The statistical indicators are extremely simple and readily grasped. The first is the linear coefficient of correlation. It proves positive in all cases, its value growing over time, indicating a reduction in the distance between the Researchers' publication vectors and the *AER* vectors. The interesting point here is that in the second cohort the coefficient of correlation measured on the *Econlit* publications makes a great leap towards unity, not followed by the coefficient calculated on all the publications, which remains almost the same as of the first cohort. In the 1994–5 cohort the Italian "internationally oriented" model shows a striking adjustment to the *AER* model, taken as standard. The non-*Econlit* publications, on the other hand, perform a powerful braking function. This move towards international uniformity becomes, however, once again questionable – albeit not to a drastic degree – in the third cohort. The coefficient of correlation on *Econlit* publications slides slightly back, but the overall coefficient, taking into account publications that do not appear in *Econlit*, stands at a level only slightly above that of the first cohort. The conclusion is that the less "prominent" publications – those not in *Econlit* – continue to hold the Italian model firmly anchored to that of the origins, i.e. of the first cohort.

The second indicator is standard deviation, the most classical measure of dispersion. It shows a drastic drop for publications in *Econlit* from the first cohort to the second, to rise again in the third. Thus the gap occurs in the transition from the 1984–5 cohort to that of 1994–5. Rather less sharp is the fall in the standard deviation calculated on publications not appearing in *Econlit* in the transition from the first to the second cohort, offering further confirmation of the fact that the publications not in *Econlit* make a decisive contribution to maintaining the difference between the Italian and *AER* models.

3.2 Comparison with the Economic Journal model

We felt it worthwhile to extend analysis to see if the typology of scientific interests of the Italian Researchers reflected only national specificities or, rather, a view to the international scene – not so much to the other side of the Atlantic as to the European picture, with the UK model taken as a reference point. To verify this hypothesis we repeat for the *Economic Journal* (*EJ*), with the same characteristics and specifications, the exercise already performed with the *American Economic Review*.

Although over a third of the articles were still by British authors in the 1980s, the *Economic Journal* has always shown a great degree of openness towards the rest of the world and independence in its editorial policy. Is this enough to conclude that the *Economic Journal* editorial policy differs significantly from that of the *AER*?

Table 19.12 differs from 19.8 only in the columns headed *EJ* in the three periods considered. (The data on the Italian Researchers' publications remain, of course, unchanged.)

If we look at the composition of the *EJ* publications, the only relevant divergences from the *AER* model are:

1   A "mild" and by no means overwhelming predominance of microeconomics. Microeconomics ("D") is the "pivot" descriptor for the *EJ*, but with a somewhat less marked prevalence than in the *AER*. In the first period its weight is below the corresponding *AER* weight (21.6 per cent as against 28.6 per cent), closely followed by the macroeconomic descriptor ("E") with 19.1 per cent. In the second, with 14.5 per cent macroeconomics eventually overtakes microeconomics, which falls to 13 per cent. In the third period microeconomics takes the lead once again, rising to 22.5 per cent, but at any rate standing well below the peak of 33.5 per cent it reaches in *AER*.

2   The weight of the history of thought and methodology ("B") is small in three cohorts, but not insignificant, as was the case with the *AER* model. In the first period the history of thought is in seventh position in terms of number of articles published; in the second it rises to sixth position, with a percentage of 9.4 per cent. The subsequent drop is sharp, to 3 per cent (but in the *AER* the history of thought dwindles almost completely away, with a mere 0.33 per cent) – a sign of the changing times, but perhaps also of the editorial policy of the journal.[23]

Table 19.12 Subjects of the *EJ* articles and of the Italian Researchers' publications by *JEL* descriptor

JEL descriptor	% EJ 1983–5	R. pub *Econlit 1984–5	R. pub All** 1984–5	% EJ 1993–5	R. pub Econlit 1994–5	R. pub All 1994–5	% EJ 2003–5	R. pub Econlit 2004–5	R. pub All 2004–5
A General and teaching	0.6	0.0	1.8	0.5	0.0	0.5	1.5	0.4	0.4
B History of economic thought and methodology	4.3	15.4	11.7	9.4	5.0	5.4	3.0	8.2	6.7
C Mathematical and quantitative methods	6.2	7.7	3.6	7.0	6.9	8.3	6.5	5.7	2.5
D Microeconomics	21.6	0.0	3.6	13.1	13.9	8.3	22.5	14.8	9.0
E Macro- and monetary economics	19.1	30.8	19.8	14.5	19.8	8.8	13.0	19.7	11.5
F International economics	9.3	23.1	7.2	14.5	6.9	2.5	11.0	5.7	3.5
G Financial economics	2.5	3.9	4.5	10.3	10.9	18.6	6.0	10.7	7.8
H Public economics	2.5	3.9	18.9	1.9	9.9	14.7	1.0	7.4	7.1
I Health, education and welfare	0.0	0.0	0.9	0.9	1.0	0.0	9.0	2.1	5.8
J Labour economics	14.2	7.7	3.6	12.2	5.9	4.4	14.0	4.5	7.9
K Law and economics	0.6	0.0	0.9	0.9	0.0	0.5	1.5	1.2	0.7
L Industrial organisation	4.3	0.0	16.2	4.7	5.9	3.9	4.5	4.5	12.5
M Business	1.9	0.0	0.0	0.5	4.0	0.0	0.5	0.8	0.4
N Economic history	0.6	0.0	0.9	0.9	0.0	0.0	1.0	0.8	0.4
O Economic development	9.9	3.9	2.7	4.7	4.0	11.8	3.0	4.1	4.2
P Economic systems	0.0	0.0	0.9	2.8	3.0	0.0	0.0	0.4	0.2
Q Agriculture, natural resources, environment	1.9	3.9	0.9	0.9	0.0	2.0	1.0	1.2	7.9
R Urban, rural, regional	0.6	0.0	1.8	0.5	3.0	9.8	0.5	2.5	7.1
Y Miscellaneous	0.0	0.0	0.0	0.0	0.0	0.5	0.5	3.7	1.6
Z Other special topics	0.0	0.0	0.0	0.0	0.0	0.0	0.0	1.6	3.0
Total journal articles	162	26	111	214	101	305	200	244	567

Notes
* Publications listed in *Econlit*.
** All publications, listed and not listed in *Econlit*.

3   International economics and labour economics have considerable weight in the *EJ* model, showing no significant dissimilarity with the *AER* model, with the exception of the years 1983–5. This is a period of great turbulence on the currency markets, with violent impact – not much different from the other countries of continental Europe – on a relatively small country like the United Kingdom. The situation is also evidently reflected in the economic research that finds prominence in the *EJ*, which still dedicates its space largely to Anglo-Saxon scholars. In the third cohort the weight of international economics falls, sinking back to the *AER* level.

Comparison between the *AER* and *EJ* models is summarised in Table 19.13.

Despite the differences pointed out above, the summary indicators offer a picture showing evident similarity. The correlation coefficient is practically the same, with very high value in the first and third cohorts. Only in the second cohort is the closeness reduced with the decreased weight of microeconomics

Table 19.13 *EJ* and *AER*: how much are they alike?

	EJ – AER 1983–5	EJ – AER 1993–5	EJ – AER 2003–05
Correlation coefficient	0.9	0.8	0.9
Standard deviation	3.0	3.1	3.3

Table 19.14 Specialisation and despecialisation of Italian Researchers relatively to *EJ*

JEL descriptor	1984–5	1994–5	2004–5
B History of economic thought and methodology	+**	–*	+*
D Microeconomics	–***	–*	–***
E Macro- and monetary economics	+*	–*	+*
F International economics	+*	–***	–***
G Financial economics	...	+**	+*
H Public economics	+**	+***	+**
I Health, education and welfare	...	...	–*
J Labour economics	–**	–***	–***
L Industrial organisation	+**	...	+**
M Business	...	–*	...
O Economic development	–**	+**	...
Q Agriculture, natural resources, environment	...	...	+**
R Urban, rural regional	...	+**	+**

Notes
+ = specialisation.
– = despecialisation.
number of stars = high, medium, low level.

and the growth in weight of the history of thought. The standard deviation shows a very low value in the three cohorts, evidencing very limited dissimilarity. Paradoxically, the dissimilarity seems to increase, albeit very slightly, in the third cohort. Thus the hypothesis we started from, namely that the *EJ*, a generalist journal, differed significantly from the *AER* model, is to be rejected. The differences are there, but not so marked as to differentiate greatly the two models in any of the three periods examined.

Given this state of affairs, we should not expect results very different from those emerging from comparison with the *AER* model in the specialisation by themes of the Italian Researchers' publications in comparison with the *EJ* model.

Table 19.14, to be compared with the corresponding Table 19.10, brings out quite clearly our specialisation pattern. Compared with the *AER* model, the differences are evidently limited, most of them concentrated in the second cohort. It was, then, in the early 1990s that a change in the model for the way of doing research – both contents and methods – took place in Italy.

Table 19.15, like Table 19.11, shows two summary indicators of similarity between the Researchers' publications and the *EJ* model.

Table 19.15 Indicators of similarity between the publications of the Italian Researchers and *EJ*

	1984		1994		2004	
	Econlit pub.	*All pub.*	*Econlit pub.*	*All pub.*	*Econlit pub.*	*All pub.*
Correlation coefficient	0.6	0.4	0.8	0.4	0.7	0.5
Standard deviation	7.4	7.2	3.5	5.9	4.5	5.3

The coefficient of correlation grows with transition from the first to the second cohort. It shows considerable growth in terms of the *Econlit* component of the publications, but hardly any at all for the "domestic" publications. Thus the most prominent publications drive research in economics towards the model that is gaining ground in the Anglo-Saxon academic markets, on both sides of the Atlantic. Transition to the third cohort sees the picture becoming stable. The diminished distance between the coefficient measured on *Econlit* and the coefficient calculated for the total of publications is a sign that the domestic publications are adjusting to the *EJ* model, which is moreover very close to the *AER* model.

A somewhat similar interpretation can be made in the case of the standard deviation. Transition to the second cohort sees a very strong drive towards the *EJ* model, particularly marked for the *Econlit* publications, far less for the others. The domestic publications still exert a braking action. In the third cohort the standard deviation for *Econlit* publications shows a slight rise, while the standard deviation calculated on all the publications declines, implying that the "internal" publications are contributing to driving the standard deviation downwards and to playing a positive role in the progress towards the *EJ* model. It is worth noting, incidentally, that in Table 19.11, referring to the *AER* model, this development is of rather less certain interpretation.

Thus, as was to be expected, comparison with the *Economic Journal* also shows that in the early 1990s a change in the model for the way of doing research – as regards both contents and methods – took place in Italy. Nevertheless, a lively interest persisted in certain fields that continue to be cultivated, even with the awareness that such research is unlikely to achieve international prominence. Some might consider this characteristic, shown also by the younger Researchers, a hangover from the past, to be eliminated, but others will see it as a resource to cultivate and a meaningful asset capable of contributing to the advance and variety of economic learning.

Appendix

Correspondence between JEL descriptors before and after 1990

	000	100	200	300	400	500	600	700	800	900
A	010									
B	031									
	036									
C	026		200							
D	021									
	022									
	024									
	025									
E	023	130		311						
				312						
				321						
				322						
F					400					
G				313						
				314						
				315						
H				323						911
				324						915
				325						917
										918
I										912
										913
										914
										920
J									800	
K							613			916
L							611			
							612			
							614			
							615			
							616			
							631			
							632			

						633				
						634				
						635				
M						500				
N	040									
O		110				620				
		120				640				
P	027					636				
	051									
	052									
	053									
Q								700		
R										930
										940
Y										
Z	011									

Notes

* University of Padua and University of Rome 2, Tor Vergata.

Earlier versions of this chapter were discussed at the seminars within the research group on "The evaluation of economic research in a historical perspective: comparing methods and arguments". We wish to thank the participants for their useful comments and criticisms. We are particularly grateful to Luigi Salmaso, for his advice on statistical matters, to Sara Pecchioli, for her precious help in building the database, to Cristina Marcuzzo, for continuous encouragement and advice. Financial support from the Italian Higher Education and Research Ministry is acknowledged.

1 The Italian "Researcher" is at the same time something more and something less than the Anglo-Saxon lecturer or assistant professor: better in having a tenure, and worse in not necessarily teaching a course with total control over it, but helping with the teaching of others' courses.
2 For the type of database used and for the fact-finding objectives we set ourselves, we applied simple tools of descriptive statistics.
3 In the literature we have tracked down only one example (Fishe 1998) of a study pursuing much the same end for those promoted full professorships in finance in a selected group of universities.
4 Alongside the growth in the number of posts to be competed for we have seen an increasing number of economics Ph.D graduates entering the academic market. This may possibly be a case in which the demand for university Researchers has not been independent of the supply.
5 The year is that in which the appointment of the Researcher took place.
6 See http://reclutamento.murst.it/bandi.html.
7 For example, it does not include the name of one of the authors of this chapter.
8 Initially all the fields of economics other than business economics came together under the one heading "group 20". Subsequently they split up into 10 categories from P01A to P01J, then reduced to 6, labelled from SECS P01 to SECS P06.

9 The birthdates of the 2004–5 cohorts were drawn from the individual personal websites of the Researchers, and so are missing in about 50 per cent of the cases.

10 However, publications dating back as early as the late 1960s are also registered.

11 We are aware that we may thus be overrating the production in collaboration. However, if, following the convention, it had simply been divided by the number of co-authors, the results would have appeared only slightly less favourable to the younger cohorts, where the number of co-authored works is far higher.

12 In the most recent years, due also to the boost coming with large-scale adoption of modern information technologies, the series of working papers have multiplied and the Researchers of the younger cohorts have exploited all the possible advantages.

13 Here we take into account all publications, including working papers.

14 This information is drawn from the Archive of the *Economic Journal* held in the library of the London School of Economics.

15 Some data on this point are to be found in Hodgson and Rothman (1999).

16 Excluded from the calculation are the items in "Papers and Proceedings", being extraneous to the normal refereeing process.

17 For in-depth study of the descriptors, classes and subclasses, see the site http://www. *Econlit*.org/subject_descriptors.html. There have been 20 since 1991; previously there were 10. For the record, the titles of the descriptors prior to 1990 are set out below:

> 000 General Economics; Theory; History, Systems. 100 Economic Growth; Development; Planning; Fluctuations. 200 Quantitative Economic Methods and Data. 300 Domestic Monetary and Fiscal Theory and Institutions. 400 International Economics. 500 Administration; Business Finance; Marketing; Accounting. 600 Industrial Organization; Technological Change; Industry studies. 700 Agriculture; Natural Resources. 800 Manpower; Labor; Population. 900 Welfare Programs; Consumer Economics; Urban and Regional Economics.

And, as from 1991:

> A – General Economics and Teaching. B – Schools of Economic Thought and Methodology. C – Mathematical and Quantitative Methods. D – Microeconomics.
> E – Macroeconomics and Monetary Economics. F – International Economics. G – Financial Economics. H – Public Economics. I – Health, Education, and Welfare. J – Labor and Demographic Economics. K – Law and Economics. L – Industrial Organization. M – Business Administration and Business Economics; Marketing; Accounting. N – Economic History. O – Economic Development, Technological Change, and Growth. P – Economic Systems. Q – Agricultural and Natural Resource Economics; Environmental and Ecological Economics. R – Urban, Rural, and Regional Economics. Y – Miscellaneous Categories. Z – Other Special Topics.

18 Some papers, even in the most recent cohort, appear in *Econlit* without descriptor on account of the editorial policy of the journal in which they appeared, which did not require indication of at least one *Econlit* descriptor. In the first cohort eight papers out of 26 are without descriptor, in the second 15 out of 101, in the third nine out of 244. We assigned a descriptor on our own judgement on the basis of the content of the paper.

19 In order to be able to compare the three different cohorts we transposed the previous system of *Econlit* classification (see note 17 above) to the present one on the basis of correspondences explained in the Appendix; consequently, we reclassified all the papers of the *AER* three-year period 1983–5 and all the publications of the Researchers of the two-year period 1984–5. The result is a database for the first cohort perfectly comparable with those of the subsequent cohorts, without, however, modifying

comparison of the publications of the cohort with its model, given the uniform classification criteria.

20 In order not to overfill the already ample Table 19.8 we did not include columns to represent the composition according to the *JEL* descriptors of publications drawn from sources other than *Econlit* – data in any case easily obtained from the table itself.

21 This is shown up implacably by more detailed analysis through the descriptors subsequent to the first.

22 The standard deviation is to be understood as a measure of the eccentricity in distribution of the Researchers' publications in relation to the *AER* model in each cohort. The higher the value, the more on average it diverges from the composition of the *AER* papers.

23 Hey, who took over as main editor in 1987, observed with satisfaction in 1989 that he had introduced a "marked change" in the editorial policy of the journal (Hey 1989, 210))

References

Artoni, R. (2004), "La valutazione della ricerca", *Economia Politica*, Vol. 21, No. 3.

Artoni, R. (2007), "Valutazione della ricerca e pluralismo in economia politica", *Rivista italiana degli economisti*, Vol. 12, No. 2.

Backhouse R., Middleton R. and Tribe, K. (1997), " 'Economics Is What Economists Do', but What Do the Numbers Tell Us?", *Annual History of Economic Thought Conference*, University of Bristol, 3–5 September.

Bardhan, P. (2003), "Journal Publication in Economics: A View from the Periphery", *Economic Journal*, Vol. 113, No. 488.

Bronfenbrenner, M. (1966), "Trends, Cycles and Fads in Economic Writing", *American Economic Review*, Vol. 56, Nos 1/2.

Corsi, M. (1999), "I concorsi per ricercatore nelle discipline economiche", in Carabelli, A., Parisi, D. and Rosselli, A. (a cura di), *Che "genere" di economista*, Bologna, Il Mulino.

Fishe, Raymon P. H. (1998), "What Are the Research Standards For Full Professor of Finance?", *Journal of Finance*, Vol. 53, No. 3, June.

Gillies, D. (2006), "Why Research Assessment Exercises Are a Bad Thing", *Post-autistic Economics Review*, No. 37.

Gillies, D. (2008), *How Should Research Be Organised?*, London, College Publications.

Hey, J. (1989), "Comment on Theodore Morgan, 'Theory versus Empiricism in Academic Economics: Update and Comparison' ", *Journal of Economic Perspectives*, Vol. 3, No. 4.

Hodgson, G. M. and Rothman, H. (1999), "The Editors and Authors of Economic Journals: A Case of Institutional Oligopoly?", *Economic Journal*, Vol. 109, No. 453.

Holub, H. W. (1989), "Comments on Theodore Morgan, 'Theory versus Empiricism in Academic Economics: Update and Comparison'", *Journal of Economic Perspectives*, Vol. 3, No. 4.

Keynes, J. M. (1936), *The General Theory of Employment, Interest and Money*, London, Macmillan.

Lee, F. S. (2007), "The Research Assessment Exercise, the State and the Dominance of Mainstream Economics in British Universities", *Cambridge Journal of Economics*, Vol. 31, No. 2.

Lee, F. S. and Harley, S. (1997), "The Case of Economics", *Radical Philosophy*, No. 85.

Lee, F. S. and Harley, S. (1998), "Peer Review, the Research Assessment Exercise and the Demise of Non-Mainstream Economics", *Capital and Class*, Vol. 66.

Morgan, T. (1988), "Theory versus Empiricism in Academic Economics: Update and Comparisons", *Journal of Economic Perspectives*, Vol. 2, No. 4.

Oswald, A. J. (2007), "An Examination of the Reliability of Prestigious Scholarly Journals: Evidence and Implications for Decision-Makers", *Economica*, Vol. 74, No. 1.

Sen, A. (2002), "The Science of Give and Take", *New Scientist*, No. 2340.

Stigler, G. J. (1965), "Statistical Studies in the History of Economic Thought", in Stigler, G. J., *Essays in the History of Economics*, Chicago: University of Chicago Press.

van Dalen, H. P. (2007), "Pluralism in Economics: A Public Good or a Public Bad?", in Groenewegen, J. (ed), *Teaching Pluralism in Economics*, Cheltenham, Elgar.

20 Sergio as a young professor

Flavio Pressacco

I met Sergio Parrinello during the academic year 1963–4. I was a freshman at the Faculty of Economics in Trieste and attending, among other courses, the first year of *Economia Politica*. Professor Manlio Resta – who ran the department at the time – was officially in charge of the course, but we never saw him because of his institutional missions; apparently he was working for the international institutions as economic consultant of one of the developing countries (perhaps Brazil or Turkey).

Lessons and exercises were held by various young people whom we referred to as assistants. They were, in alphabetical order, Depollo, Magi and Parrinello. Depollo, fresh from having taken a mathematics degree, took on the part of the course that we would now define as microeconomics, also adding heavy supplies of mathematical tools. Magi outlined only a few issues regarding monetary economics while Parrinello taught the – to my mind – most interesting part of the course, dealing with Keynesian doctrine. It was essentially an informal introduction to the theory of interaction between aggregate supply and demand and localisation of the corresponding equilibrium, not necessarily of full employment.

Parrinello was young, and rather shy; he had only just graduated in economics (at the end of October 1962, to be precise) and, therefore, as a teacher he was something of a fledgling. At the time I was not aware of his status as lecturer without tenure in *Economia Politica*. It was clear that he was doing his best given such a hard task – all the harder given the absence of Manlio Resta. This, together with his gentle disposition and mild-mannered character, earned him great popularity among the students thronging the 'Venezian' lecture hall. And it was precisely *Economia Politica* that turned out to be my first exam, although difficulties awaited me with the mathematical demands of Depollo. Luckily, I felt more comfortable in the second part of the exam, conducted by Parrinello (they were oral exams). So I passed, albeit without a brilliant mark.

My relationship with Parrinello grew closer during the following year: the second course of *Economia Politica* was indeed in scheduling. And again it was entrusted to Manlio Resta, who gave about ten lessons on Sraffa this time. However, Parrinello was in charge of most of the course, focusing very interestingly on the Harrod Domar model and the conditions that have to be satisfied by technology and the behaviour of economic agents to ensure maintenance of the full employment path. I must say that even today, 45 years later, I still look back to that course as one of the most interesting overall in my academic career. Moreover, it was undoubtedly the only one in the area of economics that succeeded in combining methodological strictness with clear reference to the way things are in the real world.

In particular, Parrinello made ample use of mathematical tools and methodologies, striving to explain the intrinsic economic significance without resorting to an intimidating barrage of symbols. This made a very positive impression on me, and I went to see him in his study as often as possible; there, in private, Parrinello was able to shed his rigid and somewhat awkward attitude. Overcoming the shyness so evident during his lessons, he became an easy, affable interlocutor.

I remember also that, at the end of the course, I had already done the exam in the first session (June 1965), getting great satisfaction and a very good mark.

Nevertheless, after the two-year period, I had no further contact with Parrinello during my university life, partly because at the beginning of the year 1966 he moved to Rome, becoming a tenured assistant professor on the research staff of Manlio Resta, who in turn moved to the Faculty of Economics of the capital city.

A few years later, however, we met again during some extemporaneous scientific initiatives organised by various institutions of Trieste, such as the Trieste Summer Schools. On such occasions, Parrinello, who had in the meanwhile become a highly prestigious professor, was often involved as organiser and coordinator. Actually he was always very happy to come back to Trieste where some of his relatives still lived including, if my memory does not deceive me, his mother, to whom he was very attached.

Moreover, on such occasions he set out to involve representatives of the Department of Financial Mathematics and in particular the Dean of the Department, Professor Luciano Daboni, for whom he had high regard, also with the consideration that mathematical instruments are very important for a correct approach to economic issues.

As a member of the Department, I had the opportunity to collaborate on some of those initiatives and I remember with particular pleasure a special number of *Metroeconomica* in honour of Manlio Resta (Special issue of *Metroeconomica* in honour of Manlio Resta, vol. XXXVI, n. 2–3, 1984), where one of my papers, on the role of life insurance in economic agents' choices of optimal decisions in a multiperiod horizon, was published.

It is also worth noting that, at that time Parrinello was editor of the journal, and in view of the period Resta spent at the University of Trieste he also enlisted for the special issue, together with a number of leading Italian economists such as Garegnani and Vicarelli, quantitative exponents of the Faculty of Economics of Trieste (Daboni, Wedlin and myself, to be precise).

Those truly profitable meetings and occasions for scientific collaboration probably had something to do with the fact that soon after, together with some colleagues such as Feliciano Benvenuti and Sergio Vaccà, Parrinello became a member of the Board of the planned Faculty of Banking and Economics, at the University of Udine, which had been established in the meanwhile, shortly after the earthquake in 1976.

As member of that Board, Parrinello began by urging me to hold the mathematics course (which, as a *friulano doc*, I was glad to do), and then included me in the trio of professors that, as from 1 November 1986, constituted the first stable group of the Faculty. During those months Parrinello and I were often consulted on the prospects for the new Faculty and I had the opportunity to appreciate the scrupulousness, sensitivity and strong sense of responsibility with which, having no particular personal interests to defend, he carried out his mandate.

Looking back to my appointment as Dean of the Faculty during the first Board meeting in November 1987, I realise now that in a sense my academic career came full circle under the influence of Sergio Parrinello, from the first exam I took as a freshman at the University of Trieste to my position as Dean of the Faculty there less than 25 years later.

I still hold dear these receding, elusive traces of the past, which are of great importance and significance for me. And, therefore, I was very pleased to meet Sergio Parrinello in Udine again in 2007, on the occasion of the celebration of our Faculty's 20 years when we dedicated to him, approaching the end of his splendid academic career, our wholehearted tribute. And, with this spirit and with these memories, I participate with pleasure in an even vaster tribute which today the whole academic community is about to pay him.

21 The smiles of Sergio

Angelo Marzollo

I would have liked to start this writing about my friend Sergio Parrinello by recalling the first occasion we met. I tried again and again to remember it, but I could not find it in my memory. I called and asked him. He did not remember. He consulted with Giuli, the same result. We concluded that we must have been friends forever.

The difference in our characters is so great that no conflict is possible, and mutual knowledge entails deep reciprocal respect. I am sure that each one of us would like to possess some characteristics of the other one. At the same time, we are amazingly similar in intellectual, moral and political visions. And, most of all, we are united by a common taste for the new, the unexplored, the starting of new initiatives, the change.

Let me recall here how this affinity brought us, coming from different academic disciplines, to work together on several occasions towards concrete goals,

This story started in the late 1960s in Poland, on a bus carrying Italian guests invited by the Polish Academy of Sciences. The important personalities in that Italian group were the economist Siro Lombardini and the system and control scientist Antonio Ruberti. They were often walking or sitting together, held at a respectful distance by the rest of us, all at an early stage of our university careers.

Two members of that group, the researcher in economics, Sergio, and that in mathematical system theory, me, had together found some well-defined common points between these disciplines, from a methodological and application point of view. We were excited by our discovery, rather unorthodox in the Italian academic world of those days, and hesitant on how to proceed in submitting these ideas to Lombardini and Ruberti. We wanted to seize that unique occasion and we did, during an unexpectedly long bus halt in Krakow, a place still emanating its great cultural heritage.

The result was good, the next days our scientific discussions were extended to our great bosses. Sergio and I promptly took the occasion to engage them to sponsor a common research group that we had in mind to promote, on system science and economics.

This we did soon afterwards, in Italy. We started by obtaining the adherence, on Sergio's side of P. C Nicola from the State University of Milan and of B. Sitzia, from the University of Pisa and on my side of S. De Julio, a pupil of Ruberti at the University of Rome and of F. Brioschi, from the Polytechnic of Milan.

The Gruppo di Economia e Sistemistica (GES – Association for Economics and System Theory) was then founded, gathering more than 100 researchers from various Italian institutions, including the research section of the prestigious Bank of Italy, where B. Sitzia had moved in the meantime. So many episodes of that adventurous enterprise, which lasted for more than ten years, come to my mind and may now look like a fantasy of mine, shared only by Sergio. But a concrete object, physically proving the contrary, is available: the book *Teoria dei Sistemi ed Economia* (System Theory and Economics) published in 1976 by Il Mulino, authored by 23 contributors and edited by A. Ruberti and S. Lombardini. Their preface does indeed put the conceptual foundations for those system theory-oriented studies which are now common in economics publications.

This book corresponds to the Proceedings of the First Meeting of GES, held in 1974 at the International Centre for Mechanical Sciences (ICMS) in Udine, and followed by second and third meetings, in 1975 and 1976.

Udine, the capital of the Friuli Italian region, was actually the birthplace of these initiatives, not only because of my position at ICMS, but also because Sergio's roots lay there. He had spent the important years of his early youth in that city and seemed to have absorbed there some aspects of his character which are well known in Italy as typical of the Friuli people: work-oriented, rather silent yet attentive to the meaning of each word and stubborn.

In some way, GES and ICMS in Udine favoured the birth of the Centre for Advanced Economic Studies (better known as 'the Trieste School'). This is also recalled by Adriano Birolo in his Introduction in this book, where he mentions that the first Conference of the Trieste School was held at ICMS in Udine in 1980. Actually, the quick local organisational start of the School was mainly due to the joint endeavour of Sergio and myself.

For the later ten years we worked together as members of the Administrative Board of that School. We now smile when remembering some stormy meetings of that Board.

On those occasions, I often wondered whether the disputes among changing coalitions of the Board's members were due to theoretical differences among various economic thoughts, or differences on strategies about the practical conduct of the School. I am now rather convinced by the first hypothesis, since it explains why only the two members of that Board, Gianpaolo De Ferra and I, who were aliens to the various, sometimes different interpretations of the thought of great founders of the science of economics, could settle those disputes among well-known, distinguished economists. According to his Friuli character, Sergio tended to keep rather silent during those discussions, taking time to think things over, and later expressing his opinions in writing or speaking with me, his friend. His ideas were as intellectually and morally uncompromising as he is.

This habit of his also manifested itself a few years later in a rather strange episode in the antechamber of the newly appointed Minister for State Participation in Economics, Siro Lombardini. He had asked Sergio Parrinello, Sergio De Julio and myself to become his personal advisers. This great academic personality was a newcomer to Italian political life and was actually empowered to appoint only three persons in the whole Ministry, until then directed by Ministers quite different from him, who were endowed with real political and economic hardcore power.

In that antechamber, while waiting for the Minister, the three of us were surprised to be surrounded by persons with an air of those engaged in dodgy deals. Being aware of the important role that the two Sergios and myself would play in the Ministry, not knowing which type of person Siro was, but probably familiar with his predecessor, they advanced proposals that we should embark on some joint venture together, one of which I remember concerned the state railways. They hinted that we would all share the profit. The three of us were looking at each other, surprised. When alone with Sergio De Julio and me, Sergio Parrinello broke his silence, telling us that it would be impossible for him to take the job. The uncompromising Sergio. Personally, I consider that episode an antecedent of the current death of honest intellectual personalities interested in participating in the compromise-dominated (or worse) current active Italian political life, where in any case no Minister with high qualities such as those of Siro Lombardini would be appointed.

The meeting of Sergio with Antonio Ruberti on that Polish bus established a relationship of great reciprocal esteem. It is a duty to recall the gratitude that every Italian person of culture owes to Antonio Ruberti for his extraordinary work as Professor of Control and System Science, as Rector of Rome la Sapienza University, as Minister for Scientific Research and Education, and as European Commissioner for Science. I wish to recall a rather unknown detail in his wide activities which proves his deep, exceptional appreciation for Sergio as a person and for his rigorous approach to economics: some years later, in 1978, Ruberti offered Sergio a newly created Chair of Economics in that Department of System and Control Science which was one of the first of Ruberti's creations and which he considered his living creature, normally reserved for his own pupils.

I do not mention here the countless occasions which found Sergio, Giuli and me together, including on long mountain treks, but I wish to conclude by visualising his various types of smile.

Actually, his rather reserved character is complemented by an almost constant smile. But there are silent smiles with rather closed lips, which he reserves for persons and situations with which his strict moral and intellectual attitudes do not agree, and in this case Sergio keeps silent, takes time for reflection, and then expresses his rather radical opinion to friends while showing his ironical, cutting smile with lips half open. There is the nodding smile when he agrees, and Sergio's lips are all open, and there is also his happy smile, which becomes an open laugh of juvenile joy.

I hope Giuli will let me know with which kind of smile Sergio will greet this note.

Index

For Product Safety Concerns and Information please contact our EU
representative GPSR@taylorandfrancis.com
Taylor & Francis Verlag GmbH, Kaufingerstraße 24, 80331 München, Germany

www.ingramcontent.com/pod-product-compliance
Ingram Content Group UK Ltd.
Pitfield, Milton Keynes, MK11 3LW, UK
UKHW020931280425
457818UK00025B/206